WAJID ALI SHAH

Early Praise for the Book

'Few descendants of legendary figures take up the mantle of writing their history with academic rigour. Dr Kaukub Quder Meerza, great-grandson of Wajid Ali Shah, did so with exemplary dedication in his PhD thesis at AMU, offering a truthful, humane portrait of a misunderstood poet–king. Now translated into English by his daughter, Dr Talat Fatima, herself an accomplished AMU scholar, this work stands as an indispensable and enduring contribution to the study of Wajid Ali Shah and nineteenth-century Awadh.' – **Irfan Habib, Professor Emeritus, Aligarh Muslim University**

'Many poets go unsung, especially those who endured the wrath of usurpers. Among them was Nawab Wajid Ali Shah—a poet–king exiled by the British, yet the foremost custodian of Awadh's culture, poetry, music, dance, and royal stage. Through poetry and verse, he gave voice to the anguish of a displaced ruler and the fading grandeur of his beloved Awadh. Equally significant is the work of Dr Kaukub Quder, his great-grandson, who carried this legacy forward at Aligarh Muslim University. By bringing Wajid Ali Shah's literary and poetic contributions into scholarship, Dr Quder ensured that the nawab is remembered not only as a ruler but also as a leading literary figure of Awadh's rich cultural landscape. Dr Talat Fatima's English translation will go a long way in bringing out the true picture of an unfortunate poet–king so much vilified by the usurpers of his thriving kingdom.' – **Muzaffar Ali, filmmaker and Awadhi culture revivalist**

'Moreover, it makes this wealth of knowledge available to a much wider audience unversed in Urdu, and will surely help to clear the many denigrating misconceptions that surround the much maligned & misunderstood King in exile. This English version of Dr Kaukub's lifetime achievement is bound to become a classic as a towering column of reference on the life, legacy and enigmatic personality of Wajid Ali Shah.' – **Dr Sudipta Mitra, historian and author of *A Nawab and a Begum***

'Long vilified and remembered only as a ruler lost in pleasure, Nawab Wajid Ali Shah was in truth a cultural visionary, prolific man of letters, and an able administrator. He reorganized his army, implemented administrative changes, and personally inspected military parades at dawn. But to the British, such independence was inconvenient. Debt, politics, and prejudice paved the way for his removal in 1856, his love for art twisted into a charge of debauchery. Poet, playwright, composer, and patron, he transformed Lucknow into a vibrant centre of art and refinement, a ruler whose openness, creativity, and connection to his people became his undoing in the eyes of empire.

This historically rich book uncovers his enduring literary and cultural legacy, challenging the colonial caricature of decadence with the reality of a king who was not allowed to reign.' – **Rana Safvi, author of *City of My Heart* and *In Search of the Divine***

'A vividly written, remarkable insider's account of the prosperous princely state of Awadh and its greatest ruler, Nawab Wajid Ali Shah.' – **Nilosree Biswas, author of *Calcutta on Your Plate***

'The narrative created by the British politicians about King Wajid Ali Shah a hundred years ago, and continued by the English and European historians for years after that, was a political gimmick to grab and retain power. He was a poet, and his third generation descendant Dr Kaukab Qadr Sajjad Ali Meerza with the help of primary sources, intelligently and comprehensively described his contribution to Urdu poetry and literature.' – **Roshan Taqui, Indian historian specializing in Lucknow and its culture**

WAJID ALI SHAH

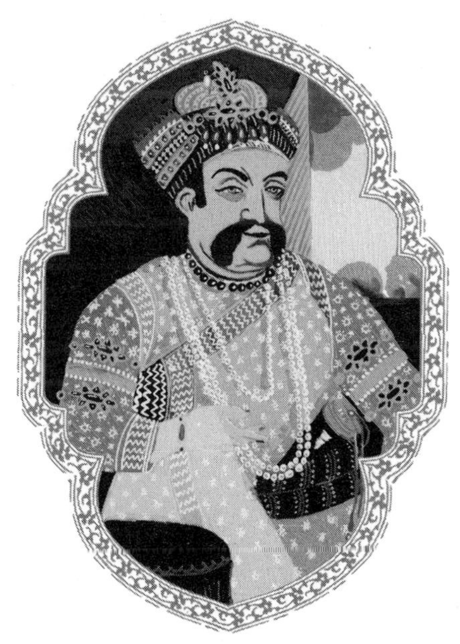

hachette INDIA

First published in Urdu in 1998 by Taraqqi Urdu Bureau

This translation first published in India in 2026 by Hachette India
(Registered name: Hachette Book Publishing India Pvt. Ltd)
An Hachette UK company
www.hachetteindia.com

1

The photographs inside the book are from the author's archive.
Cover design and illustrations by Amit Malhotra.
Wajid Ali Shah's illustration on the back cover by Harshavardhan Behura.

Hardback ISBN 978-93-5731-608-8
eBook ISBN 978-93-5731-366-7

Hachette Book Publishing India Pvt. Ltd
4th & 5th Floors, Corporate Centre,
Plot No. 94, Sector 44, Gurugram 122003, India

Typeset in Garamond Premier Pro 11.5/16.5
by InoSoft Systems, Noida

Printed and bound in India
by Manipal Technologies Limited

This treatise is dedicated to Prince Anjum Quder, great educationist and our guardian, who served as a lighthouse for illuminating with the brightness of education not only the life of Dr Kaukub Quder and Prince Nayyer Quder but for the entire generation of Birjees Quder, and whose love for education made us all what we are today. The generations remain beholden to him.

THE UNFULFILLED DREAM

The *Times of Wajid Ali Shah* by Dr Kaukub Quder was approved by Aligarh Muslim University for the degree of DLitt in 1984. Unfortunately, it could not materialize. The topic prescribed the following aspects:

- Wajid Ali Shah of English
- Wajid Ali Shah of Hindus
- Wajid Ali Shah of Muslims
- Wajid Ali Shah of Children
- Wajid Ali Shah of Women
- Wajid Ali Shah of Artists
- Wajid Ali Shah of Commentators
- Wajid Ali Shah of Critics and
- Wajid Ali Shah of Universities.

This is being presented here for those keen to learn more about the above topic. These subjects are a good place to understand the political, social, literary and cultural ambience prevalent during the period.

Contents

Translator's Note

History is never rendered obsolete. As years pass, its value is not diminished but enriched, sustained through generations of stories. Through careful study and reflection, history preserves the record of human experience. It addresses a world once peopled by the genius, the great, the prodigious and the phenomenal. It holds tales of the good and the bad, the ordinary and the extraordinary. One such remarkable, yet largely misunderstood, individual was Wajid Ali Shah, the ruler who adorned the throne of the Awadhs in Lucknow, India, in the nineteenth century. He harboured rare artistic qualities, was less of a king and more a poet, and an author and a creative par excellence. Soon he fell prey to the nefarious designs of the British and the crown fell off his head prematurely.

This book is an English translation of the Urdu book *Wajid Ali Shah Ki Adabi aur Sakhawati Khidmat* (Literary and Cultural Contributions of Wajid Ali Shah), published by Tarraqi Urdu Bureau, New Delhi, 1995. This work is a product of the extensive investigative research done by late Dr M. Kaukub of Aligarh Muslim University. It is a magnum opus, a deep dive into the realities of the the nineteenth century India, and reveals the literary excellence of a misconstrued king. Dr Kaukub's work is the most authentic study done on Wajid Ali Shah's literary persona and is a successful attempt to blow the dust off his image as a ruler who has been largely perceived as an opulence-loving character of history, and how his contribution to the literary and cultural treasures of India remains unparalleled.

Such was the influence of Wajid Ali Shah that every facet of his life, from his birth to his death, his marriages, his compositions, his literary works, is shrouded in clouds of doubt. It is difficult to say whether the king was a natural leader, a poet, a writer or a painter, a thoughtful environmentalist, or an accomplished architect. But Wajid Ali Shah, as evidence suggest, had the Midas touch and excelled in fields of art, literature, philosophy and creativity. Sadly enough, all his talents were cunningly misinterpreted and misread, and incorrect notions were propagated by the English for their shrewd and astute political gains. As a result, Wajid Ali Shah was presented before the world as a debauched king. What is more, there was no one to defend him, no one to vouch for his strengths. The dead never speak, but their talent does. Wajid Ali Shah's works of art, his formidable writings, his vast cultural contributions, his boundless poetry, leave one awestruck, dispelling the smokescreen of unsavoury reputation and disgrace.

There was a need to clear the dust and clean the glass in order to reveal a more accurate picture of Wajid Ali Shah. The one to do so was none other than his great-grandson Kaukub Quder Sajjad Ali Meerza, whose thorough research does the needful. His study presents the erstwhile ruler's work, encompassing his contributions in the field of literature and to the cultural wealth of India. Unfortunately, not only the English but some of the king's contemporaries, his courtiers and a good number of his rivals, contributed towards maligning his public image; there was no dearth of aspersions cast on his talents.

This research work revolves around two priorities: first, to clear certain widely held misbeliefs and second, and more important, to refute the charges labeled against him. Confusions abound regarding the king's date of birth, number of wives, romantic engagements, number of *Diwans*, the bulk of his work and his image. On these pages, the author rationally rebuts and refutes the doubts surrounding the authenticity of the king's work, his authorship, and clears the dust on his supposedly debauched, lewd, and hedonistic behaviour. No doubt, the king had a flair for the fantastic, was a romantic at heart, and has himself penned the details of his relationships with a number of members of the opposite sex. *Ishq Nama*, his magnum opus, apart from demonstrating his literary mastery is a specimen of his frankness, guilelessness and outspokenness where he cares least about the gossip and chinwag it creates. The author emphatically draws a parallel between the sex-laden poetry of Wajid Ali Shah and the artifacts of Ajanta and Ellora, one of the architectural marvels of India.

Though it is said about the king that he had no master or 'ustad', his library included several inspirations that made his writings informed and influential works of literature. He learned characterization in poetry from Quli Qutub Shah. Wajid Ali Shah was also a contemporary of Mir Anis and Dabir, the celebrated elegists. He was highly impressed by Anis and drew inspiration from him and had the zeal to come on par with his compositions, though he could not. Imdad Hussain was his guide but often Asir is regarded as his ustad. The great poets Aatish and Nasikh were active during his period and inculcated in him the love for poetry, though the king often regarded Barq, who lived with him in Fort William, as his ustad. Sharar claims that the king used to compose and dictate elegies while going to Imambara Sibtainabad. But his elegy writing was not a work of mastery. Nevertheless, through Wajid Ali Shah's works like *Sabatul Quloob, Tosha e Aakhirat,* and his *Noha*s, Dr Kaukub proves that all charges on the king's character were motivated, and on the contrary, he was a pious person, a devout and a fervent Muslim. Poetry was his passion but equally zealous and impeccable was his faith in Allah.

This research work corrects a number of misunderstandings, errors and confusions, often with logical interpretation, sometimes with facts from history. For instance, regarding the date of birth of Wajid Ali Shah and its corresponding date with Gregorian calendar, he beautifully relates the commencement and end of dates per the solar and lunar systems, which he regards as the main error in calculating the dates. He scientifically proves that for every lunar date there are two Gregorian dates, and for every Gregorian date there are two lunar dates. The author rectifies the miscalculation in the number of *Diwan*s, which was due to the misconception and incorrect understanding of writers and critics regarding the import of the word '*Diwan.*' The author argues that *Ishq Nama*, the king's celebrated composition, is his greatest literary contribution. This masnavi is a work of wonder; it relates not only stories about the 'pari khana' but enumerates important events of his life, birth, death of his father Amjad Ali Khan, about his clay toys, and suggested that 'the intellectuals read it with an academic attitude.' Its ill fame is mainly due to the poet's account of an opulent life, one, it is argued, is evocative of his sexual desires. A day shall come when this masnavi will be regarded as the 'king of masnavis' (*Mulook ul Kalam*) and not the 'masnavi of kings' (*Kalamul Mulook*).

Wajid Ali Shah loved writing masnavi, as it was free of the restrictions of 'radif qafia' or rhyming. His *Sabatul Quloob* is a mammoth piece of eloquent expressions and Dr Kaukub, with meticulous and painstaking calculation of its couplets, has proven that it is the longest masnavi (with 48,150 couplets) of Urdu literature; no other is even half of its size. Both *Ishq Nama* and *Sabatul Quloob* have their roots in Persian, though none can deny their originality. Both are complete though imperfect. The king was deeply engrossed by the concept of '*ishq majazi*' (temporal love) and '*ishq haqiqi*' (divine love). He composed *Ishq Nama* to express his temporal love at the age of twenty-six and wrote his masterpiece *Sabatul Quloob*, where he expressed his divine love, when he was sixty-two. Modesty in arrogance and meekness in humility are the two hallmarks of Wajid Ali Shah's compositions. He was a poet of class and exuded taste in his literary endeavors.

Dr Kaukub also proves that the letters written by 'begmats' (the wives of Wajid Ali Shah) was a myth, as he proves beyond doubt that with the exception of one or two, all the begmats were analphabetic and their letters were actually the charisma of hired writers like Ashir, Munshi Tauqeer, Mir Agha, and Ali Jaan. Consequently, the author also blows up the concept of 'Begmati language' saying that it is better to call it Lucknavi language. The king was extraordinary and had a desire to preserve his love letters for generations to come – the letters being a loud specimen of literary eloquence. He was not shy in talking about his indulgences and thus much of his reputation is due to his own account.

He was a great visionary, evident from his pioneering contributions in the field of drama, music, and dance, which were much ahead of his times. He invented the concept of 'rahas' or dance drama. He wrote the tale of *Radha-Kanhaiyya*, which is considered a pioneering work by researchers. Moreover, he not only composed the tale but also directed the artists regarding their performance and acting. He designed their costumes, adorned the stage with swags and draperies. Today, song writing, script writing, music direction and stage setting are done by different specialists but back in the day, to use modern terminology, he was a lyricist, a choreographer and a music director all in one. He not only wrote 'geets' but set their melodious tones or 'gutt'. In the field of dance, he introduced 'thumris'. It will be a rare revelation for many that the king was hard of hearing and hence he concentrated more on gestures, actions, gesticulations and movements in his rahas and plays (naqals).

The king's interests encompassed all the hues of life: laying down code of conduct for palace staff, courtiers, women, also for fish-rearing, and wrote a dictionary of near to twelve languages (though it was not a full-fledged dictionary and only words of common use were included). He had great faith and love for Hindustani art and propagated it through his fine arts like rahas, paintings, composing them in Hindi, and using Punjabi and Bengali words often. Though he had a bent towards Persian, he switched to Urdu seeing that it was the language of the masses in the Hindustan of that time. He even rejected English terminology for his army and named the regiments and laid down the code of conduct in Persian.

By the time one reaches the last page of this book, they will meet a different Wajid Ali Shah, unlike the commonly understood persona; a Wajid Ali Shah who is a bold and audacious man, a magnanimous person, a lover of nature, a patriot, a philanthropist and an embodiment of rare artistic qualities. He proved that a person can be a true believer of Allah and at the same time be secular to the core.

Today, as I sit at my desk, wrapped in this colossus work, I am awestruck. Unbelievably, the impossible has been made possible; the incredible has happened. Hard to believe that an unwise like me translated the magnum opus of two geniuses: Wajid Ali Shah and Dr Kaukub. They served like my North Star in my endeavour to shoulder this responsibility. A fusion of Persian, Urdu, Hindi, the original features the languages in their toughest form, with an ancient style replete with obsolete terms and outmoded language. I read through the treatise three to four times. As I translated this colossus, often I smiled, cried, and was left awestruck and blank. The book required knowledge of Urdu and an intricate understanding of the style of the author and also of Wajid Ali Shah. I feel honoured that my humble knowledge of Urdu which scored letter marks for me in my Higher Secondary Board Examination and hitherto remained quiescent is put to best use. Today, I feel it was a miracle; some divine hand and nothing but the blessings of the dead gave my keyboard the power to achieve this Herculean task. Though I remained meticulous and careful and gave the last drop of my humble self all through, to err is human, and I request readers to forgive me for any mistake they may come across.

None can claim to be independent, perfect, and excellent, let alone me. Some humans around me were my strength. All my brothers and sisters, especially Manzilat and Kamran, inspired me, helping me to achieve the impossible both with their words and deeds. I am also thankful to Janab Shakeel Shamsi (poet and journalist) for his timely support.

I am indebted to Rana Safvi, historian and author, who of her own volition wrote an endorsement for this book, thus giving me and the book that extra gravitas.

I remain grateful to Professor Umar Khayyam (Kolkata) and Syed Mujtaba Ali (Delhi) who helped me with their learned Persian translations.

This manuscript would not have seen the light of the day without the care given to it by Hachette India. I express my gratitude to Thomas Abraham, a fine self and a thorough gentleman who supported to encapsulate history in these pages. I am also thankful to Riti Jagoorie for her valuable cooperation. I thank Abhivyakti Singh and the editorial team for their patience in going through this long treatise which is spotted with difficult Urdu and Persian transliteration and translation.

Dr Talat Fatima
Great-great-granddaughter of
Wajid Ali Shah and Begum Hazrat Mahal
26 August 2025

Preface by the Author

Wajid Ali Shah is one of the more popular kings of India. Within and outside the country, people may not remember the empire he ruled or the period of his reign, but they do know he was a king fond of dance and music, and it was his indulgence that brought down his empire. But history is witness to the fact that if a public figure sees notoriety, there are also stories of their virtue and goodness that keep their name in good stead. If there are people who propogate false stories about Wajid Ali Shah, then there is also no dearth of narratives that draw a halo of virtues and genius around him. His life spanning almost seven decades is replete with evidence of his greatness and enormity of attributes, which to date attracts admirers and passionate fans. If for the sake of argument one admits that Wajid Ali Shah was an incompetent ruler, one cannot disregard the fact that he had an all-embracing personality, was a paragon of uprightness, and has impacted literature, religion, poetry, music, painting, dance, architecture, calligraphy and a number of other fields of creativity. The qualities and the cultural ethos left behind by his ancestors were two factors that shaped his personality. His name in the history of India will remain as a shining example for as long as the name of Lucknow and 'Luknaviyat' remains. This thesis attempts at highlighting these imprints of the great king, which due to indifference of vested interests and cruel passage of time are about to wane and vanish.

Much of Wajid Ali Shah's reputation is rooted in his political and personal life, both of which are beyond the scope of this thesis. The subject matter of this study is his literary and cultural contributions, which mark his entire life. So far, three noted works have been done on Wajid Ali Shah but none of those are concerned with his life. Dr Abul Lais Siddiqui in his thesis 'Lucknow Ka Dabistan e Shayaari' mentions the life and poetry of Wajid Ali Shah, and whatever was left out from that thesis is compensated in some of the articles and in the latest edition of his works. In the papers of Dr G.D. Bhatnagar entitled 'Administration of Avadh under Wajid Ali Shah' there is mention of his life in brevity, which unfortunately lacks necessary background. Professor Masood Hasan Rizvi's book *Lucknow Ka Shahi Stage* is the last of these series, which gives an elucidative and convincing description, but that too is not useful enough regarding his biographical account. The analysis of his contribution was not possible without a reference to his circumstances and his life. It was necessary to mention certain facts by way of his personal history. Why a person has said something, what he has said and how he has said it are important to analyze one's narrative. The first two chapters of this thesis relate to why such narration is made, the two middle chapters relate to what has been stated and the last chapter is concerned with how he has narrated.

The first chapter of the book 'The Mystification' identifies personal happenings, events and anecdotes which in a collective form journey towards a point beyond which there was once sheer disgrace and ignominy for Wajid Ali Shah. On the rise, fall and contributions of the king, there is a formidable impact of the political, social, literary and religious movements of that period. After his dethronement and then after his death, important events resulting from the intermingling of these movements come to the fore. The last chapter gives an account of these in brief so that the resulting conclusions are understood.

The important events of Wajid Ali Shah's life, which should have been recorded in one place are scattered over several books and hence there is no consensus among the writers regarding his birth, compositions, children, wives. In the second chapter there is not much scope to discuss these and hence I have mentioned and ascertained certain dates. His dethronement attracted every high and low and there was hardly any newspaper or language that did not take note of this. Wajid Ali Shah's books comprise Urdu and Persian, prose and poetry, politics, music philosophy, dictionary, letters and Hindi songs (geets). To argue and discuss all of these per their requirement and to mention the origin and sources are the obligations of those who intend to write on these points. Investigating the life of Wajid Ali Shah is an entirely different subject matter and the discussions in the second chapter are not enough to circumscribe it. They only hint at a need to do so.

The third chapter of this thesis is an important one, in which there is mention of his compositions and also analyses narratives that have been accepted as true without any proper authority. Not all the compositions of Wajid Ali Shah could be gathered in his library, neither there is any chance of it today. Many strange misunderstandings have resulted due to the rarity, unavailability and abundance of these compositions. Some commentators repeat the same points that were written almost seventy years ago and were as much incorrect at that time as they are today. Some try to bring a newness to those narratives but they too disappoint. In the first section of the chapter, I mention the opinions and discourse of the commentators and in the second section, I bring up the attributes of Wajid Ali Shah's compositions. The third section goes into the details of the forty-two compositions of Wajid Ali Shah and names other rare books. I am sure that this analysis is incomplete while also being certain that in the future no other analysis can be called 'complete'.

Wajid Ali Shah's proficient pen, which from the peak of his youth up until his death bed spilled pleasant and unpleasant stories for about fifty years, but the entire treasure of his literary offerings could not be conserved in spite of his interest in preserving them. There is no hope as these could be scattered all over the four dimensions, destroyed and lost, and hence there can hardly be any research or analysis that would embrace the entire length and breadth of his seemingly endless treasure of words. As most of the books have been destroyed, it is always advisable to at least save those which have been discovered, and this has been done at level best during my survey. This study shows that books mentioned by Wajid Ali Shah in *Bani* are all intact though they are scattered. One cannot say with certainty about the fate of the manuscripts of which there is not much mention in the list. Some books are recently discovered, though many private libraries of Asia and Europe are still beyond our reach. There is nothing available to verify the claim that Wajid Ali Shah had written hundreds of books. People have not even heard about the names of such 'imaginary' works, and it seems to be as true as the narrative that the English had published some of his books.

The bookish detail of the survey makes the thesis extraordinarily lengthy but in the absence of such explanation people would be unsure of the date of composition of the books let alone their names and titles. Mentioning the place of availability of such books, which is the most important part of this research, will help those who want to have a glimpse of the works. The thesis mentions some copies of the manuscripts bearing royal seal, which is proof of their authenticity. On printed copies there is a singular seal of the king, which as per the trend at that time is found in all the copies which were printed by Matbaey Sultani. In the explanation of the books, the mention of 'Bismillah' in the beginning and of 'Qata'at e Tarikh' at the end of the book has been purposely avoided. This is because writing 'Bismillah' was a common trend and 'Qata'at e Tarikh' are also commonly found in printed copies. There is narration of preface (tarqima) and of epilogue (khatima) in the manuscript of the books which are given a separate detail. The books are written in the Persian script and if there is any diversion, it finds a mention. The detail of the parameters and volume of the books (taqtee) is helpful in determining the size of the work and it has been mostly has been retrieved from original copies. Repeated binding of the books damages its paper. So the measurement of the size is given in centimeters, as per today's style. The details of the books also mention their uniqueness and special features, which are not found in other works. This knowledge is helpful in knowing the name and characteristic of Matbaey Sultani. This detailing will be helpful for those unable to identify the books due to the flaws in the incomplete copies of Wajid Ali Shah's compositions that are available in the libraries.

Often there is a charge that books associated with Wajid Ali Shah are, in fact, not his books. Such objections or claims are usually mere words and there is neither mention of any such research nor any proof present to support the claim. Although, when carrying out research on the works of Wajid Ali Shah, it is not proper to ignore such claims. They have disturbed intellectuals and now even important compositions have fallen prey to such baseless claims. In the fourth section of chapter three such claims have been negatively responded to, and in the positive response the characteristic features of Wajid Ali Shah's writings have been mentioned, which are comprehensive and are found in almost all his compositions thereby refuting this as nothing but impudence. Another way of disregarding such charges is to identify his writing, and the books written in that script be saved from getting destroyed. The specimen of his penmanship, which is presented by Professor Masood Hasan Rizvi in *Lucknow Ka Shahi Stage* is based on a misreading or misinterpretation. In the last section of this chapter, by comparing different specimens of handwritings, it is revealed that in Wajid Ali Shah's writing the same innovation and fervor is seen, which is found in most of his masterpieces.

In the cultural contributions of Wajid Ali Shah, right from his contemporaries up to the present writers, all have highlighted his 'Shahi Rahas' and it is common thinking that the king resorted to it by the way of entertainment. But had the intellectuals given more attention to it, they would have realized that this was not random His cultural affairs start not from drama but from the dramatic style of delivery of dialogues and the reason behind it is not due to any external factor but his impaired audibility. In chapter four, the cultural activities of Wajid Ali Shah have been highlighted in a comprehensive and concise manner in which stress is laid on this aspect of his personality. It has been shown how he gradually improvised the trends of music, dance, poetry, architecture and costume designing of his time and laid down the outline of 'rahas' and at the same time took care to keep it purged of the effects of the English theatre. Unconsciously, he adopted measures and styles which are in consonance with the present style. This part of the thesis be perused as a supplement to the book *Lucknow Ka Shahi Stage* because in it, the learned scholar advocates with necessary evidences and it is futile to repeat them.

Another aspect of Wajid Ali Shah's cultural activity is natural history. Here too the king tried his best to keep his interest and awareness distinct from the English style; he made myriad innovations, which were followed until he reached Calcutta. Historians did not bother to pay attention to the drawing and painting skills of the king and his associates, but if his drawings are inspected, one will realize that even at that time he was not unaware of the techniques that help in commercial art-making. Regarding his cultural contributions, it is sufficient to point out the before-mentioned competencies of the king. However some specimen of his drawings are included here [in the original Urdu edition] as it is not within capability of words to explain his art.

In chapter five, the contributions of Wajid Ali Shah as a writer and a poet have been analysed. With the help of some samples of his prose work and poetry, it is shown how being affected by his surroundings he gave expression to his creative abilities in different ways. Conversational tone in letters and the dramatic style in masnavis are the hallmarks of his prose and poetry writing, and thinking that he was enthused by anyone is misunderstanding the persona of Wajid Ali Shah. The mention of some tales (naqals) in *Bani* and the ghazals associated with begmats due to artificiality have secondary importance. But again, the conversational mode and dramatic style in these tales have refined the letters to some extent. These two pieces of his compositions have carved a niche for themselves in Urdu literature. The extremism in his work is manifested in the naqals which daringly narrate the unsatisfied lewd emotions that are often disliked by the readers.

The collections of Wajid Ali Shah's letter reveal an interesting point. The letters that were hitherto regarded as an expression of feminine and begmati emotions are, in fact, written by ordinary letter writers and the begmats were basically unlettered. In the beginning, this misunderstanding was inculcated by the publishers and later on a few commentators and researchers substantiated this on the basis of insufficient investigation and proof. Had the researchers given attention to the internal evidences of the letters, the statements of Wajid Ali Shah himself, and the standard of female education of that time, this reality would have been revealed long back.

Among the various compositions of Wajid Ali Shah that are mentioned in the last part of the chapter include *Sabatul Quloob*, which was written in his last days; but it is not even known in the academic circles. Of all the works of Wajid Ali Shah if only this masnavi is taken into consideration, then its magnitude of forty eight thousand one hundred and fifty verses, the work of same standard not yet produced, alone will keep the name of Wajid Ali Shah everlasting and alive in the history of Urdu language. The long masnavis in Urdu literature which have been discovered so far are not even half the size of *Sabatul Quloob* and this has been discussed with proof in the same chapter.

In the last pages of the thesis, it has been concluded that Wajid Ali Shah was born with remarkable creative abilities but it was his misfortune that he could not find a suitable environment in which these abilities could flourish to the full. When he became king and even after his dethronement, he realized that the English were not only his enemy but were the opponents of his culture too. The king was not competent to fruitfully challenge the English in matters of warfare or magnitude of their empire, but as a ruler he decided he must put up a fight. His attempts are considered immature and only a means to give way to his pent up feelings but his creative mind did its best. He outshone everybody during peacetime, but sadly enough whatever he did during the political upheavals go unnoticed. Labeling his literary and cultural contributions as his pastime is faulty reasoning because of which the genius of the king does not get its due recognition.

The drastic differences in opinions for some of the important findings and matters, and displaying ignorance in making statements when that Wajid Ali Shah's books are 'purchased', only go to show that he and his work are not taken seriously. Justice calls for the attitude that his work be evaluated and studied with reason and an academic attitude. Additionally, the flaws and shortcomings in a person with which he is born cannot be forgotten;

those qualities should not be allowed to die an unnatural death. The writer of this thesis came across certain misses in the personality of Wajid Ali Shah and they have been mentioned at appropriate places, but there is not a single flaw in him which one finds only in him and not in others. But he was an epitome of many extraordinary qualities, which are found only in him and which give him name and fame.

In the thesis of history and literature, it is desirable to present extracts in conformity of the context and in literary form, which also makes a treatise weighty and substantive. There was enough scope in the subject of this thesis to gain from this trend as this undertaking is not only a thesis of Urdu literature but an account of a king's achievements. It is also the history of the culture and civilization of a certain period in time, which is symbolized by the great king.

However, the writer of this thesis has been cautious in bringing out the correct and reliable material among a deluge of contradictory narrations, and which due to the impartiality of the writer can be considered most authentic. At places, the importance of contradictions have been given their due treatment after giving arguments in the light of available evidences, which can be helpful in accepting or rejecting a particular opinion. It is not easy for one to criticize Wajid Ali Shah by brushing aside the contradictions because often the source of contradiction are the arguments of scholars, and moving ahead without investigating their narrations will give rise to the doubt that the narration which so far has been unchallenged, was correct and the present one imperfect. While distinguishing fiction from reality, it is important that diversion from an established point or assertion of a new point must be supported by evidence or reasons. The list of sources and references is preceded by a list of English books, which are written in the English pattern with the name of the author, and the list of Urdu and Persian books entered with the name of the books, and these are listed in the same pattern in the footnotes. A short index [as in the original Urdu edition] is also present, in which other than the names of noted people and events, the names of even prominent writers from whose opinion there has been some diversion or on whose opinion further additions are made, are also included. The dates of important events of Wajid Ali Shah's life are written in the Hijri era and they are proved to be authentic. At places, the dates are given as per the Gregorian calendar and the mistakes, if any, are not of more than a difference of two or three days.

The thesis writer started collecting material from 15 January 1964 and in March 1967 these concluding lines are being written. A period of thirty eight months is not less but it is not enough for an extensive subject like this, the different parts of which are scattered all over India and in the possession of those who give scant regard to the hardships of the researcher and are more pre-occupied with their own schedule. Many doors remained unopened and several books though seen once could never be perused again. Maybe by the time these doors are opened or those books come to the fore, some narrations get more explanations or are deleted. However, the writer can say this much that whatever is already written is written with full responsibility and faithfulness in this study, based on reason and rational arguments. The sagacious can decide as to where an informed assumption is made and where it is thoroughly logical.

It was not an easy task for a humble person like me to write something on an ill-famed ruler like Wajid Ali Shah and if I say that Professor Ale Ahmed Suroor (Head of the Department), gave me the courage to do it then it may also malign his choice of subject. When it comes to thanks, then wholeheartedly I am pleased to start the list with his name on the top thinking that while other universities did not heed to this subject , he not only laid stress on the need to write it but also provided resources without which my journey to complete the work would not have been possible. The supervision of this work was done by learned Dr Khalilul Rehman Azmi. Coming across some rare document related to my subject was not as much heartening as it was to work under the learned and knowledgeable guidance of Professor Azmi. I was introduced to Suroor Sahab and Azmi Sahab by my younger brother Nayyer Quder Wasif Ali Meerza as his attachment with the subject and with the university was so intense that at the time of leaving for

London for his Bar at law course, he entrusted me with this responsibility. Had there been a tradition to dedicate the thesis to someone then I would have preferred his name for this.

Many other people cooperated with me in compiling this work. It would be improper if I don't include their names in my list. Nawab Inayat Jung Bahadur (Hyderabad), Qazi Abdul Wudud Sahab and Professor Syed Hasan Askari Sahab (Patna), Mahrajkumar Md. Amir Haider Khan (Mehmoodabad), Dr Momin Moiuddin (Bombay), Maulana Kalbe Sadiq Sahab (Lucknow) and Murshadzada Rafiul Quder Bahadur (Calcutta) top the list. I remain indebted to Nawab Sahab, Qazi Sahab, Professor Sahib, Maharajkumar Sahab, Dr Sahab and Maulana who not only offered me their valuable advice but also gifted relevant and precious books to me. Murshidzada Sahab very generously gifted to my humble self those handwritten and printed books, and pictures from the libraries of his grandfather Late Sir Mirza Jahan Quder and late Shehzada Aasman Jah, which are rarely found in any of the libraries of India. Research work cannot be completed without the help and cooperation of the staff of various libraries. For me, naming only a selected few would not be proper hence I indiscriminately and wholeheartedly thank all of them who were so cordial and helpful in providing me with the required support.

Kaukub Quder Sajjad Ali Meerza
Department of Urdu
Aligarh Muslim University, Aligarh
21 March 1967

POST SCRIPTUM

At the time of printing, my dear Dr Qamrul Huda Faridi, Senior Research Fellow, Department of Urdu, helped me in the text's proofreading and in the compilation of [the original] index, and my brother Farhatullah Khan Sahab, Reader Incharge, University Polytechnic (Electrical) helped me in typing of the English part, I am thankful to both of them.

ONE

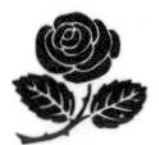

Background and Milieu

Before embarking upon the life and contributions of Wajid Ali Shah, it is necessary to identify those traditions which shaped the cultural school of Lucknow and gave it a unique identity, at the same time heralding the era spreading over the life of Wajid Ali Shah.

TRADITIONS ESTABLISHED BY ELDERS

Meerza Mohammad Muqeem, the heir of Wajid Ali Shah, was the son in law of one Mir Mohammad Musavi.[1] Both of them were Shias and were born in Nishapur.[2]

In 1722, the King of Delhi, Muhammad Shah, bestowed the title of Nawab Saa'dat Khan Burhan ul Mulk Bhadur Jung, as well as the Subedarship of Avadh, upon Mir Mohammad Ameen. This was in acknowledgement of

1. Wazir ul Sultan Mohammad Amir Ali Khan Amir; *Wazirnama*, Publication Nizami. Kanpur (1293 hijri) pp. 26–27.
2. A.L. Shrivastava; *The First Two Nawabs of Oudh*. Lucknow (1933). pp. 1–3 and 87–89.

his great services in defending Delhi from the conspiracies of outsiders. Subjugating the rebellious Sheikhzadas and Rajputs was Burhan ul Mulk's most commendable achievement. In 1739, when Burhan ul Mulk died, his son-in-law gifted two crore rupees to Nadir Shah. In return for his loyalty to the Delhi Durbar, he not only got the Subedarship of Avadh,[3] but also earned the title[4] of Waazir ul Mumalik Mansoor Ali Khan Bahadur Safdar Jung. Due to his strong bond with the Delhi Durbar, he was envied by all the other subedars. The King adopted Subedar Gujarat's daughter and got her engaged to Safdar Jung's son. Ultimately the daughter got massive dowry not only from the King but from Mautum ud Daulah who was the Subedar of Gujarat and also from all the other Subedars of Hindustan at that time. Acting as both a father and a king, Mautum ud Daulah and the owner of Gujarat he gave an an unlimited dowry. Following his example, all the other subedars at that time also contributed immensely towards the dowry.[5] This wealth contributed directly to the formation of Faizabad and indirectly to the formation of Lucknow. However, due to unfavourable circumstances, this bond of love and affection could not last long. But so long as the relationship continued, the people of Delhi rightfully claimed help and cooperation from them and their children, and the latter dutifully served the people of Delhi.

The activities of Burhan ul Mulk and Safdar Jung within Avadh were limited to strengthening the empire.[6] They lived the hard life of a soldier and preferred to be nomadic. This is evident from the fact that in the thirty-two years of their rule, they did not build a permanent abode for themselves. They spent their lives in army cantonments and died in Delhi, where they were buried.[7] Though Iranians are by nature opulent, their simplicity and austerity earned[8] these two a place of distinction among all the rich and mighty of

3. Supra note 2 at pp. 91, 92.

4. Supra Note 1 at pp. 33, 34.

5. *Tarikh-e-Lucknow (Manuscript)* at p. 306, 308

6. A.L. Shrivastava; *The First Two Nawabs of Avadh*. Lucknow (1933) at pp. 260–263.

7. W. Hoey; *Memoirs of Faizabad*. (1988) Volume 2. p. 3 & 4.

Shahjahanabad.[9] Safdar Jung was a generous person, which is evident from the fact that he granted 50 'ashrafis' to anyone with whom he held some conversation. If he was impressed by a soldier, then he used to increase his salary by 10 rupees. The poetry of Burhan ul Mulk[10] and its appreciation by Safdar Jung[11] depict their literary interests. But more than patronizing the subtle arts, they were dedicated to administration. In this, their Iranian origin and beliefs were never an impediment. Due to their secular and non-communal approach, they were quickly able to gain the confidence of the masses. Soon, even the most rebellious and mulish people submitted before them.[12] Burhan ul Mulk's empire was full of renowned Hindu pilgrimages, like Mathura, Prayag, Kashi, and Ayodhya. In the Zamindar community, there were many aggressive Hindus.[13] The majority of the Muslims were Sunnis. From the viewpoint of race, both the rulers were different from the governed class. However, they enjoyed the submission and goodwill of both Hindus and Muslims so much that the people in Delhi thought that Safdar Jung was a Hindu.[14] The good faith of the Sheikhs was so deeply rooted that, after driving out the Rohillas from Lucknow, they invited Safdar Jung to rule.[15] This healthy legacy of unity and harmony among Hindus and Muslims, and among Sunnis and Shias, was carried forward to the era of Wajid Ali Shah.

Even after the incident of HanUmangarhi, the events of 1857 clearly proved that the people of Avadh were true loyalists of this family. HanUmangarhi was granted to Wajid Ali Shah by Safdar Jung through a

---

8. Supra note 1 at 253.

9. *Sabat ul Qulub*(Manuscript. Volume 1. at p. 19.) and Supra note 1 at p. 252.

10. A.L. Shrivastava; *The First Two Nawabs of Avadh*. Lucknow (1933) at 77.

11. *Ibid.*

12. *Ibid* at 255–96.

13. *Ibid* at 263–67.

14. *Ibid* at 256.

15. *Ibid* at 127–28.

deed,[16] and Wajid Ali Shah tried to maintain the status quo up to the end.[17] The legacies of language, literature, culture, religion, and good governance, which were brought by Burhan ul Mulk from Delhi in his quest for welfare and solicitude, faced tremendous rebellion on the soil of Avadh. Some of these healthy legacies stood the test of time for fifty to a hundred years, while some died out after only ten to twenty years. Before the birth of Wajid Ali Shah, even the titular relationship between Delhi and Lucknow, which had been maintained against all odds, had ended. After royal declaration, the futile attempt to keep alive the pomp and opulence of the erstwhile rulers on the one hand, and the expression of regret and ironic comments on the other became the hallmark of the forthcoming era of history. However, the formidable changes which took place during this time had surfaced before the birth of Wajid Ali Shah. These changes gained strength and vigour, and not only impacted Wajid Ali Shah's life, but served as his cradle. He was bound to work for the advancement of such changes.

THE DECISIVE WARS

From subjugation to self-reliance, from military expertise to royal splendour, from battlefield to luxurious chambers, and from Islamic traditions to Indian ethnicity, the kith and kin of Safdar Jung showed great promptness in this changeover; his son became its first remarkable example. Burhan ul Mulk and Safdar Jung grew beards and wore the attire of the Delhi court. Shuja ud Daulah grew a moustache of the Indian style and his beard disappeared.[18] Asaf ud Daulah wore formal shoes, and Nasiruddin Haider was fully drenched

16. Maulvi Najmul Ghani Khan has presented this deed along with other episodes in his Book *Tarikh e Avadh*. Publication: Munshi Naval Kishore, Lucknow (1919). Volume 5. at p. 20.
17. G.D. Bhatnagar; *Administration of Oudh Under* Wajid Ali Shah. Thesis for Ph.D. of Lucknow University. This statement was recorded on the basis of Resident's reports. p. 175–177.
18. A.L. Shrivastava; Shuja ud Daulah. Lahore (1945) Volume 2. p. 294–95.

in English chic.[19] Such changes were also witnessed at the administrative level. The affluent Hindu class was the confidant of Burhan ul Mulk and Safdar Jung,[20] while Shuja ud Daulah and Asaf ud Daulah often gave this honour to both the Hindus and the Muslims. From the period of Saa'dat Ali Khan, Muslims were regarded as worthy of administration. Hindus were given only the position of Diwans.[21] During the reign of Shuja ud Daulah, many reasons manifested for this change. Only those incidents which had far-reaching ramifications are mentioned here. At the time of the crowning of Wazir ul Mumalik Shuja ud Daulah Abul Mansoor Khan Bahadur Asad Jung (1754), the Mughal Empire was surrounded by formidable dangers. The Battle of Plassey (1757) had crippled the empire, in addition to existing Maratha aggression.

"The Marathas blockaded Delhi with a formidable strength of about twenty to twenty-five lakh strong army, whose ultimate motive was to conquer Delhi and cause devastation thereof."[22]

Shuja ud Daulah was present at both these fronts, and "the fates of two forceful communities of the world were decided before his eyes."[23] First, there was the Third Battle of Panipat (1761) in which there were Agha Haju Sharf, Shuja ud Daulah and the armies of other Chiefs while on the other hand there was the battalion of the Marathas. This battle decided in just one day that if Hindustan does not belong to Muslims, it also cannot belong to the Marathas.[24] Shuja ud Daulah, fully engrossed with the victory, vehemently challenged the growing power of the English, gearing up for

19. See pictures in *Qaisar ul Tawarikh, Tawarikh e Nadir ul Asar, Boostan e Avadh*, and *Guldasta e Lucknow.*

20. Supra note 20 at 255.

21. Refer to Rulers of Avadh in *Tawarikh e Nadir ul Asar* and *Boostan e Avadh etc.*

22. Munshi Naval Kishore; *Tawarikh e Nadir ul Asar.* Publication: Munshi Naval Kishore, Lucknow (1863), 62.

23. Maulvi Abdul Halim Sharar; *Guzishta Lucknow. Publication*: Nasim Book Depot, Lucknow, 33.

24. *Ibid.*

the Battle of Buxar (1764).[25] In this battle, the well-organized army of the English was on one side, and the battalion of Hindustani and Mughal leaders was on the other. The Battle of Buxar decided within twenty-four hours that Hindustan does not belong to the Muslims, it belongs to the English.[26] Despite their military might and political manoeuvres, the English traders were not willing to shoulder such a great responsibility. They needed the able leadership of the ambitious Shuja ud Daulah and were willing to proceed gradually under his leadership. Hence, they were willing to maintain cordial ties with him.[27] Defeated, overpowered and saddened by the hollow encouragements of friends in whom he confided,[28] irritated and disheartened by the selfishness of his Wali Naimat who harboured the nasty plans to hand over his administration to others,[29] Shuja ud Daulah submitted before the English. Though the conditions laid down by the English aimed to please Shuja ud Daulah and solicit his cooperation, the result of this apparently generous treatment was that Avadh, a great power centre of Hindustan, was severed from the politics of the country.[30] Under the guise of helping and cooperating with Shuja ud Daulah, the shrewd English started uprooting the neighbouring states one by one. It gave material and political mileage to the English, though it apparently also gave power to Shuja ud Daulah coupled with disrepute, as the boundaries of Avadh were enlarged.[31] The military activities of Shuja ud Daulah started gaining momentum, and the English became anxious[32] that this predicted some sort of vengeance by Shuja ud Daulah. Haider Naik, the Ruler of Mysore, who was fighting under the

---

25. *Company Ki Hukumat*, 105–6.
26. Supra note 25 at 33.
27. Shrivastava; Shuja ud Daulah. Lahore (1945) Volume. 2, 3.
28. *Id.*, at 1 & 2.
29. *Id.*, and *Qaisar ul Tawarikh* Volume 1., 63, 66 & 68.
30. Syed Kamal Hussain Haider Alias Mir Zair; *Qaisar ul Tawarikh*. Publication: Munshi Naval Kishore. Lucknow. (1907) Volume 1. 63, 66 & 68. Supra Note 29 at 18–20.
31. *Ibid* at 308–9.
32. *Ibid* at 54–60.

French flag, asked for Shuja ud Daulah's help. Through a secret reply, he refused to help him, saying that he is the friend of English and enemy of their enemies. This was enough to dispel the fears of the English that Shuja ud Daulah would betray them.[33] He was allowed to keep as large an army as he desired, and they held that there were no restrictions on him.[34] There was no end to the ambitions of Shuja ud Daulah, who was highly determined. Thus, instead of becoming the minister (*wazir*) of the King of Delhi, he was keener to accept the ministership (*wazarat*) of England.[35] Therefore, had he lived longer, or had his heirs shared his mentality and temperament, the history of Avadh would have taken a different turn. Secured within the four walls of his state and away from the internal rift of Hindustan, Shuja ud Daulah bade farewell to this world in 1775, at a time when the expansion of the empire had reached its zenith,[36] and its annual income was at three crore and sixty lakh rupees per annum.[37]

DAWN OF CULTURAL LUCKNOW

Shuja ud Daulah was as much a lover of fine arts and an adMirer of the fairer sex as he was interested in the strategic and administrative affairs.[38] Asaf ud Daulah inherited his educational and literary taste from his father and tired of the intricacies of administrative affairs, soon assigned to those who were most wishful for the same. Deeds of agreement were concluded between the English and *Nawab* Shuja ud Daulah ended with his death.[39]

---

33. Khan Bahadur Moulvi Md. Musseehooddeen; *Oude, Its Princes and its Government, Vindicated*. London (1857) at 5, 6.

34. Supra note 29 at 86.

35. *Id.* at 9, 30.

36. Id. at 413.

37. Id. at 326. According to the manuscript *Maraatul Awza* (Handwritten at p. 10) the income was one crore twelve lakh rupees during the reign of Wajid Ali Shah.

38. Supra note 29 at 297–308.

39. Supra note 35 at 10, 11.

This included the deeds related to residence[40] in Avadh, tax free trade, and maintaining a helpful army.[41] With the new settlement (1775), the English expanded their power and prepared Asaf ud Daulah to dismiss the army,[42] and to engage foreign employees only on the approval of the East India Company.[43] In order to gain prosperity for the commercial activities of the Company, it was thought that there must be an increase in the concessions given to it. Asaf ud Daulah was "subservient to his Western friends, he acted at their behest and would never listen to anyone before them."[44] But Asaf ud Daulah was helpless before his experienced and veteran mother Bahu Begum Sahiba. Immediately after his crowning (Masnad Nashini), he declared Lucknow as his final abode in 1775.[45] Even the mixed culture of Iran and Hindustan, which was the gift of Faizabad, had been touched by English influences by the time it reached Lucknow. The structure of the Lucknow Residency was built by Asaf ud Daulah.[46] But it was he who had to face its dire consequences. It was the duty of the occupants of the Residency to make arrangements for the entertainment and amusement of Asaf ud Daulah. The Nawab showed tremendous interest in English toys, watches, and other goods.[47] English traders charged extravagantly for such goods. Following their wishes, the Nawab often had to purchase goods he did not even require, merely for the sake of his residence. Additionally, servants were recruited from the lowest levels of English society.[48] The best way to please the Nawab was to be a partner in his entertainment

40. Supra note 29 at 222.

41. Supra note 35 at 12.

42. Maulvi Abdul Halim Sharar, *Guzishta Lucknow*. Nasim Book Depot. Lucknow. at p. 34, 35.

43. H.C. Irwin; *The Garden of India*. London. 87, 88.

44. Id at 87. *Guzishta Lucknow*, 34.

45. Id at 17, 34.

46. Id at 97, 98.

47. T.G.P. Spears; *The Nabobs*. London. (1932). 83.

48. Hon. F.J. Shore; *Notes on Indian Affairs*. London. (1837). Volume 2., at 83.

pursuits.[49] It is said that the huge amount spent on the Nawab's pets was sufficient to maintain a whole army, and there is also a mention of about 1000 dogs,[50] which were mainly influenced by foreign factors.[51] Soon the Nawab realized that in the name of hospitality for his honourable guests, he was being plundered. When he petitioned the Central Rulers about this, he was given some aid. But by that time, it was too late.[52] The dilution of western aroma in Lucknavi fragrance had begun, and soon Lucknow became the largest junction of Western and Eastern cultures. Out of the precincts of Avadh, there was bloodshed and devastation all over Hindustan, but within Avadh the atmosphere was one of peace and serenity. There was an abundance of wealth, luxury, and enjoyment; thus scholars, artists, and lovers of art were given a warm welcome here. Even the common man who entered the place had no worries for his livelihood. The phrase 'He who does not get from the Almighty, gets from Asaf ud Daulah' (*Jis Ko na de Maula uss ko de* Asaf ud Daulah) bore some reality in this period.[53] Faizabad could not become Shahjahanabad due to the untimely death of *Shuja-ud Daulah*, but his son

> "within days gathered all the paraphernalia and embellishment within his area (Lucknow), his only ambition being that whether it is the Nizam of Hyderabad or the courtyard of Tipu Sultan, neither the people nor the pomp or magnificence should exceed that of his own."[54]

Consequently, not only the pupils but even the princesses of the Mughals reached his court without any invitation. Asaf ud Daulah even

---

49. Emma Roberts;*Scenes and Characteristics of Hindustan*. London. (1837). Volume 2., at 353; Moreover there is a painting by Asaf ud Daulah's court painter *Zofani* which depicts the crowd engaged in chicken fight. (M. Edwards;*The Orchid House*. London. (1960). p.48).
50. W. Hoey; *History of Asafuddaoulah*. Oudh Government Press (1885) at 37, 38.
51. Supra note 49. at 83.
52. Supra note 45. at 97, 98.
53. The phrase is also understood as "Asaf ud Daulah gives to those who are recommended by the Almighty (Maula)".
54. Maulvi Abdul Halim Sharar; *Guzishta Lucknow*. Nasim Book Depot. Lucknow. at p. 15 citing *Tarikh Farah Baksh*.

fixed precious grants for them.[55] In exchange for the financial aid given to the Delhi Durbar,[56] the title[57] of *Wazir ul Mumalik* Asaf ud Daulah *Nawab Mohammad Yahya Khan* Bahadur *Huzbar Jung* was bestowed on him. The legacy established by Asaf ud Daulah carried on even after his death. Saa'dat Ali Khan gave a warm and affectionate welcome to all the Princesses who came [to his court]. The fact that he took care of their comforts personally demonstrates that, in spite of the baneful effect of the English, the rulers of Avadh still gave the deserving what was due. The elite treated the Princesses with princely treatment and the poets applauded the poets in a poet-like manner and never let anyone feel that they were migrants who came in need of their favour. This politeness and demureness of the people of Lucknow in dispelling the worries of strangers was exemplary, unmatched over the course of time. It was the individual opinion of those suffering from superiority complex who still spoke ill about the ambience in Lucknow.[58] Gradually, as a reaction to this egoistic behaviour, and in the quest for a luxurious lifestyle, inventions and discoveries were made in language, poetry, literature, costume, food, style, and fashion – in every aspect of life. Khan Aarzoo, who had brightened the literary world of Delhi, held the foremost position among the newcomers in Lucknow.[59] Poets like Sauda, Mir, Soz, Mir Hasan, Insha, Jurrat, MuShafi, and dozens of their contemporaries came to Lucknow and contributed to making or spoiling the literary ambience of Lucknow. Conflict came to an end due to the English, but to prove one's supremacy is human nature. To satisfy this instinct amidst the tumultuous

55. Supra note 52., at 80 and 89.

56. Supra note 45., at 87.

57. Wazir ul Sultan Mohammad Amir Ali KhanAmir; *Wazirnama*,Publication Nizami. Kanpur (1293 hijri) at 42.

58. Supra note 51. Volume 2. at 255–56. and D.D. Heber; *Narrative of a Journey Through Upper Provinces of India* (1824–25). London (1829) at 63.

59. Supra note 56. at 96.

atmosphere of KashMiris and poets, the Lucknow people distinguished themselves in the field of kite-flying and bird-fighting, which ultimately sowed the seed of Lucknavi culture.

The Rise of Shii'te

The propagation of Shii'te beliefs had a mentionable role in shaping the Lucknavi culture and Imambarah Asaf ud Daulah. The elegies by Mir Anis owe their existence to this historical movement. Lucknow, which is still regarded as the epicentre of Shii'te and the fountain of Shia beliefs and learnings, remains indebted to this movement. There were no clergymen (*Shia Mujtahid*) until the period of Asaf ud Daulah.[60] There was no separate congregation for namaz, and there was no remarkable difference in the maintaining of a replica of Imam Hussain (*Taaziadaari*[61]). There were Shia states in South Gujarat and Murshidabad, but they lacked the enthusiasm to propagate their beliefs. Perhaps nature had reserved this honour for the soil of Avadh: when Asaf ud Daulah steps upon this soil, then *Maulvi Dildar Ali* (Al Matufi 1235 A.H./1820) will come from Nasirabad, and under the patronage of this Darbar, after completing his own religious learning, would propagate *deen*:

> "All such services (purification of Shii'te beliefs, management of Shii'te groups, and giving a logical reply to opponents), rendered personally by *Ghufran Maa'b*, could be the lifetime achievement of any one person, but collectively rendering these services was the prerogative of this genius and which was not possible without the Divine blessings. Wherever there is knowledge and learning in Hindustan, it definitely reaches its culmination up to *Ghufran Maa'b Taab Sarah*."[62]

---

60. Maulana Syed Ali Naqi Sahab; *Janab Ghufran Maa'b*. Sarfraz Qaumi Press Lucknow (1378 hij.) at 4.

61. *Hindustan Mein Shiite Ki Tarikh*, at 19, 20.

62. Maulana Syed Ali Naqi Sahab; *Janab Ghufran Maa'b*. Sarfraz Qaumi Press. Lucknow. (1959) at 9, 10.

The first congregation of Namaz[63] under the Shia organization took place on 13 Rajab 1200 A.H. (1786), and the first Friday Prayer is reported to take place on 27 Rajab 1200 A.H. (1786).[64] The present form and popularity of *Taaziadaari* owes its origin to Janab *Ghufran Maa'b*:

> " ...and these rituals became so popular that it reached every doorstep, all the roads were flooded with *Taazia* processions, and in this way he gave a new identification and trend to *Shia Taaziadaari*, segregating it from common Muslims. Consequently he speeded up religious propagation, community organization, and advancement of *Shia* culture."[65]

Even today the ruins of Lucknow are reminiscent of the strong convictions of the townsmen of yesteryear, and are living evidence of the surging wave of Shii'te. There are hardly any places of pilgrimage in Iraq, Najaf, or Kaazmain, replica of which was not built in Lucknow. Up to the period of Asaf ud Daulah, his courtiers and other members of the elite class had mausoleums constructed for their final abode. Asaf ud Daulah (d. 1212 A.H./1797) was buried in his Imambarah (Constructed 1205 A.H./1791) and thereafter this tradition was followed by his descendants. Instead of building mausoleums, they constructed Imambarah*s* which, during the days of mourning (Muharram), encouraged the entry of crowds of believers who lit candles and witnessed religious fervour and brightness all around, thereby also giving a boost to the family prestige. The *Shia* sect was guided by two principles: '*tawalla*' meaning affection towards the family of the Prophet, and '*Tabarra*' meaning hatred towards the enemies and opponents of the Prophet's family. Although these took the form of traditions through Asafi Imambarah, due to pretensions and artificiality, they soon fell victim to

63. The Asafud Daulah era has special distinction of holding first Shia Namaz of Hindustani Shias. *Qudsi Jaisi.*

64. Zia Paash Sahab Posh; *Hindustan Mein Shiite Ki Tarikh*. Darul Tasnif. Karachi (1957). at 17.

65. Id. at p. 20.

profanation (*Bidaa't*). In poetry, *tawalla* is expressed in various forms, but the art of poetry which became immensely popular was elegy. Similarly, *tabarra* was also expressed in different forms, but *Harzia goi* was the hallmark of Lucknow poetry.[66] Sufism has no place in Shia belief. In the religious poetry of Lucknow, Sufism was presented in the form of '*tawalla*' and '*Tabarra*'. If the father dies in the lifetime of the grandfather, then the grandchild is devoid of inheritance. With the progress of Shii'te, the English – for their own political gain – gave special importance to this principle. Thus, during crowning ceremonies their decisions were always a matter of concern for the royal family.[67] *Mutaa* marriage has always been controversial, but was well accommodated in Lucknow culture. As per Shia belief, *Mutaa* and polygamy became popular. At the evolutionary stage of the rise of Shii'te, it was not possible to exceed the permissible limits, nor is there evidence to refute this statement. The participation of Asaf ud Daulah in the Holi festival[68] and the construction of the magnificent Imambarah by Jhau Lal[69] is a reflection of the religious harmony which originated at the time of Burhan ul Mulk and Safdar Jung. After Ghufra'n Maa'b and Asaf ud Daulah, religious harmony and impartiality started degrading. Up to the period of Nasiruddin, germs crept into Lucknow culture which bloomed under the banner of religion, and proved fatal for humanity and politics. Apparently, this was taken as religious advancement;

"Many Hindus were converted to Muslims and many Sunnis to Shias."[70]

The King was also not untouched by this. When furious, the King often passed orders that the house of the clergyman of the time be blown up

---

66. Maulvi Abdul Halim Sharar; *Guzishta Lucknow*. Nasim Book Depot. Lucknow at 107–9.
67. *See* the treatise of Captain White; Mirza *Kaiwan Jah*. London (1838) and *The Prince of Oude*. London (1838) Burgess.
68. W. Hoey; *History of Asafuddaulah*. Oudh Government Press. (1885) at 37.
69. Even to date the ruins of Jhau Lal's Imambarah are still famous and on *"Yauom e Gham"* (First of the month of Safar the religious processions are taken there).
70. Munshi Naval Kishore; *Tawarikh e Nadir ul Asar*. Publication: Munshi Naval Kishore at 112.

with a tank. Thus, the townsmen, following his dictates, managed to aim a tank at the clergyman's house, with the intention that the house of the religious head be blown up, while the house of the head of the state remains intact.[71] But in reality this progress was not the progress of religion – it was the fanaticism which had weakened the foundations of the Mughal Empire, and now it was Avadh's turn. To address the heads/rulers of non-Muslim states as low and vile[72] was a move to instigate the rulers to appoint Muslims to all high posts of the state, and its responsibility to be carried by the English. During the reign of Asaf ud Daulah, Raja Jhau Lal was forced to step down from his post, and it is said that Asaf ud Daulah was so shocked by this that it resulted in his death.[73] Allama Taffazul Hussain Khan was appointed as Jhau lal's successor.[74] Taffazul Hussain's first move was the dismissal and devastation[75] of Wazir Ali Khan, and his second move was to divide the state in the reign of Saa'dat Ali Khan. Soon Saa'dat Ali Khan "sent Taffazul Hussain to Calcutta as a lawyer, and in the same manner, he slowly and gradually punished those who were guilty of hurting and agonizing."[76]

However, the successors of Saa'dat Ali Khan lacked farsightedness, as if it had become a tradition to be devastated at the hands of minister.

SUBMISSION TO THE ENGLISH

Up to the pinnacle of Mughal Empire, issues of succession were resolved through the sword. By the time this tradition ended, the conspiracies in the court had caused the fracturing of the empire. Despite the bloodshed

71. Maulana Syed Ali Naqi Sahab;*Janab Rizwan Maa'b* Sarfraz Qaumi Press. Lucknow (1959). pp. 11, 12.

72. W. Hoey; *History of Asafuddaoulah*. Oudh Government Press (1885) p. 2, 3.

73. Munshi Naval Kishore; *Tawarikh e Nadir ul Asar*. Publication: Munshi Naval Kishore. pp. 70, 72.

74. Id.

75. Id., at 73, 75.

76. Id. at 78.

caused by this internal strife, the unity of the empire remained intact. Even the most rebellious official would submit before one who claimed to be skilled in swordsmanship. In Avadh, those who aspired to the throne were never powerful or mighty enough to fight for their rights. They used all their resources to please their superiors and benefactors. Conceding to any conditions set by the English was considered a good way to achieve their goals, and they were ready to pay an exorbitant amount of wealth to them.[77] The well-wishers of the empire were also not so loyal as to prefer selfless service to personal gain. It was very easy for the powerful to prove an upright officer as dishonest and a legitimate child as illegitimate. These unpleasant events started to surface from the time that Asaf ud Daulah was crowned. The more power-hungry the contenders became, the more significance the crowning ceremony gained. Asaf ud Daulah had the right,[78] but not the ability,[79] to rule over the empire. He was apprehensive about his brother Saa'dat Ali Khan. The Company Bahadur was successful in soliciting both an agreement and a grant from him. Later, his son, Wazir Ali Khan, acceded to the throne, but the English soon realized that he was not a puppet. To dismiss him from power, they did not collect even the amount of evidence that is required to evict a tenant.[80] This was because Saa'dat Ali Khan was ready to surrender two thirds of the empire in order to gain one third of it. Saa'dat Ali Khan managed his remaining empire with administrative acumen and was regarded the best administrator of his times – though his critics say that his period was the most indolent era.[81] However he was so harassed himself that, like Asaf ud Daulah,[82] he decided to get rid of the administration.[83] These early

77. For details see Captain Bird's Book; *Dacoitee in Excelsis*. London. (1857).

78. A.L. Shrivastava; *Shujaud-daulah*. Lahore (1945). Volume 1., at 293.

79. Syed Kamal ud din Haider Alias Mir Zair; *Qaiser ul Tawarikh*. Publication: Munshi Naval Kishore. Lucknow. Volume 1., at 91–92.

80. H.C. Irwin; *The Garden of India*. London., at 100.

81. Id., at 103–110.

82. Id., at 90. and supra note 73 at 70.

83. Id., at 103–104.

submissions to the English are sufficient to make clear that the lost country was not restored to Shuja ud Daulah with the aim that his descendants would continue to rule undisturbed. As head of the administration, the English did not want to lose a single opportunity to expand their authority and to undermine, weaken, and disrepute the rulers of Avadh.

SEVERANCE FROM DELHI

The *subedari* of Avadh or any other state did not imply it as the personal asset of the *subedar* which could be passed on to his successors. In fact, it was the prerogative of the central government to bestow it on anyone they wished. Safdar Jung acquired it through the payment of two crore rupees.[84] This was the reason that the empire of Avadh was regarded as the purchased personal property[85] of the buyer. Shuja ud Daulah did not need confirmation from the central government. The central government had become so weak that it, in fact, needed Shuja ud Daulah. Hastings even advised him to declare his emperorship, but he bluntly refused to do so.[86] It was his policy that he should not do something which benefits others, but where he himself would gain nothing but a meaningless title. By the time of Ghaziuddin, circumstances had changed; there was neither a state nor an army. In such a situation bestowing kingship was thought as the best way to ruin someone who aspired to become a King. Before becoming King, Ghaziuddin Haider had already granted two crore rupees and huge military assistance to the English.[87] There was still a huge amount of accumulated wealth from his father in the state exchequer.[88] This amount was enough for royal pomp and pageantry. Thus, on 9 October 1819 (1235 A.H.), Ghaziuddin Haider

84. A.L. Shrivastava; *The First Two Nawabs of Avadh*. Lucknow (1933) at 92.

85. Israr e Wajidi (Handwritten) p. 494., and *Khulasai-Tarikh*. at12.

86. A.L. Shrivastava; *Shujaud-daulah*. Lahore (1945). Volume 2. At 223.

87. M.T. Ahmed; *Tarikh Badshah Begum*. Lucknow at 49–54.

88. Supra note 83 at 11; and *Tarikh e Aftaab e Avadh* (Handwritten) at 94.

was declared King.[89] The crown and the attire sent from England was such an honour[90] that his flattery and appeasement of the English was no longer a surprise. But apart from this temporary appreciation, and, as quoted by some, the revengeful action of Lord Mayra,[91] the nominal relationship with Delhi, which had been beneficial for both, came to an end. The Avadh people thought that the English were well-wishers of their empire hence the empire would only prosper if English too exist. However, the empire did prosper but this progress was of luxury, of pomp and of hostility. The influx of educated men from Delhi came almost to an end during Ghaziuddin Haider's time, and those who were born in Lucknow began drifting from those arts and artifacts which carried the flavour of Delhi.[92]

SUBJUGATION AND CAPITULATION

The gradual and indiscernible movement to subjugate the rulers of Avadh in the name of their welfare and that of the people of Avadh continued. The only difference was that, as per the Agreement of 1775, this was done covertly, under the guise of friendship. The English changed their style, from friendship they apparently changed to guardianship and from 1837 they openly started getting hold of the empire. All the levels of the state administration from royals to ministers were deserving as well as undeserving. . There were often parochial-minded, ambitious, and shrewd Governor Generals, who implemented the policies of the Company. But one thing which did not change was the subjugation, helplessness, and submissiveness

89. Wazir ul Sultan Mohammad Amir Ali Khan Amir; *Wazirnama*. Publication Nizami. Kanpur(1293 hijri) p. 62.

90. Id at 61.

91. Syed Kamal ud din Haider Alias Mir Zair; *Qaiser ul Tawarikh*. Publication: Munshi Naval Kishore.Lucknow. Volume 1. pp. 91–92.

92. D.D. Heber; *Narrative of a Journey through the Upper Provinces of India*.(1824–25). London. (1929) p. 69. and Emma Roberts; *Scenes and Characteristics of Hindustan*. London (1837). pp. 365–66.

of the rulers of Avadh. To remain subservient to the English had become characteristic of the Kings of Avadh.[93] If any ruler ever thought of protesting, the conspiracies of the court stood in their way.[94] The involvement of the King in pastimes which did not impede the authority of the English was provided solace to every rival, and there was an attempt to maintain a congenial atmosphere, so that it did not give an opportunity to any rival to complain against. Human beings are, by nature, easily attracted to religious and cultural pursuits. These are not harmful for anyone. The inhabitants of Hindustan had a natural liking for feasts, congregations, fairs, and plays[95] and special blessings of religion and luck enhanced this. Thus, to keep the enthusiasm of both rulers and subjects alive, many options were explored, which were otherwise not possible. Religious leaders like Sultan ul Ulema Syed Muhammad Sahab, kings like Wajid Ali Shah, loyalists like Rajab Ali Beg Suroor, elegists like Mir Anis, writers like Nawab Mirza Shauk, poets like Aatish and Nasikh, and dancers like Kalka and Bindadin, were the creations of Lucknavi culture, without which these masterpieces, which have a place of pride in the culture and civilization of Hindustan, would have died before their birth. The services of these great men were an indispensable part of life for over a hundred years. They spanned every facet of life, including religion, etiquette, cordiality, conversation, and daily living, reaching the pinnacle of subtlety and delicacy.

The impact of a country's politics on its culture is not a new phenomenon. If there was something new, then it was that the King's nominal character. Though the administration was carried in his name, but the Resident acted according to his own whims and caprices. Such a dual system caused maladministration, ruining reputations of both. Collaboration between the

---

93. The Books of Masihuddin and Bird, Bluebook and English magazine "The Calcutta Review"(Volume 1, 1844) and the Essays of Sir Hans Lawrence (Volume 3, 1845) are enlightening on the subject. Details are obviously avoided.

94. Supra note 95 at 79, 80.

95. Read *The Travellings of Roberts and Parks.*

Resident and the King was possible only if both were acting in good faith, and looking at the political conditions of the country; this rarely happened.[96] In the face of discord, it all depended on the nature of the issue, whether the King would withdraw or the Resident would remain adamant in his decision. The King was left with no choice but to silently submit to the desirable or undesirable interruptions. The Kings of Avadh, by resorting to such traditional compliance and by making all sorts of sacrifices, saved their empire.[97] During the imperialism of Lord Dalhousie, when small states were being devastated under petty pretexts, the English were not in need of sacrifices, but of empire. The upheaval of the Avadh empire anticipated a great revolution both in the life of the King and his subjects. But in the face of helplessness and compliance, this incident was also no less than what had already occurred in the past. The only difference was that the King and his supporters neither protested against it nor did they accept it. In respect to not protesting, they followed the people of Delhi, but in not accepting it they proved that in spite of being lovers of luxury and lavish lifestyles, they still cared for the empire as their own, and wished for its survival. The boundaries of the Mughal empire, which once extended from Arabian Sea to the Bay of Bengal, with the favours of the English, were shrivelled up to the walls of Red Fort. There was a common feeling among the supporters of the empire that somehow the throne must remain intact.[98] Before the patronizing of English, the boundaries of Avadh had the Ganges and the Yamuna in their bosom, but under the influence of this foreign power, they too were reduced to the banks of Ghagra and Gomti. Had Wajid Ali Shah desired, this would have been circumscribed up to the four walls of Qaiser Bagh, but this was neither acceptable to him nor to his subjects.

---

96. H.C. Irwin; *The Garden of India*. London at 95.

97. Hon. F.J. Shore; *Notes on Indian Affairs*. London. (1837) at 84.

98. Akhbar Rangeen at 5–19.

REVOLT AND END OF LUCKNOWISM

The turmoil of the empire was expected. In August 1855, some two hundred powerful individuals held a secret meeting and decided that to prevent the upheaval, one and a half lakh pounds should be given to satisfy the greed of the employees of the East India Company. Their unanimous verdict was that "*Firangis* love gold and the people of Avadh like their freedom more than it..."[99] To implement this declaration, they published secret pamphlets and got busy revolting against the British and safe-guarding Avadh.[100] Wajid Ali Shah did not encourage such people.[101] However this movement continued without his support. In the upheaval of 1857, these covert movements became public. The Residency's building was destroyed in their fury. The narrator writes that the flag bearers of freedom had the wish "to dig it into a pond."[102] But before their wish could materialize, the factors which had made Wajid Ali Shah bear all excesses with silence were ultimately revealed;[103] more than half of Lucknow was turned into debris,[104] ancient dynasties were

---

99. J.M. Ludlow; *British India*. 2 Volumes. Cambridge. 1858. Volume 2 at 208.

100. G.D. Bhatnagar; *Administration of Oudh Under* Wajid Ali Shah. Thesis for Ph.D. in Lucknow University, at 198–99.

101. Supra note 94. Volume 2. at 174–75.

102. Id. at 233.

103. Sabatul Quloob (Manuscript) Volume 1., at 26, 27. This devastation in the words of *Anis* is as follows:

The door which enriched the whole world
Is destroyed and the house is devastated
Neither the inmates nor the house remained
earth is uprooted the change is so formidable
O! destiny the lightning struck that field where I had one grain of my fate

104. Khwaja Arshad Ali Khan Qalq. Publication: Karnama. Lucknow. (1289 hij).

More than three part of the city is excavated
As far as one can see it is all haunted
There where hundreds used to stroll
People stumble down all over
They loiter like strangers
even the residents don't find the way

ruined,[105] the worth of poetry and literature were changed,[106] and the revolution which was to reveal itself slowly carried away that which is called "the last specimen of eastern civilization"[107] in its furious deluge.

105. *Tarikh e Firaq* (Manuscript). p. 194–96

106. Munshi Amirullah Tasleem;

Tasleem !*Poetry continued up to the royal era*
now in what hope to expect appreciation of art

Mir Anis;

Not only one portion of Lucknow is uprooted
There is revolution also in the world of poetry

107. Maulvi Abdul Halim Sharar; *Guzishta Lucknow.* Nasim Book Depot. Lucknow. at 5.

TWO

Biography

BIRTH

There is a difference of opinion among historians not only about the personality of Wajid Ali Shah, but also regarding his name, date of birth, and death. In history books, the popular name is Wajid Ali Shah, although his true name was Mohammad Wajid Ali[1] – with the addition of Shah, this became Wajid Ali Shah. This style is seen in royal manuscripts and writings.[2] People use Wajid Ali Shah for the sake of convenience. According to his courtyard commentator, Saqib, his date of birth is 10 Rabi ul Sani 1243 A.H.[3] From the autobiography written during the beginning of Wajid Ali Shah's reign, from self-written manuscripts, and from other statements, it is evident that Saqib was mistaken, and Wajid Ali Shah was

---

1. *See Guldastan e Aashiqan-* Title Page Meerza Md. Wajid Ali Shah Akhtar Muhammadi Publishers. Lucknow (1259 A.H.) (Anjuman Khuda Baksh).
2. In the India Office Library list the Writings are entered under the term "Muhammad."
3. In Bhatnagar's Thesis with reference to and contradicting Zehd ul kawaif (Manuscript), Compilation 1276h.

born much before the given date. Some writers regard 10 Zeeqad 1237 A.H. as his date of birth.[4] In present times, this is regarded as the correct date.[5] But had this been correct, Wajid Ali Shah would have been aged twenty-six at the time of his coronation in 1263 A.H. But, other than Mirza Rajab Ali Beg Suroor,[6] commentators mention he was twenty-five.[7] There is strong evidence favouring this age (twenty-five) as correct. Wajid Ali Shah was born in Lucknow[8] on 10 Zeeqad 1238 A.H., corresponding to 19 July 1833.[9] Hence, he was coroneted in the beginning weeks of his twenty-fifth year.[10]

---

4. Manuscript: *Sultan ul Nikayat-* 475. *Qaisa rulTawarikh-* Syed Kamal Hussain Haider Alias Mir Zair; *Qaisar ul Tawarikh.* Publication: Munshi Naval Kishore. Lucknow. (1907) Volume 2, 6.

5. *Lucknow ka Shahi* Stage, Prof. Syed Masood Hasan Rizvi Adeeb, Kitab Nagar Lucknow. 1957 13 and 66: Bhatnagar G.D.: *Administration of Avadh Under* Wajid Ali Shah. (Article) Ph.D. Thesis, Lucknow University (Tagore) Article, 1 as referred to in Mir*at ul Avadh,* 475.

6. *Fasan e Ibrat,* Mirza Rajab Ali Beg Suroor, Published by Najmul Uloom Karnama, 1884, 57.

7. *Iqtidar ud Daulah Muhtashamul Mulk Mehdi Ali Khan* Bahadur: *Tarikh e Iqtedaria* (Manuscript): Vol. 2, 227; Mirza Md. Taqi: *Aftab e Avadh,* (Manuscript) 1874–75, 143; Munshi Zahiruddin Bilgrami: *Israr e Wajdi* (Manuscript)1266–78 A.H. (Tagore), 302; Munshi Ram Sahay Tamanna: *Ehsanul Tawarikh,* Tammanai Publication, Lucknow, 1259 A.H., 4; Munshi Ram Sahay Tamanna: *Afzal ul Tawarikh,* Tammanai Publication, Lucknow, 1879, 98; *Kanwar Durga Prasad Sandelvi: Boostan e Avadh,* Ahmedi Publication, Lucknow 1892, 137; *Abbas* Mirza*:* Manuscript *Alhasnul Mateen fi Tarikh ul Salateen*, 1281 A.H. (Society)164b; Mirza Md. Zaki Ali Khan Zaki Lakhnavi: *Akhtar Jinan,* Lucknow, 1305 A.H. Jafri Publication, 45

8. Munshi Zahiruddin Bilgrami: *Israr e Wajdi* (Manuscript) 1266–78 A.H. (Tagore), 302; *Abbas* Mirza: Manuscript *Alhasnul Mateen fi Tarikh ul Salateen* (Manuscript)1281 A.H.(Society)*164b*; Syed Kamaluddin Haider Alias Mir Zair (Compiler/Translator): *Taqweem e Sultani Sultani Publication, Lucknow* 1265 A.H., 68; Mirza Md. Zaki Ali Khan Zaki Lakhnavi: *Akhtar Jinan,* Lucknow,1305 A.H. Jafri Publication. 45; Maulvi Md. Najmul Ghani Khan: *Taree kh e Avadh,* Munshi Naval Kishore Publication, Lucknow. 1919. Volume 5, 45; Md. Taqi Ahmed: Wajid Ali Shah, Adabi Press, Lucknow, 1945.

9. In the forthcoming sections wherever there is mention of A.H. and A.D. in bracket it is as per Taqweem. A.H.; and A.D. Published by AnjumanTarraqi e Urdu (Hind) Delhi. 46;

10. At page 5 in *Majmuey Wajidia Sultani*–Muhammad Wajid Ali Shah Akhtar Publisher Sultani – Lucknow 1267 A.H. (Avadh, Tagore) King's age is referred to as twenty-nine in 1267 A.H. This is possible only when his date of birth is 1238h.

FAMILY

Amjad Ali Shah was Wajid Ali Shah's father and Malka Kishwer was his mother. At the time of Wajid Ali Shah's birth, Ghaziuddin Haider was the ruler of Avadh. He was his grandfather, Muhammad Ali Shah's, elder brother. During the reign of Saa'dat Ali Khan, Muhammad Ali Shah, who was his father's *Naib*[11] (representative), and Ghaziuddin Haider, who was his heir, were devoid of their father's attention.[12] It was a repetition of history; like the hostility between *Asaf ud Daula* and his younger brother Saa'dat Ali Khan after *Shuja ud Daula's* death, the same animosity was seen between Ghaziuddin Haider and his other brothers after the death of Saa'dat Ali Khan. This bitterness increased so much that one of the brothers migrated to Benares.[13] Although the other brother preferred to stay in Lucknow, he was not involved in governmental affairs, nor did he receive any grants from the royal treasury.[14] Until Rabi ul Sani 1253 A.H. (1837), when Nasiruddin Haider died, there was little hope that Muhammad Ali Shah could ever become the King of Avadh, or that Amjad Ali Shah would be his successor.

Wajid Ali Shah was the eldest son of his parents,[15] and thus he was their dearest. His mother had dressed him like a monk at the time of his *Chhahti* (6th-day ritual after birth).[16] Their bond was so strong that at the time of

---

11. Syed Kamal Hussain Haider Alias Mir Zair: *Qaisar ul Tawarikh.* Publication Munshi Naval Kishore. Lucknow. 1907 Vol.1., 156; Munshi Naval Kishore: *Tawarikh Nadir ul Asr,* Munshi Naval Kishore Publication, Lucknow 1863, 87.

12. Heber, D.D.: *Narrative of a Journey through the Upper Provinces of India.* (1824–25) London. 1829, 77.

13. *Qaiserul Twarikh* Syed Kamal Hussain Haider Alias Mir Zair; *Qaisar ul Tawarikh.* Publication: Munshi Naval Kishore. Lucknow. 1907. Vol. 1., 215.

14. Nijat Hussain Khan Azimabadi: *Sawaneh Lucknow* (Manuscript) 1259 A.H. Patna University Library, 371.

15. Syed Kamal Hussain Haider Alias Mir Zair; *Qaisar ul Tawarikh.* Publication: Munshi Naval Kishore. Lucknow. (1907) Vol.1, 12.

16. Munshi Naval Kishore: *Tawarikhe Nadir ul Asr*, Publication: Munshi Naval Kishore, Lucknow 1863, 126.

the upheaval of the empire, his mother was at his side and personally visited London to advocate for his cause. Wajid Ali Shah's younger brother, Meerza Muhammad Jawad Ali, accompanied her. Both of them died in Europe and were buried in Paris.[17]

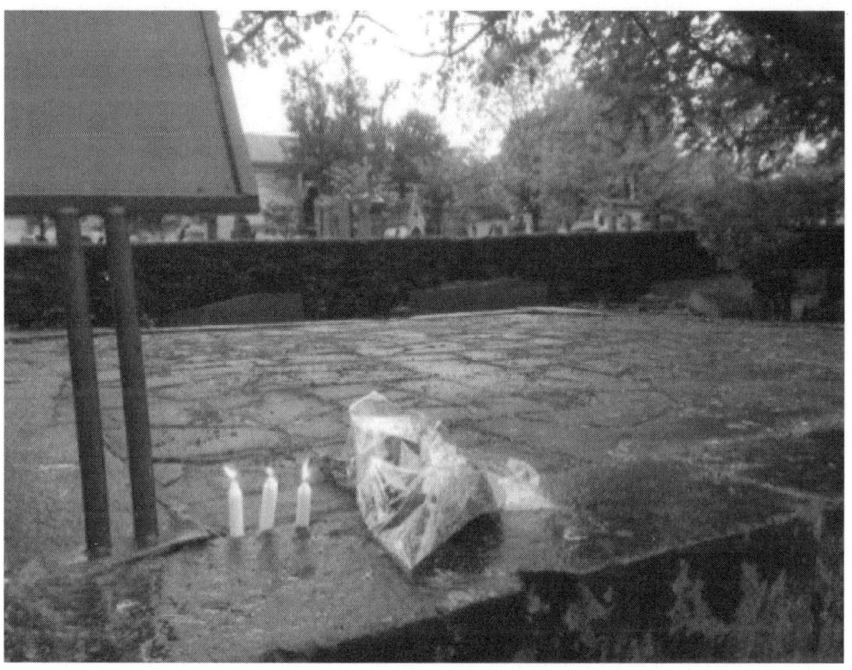

Grave of Malka Kishwer in Père Lachaise Cemetery, Paris, France.
Photo Courtesy: Aman Ahsan Khan, great-great-great grandson of Wajid Ali Shah. (May 22, 2016. On the occasion of Shab e Barat)

Wajid Ali Shah also had a sister, who was younger than the brothers, and was buried at her father's side in Lucknow. Historians have particularly appreciated the looks and personality of Amjad Ali Shah and Malka Kishwer. Wajid Ali Shah inherited all the attributes of his parents. Like his elders, he

17. Maulvi Masihuddin Khan: *Safeer e Avadh*, Al Nazir Press, Lucknow, 1929, 101–102.

was a religious person, a flag-bearer of tradition, handsome, kind-hearted, and the embodiment of acceptance and compassion.[18]

EDUCATION

Wajid Ali Shah was brought up with great indulgence and amidst lavish surroundings. Historians have recorded his childhood incidents in a perfect manner, though he was not given due importance during his childhood. Nevertheless, the genius of the King was revealed during his early years. The compiler of the *Wazir Nama* explains thus:

> In a very short time he studied and developed proficiency over the books prescribed in the curriculum of that time and joined his very brilliant and able teachers. Due to his extraordinary calibre, brilliance and genius he soon achieved mastery over the entire curriculum.[19]

Another historian regards it as a progressive and oriental education, and specifically mentions the ancient and modern history and literature.[20] Through the statements of other historians, it is further confirmed that Wajid Ali Shah was an intelligent man and could learn new things with little effort.[21] Among the learned teachers, only one name – Maulvi Imdad Hussain Khan – was mentioned by Wajid Ali Shah. He taught him two books, entitled *Meezan ul Tibb* and *Sharah e Asbab.*[22] On the basis of his merit and achievements, the title "Ameen Udd Daulah Amdatul Mulk Imdad

18. For further details *see* Manuscript *Israar e Wajidi*; Manuscript *Aftab e Avadh*; Manuscript *Muraqa e Khusravi* and *Jaan e Alam.*

19. Wazirul Sultan Md. Amir Ali Khan Amir: *Wazirnama*,. Nizami Publication. Kanpur 1293 A.H. 97. (Persian extract translated here).

20. Masihuddin, 79. (English phrase is liberal Eastern education)

21. Mirza Md. Taqi: *Aftab e Avadh* (Manuscript),1874–75 (Tagore).

22. Md. Wajid Ali Shah Akhtar: *Ishq Nama* (Poetry- Manuscript) 1266 A.H. (Anjuman). Hamid Hasan Qadri: *Daastan Tarikh e Urdu,* Laxmi Narayan Agarwal Publication, Agra. 1941, 15. Prof. Syed Masood Hasan Rizvi Adeeb: *Lucknow ka Shahi Stage*, Kitab Nagar, Lucknow. 1957, 13.

Hussain Khan Bahadur Zulfiqar Jung" was then bestowed upon Maulvi Sahab.[23] For his poetic pursuits, Wajid Ali Shah was under the guidance of Barq Lucknavi. In music, he received lessons from Qutb Ali Khan Rampuri.[24] Both of these great men were considered masters in their respective fields. Apart from this, Barq was an expert in equestrian sports, and Qutb Ali Khan had command over Arabic, Persian, and poetry.[25] During the royal period, they were bestowed with titles and high status, and had considerable influence over Wajid Ali Shah's personality.[26]

WIVES

The reign of Nasiruddin Haider is often called the youth of Lucknow.[27] This was also the period of Wajid Ali Shah's youth. In his self-written account, Wajid Ali Shah relates in detail both his love relations and his marriage. The marriage was likely held in the month of Rajab/Shaban, 1253 A.H. (1837), when he was fifteen. The wedding was lavish.[28] The bride was from a respected and rich family from Lucknow, and was five years elder to him.[29] Various sources claim her name was Alam Ara Begum. Her pen name was Alam, her alias was Nawab Khas Mahal, and her title was Badshah Mahal. She was a good sitar player.[30]

This marriage heralded a promising future for Wajid Ali Shah. With the death of Nasiruddin Haider, the family's hardships from living an artificial

---

23. Lalji Wald Seetal Prashad: *Sultan ul Hikayat* (Manuscript), 1270 A.H. (Raza), 427.
24. Md. Wajid Ali Shah Akhtar: *Ishq Nama* (Poetry-Manuscript), 1266 A.H. (Anjuman). *Daastan*, 17.
25. *Ibid.*
26. *Ibid*; Mirza Rajab Ali Beg Suroor: Sarwar *Sultani*, Maseehai Publication, Lucknow 1268 A.H., 4–5: Lalji Wald Seetal Prashad: *Sultan ul Hikayat* (Manuscript), 1270 A.H. (Raza), 487.
27. Md. Ahad Ali: *Shabab Lucknow,* Al Nazir Press. Lucknow 1912. 2, 33–38.
28. Md. Wajid Ali Shah Akhtar: *Ishq Nama* (Manuscript; Poetry Persian) 1265 A.H. (Mahmoodabad); *Daastan Tarikh e Urdu,* Laxmi Narayan Agarwal Publication, Agra. 1941, 5.
29. Oudh Pension Papers, B.S. Press, Calcutta 1913, 5.
30. Maulvi Abdul Ghafoor Nisakh: *Sukhan Shoara,* Munshi Naval Kishore Press, Lucknow, 1874, 576.

social life came to an end, and Muhammad Ali Shah was coroneted. After marriage, Wajid Ali Shah gained the freedom which he had aspired to for so long. This freedom nurtured his love for poetry and gave him a life of opulence and luxury. When Amjad Ali Shah became the successor, he fixed a five-hundred-rupee monthly allowance for his son and a four-hundred-rupee allowance for his daughter-in-law.[31] This amount was enough for a lavish lifestyle, and Wajid Ali Shah was not hesitant to spend it accordingly.

Within five years of marriage, four children were born from this union.[32] In addition, Wajid Ali Shah contracted other *nikahs* and *mutahs*, and more children were born.[33] The *Nikah* which is mentioned in many historical treatises was contracted with Wazirzadi Nawab Raunaq Ara Begum on 5 Shaaban, 1267 A.H. (1851). She was the cousin of Wajid Ali Shah's first wife, Alam Ara Begum, and the King bestowed upon Raunaq Ara Begum the title of Akhtar Mahal.[34] Alam Ara Begum's father was Nawab Ali Taqi Khan,[35] and Raunaq Ara Begum's father was Nawab Ali Naqi Khan. Both were the sons of Ashraf ud Daulah Nawab Ahmed Ali Khan and the grandsons of Madarul Maham Madar ul Daula Mukhtar ul Mulk Nawab Syed Yusuf Samsam Jung.[36] Akhtar Mahal was a minor at the time of her marriage, and gave birth to only one child (male) after the fall of the empire,[37] who died during the lifetime of Wajid Ali Shah.[38]

31. Md. Wajid Ali Shah Akhtar: *Ishq Nama* (Manuscript; Poetry Persian) 1265 A.H. (Mahmoodabad); *Daastan Tarikh e Urdu,* Laxmi Narayan Agarwal Publication, Agra. 1941, 5.

32. *Ibid* 7, 8, 10 and 12.

33. For detail See, Md.Wajid Ali Shah Akhtar: Behre Mukhtalif. Mustafai Publication. Calcutta. 1277 A.H. (Avadh)

34. Syed Md. Azmat Ali alvi Naami Kakorvi: *Murraqa e Khusravi* (Manuscript) 1286 A.H. (Tagore), 195.

35. Mirza Fida Ali Khanjar: *Mahal Khan a e Shahi,* Nami Press, Lucknow, 1934, 13. (In other books only Nawab Ali Khan is mentioned).

36. Wazir ul Sultan Md. Amir Ali Khan Amir: *Wazir Nama,* Nizami Publication, Kanpur. 1293 A.H., 6.

37. Md. Wajid Ali Shah Akhtar: *Huzn e* Akhtari,Sultani Publication, Calcutta 1276 A.H. (Azad,Avadh National Library, Calcutta), 84–85.

38. Oudh Pension Papers, B.S. Press, Calcutta 1913, 5.

CHILDREN

After Shuja ud Daulah, Wajid Ali Shah is said to have the largest number of children. For brevity, names of only those princesses who became famous are mentioned here. Of these, four princesses, including Meerza Khush Bakht Bahadur, died in the lifetime of the King, and there were no issues related to inheritance. Some princesses had titles, and also produced compilations of their written works. Out of these, the compilations of Kaukab, Huzbur, and Anjum have been published. Some of the Ghazals are famous even today.

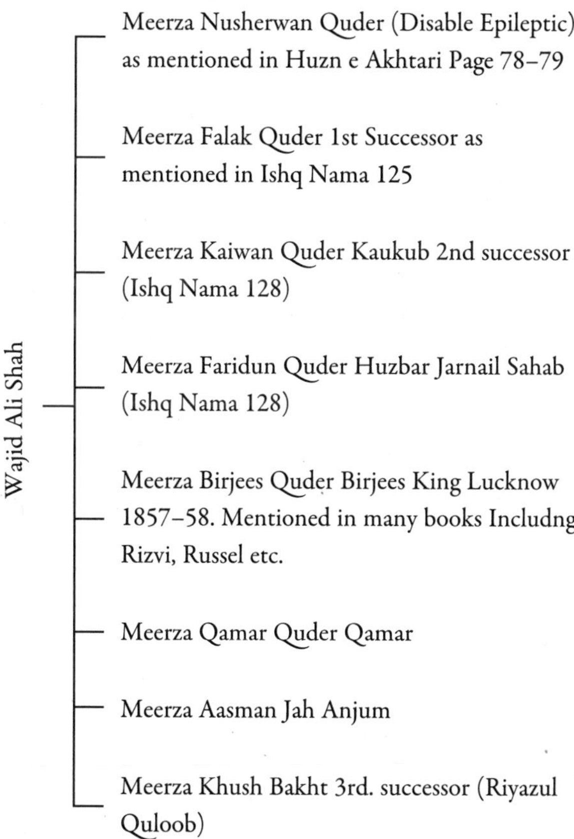

Table A – Showing Children of Wajid Ali Shah

SUCCESSION

On 10 *Rabi ul Sani* 1258 A.H. (21 May 1842), after the coronation of Amjad Ali Shah, Wajid Ali Shah was given the title of Abul Mansoor Sikander Jah Sulaiman Hasham Sahab Alam Wali Ahad Meerza Muhammad Wajid Ali Bahadur, and assumed new responsibilities.[39] Barq has analysed these responsibilities as ministerial affairs.[40] Wajid Ali Shah himself regarded them as a royal service.[41] Every day after the Morning Prayer, he was present in the courtyard, heard petitions, passed orders, and listened to the pleas of his subjects.[42] He also gathered knowledge about governmental affairs and utilized his own abilities accordingly, which was not an easy job. In the works of contemporary historians, there is no mention of the fact that Wajid Ali Shah was in any way reluctant to perform his duties or that he defaulted in his responsibilities.

During his formative years, Wajid Ali Shah's personal life did not change much; in fact, he had sufficient funds and full freedom to pursue his interests, and to achieve his goals. Those who were hopeful and optimistic about his succession had an opportunity to rise in the eyes of the new heir, and did a lot to achieve this. In his autobiography, Wajid Ali Shah mentions specific anecdotes relating to this. The work of *Parikhana* and the appointment of its staff,[43] meeting with *Ali Naqi*,[44] the organization of meetings and fairs,[45] and educating army units on the rules (in Persian)[46] were some of the practices

39. Lalji Wald Seetal Prashad: *Sultan ul Hikayat* (Manuscript), 1270 A.H. (Raza), 426.
40. Md. Wajid Ali Shah Akhtar: *Sabatul Quloob* (Manuscript), 1304 A.H. (Avadh) Volume 1, 26.
41. *Ishq Nama* (Poetry Manuscript), Daastan, 23.
42. Prof. Syed Masood Hasan Rizvi Adeeb: *Lucknow ka Shahi Stage,* 13 (as referred to in Tazuk e Shahi (treatise 1265h.) Kitab Nagar, Lucknow 1957.
43. Supra note 32. *Daastan Tarikh e Urdu,* Laxmi Narayan Agarwal Publication, Agra. 1941, 26–27.
44. *Ibid*, 25.
45. *Ibid*, 87, 89, 95.
46. *Ibid*, 63.

which were associated with excellence and artistry, and yielded perfect results during his reign. Poetry and music reached new heights during this period. The King mentioned that he invested lakhs of rupees in nurturing these interests.[47] However he also mentioned that his income was insufficient when compared to these expenditures.[48] Though he had full control over the royal treasury, there was paucity of funds with respect to his ambitions.

ROYALTY

Wajid Ali Shah was coroneted on 13 February 1847 at about 9 PM.[49] The initial period of Wajid Ali Shah's reign is significant as he sent an alarming message to his opponents.

> *In the beginning he used to indicate such intricacies in the title deeds and financial papers that even the sharpest minds were awestruck.*[50]

He also showed generosity of the highest order as seen below:

> "That day (while going to Dargah) he had thrown one lakh ten thousand rupees"[51]

In matters of justice, other than "*Mashgalae Sultani Adl e Nausherwani*",[52] he received great appreciation not only for content but also for language, style of writing and way of presentation. Whenever he met a complainant, he

47. Mirza Fida Ali Khanjar: *Mahal Khan a e Shahi*, Nami Press,Lucknow, 1934., 108–109, 115.

48. Ibid, 73.

49. Syed Kamaluddin Haider Alias Mir Zair (Compiler/Translator): *Taqweem e Sultani*, Sultani Publication, Lucknow 1265 A.H., 68.

50. Mirza Md. Taqi: *Aaftab e Avadh* (Manuscript)1874–75.(Tagore), 143–144.

51. Iqtidar ud DaulahMuhtashamul Mulk Mehdi Ali Khan Bahadur: *Tarikh e Iqtedaria* (Manuscript): Vol. 2, 228.

52. Supra note 50 at 143.

would immediately give him his undivided attention.[53] Usually, subjects pay this kind of attention to their king. This quality made him popular among all, regardless of status. His popularity continued because whenever he came across his subjects, he continued with his usual decent manner of dealing with them.[54] His style of administration and goodwill towards the people was irreparably harmed by sycophants who pretended to be well-wishers. One such group consisted of politicians, whose shrewdness caused the King to slowly drift away from governmental affairs. Another group consisted of a handful of luxury-loving people, who began to behave arbitrarily after receiving the titles, positions, and status that they had been waiting for since his coronation. The former group was sincere, but they were not aware of King's nature. The latter group showed arrogance and lacked knowledge.

As a result of the conspiracy of this second, self-indulgent group, which was headed by Qutb Ali Khan Rampuri and the head of state affairs, Maharaj Bal Krishan,[55] Nawab Ali Naqi Khan was appointed as minister in place of Nawab Amin ud Daula on 5 August 1847. *Nawab Ali Naqi* was an inexperienced man. After his appointment, mismanagement led to a strange and bitter relationship between the King and the Resident, which ultimately resulted in the devastating end of the empire.[56] Being naïve, the Nawab failed to run the administration smoothly, and concentrated mainly on three things: firstly, on how to please the King, who was hard-headed and did not care a straw for anyone when keeping his words;[57] secondly, on satisfying the Resident, who was unhappy about his appointment; and thirdly, on how to keep the group responsible for his appointment busy with their own selfish recreations.

---

53. Munshi Ram Sahay Tamanna: *Afzalul Tawarikh*: *Tamanna*: *Publication Tamni, Lucknow, 1879,* 103.

54. Supra note 50 at 144.

55. Syed Md. Azmat Ali Alvi Naami Kakorvi: *Muraqa e Khusravi*, 1286 A.H. (Tagore), 177–178.

56. Bhatnagar G.D.: *Administration of Avadh Under* Wajid Ali Shah. (Article) Ph.D. Thesis, Lucknow University (Tagore), 51.

57. *Ishq Nama* (poetry/manuscript) Dastan 88.

Although, he did not succeed in any of his pursuits, he held this position as long as the King's rule lasted.

In the beginning of his rule, Wajid Ali Shah drifted away from engaging in governmental affairs. Apparently, the main reason behind this was that physicians advised the King not to take too much mental pressure due to the various maladies he was suffering from.[58] The expert physicians were well aware of his illness and its causes. From the very beginning, the King remained connected with those affairs which befitted his stature. This was lauded by the masses, but frowned upon by the sycophants who surrounded him. Management of military affairs along modern lines and equipping units with the latest technology was one such engagement. The King took over upgrading the forces on a larger scale. Based on the information given by the Governor General, there were four hundred cannons, five thousand cannon operators, and forty-four thousand infantry men.[59] The King himself named them as Akhtari and Nadri, and stated that there were three thousand riders. The Rule Book in English was not to his liking.

The rules were written in Persian[60] and many hours each day were devoted to composing them.[61] The Resident did not like this, and when the King came to know about this, he drifted away from the task.[62] By the end of the year, the King had given up the idea of becoming the Sultan e Alam, and was more interested in becoming Jan e Alam. This is evident from the fact that he drifted away from the management of the forces. Whenever the King tried to overhaul and upgrade the Akhtari and Nadri units, the Resident and Governor General would interfere under the pretext of sharing their

---

58. Wazir ul Sultan Md. Amir Ali KhanAmir: *Wazir Nama*, Nizami Publication, Kanpur, 1293 A.H. 152–154.

59. Supra Note 55, 58–59. Referring Foreign Department PC. No. 200. Dated 11th December 1847.

60. *Sabatul Quloob* (Manuscript). Volume 1, 26.

61. Metcalf C.T.: *Two Narratives of the Mutiny*, London, 1865. 32–33.

62. *Aaftab e Avadh*, (Manuscript), 152, *Tawarikh e Nadir ul Asr*, 122, *Ahsan ul Tawarikh*, 44.

wisdom. Until the return of Resident Richmond on 25 November 1848,[63] such interference continued, and disappointed the already hurt King. With the arrival of Resident Solomon, the King was insulted and snubbed by petty excuses.[64] At this point in time, the King became seriously ill.[65] He wanted to appoint his successor, but the people did not like this.[66] Ultimately, Nawab Ali Naqi Khan (the King's father-in-law) was appointed as Minister. A book of directions, titled *Dastur e Wajidi*, was handed over to him and the King himself became busy with dance, music, and composition.[67] With the story of his ill health, the direct rule of Wajid Ali Shah came to an end in 1849.

In Ramadhan 1266 A.H. (July 1849), *Qutb Ali Khan* and his companions were expelled from the city for their undesirable behaviour.[68] This displeased the King;

> "(He)...became frustrated, now became aware of Nawab Ali Naqi Khan's cleverness, due to whose negligence there was apprehension about running of the government. He tried to divert his mind and got engaged in entertaining pursuits like kite flying, poetry composition etc. in which Begum Nawab Khas Mahal played an active role."[69]

Rashk has composed a *tarikh* (chronological poem) about five poets receiving the honour of 'Khila'at', but does not mention their names.[70] The editor of the Residency mentions the names Fateh ud Daula Barq, Maqbool ud Daula Qubool, Aftabud Daula Qalq, Mehrud Daula Mir Zaki,

---

63. *Sultan ul Hikayat* (Manuscript), 562.
64. Musseehoodeen, Khan Bhadur Moulvi Md.: Oudh, *Its Princes and its Government, Vindicated*, London, 1857. *Masihuddin*, 79, 80.
65. *Taarikh e Iqtidariya* (Manuscript), Volume 2, 244.
66. *Sabatul Quloob* (Manuscript). Volume 1, 342.
67. Wazir ul Sultan Md. Amir Ali KhanAmir: *Wazir Nama*, Nizami Publication, Kanpur, 1293 A.H. 152–154.
68. Solomon. Volume 1, 46–47.
69. Supra note 55 at 190 *Alif.* Syed Md. Azmat Ali Alvi Naami Kakorvi: *Muraqa e Khusravi*, 1286 A.H. (Tagore), 177–178.
70. Mir Ali Ausat Rashk: Diwan e Rashk (Manuscript III), (Azad) 77 b.

and Tadbirud Daula Aseer.[71] Apparently, the appreciation of singers and musicians and the rise of poets was a pleasant change. In addition to poetry, the King presented his three epics in the form of a drama. He organized the marriages of some of his children, and performed *nikah* with *Ali Naqi Khan's* daughter. Perhaps the masses were not happy with this.

Although Nawab Ali Naqi Sahab was a minister, in reality he ruled the state. No minister got as high a position and stature as him. But all these niceties were an eyesore for Bare Sahab (Resident Solomon).[72]

Bare Sahab or Resident Solomon was a frequent visitor to such events, but had some ulterior motives. *Ali Naqi Khan* played a shrewd role in presenting a prolonged list of baseless charges against the King.

THE DEBACLE

The new Resident of Avadh, Colonel Outram, took charge on 5 December 1854. He was specifically appointed to scrutinize the reports submitted by Colonel Solomon. When Outram investigated, he found that there was considerable progress in governmental management.[73] But perhaps the Central Government did not require such reports. Outram based his reports on the documents left by Solomon and dispatched them within three months, but it is believed that in these reports only the words were Outram's, while the real facts were those collected by Solomon.[74] Following this report and Lord Dalhousie's wishes, the acquisition of Avadh was allowed on 1 November 1855, and a document was prepared in which the King was assured that if he agreed to all the conditions given there, his title and his right over the royal property would continue, he would be given twelve lakhs per annum for his personal expenses and three lakhs for the maintenance

71. Lalji Wald Seetal Prashad: *Marat ul Auwza* (Manuscript) (Raza), 72–73.

72. Supra note 69 at 199 b.

73. Bhatnagar G.D.: *Administration of Avadh Under* Wajid Ali Shah. (Article) Ph.D. Thesis, Lucknow University (Tagore) 131, 137.

74. *Ibid* at 138.

of his staff, and the same would continue with his successors. To obtain the King's consent, the Resident was given the power to increase his allowance according to his demands, and also to fix better allowances for the King's mother and other ministers.[75]

On 4 February 1856, the Resident met the King. In front of his ministers, brother, mother and some other dignitaries, the King asked Sahab ud Daula Bahadur to read out the document of accession. He was emotional, and could not read it for long. The King took it from his hands and started reading himself. The King then reacted in the following words:

> "Agreement is signed among the equals, but if I am no longer the King, then how can I have a right to have an agreement with the British Government? I will go to Britain and will request that the Crown reconsider it."

In spite of strong insistence from the Resident and the minister, the King refused to sign the document. His subjects had already been directed to remain silent, and his forces were asked to surrender. Ultimately, the King laid his turban in the hands of Resident and wistfully reminded him that it was the British Government which had crowned his grandfather and that if the Crown now wished that he should be reduced to a non-entity, then it is futile to sign any agreement as he has already been stripped of his position and grandeur.[76]

JOURNEY TO CALCUTTA

On 13 March 1856 at 8 PM, the King started for London via Calcutta.[77] In spite of the King's orders that nobody should accompany him, some of his loyalists, Begums, and well-wishers went with him up to Kanpur.[78] Some

---

75. *Rizvi* A.A.: *Freedom Struggle in Uttar Pradesh, Lucknow*. Volume. 1, 105. *Qaiser ul Tawarikh* Volume 2, 30. Also in Bhatnagar (Article) in section relating to Advisory to the Resident.
76. Report of this meeting as related by Outram; Rizvi A.A. Volume 1, 95–98.
77. *Rizvi* A.A.: *Freedom Struggle in Uttar Pradesh, Lucknow*. Volume. 1, 109.
78. Ibid at 103.

of them were not allowed by the Resident to accompany the King, while some returned from Kanpur.[79] The King travelled in buggy up to Benares, and from Benares he sailed to Calcutta in steamer.[80] After two complete months, the King reached Calcutta on 13 May 1856.[81] In Mochi Khola, the house of Maharaja Burdwan had already been hired for five hundred rupees per month. The King resided here.[82] In the beginning, this appeared to be a temporary residence, but after thirty-one years, from the same house of exile, the King's body was taken to its final rest.

Due to the exertion of the journey, incompatibility with the wet weather of Bengal, the financial burden, and the emotional disturbance, the King fell ill. It was necessary for the delegation to leave for England. Hence, on 18 June 1856, the King bade farewell to his mother, brother, and successors who left for England with precious and valuable gifts.[83] He himself was engaged in the writing of *Jawab e Blue Book* and in defending his case of Lucknow.[84] There was no limit to his expenses, and in spite of all his miseries, the King wished that all his companions remain with him. He gave them whatever he could for maintenance, but some of his compatriots left. The fact that Aseer stayed back in Lucknow[85] and Qalq departed Calcutta[86] irked him a lot. But it was not possible for the King to pamper them anymore, nor were those

---

79. *Ibid* at 109–114. Syed Kamaluddin Haider Alias Mir Zair: *Qaiser ul Tawarikh*, Munshi Naval Kishore Publication, Lucknow. 1907. Volume 2, 160–164.

80. Md. Wajid Ali Shah Akhtar: *Shev e Faiz*, Sultani Publication. Calcutta 1277 A.H., 4–7. (Avadh, Tagore, Murshidabad, Khuda Bakhsh)

81. Statesman (Calcutta) Dated 23.9.1887 referring the newspaper Englishman.

82. Supra note 80 at 8.

83. Maulvi Md. Masihuddin Khan: *Safeer e Avadh*, Al Nazir Press, Lucknow, 1929, 94.

84. Supra note 61 at 240–42. Wazir ul Sultan Md. Amir Ali Khan Amir: *Wazir Nama*, Nizami Publication, Kanpur, 1293 A.H. 240–42.

85. Md. Wajid Ali Shah Akhtar: *Bani*, Imambarah, 1292–24.A.H., 236–37.

86. Iqtidar ud Daulah Muhtashamul Mulk Mehdi Ali Khan Bahadur: *Tarikh e Iqtedaria* (Manuscript): Vol. 2, 427–28.

companions interested in materializing their tall claims[87]. In Rabi ul Awwal 1273 A.H. (November 1856) he asked for a loan of seventy lakh rupees from Nawab Ali Naqi Khan. But he did not provide this, nor did he make any promise to do so. [88] The King was very much disheartened with this; he was already unwell when suddenly another setback overcame him.

HOUSE ARREST

The First War of Independence was heralded in Meerut (10 May 1857). Between 21 and 28 May 1857, a Calcutta lawyer named Amir *Ali Khan* informed the government that the King was conniving with the rebels.[89] The fears of the government were further confirmed by the visits of soldiers to *Mochi Khola*, and thus they decided to place the King under house arrest.[90] Meanwhile, the King recovered from his long illness, and in the evening of 14 June 1857, there was celebration of the King's health (*Gusl e sehath*).[91] In the early morning of 22 Shawwal 1273 A.H, (15 June 1857) with the call of *Azaan*, *Mochi Khola* was surrounded by warships on the waterway and by the English forces on land.[92] They wanted to take only the King, but due to their closeness with the King, a total of twenty-four people, including his loyalists and servants, accompanied him.[93] The King was thankful to those

---

87. *I am unable to bear the pangs of separation*
Here only I wish to die
I should not be deprived of services at once
I want to perish in love
I wish to relive my empire
I want to have salvation. (Aseer, *Durrat ul Taj*, 232.)

88. Supra note 86 at 426.

89. Kaye JW: A History of the Sepoy War in India. London. 1876. Volume 3, 32.

90. *Ibid.*

91. Md. Wajid Ali Shah Akhtar: *Huzn e* Akhtari, Sultani Publication, Calcutta. 1276 A.H. Azad, Avadh, National Library, Calcutta. 35–38.

92. Kaye J.W.: A History of the Sepoy War in India. London. 1876. Volume 3, 32.

93. Supra note 91 at 35–38.

who accompanied him, but after house-arrest in Fort William (Calcutta), they could not spend even twenty-six months.[94] In the words of the King;

> "When the King was imprisoned groundlessly
> The Black fairies flew away, the whites stayed back
> Some were reminded of Hajj while some went crazy
> Companions deserted, only Akhtar was left in the prison."[95]

Fatehudd Daulah Barq, in spite of old age and restrictions, remained with the King in Fort William. He died on 28 Safar 1274 a.h. (18 October 1857).[96] The King has regarded the following couplet as the last gift from his master;

> "At last Barq did what he wished to
> Sacrificed his life at your doorstep."[97]

Forgetting the harassment at the beginning of his house-arrest, the King devoted his time to composing poems, reading, and writing, which resulted in a voluminous treasure of letters, poems and other writings. If one peruses the collections of the King's letters, one will find that most of the time the King lamented the misfortune which had befallen him. During the final period of his arrest, the King could not take time to peacefully write letters even to his Begums. Thus, Zulfiqar ud Daulah was entrusted with this work. On 7 Zilhij 1275 a.h. (9 July 1859), when the King was bidding farewell to the Fort,[98] *Zulfiqar ud Daulah* was involved in his work, and the King was busy in collecting his compositions.[99]

---

94. Md. Wajid Ali Shah Akhtar: *Tarikh Mumtaz*, (Compiler: Dr. Md. Baqar), Urdu Markaz, Lahore, 1952, Azad. 45.

95. Md. Wajid Ali Shah Akhtar: *Shev e Faiz*, Imambarah, 1276 a.h., 50.

96. Supra note 91 at 42.

97. Md. Wajid Ali Shah Akhtar: *Bani,* Imambarah, 1292–24 a.h., 239.

98. Supra note 94 at 61.

99. Last letters of Wajid Ali Akhtar:*Tarikh e* Ghazala (Compiler Wasi Bilgrami)Mufeed e Aam Publication, Agra. 1914. (Azad) and Md. Wajid Ali Shah Akhtar: *Tarikh Mumtaz*, (Compiler: Dr. Md. Baqar), Urdu Markaz, Lahore,1952, Azad.

EXILE

On reaching Calcutta the King had resolved:

> "I have no intention to come to Lucknow without regaining my empire. Of course, if I regain it, only then will once again be in your company. Otherwise, I will long remain in someone's house."[100]

After the upheaval of 1857, all Indians, especially the people of Avadh, deserved no sympathy.[101] In spite of reductions in the King's expenses, there were still expecting eyes of the public while there was no giver. Because of the untimely demise of his mother and brother, the King's resolve to not accept the offers made by the English was further weakened. Ultimately, the King became completely resigned to his fate, and in order to meet his requirements, started accepting their payments.

The British Government had decided that, as per the Agreement of Accession of 1857, no other grants would be considered in addition to the payment of twelve lakh rupees per year. However, these twelve lakhs were not exempt from tax and, in spite of the King's request, there was no change.[102] All those to whom the King had made monetary grants still lived lavishly, while the King himself had no source of income. Those who were still in Lucknow were unemployed and still expected the King's return. Ultimately,

---

100. Dr. Syed Noorul Hasan Hashmi: *Adab ka Maqsad*, Hindustan Kitab Ghar, Lucknow, 1956. 186, as referred to in *Tarikh e Mazzahab.*

101. Khan Bahadur Sheikh Siddiq Ahmed: *Tarikh e* Anjuman *e Hind Avadh*, Naval Kishore Press, Lucknow, 1937. Volume 1, 14–18.

102. As per Avadh Pension Papers, 2, from the same amount the Government had fixed allowances to some of his sons and thus the King's income was further reduced. Thus the King complained against this in the following words: (*Sabatul Quloob* [Manuscript] Volume 1, 343).

The few coins which were my income
Were plundered by others
This loot reduced my income to seventy four, seventy five.
But I give receipt of one lakh and suffer terribly.

they became hopeless and started moving to Calcutta. It was due to the King's attachment and affection towards his subjects that he did not drive them back. Apart from this, the King's own lifestyle and his urge to construct buildings to beautify the Sunderbans required extra funds.

> "In this state of exile there were about twenty thousand acquaintances and associates who were still treated in the same way as they were during his rule. Sultan e Alam had a craving for all the good things of the world, and by the grace of Allah all his wishes were fulfilled."[103]

Even the treasure of Qaroon[104] was emptied; hence a pension of one lakh rupees was nothing.

> "The day the pension used to be received, that very day it was distributed among the staff and nothing remained. Other daily expenses were met by selling off jewellery."[105]

It is not clear what the King carried when he left Lucknow, but it is certain that by that time he had nothing left in Lucknow. Had the lost treasure of royal times existed, the King would not have resorted to loans. After 1857, the English rulers had sent jewellery worth approximately twenty-five lakh rupees,[106] but this amount was not sufficient for more than a year or two. This is obvious from the fact that, during Eid, the Begums were gifted jewellery, just as they were during the royal period.[107]

---

103. Lala Sri Ram: *Kham Khana e Javed,* Mukhzan Press, Delhi Volume 1, 208.

104. *Qaroon* also known as Croesus is one of the richest men in history. He was an Israelite, lived in Egypt was a haughty and arrogant man who disobeyed Prophet Musa (Moses).In contrast of the suffering humanity Qaroon lived in sea of gold and precious stones, took pride in his high and opulent status. In a severe earthquake Qaroon was buried under his riches. Rekhta. https://www.rekhta.org/allusions/qaroon-croesus (By Translator).

105. Maulvi Abdul Haleem Sharar: *Jaan e Alam,* Idara Farog e Urdu, Lahore, 1951. 191–92.

106. Mirza Md. Taqi: *Aftab e Avadh* (Manuscript) 1874–75, (Tagore), 155–56.

107. *Majmu e Maroozat Madarulham, Lasanul Sultan, Wafa ShuuarMahmood ud Daula Hamidul Mulk Munshi Md. Safdar Ali Khan Sultan* Bahadur, 1281 A.H. 66.

Wajid Ali Shah and his associates gave crores of rupees to the Company, and thus they received allowances and emoluments from the interest on this amount.

At the time of the fall of the empire, more than one crore and eighty lakh rupees were due to the Company. After the overthrow of the empire, the rulers seized not only this amount, but also Kheri Garh in Nepal, which was considered the personal property of the King.[108] Due to his increasing expenses, the King wanted this amount be returned to improve his situation. This matter was taken before the British Parliament, but it was futile.[109] Adding to his misery, the King's most-trusted people, whom he helped and supported for years, betrayed him and filed a suit on the grounds that the King is indebted to them, and that they are owed about one crore rupees. However in March 1867, the King engaged a lawyer who had been his opponent in 1857. Due to the lawyer's judicious advocacy, amount of only seven lakh rupees was found due. The King was much pleased by this, and in 1275 A.H. (1868), he gave him the title of Wazir ul Sultan Muhammad Amir Ali Khan Bahadur.[110] Up till his death, *Wazir Sultan* remained his advocate and confidant.[111] *Wazir Sultan* also wrote the *Wazir Nama*, which is the King's biography.

During his exile, apart from some personal and financial hardships, the king had no major issues to distract him from engaging in creative and cultural pursuits. In *Mochi Khola*, a literary institute (Matba e Sultani) was the first milestone in this direction. The incoming of talented people, literary events and gatherings helped the king to overcome the grief and pain from which

108. Syed Kamaluddin Haider Alias Mir Zair: *Qaiser ul Tawarikh*, Munshi Naval Kishore Publication, Lucknow, 1917. Volume 2, 181.

109. Letter dated 15th August 1875 addressed to the King of Avadh by Home Political Department. As published in Memorial 1939.

110. Wazir ul Sultan Md. Amir Ali Khan Bahadur Amir: Amir *Nama*, Calcutta. 1870. 95–188.

111. Md. Wajid Ali Shah Akhtar: *Bani*, 1292–94. Imambarah, 339.

he had suffered at the time of his departure from Lucknow. His hopes and prayers to regain his lost empire were still alive, but people appeared to be satisfied with their new living conditions. Wajid Ali Shah's books, which were written during this period of his exile, are a clear depiction of the fact that the great King had full faith in the Almighty, and took everything as a divine decision.

DEATH

There is some disagreement regarding the date of Wajid Ali Shah's death. Saqib states that it was 20 September 1887:

> "It was the 20th day of September, the 3rd day in the month of Muharram during midnight.[112]
> It was the tragic night of the month of September.
> It was midnight of Wednesday, Third of Muharram,
> As it is revealed from the English Date."
> (Translated from Persian)

According to Maulvi Najmul Ghani Khan, whose writing on this topic is considered authoritative, the date of the King's death was 3rd Muharram 1305 A.H. (corresponding to 21 September 1887) at 9 PM.[113] He also writes:

> "As per the letter of a person named *Sarfraz Ali Khan* who was present there at the time of the King's death, the date is 2nd. of Muharram who certifies that the King was buried on the third day of his death in his self-constructed Imambarah Sibtainabad."[114]

Writers disagree on the date as they seem to be unaware of the time that the date changes. In a lunar month, the date changes with the appearance

---

112. Syed Md. Sajjad Hussain Rehmani: *Savaneh Shah e Avadh,* Tuti Hind Publication, Meerut, 1887, 89–90.

113. Maulvi Md. Najmul Ghani Khan: *Tarikh e Avadh* (Second Edition), Publication Munshi Naval Kishore, Lucknow, 1919, Volume 5, 282.

114. Ibid.

of the moon, at the time of *Azaan* of *maghrib*. In a solar month, the date changes at twelve o'clock, or at midnight. Due to the difference of a few hours in the timing of the date change, a difference between the dates of solar and lunar months is inevitable. This is because every solar date includes two lunar dates, and every lunar date includes two solar dates. Thus, if any event takes place between the evening time and midnight, there is a strong possibility that there is a difference in dates. For this reason, it was traditional to write the A.H. date along with corresponding A.D. date, and not merely because it was entered in a calendar (*Taqweem*). Thus, any dates that are mentioned in history books or special couplets cannot be fully trusted, as they may suffer from incorrect calculations based on automatically prepared calendars. About a century ago, a common Indian would have been unaware of the timing of the change in solar day or year, as today one is unaware of the changes of date in the lunar calendar. In the above couplet by Saqib, only the date of the solar month (20 September 1887) appears to be wrong. Because the King died at two in the morning,[115] the corresponding solar date is 21 September. But in the case regarding an event, such as Wajid Ali Shah's coronation, which takes place at the time of *Isha*, the solar date will remain the same as it was at the time of *Asar*, but the lunar date will change by the evening (*maghrib*). Thus, if the date of Wajid Ali Shah's coronation is given as 26 Safar 1263 A.H. (13 February 1847), it is incorrect. This is the date of the death of Amjad Ali Shah, on which there is consensus among historians. Thus, Wajid Ali Shah was coronated on 27 Safar 1263 A.H. (13 February 1847), as mentioned in *Afzalul Twarikh* and in the wordings of Wasiq's couplets, *Qatae Tarikh*.[116] Although Najmul Ghani Khan had imitated the date at the same time he had

115. Newspaper; *Indian Daily News*, Calcutta, Dated Thursday 22.9.1887.

116. Chronological poem in Urdu in which the poem is composed taking care of the Abjad Numerals in which 28 letters of Arabic are assigned numerical values. A *Tarikh* poem in Urdu uses such alphabets with numerals arranges them in such an order to form words which indicate the year of a particular event like birth, death, coronation etc. (Translator)

expressed doubts[117] in *Afzalul Tawarikh.*[118] Maulvi Sahab has expressed the same doubts regarding his date of death, but did not remove the discrepancy.

In sum, Wajid Ali Shah breathed his last on 3rd. of Muharram 1305 A.H.[119] (21 September 1887) at 2 in the morning. Consequently, he was buried after twenty-one hours, on 4th. Of Muharram 1305 A.H. (21 September 1887) at 11.00 in the night. He was buried in his self-constructed Imambarah Sibtainabad Mubarak, Metiaburj, Calcutta.[120] Munshi Sirajuddin Ahmed says:

> His year of death is clear from this statement
> Alas! the name of Lucknow has vanished from Calcutta. 1305 A.H.

---

117. Maulvi Md. Najmul Ghani Khan: *Tarikh e Avadh* (Second Edition), Publication Munshi Naval Kishore, Lucknow, 1919, Volume 5, 120.

118. Munshi Ram Sahay Tamanna: *Afzalul Tawarikh,* Tamannai Publication, Lucknow 1879., 98.

119. As per Taqweem of A.H. and A.D. published by Anjuman Tarraqi e Urdu (Hind) 21st. September 1887 fell on 3rd of Muharram 1305h. But the corresponding date of 13th February 1847 instead of 27th Safar, 26th Safar is written. The reason of this difference has been explained above. But 13th February 1887 corresponds to 26/27 Safar 1263 h. In calendars for the sake of convenience only that one lunar date is written which is equivalent to eighteen hours of that corresponding date hence this kind of confusion is bound to take place.

120. Newspaper; Statesman, Calcutta Dated 23.9.1887.
The King of Lucknow is buried in a strange place
Had there been flowers then even the spring of Lucknow would have been attracted. (Shair Lucknavi)

THREE

Writings

WRITINGS DISCUSSED

As per various sources, the number of Wajid Ali Shah's writings could be twenty to twenty-five,[1] forty,[2] fifty,[3] sixty,[4] seventy[5] or even hundred,[6] all of which have great fan following. These take the form of both manuscripts and publications. His publications are all listed by *Bani*.[7] Even if the books are not available, regarding them as non-existent is not proper.[8]

---

1. *Yaadgar Zaigham Md. Abdulah Khan Zaigham 1303.* (Manuscript) 21.
2. Khamkhanaey Javed Volume I, Lala Sri Ram. (5 Volumes) Mukhzan Press. Delhi. 209.
3. *Urdu Adab ke Aath Saal,* 166.
4. *Lucknow Ka Shahi Stage*. Prof. Syed Masood Hasan Rizvi Adeeb. Kitab Nagar Lucknow. 1957. 17.
5. *Hamari Zaban*, (Weekly, Aligarh), Different Issues from 1964–67.
6. Kidwai-28, *Lucknow Ka Shahi Stage*. Prof. Syed Masood Hasan Rizvi Adeeb. Kitab Nagar Lucknow. 1957. 17.
7. *The Raj Herald* (Monthly, Lucknow) November 1934, 82.
8. *Lucknow Ka Dabistan e Shayeri*. Lucknow Ka Dabistan e Shayeri, Dr. Abullais Siddiqui. Gilani Press. Lahore. 1955. 63.

Misunderstandings such as the idea that there are only six Diwans[9] of the King, that *Bani*, *Najo* and *Dulhan* are long poems,[10] that *Ishq Nama* is a Sufi creation, or that *Saut ul Mubarak* is a book of economics[11] are regarded as true even by the matured and educated class. While no discussion can be regarded as totally wrong or unacceptable, only those statements are trustworthy which are based on the maker's personal knowledge. The scope becomes all the more narrow when out of the ancient and modern reviews, only those that were used to either guide or mislead others are taken into consideration.

Reviews like *Khush Maarka e Zeba*,[12] *Sarapa Sukhan*[13] and *Sukhan Shooara*[14] showed interest only in compilations and poetry. At the time of their compilation, Wajid Ali Shah was not more than 34 years old, thus in these reviews the mention of his writings is fully ruled out. The statements and poetry mentioned in these reviews only indicate that, by the time these reviews were written, this kind of poetry was published, and thus they can be helpful in calculating the time period when these were published. Instead of writing a review, Safir ud Daula Maulvi Masihuddin Khan had written and published something in support of the King, in English.[15] This work indicates that in addition to poetry there were several prose books by the King, which were stored in well-known book houses in Europe. There can be no exaggeration in the words of Maulvi Sahab because that book, which was

---

9. *Khamkhanaey Javed* Volume I, Lala Sri Ram. (5 Volumes) Mukhzan Press, Delhi. 209.

10. *Tarikh e Adab Urdu*-Ram Babu Saxena (Translator)Mirza Md. Askari. Naval Kissore Press. Lucknow. 1937. 258.

11. *Mushair e Alam e Arwah,* Syed Murtuza Hussain, Naseem Book Depot, Lucknow. 1955. 254–255.

12. *Khush Maarka e Zeba* (MS).

13. *Sarapa Sukhan*- Syed Mohsin Ali Mohsin - Pubication Munshi Naval Kishore - Lucknow 1874. 4–8.

14. *Sukhan Shooara*- Maulvi Abdul Ghafoor Nassakh- Publication, Munshi Naval Kishore, Lucknow. 1874. 16.

15. *Masihuddin* – 79.

published in 1857 in Europe, was written in protest against the oppressive ruling of the English. Once it was among them, it was not possible to keep the people there under bewilderment. Garsaan and Taasi also mentioned in their writings that the King was a writer and a poet, but the books on the basis of which such conclusions were drawn are unknown and untraceable.[16]

From 1292–93 A.H. (1875), review and discussion became clearer. This is because in the same year, both Wajid Ali Shah[17] and Wazir ul Sultan Nawab Muhammad Amir Ali Khan Bahadur[18] mentioned the titles and characters of these books, only to the extent that was necessary for discussion. Both these writings are insufficient; one cannot mention writings which were written after the statements were made. Even people who made such statements did not claim that they were based on works which had been written before them. The fact is that those who wrote later should have examined how far these statements substantiate or disprove each other. But they apparently did not give any importance to the statements in *Bani* and hence, the *Wazirnama*, which was written to give direction, actually became a cause for misinformation. The inferences made from the *Wazirnama* caused misunderstandings that were not easy to correct:

a. Firstly, Lala Sri Ram compiled his discussions with reference to the *Wazirnama.*[19] Consequently, six Diwans of the *Wazirnama* were included in Urdu for the first time. He gathered many of the King's books after much effort, which is evident from the fact that the selections which are found in *Kham Khana-e Javed* are exclusive, and are found nowhere else.

---

16. *Khutbaat e Gaarsan wa Taasi*, Maulvi Abdul Haque-(Compiler), Anjuman Tarraqi Urdu Hind, Aurangabad, 1935. 97–98, 124–143.

17. *Bani* (Manuscript) – 219–20, Md. Wajid Ali Shah Akhtar (MWASA) Sultani Publication. Calcutta, 1877. (Khuda Baksh, Avadh). 242–43.

18. *Wazir Nama*, Wazir ul Sultan Md. Amir Ali Khan Amir. Publication Nizami- Lucknow. 1293. 219–318.

19. *Kham Khana-e-Javed* Volume 1, Lala Sri Ram. (5 Volumes) Mukhzan Press. Delhi. 12–204

b. Ram Babu Saxena however has not mentioned these extracts,[20] which are actually from *Khamkhana-e-Javed* and some other books. The *Wazirnama* has no mention of the King's long epics. Lala Sri Ram mentioned the names *of Huzn-e-*Akhtari, *Bani*, *Najo*, and *Dulhan* as musical art in Persian and Urdu.[21] Saxena, in addition to these, referred to the epics *Huzn-e-*Akhtari, *Khitabat-e-Mahallat,*[22] *Bani,*[23] *Najo,*[24] and *Dulhan*[25] as epic in the art of music and *Darya-e-Taashuq...*" Saxena could not have accessed the books titled *Bani, Najo* and *Dulhan*, else he would have discovered that there are no epics (*masnavis*) in these books. The flaws in the language of *Khamkhana-e-Javed* were bound to cause some misunderstanding. The *Ishq Nama* and *Haibat-e-Haidari* are epics but both Lala Sri Ram and Ram Babu Saxena have regarded them as part of some different poetic genre. Saxena inferred the wrong names of *Khitabaat-e-Mahallat* and other elegies from Munshi Naval Kishore's *Huzn-e-Akhtar.*[26] After much research, it was found that many incorrect names were adopted after the publication of this book. Like *Khamkhana-e-Javed*, in the Urdu writing *Tarikh-e-Adab*, there is mention of only six compilations (*Diwans*) which appear to have been taken from the *Wazirnama.*

c. Like Saxena, if any writer is not aware of *Bani* and remains confined to the *Wazirnama*, his sayings and discussions are not trustworthy.

---

20. *Tarikh e Adab Urdu,* Ram Babu Saxena (Translator. Mirza Md. Askari. Naval Kissore Press. Lucknow. 1937. 256–60.

21. *Khamkhana-e-Javed* Lala Sri Ram. Volume I (5 Volumes) Mukhzan Press. Delhi. 209.

22. *Tarikh-e-Adab Urdu,* Ram Babu Saxena (Translator. Mirza Md. Askari. Naval Kissore Press. Lucknow. 1937. 258.

23. *Huzn-e-Akhtar, 147–48 Huzn e Akhtar-* Md. Wajid Ali Shah Akhtar- Md. Ali (Compiler), Daeraey Adabia. Lucknow 1922. 147–48.

24. *Tarikh e Avadh,* Maulvi Md. Najmul Ghani Khan. Munshi Naval Kishore Publication. Lucknow. 1919. Volume 5–94, 101, 103, 113, 117.

25. *Id*, 109–111.

26. *Huzn-e-Akhtar*, 147–48.

However, if any historian refers to *Bani*[27] but then switches to discussion of the *Wazirnama or Khamkhana-e-Javed*,[28] leaving aside *Bani*, then it would appear that *Bani* has been left out deliberately. Maulvi Najmul Ghani Khan did exactly the same. Maulvi Sahab was not interested in the Moradabad publication of this book. That statement under the title "*Thoughts behind* Wajid Ali Shah*'s poetry*" was given on Page 11 of Munishi Naval Kishore's present edition.[29] In his composition there were no Ghazal couplets. Couplets with some flaws are taken from Munshi Totaram's book entitled *Tilisme Hind*, which forms the outcome of this history.[30] The book named *Majmua-e-Wajidia* was in the knowledge of Maulvi Sahab,[31] but there is no mention of it. The language of *Khamkhana-e-Javed* has been copied in full, and that is why the six diwans got so much fame. Maulvi Sahab should have expressed his views regarding *Bani*, which would have been much more acceptable than just copying it. The present work lacks newness and comprehension.

d. The first impression of the amalgamation of *Bani* and the *Wazirnama* is found in *Khwaja Abdul Rauf Ishrat's* discussion. *Khwaja* has mentioned the six diwans,[32] and the *Diwan-e-Mubarak*, which is found only in the list in *Bani. Khwaja Sahab's* statement is based mainly on his personal studies and thoughts, and his discussions about the books are preferable to those discussions which are more popular but are based on the extracts of other writers rather than on the commentator's own research.

27. *Supra note*. 24.

28. *Id* at 109–111.

29. *Tarikh-e-Avadh* (Moradabad Publication) Volume 4 (Print 1) Maulvi Md. Najmul Ghani Khan, Matbaul Uloom. 52–53.

30. *Hamari Zaban-* (Weekly, Aligarh) - 8/2/1966 Edition.

31. *Supra Note* 29.

32. *Aab e Baqa*, Khwaja Abdul Rauf Ishrat Naami Press, Lucknow. 1918. 161.

At present, research has moved beyond the point where *Khwahja Ishrat* had left off. There are people who carry the legacy of Lala Sri Ram or Ram Babu Saxena, but there are others who have centred their studies on the statements of *Bani*.[33] They are perplexed on whether to substantiate the *Wazirnama* or to rebut it. This could be resolved by going through the statements regarding six diwans. The question then arises as to where these diwans in the true sense of the term?

SIX DIWANS – A MYTH

Since the writing of the *Wazirnama*, various commentators have unanimously associated six diwans with Wajid Ali Shah: *Shevai-e-Faiz*, Qamar Mazmun,[34] *Sukhan Ashraf*,[35] *Guldasta-e-Ashiqan*,[36] *Akhtar-e Mulk*, and *Nazm-e-Namvar*.[37] There is no doubt regarding their titles, as all six titles are mentioned in *Bani*.[38] But a question is often raised as to whether these are actually diwans. Moreover, there is also doubt regarding their number and the chronological order in which they are presented. With this uncertainty, it is unfair to associate them with the King. This is also evident from the fact that, before mentioning their number, the King had clearly declared that;

> *"Instead of choosing, I am giving a list of some magazines,* Diwans *and books"*[39]
> (Translated from Persian)

---

33. *Lucknow Ka Dabistan e Shayeri*, Dr. Abullais Siddiqui. Gilani Press. Lahore. 1955. 62–63, 80.

34. *Wazirnama* 317, *Khamkhana-e-Javed* -Volume 1, 209, *Tarikh-e-Avadh* Volume 5, 110, *Tarikh-e-Adab Urdu* 258, *Intikhab e Zarrin* 130.

35. *Bani* - MWASA- Sultani Publication. Calcutta, 1877. (Khuda Baksh, Avadh).236. (Manuscript) 241–43.

36. *Wazir Nama*, Wazir ul Sultan Md. Amir Ali Khan Amir. Publication Nizami- Lucknow. 1293. 317.

37.

38. *Bani*, 241–43.

39. *Wazirnama*, Wazir ul Sultan Md. Amir Ali Khan Amir. Publication Nizami Lucknow. 1293. 317.

After making this statement, Wajid Ali Shah was alive for a long time and commentators could have included the changes or additions he made, but somehow this did not happen. Thus, the questions remain regarding the name a particular Diwan was associated with, whether there were more Diwans, and what is the sequence of his Diwans and other collections.

Introduction of the Word Diwan

There are many shades of meaning of the term '*Diwan.*' Ascertaining a particular meaning is thus necessary to identify his books, so that it is easy to clarify whether a particular book falls into the category of Diwan. The various meanings as given in different dictionaries are as follows;

Arabic Dictionary:

1. *Collection of books 2) Collection of books in which eulogies are given.*

Persian Dictionary:

1. *A book in which a poet's collection of poetry are given and which are arranged alphabetically.*

Urdu Dictionary:

1. *In Arabic it means a book of verses, in Persian it means a book of* Ghazals *(*Noor *ul Lugat)*
2. *A Book of* Ghazals *(Firhang* Asfia, Nasir*ul Lugat Translation, Ghayasul Lugat, Karim ul Lugat, Moeen ul Shoara, Lugat Heera-Urdu Hindi Dictionary).*
3. *A book of* Ghazals *(Firhang Dasturul Sabiyan-Firhang Dastur ul Shoara).*
4. *Collection of a poet's compositions. (Firhang Amera, Urdu-Hindi Dictionary).*
5. *Diwan is the collection of a poet's compositions. (Urdu Encyclopaedia)*

English Dictionary:

1. *Collection of poems which are arranged alphabetically as per rhymes.* (Translation *Firhan Jama-e Farsi, English-Tehran, Published 1312 A.H.)*
2. *It is a collection of poems or* Ghazals *of a poet which are arranged alphabetically as per rhymes. It is also a collection of an author's writings. (Dictionary of JB Plots - A Dictionary of Urdu Classical Hindi and English).*

From the above it is not wrong to infer that in Arabic the term Diwan had no special meaning, thus it could be a collection of eulogies, of verses, or of elegies. But in Persian the meaning is narrow, and it is understood to be only a collection of Ghazals which are arranged alphabetically as per rhythmic order. However in some usages there was no restriction on arrangement as per rhyming of '*radif*' or alphabetical order. But in Urdu the generalization did not continue, and under it, it is understood to be a collection of Ghazals which must be arranged alphabetically, and every letter of the alphabet must have a Ghazal. After passing these tests, it was a matter of pride to be an owner of a *Diwan* (*Sahib-e-Diwan*), and if there was no first verse (*Matla*) or last verse (*Maqta*) then it was considered to be a flaw. A rival of Ghalib, on the publication of his Diwan, reflected this idea while making a sarcastic remark that:

Matla and Maqta are nowhere
Ghalib*! It is difficult to become owner of a Diwan*

In the 19th Century, Garsaan and Taasi describe the difference between a *Diwan* and a collection of poetry in the following words:

"In the beginning, in Arabic, Diwan meant a simple collection of poems like *Diwan-e Mutnba*, *Diwan Ibn Farid*, and *Diwan Amarul Qais*, which were the collections of famous poets. But now in some other eastern languages like Hindustani, Pashto, and Turkish, *Diwan* means a collection

> of Ghazals, which according to rhythm, are arranged alphabetically. When poems of other genres are included, then it is called a compilation or *Kulliyat.* This means that *Diwan* and *Kulliyat* are words which are used for the compositions by the same poet. Collection of poems and *ashloks,* which are written in Devanagari, are not known by the term *Diwan.*"[40]

On the whole, the difference between a *Diwan* and *Kulliyat* is the same as that followed by Wajid Ali Shah and others. There is another term called *Majmua-e-Kalam*, but it does not appear in the above extract from Garsaan. The three terms *Diwan*, *Kulliyat, and Majmua-e-Kalam* are prevalent in the Urdu language with their own attributes. Following is a clarification on how a book can be termed as a *Diwan* but not a *Kulliyat or Majmu e Kalam.*

a. By *Diwan* is meant a collection of poems in which there is a single genre of poetry, which is arranged alphabetically. If, as per Arabic terminology, every collection of poems is called a *Diwan* then it would not be proper to say that "Wali was the first *Sahibe Diwan* poet" or "*Md.* Quli Qutub Shah was the first *Sahib-e-Diwan* poet." By this analogy, even today when there are abundant collections of various poetic genres like *nohas* or Ghazals which do not have rhymes (such as *Radif* – the repetition of a word in a poem or Ghazal) would be categorised as a *Diwan.* As per Persian terminology, a *Diwan* is not necessarily a collection of Ghazals. In Urdu there are plenty of examples where collections of poems praising the Prophet (PBUH)[41] or of *nohas*,[42] are known as Diwans. A collection of eulogies and quatrains can also be termed *Diwan*. The alphabetical arrangement of rhymes is by itself excluded in that genre of poetry which by nature

40. *Khutbaat e Garsaan wa Taasi,* Maulvi Abdul Haque (Compiler) Anjuman Taraqqi Urdu, Aurangabad. 1935. 121–22.

41. Asir's Diwan is named by Asir as *Guldasta-e-Imamat. See* Guldastaey *Imamat-* Munshi Muzaffar Ali Khan Asir, Matbaey Sultani Lucknow - 1271. 483.

42. Hashim Burhanpuri's collection of *nohas* and *Salams* is named as "*Diwan-e-Hussaini.*" See *Hindustani* (Magazine, Allahabad) July 1931, 230–31.

do not have *radifs*, such as *masnavis* (epic poems relating a story or chain of events) or elegies.

b. *Kulliyat* means a collection in which one or more of Diwans or collections of quatrains, eulogies, or elegies are compiled. Wajid Ali Shah has not called his elegies *'Kulliyat-e-Marasi'* (See title page of *Tosha e Aakhrat* and *Riyaz ul Uqba*) because they do not contain a Diwan. However, it is a common understanding that when all a poet's compositions are compiled, it is called a *Kulliyat* whether it includes a Diwan or not.

c. *Majmu-e-Kalam* denotes a collection of poems composed by a poet. It has no restriction of rhyme or poetic genre. The collection of *Thumris* can also be termed as *Majmu-e-Kalam.* Collections of modern-day free poems can also be called *Majmu-e-Kalam.* The inclusion of various poetic genres or the bulky features in a book cannot be referred to as a *Kulliyat* because in a *Kulliyat* as per common understanding there must be the inclusion of a *Diwan.* Most of present-day collections fall under this category. In Wajid Ali Shah's poetry there are some such collections, but these are not termed as *Diwan* or *Kulliyat.* "*Akhtar Mulk*", which is known as a *Diwan*, is described by the compiler, Sultani Publication as:

"Book is excellent compilation of His Excellency's compositions"[43]

And the chief of Royal Library has described it as:

"His Excellency the King has written a rich and eloquent book which is a collection of great knowledge and data."[44]

d. Names of Diwans:

---

43. *Mulk e Akhtar-* Md. Wajid Ali Shah Akhtar, Matbaey Sultani, Calcutta. 1296. 1

44. Id at 205.

1 and 2 . Qamar Mazmun and Nazm Namvar are the names which are given in the publications of Sultani Publication, by which these books are identified.

3. There is another book by Sultani Publication which has the name *Mulk e Akhtar. Wazir ul Sultan* has termed it as *Akhtar Mulk*, while Wajid Ali Shah has named it *Akhtar-e-Mulk*. There are continuous differences in the names, but it is better to regard the last name as the correct name of the book. In the last name – that is *Akhtar-e-Mulk* – the chapters are called *subas* (provinces), which is in line with the term *mulk* (country).[45]

4. During his princely days, a *Diwan* was published which had the seal of the writer, the publisher's name, and date, but instead of the title of the Diwan the King's name appeared within a circle. At the end, Maulvi Karamat Ali Azhar inserted the date (*tarikh*) in Persian.[46]

The King composed beautiful verse which is written by Azhar in a fine writing.
(The date given is 1259 A.H.).

For quite a long period, this *Diwan* was called a *Diwan*, but when there was a collection of many Diwans, instead of referring to them as First and Second, the terms were taken from the above stanza of *Azhar*, which was quite suitable. Though the words "*Selected from Intikhab az Guldasta-e-Ashniqan*", mention the twelve verses in the discussion of Lala Sri Ram, they are taken from the same Diwan.

5. Out of the published Diwans of Wajid Ali Shah, there is one *Diwan* which has poetic letters and some other poetry in the

---

45.

46. *Guldastaey Aashiqaan-* (Mirza), Md. Wajid Ali Shah Akhtar- Matbaey Muhammadi. Lucknow. 1259. 221.

beginning, and the Ghazals found in the end have rhymes in the names of his Begmats (wives). It lacks a title page as do all the copies which were available; they all start from page 3, which means that only the title page and page 2 were missing. Luckily, the manuscript and sealed copy of this Diwan is preserved in the Royal Library. On it are scripted, likely in the pen of the librarians, only two words: *Sheva-e-Faiz.* The 1276 A.H. figure is also found, which is the year of its compilation.[47] It is thus understood to be the correct name of the *Diwan*, as no other title is more suitable for it because it contains those poetries and Ghazals which were addressed to the Begums.

6. Out of the six Diwans indicated by Wazir ul Sultan, only one is found in the libraries.[48] The title page has a picture of the royal court and in the last line is the name of the writer. The expressions given in all the published manuscripts are in the same handwriting, hence it is concluded that it is actually *Sukhan-e-Ashraf Diwan.* This is further corroborated by the fact that the copy which is under the possession of *Sir Meerza Jahan Quder* contains the two words *'Sukhan-e-Ashraf'.*[49] These two words have the figure 1291 A.H. but it was published much before this (1278 A.H.), which is included in *Kulliyat-e-*Akhtari.

An interesting fact regarding the titles of the Diwans is that up to 1278 A.H. (1861–1862 A.D.), Wajid Ali Shah showed no interest in naming his Diwans. Had he given them these titles in the beginning, or before the publication of *Kulliyat-e-*Akhtari, then these names would have been found in the above-mentioned Diwans. Wajid Ali Shah himself has addressed

---

47. *Sheva-e-Faiz,* Md. Wajid Ali Shah Akhtar. Publication Sultani. Calcutta 1277. 424–25.

48. One copy of *Sukhan-e-Ashraf* is also available in Maulana Azad Library, Aligarh.

49. This copy of *Sukhan-e-Ashraf* is under the possession of Yateem Khana Islamia, Calcutta.

these Diwans as First, Second, and Third hence these names are not found anywhere before 1281 A.H. Thus it is quite possible that when the title of *Sheva-e-Faiz* was given, then simultaneously titles were given even to those Diwans that were published much earlier, as well as a name for a Diwan which had not even been compiled yet. Qamar Mazmun has 1276 A.H. (as year of compilation) and it is proved that the compilation of this Diwan had started by 1276 A.H., although it would have been published only by 1281 A.H. Qamar Mazmun is the first Diwan which has been properly named so and the name appears on the title of every copy.

Garsaan and Taasi, in their fifth statement (1271 A.H./1854 A.D.) said that in special cases the Diwans were given a title, and cited the example of *Diwan-e-Akhtar* (1259 A.H.) and said that its title was *'Faiz-e-Banyan'*.[50] However, as mentioned earlier, this is not true as during that period Wajid Ali Shah was not interested in giving names to his Diwans. As Garsaan and Taasi were not well versed in our language,[51] they may have made this mistake because they inferred it from the sentence "...thankfully this *Diwan-e-Faiz Banyan* as written by Prince of Hindustan..."[52] which was written on the title page.

Search of Diwans

Apart from the six Diwans of the *Wazirnama*, there are three more collections which lack a title. Like *Guldasta-e-Ashiqan* and *Sukhan-e-Ashraf*, these two are part of the *Kulliyat-e-*Akhtari. The list from *Bani* can assist one in identifying these collections by name. There are three names: *Diwan-e-Mubarak, Daftar-e-Humayun, and Daftar-e-Pareshan*, and in the

50. *Khutbaat e Garsaan wa Taasi,* Maulvi Abdul Haque (Compiler) Anjuman Taraqqi Urdu, Aurangabad. 1935. 142.

51. In June 1965 in the Tagore Library of Lucknow University this name appeared on its Index card. But in other Libraries neither this name was given nor *Guldasta-e-Ashiqan.* It was only written as *Diwan-e-*Wajid Ali Shah.

52. *Guldastaey Aashiqaan-* (Mirza), Md. Wajid Ali Shah Akhtar- Matbaey Muhammadi. Lucknow. 1.

absence of any solid evidence, one can name these Diwans on the basis of the following reasoning:

1. *Diwan-e-Mubarak*, with different names of *Sukhan-e-Ashraf, Sheva-e-Faiz*, and Qamar Mazmun appears on the headings of poem *'Namvar'* and in *Kulliyat-e-*Akhtari as per the alphabetical arrangement.[53] Perhaps it was done according to the royal etiquette. Thus, in the other places, the two words '*Diwan-e-Mubarak*' also appear every now and then. But these words are more than a form of address, as they are also listed in *Bani.* No other book has this name; hence it should be attributed to the *Diwan*, which is found under the title of *Diwan Saalis Tasnif Mubarak, Kulliyat Soom and Diwan-e-Mubarak Soom* in the *Kulliyat-e-*Akhtari. One can raise the objection that when one *Diwan* is included in *Diwan-e-Soom* and *Kulliyat-e-*Akhtari under two different titles, then it should not be counted separately. But this objection can be answered by the fact that *Guldasta-e-Ashiqan* and *Sukhan Ashraf* are part of the *Kulliyat-e-*Akhtari and still have their separate identities. Similarly, *Diwan Mubarak* is also part of the *Kulliyat-e-Soom*, and it also has a separate identity, and the *Kulliyat Soom* in turn is part of the *Kulliyat-e* Akhtari. [54]
2. Another collection called *Diwan Mubarak Chaharum* is also part of the *Kulliyat-e* Akhtari.[55] But the use of the word *'Diwan'* for this collection is not proper. There is no Ghazal found with the letters *be, pe, te, tay, say, jeem, chey, hay, khay, daal, zaal, ray, zay, seen, sheen, suad, zuad, toey, zoey, aain, ghain, fay, qaf, kaf* and *lam.*

53. *Sukhan-e-Ashraf-*2, *Sheva-e-Faiz-*3, Qamar Mazmun-259, Nazm Namvar-1, *Kulliyat* Akhtari-1, 59, 132, 178, 200, 289.

54. In this book details of the above-mentioned books are given.

55. *Kulliyat e* Akhtari, Md. Wajid Ali Shah, Matbaey Sultani Calcutta. 1278. (Found in Khuda Baksh, Salar Jung, Raza, Azad Libraries). 132.

3. In *Diwan-e-Chahrum*, the dates of compilation of *Sheva-e-Faiz*, *Kulliyat-e-*Akhtari, and Qamar Mazmun are the same. It is possible that at the time of compilation of *Kulliyat-e-*Akhtari, Wajid Ali Shah must have thought that the Ghazal*s* of *Sheva-e-Faiz* and Qamar Mazmun were included in the *Diwan*, but when *Sheva-e-Faiz* was compiled separately and the publication of Qamar Mazmun had stalled for some reason, another compilation under the name of *Diwan Mubarak Chaharum* was made, and in this way it came before us under a new name. It cannot be ruled out that this collection was later compiled either as a manuscript or in the form of publication and was probably given the title of *Daftar-e-Humayun.*
4. The collection of *Malazul Kalmat* has no name.[56] In this collection there is poetry titled 'Chanchal', a poetic letter, a *harzia* (a frivolous talk), some Ghazal*s*, and a variety of verses and quatrains. There is mention of a *harzia* even in the the list of *Bani.*[57] Such a collection must not be without a title, and thus in the list of *Bani*, the title *Dafter Pareshan* is given, which is probably a suitable name for this collection. We can also call it *Daftar Humayun*, but the word *pareshan* (disturbed) cannot be applied to it because despite some flaws it is well compiled. That means that it is applicable to the fourth Diwan of the *Kulliyat-e-*Akhtari, which was not in systematic order and more resembled a dictionary, had no proper arrangement, and was regarded as a supplement for a book which was not a collection of poetry but a dictionary. It is correct that in the *Wazirnama*, *Daftar Pareshan* was regarded the first divine description of the tragedies of '*Imam Hamam* (a.s.).'[58] But at the time of the compilation of

56. *Malazul Kalmat*, Md. Wajid Ali Shah Akhtar, Matbaey Sultani, Calcutta. 1297. (Azad Library). 690.

57. *Bani*, Md. Wajid Ali Shah Akhtar (MWASA)- Sultani Publication. Calcutta, 1877. (Khuda Baksh, Avadh). 242.

58. *Wazir Nama*, Wazir ul Sultan Md. Amir Ali Khan Amir. Publication Nizami- Lucknow. 1293. 317.

the *Wazirnama*, many such books were not arranged, the names of which are given in this book. For instance, the book named *Mulk e Akhtar* (which was published four years after the publication of the *Wazirnama*) or *Tosha-e-Akhirat*, *Riyaz ul Uqba* and *Imaan* (Published in 1301 A.H.) describe the Karbala episode. It is possible that manuscripts, which had long remained in the royal library under the name of *Deh Majlis Awwal* and *Deh Majlis Doom*, were published as the collection of *Wazirnama* under the name of '*Maqtal Motabir.*' Had *Daftar Pareshan* and *Maqtal Motabir* been published separately, then we could find the names mentioned in royal Diwans, but this was not so. A *Diwan* having one name in the beginning and the same *Diwan* having a different name later was not a new thing. For instance, one collection first had the name *Kashkol* Akhtari, then was later named *Gulzar Hussaini*, followed by *Akhtar Mulk*, and then lastly it was named *Mulk Akhtar.* Hence, it is true that the supplement of the *Malazul Kalmat*, which does not have much to say about the agonies of the *Imam*, is *Daftar Pareshan.* In this collection is a variety of compositions. *Nohas* and *Salams*, which were part of *Daftar* in the beginning, later[59] became part of *Imaan* (Published 1301 A.H.). The compiler of *Tazkira-e-Aab Baqa* has considered it in the category of a collection of Ghazals.[60] Even the selection of a couplet would have indicated that collection which he has associated with was the *Daftar Pareshan.*

There is no confusion regarding identification of *Najo*, *Dulhan*, and *Bani* as these names appeared on the title page. These three collections are the collections of Hindi poetry, and perhaps that is why the commentators refrained from calling it a collection of *kalams* (compositions). However,

---

59. The details regarding it are found in *Imaan.* Md. Wajid Ali Shah Akhtar. Matbaey Sultani. Calcutta. (Two Edns. 1288 & 1301).
60. *Aab-e-Baqa*-Khwaja, Abdul Rauf Ishrat. Naami Press. Lucknow, 1918. 166.

since they are a collection of poetry, when one is reviewing the poetic treasure of Wajid Ali Shah there is no reason to overlook them. Collections of compositions (*Majmua-e-kalam*) have a scope that includes all sorts of poetry. Somehow in these collections, the compiler has included the compositions of not only Wajid Ali Shah but also of other poets.

Number of Diwans

In light of the above discussion, we can conveniently say that *Guldasta-e-Aashiqan*, *Sukhan Ashraf*, and *Diwan Mubarak* are only Diwans, as this is also mentioned in them. (Figure 1). *Kulliyat Soom*, *Sheva-e-Faiz*, *Kulliyat-e*-Akhtari, Qamar Mazmun, *Nzam Namvar*, and *Imaan* are *Kulliyats*, as is also mentioned. (Figure 2) Sheva-*e-Faiz*, Qamar Mazmun, Nazm Namvar are rightly categorised as Diwans, although they also contain some poems, verses, and quatrains. In this way the count of Diwans goes up to seven. *Daftar Humayun*, *Najo*, *Dulhan*, *Nabi*, *Mulk Akhtar*, and *Daftar Pareshan* are collections of compositions (*Majmua-e-Kalam*) (Figure 3). When one refers to all the poetic treasure of Wajid Ali Shah in short, it is enough to refer to the *Kulliyat* and Collection of Compositions. The Diwans are included in these *Kulliyats*. The epics and long elegies which are in the form of a book are not included in this.

The conclusion regarding the categorisation of Wajid Ali Shah's compositions is shown by the following graphs: (Translator)

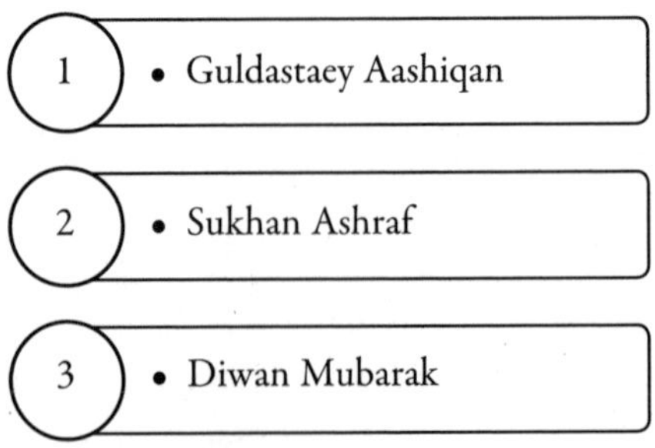

Figure 1: The Three Diwans (As also mentioned on original Diwans).

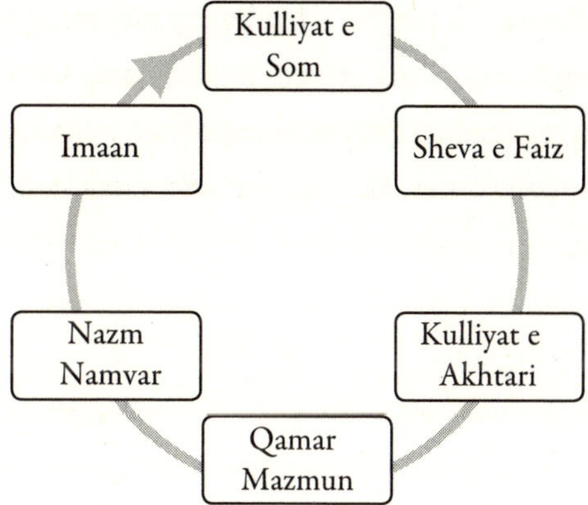

Figure 2: 6 *Kulliyats* (As Written on Them) – Often Sheva-e-Faiz, Qamar Mazmun, Nazm Namvar, and *Imaan* are called Diwans.

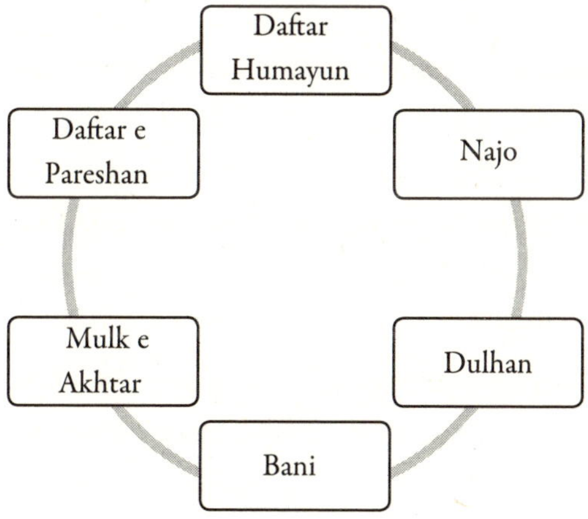

Figure 3: *Majmuey Kalam* (Collection of Compositions)

Wazirul Sultan Bahadur wrote his comments in Persian, and thus from his viewpoint it was not wrong to regard *Mulk e Akhtar* as a *Diwan.* He defaulted in not including other collections in his discussion. Our commentators were translating these statements into Urdu, in which since the times of *Wali*, a *Diwan* was understood to mean a special type of collection and *Wazir ul*

Sultan must have been aware of this. Had he actually seen the books regarding which he was giving his opinions, then he would have surely reached the same conclusion that every reader of Urdu would have reached.

By ignoring the direct and simple option, and adopting a complex method, if we set aside long-standing facts then we are bound to end in confusion. If Arabic terminology is correct and every collection of compositions is a *Diwan*, then all the books which are numbered must be included in the six Diwans of the *Wazirnama.* And if we conclude that Persian terminology is correct and believe that the collection of Ghazals is a Diwan, then also the *Wazirnama* is incomplete. *Diwan Mubarak* and *Daftar Humayun* should be included in those six Diwans. The Diwans of *Nohas* and other collections are excluded from this.

Compilation of Diwans

Wazir Sultan Bahadur though presented and numbered the Diwans serial wise but while doing this he did not follow any particular system. Thus, it was neither done chronologically nor alphabetically. This is evident by the fact that if done alphabetically, then *Sukhan Ashraf* should have come before *Sheva-e-Faiz*, but it was instead set after Qamar Mazmun. And if done chronologically, then *Akhtar Mulk* (1287 A.H.) and Nazm Namvar (1287 A.H.) are the names given according to date (Tarikhwar), which should have been set accordingly. At the time of the compilation of the *Wazirnama*, Nazm Namvar was published, and the compilation of *Akhtar Mulk* was not yet complete, hence *Akhtar Mulk* should have come after Nazm Namvar. Due to unavailability of the books, the commentators neither followed the chronological order nor the alphabetical order.

For a student of criticism and review, it is important to know the correct order of the aforementioned books. This is because it gives an understanding of the primary stage of the compositions and because Wajid Ali Shah's verses are mostly of biographical importance, if the correct year of their composition is not known, then it is quite possible that the reader will infer meanings which were not intended by the poet.[61] In the previous pages, Diwans, *Kulliyats*, and the collection of compositions are presented in the most apt manner. To present it in correct order is the best way to escape criticism. Determining the time period is difficult, but not impossible. If it lacks reason at any point, then it weakens the entire expression. The earlier Diwans have no date of publication; hence there is no option but to depend on reason and logic, unless some solid evidence is available, by which such a period can be fixed which is near the correct one.

Mixed Arguments

There is much contradiction regarding the above-mentioned order. After spending 26 months in prison, when Wajid Ali Shah came out of Fort William he had many manuscripts. Qamar Mazmun, its date-wise name (*Tarikhi naam*) and some *tarikhi* segments (*Qata'at*) indicate the timing of the composition and publication of these manuscripts. *Mahtab ud Daulah* Bahadur Darakshan was one of the close companions of the King, and he is said to have better knowledge of all his compositions and publications. His following verses indicate the same:

Three special Diwans *were published first*
See the greatness of Khusru-e-Hind
The King then published them together
It was the luck of the Companions Khusru-e-Hind
Some other writings were also included
And in this way
All were taken together by Khusru-e Hind
With much labour there was the publication of the fourth one

61. For instance, Lala Sri Ram by inferring the meaning of this verse; *I endured the pains so much; I lost my clan.* (Commented in the Margin); "This indicates the disaster of the Royal clan which went to England for the annulment of the empire."(*Khamkahna-e-Javed*-Volume 1–221).

There is name of Khusru-e-Hind everywhere
Read the line of date (1281h)
Four Diwans *of Khusru-e-Hind.*

If the claims of *Mahtab ud Daulah Bhadur* are correct, then our claim that Qamar Mazmun is a *Kulliyat* or a fifth *Diwan* is wrong. But the controversy does not rest there. In the last part of Qamar Mazmun, there are fifteen *Qata'at-e-Tarikh* (date-bearing verses) out of which two verses have no indication whether it is a *Diwan* or *Kulliyat*,[62] five of the verses regard it as a *Diwan*,[63] while eight verses regard it as a *Kulliyat*.[64] The last *Qata'a* is of the compiler Zargham ud Daulah Mehdi Hasan Khan Bahadur, and is as follows:

The composition of the King is published
Everyone is looking forward to it
Words fall short of appreciation
What to say what collection it is
The verses are doubtlessly lucid
It is a selected Collection which is published[65]

Kulliyat can be termed as a collection, but a collection cannot be called a *Kulliyat*. (1281 A.H.). In the beginning, to refer to a *Kulliyat* as a collection is

---

But this verse is given in *Diwan Sukhan Ashraf* (p.190) which was published during the ruling period. Possibly it was composed before the coronation. At that time, it was even unthinkable that he would be dethroned, and his family would have to visit England. (Such is the importance of knowing the correct timing of any verse).

62. See One Verse of *Mahtab ud Daulah* which infers date and another of *Jaygopal* Saqib- *Qata'a* 4 & 15.

63. One more *Qata'a* of *Mahtab ud Daulah* and other *Qata'as* of *Zulfiqar ud Daulah,* Syed Ali Hussain Faarig, Mirza Ali Jaan Shafaq and *of* Mirza *Md, Shaaz*. (*Qata'at*; 1, 2, 8, 12 & 13).

64. *Qata'ats of* Mirza Muzaffar Ali Hunar, Inayat Hussain Adil, *Ali Hussain Faarig,* Mirza Masita Aish, *Syed Hasan Jaan Zia,* and *Mizgham ud Daulah*. (*Qata'ats*; 5, 6, 7, 9, 10, 11, 14 & 16).

65. Qamar Mazmun- Md. Wajid Ali Shah Akhtar. Matbaey Sultani. Calcutta.1281. 476.

due to the date given there. After this proof that Qamar Mazmun is *Kulliyat* there is no need of further evidence. It is evident from the following three things that those composing the dates were not aware of the fact that they were saying the date verse (*Tarikh*) for a *Diwan* or *Kulliyat* which had both prose and poetry:

a. In some of the collections generally the word "*Diwan Mubarak*" or "*Kulliyat Mubarak*" is used in the beginning and in the end also but in the case of Qamar Mazmun the word "*Tasnif Mubarak*" is used.[66] Thus this statement would not have been wrong had there been the inclusion of prose in the *Kulliyat*.
b. The addressing of it by various poets often as *Diwan* and often as *Kulliyat* is not so astonishing as when it is said by one poet. Thus, Syed Ali Hussain Faarig says in these following verses;[67]

   Jan-e-Alam composed such a Diwan
   Each verse of which is a valuable gem
   No poet can (has the ability to) appreciate it
   No one has ever or will ever compose like this
   When my heart thought of composing a date for it
   It thought whether it is Diwan or a creation (mazmun) which is published (1281 A.H.)

   Later when *Faarig* realised that there are also epics, elegies and quatrains in it then he went on to say:

   Faarig! Such a Kulliyat is composed by the King
   That it will be appreciated forever

---

66. *Mahtab ud Dulah* or any other poet who has composed date verse and has regarded Qamar Mazmun as a *Diwan* has not mentioned as to what are the contents of the *Diwan*. Contrary to this those who regarded it as a *Kulliyat* have also mentioned that it contains *Salam* and epics.
67. Qamar Mazmun. Md. Wajid Ali Shah Akhtar. Matbaey Sultani. Calcutta. 1281. 475.

It is better to write a date for it
What better can be composed by anyone. (1281 A.H.)

c. In the collection *Mulk e Akhtar* there is both poetry and prose. It was published in 1296 A.H., but it was compiled in 1291 A.H. The King has himself mentioned this in the Preface;

"And the name of this collection is titled 'Mulk e Akhtar.' Out of many dates I selected 1295 A.H." [68]
(Translated from Persian)

There is no such preface in Qamar Mazmun but the '*Tarikhi*' (date-wise) name is evident based on the fact that the verses of *Baab Soom dar Ilm e-Urooz*,[69] which for some reason could not be included in *Sheva-e-Faiz*, were composed during the period that *Sheva-e-Faiz* was being written.[70] Muzaffar Ali Hunar, by making a slight change in the name of Qamar Mazmun, has composed this date verse.

The vision of Hunar *nicely*
Has been entered in the Qamar Mazameen (1281h).[71] (Translated from Persian).

It is possible that in the beginning there was an intention to publish the *Diwan*, hence those associated with it wrote date verse for the *Diwan*. Later there was the idea to include other genres of poetry as well, hence more *qata'as* came up, but the majority regarded it as a *Kulliyat* which was quite proper.

The part of *Mahtab ud Daulah* Bahadur's verse which he regards it as a Fourth Diwan must be based on some misunderstanding which is not known.

---

68. *Mulk e Akhtar*. Md. Wajid Ali Shah Akhtar. Matbaey Sultani. Calcutta. 1296. 7.
69. *Sheva-e-Faiz*. Md. Wajid Ali Shah Akhtar. Publication Sultani. Calcutta. 1277. 409.
70. Read the details of writing of Qamar Mazmun and *Sheva-e-Faiz*.
71. Qamar Mazmun. Md. Wajid Ali Shah Akhtar. Matbaey Sultani. Calcutta. 1281h. 5.

The same mistake was made by Hunar, where he regarded Qamar Mazmun as a second *Kulliyat*;[72]

Learned people are convinced of King Akhtar's compositions
*Like Saib, Urfi, Khaqani, Wa*Hali *and Salim*
The Second Collection (Kulliyat) which has been published now
Is more eloquent than the first one
Hunar *has retrieved its year and date (1281 A.H.)*
This composition is highly acclaimed (Translated from Persian)

Qamar Mazmun is neither a Fourth Diwan nor a Second *Kulliyat.* It was in the knowledge of *Mahtab ud Daulah* Bahadur that three Diwans were published separately and later they were collectively included in the '*Kulliyat-e*-Akhtari.' The Fourth Diwan *Sheva-e-Faiz* is present in published form. We cannot set it aside by regarding it as a collection of compositions. This is because the *masnavi* (epics) pages and the pages of Diwans are counted separately. The *Diwan* begins as follows;

"Chapter four of Diwan Mubarak which is the creation of Sultan Alam Akhtar."[73] (Translated from Persian)

If names of Begums are used as rhymes in most of the Ghazals, and this cannot be a flaw on the basis of which it should be denied the status of *Diwan.*

While denying Hunar one cannot deny the status of *Sheva-e-Faiz* as a *Kulliyat*. Wajid Ali Shah's statement in *Bani*[74] and the existence of *Kulliyat Soom* and *Kulliyat* Akhtari are enough evidence for the fact that Hunar was

72. *Aish* has also written Qamar Mazmun as- "Second Kulliyat as published in Urdu". *See,* Qamar Mazmun- 475–76.

73. *Sheva-e-Faiz* (Ghazal portion). 1.

74. *Bani*, - MWASA- Sultani Publication. Calcutta, 1877. (Khuda Baksh, Avadh). 220–43.

perhaps either unaware of *Kulliyat Soom* or that he was unmindful of it. *Kulliyat Soom* is in fact the *Kulliyat Awwal* (First).

Although such flaws found in the statements of close associates of the King are surprising, one would see that a person for whom so much effort was made to appreciate him was himself not single-minded about things.[75] It is quite possible that our misunderstanding is baseless. For instance, to clarify. *Mahtab ud Daulah's* clear narration is given in the last part of *Sheva-e-Faiz*, as below:

> *"By* Allah*'s grace the Collection of the great poet through the order of Zargham ud Daulah Mehdi Hasan Khan* Bahadur*t was published by Matbaey-Sultani at Mochi Khola, Calcutta under the aegis of the loyal servant Muhammad Hussain on the auspicious day of 27th Ramadhan 1277 A.H....*"[76] (Translated from Persian)

Here the term *Majmua-e-Mubarak* is not used mistakenly. It is further consummated by the fact that immediately after the statement, the three *Qata'ats* of two poets – Amir Ali Khan Hilal (in charge of *Matbaey-Sultani*) and Md. Abdul Rehman Ahsan (the writer) – which are in Persian and Urdu have not mentioned it as a *Diwan* or a *Kulliyat*. This is clear from the following stanzas:

This time this moment is so auspicious
When this collection is reverently published
It is not in need of any proof or reasoning
No king ever composed so Mir*aculously*

---

75. In the manuscript *Tarikhe-e-Firaq* (pg. 347) Navrozi Begum writes to the King; *"Like you I too am not single minded and am restless all the time."* The proof of King's fickle mindedness is found at many places in his compositions. To get a proof of this and the continuous change of names, additions here and there, taking out of the published pages and adding more pages in between one can see Chapter 4 of this Book especially the review of *Kulliyat-e-*Akhtari, *Naj*o and Nazm Namvar.

76. Ghazal*iyat* Part-*Sheva-e-Faiz*. Md. Wajid Ali Shah Akhtar. Publication Sultani. Calcutta. 1277. 425.

He is the fountain of eloquence, knowledge and art
He is so sagacious, learned and intellectual
He is the emperor and an efficient ruler
So popular and graceful the Star of Hindustan
Who every year expresses his feelings in his expressions
Hilal*! He is monarch of this world*
Even the Khaqani does not have such poetic taste
Who is the god gifted and is the crown of all poets[77] (1277 A.H.) (Hilal)
(Translated From Persian)

Urdu Verses

What to say about the poetic style
King of Oudh's style is the sweet song of robin
There is newness in his thoughts
The King of Oudh's style is royal
Ahsan write the date of the collection
Published in the time of King of Oudh (1277 A.H.).

Thus, this is not a *Diwan* or *Kulliyat* but only a collection, though *Mahtab ud Daulah* Bahadur referred to Qamar Mazmun as a fourth *Diwan*. However, the headings and in the manuscript seal of the published *Sheva-e-Faiz* confirm my claim that in the beginning, *Sheva-e-Faiz* was called a Diwan, as narrated in the following paragraph;

> *"By* Allah*'s grace... this eloquent, articulate, lucid, and classy Diwan was completed by His Excellency on the auspicious and fortunate day of 29th Rabu ul Sani 1276 A.H. and which was pleasingly written in the hand of the humble servant Md.* Amir *Bin Ali Raza Khan."*[78]
> (Translated from Persian)

---

77. *Ibid.*
78. *Sheva-e-Faiz* (Manuscript) 424–25.

After addressing *Sheva-e-Faiz* as a Diwan, if for some reason the King changed his mind and his associates verified it, then it is not necessary that I should also follow this and not address *Sheva-e-Faiz* as a *Diwan* or *Kulliyat.*[79] Wisdom is on my side, all the discussions and books and a dictionary is before me, hence I have no reason to follow them blindly.

STATEMENTS OF WAJID ALI SHAH REGARDING HIS WRITINGS

The importance and usefulness of *Bani's* list is evident by the ongoing discussion regarding the six Diwans. This list is very valuable, as in matter of any controversy this list becomes decisive. Some important points are given in the beginning so that in the event of verifying or refuting the list one is not required to go into detail. Luckily this list is contained in the writing of the author (Wajid Ali Shah) himself.[80]

1. The first book is described as '*Akhtar Mulk*' while on the book it is written *Mulk e Akhtar.*[81] But this was a mistake because at the time of the compilation of the list, *Mulk e Akhtar* was not in book form.[82] The incomplete books are written in the last part of the list and don't have any title, and so *Mulk e Akhtar* should have been there.

79. In the treasure of Urdu literature there is also a magnanimous and rich Diwan like *Sheva-e-Faiz* entitled "*Badshah Nama*" which was completed on the King's wish by his *Begum* Sadar Mahal in 1288 A.H. In this *Diwan* the rhymes were completed with the name of the King. Apart from the *Qata'ats* of the *Badshah Nama,* Sadar Mahal herself addresses the King in expectation of some applause and says; *Congratulations! the Diwan is compiled.* If *Badshah Nama* is *Diwan* and the associates of the King also address, it as such then there is no hesitation in addressing *Sheva-e-Faiz* as Diwan. See this poem of Sadar Mahal in Chapter 5 of this book.

80. *Bani.* Md. Wajid Ali Shah Akhtar. Sultani Publication. Calcutta, 1877. (Khuda Baksh, Avadh). 219–20.

81. *Mulk e Akhtar*, Md. Wajid Ali Shah Akhtar. Matbaey Sultani, Calcutta 1296. 1 & 8.

82. *Ibid.*

Perhaps the author wanted to start the list with his own name (*Ism e Mubarak*) and hence wrote the name *Akhtar Mulk* in the beginning. The completed books did not have the starting word '*Akhtar.*' Thus, the author (Wajid Ali Shah), out of all the books which were under completion, chose that book which indicated the bent of the author's mind towards prose, poetry, Urdu, Persian, politics, religion, romance, and music. *Wazir ul Sultan* Bahadur has adopted this name from this very list. (An example of the manuscript given as Photo A). At the time of the publication of the *Wazirnama*, neither *Bani* nor *Mulk e Akhtar* had been published.

2. The first letter, *Alif*, of *Akhtar* indicates that the other books are compiled alphabetically. However, the compilation does not follow the dictionary rules because the writer has considered only the first letter. Other than some incomplete and unknown books, all the names followed this pattern, as is found in the old discussions.[83] If we address *Afsaana-e-Ishq* as *Fasaana-e-Ishq*, then this name will differ from the present pattern and will also be incorrect.[84]
3. The disarrangement of books and the statement that "...so many volumes of the book were written" clearly indicates that the writer was not aware as to how many books were written and what names would be given. Everything was written randomly; hence some omission was bound to happen. Wajid Ali Shah had been mistaken in naming his issues because the number of these was as many as the number of books, and that list was also compiled randomly.[85]
4. Those who compiled the list of the books addressed them as first, second, third and so on, and by doing this they became accustomed

83. *Sukhan Shoara, Yaadgaar-e-Zaqham, Khamkhana-e-Javed,* and *Chamanistan-e-Sukhan* are the books which though arranged alphabetically have not followed the dictionary rules.
84. Bloom Heart in his list *"Hindustani publications-British Museum"* has unknowingly used the word *Fasaana-e-Ishq*.
85. *Bani*. 336–38. *Shehzada Aasma Jah* 's name is not on the list although he was alive at that time, and he has been lovingly addressed in *Huzn-e-*Akhtari.

to two rules: one was the counting of books, and the other was alphabetical order.

دستاویز الف: بنی (قلمی) کی فہرست بخط واجد علی شاہ

٣١٩

PHOTO A: List of *Bani* in the Hand of Wajid Ali Shah

PHOTO B: List of *Bani* in the Hand of Wajid Ali Shah

The problem was that if any name came up after adding some names, then there was a possibility of distorting either the counting or the alphabetical order. *Majmua-e-Wajidia* came up after completing the list. This name is not in the manuscript list, but it is in the published one. If some names were found to be different from the alphabetical order, then they were not included in the list for fear of disturbing the arrangement. *Malazul-Kalmat* is the name of a chronogram verse (*Tarikhi*) (1293 A.H.), and the list includes this name. The book *Bani* was published in 1295 A.H. (1878), long after it was written. There were many changes and deletions, but this name was not included in the list, perhaps either because it was not given this title until that point of time, or the list was not thought of as being complete without any systematic arrangement.

5. This list was presented proudly, and it would not have been difficult for the author (Wajid Ali Shah) to include those books which were destroyed, but this was not done. This shows that those names which were included were not exaggerated but were humbly included. The author did not present other's books in his name. The King owes no responsibility regarding the *Jawab e Blue Book* and *Tarikh-e-Badr*, which were associated with his name.
6. The list is incomplete regarding the books which were written before the fall of the empire and after the compilation of the list. This is evident from the language of the list itself. This is further confirmed by the discovery of the above-mentioned books.
7. The book *Behr-e-Hidayat* is presented as *Behr-ul-Hidayat*, which appears to be a mistake, as there is no book by this name. Perhaps a revision of the list would have corrected these mistakes, but the associates were not bold enough to advise him, and it was dependent on the will of the King if he would revise it on his own. Thus, he often, without any strong reason, revised the *Diwan* in such a manner that a totally new book came into being.[86] He often deliberately left the list incomplete, which could have been a guide for others. It is not possible that the King was not attentive towards it, because without it the *Wajidia Collection* could not be extended. Perhaps he had asked the writer to extend it. Thus, it is quite clear that such extension was done at the time when the book was being corrected.

86. *See, Sukhan-Ashraf, Diwan Mubrak* and Nazm Namvar

8. In this list only the names of the books are given. Whether the books were in Urdu or in Persian, written in Calcutta or Lucknow, contained poetry or prose, and were published or a manuscript can all be decided by examining the book. But again, this need not be decisive because the books had several editions.
9. In the start of the list, he mentions that his age was 50, and the duration of his stay in Calcutta was around 20 years. He arrived in Calcutta in 1272 A.H. (1856), and the book was written in 1292 A.H. (1875). At that time his age was 55.[87]

Wajid Ali Shah in *Ishq Nama* mentions five books, though the names are not given. He writes:

> *"While expressing my feelings I wrote two* Diwans *regarding my romance with the fair sex and three masnavis but I did not disclose my heart before anyone."*[88] (Translated from Persian).

In 1275 A.H. Zaheer Bilgrami asked him about his writing, but he did not receive any specific response. He only said:

> *All the compilations and writings in various genres were present in various daily papers and in the form of biography, but all were destroyed and lost in the cruel devastation, and now there is no sign of them.* [89]

87. Regarding his age, the statement of the King appears to be correct, and it confirms the statement of Saqib. However, it appears that perhaps to please the King, Saqib may have written his year of birth as 1238 A.H. This is because, at the time of King's death, in the *Qata-e-Tarikh* composed by Saqib, he mentions his age as 67 (*See Sawaneh Shah-e-Avadh* page 89.) which can only be correct if his date of birth is taken as 1238 A.H. Towards the end, Wajid Ali Shah himself stated his age as 5 years less than his actual age, as appears from the List of *Bani* and in the verses of *Sabatul Quloob*. (Page 429–30).

88. *Ishq Nama* (Persian). Md. Wajid Ali Shah Akhtar. 1265. (Mahmoudabad). Ninth Dastaan regarding romance with Moti Khanam.

89. *Boostan-e-Avadh*- (For Persian lines). Kunwar Durga Prasad Sandelvi - Matbaey Ahmedi, Lucknow.1892. 184–85.

But in the *Tamseeli mushaira* (*Mushaira* where members dress up like some famous poet/person) of *Bani*, when the other poets were being introduced, during his turn he ultimately declared the names of his writings, which became the most trustworthy, authentic and reliable list. Though the *Wazirnama* was published much before *Bani*, as verified by '*Akhtar Mulk*' it was inspired by *Bani* and hence can be regarded as a supplement to it.

Writings of Wajid Ali Shah

In light of Modern perspective: Almost a century has passed since Wajid Ali Shah's writings were made public and in all these hundred years there are a good number of articles and some hundred libraries which have been dedicated to the 'titles' (naming) of these writings. Wajid Ali Shah's writings were and are immensely popular, but from the famous libraries of Europe to the libraries in India, from his contemporary commentators down to the present-day writers, there is not a single instance where the names of his writings and compilations are addressed correctly. Not a single writer has confidently mentioned these names. Whatever has been mentioned is inferred and inspired by certain references which have already been discussed. The authenticity of these commentators is the least reliable. The entire state of affairs is pathetic; it is very difficult to draw a reliable conclusion because not only the books are rare, but it is not clear whether the so-called books were published or were in the form of manuscripts.[90] Often if a book is found, then its title page is missing[91] or is blank.[92] Not only this, but often the title page does not have the name of the book.[93] There are often two books, one in Urdu and another in Persian,[94] that have the same title – often one is in prose and another is poetry,[95] and the different editions differ in their

90. For instance, the names given in *Bani's* list.

91. See *Sheva-e-Faiz.*

92. See, *Sukhan Ashraf.*

93. See the details given in *Guldasta-e-Ashiqan.*

94. *Ibid* in *Majmua-e-Wajidia.*

95. *Ibid* in *Ishq Nama.*

contents. The entire story is blotted with uncertainty and unreliability, which is further aggravated by missing and incomplete pages. Also, the pages which are found in one book are often not found in another,[96] and then again, the same pages are missing from another book.[97]

All this was further aggravated by the careless publishers, who continued publishing the books with minor changes or additions, but without making any reference to the original manuscripts or publications.[98] The entire condition is extremely misleading. It is futile to expect anything convincing from writers or libraries that are just performing their duties formally. This can only be done by a dedicated person who has come across these books and has discerned the anomalies within them. It has been a humble effort to sort out these irregularities and qualms in the forthcoming pages.

CHRONOLOGICAL COMPILATION OF PUBLICATIONS AND MANUSCRIPTS

In this study, the compilation is on the basis of the Hijri era. Often the verses also mention the A.D. era, but neither the titles of the books nor the publications of Wajid Ali Shah have any reference to it. There are two benefits of this sequential compilation; *firstly*, it indicates the preoccupation and mood of the writer and *secondly*, it depicts his temperament and progressive style. This further helps in identifying the subject matter of the book, which can indicate the timing when the book must have been written. Simultaneously, if such conclusions are the result of one's imagination, then it can also be helpful in its denunciation. Our writings are the reflection of our mood, our frame of mind, and our disposition, and looking at the harmonious compilation of his writings, one can conclude that even an erratic and prolific writer like Wajid Ali Shah was not an exception to it.

96. *Sheva-e-Faiz, Najo, Riyaz ul Quloob.*

97. *Kulliyat-e* Akhtari, Nazm Namvar.

98. *Ibid* at *Ruqat-e-Badr, Daftar-e-Gham, Pari Khana, Khaqan-e-*Sarwar.

The selection of the year of composition of these books is made on the basis of the dates given in the books, but if any exterior source was more reliable and trustworthy, then that has been taken as the final date. It is possible that the year of the edition of the book which is given in the list is taken as authentic, but when there is strong exterior evidence to show that the basic part of the book was written at a certain date, then it is preferable to fix the edition to the nearest date.[99] Some of the books mentioned in the list were written over a long period of time, hence the date when these were concluded is ascribed to them as the date of writing, though there is also mention of the entire period of writing to avoid any error.

As a good number of his books were spread over a variety of subjects, they could be arranged by topic. Alternatively, there could be a separate list for his Urdu and Persian books, or for his publications and manuscripts, but this would have not served any purpose other than listing these publications and manuscripts. Thus, the following compilation is done in such a manner that several books on the same subject matter can be separated very easily. In case the A.D. year is required, it can be determined with the help of a calendar. Table 1 lists the books according to their subjects:

WRITINGS AND COMPOSITIONS OF WAJID ALI SHAH IN CHRONOLOGICAL ORDER

Title of the Book	Year of Writing Hijri era	Language	Literary Style	Publication[100]	Page No. in the book
Afsaana-e-Ishq	1255	Urdu	Epic	MS/Published	113

99. It is believed that there were two editions of *Afsana-e- Ishq, Darya-e-Taashuq, Behrul Ulfat, Haibat-e-Haidari, Nasah-e-* Akhtari, *and Behr-e-Mukhtalif* out of which seemingly the second edition is available and there is no clue regarding the other editions.

100. Publication indicates those books which were published by Sultani Publication. Some other books like *Jawab-e-Blue, Nasaah-e-*Akhtari, *Behr-e-Mukhtalif, Tarikh-e-Mumtaz, Tarikh-e-Mazzahab* and *Taarikh-e-*Ghazala were published by others.

Daryaa-e-Taashuq	1256	Urdu	Epic	Published	120
Behr-e-Ulfat	1256	Urdu	Epic	Published	122
Guldasta-e-Aashiqaan	1255–59	Urdu	Collection of Ghazals	Published	125
Ishq Nama (Persian)	1263–65	Persian	Autobiography	Manuscript	127
Haibat-e-Haidari	1265	Urdu	Religious Epic	Published	132
Ishq Nama (poem)	1266	Urdu	Epic/ Biography	MS/Published	135
Majumua-e-Wajidia	1263–66	Urdu/ Persian	Collection of Different Sources	MS/Published	142
Behr-e-Hidayat	1263–67	Persian	Collection of Islamic Quandaries	Published	150
Saut-ul-Mubarak	1267	Persian	Music Rule	Published	154
Sukhan-e-Ashraf	1258–67	Urdu	Collection of Ghazals	MS/Published	159
Irshad-e-Khaqani	1268–69	Urdu	Prosody	Published	162
Jawab-e-Blue Book	1273	Urdu	History of Avadh	Published	166
Diwan-e-Mubarak	1255–73	Urdu	Collection of Ghazals	Published	171
Kulliyat-e-Som	1255–73	Urdu	Collection of Poems	Published	174
Huzn-e- Akhtari	1274	Urdu	Epic/ Biography	Published	176
Behr-e-Mukhtalif	1275	Urdu	Poetic Biography	Published	180
Nasaah-e- Akhtari	1275	Persian	Congregation Protocols	Published	184
Tarikh-e-Mazzahab	1272(73)	Urdu	Collection of Letters	Published	186

Taarikh-e-Mumtaz	1272–76	Urdu	Collection of King's Letters	Published	197
*Taarikh-e-*Ghazala	1275	Urdu	Collection of King's Letters	Published	202
*Taarikh-e-*Noor	1272–76	Urdu	Letters of Begums	Manuscript	207
Taarikh-e-Badr	1273–76	Urdu	Letters of Begums	MS/Published	215
Taarkh-e-Firaq	1275–76	Urdu	Letters of Begums	Manuscript	226
Taarikh-e-Jamshedi	1275–76	Urdu	Letters of Begums	Manuscripts	246
Sheva-e-Faiz	1272–76	Urdu	Collection of Poems	MS/Published	255
*Kulliyat-e-*Akhtari	1255–78	Urdu	Collection of Poems	Published	261
Qamar Mazmun	1276–81	Urdu	Collection of Poems	MS/Published	268
Naajo	1285–86	Hindi	Collection of Poems	Published	274
Sahifa-e-Sultania	1286	Persian	Benedictions/ Prayers	MS/Published	278
Nazm-e-Namvar	1279–87	Urdu	Collection of Poems	Published	282
Imaan	1268–88	Urdu	Collection of Poems Salaam and Noha (Elegy)	Published (Two Editions)	282
Dulhan	1289	Hindi	Collection of Poems	Published	290
Mubahis-e Bainul Nafs w Aql	1287–89	Persian	Islamic Quandaries	MS/Published	293
Jauhar-e Urooz	1290	Persian (Urdu)	Prosody (Urooz)	Published (Two Editions)	299

Bani	1291–94	Urdu (Hindi)	Collection of Prose and Poetry	MS/Published	303
Mulk-e-Akhtar	1291–95	Urdu (Persian)	Collection of Prose and Poetry	MS/Published	3011
Malazul-Kalmat	1276–97	Persian	Seven Language Dictionary	Published	316
Tosha-e-Akhrat	1267–99	Urdu	Collection of Elegies	MS/Published	320
Riyaz-ul-Uqba	Not Available	Not Available	Selection of Tosha-e-Akhrat	Published	330
Riyaz-ul-Quloob	1297–99	Urdu	Stories of Prophets	MS/Published	332
Sabatul Quloob	1300–04	Urdu	Religious Epic (Two Volumes)	Manuscript	335

Table 1: The Authentic List of Wajid Ali Shah's Writings

The 42 books mentioned above are authenticated by Wajid Ali Shah's confidential documents. The documentary proof of the books entitled *Tarikh-e-Mumtaz* and *Tarikh-e-Mazzahab* is not available, but these are mentioned in such reliable writings that there are no grounds for disbelief. All the collections of letters were compiled in 1276 A.H. and here they are listed according to their topics in the order of their writing. There is mention of some other writings of Wajid Ali Shah in some reliable documents, but these are not available in as separate books. Some of the books are wrongly associated with him. Some parts of his compositions are not only unpublished, but they are also unfamiliar. Hence, before dwelling on these intricacies, the details of the aforementioned books are given below.

ELUCIDATION OF WAJID ALI SHAH'S WRITINGS

Afsaana-e- Ishq (Manuscript)

Epic (Dastaan Masnavi)
Writing Date: 1255 A.H. Language: Urdu Printed: 1263 A.H.
Format: 24×9 Pages: 286, 7-lined
Manuscript: Nawab Salar Jung Library, Hyderabad

Composed in Urdu, this is an epic spread over 286 pages and was written in 1255 A.H.

In the beginning the poet says:

My tongue is drenched in Allah*'s praise*
Every tongue praises him
It is better to praise the Almighty
And this sharpens my tongue
Why not I praise him
My heart is brimming with his adoration
In the end he says;
Now the epic is nicely ending
It is the result of my deep thoughts
It is as valuable as a diamond string.
Every line is heavenly
Every verse blooms like a garden.

The writer who compiled the list praised the quality of the paper in his article,[101] but he forgot to mention three important things, which are presented below:

a. The manuscript is written on imported paper in the shade of ebony, the margins are adorned with beautiful plants, and the image of Cupid

101. *Naya Daur* (Monthly). May 1959. Lucknow. 304.

playing the flute at the side of a pond is inscribed in some places. There is also some writing in Italian, and the entire work seems to be the creative work of some foreign expert. The handwriting is impressive and attractive.

b. There is another peculiarity in the manuscript which is indicative of the fact that there was some expectation that it would be printed using lithography. This is evident from the fact that after every line, numbers are given in ascending order from 12 to 301, which is in the style of writing for litho printing. One heartening fact is that the writing style used in the manuscript is followed in the published form. In the MS, the epic begins from page 12. From pages 1–11, Allah is eulogised, there is adoration for the Prophet, and the personal activities of the King are related. This protocol is followed in the printed form. The King followed the same style in other MS,[102] which shows that perhaps the writer was aware of the temperament of the King.

c. The manuscript is scripted in beautiful handwriting, but in places verses have been inserted in the margin. Presumably these are in the King's hand as it is the manuscript of the royal library,[103] in which no one had the authority to inscribe something. This is further supported by the fact that it was in the King's thoughts that the manuscript should be printed, hence the changes were made only by him. The writing also resembles the King's handwriting and moreover, the corrections reflect his style.[104]

Page 8 is left blank. Regarding this the writer says:

---

102. *See,* the details of *Mubahis-e- Bainul Nafs wa Aql.* (Manuscript 1). Md. Wajid Ali Shah Akhtar. 1290.

103. The compiler in his article published in *Naya Daur* (May 1959 Issue of *Naya Daur,* Monthly Lucknow, page 3 and 4) cautiously remarked that it may be from the royal library.

104. At the end of this chapter the author presents specimen of king's handwriting and according to the author this is the oldest specimen of the King's handwriting.

This place is left empty on the order of His Excellency
(Translated from Persian)

The style of address shows that by that time the King was coronated, and so the manuscript must have been written after 1263 A.H. Moreover, the Urdu lines, as given below, show that the epic was composed after his coronation:

Almighty has made me King
It is better if I am addressed as Jaan-e-Alam

Moreover, in the eighth tale of the poetic *Ishq Nama*, it is indicated that the epic was composed at a time when Wajid Ali Shah had not yet ascended to the throne. In that story he mentions his love as the spirit behind his poetry:

This dialogue happened
When I was eighteen
My heart was torn by the sorrow
This sorrow inspired my poetry
Whatever I composed it was so romantic
My wails were forceful
Every verse pierced the heart
My epic and verses are colourful
My hidden pain augmented
That sorrow made me crazy

The King turned 18 on 10 Zeeqad 1255 A.H. (1840). Hence, it is certain that the three romantic epics were not composed before that. The verses above are from the first of these three epics. This is supported by the following verses:

Thus it came to my mind
That I better compose some verses about my condition
I composed some romantic verses

And recited them loudly
I chose Hasan Yar Khan poet
As he knows the pros and cons of poetry
When I recited some verses
He appreciated it a lot and said
Compose an inspiring epic
So that it becomes famous
So that Hasan forgets all (previous) verses
And enjoys nothing else
I said what are you saying gentleman
What I have to do with poetry composition
But he went on insisting
And said think about composing epic
But I clearly told him
I have no taste for poetry
It was only an impulsive moment
That I became so spirited
Thereafter I kept silent
Though I thought of composing poetry.

It is evident from the lines above that in response to the *Sehrul Bayan* epic, the King was inspired by *Hasan Yar Khan* to begin writing poetry. He points at the love which he mentions in the *Ishq Nama*, and says:

One day it happened thus
That the love bug bit me
My heart went into pieces as if
the glass is shattered by love (brunt)
I went on relating this tale
And my heart bled badly
The composition went on day and night
And it was concluded in fifteen days.

It was the way of saying a verse
Which I wanted to finish soon
But this is not the way to compose
Fluency and rhyming cannot be done in haste.

If an amateur poet writes three epics within a year, then it is natural that there may be some missing pieces. Hence, it is possible that after some time, he revised his verses and made some literary changes. Though the facts remained untouched, he added verses that appeared to be composed during the period of his reign.[105]

Thus, the *Afsaana-e-Ishq*, which we are currently discussing, must have been compiled after this revision. After writing the manuscript, perhaps at the time it was printed, the King again revised the verses. The changes which he made at this juncture can be discerned by comparing the manuscript and the printed work. Some excerpts are given below:

1. In one place he writes:

   the shade is full of decorations
   and every curtain is weighed with rubies and pearls.

   Then he writes 'thousands' (*hazaar*) in the margin, and the verse becomes

   every curtain is full of thousands of rubies and pearls.

2. In the other line it is said:

   everywhere there was such fragrance
   that flowers never had such smell

   But then the King corrects this in the margin and changes the second verse:

105. *Lucknow Ka Shahi Stage.* Prof. Syed Masood Hasan Rizvi Adeeb. Kitab Nagar Lucknow. 1957. 123.

that the wind blew with its joy

3. Again, in the following couplet he makes a correction:

   All kinds of dry fruits were sent
   And the ritual of "chauthi" was completed

   The King initiates a correction in the margin, and the word '*ritual*' is replaced by the word '*rite*'. (Page 285 in the manuscript and 288 in the published version). Thus, the line is rewritten as:

   And the rite of 'chauthi' was completed

4. At the end of the manuscript the last verse is:

   Every verse is heavenly
   Every line is like the beautiful plant

   But perhaps the poet was not satisfied with the concluding verse; hence two other verses are added in the margin as follows:

   Every word is like a flower
   The meaning is like the fragrance
   May it last forever
   May the printed form becomes everlasting

   Both the manuscript and the printed form ended in the same way.

Afsaana-e-Ishq (Printed)

(Urdu) Epic (Daastan Masnavi)

Writing Date: 1255 A.H. Language: Urdu Printed: 1263 A.H. Format: 29×19 Pages: 152, 13-lined

Print: By Sultani Press (Lucknow) with the support of Madad Ali (Second Ed.)

The page numbering starts from the title page. On the second and third pages tabulated information is provided, and on the third page the royal emblem is sketched. The poetry is spread over 301 pages, and on the last page there are indicators regarding corrections, which are about 34. The author's name along with his other titles is given as "*Abul Mansoor Sikander Jah Badshah Aadil Qaiser Zaman Sultan Alam...*" This epic contains about 3,800 couplets and tells a love story. In the poem, the poet describes the entire journey of love, from the birth and upbringing of a hero named *Maah Paikar* who spots a beautiful woman in a portrait and falls in love with her, his struggle to achieve the love of a heroine named *Seemtan*, to finally the happy ending. The headlines are given in beautiful Persian language.[106]

Darya-e- Taa'shuq

Writing Date: 1256 A.H. Language: Urdu Genre: Daastani Masnavi, (Epic)
Printed: 1263 A.H. Format: 29×19 Pages: 117, 13-Lined
Publication: With the support of Khana zaad Qadeem Madad Ali, Sultani Publications, Lucknow, Second Edition.

I begin in the name of Allah
Who has created us
All are incipient He is the oldest
All are ignorant he is knowledgeable
Mir*aculous are his creations*
Humans and angels all are appalled
He is seen in petals and in thorns
In stones and in the sparks
How can we thank you
We expect mercy from you
Always bestow fortune on me
Keep my enemies dishonoured and perish
Always fulfill my wishes
Always keep me happy
May this royal star keeps shining
And He rules from the moon to the ocean

106. Apart from *Haibat-e-Haidari* and *Sabaat-ul-Quloob*, all the Urdu epics of the King have Persian headlines.

This text has 234 pages and there are no blank pages in any of the available copies. There are flowers drawn on page 2 and 3, and the style of the pages is similar to *Afsaana-e-Ishq*, with the King's name at the top of the page. The verses clearly indicate that they were composed during his reign. But as mentioned in the final part of *Afsaana-e-Ishq*, it seems that only some verses were added after his coronation. The copy which is saved in a private library[107] and was published in 1263 A.H. likely does not have the verses which show that the epic was composed during his reign. The arrangement of the epic shows that it was the King's second poem which was like the first epic was composed at someone's request:

Once there was a group
Who were carefree and cheerful
They were busy composing poems
And were very enthusiastic
One of them showered blessings on me
The beauty then told me
My dear Jaan-e-Alam
I have a crush on you
Write a poem for me
No one in the world composes like you
The poem you wrote earlier
Is full of love stories
Its title is Afsaana-e-Ishq
Its beginning and end both are great
This poem must also be romantic
Which appeals to the people at large
I argued with many
And could not refuse

107. *Lucknow Ka Shahi Stage.* Prof. Syed Masood Hasan Rizvi Adeeb. Kitab Nagar, Lucknow. 1957. 123.

Then I became very excited
My intellect and wit became active
I thus composed an agonizing story
Which was liked equally by men and women
After 21 days I could finalize it
And named it Daryaa-e-Taa'shuq

There are about 3,000 verses in it which relate an intense imaginary love story. The love story develops between the King's daughter, Ghazala, and the *Wazir's* son, Gul Pairahan. Ghazala fell in love with the Prince of Mulk-e-Khatan, Maah Ru, but there was another woman named Laal Pari who had also fallen in love with Maah Ru but had put him in jail. However, Maah Ru loved Ghazala. Thus, when the King of the *Djinns*[108] (*Shah Djinn*) came to know about this, he helped unite the two lovers. This infuriated Laal Pari and there was a fight between the *Djinns* and the devils, in which the *Djinns* were victorious. However, Laal Pari, because of her failure in love, tried to end her life. This melted Ghazala's heart, and she persuaded Maah Ru to marry Laal Pari. Thus, Maah Ru married both Ghazala and Laal Pari, and ultimately the story ended happily, as they were blessed with a child which pleased everyone. The poem has romantic overtones spotted with jealousy, envy, and patience, which ultimately makes the poem an interesting one.

Behr-e-Ulfat

Writing Date: 1256 A.H. Language: Urdu Printed: 1263 A.H.
Format: 29×19 Pages: 173, 13-Lined
Publication: With the support of *Khana Zaad Qadeem Madad Ali,* Sultani Publications Lucknow, Second Edition.

108. Oxford Advanced Learner's Dictionary, 9th Edition, 2015. 449. Djinns are Allah's creature. They are invisible creatures from the pre-Islamic era and also during the Islamic period. They are like human beings accountable for their deeds before Allah. (Translator). Jinn - Wikipedia

He says:

O! My pen praises Allah
Who has created the Sun and the Moon
All the stars are adorned with it
It brightens the moon and the stars
Here move with the head down
And everyone should kneel down before Him

He further adds:

So long the stars are moving
And these twelve minarets are staring at the sky
May my splendour and strength augment
And my grandeur last forever
May my magnificence and glory lasts
And my empire continue until the Day of Judgment

This poem has many similarities with the previous ones. Most of the pages are blue, while some are also white. The King's photo appears on the title page with his long name and titles. The work is, in places, written by hand in red ink, and parts of it are printed. The date of its composition is confusing however, as the poem, when listed among the Indian titles by Bloom Heart,[109] has the title *Masnavi Meher Parvar Aur Maah Parveen,* who are its main characters. The title *Behr-e-Ulfat,* in addition to the title page, is given in the following verse

Behr-e Ulfat hua jo naam uska
Misl darya hua kalaam uska

109. *Blumharadt, J.F.* Catalogue of Hinudstani Printed Books in the Library of the British Museum, London. 1889. (Column 256).

(As its name was wave of love
Thus the composition is like the flow of a river)

The title *Masnavi Meher Parvar Aur Maah Parveen* indicates that this is likely a version of the *masnavi* which was written before it was revised.[110] The long *masnavi* was supposedly composed during the same period as the previous two *masnavis*. This one however, indicates that the King composed it with greater interest and concentration: He says:

Hear the song as per your choice
Hear the people if you like
Akhtar is well spoken
His mind is fresh now
He is in the mood to tell a story
And has some bent of mind
Let the intoxication linger
let it be a bit more frank
Then hear these magical expressions
And hear the slurs
His name is Akhtar the sweet composer
to adorn the song is his job
All the Urdu followers
Know your magical style
Your poem is unique
It is like Urdu dictionary
All the audience is fan
Some have met you

110. *Ibaadat Barelvi,* in his essay Wajid Ali Shah *ki Nadar Masnavi* (Published in *Maah Naama* Magazine March 1965, Karachi, 77–86), has made a copy of the poem (as in the British Museum) as his base work, which only indicates that he is not only ignorant about the original name of the poem but that he is also unaware that it has been published.

It pierces the heart like the love lorn
It further ignites the flame of love

By any measure, this *masnavi* is far better than the previous ones, but in places the continuity of the storytelling is disturbed. The poet, instead of showing a prince falling in love, has shown that three women named Mah Parveen, Yasmin, and Gulshan are in love with King Meher Parvar. The story goes like this: Mah Parveen was the daughter of a King, and was abducted by the daughter of a Fairy King, and was brought up by her. *Yasmin* was the daughter of a Magician King and is the sister of Gulshan (who is the rival of Mah Parveen), and she (*Yasmin*) is also secretly in love with Meher Parvar. *Meher Parvar* was haughty and puffed up with his own good looks; he was arrogant. He never gave importance to any woman, but he was attracted to Mah Parveen. The jealousy between Mah Parveen and *Yasmin* resulted in a fight between the devils and the magicians. As *Meher Parvar* was also interested in Gulshan, she came to him for help. After defeating the magicians, *Meher Parvar* came to know that Mah Parveen had been abducted by one of these magicians, who had imprisoned her in box under the sea. *Meher Parvar* ultimately freed her, and the story has a happy ending. The poet tells this story in about 4,300 verses, but the ending was not written in an expert manner.

Guldasta-e- Ashiqaan

Writing Date: 1255–59 A.H. Language: Urdu Genre: Diwan Printed: 1259 A.H. Format: 27×17 Pages: 111, 17-Lined
Publication: With the support of Mirza Mehdi Ali Qubool on the request of the author – Muhammadi Publications, Lucknow.

The Diwan was written in about four years and has many Ghazals. It starts with the following verse:

Allah *I will not shun my love for you*
I am a sinner but now will not commit any wrong

And the Diwan ends with the following couplet:

The stars are black there is so much grief
Because there is the darkness of night on the pages of my Diwan

The title page of the Diwan is well decorated with flowers and has the following name written on it:

> *"Abul Mansoor Sikandar Jah* Sulaiman *Hasham Sahab e Alam Wali Ahad* Mirz*a Muhammad Wajid Ali* Bahadur 1258 A.H."

On the last page, the final message is written in the form of a poem. The message shows that with the cooperation of Mirza Mehdi Ali Qubool (Maqbool ud Daulah), Md. Hussain issued it on 15 Shawwal 1259 A.H. (1843) from the Muhammadi Publication. The dates of completion of the publication were written in Persian by Maulvi Karamat Ali Azhar. The paper used was of good quality, and the printing of the *Diwan* was comparatively better. Two dates were printed on the title page. Two were given on the last page. The last quatrain which concludes the book is as follows:

Hazrat Kevan Janab, the favourite of all big and small
Who by the grace of Allah *completed his Diwan*
And it was pleasantly read by the humble Azhar
And which was printed by Md. Hussain (Translated from Persian)

The King composed some verses about his relationship with Moti Khanam, which is given in a Ghazal.[111] *Asir* likely referred to some Ghazals in *Durrul Taj*, written in same time period.[112] The verses of this *Diwan* were given in *Tazkira-e-khush Maarka-e-Zeba.*[113] All this points to the fact that the King

111. *Ishq Nama* (Manuscript—poetic) Eighth Daastan. Md. Wajid Ali Shah Akhtar. 1265.
112. *Durra-tul- Taj*-Md. Muzaffar Ali Khan Asir. Matbaey Sultani. Lucknow. 1270. 108–112.
113. *Khush-Marka-e-Zeba* (MS) 15300(?).

enumerated his love affairs in this *Diwan*, which is rightly named *Guldasta-e-Aashiqan*.

Ishq Nama (Persian)

Epic (Dastan Masnavi)

Writing Date: 1263–65 A.H. Language: Persian Genre: Autobiography
Printed: 1263–65 A.H. Format: 27×18 Pages: 217 9-Lined
Manuscript: Found in the personal library of Maharaja Md. Amir Haider Khan – Mahmoodadabad.

He starts the narrative with the following sentence:

The first tale is about Rahiman when I was a minor.

At the end he writes:

I have mentioned about the women
I thank Allah *for this*
Akhtar reveals its year as (1265 A.H.)
Ishq Nama is concluded today
...I have completed the tales about women

The first verse describes the reason behind its compilation, the second discusses its name, and the third one is concerned with the date. It is quite interesting to note that though this is the most famous work of the King, his reasons for writing it, its name and its date are widely misunderstood. The correct name of the book is *Ishq Nama*, and by this name only it is included in the list of *Bani.* The name '*Taarikh-e-Pari Khana*' or only '*Pari Khana*' is commonly used, which is incorrect. The reason behind this could be that the original book was not printed even once, though multiple translations spread over 50 years reached the readers with the incorrect name. Mirza Fida Ali Khanjar used the word '*Taarikh-e-Pari Khana*' in the Preface. There are five editions of the book.[114] Its oldest edition is dated 1914. It is after this that the wrong name was circulated in reviews and discussions.[115] Gradually this name continued to be used by writers, and they forgot the correct, original name. *Tehseen* Sarwar*i* translated it anew and named it '*Pari Khana.*'[116] This work is less related to the original book. Both the translators were aware of the second verse and also knew that *Pari Khana* was the name of a building as found in the 28th Daastan. Giving a name to his work is the prerogative of every author and the name *Ishq Nama* is the most suitable and verified name, while the titles *Taarikh-e-Pari Khana* or *Pari Khana* are not.

The third verse (*Qata'a-e-Tarikh*) contains the date when the work was completed, which is 12 Zeeqad 1265 A.H., although the events which are related in the last two Daastans (the death of *Jahan Ara Begum*) are dated 10 Zilhij and 19 Zilhij (the month after Zeeqad). Actually, these *Daastans* and the one in which *Kevan Quder* is nominated as his successor are extended *Daastans*, and the actual book ended after describing the infidelity of women and a note of advice.[117] In the poetic *Ishq Nama* this advice is given as the supplement. The compiler had no intention to publish the prose part of the *Daastan*, hence the advice is rightly given in the last part of the poetic autobiography.

The compiler enumerates the incidents up to 19 Zilhij 1265 A.H. (5 November 1849), which indicates its date of completion. Instead of giving the date he began working on the *Ishq Nama*, the compiler instead gives his age to indicate the period. 10 Zeeqad 1238 A.H. is Wajid Ali Shah's date of birth. On 10 Zeeqad 1263 A.H. he reached 25 years of age. Most probably the writing of his autobiography started during this period. This is evident not only from his own writing, but in the 6th *Daastan* he uses the word "*Jannat*

114. *Hamari Zabaan* Weekly. February 15. 1966. Aligarh. 8.

115. *KhamKhana-e-Javed.* Volume 3. 1927. Name first appeared on page 59.

116. *Pari Khana.* Tehseen Sawari. (Translator). Publication; Naya Raahi, Karachi. 1958. (Pakistani Edition) 1.

117. *Ishq Nama.* (MS: Persian). Dastan 129.

makani" (late) for his father. If Wajid Ali Shah was born in 1237 A.H. and his *Daastan* was written between 10 Zeeqad 1262 A.H. and 26 Safar 1263 A.H., then why would he have used the phrase *Jannat Makani*, (or late) or written this autobiography at all? The frankness with which he composed the verses would have been detested by his father. Therefore, this proves that *Ishq Nama* was composed after his coronation, and it was compiled between Zeeqad 1263 A.H. and Zilhij 1265 A.H. The compiler, instead of writing the autobiography during a single period, in spite of his preoccupation continued with the work over a longer period. The period around 1265 A.H. was the time when he was unwell and was busy translating *Hamla-e-Haidari*, and hence writing his autobiography in prose was not an easy task which could be completed in a period of a few weeks. As per the compiler's own accounts, the autobiography apparently relates to events spread over a period of 18 years, but in fact the events relate to a period of 20 years. If something is recalled from memory, then the older the event the more unreliable the information becomes. If we consider *Ishq Nama* to be an autobiography, then we will have to consider both the period of events and the time taken to write it.

The first few verses of *Ishq Nama* denote the urge to compile it and refer to the *Sura-e-Yusuf* of the Quran, which reminds the reader about the beauties of Egypt and the Egyptians' deceptive and shrewd attitude. The compiler draws a parallel between the story of Yusuf and his own, and considers himself to be like *Yusuf*, surrounded by the deception and trickery of women like the ladies of Egypt. The subject matter of the book is quite evident from the name and the ending notes. Though *Ishq Nama* is an autobiography, strangely enough instead of recollecting past events, the book revolves round romantic encounters with women. Though it mentions his birth, coronation, architectural feats, and death, which reflect on the background, instead of relating a chain of similar events it is studded with a mosaic of happenings. It has 132 *Daastans*. The translators, either because of the variety of writings, or for the sake of better compilation under the 127 or 128 headings (*Khanjar* in *Mahal Khana e Shahi* and *Tehseen Sarvari* in *Pari Khana* respectively), have mentioned those events which are given in the book. Some additions are made in the poetic *Ishq Nama* where two *Daastans* have been combined into one.

Haibat-e-Haidari

Writing Date: 1265 A.H. Language: Urdu Genre: Religious poetry Printed: 1292 A.H. Format: 26×17.5, Pages: 149, 11-Lined
Manuscript: Found in the personal library of Maharaja Md. Amir Haider Khan – Mahmoodadabad.

I start in the name of Allah*'s praise*
My entire self is all praise for Allah
Allah *is the owner of everything*
He shines in the world and on earth
He is the Creator of sky and moon and time
He is the creator of Stars and the Sun

The above lines are the initial verses, and the text ends with the following verse:

He is freed from prison
And met his Healer
Became dignified like Sulaiman
Became devout and generous
He was beautiful from inside and outside
He was one among thousands

The title page starts with the name of the Prophet (PBUH) and has other details regarding the book, with the statement that it is the marvelous creation of Hazrat Sultan e Alam. The date of printing is the month of Ramzan 1292 A.H. It contains attractive sketches, and the poem spreads over 292 pages. In the *Qataa't e Tarikh* there are verses by Mehtab ud Daulah Bahadur Darakhshan, Taa'yeush ud Daulah Bahadur Aish, and Atar ud Daulah

Muhammad Ali Mohsin. Darakhshan has written the dates of the Gregorian, Hijri Sambat, and Bengali calendars in every line of the *Qa'taa*. On the last page is given another *Qata'a* by Aish and explanations of important points and words are given in the margin. There are some errors in the inscriptions, and in places the relevant corrections are also given.[118] The subject matter of the book is the Persian *masnavi* of Mulla Bamaan Ali Kirmani (pen name Raji). The original epic of Raji related all the events from the Prophethood of Muhammad (PBUH) up to the era of *Hazrat Ali*, spread over 30,000 pages. Wajid Ali Shah mentions only the events from the original *masnavi*, while about 3,000 verses are recomposed in Urdu. He says:

O Critic! this composition was done
In the year twelve hundred sixty-five
I was unwell and could not expand it more
I took more interest in composing
Lest my mood becomes more gloomy
Thus in such a state of restlessness
It suddenly struck me
That I should do something substantive
And thus I started reading "Hamla-e- Haidari"
It was a Persian Poem
That was about the Imamat
Then it came to my mind
As I was fed up of melancholy
That I shud use beautiful expressions
And that I should translate it into Urdu
That it should be expressive
Endorsing the words of Allah
That it should become popular
So that all big and small should enjoy it

118. As given in the copies found in the Library of Tagore University Library, Lucknow.

When I thought of its title
"Haibat-e-Haidari" came to my mind

In this poem, after stating the name of Allah, heavenly prayers, and the reason for its compilation, the poet, in about 36 Urdu titles, sings the glory of the Prophet up to First Hijri era. He expresses his desire to write more in the following words:

If I live more - I will write more on that

However, the epic could not be completed. The title of the epic does not explain its subject matter. Thus, the weekly paper of that time, *Asad ul Akhbar*, commented as follows:

> *"These days the King is more bent upon writing poetry and thus he is interested in writing 'Hamla-e-Haidari' in Urdu. For this many intellectuals and writers are engaged to do the work of making a fair copy of it."* [119]

This statement is further verified by the *Safar Nama* by Sulaiman[120] and the epic (*Masnavi*) by Asir.[121] A major part of the epic was completed in 1265 A.H. (1849), but it was still incomplete, as evident from the present condition of the writing. This is further verified by the comment of Atar ud Daulah Mohsin, the head of the Royal Library, as he writes in his *Qata'a* "The date of completion of the epic *Haibata-e-Haidari*".[122] However, there were some additions to it made in 1292 A.H., though it still did not suit the title. The present edition of the epic does not indicate that there was any other edition before it. However, if it is considered a second

---

119. *Asadullah Akhbar,* Agra –Edition 118-(1265h). As Quoted by *Masir* (Patna). Volume 4. 1942, 23.

120. Sulaiman, Volume 1, 73.

121. *Durr-ul-Taj* - Md. Muzaffar Ali Khan Asir. Matbaey Sultani. Lucknow. 1270. 231.

122. The same *Qata'a* is written in the end of *Mazaaq-e-Muhabbat* (p. 262) though under a different heading.

edition,[123] then there can be no opinion regarding the changes made or about the additions unless one peruses the first edition.

Ishq Nama (Poetry)

Writing Date: 1266 A.H. Language: Urdu, Genre: Epic or Masnavi (Poetic Autobiography) Printed: 1266 A.H. Format: 29.5×19 Pages: 191 13-Lined Draft (Mussavida) in the hands of the writer: Property of Anjuman Tarraq-i-Urdu Hind[124]- Aligarh

There are two copies of this *masnavi* one in the hand of the King, which is incomplete, and another which is complete, and is an antique and well-decorated piece. The start and end of the *masnavi* is evident from the following verses:

I start in the name of Allah
Who is omniscient and all merciful
Then I welcome Muhammad (PBUH)
And then I salute His family
Prophet who is friend of Allah
Both of them know Each Other well
(End)
Its Allah*'s ordain to remember Muhammad (PBUH)*
The hijri year is ending
And so I end the love story of women[125]

---

123. *Lucknow Ka Shahi Stage.* Prof. Syed Masood Hasan Rizvi Adeeb. Kitab Nagar Lucknow. 1957. 11.

124. There is no evidence as to how and when this manuscript came into the possession of the Library. It is entered in the name of "*Masnavi* Wajid Ali Shah". In the fourth section of this chapter, it is explained how far it is correct to regard this handwritten copy as a manuscript and what its importance is.

125. 1266h = 481,96, 210167 470 31. These are the value of Urdu alphabets as per the metrical pattern of *Tarikh* by which the year of a particular event like birth, coronation, death etc. is deciphered from a couplet. (Translator).

When I reached the end
The endnote Taarikh came to my mind (1266 A.H.).

The writing starts with the last verses of the 25th *Daastan.* And before the completion of the129 Dastan, it ends abruptly. The pages are counted as per the writer's hand, which starts from page 132 and ends at page 518. In this way, though there should have been 387 pages or 193 leaves, in fact it is not so. The reason is the loss of two pages and the mistakes made by the writer while counting the pages. The writer wrote 192 after 190 and continued this mistake until page 208. He then wrote the number 208 twice and though it was corrected, he again wrote 212 on page 211. This mistake continued up until page 363, where he again made the same mistake, writing 365 instead of 364. In this way, two pages were mistakenly added. The last page should have been page 455, but instead 454 was repeated. In this way, though two pages were added, one was then deleted. Thus, though on pages 193 and 194 and 495 and 496 on which *Daastan* 124 (complete) and last verses of Daastan 123 and 125 respectively should have been there are somehow missing.

The author only wants to say that some pages and consequently the related Daastans are missing from the original manuscript.

Some styles of the writer, like the vivid lines and the neat and clean pages, indicate that he must have followed a book, and most of the evidence indicates that he was not a professional writer. He abruptly continued his writing of the manuscript, unmindful of the mistakes, and sometimes the writing contains scribbles, while sometimes it is perfect. There is irregularity in the spacing of lines.

Of all the available manuscripts of Wajid Ali Shah, only this one is in his handwriting from beginning to end, and some portions also depict his painting.

Ishq Nama

(Manuscript)

Writing Date: 1266 A.H. Language: Urdu Genre: Epic or Masnavi (Poetic Autobiography) Printed: Ancient/Classical, Format: 12.5×26.5 Pages: 225, 15-Lined
Manuscript: Proprietor, Maharaj Md. Amir Haider Khan, Mahmoodabad

The first and the last pages were destroyed by moths; hence the numbering starts from Page 2. There are about 448 pages. The headings are given in red, while some short margins are also found. The Librarian Janab Syed Sibte Hasan Hanswi has written the foreword of the manuscript, in which it is said to be near the date of composition.

The Persian *Ishq Nama* is said to be completed in 1265 A.H. during which the King, though unwell, was busy in poetic translation of *Hamla-e-Haidri.* The incomplete condition of *Haibat-e-Haidri* and the last verses of *Ishq Nama* (Persian) indicate that most probably after regaining his health the King discontinued the translation of *Hamla-e-Haidri* and lured by the subject matter, preferred to give his attention to the Persian version of *Ishq Nama.* There were 132 *Daastans* in the Persian version, and 131 *Daastans* and 6,500 verses in the *Ishq Nama Masnavi.* As this was a personal expression and autobiography, the King did not strictly follow the Persian literature. The following examples show this:

a. In Persian literature, the year of composition was given, while it is not mentioned in the Urdu version.
b. In the Persian version, the date of his '*Manjha*' (pre-wedding ceremony) is given as 15 *Shaban* 1253 A.H.

   But in the Urdu version the following words denote a different date:

   All the previous ones became a matter of the past
   My parents gave their consent to it
   The Manjha ritual was performed

And my wedding was solemnized
One thousand two hundred and fifty-three This made us all happy
It was thirteen of Rajab *month*
The stars (Venus & Jupiter) were close
When the manjha ritual was observed

c. In the seventh and eighth *Daastan*, the birth of *Nausherwan Quder* and *Falak Quder* were separately mentioned in the Persian version. In the Urdu version both these events were jointly mentioned in the eighth *Daastan* titled 'Moti Khanam *ke Ishq*.'
d. Playing the tabla on Yasmin Pari's wish is mentioned in the sixth and seventh *Daastan* of Urdu version while it is not mentioned in the Persian version.
e. When there was a controversy over the illegal pregnancy of Haideri Kaneez, it was written:

   She started talking shamelessly
   which was heard by Aazam Bahu

   This mention of Aazam Bahu is missing from the Persian version.

f. In the fifth *Daastan* of the Persian version there is a mention of the delay in marriage and of one more fact. The lines go as such:

   In Manjha a thought came to my mind
   That the days of reunion are close by
   I am not aware of the worldly traditions
   And I am a stranger on this path
   'Sandal' named maid of my grandmother
   Was very well-versed in this matter
   She was forty with good height
   And she had smallpox marks on her face
   She learned the good art
   And many got the right target

g. In the 72nd Dastan there is mention of Hoor *Pari's* pregnancy, childbirth at seven months, and then the child's death. There are some other facts in it, for example:

When seven months of pregnancy were passed
Son was born
There was no idea of immature days
As there was uncertainty regarding full term
When I recollected
I solved this with experience
There was much difference
And I realised that it was not my child
I was deeply pained
But I kept it as a closely guarded secret
At last Allah *was beneficial*
The child expired within forty days

h. In the Persian version, in the 73rd *Daastan* some surprise is expressed at the pregnancy of Haideri Kaneez. By the 72nd *Daastan* of the Urdu version, it appears that the King was waiting for this opportunity. He says:

The second maid 'Haideri'
Was included among the special ones
She was only in the service all the time
And never had the opportunity to share seclusion
The reason of this seclusion was that
It was a testing time
'Pari' was conversing with 'Hoor'
There was some problem in pregnancy
I was very curious and inquisitive about it
And wanted that the truth should be revealed
And that the culprit be brought to book

i. In the Persian version, immediately after the above-mentioned episode, the story of driving out of *Bilquis Pari* on the charge of theft is mentioned.
   In the Urdu version a full chapter is found which consists of 25 verses. There is no mention of such an episode in the Persian version.
j. In the Persian *Ishq Nama, Daastans* 80 and 81, with minor changes, are the *Daastan* 80 and 82 of the Urdu *Ishq Nama.* Apart from *Daastan* 81 of the Urdu *Ishq Nama*, there are 41 verses in which there is a mention of the illegitimate relations of women. This is missing in the Persian version.

For the sake of brevity, only a few such differences are mentioned here. A comparison of the prose and poetic sections reveals that there are many things which are found in one version but are missing in the other. This is not surprising because when a poet composes a poem, then with his power of imagination he includes things which are not found in the prose version. If the biographer and the poet are one and the same person, like in the case of *Ishq Nama*, then there is no doubt in accepting the difference, but if these are two different people, then the writer's expressions will be regarded as self-story and that of the poet only as a story which should be authenticated. [126]

In the present times, people have started addressing this *Masnavi* as '*Tarikh Pari Khana Manzoom*' or '*Khaqan-e-* Sarwar', but this is not backed by any authority. In the *Masnavi*, in the *Tarikh* section, the poet has clearly mentioned the name of the *Masnavi*:

I have completed the story of lady love.
(31,470 167,21 96,481 = 1266)

---

126. This becomes relevant when often *Ishq Nama* is regarded as the composition of *Asir* or any other writer.

To discern the year, some more words were inserted. In case there is any doubt in this regard, the statements of *Wazir ul Sultan* Bahadur and Wajid Ali Shah are available. *Wazir ul Sultan*, while discussing the examples of the King's Urdu poetry, indicated some portions of this *Masnavi*, and named it *Kitab-e-Lajawab Mausoom ba Ishq Nama-e-Mubarak.*[127] However, Wajid Ali Shah, in his *Bani* list and in *Chanchal Masnavi*, has named this autobiography only as *Ishq Nama.*

> *Whosoever wants can read Ishq Nama - And learn about union with beloved*[128]

The *Ishq Nama* in the *Bani* list indicates a Persian prose book, while the above mentioned *Ishq Nama* refers to poetry. This is further confirmed by the fact that the *Masnavi* mentions the publication of *Saut ul Mubarak* and also confirms that the book is present in the library where anyone can access it.[129] The mention of *Ishq Nama* in the above verse is not about its Persian version.

Kar Khatma is the free translation of Wajid Ali Shah's self-written Persian version of *Ishq Nama*. Later on, in the *Masnavi Ishq Nama*, some additions continued.[130] But the added verses are not found in the Persian version. The *Masnavi Ishq Nama*, which included the added verses, has been published, though it is rarely found.[131]

---

127. *Wazir Nama.* Wazir ul Sultan Md. Amir Ali Khan Amir. Publication Nizami- Lucknow. 1293. 311.

128. *Malazul Kalmat.* Md. Wajid Ali Shah Akhtar, Matbaey Sultani, Calcutta. 1297. (Azad Library). 715.

129. *Ibid*, 728.

130. *Lucknow Ka Shahi Stage.* Prof. Syed Masood Hasan Rizvi Adeeb. Kitab Nagar Lucknow. 1957. 173–74. 186.

131. Only two copies of *Ishq Nama* (Poetry) are available but both of these are incomplete. The author is unable to give any opinion regarding these as he had no access to it.

Majmua-e- Wajidia (Persian)

Writing Date: 1263–66 A.H. Language: Persian Genre: Book (containing writings from many sources) Printed: 1266 A.H. Format: 25×17 Pages: 183 9-Lined
Published: Matabaey Sultani (Lucknow) with the support of Captain Maqbool ud Daulah Mirza Md. Mehdi Ali Khan Qubool

The first page is blank. On page 2, instead of the seal of the King, '*Bismillah*' is written, and then up to page 4, there are verses in the glory of Allah and the Prophet (PBUH). The main subject starts from page 4, while page 5 is blank as perhaps it was intended for some painting by the author. The title of page 6 reads '*Ibn Hazrat Jannat Makan Shah Amjad Ali Ibn Hazrat...*' There is a picture of the King holding a sword in his hand, with a studded chair alongside him and a well decorated cap on his head. The artist shows a halo around his face and in the margin his name is inscribed with the official stamp that is found on all pages. There are also brief headlines regarding the text. The Arabic statement is written in Arabic script with vowel indications. The poetry is written in poetic style. The lines continued in harmony up to the end, while the ink is not changed for the headlines. Alas! With the advent of time the paper was damaged, and the first page itself from where these details are gathered is incomplete.

Majmua-e-Wajidia (Urdu)

Translation: 1266 A.H. Language: Urdu Book: (containing writings from many sources) Publication: 1267 A.H. Format: 28×18 Pages: 204 9 Lined
Published- Matabaey Sultani (Lucknow) with the support of Captain Maqbool ud Daulah Qubool

The first page is blank on pages 2 and 3 there are decorated words in the centre and the margins, and in the official stamp is written '*Dibach Mubarak*' (Preface). On Page 5 there is a picture on which are the words '*Chhupi in baton ki guchhi Chunni wala – Sultan Alam Md.* Wajid Ali Shah *Badshah Takullus Akhtar.*' This continues on the next page where it is written '*Beta*

Hazrat Jannat makan Md. Amjad Ali Shah *Badshah ka aur pota Hazrat...'* Details of the picture are given in two different official stamps, in which it is written '*Shabeh Mubarak Hazrat Sultan Alam Md.* Wajid Ali Shah *Badshah Ghazi Khuld* Allah *Malka wa Saltanat.*'

On the second stamp are the words 'Age 29 years, 1267 A.H.' There are remarkable differences in the pictures as compared to the previous ones. *First*, a crown replaces the cap, *second*, in his hand a royal document replaces the sword and *third*, a sitting position is seen. In the handwritten *Bani* list this book is missing. In the published *Bani* it is named Matbua-e-Wajidia. In the Persian version, in the text and in the endnote, it is named '*Majmua-e-Wajidia Sultani*', and in the Urdu version it is also written as '*Majmua-e-Wajidia Sultani*', while in the endnote only '*Wajidia Sultani*' is written. Out of these three names, the one mentioned in the *Bani* list must be taken as authentic because the titles of most of the King's writings are two-worded.

The original book is in Persian and is written by the King. Most probably the King himself did not translate it into Urdu. This is because had he done it himself, there would have been no need to replace '*Nuskha-e Mutabarka*' with '*Risala*', '*Majmua-e-Wajidia Sultani*' with only '*Wajidia Sultani*', and '*Tasnif Mubarak*' with '*Hasbul Hukm.*' The endnote could have been written verbatim. Most probably, Aminuddin translated it on the King's order and under the supervision of Qubool. The King was not very interested in prose, hence, to associate the translated version with the King is not acceptable without any authority. The dates of the compilation and printing of these two versions are not given, nor does any verse indicate them. There are also no external factors to verify this. However, these dates can be verified from any verse or statement from the versions. For instance, while referring to *Imam Akhiruzz Zaman* he writes:

> *"Age of Hazrat up to 1245 A.H. appears to be 909 years. And whereas the book is written in Urdu in 1266 A.H. in the month of Safar, thus according to this date his age appears to be 1,011 years."*[132]

---

132. *Majmuay Wajidia Sultani*. Md. Wajid Ali Shah Akhtar (Amir). 40–41.

This book is translated from Persian to Urdu, hence by this calculation the Persian version must have been compiled around 1263–66 A.H. and the Urdu translation, as appears from the above statement, was written in 1266 A.H. The preface must have been written in or after 1263 A.H. because in it the writer mentions himself as King and Amjad Ali Shah is mentioned as 'late.' In the picture given in the Urdu version the King's age is mentioned as 29 years. In other words, the year of its publication must be 1267 A.H., and the publication of the Persian version must have been in the same year, or possibly a year or two before.

The subject matter of the book is theology, history, literature, geography, medicine, handicraft, and trade. The materials related to these topics were collected by the compiler during his formative years and were well-preserved. The book is divided into 27 sections and is named '*Afsar.*' The compiler says that the book is meant for the pleasure of the readers so that the poet learns to compose, the fortune teller learns the art of foretelling, the one who innovates enjoys it, and the ill becomes healthy.

First Section: Name, patronage, birth, and martyrdom of the 14 '*Masoomeens.*'

Second Section: Details of auspicious and inauspicious dates.

Third Section: The benefits of '*Sura-e-Yaseen*'

Fourth Section: Nikah and details of sexual intercourse

Fifth Section: Prayers and '*aayats*' regarding love and romance

Sixth Section: Prayers and '*aayats*' regarding enmity and discord.

Seventh Section: Prayers and acts to achieve health and well being

Eighth Section: Prayers and acts to diffuse djinns, fairies, and ghosts

Ninth Section: All kinds of prayers

Tenth Section: Sketches to lure others

Eleventh Section: Sketches to spread enmity among friends

Twelfth Section: Sketches to diffuse *Djinns*

Thirteenth Section: Different types of sketches

Fourteenth Section: As per *Hadith, aayats* to inscribe on gems

Fifteenth Section: Tricks by which *Djinns* can be made to appear

Sixteenth Section: Good deeds which bring prosperity

Seventeenth Section: Bad deeds which bring poverty

Eighteenth Section: Names of the martyrs of Karbala and their killers

Nineteenth Section: Prescriptions to increase potency

Twentieth Section: Techniques to make fireworks

Twenty-First Section: Different types of prescriptions

Twenty-Second Section: Reigning periods of Kings, Mughals

Twenty-Third Section: To memorise the meaning of words, instructions to remember their synonyms, for examples for words like 'officials', 'food', 'kebab', 'bread', 'robe of honour', 'music', 'song' and 'singers', 'letter', 'clothes', 'beasts', 'tents', 'birds', 'gems', 'jewelry', 'dry fruits', 'flowers'.

Twenty-Fourth Section: Puzzles, riddles, and enigma

Twenty-fifth Section: Alphabetical orders of Hindi and Persian

Twenty-Sixth Section: Terminology of the Army

Twenty-Seventh Section: Classic fables

An eye-catching handwritten copy of the Urdu translation of the above book was available in Amir ud Daulah Public Library, Lucknow until May 1955. The title page was decorated with golden art and was in the hand of the writer Aminuddin. It had 207 pages. Presently, the handwritten copy has been replaced by a printed one with 204 pages.[133] On the title page, the former proprietor of this book gives an account which contains information about the book. It reads as follows:

> "Property of Abdul Zalil Ahmed Artaza Hussain Ibn Haider Hussain Gafrullah purchased from Janab Hakim Nawab Mirza Sahib for three rupees eight annas on Sunday 14 Ramazan 1270 A.H...."
> (Translated from Persian)

The writing appears to be antique, contains a seal, and shows no possibility of forgery and hence appears to be trustworthy. The books of *Matbaey-Sultani* were often gifted to special and distinguished courtiers. The booklovers who did not have access to the court had no choice but to either take them from the courtiers or have it copied by professional writers. Artaza Hussain purchased it at a high cost. The buyer also named the courtier through whom the purchase was done. Regardless of whether the book was the property of Hakim Nawab Mirza or if it was purchased through him, this fact is reliable because during the Ahd-e-Wajidi (period of Wajid Ali Shah) there was a person by the name of 'Mirza Sahab' who was quite well-known, as is evident from the following verse:

I think what is the reason
Only You are Nawab Mirza
You are mentioned in all the writings
Your existence is exemplary

After being separated from the courtesans (*Waziran*), Wajid Ali Shah also mentions the name of Nawab Mirza in *Ishq Nama*;[134]

---

133. *Majmua-e-Wajidia*. Propriety: Amir ud Daulah Public Library, Lucknow-No. RU891.43108/A28M. G.D. Bhatnagar must have seen this handwritten copy as he mentions it in the Bibliography of his Thesis.

134. *Ishq Nama* (Poetry). Wajid Ali Shah Akhtar-Dastan- 28p. 1266. (Anjuman). 28.

Maintained relation with Ali Baksh – Often romanced with Nawab Mirza.

Moreo Agha Haju Sharf ver, Agha Haju Sharf also mentions *Nawab* Mirza while discussing the well-known courtiers of *Darbar-e-Wajidi*:

Honoured Nawab Mirza *Hakim*
Is an old physician of the King
He is like a second Isaa
And is well-known and professional
His treatment is world famous
His clinic is a health centre
He is Isaa for the sick ones
And is quite experienced
He was active during Khilafat times
And is distinguished among the elite
He is a famous pupil of 'Aatish'
He was witty, well informed, and cultured
The sick who were apprehensive of death
Gained recovery at his hand[135]

Sharaf himself was a court visitor and the pupil of Aatish. Thus, it is not proper to doubt his statement regarding account of his contemporary master. Consequently, it is not correct to say that Shauqq did not have access to Wajid Ali Shah's court, though he wished to be there. *Hakim Ahsan Sahab Lucknavi's* (the grandson of Shauqq) statement that Shauqq was as a servant in Wajid Ali Shah's court is beyond belief. No history, writing, anecdote, or tradition supports this argument."[136] In *Masnavi Huzn-e-*Akhtari, Wajid Ali Shah confirms that there were about 500 physicians,[137] and to say that

135. *Afsanaey Lucknow.* Syed Jalaluddin Haider Ali*as* Agha Hajju Sharf. 1290. 169.
136. *Tazkira-e-Shauqq.* 43–44.
137. *Huzn-e-Akhtari.* 71.

Shauqq was not one of these is equivalent to saying that either Shauqq felt indignation at working with the King or that he was worse than all these physicians.

Behr-e- Hidayat

Compilation: 1263–67 A.H., Language: Persian, Genre: Majmua e Masail e Fiqh, Publication: 1267 A.H. Format: 30×20 Pages: 56, 9-lined Published: Matabaey Sultani (Lucknow) with the support of "Namak Khwar wa Jaannisar-e- Qdeem" Captain Maqbool ud Daulah Qubool.

The title page speaks highly about the printing excellence of *Matbaey-Sultani.* In the artistic title page, within the square is an oval within which is inscribed '*Bahr-e- Hidayat*' and 1267 A.H. – the year of its compilation and printing. Above the title, the words '*Risala-e-Haza Taleef Mubarak*' alongside the king's name and royal address were written. The names of the printer and that of the person under whose supervision the work was done (*Captain* Maqbool ud Daulah *Qubool*) were also given. On page 3 and 4, the royal seal of a nymph is also given. The main book starts from page 5, after the preface. The *aayats* and one-word headings are given in Arabic script. The lines continued up to the last page. Up to this part, the explanation of the content given on a page was placed in the lower margin. There is no such indication on page 112 nor is there any proof of corrections.[138]

Since childhood I was enlightened of the quandaries of Fiqh from my honourable father, which was in the form of queries the answers to which were written by the erstwhile Mujtahid ul Asr. These were in a scattered form

138. This detail of *Bahr-e-Hidayat* is an excerpt from a damaged copy of the manuscript. In it there is seal of Zulfiqar ud Daulah Bahadur on the margin of page five though the seal out sized the margin and is hence incomplete. Had there was no printing of the title page or if there was some blank page after page 112 then this seal could have been put there. The fact that the seal was on page five is pointer to the fact that the book had only 112 pages. The copy which is there in the Library of Tagore University (Lucknow) also further confirms that the book has only 112 pages.

which was composed in the form of a poem so that they are well secured. I was sure that everyone will be benefitted by this narrative, and the writers will be honoured and rewarded by Allah. *As it was in the form of scattered parts, these were not divided into chapters, in fact they were written as per the instructions of His Excellency.*
(Translated from Persian)

It is quite clear from the above statement that it was written after the death of Amjad Ali Shah. The main purpose behind this compilation was to recollect the problems which, on the advice of Amjad Ali Shah, were often put before Sultan ul Ulema Maulvi Syed Md. Sahab Aalallah Maqama Ibn Maulvi Syed Dildar Ali Sahib Ghfranma'ab.[139] The questions and responses of both the compiler and author were shown, as both of them deserved blessings. Like *Majmua-e-Wajidia Sultani*, here also the title of the book is reported as *Bahr-ul Hidayat Sultani.* The word '*Sultani*', like the word '*Mubarak*', is only a formality, and the correct name is that which is given on the title page of the book and in the *Bani* list.[140]

The person who posed such questions and the one who responded were all from the *Ithna Ashri* (Shia) sect, and hence all 163 such problems reflect their faith and beliefs. The book contains clarification and authentic Islamic opinions on subjects like *Nama*, *Khums*, *Zakaa't*, *Nikah*, *Mu'ta*, cohabitation, *Halal*, *Haram* and *Makruh*, slavery, interest, unfair livelihood, and Sunni and Shia followers. Such learned opinions reflect the mental caliber and worthy competence of such scholars, but had they mentioned the dates alongside such queries, then this would have been more beneficial. Some of these subjects which are of general interest are presented here.

139. At five places in *Behr-e-Hidayat* (at pages 47, 58, 78, 88, and 94) there are signatures of the person answering such questions. His title was *Sultan ul Ulema* while his name was Syed Muhammad. (Janab Rizwan Maa'b page 22).

140. In the *Bani* list the word '*Behr ul-Hidayat*' is given (See page 103), and in the text the same term is also used. But on the title page the word *Behr-e-Hidayat* is used, which is also eloquent and is hence preferable.

a. Query: What is the extent of the right of parents over the children? What is the extent of a child's obedience towards his parents? Answer: As per the available knowledge, both have rights, but it is incumbent upon a wife to obey her husband and thus obeying the father is mandatory. No further detail is required. (Pages 37–38).
b. Query: If a person wants to visit a disreputable place, though he has no bad intentions, for example visiting the bar not to drink wine, but to buy vinegar, then is it alright for him to visit such a place? - Answer: Keep away from disreputable places. (Page 56 *Hadith*).
c. Query: Is it alright to give non-believers gold and silver coins on which some sacred names and *Kalma* are inscribed? Can these be converted into jewellery? Answer: It is better not to give such coins to non-believers. A prohibition against converting these into jewellery is not backed by any authority. (Page 71)
d. Query: Is it proper to perform *Nikah* or *Mu'ta* with a prostitute without any information about her *Idda* (separation period of a widow or divorcee) and without any investigation? Answer: It is better to be cautious.
e. Query: Is it proper to perform *Namaz* in the flannel material which is very trendy nowadays? Answer: If it is unclear whether the wool is of an edible (permissible) animal or non-permissible animal, it is better to keep away from it. But if the material comes from a Muslim country or if a Muslim delivers it without knowing its origin, then there is no harm in using it.
f. Query: It is permissible (*makruh*) to say '*sher*' or verses while fasting even though it is in the glory of the Prophet's family (*Ahl-e-bait*)? In such a case is it also *makruh* to recite 'elegy' regarding *ahl-e-bait?* Answer: It is *makruh*, which means that there will be less '*sawab.*' If the elegy is recited in prose form, it will definitely attain more '*sawab.*' (Page 82).

Such queries by the compiler not only came from his perplexed mind, but also came to his attention while he studied books and documents like

Hadiqul Muttaqeen, Jama-e-Abbasi, Hayat-ul-Quloob, Maqna-wa-Amaali, Tehzeeb ul Ahkam, Kitab-ul-Ashraaf-o-Ikhtiyar, Mafatih, Shahab Saaqib, Jami-ul- Maqasid, Sharhe-lama, Tanqeeh, and *Shaara-ul Islam.*

Saut-ul- Mubarak

Compilation: 1263–67 A.H. Language: Persian Genre: The art of Music, Publication: 1269 A.H. Format: 22×13 Pages: 82, 11-lined Published: Matabaey Sultani (Lucknow) with the support of Amir Ali Khan Hilal

The first page is blank. On pages 2 and 3 there are decorated columns, on page 2 is the seal of the King and below it, *Bismillah* is written. The lines continue uninterrupted and headings and other important content are in bold letters, though there are some printing mistakes.[141] The pronunciation of Hindi words is as per the old dictionary. At the end page 163, Amir Ali Khan Hilal writes a '*qata'a*' in seven verses. Hilal was the manager of *Matbaey-Sultani*,[142] and thus it is quite possible that the book was published under his supervision. The above-mentioned details of the book are gathered from a very damaged copy, the existence of which stands witness to the fact that the book-lovers took good care of it.[143] Even 100 years ago this book was so rare that Wajid Ali Shah mentioned it in the following words:

Dear if you are interested in music
Then young man! read Saut-ul-Mubarak
It is about this fine art
But now it is rare like a Mirage
During my times it was available freely

141. Read page 131 and 137 of Saut-ul- Mubarak, (Md. Wajid Ali Shah Akhtar, Lucknow 1269 A. H. (Raza Library); instead of 131 and 137, only 31 and 38 is written.

142. *Bani* - 233–34.

143. Janab Imtiaz Ali Arshi, the Librarain of Raza Library (Rampur) gathered from the entries of the register that the book was included in the Library a little before 1889. In 1962 the National Archives (Delhi), by laminating every page, has preserved the book in the library.

It is now rare since the plundering
It is found in my library
It is scarce elsewhere[144]

The first and last pages are incomplete from the binding side, and the *Qata'a-e-Tarikh* of Hilal was also damaged. Only the second lines are legible, but it is not clear whether the dates pertain to its writing or printing. The verses are as follows:

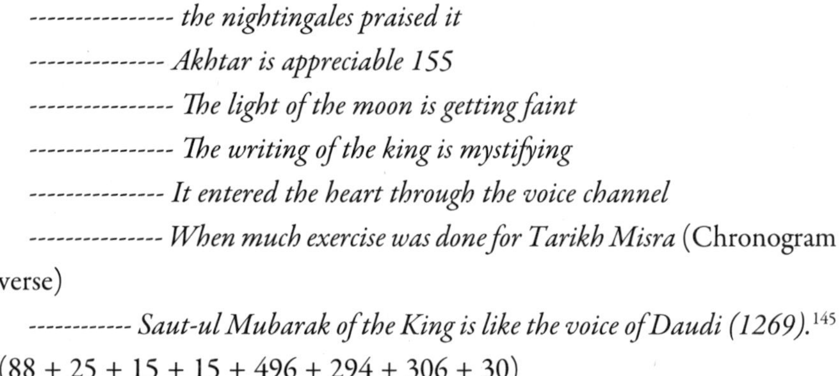

---------------- *the nightingales praised it*
--------------- *Akhtar is appreciable 155*
---------------- *The light of the moon is getting faint*
---------------- *The writing of the king is mystifying*
--------------- *It entered the heart through the voice channel*
--------------- *When much exercise was done for Tarikh Misra* (Chronogram verse)
------------ *Saut-ul Mubarak of the King is like the voice of Daudi (1269).*[145]
(88 + 25 + 15 + 15 + 496 + 294 + 306 + 30)

Most of the poets of the court had composed '*Tarikh Qata'at*' for the year of printing, thus here too the date 1269 A.H. could be the date of printing. The date of its composition was probably 1267 A.H. or 1268 A.H. Mirza Mehdi Ali Qubool used to write '*Qaseedas*' to glorify Eid, *Navroz*, or *Eid-Gadeer.* One of his compositions (*Mukhammus*) is below:

Among the experts of music there is a buzz
You are the King and we are all your subjects
You know so well about this art

---

144. *Malazul Kalmat* page 728. (Excerpts from Masnavi 'Chanchal' written in 1295 A.H.).
145. The starting letters are incomplete. Only page 69 is legible; with the help of this the verse was completed.

Your impressive writing is given here.
Whosoever sees is never tired of it.[146]

In Hilal's *Qata'a* a name is given, but ignoring the name of the book by *Qubool* is doubtful. The subject matter of the book is a brief account of Indian music. From the viewpoint of sounds, the various terminology of music has been divided into subheadings spreading from pages 2–9. The compiler admits that since childhood, he was attracted to music, but he had no opportunity to express it. People who had knowledge of this art were greedy and narrow-minded, and the books written by them including *Naghmat-e-Aasfi, Khulasatul Aish and Sang-e-Darpan* were not satisfactory. With immense indulgence and effective hard work, this book is written so that others are also benefitted by it.

The book is divided into six chapters, and each chapter is called '*Hijab*'. It is further divided into sections which are called '*parda.*' In the first chapter there are 17 sections spread over pages 9–53. In this chapter, there are descriptions of melodies and songs. This includes the details of melody, the meaning of the word '*mausaqi*' (music), and also the identification and division of melodies, the degree of expertise in music, and the profile and services of previous experts. In the second chapter (pages 53–78) there is an explanation regarding the tune and tone, their different shades, and how a change in them changes their effect. In chapter three (pages 79–82) there is a description of four types of musical instruments, namely *Tat, Batat, Kathan,* and *Sukhar*, along with the details of their inventors. In chapter four (pages 83–92) there is an appreciation of dances, and the book mentions 14 types of '*gutts*' or musical quavers, which are as follows:

a. *Pari Gutt*
b. *Salami Gutt*

---

146. *Zikrul Masoomeen*, Mirza Muhammadi Ali Khan Qubool, Matbaey Sultani, Lucknow, 1272 A.H., 78.

c. *Faryad Gutt*
d. *Mukut Gutt*
e. *Aanchal Gutt*
f. *Muskurati or Khanda Gutt*
g. *Moaddab Gutt*
h. *Husn Gutt*
i. *Ghoonghat Gutt*
j. *Mehboob Gutt*
k. *Naaz Gutt*
l. *Ghamzada Gutt*
m. *Ada Gutt*
n. *Nek Gutt*

Towards the end of the chapter the delicacy of *Bhav* (gestures during a dance) and the unfamiliarity of people with this *Bhav* are also mentioned. In chapter five (pages 92–108), through the medium of 24 fables, the lives of some distinguished musicians, their services, and their amazing contributions are discussed. In chapter six (pages 108–162), there are two sections. In this chapter the dance style, as invented by the compiler himself, called '*Rahas Mubarak Sultani*' is discussed. In the first section (up to page 139), there is a mention of 17 *Rahas* (Dance Drama) as listed below:

1. *Rahas Salami*
2. *Rahas Seedhi Hath Jodi*
3. *Rahas Seedhi Gal Bhaiyyan*
4. *Rahas Mor Pankhi*
5. *Rahas Morchhal*
6. *Rahas Khewa*
7. *Rahas Hath Jodi Chakkar*
8. *Rahas Gul Bhaiyyan Chakkar*
9. *Rahas Chandra Mukhi*

10. *Rahas Suraj Mukhi*
11. *Rahas Akaas Mukhi*
12. *Rahas Chau Ghada*
13. *Rahas Chau Mukha*
14. *Rahas Taj Mubarak*
15. *Rahas* KHali *Joda*[147]
16. *Rahas Rahas Palta*
17. *Rahas Kunj Galyan*

In the second section the following 15 *Rahas* are mentioned:

1. *Rahas Mujra*
2. *Rahas Ghoonghat*
3. *Rahas Mor Chhatri*
4. *Rahas Chomak*
5. *Rahas Nayya*
6. *Rahas Raj Mukhi*
7. *Rahas Pran Mukhi*
8. *Rahas Achpal*
9. *Rahas Jia Sakhi*
10. *Rahas Chitra Mubarak*
11. *Rahas Gyan Sakhi*
12. *Rahas Sogna Mukhi*
13. *Rahas Kandar*
14. *Rahas Mor Chaal*
15. *Rahas Nain Sakhi*

The details regarding the number of participants, their words, and other important aspects in all these *Rahas* (Dance Drama) are elaborately discussed.

147. In the list of *Saut ul Mubarak,* the order of KHali *Joda* and *Rahas Palta* is the same. However, on page 137–38 this order has been reversed.

The Urdu translations of the fourth[148] and sixth[149] chapters are included in *Bani* with the necessary changes and additions. The poetic Urdu translations of chapters one and two are included with omissions and additions under the name *Masnavi 'Chanchal'* in the supplement of *Malaz ul Kalmat.*[150] In the manuscript of *Bani*, a verbatim translation of chapter six under the title '*Tarjuma Rahas Mubarak Mundarja Saut-ul-Mubarak*' has been included, which to some extent compensates for the damage found in the present published copy.

Sukhan Ashraf

Writing: 1257–68 A.H., Language: Urdu, Genre: Diwan Publication: 1269 A.H. Format: 39×27 Pages: 145, 9-Lined Published: Matabaey Sultani (Lucknow) with the support of Sheikh Madad Ali KhanAzad Qadeem Aminuddin Tehrir .

Every King becomes a pauper in your love
Why did my heart become disobedient
No other claim of Khudai except on You
That Beauty will scorch me like 'lala' (flower)
The one who is hurt in love is good
It was compensated when Akhtar saw your face
My dear You abused me and you were rude

The first page of this printed copy is blank, like the other manuscripts. The second page is regarded as the title page. On this page *Bismillah* is inscribed with decorative paintings on three sides and a picture of the King in the centre, surrounded by courtiers. In the front a dancer is presenting *Mujra.* Above the picture is written '*Picture of the Writer of Diwan Sultan Ibn*

148. *Bani*, There are details of *'Pargat'* with pictures. 41–68.

149. *Ibid*, 69–85.

150. *Malazul Kalmat*, Md. Wajid Ali Shah Akhtar, Matbaey Sultani, Calcutta. 1297 A.H. (Azad Library). 715–30.

Sultan Khaqan Ibn Khaqan Al mutakhallus Akhtar.' Below the picture are the words '*start of* Ghazal *from the Diwan written by Hazrat Abul Mansoor* Nasiruddin *Sikander Jah Badshah Adil Qaiser Zaman Sultan Alam Md.* Wajid Ali Shah *Avadh Ghazi Khuld* Allah *Malka wa Sultanat o Afaz Ali ul Alameen barah wa ehsana.*' These words are written in red ink. In the last verses, his *Takhallus* (pen name) and the rhyming words are also written in red. The details regarding the Ghazal are given in a well-decorated seal, and the number of verses is also mentioned, though the possibility of incorrect numbering is not ruled out.[151] There are also many printing mistakes and corrections are given only in one copy of it.[152] There are no headlines in it; some 49 corrections are made. The printing of the corrected copy is in good handwriting and the name of the writer, and the supervisor is given on the last page (page 288). In one line is Persian script, while the remaining part is left blank. In one copy, the three words 'Mir *Banda Hasan*' are found, and there is no further explanation about them. The last page of the book is blank, and the seal of the royal library is not found anywhere.The printed copies are on white, green, and blue paper. Only Ghazals are found in this copy, and out of all the writings of Wajid Ali Shah, this one is in the largest format. In the poetic *Ishq Nama*, the King referred to one of the Ghazals of this Diwan, which was often sung by Sahab Khanam:

Often she used to sing my Ghazal
Its first verse is exemplary
There are shackles of love around the feet
It is bad for me but good for love

151. Please check pages 188 and 195 of *Sukhan Ashraf.* Here the page numbers are wrong, as in place of 8, the number 9 is written while on page18, the number 8 is written.

152. Copy in the Maulana Azad Library, Aligarh Muslim University, Aligarh. No. Habib Ganj Urdu 54/103.

His relationship with Sahab Khanam happened after the birth of Kaiwan Quder.[153] The writing of *Sukhan Ashraf* must have started in 1257 A.H. It was completed in 10 years. The compiler of *Sarapa Sukhan*, who was in search of a Ghazal, was found in the second Diwan (i.e. *Sukhan Ashraf*):

Love is like a heavy burden on the head
On whom the young and the old throw stones

Tazkira e Sarapa Sukhan was completed in 1269 A.H. This Ghazal was composed for the *Tarhi Mushaira* (Mushaira with given rhyme and meter) of Mir *Asad Sabar* in 1267 A.H.[154] The person who organised the *tazkira* regarded the Ghazal as being extracted from the *Diwan* and not from the *Mushaira.*[155] From this we can say that *Diwan Sukhan Ashraf* was almost completed by 1267 A.H. and was published in 1269 A.H.

Up till 21 May 1955, a handwritten copy of this *Diwan* was available in Amir *ud Daulah Public library*, Lucknow, and had about 1,400 pages. On the title page, a golden weed was inscribed and above every Ghazal, the number of verses and other details were written in golden script. In the compilation details, there was no date of printing, but the writer's name Aminuddin and the name of the compiler *Sheikh Madad Ali* were mentioned.[156] Now in place of this gold-plated copy there is a printed copy of *Sukhan Ashraf* on blue paper,[157] which shows a faint effort to gold-plate it using golden powder. The previous gold-plated copy was the first one of *Sukhan Ashraf.*

---

153. *Mahal Khana e Shahi,* Mirza Fida Ali Khanjar. Naami Press. Lucknow. (1934). 16–17.
154. *Lucknow Ki Aakhri Shama.* Dr. Abulai Siddiqui and Maulana Abdul Salam Nadvi. Educational Book House, Aligarh. 27.
155. *Sarapa Sukhan.* Syed Mohsin Ali Mohsin. Pubication Munshi Naval Kishore. Lucknow 1874. 7.
156. Shri G.D. Bhatnagar, Scholar Lucknow University must have seen this handwritten *Diwan,* as it is entered as a *Diwan* of Wajid Ali Shah in the handwritten list of references.
157. Copy No. RU891.431/A28D.

In the present printed copy, some of the verses were copied from that and the flaws are easily discernable.

Like *Guldasta-e-Ashqan*, *Sukhan Ashraf* is also part of a *Qata'a-e-Tarikh*, as the year 1291 A.H. is discernable from it. But most of the Ghazals of *Nazm Namwar*, which was completed in 1287 A.H., are copied from *Sukhan Ashraf.* This name is verified from the copy, which was owned by the King's nephew, *Sir Meerza Jahan Quder*, though it is difficult to infer when this name was written on it. *Sukhan Ashraf* is the second *Diwan* of the King. When the poems of this *Diwan* were being shifted to *Kulliyat-e-Akhtari*, it was addressed as the Second Diwan. There are 245 Ghazals and 2,151 verses in this *Diwan.* These Ghazals underwent a change, and there were also some additions or deletions when they were published in *Kulliyat-e-*Akhtari. When again, for the third time, these Ghazals were published in *Nazm Namwar*, some more changes were made. A comparative study of the three variations gives a good understanding of the entire composition of the King.

Irshad Khaqani

Writing: 1268 A.H. Language: Urdu, Genre: Art of Prosody, Publication: 1269 A.H. Format: 27×18 Pages: 62, 11-lined Published: Matabaey Sultani (Lucknow) with the support of Jaan Nisar Captain Maqbool ud Daulah Mirza Md. Mehdi Ali Khan Bahadur Qubool

In the beginning, on the printed title page, two lines of the name of the King are inscribed '*Risala Haaza Tasnif Mubrak.*' At the end, the name of the printer and the compiler are given, while in the centre the name of the book is written. The columns on pages 1–3 are decorative. On page 2 is the seal of the King and *Bismillah* is written. In the text, the one-word headlines are underlined. At the end, on pages 119–123, there are *Qata'at Tarikh* and endnotes. Page 124 is blank. In the *Qata'at e Tarikh*, the first *Qata'a* of two verses is by *Munshi Muzaffar Ali* Bahadur *Jung* (*Asir*):[158]

158. In the same book the King has regarded Barq as an expert of this art. There is only a Qata'a of Asir with incomplete addressing.

Shamsuddin is writing the prosody
It is the translation of the King's work
Asir has its date of composition
Name of Faqir is alive due to His Excellency the King (1268)
(Translated from the Persian couplet)

It is not clear whether the above translation shows the date of translation or of printing. It is clear from the *Qata'ats* of Amir Ali Khan Hilal, which were composed separately for translation and printing, and which were entered after the *Qata'at* of *Asir.*

(A)
The Takhallus Akhtar is enlightening
So much that the Moon is embarrassed
When Hilal *searched for the Year of printing*
He is humbled before His Excellency
Then Isaa (Prophet) gave him a call from the sky
The King of Hind has given life to Faqir (Takhallus) 1268.

(B)
Wajid Ai Shah is the monarch of eloquence
He has established himself in Urdu literature
The work of the humble self was of an ordinary level
This has received honour
His poetry and prose both are fluent
Every page of which raised the standard of Urdu
This created a niche for itself in the royal print house
And this treasure was published in Urdu circle
Hilal *has calculated the Hijri year*
This is like a rose in the garden of Urdu literature (1269 A.H.)

From the two Persian *Qat'a'ats* of *Qubool,* it is now clarified that the translation of this book was done in 1268 A.H. and the printing in 1269 A.H. Other than Irshad Khaqani, *Tarbiyat-e-Nama-e Sultani* is the *Tarikhi* name of this translation. '*Tawaul Azhan*', '*Tehzib ul Asal*', and '*Hukm-e-Akhtar*' are the three names which are related to the printing of the book. In the endnote the name of the writer is given as *Md. Khursheed,* and the correction of the printing was done by Amir Ali Khan Hilal.[159]

In the title, endnote, and headings of the *Qata'at,* this book is referred to as the writing of the King. But in fact, as evident from the *Qata'at* and the Preface of the book, it is not his original writing but a translation. This is clear from the following lines from the Preface by the King:

> *"Now the humble Akhtar who is the translator of the writing of* Mir *Shamsuddin Faqir humbly says that the lovers of poetry must have the knowledge of prosody and rhyming. The Persian poets translated these two arts from Arabic to Persian, but they gave less importance to these two arts and these arts started fading away. Now this modest person who is the emperor and by* Allah*'s grace attained the age of almost thirty years is attached to poetry composition since the times of Hazrat* Amjad Ali Shah Noor*ullah and had no other pastime other than poetry composition, which without the knowledge of prosody and rhyming was futile. Then Fateh ud Daulah Bakshi ul Mulk Md. Raza Khan* Bahadur *Fateh Jung, who had the penname* Barq, *appeared. Hardly three years passed that once again the art of poetry was revived. Truly speaking,* Barq *was an expert in this art. The compiler also developed an interest in the art of prosody and rhyming and had the urge to try this in the Urdu language as we are the only followers of this great language. I wanted to write something on this so that anyone who wants to learn these arts need not consult any other book. Doubtlessly it may prove beneficial for the scholars of poetry and the intellectual and they may find a reason to remember me. The basis of this book was its Preface (muqadma) and two verses, and it was given the title of "Hukm-e-Akhtar."*

---

159. Copy of Irshad Khaqani is in Maulan Azad Library, AMU, Aligarh and one in National Library Calcutta.

In the above mentioned two *rukn* (last part of a verse), each *rukn* had a preface (*muqadma*) and multiple sections (*fasal*). The first verse is about the details of prosody. In it there is appreciation of the verse for which the intention of first person and its *wazan* (valuation of words) is made mandatory. The *afaeel* (rules of meter) are appreciated for the balancing of words, and the rules of rhythm, explanation and the detailed account of metrical variation are given over 87 pages (pages 6–93). In the second part there is an appreciation of rhyming, and in various sections, the various kinds of rhymes are explained with illustrations. Though Irshad Khaqani is the translation of the treatise of Mir Shamsuddin Faqir, the translator has not strictly followed the original wording, but has recounted the details of other prosodies as per his own taste and style, and has even disapproved of *Faqir* in places.[160] In the Urdu prose book, Persian verses looked out of place, hence the translator mentioned very few Persian verses and instead used his own verses. It is difficult to remember uncommon names, so the compiler used them in the form of verses.[161] After many years of compiling the Irshad Khaqani, the compiler had the intention to write the whole book in poetic form. But due to metrical variations, he left it incomplete. Chapter three of *Sheva-e-Faiz* and the various verses of *Qamar Mazmoon* (Manuscript) are reminiscent of these efforts.

Jawab e Blue Book

Translation: 1273 A.H. Language: Urdu, Genre: About History of Avadh
Format: 30×20 Pages: 62, 21-Lined
Publication: Unknown

Brother Mirza *Sikander has been directed to London with a plea. Thereafter the printed Blue Book is received in Hindustan. After being translated, when I*

160. See *Irshad e Khaqani*- Md. Wajid Ali Shah Akhtar- Matbaey Sultani, Lucknow, 1269. (Azad Library, National Library). 37.

161. Irshad Khaqani. Kinds of Rhymes. 94

perused it, I realized that some people have unreasonably plundered my country and caused havoc. (1854, 1855, 1856).

The title page is blank and there is no endnote on the last page. There is no mention of printing, the author's name, or the date of publication. On page 2, the words '*Tawakulto ali* Allah' are written in an ornate style, and below them '*Bismillah*' is written. There are brief headings in the text and in the margin. The printing is not as perfect as Matbaey Sultani, but it is acceptable. Perhaps in haste many mistakes were not corrected. Through the use of a first-person style and other indications it is not difficult to identify the compiler of the book. The construction of sentences indicates that though they are written in Urdu, they have been translated from another language. The last sentence of the final section has not been translated, as it was thought to already be in Urdu usage. This proverb shows that perhaps the other language is Persian. In the Preface, the purpose of compilation and the details of the chapters are given. In this description, there are also more indications that this was a translation. These are given below.

The first chapter is about the reality of obedience to the 'Sarkar Company'. The second chapter mentions that the Sarkar Company concealed the details of the agreement. The third chapter is about the details of those facts on which Colonel Sulaiman Sahab and General Outram Bahadur defamed the empire. The fourth chapter is about the differences between Lord Dalhousie Sahab Bahadur, General Outram Sahab Bahadur, and other members of the Council. The fifth chapter is about the management of the Avadh Empire. The sixth chapter is dedicated to the fact that the agreement which was made between the rulers was not easy to violate. The seventh chapter is about bloodshed and riots, which was the working style of the English. In these seven chapters the writer limits himself to criticising and explaining the charges which were made in the Blue Book or Parliamentary Papers during 1855–56. This book was written to seek justice from Queen Victoria and the British Parliament. For this there was no need to invoke irrelevant debate, and everything was written in good faith. In its printing, there was a reference to a newspaper *Jaam Jahan Numa* dated 24 October

1856, in which 25 October 1856 is written as the last date to present an application during the visit of the Commissioner to Allahabad. The King was in Calcutta at that time; hence the dates were written during that time only. The arrangements in Lucknow were in chaos and *Kalan Kothi*, which once housed Matbaey Sultani, was bombed.[162] Hence it is quite possible that this book was printed by some local Press in Calcutta, and because both the compiler of the book and its subject matter were against the English rulers, the details of the printing press were deliberately concealed.

In many places in this book, there is mention of a book called *Jawab-e-Blue Book*, which was written before this.[163] If that book is *Jawab-e-Blue Book* then also addressing this book as *Blue Book* is objectionable. But *Blue Book* is not the name of any book. In fact, it is a synonym for a collection of reports from different departments for the appraisal of Parliament. Reports about Avadh were called *Avadh Blue Book*. Hence, whenever any response is given to such a book, it is called *Jawab-e-Blue Book*. The compiler was not aware of the English language, and so it was important to have it translated before he could give his response to it. At that time, though Urdu was not the language of discussion, after two years when Sir Syed Ahmed Khan picked up his pen to write his questions and answers, he did it in Urdu.[164] Wajid Ali Shah was impressed by the Persian language, and so perhaps he responded in Persian. Avadh Blue Book became popular both in England and in India and was equally popular among those in power and the masses. It was necessary to have the response written in English, and if possible, in Urdu. The Persian version was destroyed, but we have the Urdu version. There is also proof that the English version was published and reached readers in Europe. The names of the English and Urdu translators are not known, but it is true that

162. *Jawab e Blue Book*, MWASA, Published from Under Beni Prasad Nawaz Ganj, Lucknow. 4 and 89.

163. *Ibid.*

164. *Risala-e-Asbab-e- Baghawat Hindustan*. See *Hayat-e-Javed-* Khwaja Altaf Hussain Hali - Academy Punjab-Lahore. 1957. 145–49.

the translations were done.[165] The owner of *Qaiser ul Tawarikh* verifies that some 300 copies were sent to England.[166] These were surely not of the Persian or Urdu versions. In his book, *Maulvi Masihuddin Khan* wrote a one-page extract of the English printed version and mentioned that the book was published in Calcutta. Another authority comes from Dr. V. Hoffmann, a prose writer from Germany who wrote in a letter dated 24 September 1864 to Wajid Ali Shah that 'after reading your and your envoy's books, I am so deeply impressed by you and your family that I translated your envoy's book in Germany, and at present I am translating your book.'[167] We are very far away from the German language, and *Maulvi Masihuddin Khan's* book was translated and published, but we are still unaware of it. It is distant possibility to find the translation of *Jawab-e-Blue Book* in Germany.

There is one more edition of *Jawab-e-Blue Book*, on its last page are the words:

> *"This book is printed with the support of Beni Prasad, Moh*Allah *Nawaz Ganj, Lucknow."*

The '*ayat*' before '*Bismillah*' is not found, and the words "The End" are written on the last page. There are no page numbers, though there are 36 pages. Other than slight differences in the printing of these two editions, there is no other notable difference.[168] The details of this book were also published separately in small format.[169] The compiler of '*Zia-e-Akhtar*' had copied almost the entire book in his compilation.[170] It is quite possible that

---

165. *Wazir Nama*- Wazir ul Sultan Md. AmirAli Khan Amir. Publication Nizami. Lucknow. 1293. 241–42.

166. *Qaiser-ul-Tawarikh*, Syed Kamaluddin Haideralias Mir Zaair. Publication Munshi Nawal Kishore. Lucknow 3rd. Edn. 1907. Volume 2, 391–92.

167. Ahmed (Safi). 156–57.

168. Both these editions are available in Salar Jung Museum, Hyderbad.

169. Propriety: Nadar Library, Lucknow.

170. Propriety: Malvia Pustakalaya, Aligarh.

the book was also translated into other Indian and foreign languages, as it is mentioned in the *Wazir Nama* that many benefitted from this book.[171]

Diwan Mubarak

Writing: 1255–73 A.H., Language: Urdu, Genre: Diwan, Publication: 1273 A.H. Format: 26×16 Pages: 71, 13-Lined Published: Matabaey Sultani (Lucknow) with the support of Jaan Nisar Captain Maqbool ud-Daulah Mirza Md. Mehdi Ali Khan Bahadur Qubool.

The first and last pages are blank. The Diwan starts from page 2. After '*Bismillah*' is the addressing of Allah and the name of the King with a long title (in Persian). At the top of every Ghazal is written '*Wala Khuld*Allah *malka-o-Saltanata*'. The Ghazals have been arranged based on the last letter of the rhyme (*Radif*). The last Ghazals are in Urdu. There is no mention of the publisher, and the paper, writing, and printing are of ordinary quality. Had the first three lines not existed, then it would have been really difficult to determine who composed the *Diwan*.[172] The reason behind addressing the '*Diwan-Salis*' as '*Diwan Mubarak*' has been explained earlier. In the radif of '*alif*', there is a Ghazal which has been associated with *Nawab Raunaq Ara Begum*, daughter of Nawab Ali Naqi Khan. It goes as such:

Name of Akhtar Mahal *should adorn the skies*
This is the good reward of Akhtar Mahal.

This Ghazal can guide us towards ascertaining the date of the *Diwan*, as it was in the year 1267 A.H. that Akhtar Mahal was married to the King.[173] This Ghazal could not have been composed before her title (Akhtar Mahal)

---

171. *Wazir Nama*, Wazir ul Sultan Md. AmirAli Khan Amir. Publication Nizami, Lucknow. 1293. 241–42.

172. Only one copy of this *Diwan* is available in Salar Jung Museum, Hyderabad which was sold to the museum by Syed Ghulam Hussain Tajir on 21.8. 1350 A.H. for 8 annas.

173. *Faizan-ul-Fikr*. Mirza Mehdi Ali Khan Qubool-Matbaey Sultani. 1272. 520.

was bestowed upon her. The compilation of the *Sukhan Ashraf* took place during this time. Thus, the beginning of '*Diwan Mubarak*' must be calculated from this period. The paper and printing of the *Diwan* indicates that it is not the job of Matbaey Sultani, and printing by any other publisher is fully ruled out, as Matbaey Sultani was working well until 1272 A.H. (1857). The *Masnavi* of Maqbool ud Daulah Mirza *Mehdi Qubool* titled '*Zikrul Masoomeen*' was published by this publisher in the same year. The *Diwan* was thus not printed in Lucknow, but in Calcutta, though at such a time when there were no funds to bear the expenses and no loyalists to supervise the work of printing. The period was after the publication of *Jawab-e-Blue Book*, which was in Shawwal 1273 A.H. (1857). It was a period which is marked by the abject and miserable condition of the King.[174] It is during this period that the King started composing Ghazals for his wives (*Begmat*).[175] Ghazals associated with Akhtar Mahal and *Mehbooba-e-Alam*,[176] which should have been in *Sheva-e-Faiz*, are part of this *Diwan*, likely because they were his first attempts at Ghazal composition.

Diwan Mubarak is the King's third diwan, and as is mentioned on the head of the diwan, it was first called '*Diwan-e-Saalis*', and when it was again published in *Kulliyat-e-*Akhtari, it was called '*Diwan-e-Soom*'. In '*Tazkira-e-Sarapa Sukhan*', we find the mention of three Diwans of the King.[177] If we take the statement regarding *tazkira* in or before 1269 A.H., then the compilation of '*Diwan-e-Mubarak*' must have taken place around 1269 A.H. But the proof of publication of the *Diwan* is not found in the *Diwan*, but the publication of the second *Diwan* was mentioned in *Tazkira* as if it had

174. *Tarikh -e-Iqtidariya*, Iqtidarud Daulah Mohtishamul Mulk Mehdi Ali Khan Bahadur. 1280. 2 Volumes. (Asfia, Andhra Pradesh State Library, Hyderabad). 427.

175. See the Ghazals of *Tarikh Mumtaz*. Md. Wajid Ali Shah Akhtar. (Compiler; Dr. Md. Baqar). Urdu Markaz. Lahore. 1952 (Azad).

176. *Mehbooba-e-Alam is the head of all - Mehbooba-e-Alam is so intelligent* (Couplet).

177. *Sarapa Sukhan*. Syed Mohsin Ali Mohsin. Pubication Munshi Naval Kishore. Lucknow 1874. 8. This was completed in 1269 A.H. and was published in 1277 A.H.

come to his knowledge during the writing of *Tazkira*.[178] But it is not clear from this writing what the time period between the publication of the second and third Diwans was, but it can only be imagined that perhaps the third *Diwan* was mentioned at the time when *Tazkira* was published.

There are strong reasons for the origin of the so-called '*Third Diwan*'. On the head of the *Diwan-e-Salis*, the King, in his own verse, says:

May Khuda give it a perfect ending
Because this Diwan is the beginning of Akhtar's (poetry)

Thus, it is doubtful that he called his first Diwan '*Diwan-e-Salis.*' It is most probably the result of the king's first attempts at poetry composition, which he did not destroy. His two Diwans reached the public during his reign, perhaps to give a strong impression regarding his caliber. The third *Diwan*, which in reality was his first *Diwan*, was a manuscript at that time. It was probably published when the kingdom was doomed. The Ghazal*s* of *Diwan Mubarak* are found in *Kulliyat-e* Akhtari and also in Nazm Namvar. In *Kulliyat-e-*Akhtari, all the Ghazals were entered with minor changes, while in Nazm Namvar, the Ghazals with 'alif rhyming (*radif*) were included with care. There are 103 Ghazal*s* (518 verses or *shers*) in *Diwan-e-Mubarak*, and there are no Ghazals with the *radif* of 'ze'. Perhaps *Diwan Mubarak*, despite being part of *Kulliyat-e-Soom*, was published separately because had it been published with '*kulliyat*', then there would not have been a separate numbering of the pages. Its arrangement would have followed the pattern of *Sheva-e-Faiz* or Qamar Mazmun.

Kulliyat-e-Soom

Writing: 1255–73 A.H., Language: Urdu, Genre: Diwan (Kulliyat)
Publication: 1273 A.H. Format: 26×16, Pages: 71, 13-Lined
Publisher Not known

178. *Ibid*, 7.

Your face is like a bright morning for me
O Heaven! Show me Beauty
He is burned and buried out of jealousy
The enemies are being burnt under the ground
Live life in such a way
Embrace her love
Though smile is the real advice
But this is beneficial

Only one complete copy of *Kulliyat-e-Soom* is available. It's writing and printing is not much different from *Diwan Mubarak.* There is no mention of the name of the compiler and other details. Four different essays are of the same size and writing, and every essay is numbered differently. Those readers who have come across these separated parts have regarded them as four different writings, but the original form of the *Kulliyat* indicates that it was one complete treatise.[179] At most, *Diwan Mubarak* can be treated separately, as the author himself has listed it in *Bani*. Following are the details of this arrangement, as given in *Kulliyat*;

A. There are 37 pages in the first essay. The first and last pages are blank, though the numbering starts from the first page. This part is a collection of the following compositions:[180]

   a. *Tumhare chehre se hota hai mein* Rashk *e Subah bellor* (Praise of Prophet)
   b. *Chunn shudd wa hamd e Khudawandjahan az mann bayan*
   c. *Salami kehte the shay apne gardan ki safai hai (Salaam)*

---

179. Nasiruddin *Hashmi,* in his article published in *Naya Daur* (Monthly) Lucknow in May 1959. (People's Library, *Qila-e-Nizamat,* Murshidabad) has regarded these essays as different, because in the Library of Salar Jung Museum these are entered as different essays with separate numbering.

180. These are the headings of the compositions; hence they have not been translated here.

d. *The sorrow makes my heart restless (Salaam)*
e. *Salaami kehte they sheh apni gardan ki safai hai (Salaam)*
f. *Wo mor ko Chhahein toh* Sulaiman *kar dein-(Rubai)*
g. *Zahid ko maza jo parsai se mila (Rubai)*
h. *Sooey behasht peambar ka* Noor-*e-ain gaya (Elegy)*
i. *Bemisl-o-lajawab hai dil band-e-murtuza (Elegy)*
j. *Duniya mein koi bhai se bhai juda na ho (Elegy)*
k. *Sar peet ke ye kehti thhein ye Zainab-e-muztar hai hai mere bhaiyya (Noha)*

These works, which were composed out of affection for the Prophet's family (*Ahl-e-bait*), also became part of the other collections, and the first examples of this genre are found in *Kulliyat-e-Soom.*

B. The second part is '*Diwan-e-Saalis*' (71 pages). The first and last pages of this are blank, and the numbering starts from the first blank page. '*Diwan Mubarak*' is the name of this *Diwan*, which is discussed under the same heading.

C. The third part is a collection of '*rubayat*' (quatrain) and has 12 pages. Again, the first page is blank, and the numbering starts from this blank page. Other than these *rubayats*, there is one '*musaddas*', one *Masnavi*, and one '*mukhammas*'. The masnavi enumerates a Miracle. *Qamar Mazmoon* seems to be the improved form of this *Masnavi.* The remaining compositions were later published in *Kulliyat-e-*Akhtari.

D. The fourth Part is the *Masnavi* '*Ganna*' comprising nine pages, of which the first and last pages were blank. The *Masnavi*, which consisted of 200 pages, was again published in *Kulliyat-e-*Akhtari. The composition was published in *Kulliyat-e-*Akhtari without any changes, which only confirms the fact that writers have unnecessarily increased the number of these writings by considering '*Ganna Tawaif*' and other parts as separate compositions. The author himself has considered it one collection, and whether it is '*Kulliyat-e-Soom*' or '*Kulliyat-e-*Akhtari', the spoiled or disarranged pages cannot

> regard it as separate. The term '*kulliyat*' will lose its meaning if the compositions are regarded as different and separate.

'*Kulliyat-e-Soom*' is the first *kulliyat* of Wajid Ali Shah. The books which were published before this were either only *Diwan* or long *Masnavis.* It's quite possible that the King must have made attempts at other genres of art, but any solid proof of this exercise is not available before '*Kulliyat-e-Soom.*' There are *salaams, Nohas, Mussadas, Mukhammas, and Rubayat* in *Kulliyat Soom* and the *masnavis* show their rudimentary style. All this evidence indicate the possibility that *Kulliyat-e-Soom* was composed much before the period as shown here, but there is no other satisfactory evidence to confirm it.

*Huzn-e-*Akhtari

Writing: 1274 A.H., Language: Urdu, Genre: Masnavi (poetic autobiography) Publication: 1276 A.H. Format: 31×21 Pages: 77, 13-Lined Published: Matabaey Sultani (Calcutta) with the support of Md. Hussain in the hand of Md. Abdul Rehman Ahsan

My pen starts flowing
And is drenched with the glow of Allah
Allah *is the creator of the world*
He is manifested like a flower but hidden like its smell
The dark nights are illuminated with it
There is no one other than Him who can do this

The end is at page 153 with the following words:

As I gave my verses the name of Huzn-e-Akhtar
I end it with same name
May all the people of Hind remain happy
May all the youth of Hind flourish
This masnavi ends on this note
Salam Alaikum Alaik us Salaam

The first page is blank. There is a decorative plate on page 2 where below the seal '*Bismillah*' is written. After this there are three verses in Allah's glory (*Hamd*), four verses for '*naat*', and nine in *Manqabat* (Prophet's glory). The fourth page has the words '*Saaqi Nama and the Plight of my old age in prison.*' On every page there are about two-inch wide patterns decorated with a centimeter-wide delicate design of creepers, which kept on changing thoughout the treatise. At places, same design is spread over two pages. There are some printing mistakes too,[181] though there are no corrections attached. But this attractive printing is rarely found even in the books printed by Matbaey Sultani (Lucknow) and it is hardly found in the copies printed by Matbaey Sultani (Calcutta). The headings are in Persian and in bold letters. On page 103, at the completion of the *Masnavi*, the name of the Masnavi, '*Tarikh Huzn-e-Akhtar*', the date of printing (19 *Shabaan* 1276 A.H.), and the names of author, writer, and compiler are given. At the end, a *Qata'a e Tarikh* by *Md. Abdul Rehman Hasan* is given as below:

His Excellency Sultan e Alam
Akhtar is genius and brilliant
He penned down masnavi Huzn e Akhtari
Really his poetic excellence is commendable
Ultimately on His order Ahsan has got it published
I am composing this 'Tarikh e Akhtari'
(Translated From Persian)

These words, along with another Urdu line meaning '*what glory is brought to poetry*' (*Kya Jila di Gauhar-e-Mazmoon ki*), are inscribed in the margin. Both the compositions indicate the year of its publication

181. The copies are found in the National Library, Maulana Azad Library (SubhanAllah Collection, Aligarh) and in Salar Jung Museum, Hyderabad. These were printed by Matbaey Sultani, and they are complete. In these copies for corrections see page 28 (Zangi), 35, (Poshak Doz), 72 (One) 78 (Lal).

(1276 A.H.).[182] Three names for the *masnavi* ('*Huzn-e-Akhtar*', '*Tarikh-e-Huzn-e-Akhtar*', and '*Huzn-e-*Akhtari') are found in the above statements. Of these, '*Huzn-e-Akhtar*' is the most popular, but after the printing of the writings of Wajid Ali Shah[183] and *Wazirul Sultan* Bahadur,[184] the name '*Huzn-e-*Akhtari' is found, which should be taken as the correct one. In the last verses the name '*Huzn-e-Akhtar*' confused the intellectuals. *Maulvai Abdul* Hali*m* Sharar was doubtful that the *masnavi* was composed in 1266 A.H.[185] because from '*Huzn-e-Akhtar*' *by* the calculation of '*Abjad*' (the table for calculating figures/valuation from words) this figure is yielded (1201 + 65). But *Maulana Hasan Marharvi*, with evidence from the *masnavi* itself, disproved the claim and was assured that 1266 A.H. is connected with the number of verses, and not with the year of composition. The year of composition is revealed from the 74 headings of the *masnavi.*[186] *Maulana* had considered the edition by Matbaey Sultani.[187] The number of verses in this edition is 1239. Up to "*rakha Huzn-e-Akhtar jo heron ka naam*", there are only 1236 verses. Had the King mentioned some specialty (*sanat*) in the name '*Huzn-e-Akhtar*' then he would not have given preference to the name '*Huzn-e-*Akhtari.'

---

182. A set of words in which numbers associated with each letter are added together to yield a certain year. *Oxford Urdu English Dictionary*. page 260. (Translator).

183. *Bani* (Manuscript). Md. Wajid Ali Shah Akhtar. Sultani Publication. Calcutta. 1877. (Khuda Baksh)

184. *Wazir Nama.* Wazir ul Sultan Md. Amir Ali Khan Amir. Publication Nizami- Lucknow. 1293. 318.

185. *Huzn-eAkhtar* p. 7. *Jaan-e-Alam* p. 74. While popularizing the term 'Huzn-e-Akhtar Sharar did not consider that in the *Tarikhi* name the letter 'ye' is included. Not a single writer in the nineteenth century addressed it as '*Huzn-e-Akhtar*' and this trend continued up to Saxena's Book. '*Tarikh-e-Adab Urdu.*' (Published 1929, page 257 and 258). This tradition of writing '*Huzn-e-*Akhtari' was so forceful that in the collection '*Begmat-e-Avadh ke Khutoot*" allegedly Wajid Ali Shah, violating this, wrote '*Huzn-e-Akhtar*' in one of his letters (page 73) but after much investigation it was revealed that not only the particular letter but some other letters were also forged. (page 12).

186. Hindustani (Risala-Allahabad) April Issue. 1931. 265–66.

187. He has referred to this edition everywhere in his article.

The second name of the *masnavi* indicates its subject matter. The poet himself in one place has regarded it as its poetic '*Tarikh*.'[188] After being deposed, Wajid Ali Shah lived in exile in Calcutta, and was unwell for several months. After the turmoil of 1857, the English rulers, out of caution, imprisoned him in Fort William, Calcutta on 22 Shawwal 1273 A.H. (15 June 1857).[189] In this *masnavi* the King relates his pain and suffering, the loyalties and disloyalties of his own people, and also the small events from the two years (1856–57/1273–74). The poem starts with a prologue on the fall of his empire, and in the end, he prays for his freedom from the confinement. As it is a '*Tarikh*', the dates and details regarding the people is given importance. But alas, the writer did not take much care, and not only are some explanations and details incomplete, but in some places even the dates are irrelevant and doubtful. For instance, at one place it is written that when he took a bath of recovery, on the second day he was confined:

Then the year changed to seventy-two and I recovered and gained health

After some pages he correctly writes the year:

There were seventy-three plus twelve hundred days
When I entered the prison

Thus, in places, months are given but the dates are missing and where months are given the year is missing. To ascertain the period of composition he mentions different dates of *masnavi* while the last date that is given is probably correct. It goes as follows:

Today is the twenty sixth day of Zeeqad
Write something about post prison days

---

188. *Huzn e* Akhtari, MWASAA- 1306 (Raza Library, Rampur). 29.
189. K Volume 3, p. 35.

Now there are seventy-four plus twelve hundred days
In this year composition bloomed
This day of Friday is good for you
As it will give you the age of Khizr[190]. *(Very long life).*

The fact that only 12 people remained out of 24[191], the death of Dildar Mahal,[192] and the desertion by *Mujahid ud Daulah*[193] are not mentioned in the *masnavi* because it was completed by the end of 1274 A.H., and these events took place in 1275 A.H.

There are two more editions of the *masnavi.* One was published with a foreword by Maulvi Abdul Haleem Sharar in 1922 by *Daira-e- Adibia*, Lucknow.[194] The second one was published with Sharar's comments by *Farogh-e-Urdu* , Lahore in 1951.[195] Also, the English translation of this book with a poetic translation of some of the verses and the foreword was issued from Calcutta.[196] In some libraries the manuscript copies of this *masnavi* are also found, but these are copies of the printed edition. The copy of the *masnavi* of that period or of the royal library is not found in any of the big libraries.

---

190. Th name appears in *Surah Al kahaf* of Quran where he is described as the righteous servant of God who has great wisdom and mystic knowledge. As per some Islamic and non-Islamic traditions he is described as an angel, a prophet and as a Wali. Though often called as being ageless or being immortal (of long life) but this is not backed by any authority. Khidr - Wikipedia (Translator).
191. *Tarikh Mumtaz,* (Written on 14.6.1275) Md. Wajid Ali Shah Akhtar (Compiler; Dr. Md. Baqar). Urdu Markaz. Lahore. 1952 (Azad). 45.
192. *Ibid* at 48 (Written on 7.7.1275h).
193. *Ibid* at 58 (Written on 17.11.1275h).
194. *Huzn-e-Akhtar*. p. 1. The name *Huzn-e-Akhtar* (instead of *Huzn-e-*Akhtari) was popularized after this edition of the book.
195. Jaan-e-Alam Press, Lahore.
196. Propriety of National Library, Calcutta.

Behr-e-Mukhtalif

Writing: 1275 a.h., Language: Urdu, Genre: Masnavi, Publication: 1277 a.h., Format: 23×15, Pages: 28, 15-Lined

On top of the title page "*asa* Allah *ul ali ul azeem Itba-e- rasul ul kareem*" is written alongside the name of the *masnavi* and publisher. On top of page 2 is the seal of **Wajidi,** which is different from the seal of *Matbaey-Sultani*. After '*Bismillah*' the subject matter of the *masnavi* was written in the title. The names and titles of people are composed in verses. A metrical analysis of the verses is given in the last pages. On page 53, after the completion of the poem, the name of the author, his royal title, and the date of completion of the *masnavi* are given. But the name of the composer of the "*Qata'a tarikh etasneef*" is not given anywhere. The *Qata'a* is in Persian.

Every corner is illuminated with the beauty
Everywhere there is benevolence of the King
You the Great Akhtar! You are the brightest star
Everyone is benefitted by your blessings
There is no other like You the Great King!
Everyone is blessed by You as per his needs
My King has written a book which can be termed as a bowl
This is illuminated like the blaze of the Kings
Alas! Upheaval befalls his fate
That everyone is ashamed before Him and His family
His plight which is made known by others
May perhaps solve these problems
I enumerate the year through this couplet (1275)
May these words befit his family

Towards the end, a sketch of a flower is used to fill the blank space, while the last page is empty. This book has been considered a *masnavi* because it has the *behar* (poetic metre) of a *masnavi*, otherwise there is no continuity in the verses. Its literary importance is not so strong, but it has historical importance because it mentions the names of the women, the number of whom was often referred in the hundreds[197] and thousands. [198] Wajid Ali Shah's statement is brief and authentic when he mentions:

My pen counts the Mahals as sixty or seventy
Out of these, five or six came to Calcutta.[199]

However, the King has often mentioned the number of thousands by way of sarcasm in his poetry. He says:

Alas! When once I wore royal head gear
I was once upon a time the King of Avadh
I had hundreds and thousands of servants
The amblers were at my beck and call
There were some seventeen hundred writers
And some five hundred physicians
There were fifteen hundred gatemen
And Countless subjects

These verses of the King seem to explain reality. He did not exaggerate. Those who give hypothetical, imaginary, and exaggerated accounts must learn

---

197. Page. 54.
198. For instance on page 155 of the book '*Tazkira-e-Shauq*' by way of proof a verse of Hakim Md. Sami Iradatullah's verse is mentioned (See, Margin at page 182.) which says ; *Had I the chance to be King Wajid Ali for some days- I would have had some hundred wives in a month.* The same figure reaches up to thousands on page 307–8 where it is mentioned "As per Wajid Ali Shah himself there were some three four thousand women in the royal courtyard." When such statements are mentioned unauthorized, misunderstandings and wrong conclusions are bound to take place. The statement of Wajid Ali Shah in *Behr-e-Mukhtalif* is self-evident which endorses the facts mentioned in *'Ishq Nama.'*
199. *Huzn e* Akhtari. MWASAA. 1306 (Raza Library, Rampur). 71.

from the factual statements of the King. In 1275 A.H. the King recounted 80 names of the 'Begmats' and '*Mahlats*', including even those Begmats who were employed to serve the King[200] and had not been elevated to any higher position.[201] There were 31 who had been divorced or alienated by the King, and 13 who had died by the time of the composition of the *masnavi.* These have been mentioned along with names and their titles, though there is a possibility that the names of some of the women and their children were omitted or missed, but the final number is undisputable. The King has mentioned almost all the names of the women who, up till the composition of the *masnavi* (1253–75 A.H.), were included as his 'wives.'

Nawab Dildar Mahal Saheba *died* on 3 Rajab 1275 A.H.[202] Hence, it is presumed that the composition of *Behr-e-Mukhtalif* must have been completed before Rajab 1275 (January 1859), which mentions the lifetime of the late Nawab Dildar Mahal Saheba. *Huzn-e-*Akhtari was completed in Zeeqad 1274 A.H., though the King does not mention his imprisonment here. Maybe because the topic, which was dealt with in *Behr-e-Mukhtalif*, was the same as in *Huzn-e-*Akhtari, which was abruptly ended.

*Masnavi Huzn-e-*Akhtari was published by Matbaey Sultani in Calcutta in 1276 A.H. *Behr-e-Mukhtalif* was published in 1277 A.H. If Matbaey Sultani was established by then, the reason behind its publication by another local press would have been that the work of Matbaey Sultani, though perfect, was slow. There is a possibility that *Sheva-e-Faiz* and *Kulliyat-e-*Akhtari were in the process of being printed. Probably the King was in a hurry, and due to the amount of work, *Behr-e-Mukhtalif* was handed over to a different press under the supervision of another person, who did not consider the intricacies which were characteristic of Matbaey Sultani. There is only one copy of

200. The names of those women which are mentioned in '*Huzn-e-*Akhtari' as tailors, '*khasdann lifters*' etc. are mentioned as the '*Mamtua* Begmats' in *Behra-e-Mukhtalif.*

201. In Avadh Pension Papers See names of Class C (p. 34) and Class D Begmats (p. 41).

202. *Tarikh-e-Mumtaz.* Md. Wajid Ali Shah Akhtar. (Compiler; Dr. Md. Baqar). Urdu Markaz. Lahore. 1952 (Azad). 49.

Behr-e-Mukhtalif available. The title given in the *Bani* List is correct. Those who name it as *Khitabat-e-Mahlat* did not indicate that it was published by Matbaey Sultani.

Nasah-e-Akhtari

> Language: Persian, Genre: Aadab e Majlis, Publication: 1275 A.H. Format: 22×14 Pages: 8, 11-Lined, Published: After Correction, Md. Shafi Rizvi, Ghazanfar Ali Tanveer, Publication by Munshi Naval Kishore Publishing House, Lucknow

On the printed page, in the three starting lines, the appreciation of Allah, magazine, and author is given and in the last three lines there is mention of the press and the people who contributed to printing. The name of the magazine is given in the middle of the design. On page 2 is given the word Allah in ornamental wording, while the entire book spreads over 12 pages. On page 13 is given the epilogue, and thereafter, on two pages, are given the Persian '*Qata'ae Tarikh*' of Mir *Abbas Salim*, *Ashraf Ali Ashraf* (Writer of the Magazine) and three Persian *Qata'ats of Khwaja Md. B*Asheer.[203] In these *Qata'ats*, the date of composition given is 1275 A.H. Page 16 is blank, while there are many mistakes in writing and printing. On the title page the book is described as "*Risala-e-Haaza aur ilm o Adab Tasneef Mubarak.*" With the name of the King instead of the phrase *Khuld ullah Malka*, which was commonly written, is replaced by the words *Khuldullah Dula. Md.* Shafi *Rizvi* is probably the same person about whom after 20 years the King wrote as follows:

> *"Rafat ud Daulah Rafi ul Mulk Katibul Mulook Munshi Syed Md.* Shafi *ul Rizvi is a confidant. All the papers are original and well signed."*[204]

---

203. Nuskha-e-Mamluke, Maulana Azad Library, Aligarh.

204. *Bani*. MWASA. Sultani Publication. Calcutta. 1877. (Khuda Baksh, Avadh).236. (Manuscript). 341–42.

The explanation and analysis of this book is his masterpiece. The detailed explanation of "*Sharah Nasah-e-*Akhtari" is in Persian.[205]

In the Preface, the author writes that the book was written during his imprisonment:

> *"The King of Avadh, pen name Akhtar... has written this amidst abject and miserable conditions, when he was confined in the prison of the enemy, Fort William at Calcutta."*

The above extracts indicate that the King managed to get this book printed through correspondence and thus of all the books which were written during his captivity in Fort William this was the first book which was published before he left the Fort.

*Nasah-e-*Akhtari is divided into four sections. In the first section are given those mannerisms which are to be followed by the young people. In the second section are those etiquettes which are to be followed before the King. The third section talks about those codes of conduct which are to be followed by the head of the family. In the fourth section those manners and decorum are explained which are to be followed when people meet the ladies, youth, kings, elders, or friends. This book has been fully copied in the *Wazir Nama*,[206] and perhaps its Urdu translation has also been published.

Tarikh-e-Mazzahab

Writing: 1272–73 A.H. Language: Urdu, Genre: Collection of Letters, Publication:1276 A.H. Format: Foolscap, Pages: 56, 7-Lined, Manuscript: Proprietor; Md. Hadi Sahab, Resident of Katra Abu Tarab Khan, Lucknow.

---

205. There is only one copy of the explanation of *"Nasah-e-*Akhtari*"* which is incomplete and is available in *Safi Darul Mutalea* (Lucknow). It has 109 pages and was published by Avadh Gazette, Gola Ganj Lucknow.

206. *Wazir Nama.* Wazir ul Sultan Md. Amir Ali Khan Amir. Publication Nizami. Lucknow. 1293. 304.

She arrests the beautiful bird in her talking style
Shaida Begum *is so amazing*
Never seen this beautiful face[207] *before*
Beauty of Shaida Begum *is God-gifted*

"*Dear I am pained to hear about the damaged house. The already broken heart was further broken. Surely the décor of the house is due to the presence of the owner, a garden without gardener is incomplete... O' dear*" (The line is incomplete). The incomplete collection of this love letters addressed to Shaida Begum were under the possession of a destitute elderly person named *Md. Hadi Sahab* in 1958. The man lived in the suburbs of Lucknow and often visited Lucknow. He wanted to sell the letters for 200 rupees, but there were no buyers. Only this much is related by the people, and nobody knows the fate of the letters. Luckily someone preserved a copy, and he relates it as follows:

> "Wajid Ali Shah*'s letters to* Shaida Begum... *These are the letters written in 1272 and 1273 A.H. and are arranged by date. The total number of letters is 38, but as the first and last pages are missing, it is difficult to say as to what the final number of these letters was. There are eight letters written in 1272 A.H., out of which the first one is incomplete. Out of the 30 letters written in 1273 A.H., the 21st, 27th, and 30th letters are incomplete. The letters from 22 to 25, and the 28th ones are missing. Ultimately the final number of letters is 19. These letters are written over 56 pages and have impressive golden words. I have not seen such a perfect and impressively gold-plated manuscript. There is a two and a half inch wide golden pattern around the page and the pattern changes after every four pages. It is also bound with a decorative golden pattern. There are seven lines on every page which are filled with gold liquid. The entire setting seems to be a creative masterwork of the writer, which is very beautiful and eye catching. The pattern includes sketches of beautiful birds, animals, flowers, and fruits, and also sketches of the royal carriers and famous buildings of Lucknow. Probably this copy was prepared*

207. In *Sheva-e-Faiz at* p. 181 the word "*Chehra-e-Khush*" is written while here it is written "*Chehra-e-Khoob.*"

> *especially for* Shaida Begum. *Alas! This copy was not well preserved and would be destroyed soon if not taken due care of. In the original copy the date, title and name of* Shaida Begum *is written in red ink, while the word 'Jaan-e-Alam' is sometimes written in golden words and sometimes in red ink."* [208]

Some of the following points are notable in the above extract:

A. The first page of the manuscript is reported missing, while it was written with the help of *Kitabat* (handwritten). This is inferred by the commentator. The letters are numbered, and after the first incomplete letter the following letter is given the title of '*Muhabbat Nama Second.*'[209] This led to the conclusion that the letter, which was incomplete, must have been the first and must have occupied only the first page of the manuscript, as the complete letter is also of the same length. The critic disregarded the fact that all the collections of letters which were discovered had a Preface which contained the details of the collection, such as its title. This collection must also have had a Preface which was destroyed. All this leads to uncertainty regarding the number of pages.

B. All the collections of letters had a title, and like *Tarikh-e-Badr*, these are included in the list of *Bani*. As the original title is not known, these are renamed *Khutoot-e-*Wajid Ali Shah *bnam* Shaida Begum. However, the real name can be found in the list of *Bani.* In this list, from the unnamed collections, *Tarikh-e-Mazzahab* seems to be the suitable one. Although the commentator is unaware of the original name, he has somehow given it a title. It is unacceptable that, like *Tarikh-e-Badr*, the writer of the marvellous piece of writing must have forgotten to give it a title.

---

208. *Adab Ka Maqsad*, 181.Dr, Syed Noorul Hasan Hashmi-Hindustan Kitab Ghar. Lucknow. 1956. 159–61.
209. *Ibid.*

C. The commentator is of the opinion that the manuscript must have been written for Shaida Begum.[210] But the author of this book does not agree with him. If the first page was available and had the seal of the Royal library, then it could have been concluded that such a magnificent work was done to satisfy one's quest to be the best. In the month of Zeeqad 1275 A.H., the King had sent letters to two of his Begums, in which he asked them to prepare the love letters in well-decorated gold-plated form and send them back to him.[211] The Begums followed him. There is little doubt then that the King must not have wished the same from Shaida Begum. The fact is that these letters were damaged in the consequent plundering and carelessness. Hopefully in the present manuscript, things were copied down carefully. My opinion is based on the printed copy of the collection of letters in which the dates and sequence is not correct. This can be proved with the help of other letters but for the sake of brevity, this claim is based on the following grounds:

a. In the first four letters the dates '4 Rabiul Awwal 1272A.H.', '6 Rabiul Awwal 1272 A.H.', 29 Rabiul aakhir 1272 A.H.', and '8 *Jamadiul awwal* 1272 A.H.' are given respectively.[212] The point is that the letters to the Begums could not have been written before 5 Rajab 1272 A.H., because up to this date the King had been in Lucknow.[213] He neither had the occasion nor the need to write such letters.

---

210. He has also given a wise ground for this in his article saying that "who could get prepared such a beautiful and gold-plated manuscript." Aajkal Monthly. April 1955. Delhi.

211. *Tarikh-e-Mumtaz* p. 58. *Tarikh-e-*Ghazala p. 41.

212. *Adab Ka Maqsad*, 181. Dr. Syed Noorul Hasan Hashmi-Hindustan Kitab Ghar. Lucknow. 1956. 121–25.

213. Letter of Chief Commissioner (Avadh) dated 15.3.1856 addressed to Secretary Government of India. Rizvi – Volume I - 109.

b. On the above four letters the words first (Incomplete), second, third, and fourth are written respectively. In every letter he expresses pleasure in receiving the letters from Shaida Begum, but in the '*Muhabbat Nama Panjum*' he writes:

> "Nawab Shaida Begum should know that five months have passed but I have not received any news regarding your whereabouts. I wonder as to what is my fault that none of you has written a single letter. Please write in detail about your good health and whether there is any pregnancy or not. Also write about the reason as to why you did not write to me all these days. Worrisome, Jaan-e-Alam. Second day of Zeeqad 1276 A.H. (5 July 1856)."

Had the sequence of the above-mentioned letters been correct, then there would not have been the expression of pleasure at receiving the letter or displeasure for not receiving the letter. Thus, it is evident that not only the dates, but the sequence is also wrong. The above-mentioned letter is the first letter of *Tarikh-e-Mazzahab* hence there is no reason for it to be incorrect. From Rajab to Zeeqad there are five months, and all the Begums of Lucknow kept silent up to 2 Zeeqad 1272 A.H. The pregnancy mentioned above is expressed in different versions in the forthcoming letters and on the basis of it the sequence of letters can be arranged.

Shaida Begum was '*mamtua*' wife of the King.[214] With English features, she was of fair complexion and often dressed up like the English.[215] Her father's name is written as *Hussain Ali Khan*.[216] Up till 1857, her parents were alive and were under her maintenance.[217] At the time of the downfall of the empire, she was pregnant.[218] She gave birth to a girl on 3 Rabiul Awwal

214. *Behr e Mukhtalif.* Md. Wajid Ali Shah Akhtar. Publication Mustafai. Calcutta. 1277. 18–19.

215. *Adab Ka Maqsad,* 181. Dr. Syed Noorul Hasan Hashmi-Hindustan Kitab Ghar. Lucknow. 1956. 172, 180. and Ghazals of *Sheva-e-Faiz.*

216. *Adab Ka Maqsad*, 159 & 180.

217. *Ruqaa't e Begmaat*, 53.

218. *Sheva-e-Faiz-* Md. Wajid Ali Shah Akhtar. Publication Sultani. Calcutta1277. 14

1272 A.H. The girl was named *Nageen Ara Nawab Ruqaiyya Begum.*[219] At the time of delivery, Shaida Begum wished to have a silver bed, and like her other wishes, this wish was also fulfilled by the King.[220] After the delivery, there were many demands on various occasions, like '*kheer chatai*', '*doodh badhai*'.[221] Due to these constant financial demands, she lost her dignified status.[222] She also kept changing her residence under the pretext of the house being haunted or dilapidated.[223] At the time of the devastation of Qaiser Bagh, she was residing in Hazrat Bagh. She was devoid of her fortune and hence went to live in Karsi. During the journey, the little girl could not be taken good care of, and she died on 17 *Ramadhan* 1274 A.H.[224] Though the King was not hesitant in extending a helping hand to her, after some time she was more interested in getting her sisters married. This was not liked by the King.[225] In some of the letters she was addressed as Shaida *Mahal.*[226] Probably she was bestowed with this honour on the birth of the girl child. There is no account of her life after 1275 A.H. There is mention of a '*mamtua*' *Begum* as Shaida Begum at the time of compilation of *Bani.*[227] Perhaps this was the same familiar Shaida Begum.[228]

Shaida Begum has effortlessly been accepted as a poet and a writer.[229] Although she was famous due to the collection of letters, at the same time

---

219. *Adab Ka Maqsad*, 183–85.
220. *Adab Ka Maqsad*, 186.
221. *Ruqaa't e Begmaat*, 9–36.
222. *Tarikh e* Ghazala. Md. Wajid Ali Shah Akhtar (Compiler Wasi Bilgrami). Publication Mufeed e Aam. Agra. 38.
223. *Adab Ka Maqsad*, 190–93.
224. *Ruqaa't e Begmaat*, 53–54.
225. *Sheva-e-Faiz,* 262–63.
226. *Adab Ka Maqsad*, 187–88, 192–93.
227. *Bani* - MWASA- Sultani Publication. Calcutta, 1877. (Khuda Baksh, Avadh). 236. (Manuscript) 335.
228. There is no mention of Shaida Begum's name in Oudh Pension Papers. Perhaps she died in the King's lifetime.
229. *Tarikh e Avadh*, Maulvi Md. Najmul Ghani Khan. Munshi Naval Kishore Publication. Lucknow. 1919. Volume 5, 102.

it was the content of these letters which disclosed her being illiterate as is obvious from the following lines:

"I got your letter written on 17th when I was eagerly waiting for the same. I was moved when Asheer *read out to me its contents.*

The sky was cruel to me
I was estranged from you in full youth.
My heart is under your arrest
As Asheer *says*
I am inconsolable
I cannot get rid of your thoughts."[230]

Had Shaida Begum been literate, then the other person would not have read out the letters to her, and had she been a poet then she would not have copied the verses of Asheer. This is further verified by the fact that the person for whose pleasure she wrote all this was also not unaware of the reality. Hence, the King often sarcastically remarked;

a. *"I got your verses (masnavi)... every line was of honour, every line was spreading fragrance, it was not a masnavi but it was like a* Hoor *or pari."*[231]
b. *"How to praise your* Ghazals*, my tongue is unable to appreciate it, what to give you, I only have my life to gift."* [232] He was often more candid and hence said "Ghazal *what to say you can ask anyone to compose it for you..."*[233]

---

230. *Ruqaa't e Begmaat* ,5. *Khat bnam* Wajid Ali Shah dated 26.2.1273.
231. *Adab Ka Maqsad.* Dr. Syed Noorul Hasan Hashmi-Hindustan Kitab Ghar. Lucknow. 1956. 171.
232. *Adab Ka Maqsad*, 180.
233. *Adab Ka Maqsad*, 188.

In 1275 A.H. Asheer started writing letters and Ghazals on behalf of *Naurozi Begum.*[234] In 1273 A.H., his services were reserved for Shaida Begum. Other than the demands which are found in the letters of both the Begums, there are many examples of similarity in the prose and poetry. The first letter of *Tarikh-e-Mazzahab* does not rhyme, either in prose or in poetry.[235] It has been presented in plain, daily language. The reason is that this letter was not written in response to any letter, but when Shaida Begum started responding to the letters then there was a change in the style of writing – casual language was replaced by formal address. The beloved was addressed as the beautiful damsel, was compared to the most beautiful creatures of Nature, to the Sun of the morning, and all sorts of superlative words were used to describe her amazing beauty. It also contained some phrases in Persian. In this way, slowly and gradually, Persian expressions were included in the Urdu letters. In Shaida Begum's letters there was simplicity coupled with good expression, which was appreciated by the King in the following words;

> *"Received three of your loving letters, what to say reading them I could enjoy your closeness. I read them a hundred times, my patience was tested, and I was much delighted. It was not a letter, but it was like meeting you and it also eased the pangs of separation. Always be so constant in writing and keep me happy always."*[236]

He himself started using conversational language in his letters, and the letters of *Tarikh-e-Mazzahab* are very valuable. Compared to the other collections, this collection gives importance to brevity and has delightful language. The King's 12 letters addressed to Shaida Begum were also included in *Ruqaa't-e-Begmaat*. Had *Tarikh-e-Mazzahab* been completed, then these

---

234. *See* the details of *Tarikh e Firaq*, Md. Wajid Ali Shah Akhtar, 1276 A.H. (Khuda Baksh Library).

235. The author has taken down the fifth letter of *Tarikh-e-Mazzahab* from page 165 of *Adab ka Maqsad,* which has been regarded as the first letter of *Tarikh -e-Mazzahab* and has been presented in Chapter 3 of this book.

236. *Adab Ka Maqsad*, 193.

letters would also have been included in it. The letters of Shaida Begum, which were sent in response to these letters, are found only in *Ruqaa't-e-Begmaat*.

The poetic part of Shaida Begum's letters is very well arranged. Two of the letters are in the '*masnavi*' style. Examples of some of the poems and Ghazals which are found among the prose letters in *Ruqaa't-e-Begmaat* are noted below:

1. *Since You left My dear Akhtar*
My fate is hanging in uncertainty since (13 Couplets)
2. *Jaan-e-Alam return soon from your journey*
Jaan-e Alam show me your beauty (18 Couplets)
3. *Patient of separation is left alone*
You are not giving me any relief (13 Couplets)
4. *Nobody cares about my oppression*
Nobody appreciates my patience (9 Couplets)
5. *My loving heart is not a useless thing*
Just give me some patience (12 Couplets)
6. *My soul wants to fly during the night*
My soul is like an impatient bird (8 Couplets)
7. *Don't be so cruel to the departed ones*
Don't give me the pain of separation anymore (11 Couplets)
8. *I neither want rose nor spring*
I just yearn for a kiss on my love's cheeks (11 Couplets)
9. *The separation of love and beloved is strange*
The dawn of Eid turns into night of sorrow (8 Couplets)
10. *I wish for garden, spring and my love*
I wish you were at my side with dignity (12 Couplets)
11. *No one yearns like me in your separation*
And no one is unaware of this like you (9 Couplets)
12. *Spring is here where are you the Quencher*
All the time I am thinking of you (16 Couplets)

13. *I am a great lover of the face of my love*
I am a victim of bad times (11 Couplets)
14. *King of Hind the face of Moon Jaan-e-Alam*
Favour me with your loving looks (11 Couplets)
15. *Due to your separation I am in great pain*
How you have thrown me in such a mess (10 Couplets)

Following are the Ghazals and poems which for some reason could not be included in *Ruqaa't-e-Begmaat.*[237]

1. *God show me soon face of my Jaan-e-Alam*
The separation becomes intolerable for this beloved
2. *I am counting the stars the whole night*
3. *While by* Allah*'s grace Akhtar is blooming*
4. *I am unable to see your face*
5. *Your favours should continue*
6. *Akhtar was always at my side*
7. *I find resemblance of Jaan-e-Alam in flowers*
8. *Akhtar the sorrow heart looks towards the sky*

Wajid Ali Shah responded to the Ghazals of Shaida Begum in the language of Ghazals, though in limited number. Some of these are as follows:

1. Shaida Begum *is not a human but a fairy*
Shaida Begum *is the killer of my heart (12 Couplets)*
2. *What to relate my plight in your love*
Show me your beautiful face in style (5 Couplets)
3. *Smile in my garden you smiling flower!*
My heart! I am your lover (14 Couplets)

237. *Adab Ka Maqsad*, 164, 178, 180, 182, 184, 185, 186, 187, and 191.

4. *You are my fairy and I have a crush on you*
I am wounded now come and meet me (12 Couplets)
5. *I am restless being away from you*
I can neither eat, nor drink, nor sleep (12 Couplets)
6. *Put your chest on my chest*
Put your lips on my lips (12 Couplets)

The last seven verses of the first Ghazal are found in *Tarikh-e-Mazzahab.*[238] The second and third Ghazals are also found in *Tarikh-e-Mazzahab.*[239] The fourth, fifth and sixth Ghazal is found in *Sheva-e-Faiz.*[240] A poetic letter[241] of *Tarikh-e-Mazzahab* is not in *Sheva-e-Faiz.* While two poetic letters[242] of *Sheva-e-Faiz* are not found in *Tarikh-e-Mazzahab.* This irregularity is due to the fact that the letters of *Tarikh-e-Mazzahab* were likely written before 1273 A.H. – the King did not have the idea or mind to collect the letters or Ghazals until the upheaval of 1857, when most of the letters were destroyed. Some of these which were saved in the collection were later lost in the damaged manuscript.

Most of the letters of the King and Shaida Begum which are found in "*Begmaat-e Avadh ke Khutoot*" are the damaged copies of *Ruqaa't e Begmaat.* And the letter is found intact on pages 72–73.[243] The person who had inserted the letter tried to convince through the verses of *Ishq Nama* that it is the style of the King, but when the style does not conform to the familiar style of the King, and the continuity of events and arrangement of verses remains the same in 1273 A.H. as it was in 1265 A.H., it is unconvincing that the writer who was so fond of innovative styles would have wasted his time over an old

238. *Adab Ka Maqsad,* 161.
239. *Adab Ka Maqsad,* 168 & 175.
240. *Sheva-e-Faiz* 49, 233, 236.
241. *Adab Ka Maqsad,* 166.
242. *Sheva-e-Faiz.* Md. Wajid Ali Shah Akhtar. Publication Sultani. Calcutta. 1277. 100, 262.
243. *Hamari Zaban* (Weekly, Aligarh) Edition dated 15.2.1966. Article: '*Ishq Nama.*'

Daastan, and this must be in the knowledge of the writer of '*Begmat-e-Avadh ke Khutoot.*' Some other letters of the collection also indicate the superficial knowledge of the one who presents these letters, hence how can one believe that these letters are free from any craftsmanship.

Tarikh-e-Mumtaz

Writing: 1272–76 A.H. Language: Urdu, Genre: Collection of Letters, Publication: 1276 A.H., Format: 25.5×15.5, Pages: 80, 7-Lined, Manuscript Proprietors: British Museum, London. No. OR 5288.

In the Name of the Most Special, the Emperor, Pardon me
You the Owner of the Universe!
(This letter) Written by Mir *Md. Safdar Ali On this 7th. Day of the month of Safar 1276 A.H.*

Wajid Ali Shah's two letters to Mumtaz Jahan Begum, though lying miles away from this country, are complete and safe. People who valued their importance published them to satisfy the quest of readers, but the description of the book in the following words has only ignited a greater desire to have a glimpse of the original manuscript. The words describe it as such:

> *"... the margin is gold-plated and the entire text is in such a decorative writing that the book itself looks like a jewel. The glamour and style loudly spells that the book is definitely written for some royal personality."*[244]

As the book has been perfectly published,[245] with an introduction and details, some important points about it are presented here;

244. *Tarikh-e-Mumtaz.* Md. Wajid Ali Shah Akhtar (Compiler; Dr. Md. Baqar). Urdu Markaz. Lahore. 1952 (Azad). 4.

245. Mr. Saxena claims that the book was published in 1276 A.H. (See *Tarikh-e-Adab Urdu,* 259) but the statement requires further verification as no such book has been discovered so far. The above details of *Tarikh-e-Mumtaz* are retrieved from its Pakistani Edition.

1. The manuscript has been published from Page 4–79, upto page 157, and the picture on page 26 has been indicated.[246] There is no explanation regarding the first three pages (Page 1 *Alif/bay*, Page 2 *Alif*, and page 79 *Bay*), and whether these are blank or have an inscription on them. Usually, these pages contain the royal seal. The compiler says that there are 80 pages.[247] The librarian, to evaluate the book, has regarded it as 160 pages.[248] Thus, other than the above mentioned four pages, two more pages were found which are silver and gold-plated, but the printed letters are silent about the contents of the pages.
2. There is no date given on the two letters of the published copy.[249] However the compiler of the list has dated these letters as 5 Zeeqad 1275 A.H. and 5 Zilhij 1275 A.H. [250]

The historical part of the introduction was written by the compiler after much research and findings, but as it is based on some unreliable references, often the conclusions drawn are incorrect. Thus, he claims that 23 people were confined with the King, out of which six were 'Begmats.'[251] However, the number of confined persons was 24[252] because *Tabib ud Daulah* escaped on the very first day.[253] There were only four women with the King during his confinement,[254] and though it was true that they were his '*Mutai*' wives,[255]

246. *Tarikh-e-Mumtaz.* Md. Wajid Ali Shah Akhtar (Compiler; Dr. Md. Baqar). Urdu Markaz Lahore. 1952 (Azad). 3.
247. *Ibid*, 4.
248. *Ibid*
249. *Ibid*, 54–57, 60–61.
250. *Ibid*, 9. (Letter 13 & 18).
251. *Ibid*, 3.
252. *Huzn e* Akhtari, MWASAA - 1306 (Raza Library, Rampur). 28–32.
253. *Ibid*, 29–30.
254. *Ibid*, 34–35 & 46.
255. *Behr e Mukhtalif.* Md. Wajid Ali Shah Akhtar. Publication Mustafai. Calcutta. 1277. 26–27.

as they were dedicated to the King, they were taken along.[256] It is claimed that Mumtaz Jahan Begum was given the title of '*Zeenat Mahal*',[257] but this is unverified. *Nawab Mujahid ud Daulah* was the paternal uncle (*Phupa*) of the King. During the last leg of his imprisonment, he also deserted the King, left the Fort, and chose to reside in Metiaburj.[258] The compiler claims that he died there.[259]Mir *Nawab* was the companion of *Nawab Mujahid Daulah*[260] but the compiler has mixed up the statements of both the master and the companion.[261]

Mumtaz Jahan was the '*Mutai*' wife of the King.[262] Her real name was *Zainab Begum* and her title was *Aklil Mahal.*[263] Her parents were alive and were under her maintenance.[264] Like the other Begums, *Zainab Begum* also made several monetary demands, but the King agreed only to 50 rupees per month for her mother. He wrote;

> *"...Listen I will only take care of your mother and not any of your relatives. Next time don't write about anyone else. My reply is clear."*[265]

The King had sent about 4,000 rupees other than studded jewellery during a span of five months (From Jamadiul Saani to *Shawwal*) to *Khas Begum Saheba*, but her demands were unending. At the time of the king's death, the name of *Zainab Begum* was not found among the Begums who received a pension. Perhaps she died before that.

---

256. *Supra Note* 252 at 34–35.
257. *Tarikh-e-Mumtaz.* Md. Wajid Ali Shah Akhtar (Compiler; Dr. Md. Baqar). Urdu Markaz. Lahore. 1952(Azad). 3.
258. *Ibid*, 58. (Letter 15)
259. *Ibid*, 17.
260. *Huzn e* Akhtari. MWASAA- 1306 (Raza Library, Rampur).34.
261. *Tarikh-e-Mumtaz.* Md. Wajid Ali Shah Akhtar (Compiler; Dr. Md. Baqar). Urdu Markaz. Lahore. 1952 (Azad). 17–18.
262. *Behr e Mukhtalif.* Md. Wajid Ali Shah Akhtar. Publication Mustafai. Calcutta. 1277. 13.
263. *Supra Note* 261 at 41.
264. *Ibid*, 50.
265. *Ibid*, 53.

Zainab Begum was not totally illiterate. It is evident from the King's letters shown below that, apart from having a love for music, she was partially literate. He says;

> *"The second* Ghazal *regarding the pangs of separation has been composed in your old name; you can read and sing the same."*

However, her letters, like the letters of the other Begmats, had been written by professional letter writers, as is obvious from the following;

a. *"Two love letters one by* Mir *Abad Ali and the other by an old writer have been received..."*
b. *"... O Dear the writer who wrote your letter is incomparable and emotional. You should ask him to write your letters. I don't like the one who writes regularly, he commits spelling mistakes and is not good at expressions." (Page 53).*
c. *"...The poet who wrote your reply is unique. Many times I asked you to get your letters written only by him, but perhaps you have not received such letters of mine."*

All the above comments indicate that *Zainab Begum's* letters were drafted by different writers. Of these, the poems and prose of *Munshi* Tauqeer *Ali Khan* were appreciated by many, and he was also chosen to write the Preface of *Tarikh-e-Mumtaz.* This preface is the only available example of *Munshi* Tauqeer*'s* authorship. Perhaps he started drafting the letters from *Ramadhan* 1275,[266] but today not a single letter of his is available. The King's letters reveal that some of the letters were in poetry form, while others were in Ghazal and *Mukkhammas.* (Five stanza form).

The starting lines of two of his Ghazals are as follows:[267]

266. *Ibid*, 53.
267. *Ibid*, 59–60.

Wow at what a (suitable) time you remembered me dear
My heart again demands your memoirs

Out of the 29 letters of *Tarikh-e-Mumtaz*, the first letter is dated 5 Zeeqad 1272 A.H., and the last one is dated 7 *Safar* 1272 A.H. Other than the last five letters, which were written by *Zulfiqar ud Daulah*, Mir *Agha*, and Mir *Md. Safdar Ali*, and which also depict their writing skills, all the rest were written by the King himself. These letters are a mixture of formal and informal language and show the pristine style of writing. The letters also contain the Ghazals written for *Zainab Begum*. These are found in *Tarikh-e-Mumtaz*[268] and also in *Sheva-e-Faiz*:[269]

1. *Aklil Mahal is full of luminous rays*
And why not Aklil Mahal is like a pearl (Couplet 12)
2. *Mumtaz your style is beautiful*
Your voice is like the (tingling) of glasses. (Couplet 12)
3. *Zainab Begum is a good human and has attributes of a* Hoor
Zainab Begum is shining like a Mirror *(Couplet 12)*
4. *Zainab Begum is well behaved and killing*
She is the master of love (Couplet 12)
5. *One wish of Musa (Prophet) on the Tur (mountain) remains unfulfilled*
The eyes still want more (Couplet 15)
6. Allah*! Make me an idol (statue) of mud*
And for these idols make my heart as hard as stone (Couplet 15)

However, in the fourth Ghazal of *Sheva-e-Faiz*, the rhyming word is *Dildar Mahal* instead of *Zainab Begum*. The number of verses is the same as it was

268. *Ibid*, 38, 39, 40, 42, 45, 51.
269. *Sheva-e-Faiz*. Md. Wajid Ali Shah Akhtar. Publication Sultani. Calcutta. 1277. 124, 155, 212, 249, 310, 371.

in *Tarikh-e-Mumtaz*, but in the arrangement the seventh verse of *Tarikh-e-Mumtaz* was made the sixth, and the sixth was arranged as the seventh; the rest is the same as *Tarikh-e-Mumtaz.* The manuscripts of *Tarikh-e-Mumtaz* and *Sheva-e-Faiz* were both compiled in the year 1276 A.H. *Dildar Mahal* died in Metiaburj on 3 Rajab 1275 A.H.[270] There is no other Ghazal in the name of *Dildar Mahal* in *Sheva-e-Faiz*. Perhaps for the sake of including the Ghazals connected with all the '*mahlats*' (wives) in *Sheva-e-Faiz*, the King included the Ghazal for *Zainab Begum* by changing the rhyming word to '*Dildar Mahal.*'

Tarikh-e-Ghazala

Writing: 1275 A.H. Language: Urdu, Genre: Collection of Letters, Publication: 1914 A.D. Format: 22×13 Pages: 22, 21-Lined, Published: Mufeed Aam, Agra. Compiler; Syed Wasi Bilgrami.

The collection starts with the following prayer:

> *I thank the great Almighty who is the creator of humans and all souls (jinn), in Whose Service angels are ready and all the angels are dumb struck in awe and reverence like a photo.*
> *Now I pray that Khuda help us in uniting, that we sit together, fulfill our wishes – In the hand of Md. Abid Hasbul Hukm- 17 Zilhij 1275 A.H.*

There were some hand-written letters by Wajid Ali Shah in the family library of *Saadat Bilgrami*, and among these were *Tarikh-e-*Ghazala. The compiler had it published with an introduction of about 12 pages. A major part of introduction is dedicated to clarifying the position of the King and in refuting the charges made by him, along with some personal impressions of the compiler. The introduction does not contain any information regarding the original manuscript. One cannot say how far the printed form is the true copy of the original manuscript. The compiler credits him for

270. *Supra Note* 261 at 49.

the work of compilation he has done.[271] The King writes to the addressee as follows:

> *"Send me the collection of love letters which have been arranged by you date wise, which should be gold plated with good writing, well decorated and in the same way as you have arranged the poems and prose. The preface should be written by you in which you should mention that the letters of Jaan-e-Alam have been affectionately collected and compiled by me and give it the title of Tarikh-e-Ghazala. Thereafter get it bound and send it to me. I will bear all the expenses."*[272]

The changes from first person (*hum ne likha hai*) to second person (*tum ne likha hai*) were probably done by the writer or the compiler himself because the same words were used in the order addressed to *Zainab Begum* to compile *Tarikh-e-Mumtaz*, which is available in its original form.[273] It is not possible that *Tarikh-e-Mumtaz* and *Tarikh-e-Mazzahab* were gold-plated and that *Tarikh-e-Ghazala* would not follow the same pattern. In the introduction there are certain omissions, connecting the arrangement of the book with the compiler's name, and are based on some reasons known to the compiler. Perhaps the original manuscript still exists.[274] Once the original copy is publicised, only then will it be solved as to what has been omitted or added.

*Tarikh-e-*Ghazala contains 20 such letters, which were sent to Nawab Malka Ghazala Saheba from Calcutta to Lucknow. The first letter is dated 28 Rajab 1275 A.H., and the last one is dated 17 Zilhij 1275 A.H. The last two or three letters were written on the King's order by some other people. The arrangement of letters, dated *Ramadhan* and *Shawwal*, is incomplete, as

---

271. *Tarikh e* Ghazala. Md. Wajid Ali Shah Akhtar (Compiler Wasi Bilgrami). Publication Mufeed e Aam. Agra. 1914. (Azad) 12

272. *Ibid*, 14.

273. *Tarikh-e-Mumtaz* 58–59.

274. *Tarikh-e- Jamshedi* was discovered from the family library of Bilgramis. The person who collected this says that *Tarikh-e-*Ghazala *is* still there.

date-wise the letters which were written later were placed in the beginning and those written earlier were arranged later on.[275] The poetic letter dated after 23 *Shawwal* has 47 verses.[276] The letter starts thus:

My Ghazala *Beautiful!*
Shining and blooming like spring
Strange her age is fourteen years
It is the onslaught of youth [277]

In *Sheva-e-Faiz*, 24 verses of this poetic letter were in appreciation of Nawab Jafri Begum Saheba,[278] and interestingly, the date given in the verses is 22 *Shawwal* 1275 A.H.[279] The similarity of verses indicates that perhaps Malka Ghazala's real name was *Jafri Begum*, but this is not true because in *Behr-e-Mukhtalif*, Malka Ghazala and *Jafri Begum* were counted as two people.[280] *Jafri Begum* was with the King during his journey to Calcutta, and at the time of imprisonment she resided in Metiaburj.[281] Malka Ghazala was of the same age as *Jafri Begum*. At the time of the upheaval of 1857, she was in Lucknow, and before the disaster the King had sent several letters to her, which were later destroyed.[282] She was separated from her parents and was looked after by the King.[283] She expressed her wish to be maintained by

275. In *Tarikh-e-*Ghazala the last letter of 3 *Shawwal* is placed in the fourth section, and the letter dated 23 *Shawwal* is placed in the first section.
276. *Supra Note* 271 at 29–31.
277. In *Sheva-e-Faiz* at page 177–78 the first line is different. Present tense is used instead of past.
278. *Ibid*, 177, 80.
279. *Ibid*, 185.
280. *Behr e Mukhtalif.* Md. Wajid Ali Shah Akhtar. Publication Mustafai - Calcutta. 1277. 19, 21.
281. *Sheva-e-Faiz.* Md. Wajid Ali Shah Akhtar. Publication Sultani. Calcutta. 1277. 5–8,185.
282. *Tarikh e* Ghazala. Md. Wajid Ali Shah Akhtar. (Compiler Wasi Bilgrami) Publication Mufeed e Aam. Agra. 1914. (Azad). 17–18.
283. *Ibid*, 34–35.

the King in her letters. Between the six months of Rajab and Zilhij, she was sent 5,000 rupees under different headings along with other valuable rings and jewellery. On her request, 1,000 rupees for '*kanyadan*' and 15 rupees per month were fixed for two *Saidanis* (women from the Prophet's PBUH family/descend). These women had given shelter to Malka Ghazala during 1857–58.[284] Malka Ghazala regularly made demands for money, and the King was very displeased at her impatience.[285] In the letters, no name other than that of Malka Ghazala is found. During the royal period of Lucknow, there was a heroine named Ghazala in the poem '*Darya-e-Taashuqq.*' The *Mutai* wife *Begum* Malka Ghazala was very fond of dance and music, but during the royal period she was very young.[286] It is unimaginable that such a young girl could have played the role of Ghazala in *Darya-e-Taashuqq*. At the time of the compilation of *Tarikh-e-*Ghazala, Malka Ghazala was in Metiaburj, and the preface was also written at that time.[287]

Like other Begmats, there was a writer appointed for Malka Ghazala:

> *"O* Ghazala *on your wish I have appointed one Ali Jaan* Shafaq *at 20 rupees per month to write letters for you."*[288]

The letters of *Tarikh-e-*Ghazala were in response to the letters written by Shafaq, and the King even appreciated him at times:

> *"In the fifth letter of Shawwal ul Muazzam* Shafaq *has shown good taste, Subhan*Allah, *Bravo!"*[289]

Shafaq was the pupil of *Sheikh Imdad Ali Behar*. He went to Calcutta with Malka Ghazala. His compositions (*Qata'at*) are found in *Kulliyat-e-*Akhtari,

284. *Ibid*, 21, 32.
285. *Ibid*, 33.
286. *Ibid*, 26, 39.
287. *Ibid*, 19.
288. *Ibid*, 24–25.
289. *Ibid*, 31–32.

Qamar Mazmun, and in other publications of Matbaey Sultani. He died in Calcutta in 1295 A.H.[290] It is revealed from the receipts of *Tarikh-e-*Ghazala, that about 31 letters were drafted by Shafaq on behalf of Malka Ghazala. Not a single letter is now available. The preface of *Tarikh-e-*Ghazala is probably an example of his authorship. as he was the writer of the letters, the Preface must also have been authored by him. The letters of *Tarikh-e-*Ghazala show that Shafaq used to send some *masnavis* and Ghazal*s* along with the letters. However, none of these are available now. In the letters of *Tarikh-e-*Ghazala, the first lines of the two Ghazal*s* by the King are found,[291] and are as follows:

1. *This is my condition in separation*
2. *One handsome and graceful out of lakhs is Akhtar dear*

The two Ghazals sent by the King to Malka Ghazala can be identified:

1. *This is the place (forest) of* Ghazal*s* Ghazala
My shrieks reach the sky (Couplet 12)
2. *She is my life* Malka Ghazala *Saheba*
She is a story (afsana) Malka Ghazala *Saheba (Couplet 12)*

In *Tarikh-e-*Ghazala, only 11 couplets of the first Ghazal are available. The second Ghazal was either entered with the letters of 1273 A.H. and was destroyed with it, or the compiler omitted it. Both of these Ghazal*s* are saved in *Sheva-e-Faiz.*

The letters of *Tarikh-e-*Ghazala, regarding the expression of emotions, are a masterpiece. The style of conversation, which was still developing in *Tarikh-e-Mazzahab*, perhaps after two years had reached maturity and improved. The writer tries to express it himself in a formal and novel style. The style of sarcasm and cynicism are novel. But it is disappointing that the

290. *Yaadgar-e-Zaigham* (Handwritten), Md. Abdullah Khan Ziagham. 360.
291. *Supra Note* 282 at 39, 40.

copy is incomplete. In the second letter of this copy, it is mentioned that previously two letters had been sent, but only one out of these was included in the printed copy. In most of the letters, the date they were sent is not given. If the sender omitted the date, then this collection is one of a kind, because Wajid Ali Shah was in the habit of putting dates on even casual papers.

*Tarikh-e-*Noor

> Compilation: 1272–75 A.H., Language: Urdu, Genre: Collection of Letters, Publication: 1276 A.H. Format: 32×21.5 Pages: 98, 11-Lined, Manuscript: Proprietor: Khuda Baksh Oriental Public Library, Patna

The collection starts with this eulogy:

> *The nightingale says that* Allah *is praiseworthy and supreme.* Allah *is the* Mir*aculous. He is the Creator of the earth and the sky...from the moon to other wonders and the fish, there is an amazing world with colourful marvels created by Him. The pious and the worshipers wish for your welfare. She is a disciple of Imam and praises him five times during Namaz, that* Allah *will bestow good deeds (sawab) on you...*

On the plain title page there are two seals of the royal library and also the rubber stamp of the present library. The printing starts from the second page, where there was praise of the Almighty (*hamd*), which is now missing. Other parts of the manuscript were also torn and damaged but have now been repaired. At the time of repair, some of the pages were arranged incorrectly. If one reads continually, then it appears as if some more pages are incomplete or missing, but as per the explanation given on the even pages, if one looks for odd number of pages then, except for the second page, all the other pages are intact. Presently there are 98 pages, and from the 99th page the manuscript is incomplete. There were not more than three or four missing pages based on the information given in the preface. It has letters up to Zilhij 1275 A.H. 48 letters have a date up to 20 Zilhij 1275 A.H. Letters were written at intervals of four or five days. This last letter was written in the last week of Zilhij, hence there is hardly one letter which is not included in this manuscript. The writer writes the name and address in red ink, while the letter is in black ink. The pages have not been counted, though in the library they were supposedly counted and numbered. However, the numbering was done in pencil and is not reliable.[292]

This is the collection of the letters of Noor Zaman Begum. The letters were arranged by Wajid Ali Shah himself, and in the Preface, spread over eight pages, *Hamd*, *Naat*, and *Manqibat* are given. After this he writes:

> *"...destiny got me in Calcutta, but I did not get any peace...for quite a long time I was in trouble, I was away from the beautiful fairies, the communication was stopped, I was sad and pained and ultimately I was freed. I was relieved of troubles; I started getting letters from dear ones. I regarded them as the wealth of my life and hence collected them, secured them. Then it came to my mind that I should sort out the letters of dear ones and bind them separately. Hence, I write these letters to my beautiful, pretty, pride of beauty, gorgeous and beloved* Nawab Noor Zaman Begum *Saheba, bind them in one collection, and I name it Tarikh-e-*Noor*, which comprises of three chapters"*

In the first chapter there are three letters written in 1272 A.H., in the second chapter there are 15 letters from 1273 A.H., and in the last chapter[293] there are 31 letters written in 1275 A.H. It appears from the Preface that these letters were written after the King was freed, but there are only five such letters. Perhaps this discrepancy appeared due to an urge to write something new. In every collection there is a separate Preface, and hence, for the sake of writing something new, every time there are differences in the statements given in different Prefaces. In other collections, Zilhij 1275 A.H. is the date of compilation, but here no such date is given because it is on the seventh of this month that he was freed.

---

292. Here the numbers of the pages of *Tarikh-e-*Noor are correct, based on the research of the author, and it is not bound by the wrong numbers given on the manuscript.

293. While counting the letters of this chapter the writer (The King) has mistakenly written nine after seven. This mistake continued up to the end.

In Behr-e-Mukhtalif, Nawab Noor Zaman Begum*'s* name is the same.[294] This *Begum* was from a well-off family from Lucknow, and her parents were alive. In the letters, the name of her elder sister is written as Achchi Begum, and that of her brother as Agha Ali. People who know the history of Avadh even casually are not unaware of the *Begum's* real maternal uncle (mamu) who was Syed Kamaluddin Haider Alias Mir Zair. This is because his two books, *Sawaneh Salateen-e-Avadh* (*Persian*) and *Qaiser* Noor *ul Tawarikh* (*Urdu*), are highly valuable. Noor Zaman Begum became the King's *Mutai* wife four years before the downfall of the empire. Before 1857, everything was fine. There were attendants, helpers, maids and even her family members were under her maintenance. However, she was interested in more concessions and allowances:

> *"... the caretaker (*Gulshan *Khwaja Sara) told me that very few animals are left, and to feed others these should be auctioned. Since I heard that sixteen elephants and some horses are left, and they cannot be fed, I am broken. Jaan-e-Alam! I swear on my head that you should write to Hasam ud Daulah* Bahadur *that he should take the elephants to* Noor Zaman Begum. *By the time* Allah *brings you back in any condition I will feed them because you once rode them, I will sell my house and everything to feed them, I will not leave them. May* Allah *give you a long life so that you once again ride them."* (Page 66–67).

This description pertains to 25 Rabiul Awwal 1273 A.H. when the English rulers were plundering the wealth and valuables, which were handed over through generations. They were also selling the animals in royal custody at throw-away prices.[295] The revolution of 1857 devastated everything:

> *"... The house was plundered, uprooted, we were thrown on the road, our eyes saw something we never imagined in our dreams, only life was continuing,*

294. *Behr e Mukhtalif.* Md. Wajid Ali Shah Akhtar. Publication Mustafai - Calcutta. 1277. 24.

295. *Qaiser ul Tawarikh.* Syed Kamaluddin Haider Alias Mir Zaair. Publication Munshi Nawal Kishore. Lucknow 3rd. Edn. 1907. Volume 2, 170–72.

> *there is an acute paucity of funds, and we yearn for food, our creditors trouble us, poverty and destitution is everywhere, take care of us, get us out of this trouble"*
> (Letter dated Jamadi ul Saani 1275 A.H., page 74–79).

In response to this, the King sent 5,500 rupees over a period of six months. This *Begum* appeared to be an accomplished and decent lady, and in her letters her demand for money was not as open and forceful as it was in the letters of other Begums. In her last letter, she requested a job for her uncle, but this was likely not met as the King was unhappy.[296] Other than these collections, there is no mention of Noor Zaman Begum in any other book. Nobody knows when and how she passed away. Her marital life was probably spent in Inayat Manzil and Qaiser Bagh. She wistfully remembers her days in Inayat Manzil. After the devastation of Qaiser Bagh, she resided in the "*adjacent Sarai Inayat Khan, House of* Mir *Nawab Khalaf Meerza Humayun Beg, Risaldar Matufi, adjacent to the Meerza Haider Kitchen*".[297] After two months, she vacated this place too. Then she took the house of Mirza Inayat Ali Beg near the house of Rafiq ud Daulah in KashMiri Mohallah on a rent of 15 rupees per month.[298] This was the last address where letters were received. Thereafter, nobody knows of her whereabouts.

An old saying that a black letter is as good as a buffalo (*Kaala akshar bhains barabar*) truly applies to her.The letters which she held so dear to her heart and regarded as more precious than her own life[299] unfortunately could not be identified by her. In one incident the King expressed his displeasure that Noor Zaman Begum returned his letter.[300] The *Begum* forcefully wrote that she had sent only the copy, while the original was with her. But when it was

296. *Ibid* Volume 1, 62.

297. *Tarikh e* Noor. (Handwritten) Md. Wajid Ali Shah Akhtar. 1276. (Khuda Bakhsh Library). 131

298. *Ibid*, 187–88.

299. *Supra Note* 295 at Volume 2. 170–72. 48–49, 183.

300. (Letter of *Tarikh-e-Mazzahab). Adab Ka Maqsad.* Dr. Syed Noorul Hasan Hashmi. Hundustan Kitab Ghar. Lucknow 1956. 186.

again told, then she admitted:

> *"...Its true you have got the original one. But what could I do, I had told the unfortunate writer that he should send the copy of it, but he made this mistake. He sent the copy to me, and I thought that it was the originl one... I am ignorant. It is the fault of the writer... Now by* Allah*'s grace my brother and father have returned after five years from 'ziyarat' and 'haj'. Now I ask them to write my love letters. I thank* Allah *that he saved me from conversing with a stranger."*[301]

She confirms in this last letter that the letters were written by Mir *Zair.*[302] Even though Noor Zaman Begum had not confirmed this, the use of Persian and Arabic words in abundance, the use of idioms and phrases, the Persian *masnavi* of 42 verses with one Arabic verse, and the unique style of writing love letters, are enough to show that the writer was drastically different from other writers. He writes:

> *"In response to your* Ghazal *I am writing some verses describing my present condition. These are written at the back of this letter in a new style. There are strange details in it. You have been addressed as the Sun while I am addressed as the sad crescent moon, in the centre is the sketch of the Sun, the white paper depicts our separation showing that the moon is away from the sun and expects a response from you."*[303]

For some time, Mir *Zair* was the supervisor of Rasad Khana-e-Sultani, and the calendar Taqweem Sultani 1265 (1849) was published under his guidance.

In this collection, examples of both poetry and prose are found. In the 12 letters, mostly consist of *masnavi.* At the end, some lines of greetings and wishes are also given in prose.[304] In many letters there are Ghazal*s*, but

301. *Supra Note* 297 at 52.

302. *Supra Note* 297 at 196–97.

303. *Tarikh-e-*Noor 123–24. Perhaps the letter when copied in the manuscript must have made the sketch as per the original one. 123–24.

304. *Tarikh-e-*Noor (Handwritten). See the letters on 90, 95, 105, 121, 126, 122, 135, 147, 155, 162, 167 & 172.

in some the last verse (*maqta*) is missing. In places the poet's pen name (*takhallus*) is Noor *Zaman*:

1. *My heart is in Jaan-e-Alam's heart*
My heart is sacrificed on him (Couplets 11)
2. *To quench the taste of union I want a 'Saaqi' (Quencher)*
In the night of separation my sad heart wants moon light (Couplets7)
3. *How to relate my story of separation*
My story of separation is very long (Couplets 6)
4. *Your fan is mad and impatient*
I take her to some wilderness for peace (Couplets 8)
5. *How to express the condition of my heart*
The tongue is unable to express (Couplets 6)
6. *Since my heart went to you*
It is not peaceful in any condition (Couplets 6)

In the prose letters, the use of Persian and Urdu phrases and learned expressions, speak highly about the writing skills of the letter-writer. Much hard work is put into expressing love and wishes. In places, there is a request for appreciation:

> *"I have sent a detailed letter in which the verses are very good, concentrate well and respond."*[305]

Rhyming expressions are in almost all the letters, but in places there is newness as the following words show:

> *"I am pleased to receive two of your letters on 5* Rajab *1275* a.h. *It comforted my pain of separation; hence I am responding in a pensive mood. I am writing in the triple (taslees) style in which there is a set of three phrases and lines. I have expressed my pains. It is your duty to take care of my plight. My sombre*

305. *Tarikh-e-*Noor (Handwritten), 17.

> *fate is unchanged; I pray that no one should suffer like me. There is no remedy for my malady."*[306]

There are some more pleasant verses:

> *Only my heart knows the depth of my pain*
> *Jaan-e-Alam don't question my sad condition*
> *There is no way to meet Jaan-e-Alam*
> *The painful shriek of my heart is also ineffective*

From a literary and biographical viewpoint, *Tarikh-e-*Noor is different from other collections and has a unique flavour. These letters are free from the mindless monetary demands and worldly attitude which are found in the letters of other Begmats, in fact it is valuable and precious in many respects.

In Zeeqad 1275 A.H. the King had wished that Noor Zaman Begum should compile his letters. This was done by the *Begum.* She writes:

> *"... and as you have written that I should compile the letters date wise, this is actually a very good suggestion. Actually, such a collection would be a memorable treasure for the whole world.* Inshallah *very soon I will comply with your order and will do as wished by you. Your letters are as precious to me as my life and I have secured them nicely in a qalamdan (desk)."*[307]

One can hope that this was materialised, because *Tarikh-e-Mumtaz* and *Tarikh-e-*Ghazala were compiled during the same period. This is because Noor Zaman Begum was no less enthusiastic and sincere than the other Begums. Sadly enough, the collection has not been found anywhere. Some 38 letters are said to be found in *Tarikh-e-*Noor, one of which is in poetry form. The letter has 66 verses, which are found in *Sheva-e-Faiz*[308] and are appreciated

306. *Tarikh-e-*Noor (Handwritten), 102.

307. *Tarikh-e-*Noor (Handwritten), 182–83.

308. *Sheva-e-Faiz* - Md. Wajid Ali Shah Akhtar. Publication Sultani. Calcutta. 1277. 234

for their astronomical style of writing. Some other Ghazals composed in love of Noor Zaman Begum are found in '*Sheva-e-Faiz*',[309] and go like this:

1. Noor Zaman Begum *my heart is unfulfilled*
You are the depth of affection Noor Zaman Begum *(Couplets 12)*
2. *You are least bothering but I am afflicted*
You are well behaved but I am not (Couplets 22)
3. *I was given the lessons about my plight in the school*
But the teacher did not teach me every (important) lesson (Couplets 11)
4. *The thought of your beautiful cheeks disbalanced my faith*
I got the glimpse of my darling's beauty (Couplets 14)

There are no other details of the correspondence between the King and Noor Zaman Begum, nor is there proof of the publication of *Tarikh-e-Noor*.[310]

Tarikh-e-Badr

Compilation: 1273–76 Language: Urdu, Genre: Collection of Letters, Publication: 1276 A.H., Format: 32×19 Pages: 46, 11-Lined, Manuscript Proprietor: Idara-e-Adbiyat Urdu, Hyderabad (Deccan)

The collection starts with a eulogy in the glory of Allah in the following words:

> *"What is the greatness of* Allah. *His* Mir*acle is manifested everywhere, whether it is flower or thorn, garden or forest, somewhere faith, somewhere disbelief, often union, often separation, often killing beauty, often intolerable ugliness, some are worshipping the oneness of God, some are worshipping the idol."*

And the letter starts:

---

309. *Ibid*, 7, 17, 192, 291.

310. In 1972 *Diera-e-Adab* (Patna) published the Mazzahab copy of Prof. Kalimuddin Ahmed (Proprietor) along with his Preface. It is not possible to comment on it without its comparative study.

"...I have heard that when a letter is sent from here then it is presented before you in brief, in this way how can you judge my condition. For God's sake, don't be so careless; read the letter fully, more love. Written in Safar 1276 A.H."

As a usual practice, the manuscript starts with a blank page. On this page, other than the seal of the royal library, there is an oval seal in which is inscribed '*Masdar-e-Altaf wa Inayat Hussain 1336 A.H.*' Along with this, the following statement is given:

"Message and letters of Badr-e Alam Saheba Gifted by Nawab Inayat Jung Bahadur, *Syed Mohiuddin Qadri Zor, 16 Ramadhan 1360 A.H."*

On this page is given the stamp of *Idara-e-Adbiyat Urdu.* These seals speak of the long-tiring journey through which the letters have passed, though they passed through educated people. On the last page is given an English rubber stamp, which indicates that some time ago this book was the property of one Maulvi Mirza Md. General Merchant of Bhadrak (Orissa).

One cannot say why, in spite of so many royal stamps, this book was not included in the list of *Bani.* At present, as it is shown in other collections, the copy is written in red and black ink. The writer has not numbered the pages. Much against the normal practice, on the last page (91), the name of the writer, Haseebuddin Ahmed Burdwani, and the date, 16 Jamadiul saani 1276 A.H., are written in Arabic. Of all the available collections of letters, this one is the shortest. Out of the 24 letters, the first one is written in Muharram 1273 A.H., and the last one is dated *Safar* 1276 A.H. In the beginning, the Preface spreads over five pages, in which the King gives a reason for its writing in the following words:

"When in the afternoon there was a change, and the journey of Calcutta was about to start, most of the Begams (Mahlat) remained under pardah (restrictions). Often, letters were full of sorrow but were affectionate. Out to carry forward the tradition of love, I thought that these tokens of love should not go to waste and must be compiled. Hence, in the month of Zilhij *1275 the collection of letters of* Nawab Badr Alam Saheba *was given the gift of*

compilation ... while letters of every month were divided into separate sections. It was named Tarikh-e-Badr, which consists of three Chapters."

In the first chapter there are two letters from 1273 A.H., in the second chapter are 19 letters from 1275 A.H., and in the third chapter there are three letters from 1276 A.H. It cannot be determined whether letters were all written during 1274 A.H. (or during the upheaval of 1857), or whether they were destroyed. Not only in this but in other collections also, there is no letter written during 1274 A.H.

Probably Nawab Badr Alam Saheba was the title of the '*mutai*' wife.[311] The same name is written in *Behr-e-Mukhtalif*.[312] And in *Sheva-e-Faiz*, in the Ghazal which was written for her, the same n ame occurs, as is evident from the following lines:

Badr Alam the beauty absolves me of sorrow
The moon and the box tree envy Badr-e-Alam[313]

In the beginning *Badr Alam* was the companion of *Nawab* Badshah Mahal. When the King had a crush on her then she was elevated to the status of *Begum* (*Badr Alam*). She started being jealous of Nawab Badshah Begum.[314] She was distanced and estranged from other '*Mahlats*.'[315] Her elder sister was employed in the royal (*shahi*) staff.[316] She resided in Hazrat Bagh before 1857.[317] During the devastation of Lucknow she was also ruined:

"I became homeless... had no place to sit, I lost my status, all my jewellery, belongings and dresses were destroyed. Some were lost due to Hazrat Mahal

311. *Tarikh e Badr.* (Handwritten) Md. Wajid Ali Shah Akhtar. 1276. 62.
312. *Behr e Mukhtalif.* Md. Wajid Ali Shah Akhtar. Publication Mustafai. Calcutta. 1277. 15.
313. *Sheva-e-Faiz.* Md. Wajid Ali Shah Akhtar. Publication Sultani. Calcutta. 1277. 176.
314. *Tarikh e Badr.* (Handwritten) Md. Wajid Ali Shah Akhtar. 1276. 9.
315. *Ibid*, 9–17.
316. *Ibid*, 54.
317. *Ibid*, 14.

> *and some were misplaced at the time of my departure. I sit on the floor, live in a dilapidated house, neither remained the palace nor is the garden, the heart is without any spark."*[318]

She started living in a rented house in Mufti Ganj.[319] After some time, she started living in the house of Darogah Wajid Ali in Gola Ganj.[320] When she got the news of the King coming out of the Fort, she was impatient to be with him. "*I am under a debt of 4,000 rupees, the creditor does not let me move, if the debt is paid or if someone gives guarantee then I can come.*"[321]

There was no mention of the debt in the letter of Zeeqad 1275 A.H. Up to that time, during a span of seven months, the King had sent 2,500 rupees. In Zilhij 1275 A.H. she was granted 1,000 rupees in the name of '*Eidi*' (Eid gift), along with some studded jewelry.[322] Her complaint regarding the debt continued. After the last letter, nobody knows about whether the Begum went to Calcutta or remained in Lucknow. In the list of *Bani*, her name is not mentioned among the King's survivors, nor is there any information regarding her separation from the King.

Like the other Begmats, *Badr Alam* was also illiterate. She herself writes about her ignorance in the letters as follows:

a. *"I got your affectionate letter...got it read word by word."*[323]
b. *"O dear for writing the letters I employed Munshi Syed Abad Ali as he is a Syed, is trustworthy, and is loyal to your (sarkar). It is written for information in the pen of Munshi Syed Abad Ali who is hopeful of maintenance."*[324]

---

318. *Ibid*, 19.
319. *Ibid*, 31.
320. *Ibid*, 45.
321. *Ibid*, 89–90.
322. *Ibid*, 79–80.
323. *Ibid*, 20.
324. *Ibid*, 32.

c. *"By the grace of* Allah... *the masnavi is liked by the Majesty,* Mushir *Shah e Hind's prestige is doubled, he is bestowed with wealth and gets distinguished place among the poets. I am thankful and grateful to Sultan-e-Alam that at least by writing the letters of Badr eAlam* Mushir *Shah e Hind got immense fame and name and got the title of* 'Mushir-*e -Hind."*[325]

d. *"This is not within my control. It is under the control of the writer, he can write whatever he wants. I am helpless."*[326]

Many changes were made at the time of publishing the letters in *Ruqa'at-e-Badr*, as it was necessary to drop the above B and D extracts.[327] The common eye is unaware of these mysterious changes, and people think that *Ruqa'at-e-Badr* is in fact *Tarikh-e-Badr* which was published with little change in the title.[328] The compilers of *Tazkira-e-Urdu Makhtootat* were probably not aware of any book named *Ruqa'at-e-Badr* as is obvious from the following statement: "*The collection under consideration (Tarikh-e-Badr) has probably been published...On the title page of this book below the royal seal someone has written this, which indicates that perhaps the book has been published.*"[329]

The strong proof of publication of a book like *Ruqa'at-e-Badr* are the pages of *Taarikh-e-Badr* itself, on which, with the help of pencil sketches, there is an indication of the published pages, and other than some minor changes, those parts have been omitted which mention that *Badr Alam* was illiterate. The printed copy of *Tarikh-e-Badr* and *Ruqa't-e-Badr* is as per the corrections made by the pencil. The compiler of printed copy Syed Md. Ali Arsh Malihabadi has given a brief introduction of it in the beginning of

---

325. *Ibid*, 72.

326. *Ibid*, 78.

327. *Ruqa'ate Badr.* Syed Md. Ali Arsh Nomani Malihabadi. Qasim Press, Hyerabad. 1323. 19, 47.

328. *Classical Adab*, Khwaja Ahmed Farooqui. Azad Kitab Ghar Delhi. Publication Ibrahimia Hyderabad. 1957. 121.

329. *Tazkira-e-Urdu Makhtootat.* Volume 1, 282.

the book. But it is not confirmed whether at the time of publication some changes were made. As a result, a common misunderstanding has come up. Though the statement of *Tazkira-e-Urdu Makhtootat* would be related to Dr. Zor who had already given his excuse that some of his pupils had given a statement, and due to shortage of time he could not check them. In the *Tazkira* the revision of *Tarikh-e-Badr* was supposedly done by some irresponsible person. He not only ignored the markings of the pencil, but relating the number of pages as 42 and the number of letters as 11[330] is either the mistake of the writer or of the person concerned.

Different persons have written letters on behalf of *Badr Alam Saheba*, and hence there is a difference in style. The two letters of 1273 A.H. are written by an unknown writer whose language is simple and free of Persian phrases. The '*Mahlats*', out of mutual jealousy, conspired to give a bad name to *Badr Alam*. She complains in the following manner:

> *"Now as you have asked, hence I am relating to you my condition. My water-carrier's husband was employed withChitra Mahal while her mother-in-law was working under Aklil Mahal. One day she said that both the Mahals sleep together. I instantly remarked that this is not good if Jaan-e-Alam comes to know this then he will be displeased. When the Mahals heard this through the water-carriers they were furious and wanted to have a fight with me. I keep secluded and silent, one day when I was on my terrace then they saw me and told me that you have given birth to a girl child and hence we want to see her.*[331] *Here only the baseless blame and lie of them is disproved because when I was pregnant with one month then how can I give birth to a nine-month old child?"*[332]

The letters of 1275 A.H. were probably written by Munshi Abad Ali, and they are well-written, though there is abundant use of Persian terminology, phrases, and newly composed verses. One example is as follows:

330. *Tazkira-e-Urdu Makhtootat*, 281.

331. *Tarikh e Badr* - (Handwritten) Md. Wajid Ali Shah Akhtar. 1276. 9–10.

332. *Ibid*, 16.

> *"...Can't express my plight, reality cannot be expressed in prose or poem, my consoler is away and the love patient is about to leave this world, my only consolation is your letter, I request you hand foldedly Jaan-e-Alam look at me and please send a letter, don't ignore me else I will die, I have suffered all sorts of pain, have pity on me. Pangs of separation have exhausted me, and I yearn for your letters."*[333]

After gaining the company of Darogah Mir Wajid Ali, there was a big difference in the style of writing; plain and simple words were replaced by difficult words, and lovable complaints were replaced by flattery and sycophancy. Making monetary demands along with superficial expressions of love are the hallmark of the letters of that period. The following excerpt speaks for itself:

> *"Before this I was in* Mufti Ganj, *and separation from Jaan-e-Alam shattered me. Now I am residing in a remote area in* Gola Ganj *near the house of* Darogah Mir Wajid Ali. *I am wounded by the pangs of separation from Jaan-e-Alam. I faintly feel that the fault of this sinner of love be forgiven, so that my conscience is clear and humbly hope that there is no grudge left from my side..."*[334]

Darogah Mir Wajid Ali Taskhir, whose name has been mentioned above, apart from supervising the work of the *mahlats* also had an interest in poetry composition. He was the pupil of Shiekh Gauhar Ali Mushir[335] of the famous Dabeer School.[336] He recommended Mushir's appointment as

---

333. *Ibid*, 26, 27.

334. *Ibid*, 46.

335. In Tazkira-e-Khush Marka-e-Zeba (Handwritten) the following verses are found in the name of *Musheer*:
The appreciator of Imam has come He is the pupil of famous Dabeer (Couplet).
Zameer was supposed to come but this humble has come The master did not come but the servant has come. (Couplet).

336. *Yaadgar e Zaigham.* Md. Abdullah Khan Zaigham.272.

the writer of *Zeb Mahal.*[337] The letters on behalf of *Zeb Mahal* could not be discovered but the poetic story of *Zeb Mahal* was composed by Mushir on the King's wish.[338] The letters of *Taarikh-e-Badr* indicate that one more such biographical *masnavi* of *Nawab Badr-e-Alam* was composed by Mushir,[339] which is very special. *Zeb Mahal* and *Badr-e-Alam* are the names of two different women, whom the King has mentioned in *Behr-e-Mukhtalif.*[340] I thus assume the *masnavi* (which has been discovered) is not the same as mentioned in *Tarikh-e-Badr.* Though it is not confirmed that Mushir wrote letters for *Badr-e-Alam*, as he wrote letters and *masnavi* on behalf of *Zeb Mahal* it is not surprising that he would have written letters on behalf of *Badr-e-Alam* too. Mushir was under the employment of the King around 1290 A.H., and within two or three years he died.[341]

In more than half of the letters of *Tarikh-e-Badr*, there is no mention of the dates of their writing, hence if the compiler had not divided them into chapters and sections, it would have been difficult to know which letter was written in which month. Five out of 24 letters are in poetic form. In the rest of the letters, some verses are from a *masnavi* and some from a Ghazal. In the Ghazals the pen name (*takhallus*) is *Badr-e-Alam*, but actually they were composed by Mir Abad Ali or Mian Mushir. Following are the initial verses (*Maqtas*) of the Ghazals:

1. *May* Allah *bring you here Sultan-e-Alam*
With due Honour and regard Sultan-e-Alam (Couplets 16)
2. *For the sake of the Prophet show me your face*
Akhtar! I am very sad due to separation (from you) (Couplets 8)

337. *Masnavi Musheer* (Handwritten) Gauhar Ali Musheer 1276 (Khuda Bakhsh Library), 17–19.

338. *Ibid.*

339. *Tarikh e Badr.* (Handwritten) Md. Wajid Ali Shah Akhtar. 1276. 86.

340. *Behr e Mukhtalif.* Md. Wajid Ali Shah Akhtar. Publication Mustafai-Calcutta. 1277. 12, 15.

341. *Bani,* MWASA. Sultani Publication. Calcutta, 1877. (Khuda Baksh Library) 245.

3. *Show me your face Jaan-e-Alam*
Don't irritate me anymore Jaan-e-Alam (Couplets 11)
4. *You are the Fountain of love, the great healer*
Jaan-e-Alam Jaan-e-Alam My Life (Couplets 28)

Nawab Badr Alam Saheba's fame as a writer and poet owes much to the letters of '*Ruqa'at-e-Badr*', in which many strange and meaningful changes destroyed the originality of the letters. This was seen in the book *Begmat-e-Avadh ke Khutoot.* In this book there are three letters from the King in the name of *Badr-e-Alam*, while there are nine letters from *Badr-e-Alam* to the King. The eight letters of *Badr-e-Alam* are in fact the distorted form of letters found in *Taarikh-e-Badr.* The points of change are enumerated as below:

A. The letter given on page 85 of *Begmat–e-Avadh ke Khutoot* has been extracted from the first letter of *Tarikh-e-Badr* (page 7–8), and the Ghazal with the first line '*For the sake of the Prophet show me your face*' (2 above) is extracted from sixth letter of *Taarikh-e-Badr* (page 30). The sentence 'a new Ghazal is also being included in the letter', to keep the continuity of the Ghazals, is not found anywhere in *Taarikh-e-Badr.*

B. *Tarikh-e-Badr*, on pages 22–27, is a poetic letter, at the end of which there are a few sentences, but no date is given. On page 87 of *Begmat-e-Avadh ke Khutoot*, prose is written to present a different letter, on which the date given is 11 Zeeqad 1275 A.H. Its poetic part is on pages 94–97. The date of departure is given as Jamaadi ul Aakhir 1275 A.H. In the prose section, more changes are made as compared to the changes made in the poetic part.

C. In *Taarikh-e-Badr* two letters are given in poem form (page 65) and in prose form (page 61). A letter was drafted with the last three letters of the poem, and a summary of the prose form dated 9 Zilhij 1275 A.H., which is given on page 89–91 of *Begmat -e-Avadh ke Khutoot.* In *Tarikh-e-Badr*, there is another letter with the same date (page

71). It is in response to the letter of '*Jaan-e-Alam Akhtar*', whose Ghazal has the first line:

My heart looks for the (one) O sky! where is that Beauty

Badr-e-Alam, in appreciation of the Ghazal writes:

"*The word 'Badr-e-Alam' spreads sweetness and is full of eloquence*", but it is strange because the word '*Badr-e-Alam*' is not used by the King in his expressions. This raises the question of how this discrepancy arose. In fact, the Ghazal which is mentioned in the letter is an extract from a Ghazal of '*Darya-e-Taa'shuq*', *given* on pages 104–105. The appreciation of *Badr-e-Alam* is actually about the Ghazal which is found in *Sheva-e-Faiz.*

D. In *Begmat-e-Avadh ke Khotoot*, the letter given on page 122–23 is the full account of the letter. There is no such short letter in *Taarikh-e-Badr*, and to compose verses so easily was not the practice among the letter-writers of *Tarikh-e-Badr. Badr-e-Alam* writes in the same letter: "*I have dedicated myself to composing verses, I have made myself a true lover.*" If composition means composing verses, then in *Tarikh-e-Badr*, though there are Ghazal*s* and *masnavis* with pennames, there is no such claim to compose poems. *Taarikh-e-Badr* reveals that the King had written some 14 letters to *Badr-e-Alam Saheba*, out of which one was poetic.[342] Out of these 14 letters, not a single one is found in the authoritative collections. In *Begmat-e-Avadh ke Khutoot*, the three letters addressed to *Badr-e-Alam Saheba* are all abridged or distorted from other sources. One is mentioned above, and the other two have the same flaws as given below:

   a. The poetic letter on pages 117–119 has the forms of address (*alqab*) in prose. The poetic part of Ghazal and *masnavi* is taken from *Darya-e-Taa'shuqq.*[343] The arrangement is also

342. *Tarikh-e-Badr* (Handwritten), 66.

343. *Daryaey Taa'shuqq* - Md. Wajid Ali Shah Akhtar- Sultani Publiation Lucknow. (Khuda Bakhsh Library). 8–12, (for Masnavi), 24–25 (For Ghazal).

different. Somewhere it was changed and shortened. There is no mention of the date.

b. In the letter on pages 102–108, other than the address and verses, there is no such content which is not also found in *Daastan* 75 of *Ishq Nama* (prose).[344] It was not the habit of the King to repeat the details. The second letter of '*Begmat-e-Avadh ke Khutoot*' is addressed to Shaida Begum, and is compiled with the help of the *Ishq Nama*, and in it, other than verses and the address (*alqab*), there are no new additions.[345] The compiler of '*Begmat-e-Avadh ke Khutoot*' has included another author while copying the first letter of *Badr-e-Alam*, and writes:

c. *"Two articles of Janab Syed Tamkeen Kazmi on 'Begmat-e-Avadh ke Khutoot' have come to my knowledge. This has also helped in this collection which should be mentioned here."*[346]

References are necessary when discussing important matters. The compiler cannot be absolved of responsibility by only mentioning them in the margin. It triggers guesses as to where those articles were published, and how much the compiler has inferred from them.[347] The response to such queries was incumbent upon the compiler. Had he given the reference then there would have been no room to complain.

344. See the text of the letter on pages 118–21 of '*Pari Khana*'- Tehseen Sarwari (Translator). Publishers Nayaa Rahi (Karachi).1958.

345. *Hamari Zaban* (Weekly, Aligarh). Edition 15.2.1966, 7.

346. *Begmat-e-Avadh Ke Khutoot.* Munshi Intezamullah Shahabi. Farooqui Press. Delhi (1366h). Margin, 86.

347. *Tamkeen Kazmi* (late) had published a collection of the letters of the King and Begmats for some publisher which was with his family up till 1965. There was no letter in it.

Tarikh-e-Firaq

Compilation: 1275 A.H. Language: Urdu, Genre: Collection of Letters, Publication: 1276 A.H., Format: 31×20 Pages 198, 11-Lined, Manuscript – Proprietor: Khuda Baksh Oriental Public Library, Patna.

The manuscript starts with the following eulogy in the name of Allah:

> *In the name of Him who is the Guard of the Earth and the Universe- with one of this gesturess He created the universe ...great thanks to Him who created this world...Such an artist that He adorned the sky with stars and the earth with human beings. He is so powerful that He created Heaven and Hell.*

On the title page, along with royal seals, there is a statement that the Late Khuda Bakhsh gifted this manuscript to the library on 26 April 1900. Like previous manuscripts, the printing is done in black and red ink. The manuscript is complete and is the bulkiest of all the manuscripts available. Perhaps it is for this reason that there is a close printing of words, and often the poetic part is also written as prose. Most of the time, the following letter starts immediately after the first letter, and the beginning or the end is marked in red ink, which with cursory reading, can be easily overlooked. Thus, the numbering of the letters, which was not done by the printer, was later done by a reader who marked it with pencil. Hence, he made a mistake. There are a total of 110 letters, but they are numbered as 109, and are all marked as written in 1275 A.H. From Rabiul Sani to Zilhij, letters of every month are divided into separate sections, and the headings of the sections are given in the margin. The Preface spreads over seven pages. On page 6 of the Preface, two lines are concealed with colour. There are more mistakes in the manuscript, but there is no other example of concealment.

There is a newness in the writing of *Hamd*, *Naat*, and *Manqibat*, and in the reason behind the compilation. The statement goes like this:

> *"...When I came from Lucknow, the* Begmats *and Mahlats were in a deplorable condition. They were not used to this separation, day and night they*

wept bitterly, they were restless like mercury, and consequently they started sending their love in the form of letters. Especially Malka Dehar Nawab Naurozi Begum Saheba, who was in fact very fond of me, started sending letters. Thus, the idea of collecting the letters came to my mind, whereas such loving letters remain memorable and everlasting in the days to come, so that people of good taste and those who are fans of such art must be benefitted... It is given the title of Tarikh-e-Firaq."[348]

The first letter of *Tarikh-e-Firaq* was written on 4 Rabiul Awwal, and the last one was written in the third or fourth week of Zilhij. On the previous letter, the date given is 14 Zilhij 1275 A.H. To write 110 letters within a span of 200 days, with a unique style of writng and new words in every letter, confirms the claim made in the Preface that Navrozi Begum was fondly in love with the King. Whether it was the restlessness of Navrozi Begum, whether the fans of her writing skills benefitted or not. one can say forcefully that these are beautifully written letters, and under this pretext one comes to know about the personal life of the King, his indulgences, the demands of the Begmats and other related people, and the lifestyle and social ambience of Lucknow at that time, all of which has been preserved in the letters forever.

Navrozi Begum is the real name of the writer, while *Jani Begum* was her pen name.[349] Nawab Malka Deher Saheba was the title awarded to her by the King[350] and she adopted the pen name 'Hoor' on her own.[351] Her father and mother received pensions of 70 and 20 rupees respectively during the royal period. They resided in Muali Khan ki Sara (Lucknow).[352] They left behind two daughters and a son called Mir*za Fajju*. The survivors became the inheritors of the pension, but with the fall of the empire, it was discontinued.

348. *Tarikh e Firaq* (Handwritten) Md. Wajid Ali Shah Akhtar, 1276. (Khuda Baksh Library). 8.

349. *Ibid* at 155.

350. *Ibid* at 143, 187.

351. *Ibid* at 53.

352. *Ruqaat e Begmat e Avadh*. (Raza). 90.

This family is known as '*Sharif Najib Paband-e-Waza Nasb wala Hasab.*'[353] Along with Navrozi Begum was her maternal aunt *Fatima Begum*, who also received a pension from the King.[354] In 1275 A.H. they lived in the house of Darogah Imdad Ali Ashir, situated at MohAllah Feel Khana Agha Mir, adjacent to Mosque Siyal Darogah.[355] There is no other source to identify this family, and it is not known how Navrozi Begum maintained herself after 1275 A.H.

Having a fair complexion, medium height, black hair, and a broad forehead, she was the younger sister[356] of Malka Sarosahi. In the lifetime of her sister, she maintained separation (*pardah*) from the King, as the sister did not like that she should come in front of her brother-in-law (the King).[357] At the time of the fall of the empire, Malka Sarosahi gave birth to a daughter.[358] She was named *Wihim Ara Begum*, thereafter she died.[359] Maintenance for the daughter was given to her aunt, Navrozi Begum.[360] At that time, the King was in Calcutta, and from there he initiated relations.[361] And in this way, a little before 1857 (1273–74 A.H.) '*Youm-e-Mulaqat Maktubi*' was started.[362] In *Behr-e-Mukhtalif*, the King had regarded only Malka Sarosahi as one of his *Mutai* wives.[363] There was no mention of Navrozi Begum. Either this was by mistake, or because at that time Navrozi Begum was only his fiancée,

353. *Tarikh-e-Firaq (*Handwritten), 224.

354. *Ibid*, 35, 138, 170.

355. *Ibid*, 185.

356. *Ibid*, 69–70.

357. *Ibid*, 110–11.

358. *Sheva-e-Faiz.* Md. Wajid Ali Shah Akhtar. Publication Sultani. Calcutta. 1277. 10.

359. *Adab Ka Maqsad*, 181.Dr, Syed Noorul Hasan Hashmi-Hindustan Kitab Ghar. Lucknow. 1956. 189. (*Tarikh-e-Mazzahab* Letter 21). 191.

360. *Huzn e* Akhtari- Md. Wajid Ali Shah Akhtar-Matbaey Sultani- Cacutta. 1276. (National Library, Calcutta.) 89.

361. *Tarikh-e-Firaq* (Handwritten), 111.

362. *Ibid*, 224.

363. *Behr e Mukhtalif.* Md. Wajid Ali Shah Akhtar. Publication Mustafai. Calcutta. 1277. 9.

and the King was an unknown lover.[364] The title of *Taarikh-e-Firaq* and its letters express the restlessness and impatience of both the lovers. Wihim Ara Begum died in *Ramadhan* 1274 A.H. The first letter of *Taarikh-e-Firaq* starts with this tragic news, and about the terrible condition prevailing at that time. The letter goes as such:

> *"The plight is terrible and deplorable, when all the concerned ran away with fear of life and limb, I too joined them along with the Princess. During the journey all were separated, our belongings were plundered, when again the people started returning to the town, I too came back. When I returned, I had to face the sick Princess Wihim Ara Begum, I was in bad condition. Ultimately this darling of my heart died in Ramadhan and I was left weeping. Jaan-e-Alam my plight is worse, I am left uncared for, For God's sake, after reading this letter do something for me, free me from this abject condition..."*[365]

Soon these stories and letters of misery were transformed into love letters. When the King responded, there was much encouragement and indulgence from the fourth letter. She says:

> *"Don't send my letter along with other's letters. Also send my expenditure separately and write to me every week...All your dear ones are charming and beautiful, they are your companions of love, I am worthless... Who am I? I am not pretty; you love all of them and with me you are only formal. I want to tell you that if you are with me even for one night then you would see how impatient you will become... Dear you don't value me, I have a crush on you, I am deeply in love, you adorn me hence I always fall for you. I have no jewelry left, my dress is torn, I am counted among your wives but... I don't go out... I don't socialize... I feel ashamed..."*[366]

The demands went on increasing, many wishes were expressed and gradually, one companion, two maids, two cooks, two palanquin-bearers,

364. *Tarikh-e-Firaq* (Handwritten), 194.
365. *Ibid*, 9–11. Letter dated 4.4.1275.
366. *Ibid*, 19–41 (Letter of Jamadiul Awwal 1275).

five gatemen,[367] two letter writers,[368] one physician,[369] one elegy reciter,[370] and many artists[371] were given under her service. This did not seem to satisfy her. Malka Seemtan was flourishing, and Malka Deher did not like it.

A. *"It is the old saying that the bird is sacrificed but the eater does not relish it. The same condition is yours that without you I am so broken but you are always complaining."*[372]

B. *"...the sum of one thousand rupees which you have sent for my Naurozi; listen Sahab... this is my first Naurozi...* (Nauroz a happy occasion to herald Spring) *what I will do with so much money...You better give this amount to your loved ones whom you have sent five thousand and seven thousand to each so that they may use it...I will never accept such a large amount of money for Naurozi. If you are adamant then I will tell you also..."*[373]

C. *"I am not receiving your kind letters... even if I receive one after a gap of ten or eleven days then I know there are several letters for others also. I am not afraid of anyone, hence I am telling you frankly that when an envelope is received then there is one letter for me while there are three or four letters for your other beloveds, like* Malka Seemtan. *O* Allah *am I so low in your estimation.... what is the new charm... If now it is like this then what about the future?"*[374]

Through letters it is revealed that there was hardly any carelessness on the part of the King regarding the pampering of Navrozi Begum. She was

367. *Ibid*, 267.
368. *Ibid*, 365.
369. *Ibid*, 72.
370. *Ibid*, 351.
371. *Ibid*, 172, 244.
372. *Ibid*, 43.
373. *Ibid*, 215–16.
374. *Ibid*, 222.

probably under the impression that the King was still the ruler, while only the King knew the reality, as he expressed in the following words:

> *"I am the victim of destiny and you instead of appreciating my favours are always sarcastic."*[375]

About King's fickle mindedness she says:

"I am not in a peaceful state of mind like you, I am restive all the time."[376] Navrozi Begum was considerate, and hence if she came to know that any of her demands displeased the King, she would at once withdraw it. This is obvious from the following statement:

> *"...This is not the time to get adorned with jewels, when* Allah *brings you here then I will see... at such a state of affairs I will flaunt before whom... I am only writing for bare maintenance ... and that even at the request of* Darogah Mir Wajid Ali... *it will not happen again."*[377]

She knew that once she lost her honour before the King, she would become hopeless. She started being careful in her demands, and gradually she received all that which pleases a woman the most. Like the other Begmats, Navrozi Begum had the feeling that she was unwanted, and that her letters were read out to her by others and were also responded to in the same way. The following explains this:

A. *"For three days* Ashir *is under high fever, but he still does not refuse to write letters."*[378]

B. "Ghazal *which was written in appreciation of me... was on my request read out to me up till the evening though I can't say for how many times."*[379]

---

375. *Ibid*, 319.
376. *Ibid*, 89.
377. *Ibid*, 98.
378. *Ibid*, 45.
379. *Ibid*, 172

C. *"Last night I had a dream and put it into a poem, and to decipher its meaning I have sent it to you."*[380]

"Up till yesterday I have sent some seventy-seven letters to you, and all of these are written by your pupil... all the writers which were appointed by you under Munshi Md. Shafi mark their presence before Malka Seemtan and they write letters for her. Here there is no one except Ashir."[381]

The above extracts show that all the letters were written by Ashir, and the language is typical of Ashir's style. In common letters he used the words "Ashir *the pupil, the loyal who is hopeful of advice and corrections*",[382] and whenever he faced any displeasure due to a mistake, he wrote the words "Ashir *the pupil, the loyal, the sinner hopeful of forgiveness.*"[383] To increase the enthusiasm, he did not mind using vulgar language, and if there was a mistake then he was scorned.[384] Out of flattery he talked in an amusing manner.[385] To gain favour he bragged about himself.[386] In short, he was a person who was present everywhere in *Taarikh-e-Firaq*, and to understand *Taarikh- e-Firaq* one should understand Ashir. It is not disappointing that he behaved like this, though he made good use of Navrozi Begum's position. However, it is disappointing to see that people, may be out of their simplicity or may be due to being too thoughtful, have not appreciated the writing skills of Ashir, but blame an innocent and ignorant girl for his strange behaviour.[387]

Before the upheaval of 1857, Imdad Ali Ashir used to write letters for Shaida Begum and the other Begmats. The letters of '*Ruqa'at-e-Begmat*' are

380. *Ibid*, 120.

381. *Ibid*, 242–43.

382. *Tarikh-e-Firaq* (Handwritten), after fifth letter almost at the end of every letter such sentences are found.

383. *Ibid*, 97–104.

384. *Ibid*, 240, 272–77, 298–99.

385. *Ibid*, 128–30.

386. *Ibid*, 10, 17, 23, 177, 187–88.

387. *Tazkiraey* Shauqq. Ataullah Paalvi. Savera Art Press. Lahore. 1956. 156–57.

the memoirs of those days. After 1857 he gave shelter to Navrozi Begum and reserved his services for her. In the beginning, he was given a salary of 15 rupees per month.[388] After much recommendation it was increased to 15 rupees more.[389] The same amount of 30 rupees was fixed for Amir Ali Khan Hilal who was appointed to write letters for Navrozi Begum.[390] Probably Ashir was from the Dabir *School*. His name is not mentioned in famous discussions. In *Taarikh-e-Firaq* the name *Talmiz ul Sultan* is written.[391] He was the son of *Darogha Md. Ali*.[392] It was written in the last letter of *Tarikh-e-Firaq* that Navrozi Begum had sent gifts to Metiaburj, but it cannot be said as to when Navrozi Begum and *Darogah* decided to travel to Metiaburj.

Three letters of *Tarikh-e-Firaq* are fully poetic,[393] while some of the other letters are in prose form. In the beginning Navrozi Begum used the pen name *Zulekha*. However, the King did not like it and suggested 'Hoor*a*' instead. But in the word Hoor*a* the letter '*alif*' was not acceptable to her, and she preferred 'Hoor.'[394] After 5 Jamadiul Sani 1275 A.H., in the Ghazal*s* the word 'Hoor' *is* used. The style of the Ghazal*s* of *Taarikh-e-Firaq* is unique, and they are in good number. Some of these are as follows:

1. *Where to find where is my dear*
Where is the Sun of beauty this evening (Couplets 9)
2. *What to do in this loneliness except weep*
I am losing my heart in the melancholy (Couplets 7)
3. *You should have enquired about the sad beloved*
Or you should have shown your face in my dream (Couplets 8)

388. *Tarikh-e-Firaq* (Handwritten), 44–45.
389. *Ibid*, 137–38.
390. *Ibid*, 235, 265.
391. *Ibid*, 154, 287.
392. *Ibid*, 272.
393. *Ibid*, 94, 101, 107.
394. *Ibid*, 19, 52, 53.

4. *Like a flower I wilt*

Due to separation I am dispirited (Couplets 9)

5. *O fairy! who is your companion?*

Fairy too is not contacting (Couplets 9)

6. *I cannot tolerate your separation*

I don't love anyone other than you (Couplets 15)

7. *Jaan-e-Alam! You are the envy of the moon*

You are a shining pearl (Couplets 21)

8. *I was not happy even for a moment*

I remained depressed all through (Couplets 9)

9. *O Jaan-e Alam! the sweet orator*

I am your great fan (Couplets 18)

10. *Since the flower is not found*

The Nightingale is sad (Couplets 11)

11. *I am sacrificed (sadqa) over you my bridegroom*

My bridegroom, my dear my beloved (Couplets 11)

12. *What to write about your charm, you are the envy of the moon*

Your face is like the shining Sun (Couplets 22)

13. *O! Wind the messenger give me the news of Akhtar*

Brighten my ray of hope (Couplets 9)

14. *For* Allah*'s sake let me relax*

Don't worry me so much the separation of my friend! (Couplets 16)

15. *Sahab! Come I am waiting for you*

Or at least call me (Couplets 16)

16. *Without you I spent the night in great trouble*

I remained restive like the dew drops and spent the night weeping (Couplets 9)

17. *Uneasiness prevails (in my eye) like a pointed arrow*

Again since evening I have had agony in my heart (Couplets 11)

18. *The lover is only getting oral solace*

I got the ring but where is he whose token is this (Couplets 7)

19. Allah*! Congratulations to Jaan-e-Alam for the royal celebration*

Allah*! Congrats to Jaan-e-Alam for his merrymaking (Couplets 5)*

20. *I enjoyed your enthusiasm in my imagination*
Often I felt you in my heart and often in my lap (Couplets 7)
21. *My eyelashes are piercing my heart*
My eyes are full of tears (Couplets 10)
22. *I am speaking from my heart*
And I am concluding my dialogue (Couplets 5)
23. *For quite a few days I have not received Jaan-e-Alams's letters*
What has happened to Jaan-e-Alam (Couplets 9)
24. *My heart is burning with the fever of separation*
The sorrow of separation is breaking my heart (Couplets 10)
25. *Look up and see how I am finished*
Why you are blushing... (Couplets 8)
26. *How to address you as Moon or Sun?*
Your face is unparralled (Couplets 23)
27. *The flowers dance in the garden during the night*
The breeze takes fresh turns in the night (Couplets 14)
28. *Messengrer! This letter is ending*
(Now) Take it and go soon messenger (Couplets 10)
29. Hoor*! now I can see my beloved*
Thanks Allah *I can see the* Sulaiman *of Fairies (The gorgeous) (Couplets 9)*
30. *When I went to my friend's place I could not return*
I sat in such a way that I could not take a step (Couplets 11)
31. *I could not relate the tale of separation to him*
Could not enjoy one night of union (Couplets 11)
32. *You showed stubbornness*
First you were affectionate then you became angry (Couplets 13)
33. *Lovers are not trustworthy*
I have no control even if he does not send a letter (Couplets 11)
34. *Congrats! my sad heart there is spring(descending) in the garden*
The wind of lovers' union makes me restless (Couplets 8)
35. *Beware no stranger should enter your house*
You are flower and no thorn should come near you (Couplets 14)

With the pen name *(takhallus)* of 'Hoor', the following nine Ghazals are found in *Ruqa'at e Begumat.*

1. *Dear I trusted you like my own*
I have no control whether you come or not (Couplets 11)
2. *My dear where are you*
Are you angry or are you compassionate (Couplets 15)
3. *I want to see your beautiful cheeks*
Come up I want to have your glimpse (Couplets 11)
4. *My heart is uncontrollable in friend's love*
Picture of my friend is before my eyes (Couplets 11)
5. *The good news of my friend's union is coming*
But the wish of my heart is showing something else (Couplets 9)
6. *O! The messenger of wind give me the news of my friend's arrival*
So that my restless heart gets some solace (Couplets 11)
7. *I have no respite from the pangs of separation*
My heart is sighing every time (Couplets 10)
8. *Every time I am thinking of the beautiful face*
Before my eyes appears the image of the bright Sun (Couplets 10)
9. *You don't give me a kiss*
You don't care for my impatience (Couplets 11)

Whenever the compiler of *Ruqa'at-e-Begmat* came across the word 'Hoor' in the poems and the prose, he related it to 'Hoor *Begum*', and when he did not get any such indication, he related it to Navrozi Begum.[395]

---

395. In *Ruqa't e Begmat* on page and 39 and 42 there are also two letters in poetry form with 19 and 50 verses each, in which the pen name used is 'Hoor.' The letters that are in prose form and have no Ghazals give such indications. A letter on page 89–92 has such indication: "According to the writer of Hoor what is the effect of love, Allah Allah' but inadvertently the compiler missed it. Tamkeen Kazmi, in the collection he compiled, relates it to Hoor Begum. But in his collection also one letter is related to Navrozi Begum.

Even if the existence of a *Begum* named 'Hoor *Begum was proved, there is a similarity in the subjects of Tarikh-e-Firaq and Ruqa'at-e-Begmat*'. There is only one difference between the starting verses (*matla*) of *Ruqa'at-e-Begmat* and the starting point of *Tarikh-e-Firaq* Ghazal *'aitbar kiya, ikhtiyar kiya.'* In both these collections, there are 11 verses and as is obvious from the following, there is no difference of even a single word in the last verse (*Maqta*):

How to believe that I am in your bosom
O Hoor*! What control have I over his heart?*

As for the verses, between the first and the last there is very little difference, and even if there is any then it is so minute that it appears to be a correction. *Tarikh-e-Firaq* is compiled with those letters which were sent by Navrozi Begum, while '*Ruqa'at-e-Begmat*' is a careless publication by Ashir. No one can say in what places corrections were made. For us it is sufficient to note that Navrozi Begum was ignorant, and all the letters were written by Ashir on her behalf. The letters of *Ruqa'at-e-Begmat* in the name of Navrozi Begum, with the pen name Hoor, were also written by Ashir. Style, verses, timing, and similarity of subjects endorse my claim. Perhaps here the author wants to say that the letters both in *Ruqa'at-e-Begmat* and *Tarikh-e-Firaq* were in fact the letters written by Navrozi Begum, though penned by Ashir under the *takkhallus* Hoor.

In *Ruqa'at-e-Begmat,* in 12 out of 15 letters there is no date given, and three letters have wrong dates. The reason is as follows:

A. The letter dated 2 Zeeqad 1273 A.H. given on page 88 of *Ruqa'at-e-Begmat* has the news of the birth of a girl child and of her death after the upheaval of 1857. As per the information given in *Taarikh-e-Firaq*, these events occurred in 1274 A.H., but the date given is 4 *Rabiul Akhir* 1275 A.H. There is a similarity in the sentences in these two letters (*Tarikh e Firaq* page 9–10 and *Ruqa'at-e-Begmat* page 88–89) which is obvious from the following illustrations:

My friend Jaan-e-Alam long time passed since (Taarikh e Firaq)
My friend Jaan-e-Alam... long time passed since (Ruqa'at-e-Begmat)
I am the same... obedient, I will do what you order (Taarikh e Firaq)
I am the same... obedient I will do what u order (Ruqa'at-e-Begmat)

In the above sentences there is a negligible difference in words. The gaps which are deliberately omitted also use the same words. There is consistency in the last part of *Tarikh-e-Firaq*. In *Begmat-e-Ruqa'at* it is oddly written "*what you say will be followed... this is the summary...*" after which there is the addition of one verse before concluding it. In the '*Begmat-e-Avadh ke Khutoot*' this letter has been distorted and then published. It becomes difficult to identify it.[396] To arrange it in such a way is the right of the compiler.

B. In *Ruqa'at-e-Begmat* the letter on page 92 is dated as "10 Zilhij 1273 A.H., in which there is a sentence of blessing '*be freed from the prison.*' *Badshah* was imprisoned in *Shawwal* 1273 A.H. The upheaval of 1857 was at its peak, there were many restrictions and hindrances in the communication system, and arrest rules were strict. In such a case, even if one supposes that the letters of Hoor *Begum* were well received, then the style of writing indicates that the informal and emotional expressions, which are not found in the beginning letters of *Tarikh-e-Firaq*, then how could these be in the present letter.

C. The letter on page 98 of *Ruqa'at-e-Begmat* is dated 10 of Rabiul Sani 1273 A.H. In the last part of the letter there is a mention of the destruction of the old seal and the impression of the new one. The letter mentioned in 'A' above is missing and was replaced by an odd verse. If the last lines of the letter on page 98 of *Ruqa'at-e-Begmat* are added to the letter of the above extract given in paragraph A, then the letter of *Ruqa'at-e-Begmat* will become a distorted imitation of the letter mentioned in paragraph A of *Taarikh-e-Firaq*. Ultimately

396. *Begmat-e-Avadh Ke Khutoot*, Munshi Intezamullah Shahabi. Farooqui Press. Delhi (1366 A.H.). 58–59.

the sentence which appeared odd in paragraph A of *Ruqa'at-e-Begmat* is well set in the letter mentioned in paragraph C. It goes like this:

'*My condition in your separation is beyond expression.*' (C) and in paragraph A it is said '...*I am losing my heart as if somebody is squeezing it.*' If the letter given in paragraph A is taken to be dated 2 Zeeqad 1273 A.H., then it can be considered as the oldest letter of Navrozi Begum. The letter of *Ruqa'at-e-Begmat* which is given on page 98 and 99, in which there is a mention of the destruction of the seal and the death of the girl Wihim Ara, the date could be 10 Rabiul Sani, but not of the year 1273 A.H. because the mentioned events did not take place during that time. The starting letters of *Tarikh-e-Firaq* confirm my claim. Out of these letters, the first is dated 4 Rabiul Sani, the second is 24 Rabiul Sani and the third is 26 Rabiul Sani 1275 A.H. All the three letters deal with the same topic but have different expressions. The above-mentioned letter from 10 Rabiul Sani also deals with the same topic but has different expressions. In fact, due to the trouble prevailing at that time, four letters on the same topic were sent at close intervals. In the fourth of these, there were some complaints regarding it, as follows:

> *"I wrote three letters to you but you did not respond even to one."*[397]

In *Taarikh-e-Firaq* (Handwritten) there are only two letters which were received by the King. Whether the letter of 10 Rabiul Sani was received or not is not known but it is not included in the Collection. However, the letter of *Ruqa'at-e-Begmat* compensates for this gap. This fact further confirms the claim that *Ruqa'at-e-Begmat*, which is known to be compiled by *Imtiaz Ali Najib*,[398] is in fact the manuscript of Ashir which was discovered by Imtiaz Ali Khan. Despite the mistakes which became part of the *Ruqa'at-e-Begmat*, this book is much more reliable than the book *Begmat-Avadh ke Khutoot.* Imtiaz Ali Khan found this copy of the manuscript in very bad condition.[399]

397. *Tarikh-e-Firaq* (Handwritten), 17.

398. *Supra Note* 396 at 5.

399. *Ruqaat e Begmat e Avadh.* (Raza).1.

The above-mentioned letters of A and C must be on different pages, but due to the ignorance of Imtiaz Ali Khan he connected the start of one letter to the end of another letter. There are more such mistakes in *Ruqa'at-e-Begmat*,[400] but for the sake of brevity these are being ignored here.

There is proof in *Taarikh-e-Firaq* that on 5 Jamadiul Akhir 1275 A.H. Navrozi Begum adopted the pen name (*takhallus*) Hoor.[401] Hence all the above-mentioned letters mentioned in paragraph A and B, on which the word 'Hoor *Begum*' was written, cannot be dated before 5 Jamadiul Akhir as mentioned above. These cannot be said to be forged either; though there are some changes in the verses and sentences, on the whole they appear to be the letters written by Navrozi Begum and penned by Ashir. For some reason these could not be included in *Taarikh-e-Firaq*. The *Begum* was herself doubtful as to why the King was not receiving her letters, hence she says:

A. *"O Dear! Almighty knows that except for two days I wrote a letter to you every day for the last two months but you are not receiving it. I am worried."*[402]

B. *"Yesterday I sent seventy-seven letters to you..."*[403]

The statement of above (B) is dated 29 *Ramadhan* 1275 A.H. hence the number of letters up to 29 *Ramadhan* should have been 77, but in *Tarikh-e-Firaq* there are only 73 letters. The King had instructed that every day one

400. For example, on page 89–92 of *Ruqa'at-e-Begmat* there is a letter in which there is the complaint:
"I am anxious that much time has passed but I have not received any news of your welfare." In the same letter this claim is denied in these words: *"Though there is no break in the continuity of letters... but I wish that I receive two letters in a day."* Here also there is a couplet from where the discontinuity starts. All these disparities can be solved.
401. *Tarikh-e-Firaq* (Handwritten), 53.
402. *Ibid*, 243.
403. *Ibid*, 242.

letter should be written,[404] and the *Begum* fulfilled this wish. In the 29 days of the month of *Shawwal* 1275 A.H., 22 letters were found, and in 14 days of Zeeqad, 11 letters were found. But after 14 Zeeqad, suddenly the series of letters was discontinued, and one letter from 14 Zilhij was found. One can hope that Navrozi Begum must not have stopped sending letters after 14 Zeeqad, but these were not received by the King. Perhaps at the time he moved out of the Fort, they were misplaced. The letters of *Ruqa'at-e-Begmat* can be considered as the lost pages of *Taarikh-e-Firaq* because based on topic the letters which were supposed to be in the Zeeqad and Zilhij Sections of *Taarikh-e-Firaq* are found secured in *Ruqa'at-e-Begmat.*

Regarding the mention of letters of the King in *Taarikh-e-Firaq*, the first letter is said to be dated 14 Rabiul Sani 1275 A.H., and the last letter is dated 24 *Shawwal* 1275 A.H. The previous letter was the first letter in 19 months and was received on 1 *Jamadiul Awwal* 1275 A.H.[405] The last letter was received on 8–9 Zeeqad 1275. A.H.[406] Thereafter there is no mention of the receipt of any letter, either in *Taarikh-e-Firaq* or in *Ruqa'at-e-Begmat.* The last letter was in response to the 76th letter. If the dates of receipt of all the letters are taken to be entered correctly in *Taarikh-e-Firaq*, then it can be said that the King, in response to the 76 letters, wrote 50 letters to Navrozi Begum. Some of these letters were pictorial,[407] while in some there were Ghazal*s*. The following twelve Ghazals are clearly identified:[408]

1. Allah*! Show me Lucknow ...*

In sleep also I sigh for Lucknow (Couplet 24)

2. *O the Charming face! get close to me in the garden*

So that the spring comes, my heart is gladdened, and I get rid of melancholy (Couplet 21)

---

404. *Ibid*, 85.

405. *Ibid*, 15, 22.

406. *Ibid*, 364.

407. *Ibid*, 123, 152, 238, 257.

408. *Ibid*, 74, 85, 141, 163, 173, 184, 201, 232.

3. *I am like a bird in captivity and my abode is separation*
The place of flower is in my feet and my abode is separation (Couplet 12)
4. Navrozi Begum *my heart is gone*
And it is vanished in the dust (Couplet 13)
5. *Lip does not touch lip (Couplet 14) (This is the* Ghazal *of* Qamar Mazmun *at p. 364).*
6. *The breasts are better than the apples of heaven*
It is a container of juice or sweet sugar (Couplet 18)
7. *The nipples of the breasts are like turquoise stone*
The breasts are of diamond and the nipples are objects of envy (Couplet 17)
8. *I even dream of your breasts*
Wow! Your charming style and the lovely breasts (Couplet 18)
9. *The eyebrow is pierced like an arrow due to separation*
My sigh of pain became the target of his arrow (Couplet 18)
10. *I was lost when I looked for the beauty of my friend*
All my scorch marks were washed away when I got senses (Couplet 11)
11. *My tragedy is that you don't care for me*
Dear my only disappointment is this (Couplet 22)
12. *You committed blunder by showing me your face*
You defamed me by expressing love (Couplet 12)

Of the above Ghazal*s*, only one line from the fifth one is found in *Sheva-e-Faiz.* After perusing *Sheva-e-Faiz* in search of signs, names, titles, and 'Ghazal *in search of photos*' some more Ghazal*s* have come to the fore. These are as follows:

1. *My dear your photo is in my eyes*
Your dear photo is on my chest the whole night (Couplet 12)
2. *Fair,* Hoor *and moon* Navrozi Begum
You are my life my heart Navrozi Begum *(Couplet 16)*
3. *My Queen I have no peace without you*
... I lay down my life for you

Fairies should ask me the taste of your lips
Your neck is like the moon crescent (Couplet 12)
4. *I click Your beauty*
Everybody will come to know of your beauty (Couplet 13)

Other than Ghazals, *masnavis*, 5-line poems (*mukhammas*), and '*Thumri*', along with '*Dharpad*' were sent on the *Begum's* wish. In *Sheva-e-Faiz*, Navrozi Begum's name is entered in only one *masnavi.*[409] The anonymous compositions could be related to anyone.

The letters of *Taarikh-e-Firaq* are still unpublished.[410] Only some parts of the first letter are published in *Ruqa'at-e-Begmat.* In the manuscript from page 208–210 and at other places there are some signs of changes and omissions, which indicates that more letters were likely published somewhere else, but this is unverified.

Tarikh-E-Jamshedi

Compilation: 1275–76 A.H. Language: Urdu, Genre: Collection of letters, Printing: 1276 A.H., Format: 30×19, Pages: 58, 11-Lined (Manuscript)

The collection opens with gratitude to Allah the Almighty:

"...We should at the outset appreciate and laud the Almighty Who in this beautiful world has created different types of wonders and living beings that it has adorned the earth and has given unparalleled beauty to all, the young and the old."
"...Khuda will simplify the hardships of the journey. He will fill up the glass of wishes with the liquor of hope... Written by the pen of loyalist, Muzaffar Ali Hunar *on the twenty sixth day of Muharram 1276."*

The first page of the manuscript is blank. There are small and big seals of the royal library. On the second page is written '*Ya Fattah*', thereafter

409. *Sheva-e-Faiz* (Masnavi section) 277–78.
410. By unpublished means in a separate collection.

the manuscript starts with *Bismillah.* The Preface spreads over four pages. In the Preface, as usual, the purpose behind the compilation is given in the following words:

> *"When I abandoned my familiar abode... and took on the journey to Calcutta, the Mahlats were very disheartened at this separation and they yearned to meet me, hence they often wrote endearing letters drenched in perfume. It however came to my mind that these scattered pages be collected in one place and be preserved from being destroyed by the hands of time. Hence in the month of* Zilhij *1275 the letters of Nawab* Jamshed Begum *Saheba are being compiled."*

Out of 49 letters, the last five letters are of the month of *Muharram* 1276 A.H. In this way Zilhij 1275 A.H. was the starting period of the compilation of these letters. In the Preface the name of the Collection given is '*Afsarul Twarikh*', but this name is written after deleting the word '*Tarikh-e-Jamshedi*'. One cannot say why this was done. The deleted words are still legible. In the *Bani* list this Collection is entered with its original name. There is no verification regarding the existence of '*Afsar ul Tawarikh*', nor is the name in line with the other names. In the manuscript, the headlines, dates and the King's name is in red ink. There are many mistakes in writing, and the pages have not been numbered, though the manuscript is complete.

Nawab Jamshed Begum was from a high class Lucknow family.[411] In Behre Mukhtalif and *Bani* the same name appears.[412] She was childless, hence she could not get the title of '*Mahal.*' After the King's departure from Lucknow, for some time she stayed in Qaiser Bagh. When Qaiser Bagh was devastated, she, along with *Begum Hazrat Mahal,* remained in exile for some time. When peace was restored, she came back to Lucknow and stayed at '*Khirke* Mir *Jaagan adjacent to the house of* Kazim *Ali Qawwal Mohalah Mansoor Nagar*' with her brothers. An allowance was fixed for her, but in the '*starting period of Birjis Qadar's reign Hazrat Mahal did not grant her allowance for*

411. *Tarikh e Jamshedi* (Handwritten) Md. Wajid Ali Shah Akhtar. 1276. 50–72.
412. *Bani,* 235, Behre Mukhtalif, 20.

six months.' In her first letter, dated 8 Rabiul Sani 1275 A.H. she related her hardships, theft, devastation, and debts to the King, and asked the King for help. [413] The King sent her 500 rupees.[414] From the letters it is revealed that from Rajab 1275 A.H. to *Muharram* 1275 A.H. for about seven months, 4,000 rupees were sent only for her personal expenses.[415] From the last letter dated 26 *Muharram* 1276 A.H. it appears that after getting permission she, along with her mother and elder brother, started for Calcutta. If *Jamshedi Begum* wrote any letter to the King before 1275 A.H., then it was not mentioned in the Collection. There are two Ghazal*s* in *Sheva-e-Faiz* which are connected with Jamshed Begum*'s* name.[416] The first couplets are as follows:

For ever the name of Jamshed *is immortalised*
*Jaam-e-*Jamshed *is the bowl of the covetous*
Jamshed Begum *is my companion*
(Hence) Why should she not be distinguished?

But perhaps these Ghazal*s* were composed in *Shabaan* 1275 A.H. because the letters of those days mentioned some Ghazal*s*.[417] After the King's death, Jamshed Begum got a monthly allowance of 70 rupees.[418] There is however no information regarding the death of Jamshed Begum. Among her relatives were her mother, grandmother, and aunt, and all three of them were widows. The Begum pursued for the maintenance of all of them, but when it was agreed for one of them, she complained as follows:

> "...*For other* Begums*' relatives the allowance was high but for my brother it is 10 rupees per month... why do you insult me among the rivals, you don't stop*

413. *Tarikh-e-Jamshedi* (Handwritten), 7–10.
414. *Ibid*, 17.
415. *Ibid*, 23, 47, 52, 87, 112.
416. *Sheva-e-Faiz*, 69 & 182
417. In *Sheva-e-Faiz* at page 397 three *Qata'as* are related to Jamshed Begum.
418. *Oudh Pension Papers*: Printed by B.S. Press Calcutta. 1913. 41.

bothering me, listen Jaan-e-Alam increase the allowance of all my brothers... as I heard (This behavior) was against your nature."[419]

In the letter the brothers are named as Mir Hasan Ali, Mir Inayat Hussain, and Mir Imdad Hussain. Mir Inayat Hussain had accompanied her to Calcutta[420] but at the time of the publication of *Kulliyat-e-*Akhtari (1278 A.H.) Mir *Ali Hussain* was also in Calcutta. His pen name was '*Faarig.*' In *Kulliyat-e* Akhtari there is also one *Qa'ta* by *Faarig*. In Qamar Mazmun there are *Qata'ats* both by *Faarig* and Inayat Hussain Adil. Up till then probably they were taken into royal service.

Jamshed Begum was illiterate. She could hardly read, hence no question arises regarding composing Ghazals. The following points support this claim, as she writes:

A. *"Your letter dated 17* Rajab *reached me on the 27th. Better I did not ask my brother to read those out for me. There was a letter writer (lady) sitting beside me, I asked her to read out the letter for me and also to write its reply."*[421]

B. *"... and these* Ghazals *which are composed by my brother go unresponsive by you. They complain about it to me. Better that you should comment upon them as you find them. You should even correct them and mark them as examined and approved."*[422]

C. *"In your first letter you asked me that I should get the reply written by a letter writer but she is not present here, perhaps she is moved out somewhere else. Your letter is written in such a way that I feel shy to get the reply written by my brother. I ask my aunt to read out your letter for me but she cannot write hence I am helpless."*[423]

---

419. *Tarikh-e-Jamshedi* (Handwritten), *Ibid*, 104.

420. *Ibid*, 116.

421. *Ibid*, 26.

422. *Ibid*, 28.

423. *Ibid*, 40.

D. *"...And I heard the* Ghazal *composed by you ... it is very commendable."*[424]

As per the above extracts, it is evident that all the letters of *Tarikh-e-Jamshedi,* including the Ghazals, were written by Ali Hussain Faarig, by some anonymous letter writer, and by Munshi Muzzaffar Ali Hunar, who was appointed to write letters in a befitting manner.[425] He was later appointed permanently:

> *"During that period in recognition of his abilities my clerk (munshi) was appointed for 25 rupees per month. It is true that for such honour the decent people achieve knowledge and learn art so that they are recognized and honoured by the rulers and Kings and get employment in the royal courts."*[426]

Hunar remained the King's companion up till his death. Nassakh declares him as the pupil of Mir Wazir Ali Saba[427] while King regards him as his own pupil.[428] In Matbaey Sultani Calcutta, in most of the books Hunar's *Qata'as* are found. On the King's death, there was an amazing *Qata'ae Tarikh*, which was the result of his calibre. After the King's death the English rulers fixed a monthly allowance of 13 rupees for Hunar.[429] An Anjuman (group) with the name *Guldasta-e-Ittehad* was formed by the loyals of the King, which lamented the devastation of Metiaburj. Hunar was the secretary of the Anjuman for several years and on 21 April 1896 he died and was buried in the graveyard of the Anjuman.[430] The Anjuman, as a memoir of Hunar, was still dispensing social, literary, and religious services under a new name.

---

424. *Ibid*, 50.
425. *Ibid*, 71.
426. *Ibid*, 104.
427. *Sukhan Shooara* 563, *Yadgar-e-Zaigham* on page 383 he is regarded first of *Asir* then of King's pupil.
428. *Bani*, MWASA- Sultani Publication. Calcutta, 1877. (Khuda Baksh, Avadh).246.
429. *Oudh Pension Papers*: Printed by B.S. Press Calcutta. 1913. 22.
430. The published Reports of Anjuman-*e-Muhammadi,* 1907- 10.

Due to the continuous change in letter writers, there is no harmony in the language of the letters. Most of the initial letters were written by Jamshed Begum's elder brother. The writing and rhyming style indicates that it was the work of an amateur. The education level of the brother was moderate. The King complained about it. The *Begum* herself was embarrassed to have the letters read out or written by her brother. If she had some lady letter writer, then she expressed her feelings through her words. In these letters, the sentences were simple and informal. The King not only wished to know the feelings of her heart, but he preferred formal language with etiquette and an attractive style. Hunar was the right man for this. The letters written by Hunar are easily identified by his unique style. The main feature of these letters is the purity behind them. Like other Begmats, Jamshed Begum also made demands for her relatives' allowances and maintenance, but there was no flattery or shrewdness in her letters, which was so obvious in the letters of other Begmats.

In this collection there are only two letters in poetry form which are also complete.[431] The other letters are in prose form, and in some, the Ghazal*s* comprising five verses are given for mere amusement. In the Ghazal*s*, though the pen name given is 'Jamshed', the style clearly shows that someone else composed them. The following sentences confirm this claim:

A. *"This* Ghazal *is composed by my elder brother... check it and correct it..."*[432]

B. *"Asked my brother to compose a new* Ghazal *explaining my plight ... (sending) for correction."*[433]

C. *"This new* Ghazal *composed by my brother ... for correction..."*[434]

431. *Tarikh-e-Jamshedi* (Handwritten), 55, 65.

432. *Ibid*, 22.

433. *Ibid*, 25.

434. *Ibid*, 28. The letters on page 22, 25, 28 above are written in *Rajab* 1275.

Gradually her style of expression changed:

A. *"This* Ghazal *is freshly composed."*[435]
B. *"This is a newly composed* Ghazal."[436]

And the last letters make it seem as if the *Begum* was herself a poet. She says: *Clouds came and reminded me of my darling:*

A. *"Now the emotions flew from my heart and I composed this* Ghazal *just now..."*[437]

She also expressed when she got the news of his release from prison:

B. *"I freshly composed these five verses and have sent this to you."*[438]

The credit for the difference in the previous and later expressions goes to Hunar. The pen name (*takhallus*) used in the verses is Jamshed and the expressions are in an affectionate style, but it is declared in the start that the plight of heart is manifested in words by the writer, hence the charm which is found in the original expression of the poet is missing. The Ghazal*s* of this collection are as follows:

1. *None of my heart's wish is fulfilled*
My youth is wasted (Couplet 5)
2. *In every flower I get your fragrance*
In every heart there is fancy for you (Couplet 5)
3. *If he is fragrance of flower then I am also the freshness of spring*
Like the wind I am restless (Couplet 4)

---

435. *Ibid*, 56.
436. *Ibid*, 62. (Letters of Shabban and Shawwal).
437. *Ibid*, 95.
438. *Ibid*, 99. (Letters of 95, 99 written in Zeeqad)

4. *Without you I am so bored*

My house stings me like a cobra (Couplet 5)

5. *I am thinking of You Akhtar all the time*

Show me again your charming face Akhtar (Couplet 13)

6. *The stylish walk is as piercing as a knife*

I am killed when he walks in style (Couplet 5)

7. *Now there is no pomp and splendour*

There is life left only in my eyes (Couplet 5)

8. *I am always noting the beauty of his face*

I daily practice letter writing (Couplet 5)

9. *Why you are concealing your face with your hair*

Why the morning of Eid is turned into darkness (Couplet 5)

10. *May* Allah *answer my prayers*

My Akhtar be released this month (Couplet 7)

11. *The envy of fairy is down with the pangs of separation*

The worried are more vexed (Couplet 5)

12. *What to say I am facing the evil*

I am facing the enemy, the cruel and the killer (Couplet 9)

13. *How could I tolerate the tragedy*

My heart was not under my control what to say (Couplet 9)

14. *My life is not in me since you are not with me.*

Your separation is not less than the tragedy of death (Couplet 5)

15. *I am so weak due to being separated from you*

Your ring has become my amulet (due to fragile figure) (Couplet 5)

16. *Neither my life ends*

Nor this night of wait ends (Couplet 5)

17. *The like of your eyes*

I have hardly seen them (Couplet 5)

18. *What oppression do I suffer Jaan-e-Alam*

Can't express in words (Couplet 9)

19. *The separation decayed my heart*

When my tolerance diminished, my sorrow increased (Couplet 9)

20. *There is blemish in myself and my heart weeps*
Thousands of troubles for my single self (Couplet 11)
21. *Congratulations for freedom from melancholy*
May your honour, opulence and magnificence remain forever (Couplet 5)
22. *Handsome! your distance kills me*
In the hope of reunion lies my wish to unite (Couplet 9)

Out of the 31 letters in response to which these are written, the first one was written on 17 Rajab 1275 A.H., and the last one was written on 26 Zilhij 1275 A.H. There is a possibility of mistakes in the count of 31. Most of the replies do not indicate what was written by the King, which letter she was responding to, or whether she was writing something on her own. There were often similar feelings which were repeated with different words. This collection was found recently, and none of its letters are mentioned by commentators.

Sheva-e-Faiz (Manuscript)

Compilation: 1272–76 A.H., Language: Urdu, Genre: Kulliyat
Printing: 1276 A.H., Format: 34×21, Pages: 440, 11-lined, (Manuscript)

"O my dear, My companion, sharer of my grief
Your Akhtar writes about his condition
My heart becomes emotional
How devoid I am of life and limb.
The rich are fond of buildings
But my life wants a shed of dry leaves
All my hopes are fulfilled
My last hope is that I want you Akhtar!

In *Kulliyat* only this gold and silver plated copy is available, and its binding was also decorative and in the royal style. Due to its attractive looks, such an amazing copy is found neither in the royal library nor anywhere else. On the first page of the manuscript is only the King's seal. In manuscripts, usually the seals are given on the first page, and the writing begins from the second page, but in this manuscript the second page is blank, and the writing starts from the third page. The back of the page is numbered as 2, which shows that for some reason, the third page is counted as the first. On the top of this third page is the seal of *Wajidi*, below is written '*Bismillah*' with a sketch of a crown on both sides. Below it is the heading of the section, and on both sides of this are sketches of nymphs. Below the heading are the five verses of the poetic letter. Between the lines the space is filled with gold, and a delicate creeper is drawn between the two pillars. On the three sides of the binding there is a 4–5 cm wide sketch of a creeper, and at the place of stitching, there is another creeper design. In the pattern of sprig and flowers pattern, the gold plating takes a greater part, and it is enhanced with red and green designs, resulting in an exquisite style. From the beginning up to the end, between the lines, in margins, and on blank places, there are fine designs in gold. The mastery is evident from the work: though the designs of fruits and flowers and sprigs are made on 877 pages, other than the placement of the creeper designs on each page, no one creeper resembles another. Other than the style of writing, for this reason the book can be termed a design book. The numbering of pages came later, though there are several mistakes in counting. The first page where the seal is given should have been counted as first, but this did not happen. The page where '*Bismillah*' is written is considered the first page. In the printed copy this page is counted as the third page, which is correct. Due to this difference in the handwritten and printed copies, in the *masnavi* section the handwritten pages are two pages ahead of the printed copy. In the handwritten copy, pages 1–32 are written continuously, but after 32, instead of 33 it is written 34. The mistake in an increase of this numbering continued up to page 386. After 386 there should have been 387 but the writer has written 384, and in this way, it proceeds up to page 413. After page 413 it should have been 414, but instead 415 is written, and this continues up to 419. After 419 is written 450, and in this way the first page of the first section which should have been 450, or according to the writer should have been 448, is counted as 477. This shows that perhaps some pages were missing, but as per the published copy, the pages are complete. There is a mistake in numbering. After page 450, at the end five pages in Persian are noted with the heading "*End of Masnavi Mubarak*" (*Khatma Masnavi Mubarak*). There is no page numbering on these pages, and they are not found in the published copy. In this note, the writer writes that in Muharram 1276 A.H. the King had entrusted the work of writing the *masnavi* to him. The writer has not written his name here, but in the original note which is at the end of the manuscript it is written as '*Md.* Amir *Ibn Ali Raza Khan Jawahar*', and the date of completion of the writing is given as 29 Rabiul Sani 1276 A.H. In "*Khatma Masnavi Mubarak*", after the four pages there is again one ornamental plate. Below the design '*Ya Fattah*', '*Bismillah*', and '*Chapter Four Diwan Mubarak Compositions of Sultan Alam Akhtar*' (*Baab Chaharum Diwan Mubarak Min Tasnifat Sultan Alam Akhtar*) is written. The numbering of page restarts from this plate. Up to page 424 is a *Diwan*, and on page 424–25 is the original note. Page 426 was blank. On this page is the big seal of '*Zulfiqar ud Daulah.*' Due to carelessness, the last part of the book is almost destroyed. From page 287 the golden work was vanishing. After page 400 the pages are very brittle.

Sheva-e-Faiz (Printed)

Compilation: 1272–76 A.H., Language: Urdu, Genre: Kulliyat
Printing: 1277 A.H., Format: 35×23, Pages: 437, 11-Lined
In Matbaey Sultani with the support of old loyal Md. Husain Bazman...
27 Ramadhan ul Mubarak 1277 A.H.
Start from page 2, (Masnavi Section)
Concluding Part pages 423–24. (Ghazaliyat Section)

O my dear, my companion, sharer of my grief
Your Akhtar writes about his condition
I swear on Allah *I am so moved*

(Because) I am devoid of life and limb.
The rich are fond of buildings
But my life wants a shed of dry leaves
All my hopes are fulfilled
My last hope is that I want you Akhtar

The first page is missing; the book starts from second page. On top of the title page is the seal of *Wajidi* decorated with sprig and creeper designs. Below it is written '*Bismillah*', and after it the first heading of the book is given "First Chapter… Eighth section… First section…" These words were not found in the headings of the manuscript. In the published copy, different notes of the poetic metre are indicated. At the three sides of the binding, there is a beautiful pattern of sprig and creepers. At the back of this page the numbering is 4. By this edition it is shown that the ornamental title page is apparently the third page. Had there been a first page of the book, then its topic would have been mentioned in the manuscript and that would have definitely been a part of the published copy. All the copies of *Sheva-e-Faiz* which were discovered start from this point only. The patterns on all the pages, from the start up to the end, are of ordinary creepers, in the center the headlines are given in bold letters and in the margin are the drawings of crown and umbrella. The two pages spreading over page numbers 179–80 and 181–82 are found in some copies[439] while they are missing in others.[440] Up to page 450 is the first part of the book. There are three chapters in it, and in the third chapter there is poetic detail about prosody. In both the manuscript and the published copies, the poetic explanation abruptly stops at the following couplet:

The final sentence of the compiler is as follows:

---

439. The copy which was presented by the King to an English officer, and which is found in the Khuda Baksh Oriental Library, Patna, is the complete one.

440. The copies found in People's Library, Qila Nizamat (Murshidabad) and Tagore University Library (Lucknow).

The Compiler now winds up saying that the metrical variation is unbalanced

The front page is blank, on the top '*Alif*' is written, and after '*Bismillah*' the following heading is given:

"Chapter Four Diwan Mubarak of the writings of Sultan Alam Akhtar
I considered Sahab's desires (likes) Now reward me for my loyalty"

On the three sides of the binding, like other pages, there is a pattern of creepers. In the margin, there is a crown and umbrella. At the back of the page is written 2, and the counting of the pages up to the end is done in a fresh manner. In the end there is a note in Persian, and thereafter there are three *Qata'at-e-Tarikh*. The first Persian *Qata'a* is by Amir Ali Khan Hilal. The other two *Qata'as*, one in Persian and the other in Urdu, are of the writer Md. Abdul Rehman Ahsan. In the endnote and in the *Qata'-e-Tarikh*, *Ahsan* has again[441] regarded *Sheva-e-Faiz* as a 'collection', but as mentioned earlier[442] *Sheva-e-Faiz* is not 'collection', but it is '*Kulliyat*'. In its first chapter there are three sections, and in each section, there are up to 21 *masnavis.* These masnavis are in fact the poetic letters which the King had sent to his Begmats, or the letters of Begmats which were composed by the King for mere amusement. The shortest *masnavi* is addressed to Navrozi Begum with ten verses,[443] and the longest one, with 321 verses, is addressed to *Zehra Mahal.*[444] It is not known on what grounds the sections are divided, as within the sections the *masnavi* does not belong to a single period, nor it is addressed to one person. Some *masnavis* are in Persian, and in some the writer's name or date is not given. The oldest *masnavi* is addressed to Seemtan Begum[445] and it is dated 27 *Shawwal* 1272 A.H. The last one is dated 27 Zeeqad 1275 A.H.

441.

442.

443. *Sheva-e-Faiz-* Md. Wajid Ali Shah Akhtar. Publication Sultani. Calcutta. 1277. 277–78.

444. *Ibid*, 132–61.

445. *Ibid*, 3–15.

and is addressed to Hakim Shafa ud Daulah,[446] who had left the King and gone to Faizabad.[447] The heading of Chapter Two is "Chapter Two of the Collection", in which there are a variety of compositions. In the beginning there are two five-line poems (*Mukhammas*) addressed to the Begums. There are also corrections (*tazmeen*) made by the King on the compositions of *Abu Tarabul Naskh, Saadi Shirazi,* and *Khwaja Hasan*, and in the end there are *salaams* and *nohas*. There is a poem of 49 verses in appreciation of Governor General Lord Canning, which was composed inside the Fort.[448] In the Third Chapter, he had started composing "*Irshad-e-Khaqani*", but the section is about the metric variations.[449] After appreciating them and counting the 31 metric variations (*zahafaat*), he had explained some pronouns, but the section was left incomplete.

In the second part of *Sheva-e-Faiz*, there is only one *Diwan* with 288 Ghazal*s*, comprising 4,062 verses. Most of these Ghazal*s* are the memoirs of the Fort and were addressed to the Begmats in their letters. In most of the Ghazal*s*, the name of the *Begum* is repeated after the rhyming word (*Radif*). Whenever he did not write a proper '*radif*', then in line with his prison life, he started to use words with meanings like 'imprisoned', 'restriction', 'detention', 'arrest', 'sorrow', 'sadness', 'cruelty', and 'prison'. There is no Ghazal starting with the '*daal*', '*rrey*', '*Zhey*' letters of the Urdu alphabet. However, he composed Ghazals with the letters '*tay*' (as in the word '*Eint*' meaning 'brick') and '*do chashmi hey*' (like in 'haath' meaning 'hand'). Some Ghazals are unfamiliar and some are in Persian. These Ghazals are very useful for understanding the biographical details of the King and the Begmats.

---

446. *Ibid*, 314–16.

447. *Boostan e Avadh*- Kunwar Durga Prasad Sandelvi - Matbaey Ahmedi, Lucknow. 1892. 185

448. *Qaiser ul Tawarikh*, Syed Kamaluddin Haider Alias Mir Zaair. Publication Munshi Nawal Kishore. Lucknow 3rd. Edn. 1907. Volume 2, 378.

449. *Supra Note* 446 at 445.

Kulliyat-e-Akhtari

Compilation: 1255–78 A.H. Language: Urdu, Genre: Kulliyat
Printing: 1278 A.H., Format: 27×23, Pages: 512, 11-Lined,
Under the support of Madarul Mahamul Lisanul Sultan Mahmudud DaulahHamidul Mulk Munshi Md. Safdar Ali Khan Mahamad Jung Bahadur
Start from page 2, (Qasaid Mubarak)
Concluding Part page 978 (Kulliyat Section)
Dated 2 Jamadiul Sani 1278 A.H.

With your face I envy the shining morning
I see heaven in the beautiful face
Out of jealousy the enemy was enflamed
And was buried under the earth

The first page is blank, and at the top of page two is written "*Qasaid Mubarak*", and below this is written '*Bismillah.*' The margins on pages 2 and 3 are decorative. On the margins of other pages there are small sprigs. In the part where *Qasaid Mubarak* is given, there is a *manqibat* for *Hazrat Ali*, and at the end there is a three-lined poem (*Musaddas*) which goes like this:

All my wishes have gone unheard fulfill them
Ali the reliever! solve my problem

On page 32, there are three lines of a *manqibat*, the remaining part is blank. On the opposite page, there are patterns of umbrellas and crowns, in a rectangular sketch there is an ornamental design, then '*Bismillah*' *is* written, and after that the following heading is given: "*Radif* '*alif Diwan Mubarak*, first creation *Mualla Khuldullah Malka wa Sultanata...*" The poetic metre as per the '*Abjad*'[450] principle is as follows:

---

450. The abjad numerals are an alphabetical numeral system in which each letter of the alpahabet is assigned numerical values.For instance the value of alif is 1, of bay is 2, and

Almighty! Your reverence will not be shunned by me
I am a sinner but will not commit any wrong again

On three sides of this page is a flowery pattern. On the back of the page, the number given is 2. There are sprigs in the margin. This continues up to the end of the book, and the margin is also the same. Like "*Radif 'alif Diwan Mubarak Auwal*" the headings of the second, third, and fourth *Diwan* are given differently.[451] All the Ghazals of each *Diwan* are arranged in the same manner as they were in the original *Diwan*. The *Radif* heading of 'bay'[452] and 'tay'[453] is also given. For other letters, it becomes difficult to know which Ghazal belongs to which *Diwan*. As for the arrangement, care is taken to write the Ghazal*s* of the first *Diwan* first and so on. Up to page 5, the name of the poetic metre (*beher*) and its components (*arkan*) are entered in the lines of the text. From page 6 the style changes. Now the name of the poetic metre is written in the text, while the components (*arkan*) are written in a circle made with crown and umbrella sketches. In most of the copies, these headings are written in bold letters. Perhaps there were directions to write it with chalk, but the headings written in the hand of the writer are not found anywhere. Up to page 900 of the *Kulliyat* there are Ghazal*s*, and from page 900–978 various compositions are collected. After page 978, there is a *Qat'at-e-Tarikh*. Due to an addition in the pages of the *Qata'at*, there is a

---

continuing in like manner the value of 'noon' is 50 and that of 'qaaf' is 100 and so on. Abjad numerals - Wikipedia. For instance, the celebrated figure 786 in Islam is derived through this system, which is the numeral form of Bismillah al Rehman al Rahim. The Urdu script is derived from the Persian script which is a derivative of the Arabic script. In Urdu poetry the letters are used to make a word from the value of which the year and date of some important event is derived, at the same time the words written with such letters construct a meaningful couplet. It is an ancient, complicated art, also known as Tarikh or chronogram.

451. *Kulliyat e* Akhtari. Md. Wajid Ali Shah, Matbaey Sultani Calcutta. 1278. (Found in Khuda Baksh, Salar Jung, Raza, Azad Libraries). 58, 132, 178.

452. *Ibid*, 200, 289.

453. *Ibid*, 312.

disarrangement. Between pages 984 and 985, there is a page[454] which has no numbering. On this page two *Qata'as* are by Mahtab ud Daulah Kaukabuk Mulk Syed Ali Jan Khan Bahadur Darakhsan Sitara Jung, and one *Qata'a* each is by Md. Jaan Ali Khan Laiq ud Daulah Bhadur Jaan, Nawab Aaitazad ud Daulah Moinul Mulk Syed Baqar Ali Khan Bahadur Baqar, and Mirza Imdad Hussain Tamanna. "End" (*Khatam shudd*) is written on page 988 after the *Qata'a* of Mirza Ali Jaan Shafaq. After receiving the *Qata'as* of Syed Hasan Khan Zia, Mir Mirza Saha, Hasan uz Zaman Ahsanand Abdul Latif Latif, one more page was added, the numbering of which is 989–990. At the end of page 990, 'good end' (*tamat*) is written. The copy of the *Kulliyat* is available in almost all major libraries, but these two[455] added pages are found in very few copies. In *Qata'at e Tarikh*, other than the compositions of the above mentioned poets, various *Qata'ats* of Md. Abdul Rehman Ahsan, Syed Ahmed Ali Qadeer, Mirza Masita Aish, Mirza Md. Abbas Shaz, Mir Ali Hussain Farig, Qasim Hussain Qasim, Maulvi Md. Shah and Hakim Ahmed Raza are found. Darakshan was an expert in inferring the date (*tarikh*) from every line (*misra*). From the viewpoint of art, his *Urdu Qata'at* of five verses is a distinguished work, but from the viewpoint of knowledge all three Persian *Qata'at* of the writer of *Kulliyat Ahsan* draw special attention.[456] The topics of all three *Qata'at* are similar. In the last *Qata'a*, by '*Madarul Maham*' is meant Mahmud ud Daulah Munshi Md. Safdar Ali Khan Bahadur.[457] In the starting *qat'ats* this name has been explained fully. In the early days

454. In all the copies where this page is found is between the above pages.

455. The copy in Khuda Baksh Library is complete in all respects and none of the headings there are coloured. This copy has the signatures of *Mahmud ud Daulah* Bahadur. In the copies found in Raza Library and Salar Jung Museum Library some of the headings are coloured. In the incomplete copy found in the Maulana Azad Library the seal of Barq*'s* son Md. Zafar Hussain is given.

456. *Supra Note* 450 at 978–80.

457. His full name along with the titles has been copied from the title page of *Majumuae Maroozat* (Handwritten) *Madaulalham Lasanul Sultan Wafa Shuaar Mehmoodud Daulah Hamudul Mulk Munshi Md. Safdar Ali Khan* Bahadur 1281.

of Metiaburj, he was very famous. Before the appointment of Wazir ul Sultan Amir Ali Khan Bahadaur the entire management was under him. He had a bad name for misusing his immense powers,[458] and was ultimately dismissed.[459] From the viewpoint of Ahsan, *Kulliyat e* Akhtari was the first and last book which was published under his supervision. The expense of printing of the book is obvious from its bulkiness. Hardly any other book from Matbaey Sultani Metiaburj was published with such a huge expense. There are three people who wrote this book: *Ahsan* himself, Abdul Latif Latif,[460] and Md. Hussain.[461] This Md. Hussain is probably the same person who displayed his art in *Guldasta-e-Ashqan* and in other books. *Kulliyat-e*-Akhtari is the third masterpiece of Matbaey Sultani Metiaburj. Before this, two more books were published, and are mentioned in the third verse '*Huzn-e*-Akhtari', which is the same *masnavi* discussed in earlier pages, but '*Majmua*' is no other than *Sheva-e-Faiz.* In the published copy, also it is referred to as *Majmua*. The second *Qata'a* of the *Kulliyat* is incomplete in the sense that no good information can be gathered from it. Some of the writers of the *Qata'a* did not even know which book they are writing the *Qata'as* (*Tarikh*) for, or whether it was for a *Diwan* or for a *Kulliyat.* For example:

Heading: *"Tarikh for Second Edition of Diwan Mubarak Sultani"*- Mirza Masita Aish *Shagird Hazrat.*[462]
Verse *(misra)*: *'Shukr Diwane Mubarak chhap chuka"*- Amir Mirza *Saha.*[463]

If this is *Diwan-e-Mubarak*, then what about the information given by the poets who addressed it as *Kulliyat-e-Mualla* and *Kulliyat Mubarak.* The

458. *Nigar* (Monthly, Lucknow) March 1963 Edition. p. 28–31 under the reference of Avadh Akhbar File, 1862.

459. Amir *Nama.* Wazirul Sultan Md. Amir Ali Khan Bahadur Amir. Calcutta. 1870. 189–93.

460. *Kulliyat-e*-Akhtari, 990.

461. *Ibid*, 979.

462. *Ibid*, 981.

463. *Ibid*, 990.

fact is that much time was spent in the publication of *Kulliyat*. Some poets in Lucknow heard about it and composed '*Tarikh*',[464] some were in Calcutta and did not know anything about the printing. By these *Qata'as* at least this much is known that who were the poets who wanted to please the King, and who were bestowed with titles.

The title *Kulliyat e* Akhtari is not found anywhere other than in the list of *Bani.* Wazirul Sultan Bahadur had mentioned this book, but in the *Wazir Nama* this book is entered as '*Qasaid Mubarak.*'[465] In the libraries also this book is known by this name.[466] Thus if there is any name other than this on the book then the writer has no urge to search for it. But the name '*Qasaid Mubarak*' is rightly not included in the list of *Bani.* Firstly, because the *Qasidas* are in the form of '*manqibat*', which is a very small part of a bulky book. They are kept in the beginning of the *Kulliyat* only by way of respect. The numbering of *Qasaid* and *Kulliyat* is different, hence, to add to the compositions of Wajid Ali Shah these can be considered as two different writings. It looks as if the King forgot to write one name, and his minister forgot to write the other name. But had this been the fact, then both parts of the *Kulliyat* could not have been in the same arrangement in each copy, and like the first page of *Qasaid Mubarak*, the first page of the *Kulliyat* (Ghazal section) also would have been blank, because this was the style of printing at that time. In the *Wazir Nama* and *Bani*, the entry of the same book under two names indicates that up to the compilation of the *Wazir Nama, the Kulliyat* Akhtari had no fixed name, and it was identified by the names of '*Kulliyat Moalla*' or '*Kulliyat Mubarak*'. *Wazir ul Sultan*, who addressed the three diwans of *Kulliyat* Akhtari under different names,[467]

464. There is no figure on this page. Tamanna: *Hua Chaar soo Lucknow mein ye Shohra*

465. *Wazir Nama.* Wazir ul Sultan Md. AmirAli Khan Amir. Publication Nizami- Lucknow. 1293. 318.

466. In the Maulana Azad Library, Aligarh Muslim University this book is entered with this name.

467. *Supra Note* 464 at 317.

intentionally addressed it as one such name which was printed on the book. Everyone could identify the book with that name, which is suitable for it.

When two or more diwans are collected in a *Kulliyat*, then usually the pattern of arrangement is that in the First *Diwan* the Ghazals starting with '*alif*' up to '*yey*' are entered, and then the second *Diwan* begins with '*alif*'. In this way, all the Diwans which are collected should be arranged one by one. But the arrangement of *Kulliyat* Akhtari is different from this. In this the Ghazals starting with '*alif*' are collected from all the Diwans and then from '*bay*', '*pay*', '*tey*', '*tay*', are collected in a like manner. With this new pattern, *Kulliyat* Akhtari has taken a bulky form and most of the libraries consider it a '*Diwan*'. The other common misunderstanding is regarding its year of composition, which is actually created by the King himself. The compilation of the *Kulliyat* took place during his imprisonment in Fort William. The writer, without any plausible reason, wrote words like 'the prisoned', 'detention in the prison', 'innocent King', and 'opressed Emperor' above most of the Ghazals.[468] Such words indicate that the Ghazals were composed during his imprisonment, which is not correct. The three-fourth part of *Kulliyaat e Akhtari* is from '*Guldasta e Aashiqan*', '*Sukhan Ashraf*', '*Diwan Mubarak*', and '*Kulliyat e Soom*'. Only one incomplete *Diwan*, which is named by the writer as *Diwan Mubarak Chaharum*, some single verses, and four poetic letters were published for the first time in *Kulliyat* Akhtari. Maybe this part of the composition was composed in the Fort. The third Ghazal of *Kulliyat-e*-Akhtari '*When I started imagining your photo*' and the Ghazals in the 'radif' of '*meem*' and '*chhoti yey*' (Urdu letters) are entered separately from the arrangement of '*Diwan Chaharum*'. The other part can be easily identified.

The trend of mistakes and corrections in *Kulliyat-e-*Akhtari is nothing new, but a much damaged termite-ridden copy has been recovered, in which there has been an interesting discovery that the inner pages were changed. It is thus quite possible that some pages which were found in some copies were not found in the same condition in other copies. Apparently, these differences

468. *Kulliyat e* Akhtari, 258, 322, 352.

are ordinary, but it is very strange that for some small reason, some parts of the printed copy were changed. Following are the points which describe the nature of such differences:

A. In the old copies on page 361 this couplet is given:

From where to bring the palanquin
The palanquin bearers are rare in Lucknow now

This couplet was supposed to be excluded, but by doing this the space of this couplet looked blank and odd, hence the printer had it printed again. The verses before this couplet were rewritten up to the end, and to fill up the empty space the metrical components, instead of being written in the sketches of crowns and umbrellas, were written in the empty space. In the reprinted page 361, there are no sketches of crowns and umbrellas. In another part of the same page, there is another correction. The original line was like this: "The '*kachcha taweez*' *will not be written in the start of the line.*" In the printed copy it is written as "*It will not write the* '*kachcha taweez*' *on the top of the hand.*"

B. In the old copies on page 755, a creeper pattern was made to fill up the empty space after five lines. In the reprinted copies this portion is blank. Thus, such blank lines and filling up the empty space with some patterns are seen in various copies. This decorative work in the printed copies often indicates that correction was done.

C. In the old copies on page 314, in the ninth line, the second line (*misra*) goes like this: '*Banahi tujh ko bhi seedha jo uss se saaf ulat.*' In the corrected copies, the verse is like this: '*Banai tujh ko bhi seedha jo uss se saaf ulat.*' In the reprinting of the same page, there is often a difference in the wording or the design. This means the first writer either wrote it using '*yay maroof*' and later it was written using '*yay majhool*', or two words were written together and when they were written again then they were written separately, or the page numbering was on the top of the page hence it was written in the margin. But such changes are noted only when one checks it deeply. The same page in two different copies appear to look alike. By pointing out the differences as above, the copies are intentionally referred to as 'old' or 'corrected'. [469] By comparing the different copies, it is revealed that the correction work is done intermittently. In the beginning some copies were released without correction. Then some pages were corrected with which the copy was released, and, in this way, different copies of the same book were circulated.

Qamar Mazmun (Manuscript)

Written: 1276–79 A.H., Language: Urdu, Genre: Kulliyat (Incomplete)
Printing: 1278–79 A.H., Format: 22.5×18.5, Pages: 165, 10-Lined

The Kulliyat starts with praise to Allah*:*
The Merciful the Only one
He is omniscient, divine, the creator of everything
He is omnipotent, the foreteller
He is ancient, kind, the harbinger, and the powerful
The presence and the unknown say
There is someone who is the Creator

The manuscript was written by the writer himself on pages of different colours, it is bound and complete and along with the writer some copyists have also written some portions. No page of the manuscript is blank. In some places, due to a shortage of space, the verses are mending together in the margin. The beginning section is clear, and it is a copy of the original manuscript. In this part are written *Hamd*, *Naat*, *Manqibat*, *Noha*, *Salaam*, *Elegy*, *Qata'a*, and Ghazals, but the arrangement is different from the printed

469. In view of the author, it is the oldest copy. In the Saulat Library Rampur there is also one such copy but it is hugely damaged and incomplete.

copy. The *elegies* are written in a cluster of three verses in the old style. From page 187 up to the end, there are different types of handwriting, and different experiments are conducted. In some places the writing is done from the left hand page and instead of proceeding towards left it is goes towards the right.[470] In places the writing starts from the bottom of the page while proceeding towards the top.[471] In some places the pages are divided into four columns, and some verses are written in a slanting position from bottom to top, while some are written from top to bottom,[472] or from right to left, or from left to right.[473] On one page the verses are written joined together in prose style in landscape form.[474] In some of the pages the writing is in western style music by drawing four lines,[475] and the writing is not harmonious. One part of the same Ghazal is written in the Persian script (*Nastaleeq*) but as the work proceeds, gradually the writing becomes worse, so much so that it becomes illegible.[476] The fickleness in the way of writing indicates the innovativeness and hastiness of the writer. In one place the writer himself appreciates his fast writing: "*By the pen of a fast writer Jaan e Alam, written on 24 Qadul Mukarram 1278 A.H.* (page 269)"[477] No other writing of Wajid Ali Shah is available in which along with the writing there is also a signature. In a *Kulliyat* other than this manuscript, no other complete manuscript is available.

In the manuscript, on every page there are two letters, '*swad*' for writing and "*meem*" for conformity (*mutabiqat*). If there are no such letters on any page, then that poetic part is also missing from the printed copy. This shows that the writing of the printed copy or of the handwritten copy is done from

470. Qamar Mazmun. (Manuscript) Md. Wajid Ali Shah Akhtar. Matbaey Sultani. Calcutta. 1281h. 318–27.

471. *Ibid*, 254.

472. *Ibid*, 284–85, 320–21

473. *Ibid*, 230–32.

474. *Ibid*, 329.

475. *Ibid*, 176–80, 196–200.

476. *Ibid*, 150–51, 218–19, 238–40.

477. *Ibid*, 13.

the manuscript from which the printed copy is compiled. The difference in arrangement and the absence of identification (*'swad'*/*'meem'*) in is due to the reason that whenever something was composed it was written in the manuscript on 'as is' basis. In the printed copy, the different genres of poetry, with rhyming words (*radifwar*) are arranged systematically, hence this difference between the manuscript and the printed copy was bound to appear. In the manuscript there was no numbering of pages, but when it was done it is found to be 330 sides or 165 pages. Some pages were separated at that time or later on were not found. The pages of the printed copy which are not found in the manuscript were probably either damaged or lost.

The beginning of the manuscript has been cleaned and improved by keeping in front the other copy of the manuscript. This is further confirmed by the following remark of the copyist given on page 90 where, to maintain originality, he wrote the three verses but then gave his comments: "*I know these three verses but due to a difference in rhymes and not being in conformity, I write here the original.*" There is a line drawn over the three verses, either by the King himself or on his order.[478] With the change in the rhyming word (*qafia*) all the three verses are present in the manuscript and in the printed copy. The copying of the beginning part of the manuscript must have been completed by 24 Zeeqad 1278 A.H. because the above-mentioned signatures of the King are from that date, and they are written in the margin of the original writing. This can also be confirmed by referring to pages 252–253 of that manuscript. On this page there is a *Qata'a* of 10 verses, which has the heading *'Adad Huroof Abjad'* and was published both in *Kulliyat e* Akhtari and in Qamar Mazmun.[479] In *Kulliyat e* Akhtari, the date of its composition

478. The first lines of the three verses of Qamar Mazmun given on page 90 which were struck by a line are the same as given on page 399 of Qamar Mazmun.The second lines (*misras*) are like this; (1)*The fairy who came before you became a dark flower*(teesoo)(2) *With good words the dove became silent as owl* (3)*The match maker (mushaata) became nervous before the nightingale.*

479. *Supra Note* 467 at 976–78 & Qamar Mazmun at 99–100.

is given as 2 *Jamadiul Sani* 1278 A.H. In Qamar Mazmun the date is not given, but the first verse was changed:

There is one for 'alif' two for 'bay' and 'pay'
And three for 'jeem' and 'chay' remember friend

By this it is clear that the beginning of the *Qata'a* is given in the manuscript. Perhaps in the beginning there was an intention to write it in *masnavi* style, hence 'this' in the above line was changed to 'friend' or 'yaar', and thereafter the rhyming words '*shikar*', '*shumar*', *and* '*nuqta daar*' were chosen to blend it into a *Qata'a*. This also shows that, as mentioned in the first section of this chapter, *Kulliyat-e-*Akhtari, *Sheva-e-Faiz* and Qamar Mazmun were authored more or less during the same period. In *Sheva-e-Faiz* only two metrical variations (*Zahafat*) '*azmar*' and '*asab*' were composed.[480] The poetic descriptions of '*waqf*', '*khaban*', '*Taey*', and '*qabz*' are given in the manuscript of Qamar Mazmun, but here also it is incomplete, and on these verses there is no indication like '*swad*' or '*meem.*'[481]

In the '*Majmuaey Rubayat*' of '*Kulliyat e Soom*', there is a *masnavi* of 40 verses under the heading "*Maujiza Manzoom Tasnif Mualla*", which is perhaps the beginning work of the King. At the time of the compilation of Qamar Mazmun, the King revisited it, and in the manuscript of Qamar Mazmun, by the pen of the copyist, its improved version was copied.[482] In the printed copy of Qamar Mazmun this improved version is found, while only the heading is changed to "*Dar Aijaz e Ali Ibn Abi Talib alai iss salam.*"[483] In the manuscript of Qamar Mazmun, some Ghazals including "*Tarah Mushaira Inayat ud Daulah* Bahadur" and "*Tarah Mushaira Zulfiqar ud Daulah* Bahadur" are written with a date which specifies when each Ghazal

480. *Sheva-e-Faiz*, Md. Wajid Ali Shah Akhtar. Publication Sultani. Calcutta 1277. 488–50.
481. *Qamar Mazmun* (Manuscript) Md. Wajid Ali Shah Akhtar. Calcutta. 260–62, 271.
482. *Ibid*, 293–95.
483. *Ibid*, 95.

was composed and for which function. There are some similar differences in the manuscript and copies of Qamar Mazmun, but which are not mentioned here for the sake of brevity.

Qamar Mazmun (Printed)

Written: 1276–81 A.H., Language: Urdu, Genre: Kulliyat
Printing: 1281, Format: 22.5×21 Pages: 238, 11-Lined
Published with the support of Zargham ud Daulah by the pen of Md. Amir bin Ali Raza Jawahar.

The printed document starts with the following verse in the glory of Allah:

From Qamar Mazmun and from the writings of Hazrat Sultan Alam Aidallah Malka, was Saltanat dar Masnavihat (page 2)

Glory to Allah *Who is one and the creator of the sky and earth*
the Unparallel Artist ... The Merciful The Only one
He is omniscient, divine, the creator of everything

The document ends with the following couplet (page 473)

Akhtar there is surely the news of arrival of the nightingale
So that the garden is overwhelmed now

First Verse (Matla)

The hair adorned with golden powder
As if the Stars are shining on the sky absurd

The first page is blank and has the seal of the King. On the second page is the *Wajidi* seal, but it is awkward. There is a flowery pattern in margins of the second and third pages. This design is also on page 258–59. From this point, '*Daftar e Soom Diwan Mubarak*' starts. On the other pages, only the margins are drawn with the help of straight lines. In the *Diwan*, the Ghazals are counted in words. When the '*radif*' is changed, then at the side of the heading is written '*Radif Alba*' and '*Radif Alna*'. There is a mistake in counting the Ghazals. After 'Ghazal *Seventy Five*' it should have been written 'Ghazal *Seventy Six*', but the word 'Five' is repeated again,[484] and was not corrected up to the end. There are 125 Ghazals in the *Diwan*. In the page numbers, writing 1001 instead of 101 and 2001 instead of 201, which is seen in many old books, is also seen in Qamar Mazmun and in other books of Matbaey Sultani. The *Diwan* is up to page 473, and in the end, after a single verse, the endnote is given in four lines. The last three pages are reserved for 16 *Qata'at e Tarikh*.[485] And on these pages, 17-lined and four pillared sketches are given, and the writing is hidden. Compared to *Kulliyat e* Akhtari, the printing of Qamar Mazmun is good quality, and the words are legible. The writer has made mistakes in places, but at the same time he has corrected them by deleting the incorrect words with a pen, which is difficult to identify.[486]

Qamar Mazmun can be regarded as one of Wajid Ali Shah's rare masterpieces, because even though it was published and has many copies available in the royal library, not a single copy is found in the libraries of famous Universities of India. Qamar Mazmun has been divided into three volumes. In the first Volume there are 30 big or small *masnavis* in addition to '*Qat'aey Masnavi Numa*.'[487] The first *masnavi* is a '*hamd*', the second one is a '*naat*', and the third one is a '*manqibat*'. Apart from letters written in poetic form, there are some poetic "invitation deeds" (*Dawat Nama*) which were composed by the King on behalf of other people.[488] Important parts of the poetic letters were published in the July 1910 Edition of *Lisanul Asar*. They were also published in the compilation of Khwaja Ishrat's book, titled *Khutoot-e-Aakhri Shah e Avadh*. But the compilers have not mentioned where they got these compositions from. In the Second Volume are '*Rubayats*', Elegies, *Salaam*, and *Nohas*. This part of the composition has also been

484. *Ibid*, 380–82.

485. For mentionable *Qata'ats* see Chapter 3 Section 1.

486. *Supra Note* 480 at 123. (*Taazir*), 145 (*bahadiya*), 148 (*jiss*), 423 (*ho*) are to be noted.

487. *Ibid*, 82.

488. *Ibid*, 16,19, 59, 66.

published in '*Imaan and Tosha-e-Akhrat*', and people are by and large aware of it. There are only Ghazals in the Third Volume. Some are in Persian, and in some the names of Begmats are used as '*radif*.' Some were composed after a specific incident. There are 2,116 verses, and there are no Ghazals with the letters '*daal*', '*rrey*', and '*zhey*'. For an evolutionary study of Wajid Ali Shah's compositions, this book serves as a halfway point.

On pages 59–66 of Qamar Mazmun, there is a poetic composition under the title '*Khwab Mubarak*' from 1270 A.H. In the manuscript of Qamar Mazmun, this part of the poem is missing, hence it is difficult to say when it was composed. However, it was not composed immediately after he had the dream it describes. In the handwritten copy at the royal library, titled *Bahar e Ajam*, a person has lightly described his dream on the flyleaf of this copy. After seeing the poetic details of this famous dream in Qamar Mazmun one can easily say that Wajid Ali Shah after seeing the dream wrote down its account in the fly leaf in his own handwriting. This is an important discovery in identifying the work of Wajid Ali Shah.

Najo

Written: 1285–86, Language: Hindi, Genre: Collection of Compositions
Printing: 1286 A.H., Format: 24×15 Pages: 141, 8-Lined,
Publisher[489] Matbaey Sultani (Calcutta). Suprvisor: Zarghamud Daulah.
Start page 2, end page 278.

489. Two handwritten copies of *Najo* were available but both of these were the copy of the published copy. In the Maulana Azad Library of Aligarh Muslim University, the copyist has copied from the published copy up to *"Zevar Taba Aarasta."* The writing is attractive and at the end there are all the *Qata'at e Tarikh* which were found in the complete published copies. In the copy found in Salar Jung Museum, on the title page the name of the book is given along with the *Qata'as* of four poets, and before the *Qata'ats* there is also the endnote which is found in the published copies. Perhaps by this description it was inferred that the copy was written in 1282 A.H. (See, the detailed list of the Urdu handwritten books of the Library of Late Salar Jung Museum on page 344). But there is no proof of its antiquity in the seal of the library, nor is the name of the writer given. This copy was purchased from *Syed Ghulam Hussain Tajir* of Lucknow in 1354 A.H. and in view of the author it was likely written during that period.

On the title page, the name of the book, publisher, and supervisor is given. Instead of the author's name, the line '*Composition and Compilation of Servants of Sikandar Shaan*' is written. The Preface in Persian is given on pages 2 and 3. On page 5 there is a two-inch wide creeper and a flowery pattern around the plate. The heading describes the list of chapters and sections in two columns. Such a list is not found in the other books of Matbaey Sultani. This is inspired by the English style of writing, which is evident from the use of the word '*lumbar.*' The compiler writes about his innovation in the Preface.

On pages 6 and 7 there is again a decorative margin, and on page 6 the Crown of *Wajidi* is given in a very awkward manner. From here the series of songs (*geet*) starts. After mention of every playback singer (*sada*), the heading of another playback singer is given in an ornamental rectangular enclosure. The titles of some of the songs are given in Persian. The main part of the book goes up to page 278, and thereafter, on two pages, are given nine *Qata'ats* by six poets. The page on which three *Qata'ats* of Wazirul Sultan Md. Amir Ali Khan Bhadur Amir are given is found in almost all the printed copies. On the following pages are two *Qata'as* of Mahtab ud Daulah Darakhsan and one *Qata'a* each of Gulshan ud Daulah Mirza Ali Bahar, Hamid ud Daulah Bhadur Bartar, Hamid ud Daulah Bahdur Qayas and Mirza Masita Aish is found in rare copies. Some copies of the book are printed on cream coloured paper. For correcting mistakes, instead of listing it in the corrigendum, the wrong word has been corrected directly at that place, and hence the correction, though neatly made is quite visible.[490] Out of nine *Qata'ats*, 3 are in Persian, 6 are in Urdu. 2 give the hijri year, and 7 give the sambat year. Bahar's *Qata* indicates the year of writing and the topic of *Najo*. This is as follows;

Glory to the Writer
Long live King Akhtar

490. See pages 33, 60, 61, 65, 74, 90, 105, 128, 137, 142, 143, 153, 165, 167, 207, 214, 228 of *Najo* where corrections are handmade.

The unique Najo book is printed
Congratulations! the instrument players
She is dark and charming
One gets lost at her looks
Voice and tone is sweet
There is hymn, musical tone and idea (1926 Samvat)

Wajid Ali Shah, for various genre of music like '*sadhra*', '*chitrang*', '*chachar*', '*thumri*', *and* '*sawan*', has collected various songs of his own, his Begmats, and other poets in 15 chapters so that there is no difficulty for anyone who wants to learn them. In the Preface, this is described as the purpose of writing *Najo*, in the following words:

> *Whatever I remember from my writings I write it here in the hijri year 1285 so that the readers are benefitted by it.* (Translated from Persian)

A major part of this collection consists of the Hindi songs of Wajid Ali Shah and *Nawab* Badshah Mahal *Alam.* Some are also expressed in Bengali. Apart from these two, the compiler has clarified the name of those musicians whose work is found in this collection. They are: Ibrahim Adil Shahul Matufi (1037 A.H.),[491] Pyar Khan,[492] Naik Gopal,[493] Naik Biju,[494] Tan Sen,[495] Umang,[496] Achpal,[497] Shaukat,[498] Udharang[499] Shori,[500] Sarshar,[501] Nasir,[502]

491. *Najo - Md.* Wajid Ali Shah Akhtar. Matbaey Sultani. Calcutta. 1296. 9.
492. *Ibid*, 25,72.
493. *Ibid*, 33.
494. *Ibid*, 51.
495. *Ibid*, 63,75.
496. *Ibid*, 96,106.
497. *Ibid*, 109.
498. *Ibid*, 110.
499. *Ibid*, 129.
500. *Ibid*, 144.
501. *Ibid*, 146–47.
502. *Ibid*, 154.

Jalal,[503] Manrang,[504] Hansmukh,[505] Rang Mahal,[506] Kazim,[507] and Mira Bai. The '*dohas*' of other old poets are also given.[508]

There is nothing notable in *Najo* regarding the art of music, hence it is not proper to consider it a book of musical art. If the words used in music are considered as musical art, then the Ghazal*s* and other genres of poetry will also be counted within the category of musical art. In '*Imaan*' and '*Mulk e Akhtar*', there are some verses which are written along with the names of certain tunes (*Raag/ragni*), but no one considers them to be a book of music. But at places, '*Najo*' and '*Dulhan*' are considered books of music.[509] In the list of the Library of Salaar Jung Museum, the learned compiler has considered '*Navras*' as the collection of compositions and *Najo* under music compositions,[510] although both the books are similar in the sense that both are about tunes or 'raags'. Hence it is said:

> *"Just like Ibrahim Adil Shah has written songs to be sung under various tunes (raag/ragni) in "Navras", similarly* Wajid Ali Shah *in this book has composed songs (geet) for different 'raags.'*[511]

Wazirul Sultan Bahadur has taken out the year (1926 Samvat) of compilation from '*Gairat-e-Navras.*' Either both of them should be considered as books of music, or both of them should be regarded as collections of compositions.

503. *Ibid*, 158.
504. *Ibid*, 169.
505. *Ibid*, 210.
506. *Ibid*, 237.
507. *Ibid*, 257.
508. *Ibid*, 273–78.
509. *Khamkhanaey Javed.* Lala Sri Ram. (5 Volumes) Mukhzan Press. Delhi.Volume I, 209.
510. The detailed list of Urdu Handwritten Books, Library Salar Jung Museum, at page 344, 370 & 888.
511. Professor Nasiruddin Hashmi: list of the Library Nawab Salar Jung Museum. Naya *Daur,* (Monthly, Lucknow). May 1959 Edition at 5.

Sahifa-e Sultania (Manuscript)

Written: 1286 A.H., Language: Persian, Genre: Prayer
Printing: 1287–88 A.H., Format: 29×18, Pages: 40, 8-Lined.
Published: Matbaey Sultani, Calcutta (Manuscript)
Start page 2, End page 76.

The manuscript starts with:

> *Glory to* Allah, *the Prophet (PBUH), in praise of Hazrat Haider e Karrar who is the successor of the Prophet (PBUH) and all the Imams.*
> (Translated from Persian)

On the first blank page, the words "*Jadwal bar avarda, abwab wa shumar ayat*" are neatly written in red ink. On the last page is the royal seal. From pages 2–15, the space between lines is filled with gold. Persian statements are in the Persian and Arabic script. For the sake of suitability, headings and the words of the text are written in red ink, and there is a creeper pattern about half an inch wide towards the binding of the book, and about one and a quarter inch wide at the three sides of the margin. The pattern of the creeper changes every two pages. The creeper is often made with indigo and gold work, and often a red colour is mixed. This design is only on the 15 pages of the Preface. The actual book starts from page 16, where on the top of the page is a golden flower image and in the centre of it the page number is given in red ink. The arrangement of the essays is such that first there is reference to the *ayat* (verse of the Quran) then its details, and then at the end the original *ayat* is given. *Ayat* is in Arabic script, while its translation is given in Persian script in red ink. Red and black ink has been used meticulously. The writing is clear and attractive, though the name of the writer is not given. It is quite possible that this copy was written by Syed Md. Shafi Rizvi. This has been appreciated in the printed copy.

At the end of the book, the last few words of appreciation and prayer are written by Maulvi Mirza Md. Ali, and instead of his name, his seal is given.

In the printed copy, this has been followed and, up to page 80, both the manuscript and printed copies are the same.

Sahifa-e Sultania (Print)

Written: 1286 A.H., Language: Persian, Genre: Prayer
Printing: 1289 A.H., Format: 27×17, Pages: 54, 8-Lined
Published: Mabaey Sultani, Calcutta with the support of Raeesud Daulah Zevar
Start page 2, end page 76

The start and end are the same in both the handwritten and printed copies. The appreciation note of late Maulvi Mirza Md. Ali is also the same in both copies. Only the appreciation notes of the title page and the last page are an addition. In the printed copy, there are two title pages, and the writing and printing of both were done with stone. In the first one, at the top of the page, the central part of the creeper design is cleared, and the seal of the royal library is placed.[512] At the back of the title page there is a list of essays, and in front is the page about which it is written. Its printing, like the printing of '*Behr e Hidayat*', is unparallel and unique. The title page of '*Behr e Hidayat*' is a masterpiece of Matbaey Sultani, Lucknow, while the title page of '*Sahifae Sultania*' *is* a masterpiece of Matbaey Sultani, Calcutta. Here, there is a one-inch wide creeper design at the three sides, and a delicate creeper is drawn at the side of the binding. In the centre is an attractive rectangular box, on the top of which there is an *ayat* of the Quran, and the name of the printing supervisor is written in an intricate and ornate style. The ornate writing is written with special ink, which is very apparent. Below the *ayat*, in the normal style of printing in narrow white lines, the following words are given:

512. Two copies of Sahifa-e-Sultania have been recovered, and are available in the Maulana Azad Library, Aligarh Muslim University, Aligarh, where at the place of the seal, Syed Ali Hussain (Monis ud Daulah) bin Syed Fazal Hussain has written his name.

> *"This book is the composition of Hazrat Sultan Alam. May* Allah *shower His Blessings on Him and on His empire. In the month of Jamadiul Awwal 1289 in the capital city of Calcutta."*
> (Translated from Persian)

Between the above two lines, there is a square with a circle inside it. As the square and the circle are smeared with a close-knit pattern, the words which are written below become very obvious and apparent.

> *It is known by the name of Sahifa e Sultania and its epithet is Jannat (Heaven).'*[513]

At the back of this title page, the number 2 is written in the ornamental setting, and there is a flowery and decorative margin both on this page and on page 3. The style of other pages is also different from the other books. On every page there are straight lines on the three sides, and as the lines merge with similar lines of the opposite page, there is a square-shaped sketch. At the centre of this area, leaving aside the margin, there are two rectangular shapes. At the top of these are the page numbers, and the original book is inside. Another notable quality is that at all places where there should have been a name, there is a seal in lithograph. In this way, the design of the seal, along with the address, name, and year is secured. In the book, instead of *qata'at*, there are only appreciation notes (*Taqriz*). In the seal of the writers, the following words are given:

A. *"peer o eema Masoomeen Qaimuttuddin Janab* Maulvi Mirza Md. Ali *Sahab. 1278.*[514]

B. "Rafatud Daulah *RafiulMulk Katibul Muluk Munshi Syed Md.* Shafi*ul Rizvi. 1284"*[515]

---

513. On the title, text, and everywhere... the word *Sahifa-e-Sultania* is written, only in the list of Bani (page 242) it is written as *"Sahifae Sultani."* The name given on the title page can be given preference.

514. *Sahifa-e-Sultania.* Md. Wajid Ali Shah Akhtar. Maybaey Sultani. Calcutta. 1289. 80

515. *Ibid*, 95.

C. *"Afzalul Itba Qari Mehdi Hasan...1288."*[516]

The last page is blank. And in spite of the fact that there are mistakes in the writing, they have been corrected only at those places.[517] There is no corrigendum. While describing the purpose of compilation, the compiler has first described the problems which he had to face with his trusted people, like Mahmud ud Daulah Munshi Md. Safdar Ali Khan Bahadur. Thereafter, he writes that once during *Ramadhan* 1286 A.H., while he was reciting the Quran, a thought came to his mind that if the *ayats*, which address Allah at the end, are collected together and their benefits and harms are brought to the knowledge of the general public, then they will surely benefit from it, and he himself would be rewarded by Allah (*sawab*). And this will be such a thing which so far has not come to the knowledge of the people who recite the Quran. The selection and searching for *ayats* was done with this purpose, and not only with the '*alif*' at the end as (*radif*), but also '*bay*', '*daal*', '*ray*', '*meem*', '*noon*', '*hamza*', and '*chhoti yey*'. In total, 76 *ayats*, along with their references and attributes, were collected. There is one chapter for every letter of the alphabet, and in every chapter, there are 2–33 *ayats*. There is also a translation of the '*ayats*', and a method as to how to be benefitted by them.

There is a description of 76 *ayats* over 66 pages. There is nothing other than the mentioning of *ayats*, their context, and their attributes. There was a need to give an explanation and comments about each *ayat*. This need was fulfilled by Maulvi Syed Hidayat Hussain Ibn Janab Syed Ali Naqi Sahab by writing the commentary titled *Mawahib Subhania Fi Sharah Sahifae Sultania*. His extensive labour is now preserved in the form of a bulky handwritten book. The year of compilation is not given there, but from the endnote it appears that it was presented to the King. In the prayer, two books – *Wazaif Nama e Sultani* from the period of Md. Ali Shah[518] and *Aamal ul Saleheen* from

---

516. *Ibid*, 105.

517. *Ibid*, 9, 11, 27, 48, 51, 58, and 72.

518. This was unique in the matter of printing. This copy was printed in 1254 A.H., and it has 194 pages.

the period of Amjad Ali Shah[519] – were published from Matbaey Sultani (Lucknow), but those books were written on the command of the King, while *Sahifae Sultania* was compiled by Wajid Ali Shah himself.

Nazm Namvar

Written: 1279–87 A.H., Language: Urdu, Genre: Kulliyat
Printing: 1287 A.H., Format: 26.5×17.5, Pages: 153, 11-Lined,
Publication: Rajab ul Murajjab 1287 A.H. in the Capital City of Calcutta by Matbaey Sultani (Calcutta) with the support of Zargham ud Daulah.
Start page 2, end page 282.

The document starts with:

Glory and praise to Allah *and in appreciation of Prophet (PBUH) whereas it is for the young* Mirza *Md.* Jalal Bahadur *from Nawab* Sadar Mahal *Saheba*
There is no life left in me nor any taste on my tongue
My heart comes out in my mouth

On the title page, instead of the name of the author, it is written Hazrat Sultan Alam wa Aalmiyan. Around the name of the book, writer, and compiler, as usual there is a flowery pattern, and the date of its compilation is also given. On the next page is a flowery pattern and in the margin of the second and third pages there is a creeper design. The headings are given in bold letters. On page 67, in a rectangular box, there is a heading given with a decorative pattern as "Volume II." On page 120, there is a more ornamental and formal heading for "Volume III: *Diwan Mubarak.*" At the top of this page is an ornamental pattern and a delicate creeper. The front page is devoid of any design. On the page also there is no *Bismillah.* The counting of Ghazals is as given in the book. At the time of changing the rhyming words (*radif*), one line is taken out as a heading. On page 286, after the end of *Kulliyat,*

519. In the style of printing, it was below the standard of "*Wazaif Nama e Sultani*" but it is still commendable. One incomplete, termite-ridden copy of "*Aamal ul Saleheen*" was found in the Palace Library, Fort Nizamat, Murshidabad.

from page 287–295 there are *Qata'at e Tarikh* and from pages 296–304 on the King's poetic line (*misra*) there are additions (*tazmeen*) by Mahtab ud Daulah Darakhshan and Mir Fida Hussain Qaney. On one side of the last page there is one Ghazal by Wazirul Sultan Nawab Md. Amir Ali Khan Amir on the versification pattern (*tarah*) of the King, and on the other side is the "*Qata'a dar sanat Izharul Muzmarma Tansiqul safat ba madhe Sultan*" by *Aish*. The details about the genre are given in the margin of the last page. In the lower, vacant part of the margin is the seal of the royal library.[520] The writing of Nazm Namvar is not free from mistakes, but the corrections are neatly done in the copies.[521] There appears to be similarities between Nazm Namvar and the rare copies of Volume III: *Diwan Mubarak*, but there are two prominent differences, which are as follows:

A. The decorative page 120 and the margins of the Volume III: *Diwan Mubarak* are the same, but the back of the page (119) in rare copies is blank while in the common copies it is written from first to the last line. On this page are the last 11 verses of the *Noha*: "*Sakina kehti thhein ro kar mere besar bhai.*"

B. In the rare copies, due to some mistakes, the entry at the back of page 193 is page 198, and after the following couplet: "*Kusht e Dehqan pe meri aankh se aansu na bahe – jinas (crop) ka ho gaya har shehar mein ghar ghar tora (scarcity)*", instead of the continuation of the same Ghazal, on the back page there is another Ghazal: "*Khus kharami se teri ped gire jaate hain, saro qad bagh mein waisa hi hai*

---

520. The complete and perfect copy of Nazm Namvar is available in the Publication Department of KhudaBaksh Oriental Library. In the copy found in the Maulana Azad Library of Aligarh Muslim University four pages are missing. (241–248) and some pages are wrongly placed.

521. Nazm Namvar. Md. Wajid Ali Shah Akhtar. Matbaey Sultani. Calcutta. 1287. (Raza, Ittihadiya, Khuda Baksh). 14, (*Suney walo*), 54, (*Tera bhi*), 170 (*gul hi*) 182, (*na kar*), 202, (Ghazal *mein*).

jo ke thha" which begins without a starting couplet (*matla*). These two incomplete Ghazal*s* are printed again.

The other two Ghazal*s*, Ghazal (75) "*Dhuan nikla thha aahon se jo ayyam e jawani ka*" (starting from page 194) and Ghazal (76) "*Jism e Faqir Takhta-e-Gulzar ho gaya*" (starting from page 195), are not found in the rare copies.[522] At first glance it may appear that to differentiate the *Diwan* Nazm Namvar from the *Kulliyat* Nazm Namvar, on page 119 a blank page is pasted, and the pages which are in disorderly condition are wrong additions.[523] In reality, such defects found in rare copies were from printing and not from binding. Perhaps only the *Diwan* portion was published separately, and the defect which was found was later on removed by reprinting it.

Kulliyat Nazm Namvar is divided into three volumes. In the first volume are a total of 24 *masnavis*, some poetic letters, and some invitations. One invitation is dated 19 *Shaaban* 1299 A.H. Most of the invitations are from 1279–1280 A.H. In the second volume are five-line poems (*mukhammas*), quatrains (*rubai*), *salaams*, and *nohas*. Most of this volume was republished in *Kulliyat Imaan* after a year. In the third volume are about 131 Ghazal*s* and four different couplets. The total number of verses in the *Diwan* is 1,433. There are 89 Ghazal*s* in the rhyme (*radif*) of '*alif*.' There are no Ghazal*s* in the *radif* of '*rray*' and in the *radif* of '*meem*' the name of the Begmats has been used. Of the 89 Ghazal*s* of *radif* '*alif*', 58 are taken from *Diwan Sukhan Ashraf* and 27 are taken from *Diwan Mubarak*, but there were tremendous changes in these borrowed Ghazal*s*, so much so that their form has been changed. For a student of literature, such changes can be enlightening

522. The copy of Nazm Namvar which is found in 'Ittihadiya Library' (Calcutta) is one of the rare copies and its only last page is damaged.

523. The copy of Nazm Namvar which is found in Raza Library, Rampur there is no defect in its printing and if the title page is seen in broad light, then the fact of pasting a blank page on it is clarified.

because the poet, at the time of revising his work, has made considerable improvements in expression.[524]

In *Qata'at e Tarikh* there are *Qata'ats* by 12 poets including Wazirul Sultan Nawab Amir Ali Khan Amir, Mahtab ud Daulah Darakhshan, Mir Fida Hussain Qaney, Mirza Masita Aish, Syed Sarfraz Hussain Bekhud, Gulshan ud Daulah Bahar, Mirza Muzaffar Ali Hunar, Hamid ud Daulah Bartar, Hameed ud Daulah Shauqq, Hasan Khan Zia, Mirza Md. Abbas Shaaz, and Jai Gopal Saqib. Darakshan, in his Urdu *Qata'a* of 23 verses, by way of his normal style has inferred the date of printing from every line (*misra*), but *Aish* in the chronogram style (*Tarikh nigari*) of Nazm Namvar has displayed an interesting rivalry. *Aish's Qata'a* is of 14 verses, and if there is a hijri year in one line (*misra*), then in the second line the same date is written, and if in one line there is a Gregorian year (A.D.), then it is written in another line also. This can be noted as below:[525]

1. *Akhtar You are Fair and Commanding 1870*
It is the glow and magnificence of the King 1870 A.D.
2. *He is in every art and knowledge 1287*
He is the great lover of pomp 1287A.H.
3. *Even the Sun on the sky says 1870*
He is like the shining Sun 1870
4. *By selected verse this magic is revealed 1287*
He is the magician of poetry 1287
5. *He is so eloquent in expression 1870*
He is the envy of judicious mind 1870
6. *In his appreciation I say 1287*
He is the glory of pen, a shining pearl 1287

524. For some meaningful changes see Chapter 5 of this book.

525. The verses here are strictly in Urdu and the dates are deciphered through art of *Tarikh*. But here it has been translated only for the interest of the elite readers. (Translator)

7. *Every line has the date 1870*
Yes the poetic art is shining 1870
8. *Aish is the fan 1287*
Of the candle of poetic art 1287

Imaan (Printed)

Written: 1268–88 A.H., Language: Urdu, Genre: Kulliyat Salaam
Printing: 1288 A.H., Format: 25×16, Pages: 131, 11-Lined,
Publication: By Matbaey Sultani (Calcutta) with the support of Rais ud Daulah Zevar (First Print)
Start page 2, end page 242

The book starts with the following verses:

When Abbas decided to destroy them
The skies echoed with the skillfulness of his sword
In Shabbir there is style of Hasan
Akbar is drenched in blood and Mah e Bani Hashim too
Hazrat (Hussain) is elegiac on earth and Zehra is sad in the skies.

There is a delicate flower pattern on the title page and on pages 2, 206, and 207. On the title page the name of the book, the publisher's and supervisor's names, and the date are given. Empty space is left at the top for the seal. Below the seal "*Flezahku Aqlillan wa lebaku aksira*" (Arabic) is written and below that "*Kulliyat Salamha Aur Rubayat waghera az tasnifat* Hazrat Sultan Alam wa Aalmiyan *Khuldullah Malka*" is inscribed. The book is divided into three parts. The first part, on pages 2–206, is the first volume, in which with '*radif* *Salam* is written. On pages 207–42 is the second volume, in which there is a Ghazal with some additions (*tazmeen*), two five-lined poems (*mukhammas*), 51 Quatrains, and six *Qata'as.* At the end on the King's *salaam* there is a five-lined poem by Zarghamud Daulah Bahadur. After page 242, there is no numbering. There are *qata'as* of Wazir ul Sultan Nawab Amir Ali Khan Amir, Mir Fida Hussain Qaney, and Ali

Baksh Hashim. After this, from page 243 upto the last page 260, under the heading "*Qata'haey Tarikh Taba Imaan Tasnif Bandgan sikandar Shaan*", there are *Qata'as* by Mirza *Ali Bahar*, Mahtab ud Daulah Darakhshan, Mirza Masita Aish, Hamid ud Daulah Bartar, *Hameed ud Daulah Qayas* Md. Abbas Shaaz, *Syed Hasan Jaan Zia*, and Jai Gopal Saqib. On the last page is the *Qata'a* of *Aish* titled "Qata'a *dar Sanat Izharul muzmar*". Below the line (*misra*) "*malak Zeb Shah-e-Husn e Akhtar*" the word "*Tamam shudd*" (ended) is written in the margin. There is no corrigendum, and the mistakes have been corrected at the proper places.[526]

In the first volume, the total number of salams is 99. The last one *is Salam mussallus.* In the second print of *Imaan* this is kept in miscellaneous items. After *Salaam* 94, by mistake there is an increase of one. In this way the actual number of *salaams* is 97, in which there are 1,904 verses. Other than '*Ray*' there are *salaams* with all the letters of the Urdu language. The *salams* of *radif* '*fay*' and '*lam*' are without '*radif*.' After some years, in the second print of '*Imaan*', the *salams* with '*laam*' *radif* were added. In '*Imaan*', there is no separate arrangement of *salams* and *nohas*, though the book from which these are collected did have separate arrangements. In the count of 97, there are three *salaams* and one *noha* from *Kulliyat Soom.* 70 *salaams* and four *nohas* are from Qamar Mazmun, and seven *salaams* and five *nohas* are from Nazm Namvar. While collecting the scattered compositions, there have been some slight changes in the words. The number of verses is the same as it was in the three *Kulliyats.* 60 *salams* and *nohas* for the first time came in the printed form in *Kulliyat Imaan* and it is quite possible that these were composed to complete the *Diwan.* After the '*Diwan e Hussaini*' of Delhi's Muasir Hashim Burhanpuri, perhaps it is the second *Diwan* of *Salams* and *Nohas* which has been compiled. And it is quite possible that the idea of compiling it came after studying the *Diwan-e-Hussaini.* [527]

---

526. This detail of the book has been procured from the copy of *Imaan*.For handwritten corrections pages, 25 (*daak),* 91 (*sabni*), 138 (*payambar*) can be seen.

527. Springer has mentioned *Diwan-e-Hussaini* in the list of library of *Shahan e Avadh.*

Many poets have regarded the *Qata'at e Tarikh* of *Imaan* as a *Diwan.*[528] Gopal Saqib writes in his *Qata'a*:

O! the Shadow of Khudavand The assistant of religion and the Judge
The lucky, the triumphant, the magnificient
The bright Akhtar the height of eloquence
Wajid Ali Sultan Alam the envy of Kings
(1288)

In the other mentionable '*tarikhs*', Bahar has inferred the date (year) from every second line (*misra*). These are all related to the incident of Karbala and were composed on the orders of the King. Both the *Qata'ats* of Darakhshan are in Urdu. In the *qata'a* of 14 verses, from every line the year in the hijri, Gregorian, and Bengali calendars have been inferred. In the second Qata'a it is said:

It is part of faith Darakhshan *the line containing Tarikh*
What a sacrifice deed is of the son of the Prophet
(31,710, 596, 53, 296, 66, 21 = 1288)

Imaan (Printed) (Second Edition)

Written: 1268–88 A.H., Language: Urdu, Genre: Kulliyat Salaam
Printing: 1301 A.H., Format: 31×19, Pages: 120, 15-Lined
Publication: By Matbaey Sultani (Calcutta) with the support of Rais ud Daulah Zevar (Second Print)
Start page 2, end page 242.

With some changes and additions, this is the second print of '*Imaan.*'[529] In the changes of printing the first notable one is that of the format and

528. See the Qata'at of Amir, *Bartar, Qayas, Shaaz* and *Zia* in the *Qata'at e Tarikh of Imaan.*
529. The termite-ridden copy of the second print of *Imaan* is available in Safi Darul Mutalea (Lucknow).

paper. The paper of the first print, despite a gap of many years, is still white in colour and strong too. The paper of this print has started to become yellow and brittle. From the title page, or from any other description, it is not clear which edition it is. In the year of publication and in *ayat*, there is a slight change. Around the title page there is a drawing of fish. On the second and third pages there is a flowery pattern and before the *Bismillah* tablet, in the empty space the royal seal has been put twice. Up to page 181 there are Diwans and immediately after the *Diwan* is the start of Volume II, in which there are different compositions from the first print. On page 339, after this continuation, at the end is written 'finish.' The last page is blank. The correction of words in this print was also done by hand. [530]

In the first print, in Volume I the words '*Daftar Salaamha*' were written after *Bismillah*. In the second print, this heading is not there. After the end of each *salaam*, instead of having a separate heading for each one there is a continuation of one *salaam* after another, and where the '*radif*' is changed there is a one-line heading. *Qata'at e Tarikh* and the five-lined poem (*mukhammas*) of *Zargham ud Daulah* is not given in this print. The initial verses are the same in both versions. The second version ends with the following words:

*"The Qata'ae Tarikh elegant composition of the great Hazrat Sultan Alam Khuld*Allah *Malka"*

Here there is the thought
Akhtar has added one 'alif'
I have liked his extension
O! Dear this is elegant work (1301 A.H.)

In the first version, there were 97 *Salaams*, in this one there are 118. Of the additional 21 *salaams*, 17 are taken from *Mulk e Akhtar*; (three in *radif* 'ray', two each in the radif of '*alif*', '*kaf*', '*laam*', '*meem*', '*wow*' and '*yey*', and

530. For instance, on page 174 "*Salaam 114*" is written with hand.

one in '*noon*'). There is one more *Qata'a* in the form of a *Salaam* which is taken from the Appendix of *Malazul Kalmat*.[531]

The other three *Salaams*, which include a '*Manqibat*', were probably newly composed. The first couplet is as follows: '*Khurshid ko banade Qamar Murtuza Ali...*'. With the addition of 21 *Salaams*, the number of verses in the second print is increased to 662. Volume II of the second print has increased quantitatively. But this addition is taken from '*Mulk Akhtar*' and '*Malazul Kalmat*'. In this addition is a "*Mukhhammas Barabiat* Nasiruddin *Shehenshah Mansub Iran*", which became very popular. It has 202 quatrains and 13 *Qata'ats*. For 'Soz' and '*matam*', some couplets are written with the names of '*rag*' *or* '*raagni*', and some are in the natural poetic metre of the King.

Dulhan

Written: 1289 A.H., Language: Hindi, Genre: Collection of Compositions
Printing: 1290 A.H. Format: 25×16, Pages: 69, Lined-8(9),
Publication: Matbaey Sultani (Calcutta with the support of Raisuddaulah Zevar
Start page 2, end page 81.

The book starts with a printed page. At the top of the page, space was left for the seal. It is at this point that in all the printed copies the seal of the royal library was given. On page 2 is the ornamental plate of '*Bismillah*', and on pages 2 and 3, in the margins there is a delicate creeper design while in the centre is the Preface in Persian. The design is not impressive like '*Najo*', it is awkward. From page 5 the series of songs (*geet*) begins, and this continues until the end without a break. To make the headings attractive, they have been written in bold. Up to page 81 is the main book, while from page 82 to the last page (138) there are *Qata'ats* with dates. For these *Qata'ats*, a nine-lined style has been adopted. In the main part of the book, additional

531. *Malazul Kalmat.* Md. Wajid Ali Shah Akhtar, Matbaey Sultani, Calcutta. 1297. 700. (Azad Library).

notes and explanations[532] have been given in the margins. The mistakes in this book have also been corrected with pen.[533]

The compiler, while recalling the purpose behind compiling '*Dulhan*', says that about 300–400 amateurs who were almost deaf and dumb, became very talkative after his first compilation '*Najo*'. Hence in 1289 A.H. he collected more songs and compiled them in another collection, so that their practice would continue. In line with the title '*Dulhan*', the chapters have been given titles like '*Dharpad*', '*Saadhra*', '*Sargam*', '*Chitrang*', '*Hori*', '*Khayal*', '*Tarana*', '*Tappa*', '*Thumri*', '*Dadar*', and '*Sawan*'. The last one is '*Tasveer*', which has miscellaneous songs for occasions like '*zacha khana*' and '*Sanchaq*'. Contrary to *Najo*, all the compositions in this book are by Wajid Ali Shah and Badshah Mahal *Alam*. Only in '*Dharpad*', one '*Chautala*' by his court musician Pyar Khan has been included.

In *Qata'at e Tarikh* there are *qata'ats* in Persian, Urdu, and Hindi, and years from each calendar – Sambat, Hijri, Fasli and Gregorian – have been included. Every poet has tried to give his best and has taken special care regarding the style and richness of his language, which has made it a memorable contribution. The first *Qata'a* is of Wazir ul Sultan Nawab Amir Ali Khan Amir and is in Persian. The second one is of *Mahtabud Daulah* Darakhshan, and in the 26 verses of this Urdu *Qata'at*, from every line the year 1290 A.H. can be inferred, and different intricacies are created. It is quite possible that this attempt was in response to the *Qata'ey Tarikh* of *Nazm Namzar*, which was composed by *Aish*. A few of the verses are presented here:

O! Sweet singer congratulations a unique book is printed
The joy is justified as it is the spring of tunes
She who goes fully covered among lakhs
She is coming here fully decked

532. *See,* Margins of *Dulhan*- Md. Wajid Ali Shah Akhtar-Matbaey Sultani - Calcutta.1290 A.H. at page 33, 46, 48, and 50.

533. See *"Pristanki"* on page 93 and *"Munshi"* on page 135.

Its name Dulhan has been given for this reason
It lives in the heart of all
All swing their heads in the tune of Dulhan
All the pious are restive and tearful
Yes this appreciation is enough for King's composition
With the presence of whom the party is brightened
The King's grants are continuing
The have-nots are being rewarded
Darakhshan *whom to tell the hundred wonders*[534]
See this 'Dulhan' alone but 'suhagan'
When the fifty-two dates are appearing[535]
It's given the name of "Bawan Sahba"

Some 18 poets wrote the '*Tarikh*' (date) for '*Dulhan*' other than those who composed *Qata'as* for '*Najo*'. These are:

1. *Mukhlis ud Daulah* Bahadur *Mukhlis*
2. Kazim *Hussain Tanvir*
3. *Lala Kali Charan Taskeen*
4. *Laiqudd Daulah Md. Jan Shahid.*
5. Mirza *Muzzafar Ali* Hunar
6. *Sheikh Sadiq Ali* Mayil
7. Md. Abbas Shaaz
8. Mir Hasan *Jaan Zia*
9. Jai Gopal Saqib
10. *Munshi Abdul Razzaq Wafa*
11. *Atar ud Daulah Md. Ali Mohsin*

---

534. Date is 1290 A.H., letters with nuqtas ('yay', 'yay', *'Khey', 'sheen', 'noon', 'chhoti ye', 'sheen', 'chhoti yay').*

535. Date is 1290 A.H., Persian words (*'chey', 'choti yey', 'jeem', 'bay', 'Qay', 'bay', 'noon', 'tey', 'chhoti yay' 'Khey', 'noon', 'choti yay', 'noon').*

12. *Sardar Hussain Riyaz*
13. *Lala Ram Dayal Naadim*
14. *Lala Ashrafi Lal Ramdas*
15. *Syed Zainul Abdin Waqar*
16. *Lala* Kalka *Prasad Kali Das*
17. *Khulasatud Daulah* Bahadur
18. *Lala Bhagwan Das Khushdil*

The lines (*misras*) of *Khulasat ud Daulah* Bahadur and of Hunar are well-crafted and appropriate.

Muzaffar Ali Hunar:

Now every Dulhan will be ashamed before this Dulhan:
599, 41, 205, 95, 3, 61, 95, 30, 161 = 1290 A.H.

Khulasat ud Daulah Bahadur:

Zehra played the tune from her mouth and sang this
Long live the bridegroom, sisters of the Dulhan and Congratulations Dulhan
215, 45, 531, 152, 95, 263, 11. 1312 Takkhraja[536] (1290 A.H.).

Aish inferred dates from *Nagma-e Jaan e Alam* and *Fasl Nagm*, and the book concluded with his *qata'a* "*Dar Sanat Izharul Muzzamar*" and the line "*The King Akhtar's beauty is the...*"

536. This is a form of *Tarikh* in which numbers associated with some letters are deducted from the total in order to get the correct date. (Oxford Urdu-English Dictionary). It is deciphered from the Urdu words (or letters) used, but these have been translated here for better comprehension of readers.

Mubahisa Bainul Nafs Wal Aql (Manuscript)

Written: 1287–89, Language: Persian, Genre: Religious Problems
Printing: 1290, Format: 26×16, Pages: 36, Lined- 9,
Manuscript in the hand of the copyist
Start page 2, end page 72.

Other than the published copy, two handwritten copies of this book are available, both of which are important. On the title page is written:

> *"From top to bottom it has been perused and corrected and is ready for printing on the 25th Day of* Rabiul Awwal *1290.*

In view of the above statement and the changes which are made thereof, the importance of this handwritten copy is revealed. This is the first copy of the King's manuscript in which changes were made by the King himself, and which has been corrected for printing. The printed version was a copy of this handwritten version. The first proof of this are the deletions and additions which have been strictly followed in the printed copy. Additional evidence is from the lines which were drawn by the copyist at the time the pages of the printed copy were changed. This style continued up to the last verses. The order of the printing supervisor, which is entered on the title page, also shows this. The printed copy was published 13 months after this order by *Raees ud Daulah* Bahadur. Thus, it is possible that this order must be in his handwriting. There is no numbering of pages in the handwritten copy. The headings are written in red ink while the remaining content is written in black. The statements of Persian and Arabic are in the Persian and Arabic script. In the Arabic content, a red line is drawn over it, and in the printed copy this text is written as if cancelled. The changes made in the manuscript are lengthy, but here some important points are indicated:

A. The starting part of the manuscript is from the second line. The first line was drawn later. But in this it is also written "learned saying" (*afadat*) and it has been crossed out with a line.

B. There is a sentence on page 57 of the manuscript in Persian, and this text is on page 101 of the printed copy, but the words which were beautifully encircled are missing. This act of correcting, in which there should not be any awkwardness, and the correction should be legible, is seen at different places in the document.

C. On page 61 of the manuscript, the Persian statement which was given on page 101 of the printed copy should have been written. But instead of cancelling it or correcting it, the Persian statement is written between the lines. Perhaps this was done keeping in mind that the *ayats* of the Quran, holy names, and events to show respect should not be struck abruptly; hence writing in between the lines was a solution. In this way, the copyist teaches us a good lesson.

The last three pages of the manuscript were blank. The entire manuscript was written in prose. When it was being revised, it must have been thought that it should not end without the addition of poems, and hence the last 37 verses in Persian (*munajat*) are written in free hand without any heading. Only in one place at the end, a change has been made.

The pages on which there is this '*munajat*', 10–11 lines are systematically written in a prose style, and only this part of the manuscript is in the hand of the King. As the manuscript ended with poetry, an addition of poems was also made at the beginning. But the poetic introduction of the printed copy and the *Qata'aey Tarikh* of *Aish* is not given in this manuscript.

Mubahisa Bainul Nafs Wal Aql (Handwritten/Unpublished)

Written: 1287–89 A.H., Language: Persian, Genre: Religious Problems
Printing: 1290 A.H., Format: 29×19, Pages: 71, Lined-9,
Start page 2, end page 142.

The document starts with a declaration in Persian that by Allah's grace the King has completed this work and, on His order, it has been written by Tarsiud Daulah Zamarrud, son of Ali Raza Jawahar in 1290 A.H.

In terms of content, there is no difference between the handwritten and printed copy, except that in the handwritten copy there is some marking and mentioning of the author's name in the Preface, and in the printed copy there is a *Qata'ey Tarikh* and a mention of the "*hamd...*". In spite of this, the handwritten copy is the one made by the writer of the royal library and is a masterpiece of good handwriting. The words are neatly written, giving a pearl like glow. Between the lines, from the beginning up to the end, the space is filled with gold water and the margin has a flowery pattern. On 71 pages there are 71 types of creepers which were made with indigo and gold water. At the side of the binding, these creepers are half an inch wide, while on the other three sides they are a quarter of an inch wide, and have the same design on both pages. On the pages on which there is poetry, in the columns there is a one inch wide creeper which resembles the design in the margin. For the safety of the gold-plated pages, there was a thin transparent piece of paper place in between, though the entire copy itself was devoid of any safety and was damaged due to termites.

Mubahisa Bainul Nafs Wal Aql (Printed)

Written: 1287–89 A.H., Language: Persian, Genre: Religious Problems
Printing: 1291 A.H., Format: 25×17, Pages: 57, Lined-11,
Publisher: Matbaey Sultani (Calcutta) under the aegis of Raeesud Daulah Zevar,
Start page 2, end 113.

The Persian narrative in the beginning sings the glory of Allah with great appreciation for the book. At the top of the printed page there is space for the seal, and below it the *ayats* of the Quran, a few sentences about the book, and the name of the book are given. The date of printing is given as 29 Rabiul Sani 1291 A.H. The name of the author is not given on the title page, neither in the beginning nor at the end. On pages 2 and 3, there is a decorative design in the margins, and on the top of the plate of *Bismillah*, 10 fish are decorated in a conical style. Up to page 50 is the poetic Preface. The author's name is revealed by the Preface. The actual book goes up to page 110. An explanation and summary of points is given in the margin. Out of the last four pages, on three there is a *Qata'aey Tarikh* of Mirza Masita Aish, the last verses of which contain the date of its publication as 1291 A.H.

In the '*Hamd*', '*naat*', and '*Manqibat*', after explaining his own plight in an effective manner, in the "*purpose of compilation*" there are details about his paternal and maternal family tree, and then he moves on to the main topic. With the advent of the month of *Ramadhan*, people get busy with *namaz*, fasting, and recitation of the Quran. For the satisfaction of the soul and for mental peace, this time is most suitable. The compiler who thought over such problems during this time has presented them in the form of a beautiful conversation between "*the Questions of Conscience*" and the "*replies of the mind.*" The number of these questions is 28, and these are presented under three headings. The first chapter is related to *Ramadhan* 1287 A.H., and it has nine questions. The second chapter comprised the *Ramadhan* of 1288 A.H. There are 12 questions in it. The third and last chapter is about the *Ramadhan* of 1289 A.H. and has seven questions. The questions are mainly related to religious traditions and '*Hadith.*' While perusing these traditions and *Hadith*, some doubts crop up in the mind of the reader about whether such events are possible or not. The compiler, to diffuse such doubts, has presented grounds which are named as "*Mubahisey Bainul Nafs wal Aql*". For instance, giving preference to The Last Prophet and his family must be backed by a solid argument. According to the compiler, like the father for whom the youngest child is the dearest, the Creator, who loves all human beings and his creations (*jinns*) 70 times more than the love of a father for his child, there should be no surprise if He likes the Last Prophet and his family as the dearest of all.[537]

In the poetic introduction, a brief account of the closeness with *Rafat ud Daulah* (Syed Md. Shafi Rizvi)[538] and a detailed account of the abilities

537. *Mubahisey Bainul Nafswal Aql-Copy 1-* Md. Wajid Ali Shah Akhtar. Calcutta 1290. 51. Question 2.

538. *Ibid*, 45.

and achievements of *Wazirul Sultan Nawab Md.* Amir *Ali Khan* Amir[539] are given. In the introduction and in '*munajat*', the personal annoyances are presented in a very admonitory way, and the biographic importance of these descriptions is undeniable.[540]

Jauhar e Urooz (First Print)

Written-1290, Language-Urdu, Genre-Prosody
Printing- 1290, Format: 24×16, Pages: 10, Lined- 11,
Printed: (First Print) At Matbaey Sultani (Calcutta) under the aegis of Khanzada Raeesud Daula.
Start page 2, end page 19.

Two editions of *Jauhar e Urooz* by Matbaey Sultani (Calcutta) are available, and in spite of similarities in their names, there are many differences in their subject matter.

On the printed title, other than formal details and the name of the book, the date of publication is written '*10* Rajab *ul Murajjab 1290 A.H.*' The name of the poetic metre (*Beher*) was written in the margin, but for some unknown reason these have been struck out with the help of some flowery patterns, as the two available copies indicate.[541]

The Preface is very short. After mentioning the *hamd*, *naat*, *manqibat* and the Prophet's kin, the purpose of compilation is given in the following words:

> "*Away from his hometown*, Wajid Ali Shah, *son of the late* Amjad Ali Shah, *deposed King of Avadh, without metrical variation and with his extraordinary intellectual ability has himself created this art which is a gift for the experts...*" (Translated from Persian)

539. *Ibid*, 46–48.

540. The printed copies of this book is found in the Maulana Azad Library Aligarh Muslim University.

541. Both the copies of *Jauhar e Urooz* is available in the Maulana Azad Library of Aligarh Muslim University. Out of this one was under the custody of *Md. Taqi Khan Afsar.*

Only this part of the book is in Persian. After this the lessons start, in which the name of the poetic metre is given and exemplified by a line (*misra*). To compose them in measured versus the same subject matter is kept in line with the metrical components (*arkan*). The metrical components are then indicated and are complete. There is no argument regarding metrical variation (*zahaf*). The trend continues up to the end. There are 69 traditional and original (*tab*Azad) poetic metres (*beher*). 52 poetic metres are named after the King, and some of these are historical.

In the beginning, seven poetic metres of '*Matdarak*', '*rama*', '*taqarab*', '*hazaj*', '*rujz*', '*kamil*', and '*waafar*' are arranged. For '*beher taweel*' (long metre) it is indicated that it is made with the metrical components (*arkan*) of *beher* '*mutaqarib*' and beher '*hazaj*':

Said that, read and listen to this my dear
"Faulan, mafaeylin, faulan, mafaeylin"

Thereafter, in its reverse form, while relating to himself, he has given two names of original poetic metres as below:

Ijaad Akhtar and Siraj Akhtari
Read this my dear and hear it with attention
"mafaeylin faulan, mafaeylin faulan,"

First, the familiar forms of the poetic metres of '*madeed*', '*basit*', '*sareey*', '*khafeef*', '*munsareh*', '*muzareh*', '*muhabbas,*' *and* '*muqtazib*' are explained, and then he relates their reverse form to himself in the above manner. These are named by him. Only the familiar form of '*beher qareeb*' and the reverse form of *beher e jadid*' is explained. In this way, up to the reverse (*maqloob beher*), 10 behers in poetic metres are originally composed by the King, as below:

1. *Siraj* Akhtari
2. *Dard* Akhtari

3. *Justoojuay* Akhtari
4. *Sanat Akhtar*
5. *Awurda e Akhtar*
6. *Tarz e* Akhtari
7. *Takapooey* Akhtari
8. *Ghaur* Akhtari
9. *Fikr* Akhtari
10. *Taa'mul* Akhtari *(Reverse modern poetic meter = Maqloob Behere Jadid)*

The trend of composing a new *beher* with the aid of metrical components and then composing its reverse form continued up to the end. In the beginning, while naming the origina *behers*, care was taken that the name should indicate the details of the *beher*. For example, '*modern poetic metre*' (*Beher Jadid*) is not prevalent in Urdu. Its reverse form was named '*Taa'mmul Akhtar*', but from the 19th *Beher* the sentence "*From here the names of dates* (*asma e tarikhi*) *start*" was written, and with it such names were chosen from which the year 1290 A.H. was inferred. 1290 A.H. is the date of composing, compiling, and publication of *Jauhar e Urooz*. In the *Tarikhi* names, some are very interesting, like '*Khazanaey Mafulat*', '*Khazan e Failatun*', '*bharistan shooara*', '*paasakh mafulat*', '*rukn azim*', '*dar uroozi*', '*maloomat taqarib*', '*raud e Areez*', '*rukn lafzi*', '*khusrowabiyat*', and '*darakhshan usul*'.

Jauhar e Urooz (Second Print)

Written: 1290, Language: Urdu, Genre: Prosody
Printing-1292, Format: 24×16, Pages: 18, Lined-11,
Printed: (Second Print) At Matbaey Sultani (Calcutta) under the aegis of Khanzada Raeesud Daula.
Start page 2, end page 35.

On the title page, the important change is the date of publication. In the First Print, 18 Rajab 1290 A.H. was given. Here it is written "...*Rajab ul Murajjab* 1292 A.H." Although with '*tarikhi*' names, here it is also written as 1290 A.H., but neither on the title page nor anywhere inside the book it is mentioned that it is the Second Print of *Jauhar e Urooz.* The name *Jauhar e Urooz* 1290 A.H. indicates its year of publication. In *Hamd*, *Naat*, and *Manqibat*, expression is long and formal. The number of '*behers*' and pages are more than before. On the last page is given the quatrain of *Aish* titled "*Taaeiush ud Daulah* Bahadur" in the genre of '*Izhar ul Muzzamar*', the line (*misra*) of which is comprehensive (*Jamay*): "*Eid e khush Jalsa Mubarakbada*". At the end of this quatrain, it is written 'the end'.

In the first print, the counting of *behers* as prevalent in Urdu and is given based on name. In this print there is explanation of the author's original poetic meters (*behers*), regarding which he mentioned in the Preface in the following words:

> "*I, after paying my reverence to the family of the Prophet Akhtar, Wajid Ali son of Amjad Ali who have been the Rulers of Avadh have created these new beher metres with eight-line stanzas under the art which is known to the world as prosody. The prosodic measure of which are 143...*"[542]
> (Translated from Persian)

The addition of 74 behers was done because earlier, for one name there was one beher. In the second print, for many *behers* two, three, or four parts are inferred. For instance, '*Beher zamzam Manzoor*'[543] is presented in the three forms of eight-line poems: 'Musamman', sixain, and quatrain.[544] This is as follows:

542. *Jauhar e Urooz.* Md. Wajid Ali Shah. Matbaey Sultani Calcutta. 1290 and 1293. Second Print. 4. (Azad Library)

543. *Ibid.*

544. In the first edition of *Jauhar e Urooz* the other name of '*zamzam manzoor*' is mentioned as *Fakhre Qaisari (*1290) and the component was "*mafaetan faulan, mafaeytan faulan.*" In this print there is only one name, and the component has been changed. He has followed the same style in his other original *behers.*

A. Eight-line poem: *Tell her to follow attentively*
Faelin Mustafalun Failin Mustafeen (*beher meter*)
Sixain: *Come and listen to this again*
Failun Mustafalun Failin (*beher meter*)

B Quatrain: *Come You and listen to this again*
Failun Mustafalun (*beher meter*)

The behers which were meant only for this edition have undergone the same process. Out of the single beher 'Murraqaey Faqr' (1290 A.H.), following the previously adopted pattern five forms are created as shown below:

1. Eight Line Poem: *My love story is not suitable for some verses*
   Mutafaelun, Faulan Mutafaelan Mutafaelen (*beher meter*)
2. Sixain: *My dear you are a fairy live in my heart*
   Mutafalun Faulan Mutafaelan (*beher meter*)
3. Similar one: *If You are fairy then live in my heart*
   Faulan Mutafaelan Mafaen (*beher meter*)
4. Quatrain: *My dear you are Fairy*
   Mutafaelun Faulan (*beher meter*)
5. Similar: *My dear live in heart*
   Mutafaelun Mafailun (*beher meter*)

In the end, the number of roots (*usool*) is 50 and that of its branches (*faroo*) is 93 for the same reason. Just like in the above example, '*alif*' is the root and '*bay*', '*jeem*', '*dal*' and '*chhoti hey*' are its branches. Similarly, the other 49 *behers* are the roots and the 79 that are explained in this booklet, along with their names, are its branches.

The strict literary section above has its charm in the Urdu language, but here a translated version is presented, so that elite readers may grasp the idea behind the art of prosody in Urdu. The ingenuity and extraordinary talent of the King is also revealed to the world here.

Bani (Ind the King's hand)

Written: 1291–94, Language: Urdu, Genre: Collection of Compositions
Printing: 1291–94, Format: 21.7×16, Pages: 187, Lined: 13–14
Written in Persian script in the hand of the author (King).
Start page 2, end page 35.

This copy was on ordinary paper in the author's own handwriting. It is termite-ridden, damaged without any binding, and has 159 pages, of which 28 are blank. Some pages are numbered, though some are numbered incorrectly. The font is often bold, often light, and the writing is often formal and often is in the Persian script of the writer, and there are 11–15 lines on some of the pages. It is a fact that this is the first copy, and was handwritten by the author. This is evident from the fact that it is often written informally, there are deletions and additions at places, and the words have been changed. There is no surprise then that there is such a difference between the arrangement of the printed copy and the manuscript. Due to the variety of topics, it was difficult to write it in a serial manner. Perhaps it was also not the idea of the author that everything that was written in the manuscript must be printed. Moreover, it was written at different times, which is evident from the difference in ink. The dating is also different. This is shown in the following examples:

A. On page 15 of the manuscript "*thumri, jhanjhuti, aastai*" it is written:

Gori! open your hair there is a black snake in it...
I remain restless for you the whole night
Dear get me the bangles from Calcutta.

At the time the additions were made to this page, the date was given as 5 Zilhij 1292 A.H. All three of these '*thumris*' are written on pages 18 and 19 of the printed copy.

B. The writing in the margin of page 29 is:

"*Tappa ragni khamanch stani: Ghaneri sayyan pyar milandy masendo aas...*" and the date given is 23 Rabiul Sani 1294 A.H. In the printed copy, this writing is in the margin of page 36, which surely indicates that this addition was made after the writing. Otherwise, like A, it would have been in the main text and not in the margin.

C. In the printed copy, in the margin of page 26:

"hori chachar aastai: Kya hua nandi anokhe piya ko hori khelat moh se nai ri nai..."

while in the margin of page 27 of the printed copy:

"raag pilo jangle, aastai: angia bejne chatkili sunder naar..."

This is not found anywhere in the manuscript because these additions were probably made after the writing on these pages was complete, or the pages on which such compositions were written were lost.

D. The words '77th copy' were written on separate paper and were added to take care of continuity. At the end of the copy, it is written: *"Written during sickness, 23 Ramadhan 1292 A.H."*

In the printed copy this writing is correctly written on page 272–73. In this copy some fun is made of the professional writers, and by looking at the markings it is not difficult to find out why it was written. Other than the arrangement, there is much change in the words and writings. There are many changes which are found in the manuscript, but these are sometimes present and sometimes not found in the printed copy. Moreover, in the manuscript, the style is Persian, and there is no counting of the sections. In the printed copy there are Urdu words instead. For instance:

A. "*Fasal dar Tukda ha, pehla tukda...*" is as it is in the manuscript. In the printed copy the heading is changed: "*Fasal Pehla...tukron ke byan mein jo alfaz se ada hotey hain: Pehla tukda...*" (page 38)

B. In the printed copy there is mention of 36 dance dramas (pages 69–85) while in the manuscript, after explaining these dance dramas (*rahas*), in the margin the suitable musical tones (*gutt*) are also given.

C. In the tale of Radha *Kanhaiyya* ("the poverty..."), after adding an asterisk, there is further explanation in the margin like below: "*Method: Continuously gives salutation to the giants and fairies, 11 Zeeqad 1292 A.H.*"

Perhaps these directions were for the workers and not for printing. On page 88 in the printed copy, there are no such directions. Apart from the arrangement and changes, there is one more important difference between the manuscript and the printed copy – the entire writing of the manuscript is not found in the printed copy. Hence one question regarding dance is found in the manuscript, but it is not found in the printed copy. Similarly, whatever is in the printed copy is not present in the manuscript. For instance, chapter six, concerning the addresses, is not found in the manuscript. In sum, the following pages of the manuscript match the pages of the printed copy:

A. Handwritten page 84–127 = page 62–124 of the printed copy

B. Handwritten page 148–252 = page 124–285 of the printed copy.

Bani (Printed)

Written: 1291–94, Language: Urdu, Genre: Collection of Compositions
Printing: 1295, Format: 28×18, Pages: 204, Lined-11
Printed by Matbaey Sultani Calcutta under the aegis of Raeesud Daulah
Start page 2, end page 374.

"*After the glory and appreciation of* Allah *and naat of the Prophet and Manqibat* Wajid Ali Shah *Akhtar presents before the adMirers and followers that before this, two books 'Najo' and 'Dulhan' were widely distributed, but in those there are only the preparatory piece of song ..." "...if it is well thought over then there are some good suggestions for them which will be materialised..." Dated: Safar ul Muzzaffar 1294 A.H.*

On the title page and on pages 1, 2, and 3, there is a delicate design in the margin. On the top of the title page, space is left for the seal. Below it there is one line for *Hamd* and one in appreciation of the book and the author. And it is written "*Kitab haza tasnif bandgan sikander shaan.*" At the place where the name of the book is written "*Musamma ba bani.*" The name of the publisher and the supervisor is given in the last lines. The date of writing is not given. On pages 2 and 3 is the Preface, and on pages 4–374 is the actual book. The '*ragas*' of the songs are given both in words and through illustrations. On pages 42–57 and 64–68 there is a picture on each page. "*In these pictures the dancers are male, by appearance they look like 'pathans', same type of turban, hair, moustache but as for dress they are wearing a full dress gown (pishwaz).*"[545] In no other book of Matbaey Sultani are pictures found. From page 375 up to the last page (408) there is *Qata'at e Tarikh* in a 15-lined setting (*mustar*). In the beginning of these *Qata'ats* there are 71 Qata'ats by Darakhshan which are in appreciation of the buildings which the King had constructed. After these there are *Qata'as* regarding the arrangement and writing of *Bani.* The space on the title page was insufficient for the seal. The seal was commonly found at the end of the book.[546] There are very few mistakes, and these have been neatly corrected at the right place.[547] In *Qata'at e Tarikh* this book, like '*Najo*' and '*Dulhan*', has been regarded as a book of music, and commentators also regard it as the same.[548] But this book, apart

545. *Urdu Adab ke Aath Saal-* Ishrat Rehmani. Kitab Manzil, Lahore. 145. In this book the number of photos is five, but the copies which came to the author's perusal revealed 21 pictures. These are all of male members.

546. See the copies of Khuda Bakhsh Oriental Public Library (Patna), Raza Library, (Rampur).

547. For instance, see on page 106 of *Bani* the word *"ghutna."*

548. *Supra Note* 544 at 142.

from music, has many other subjects. There are six chapters in it and every chapter is about a different art.

In the first chapter, from pages 4–37, there are 10 sections. There is a mention of "*suradhiya*" in it. With the restriction of timing and tuning, there are songs for a variety of melodies. In the second chapter from pages 37–47, there is a foreword and two sections in which are given different kinds of tunes (*taal*) and the method to pronounce them. The third chapter is in "*Nanach Addhiyya*". In this chapter, from pages 47–68, there two sections. In the first section there is the mention of 16 quavers or musical tones (*gutt*). The quavers of this section were also mentioned in *'Sautul Mubarak'*. Some were added, and some were presented with new names. In the second section there is "*Kaharvaey*" dance and its various forms. This sketching is done to bring home the explanation of this chapter. In the first section of Chapter Four, from pages 69–86, there are "*36 innovative dance dramas.*" By the word *'rahas'* is meant a group dance, and all these dances were directed by the King himself. In *Sautul Mubarak* there was a mention of 20 dances. In *Bani* there are additions, and some of these are brought home in Urdu with changed names. In the second section of this chapter there are two tales: the first is about the expression of love between Radha and Kanhaiyya from pages 86–109, and the second tale of Radha and Kanhaiyya is from pages 109–124. These tales are regarded by research scholars as the pioneer work in Urdu drama because the author has not only related the stories, but has also given important instructions regarding its play and acting. The dialogues are written both in poetry and in prose, and along with the dress and attire, in the endnote it is clarified that "*both of these tales are separately prepared and compiled along with 36 innovative dance dramas* (*rahas*)." In the printed copy of *Bani* dialogues, instructions, explanations, and other details are written in a very systematic and methodical way. But in the manuscript of *Bani*, on some pages "*Question-answers on dance dramas of Old Lucknow*" (*Sawal o jawab Rahas Qadeem Lucknow*) is written in the form of a conversation, which also clarifies which part is for dialogue and which part is for acting.

In Chapter Five, from page 124–308, there are nine sections. In the beginning there is a description of Amir Khusro Dehelvi and the joining of street jesters as his followers. After giving a brief introduction about the disciples, he then writes about those plays (*naqlein*) which came to the author's knowledge. In the first section there is mention of two female babblers, in the second section there are five *naqals* about the horses, in the third section there are five *naqals* about the fireworks, in the fourth there are five *naqals* for Bengal, and in the fifth section various other *naqals* have been collected. Their count is 78. Out of these 78, most can be shown through performance. But some of them are vulgar, while some are descriptive and need not be performed. In some of the *naqals*, the changes and addition of verses seems to be the creation of the author. In the sixth section, there are seven *naqals* about sex which are visual or audible. In the last two *naqals*, there is no count given and their importance is not more than a prank. In the seventh section there are four pranks, and in the last there are couplets (*dohars*) presented in *Najo* in the form of songs, which are as questions and answers between the boatman and his lady counterpart in the form of a skit.[549] The eighth section comprises jugglers, and the ninth is about riddles.[550] Between these two sections there is a Ghazal of eight verses.[551] Between this Ghazal and *naqal* 43 and 44, there are funny remarks without any context or heading. [552]

In the first section of the sixth and last chapter (from page 308–365), first there are details of the names of those Begmats, including their titles and allowances, who were appointed to perform in the dance dramas. There were 22 such groups and minstrels, and the name of every musician who accompanied these groups is also given. Thereafter there are the names of prominent *'mahlats'*, the names of the *'mutai wives'*, their children, and finally

549. *Najo - Md.* Wajid Ali Shah Akhtar. Matbaey Sultani. Calcutta. 1296. 78–275.

550. *Bani* (Manuscript) – Md. Wajid Ali Shah Akhtar (MWASA) Sultani Publication. Calcutta, 1877. (Khuda Baksh). 304–5.

551. *Ibid,* 217–18.

552. *Ibid.*

the names of people who were associated with the royal house and who were the recipients of titles. In the second section there are names of animals, trees, gardens, and the buildings constructed by him. There are two addendums at the end of the chapter by the heading *'Qanoon Akhtar'*, which are dated 18 Safar 1294 A.H. Out of these the first one is divided into two parts. In the first part there are eight instructions for the Begmats as to how they should behave with the servant-strangers (*na mehram*). In the second part there are instructions for the servants regarding how they should take care of the prestige of their masters. In the second addendum there are 20 instructions for the Begmats regarding their dress code, mannerisms regarding entry and exit, and other moral codes of conduct.

In *Qata'at e Tarikh* the first three *Qata'as* are in Persian by *Wazirul Sultan Nawab* Amir *Ali Khan* Amir. Then there are the *Qata'as* of Darakhshan, *Bahar, Aish*, Mayil, *Bartar, Malik ud Daulah Saulat, Qayas*, Mukhlis ud Daulah Mukhlis, Raja Ganga Prasad Badr, Khulasatul Daulah Munshi Ali Naqi Bahadur, Agha Haju Sharaf, Nudrat ud Daulah Nadir, Abdul Hakim Khawar, Mehdi Hasan Ahsan, Munshi Ali Bakhsh Hashim, Maharaja Jigo Gopal Saqib, Mir Hasan Jan Zia, Riyaz, Mir Syed Ali Humayun, Mir Kazim Hussain Jauhar, (Atarud Daulah) Mohsin, and Raees ud Daulah Bahadur in the same order. In *Qata'at e Tarikh*, as usual there are *Qata'as* in Persian, Urdu, and Hindi, and these are composed in hijri, fasli, Gregorian, and *samvat* years. An interesting point in these *qata'as* is that there are three different years – 1293, 1294, 1295 – shown for their writing and compilation. There can be no other reason behind this than the fact that *Bani* should have been published in the year 1293 A.H., but there was an extraordinary delay in printing, and hence some *qata'as* were published on the basis of the year of compilation,[553] in some the year of compilation and writing is 1294 A.H.,[554]

553. See the *Qata'ats* of Saqib and Mohsin in *Bani.*

554. See, the *Qata'ats* of Amir, Darakhshan, Hunar, *Bartar, Badr, Munshi Ali Naqi,* Sharaf, *Hashim, Zia, Jauhar* and Mohsin in *Bani.*

and in some the correct year of publication is 1295 A.H.[555] Both the *Qata'as* of Hindi are mentionable for their poetic clarity:

Long live the head with the Crown,
Charming and attractive bride is so endearing
Bartar (name) has saved the date with constant talks
Dear! The bride is all smiling, gorgeous endearing
(65, 65, 13, 62, 320,10, 295, 204, 251 = Fasli 1295 A.H.)

The *Qata'a* is of Hamid ud Dulah Syed Mahmud Ali Khan Bartar. Another *Qata'a is* by Raees ud Daula Bahadur: *'Make a charming bride and show her to me.'*

Mulk e Akhtar (Manuscript)

Written: 1291–95 A.H., Language: Urdu, Poetry/Persian Prose
Genre: Collection of Compositions
Printing: 1295 A.H., Format: 28×17.5, Pages: 101, Lined - 11
Start page 2, end page 199

The manuscript starts with praise to Allah *the Creator of All the World.*

In the manuscript there is no seal from the beginning to the end. But the following two lines, written neatly on the first page of the manuscript, are more valuable than the royal seal. The words not only reveal the timing of the printing of the work or which copy it was printed from, but the eloquent expression and clear instructions indicate whose style of writing this is. This handwritten copy of *Mulk e Akhtar* was compiled for the printing press, and it is written clearly in red and black ink. Up to page 34, the pages of handwritten and printed copies are the same. On page 35 and 36 the poetry is written in the style of prose. In the following pages, there are very slight differences. The changes which were made in the handwritten copy were

---

555. See the *Qata'ats* of Amir, Bahadur, *Aish,* Mayil, *Bartar, Saulat, Qayas, Mukhlis, Nadar, Khawar, Hashim, Riyaz* and *Humayun* in *Bani.*

followed in the printing copy. But there were some changes made in the printed copy for which there are no instructions found in the handwritten copy. The following examples clarify this:

A. The final sentence of the handwritten copy "*Barai takhliya makaan... (ta)... zabardasti nashud*" is not found in the printed copy, nor is any instruction to delete it given in the handwritten copy. [556]

B. In the handwritten copy there is a heading "*Suba doom dar rubayat dar matam* Imam Hussain *Alaiss salam.*" In the printed copy, the heading is in different words. "*Suba doom dar rubayat wa qata'at wan ek sad and.*"[557]

C. In the printed copy the words "*naql shrah wa dastkhat khaas*" were and there is an explanation for them afterwards, but in the handwritten copy there[558] are only the four words.

From the above-mentioned examples, it would not be wrong to infer that the writing of the printed copy was likely done by keeping this copy in front, and the changes which are seen in the printed copy must have been the result of proof-reading by the author. At the end of the handwritten copy, there are instructions in Urdu with the heading "*Aabdust lene wale ke ahkam saat dafa*", the date of which is 6 *Jamadiul Awwal* 1295 A.H. In the printed copy, there are no such instructions. There is also a *Qata'e Tarikh* which is not found in the handwritten copy.

Mulk e Akhtar (Printed)

Written: 1291–95 A.H., Language: Urdu, Poetry/Persian Prose,
Genre: Collection of Compositions,

556. *Mulk e Akhtar*, (Handwritten) Md. Wajid Ali Shah Akhtar. Matbaey Sultani. Calcutta 1296. 199 & 204.

557. *Ibid*, 20.

558. *Ibid*, 196 & 201.

Printing: 1296 A.H., Format: 24×16, Page: 103, Lined - 11,
Printed: Badarul Imarat Calcutta during Ramadhan 1296 A.H. in Matbaey Sultani with the support of Jaan Nisar Raeesud Daulah.
Start page 2, end page 204

In the margin there is a flower pattern, and in the four initial lines the name of the author and the date of publication are given. In the centre of the title page, with the help of flowery plates, the name of the book along with the date is given. On the second and third page, as usual there were ornamental margins and before the *Bismillah* plate, there is a flowery arched niche. In the poetry, the names of the poetic meter (*beher*) and components are written in one line, in bold letters. Up to page 160 is the poetry part of the collection. In the following pages, there are some writings in prose. In the last part, on page 205, there are two Persian *Qata'at e Tarikh* by the *Darogah* of Royal library (*Atar ud Daulah*) Md. Ali Mohsin. From the two *Qata'as*, the dates of 1295 A.H. and 1294 A.H. is inferred from the first and second *qata'as* respectively. The book was published during the middle of 1296 A.H. The difference in dates is perhaps because the book was supposed to be published in 1295 A.H., but for some unknown reason the year passed by, and it could not be published. The last page of the book is blank. On this page in the printed copies, there is the seal of the royal library. There are mistakes in the writing of *Mulk e Akhtar* and these were not corrected properly.[559] In the Preface, after the formal expression of *hamd*, *naat*, and *manqibat*, the author writes in detail his lineage, the reason behind the historical name of the book, and a brief account of various chapters.

"I, the humble and meek, who is so small before the Almighty Allah *at the pleasure of* Wajid Ali Shah *(May* Allah *bestows His benevolence on him) collect the trove of my humble prose and poetry in the month of Muharram in the year 1295 so that my companions are pleased, that by* Allah*'s grace I have divided this writing into six Chapters and have given it the chronogram*

559. See, *Mulk e Akhtar* pp. 37,39,135 & 170.

> *name (Tarikhi naam) of Mulk e Akhtar that there were different years in it... now I am absolved of the anxiety regarding the date and year."* (Translated From Persian)

In the six parts (*suba*) as mentioned in the Preface, five are in poetry, and one is in prose. In the first part there are 44 *qata'as* for dirge chanting (Soz). They are written with *rag raginis* which should be followed while reciting the dirge. In the second part there are 101 *qata'as,* out of which 95 were probably composed for reciting in the *majlises* (congregations). The last few *qata'as* in which the names of the Begmats are used as a '*radif*' are surprisingly included in this part. In the third part there are all sorts of incomplete and varied compositions. In this part only the first couplets (*matlas*) are in the name of the Begmats, and "*Mukkhammas Barabiyat* Nasiruddin *Shenshah Mansoob Iran*" (11 verses) is one of the 45 ill-assorted and mismatched parts (*zila*). In the fourth part there are first 70 *salams*, then 24 Ghazals in the *radif* of '*alif*', '*bay*', '*dal*', '*ray*', '*noon*', '*wow*', and '*chhoti yey*' are collected. Among *Salams*, one is in the famous line (*tarah*) of Mir Anis: "*hum aasman se laye hain in zaminon ko.*" In the second part of *Kulliyat Imaan*, all these *Salams* are collected. There is no proof of the re-publication of the Ghazals. In the fifth part there are 13 *masnavis*. Among these the heading of the first *masnavi* is '*tars o beem*' which is in Persian. The remaining are the letters written to the Begums. In the beginning of the sixth part there are five writings in prose. The first is advice and suggestions in Persian, dated 3 Rabiul Awwal 1292 A.H., and the second is rules and regulations for the caretakers of fish. The third contains different types of instructions for servants, in Urdu, and is dated 6 Ramadhan 1294 A.H. The fourth is *Andaz* Akhtari, in the pattern of '*Nasah e* Akhtari', which is written in Persian and describes the code of conduct in congregations and parties. The fifth is a copy of orders in the name of Zulfiquar ud Daulah Bahadur, dated 6 Shawwal 1275 A.H., which, because of the good authorship in Persian, have been included here. The questions asked by the King in terms of religious problems (*Sharai*) before Maulvi Mirza Md. Ali *Sahab* and the replies of Maulvi Sahab *Maghfoor*, in the pattern of *Behre Hidayat*, are included in this part (*suba*). There are 42 of these questions. As per the Preface and the information given in the sixth section, the book should have been concluded here, but there were two more additions. The first is the agreement (comprising 26 sections) about the royal zoo which is addressed to Haider Ali *Jamadar*, dated 29 Rabiul Sani 1295 A.H. The second one is a document addressed to Mirza *Jahan Quder*, in which he mentions the oppression by the British rulers, and his own humbleness and humility is written in brief. There is no signature and date on it. In the addendum of *Riyaz ul Quloob*, these complaints are explained in detail.

In the manuscript titled *Gulzar e Hussaini* there are *salams*, *qata'a*, and *nohas* composed by the King. At the end of this copy, many pages are blank, and the compositions are not arranged well. In one place, there are some *qata'as* before which is written "*Ibtidaey Kashkol* Akhtari", and in some places the names of *raag raginis* are written in the hand of the King. In these different types of compositions, there is a symbol like a '*swad*' (page 315); perhaps this is an indication of copying. The main part of the first two sections (*subas*) of *Mulk e Akhtar* (Handwritten) is taken from this same '*Gulzar e Hussaini.*' In *Mulk e Akhtar*, the mismanagement of sections and the continuous change of names indicate that this book started with "*Kashkol* Akhtari", and when the *nohas* and *salams* were added then it was renamed "*Gulzar Hussaini.*" When the Ghazals and poetic letters were added, then it was called "*Mulk e Akhtar*" as included in the list of *Bani.* When this collection was about to be published, on the title page and in the Preface was written *Mulk e Akhtar*, which is its last and correct name.

Malazul Kalmat

Written: 1266–97 A.H., Language: Urdu, Persian, Genre: Dictionary
Printing: 1297 A.H., Format: 33×22, Pages: 373, Lined - 15,
Printed: At Matbaey Sultani (Calcutta) with the support of Raees ud Daulah Zevar
Start page 2, end page 689.

On the title page, in very fine print, the name of the book, the author's name, the publisher's name, the name of the supervisor of printing, the date of publication, and other related details are entered. On pages 2 and 3 there is an attractive margin and on page 2, below the *Bismillah* plate, *hamd* and the Preface start. There is an appreciation of Allah and after the *manqibat* on pages 4 and 5 the reason behind the compilation is explained. From the last line of page 5, the dictionary starts. The first word is '*abaat*'. Words are written in the old style in bold. To make the search easier, some words are also written in the margin. The arrangement of words should have been in alphabetical order, and the chapters and sections on the basis of the alphabet were intended for this, but the changes which were made later left them in disarray. After '*khurd*', '*haram*', and after '*haram*', '*jurm*' are such examples which are frequently seen. At the end, on page 689, there is a portion under the heading '*Zamimaey malazul kalmat*', which is the poetry section. In this part, first only in the *radif* of '*alif*' there are some Ghazals, then a poetic letter to his sister *Afsar Bahu Begum.* After this there are "*Qata'at, Quatrains and Quintuple*", *masnavi* '*Chanchal*', and finally the '*harziaa*' of 64 verses. On the last three pages, there are four *qata'as* by *Shahzada* Mirza *Md.* Jalal *Sabir, Aatar ud Daulah Mohsin*, *Maharaja* Jai Gopal Saqib, and *Syed Md. Ismail Hafiz.* At the end is the seal of the royal library.

Shehzada Mirza Jalal was the son of Sadar Mahal *Sadr.*[560] His penname was Jalal.[561] In the beginning perhaps his pen name was *Sabir*. In the list of *Bani*, the dictionary with the title of "*Lugat Haft zaban*"[562] is the same as this dictionary. But at that time, this book was incomplete and was not given a title. By the time it was completed, words of five or more languages were included, and on the suggestion of one of the students of the compiler, the

560. Printed by B.S. Press Calcutta. 1913. 36.

561. Shehzada Mirza Jalal died in 1906. He left no child behind. (Geneological Tree of Avadh Family, 11). One of his '*Ishqiya masnavi*' "*Nagma-e Dardul Maroof ba Sarguzasht hijr*" has been published. In it his pen name was Jalal.

562. *Bani* (Manuscript) – Md. Wajid Ali Shah Akhtar (MWASA) Sultani Publication. Calcutta, 1877. (Khuda Baksh). 243.

title chosen was "*Malazul Kalmat*".[563] The date indicated by the name was 1293 A.H. Based on the date of printing, which was 1297 A.H., one could say that the compilation work was done between 1293–1297 A.H., but this is not true. The compilation work started much before 1293 A.H. In *Bani* (Handwritten), it is mentioned in the same way as it was in *Bani* printed. In *Bani* (Handwritten), the list was written in 1292 A.H.[564] In this way, the idea to write a dictionary and a major part of its work must have been done before the compiling of the *Bani* list, otherwise there would be no mention of it in 1292 A.H. But its name was suggested after the publication of *Bani*, because in *Bani* the name of the dictionary was not given. Instead, it is addressed as "*Lughat Haft zaban*". The date-wise name (*tarikhi naam*) was mismatched, hence it was necessary to fix the date of compilation, but there is no explanation pointing towards this fact. In *Malaz ul Kalmat*, in places there is proof of *Bahar e Ajam*. The handwritten copies of *Bahar e Ajam* were under the King's perusal for quite a long time, and he continued writing notes in its margin.[565] In places, he differed from the 'proof', while in places he supplied the 'proof'. Thus, his inclination and interest in writing a dictionary is evident from the writing given in the margins of *Bahar e Ajam*. In this *Bahar e Ajam* there is a description of a dream which is mentioned on page 124 of '*Ishq nama Manzoom*.' Based on this evidence, it can be inferred that some work, whether intentionally or by way of interest, had started before 1266 A.H., and was presented in the form of *Malazul Kalmat* in 1297 A.H.

In spite of the fact that the dictionary pertains to 12 languages, the important words of any language are not found in it. The pronunciation of words, instead of being on the principle of vowels, was only verbal, and at

563. *Malazul Kalmat*- Md. Wajid Ali Shah Akhtar, Matbaey Sultani, Calcutta. 1297. (Azad Library). 5.

564. *Supra Note* 561 at 219–20.

565. The four copies of *Bahar e Ajam* on which there is seal of the royal Library (Calcutta) and there is written '*Asad Manzil*' are at present in the Ittihadia Library Calcutta. The writing on the third copy explains that it was written on the desire of *Fatehud Daulah* Bahadur, signed by Mir Hamid Ali on 24th of *Shawwal* month 1264.

places name of the dictionary from which they are retrieved is mentioned. From the language of the Preface, it is obvious that the compiler was aware of his limitations:

> *"My humble self has some share in the Urdu language. I felt that I should also try other languages, as many languages are on my mind."*

The author included the words of 12 languages because he was the follower of *Twelve Imams* (*Ithna Ashri*) *and* regarded the figure of '*twelve*' as a good omen. The 12 languages of *Malazul Kalmat* according to the compiler are as follows:

1. *Taazi (Arabic)*
2. *Combination of Arabic & Persian*
3. *Persian*
4. *Turkish*
5. *Italia*
6. *Sanskrit*
7. *Bhakha or Kohi (Brij)*
8. *Punjabi*
9. *Ethiopian (Habshi)*
10. *Bengali*
11. *Kash*Miri
12. *Urdu (Mualla)*

After knowing the motive behind compilation of *Malazul Kalmat*, it is futile to complain about its shortcomings, but its usefulness deserves attention. In it there are only hearsay words of foreign languages, hence their number is low. By '*Italia*' is perhaps meant Italian or Latin, but the words found in the dictionary are from the English language, for example 'Dog', 'Miss', 'my Dear', 'March', 'Finger', 'From', 'Come', 'Camp', 'Committee', and 'Company'. To explain the meaning of these words, it was not necessary to have good command over the language. Today, these words are in common use but including them in the dictionary shows that even 100 years ago, these words had entered the common parlance. Hence, it was necessary to give their meaning. The compiler did not write this dictionary for the sake of writing a dictionary; its purpose was to benefit others with his own knowledge, and its importance and distinction lies in the fact that the words which are usually neglected and overlooked by the writers of other dictionaries were given importance by the compiler of *Malazul Kalmat.*

Before Wajid Ali Shah, another King, Ghaziuddin Haider, had compiled a dictionary titled *Haft Qulzum*, where in the context of the Red Sea (*Qulzum*), its different parts such as lake, waves, stream and bank were included. Apart from these words, he had also collected other knowledge. This voluminous book was in fact the encyclopedia of that time, and was published by *Sultan ul Mutabey* in October 1820 (*Muharram* 1236 A.H.).[566] An English traveler, Heber, mentions that this book was much valued in Europe.[567] Quite possibly, this *Haft Qulzum* inspired Wajid Ali Shah to write *Lughat Haft Zaban.* In the Preface of *Malazul Kalmat,* along with other books, *Haft Qulzum* is mentioned:

> *"Even Haft Qulzum before the art of dictionary writing is equivalent to a drop."*
> (Translated from Persian)

But *Malazul Kalmat* is only a dictionary, and due to the indulgence of the compiler, instead of seven languages it contains 12 languages.

---

566. It was published in large format. A termite-ridden copy of this voluminous book is found in the Palace Library of Murshidabad. On every page is printed the crown of Ghaziuddin Haider and its printing is excellent. Perhaps for this reason the type of the book was brought from London. This book could not be found in other libraries in India.

567. The appreciation of *Maulvi Qubool Muhammad* and *Qazi Md.Sadiq Khan Akhtar are* seen in *"Haft Qulzum."* Maybe these people worked with him. The trustworthy Captain of Ghaziuddin Haider, Locutt, had assured his guest Heber that there are competent people who could compile such a comprehensive book. (*See Heber D.D.*: Narrative of a Journey through Upper Provinces of India. (1824–25). London. 1829. 75.

Tosha e Akhrat

The above-mentioned book is *Tosha-e -Akhrat.* Its 4 handwritten parts were recovered from the sealed treasure of Imambarah Sibtainabad Mubarak in Calcutta under the name *Deh Majlis.* At the time of the publication of *Bani,* it was not named as such. But it is entered in the list of *Bani as* "...four or five books of poetic elegies and misfortunes of the *Martyrs of* Karbala which have not been counted." [568]

However, the account of the book is given here under the name with which it was known at that time – *Deh Majlis.*

Deh Majlis, Volume I Language: Persian, Handwritten, Format: 24×15

In this beautifully written copy, in the format of 24x15, in the three vertically drawn margins three verses are written in a slanting direction. Above each elegy, the heading and date is given in a golden, ornamental pattern. After this there is a note in Persian which explains the purpose of writing this treatise. The elegies with the following first lines are found in it.

	Elegy Heading	**Topic**	**Year**	**Verses**
	Instead of food and water Hussain suffers arrow	About Hazrat Abbas	1277	54
	Subjects of Allah are aware of the mysteries of Allah	About Hazrat Abbas	1278	89
	Ask the Nightingale about the mysteries of the Garden	About Hazrat Ali Akbar	1279	136
	The old sky mourns the death of young Akbar	ImamHussain	1280	102

568. *Bani* (Manuscript). Md. Wajid Ali Shah Akhtar (MWASA) Sultani Publication. Calcutta. 1877. (Khuda Baksh, Avadh). 243.

	Due to the injured army the world mourns	Hazrat Abbas	1281	128
	Heart does not get rid of Hussain's mourning	Imam Hussain	1281	94
	The old sky mourns the death of youngsters	Hazrat Abbas	1282	117
	The mention of Al e Aba pains the heart	Hazrat Ali Akbar	1282	105
	God's friend is the King of all	Hazrat Ali Akbar	1283	115
	The pious book which is...	Arrest of Family	1284	95

The above arrangement appears to be based on the year of composition. In *Tosha e Akhrat* there are separate elegies. The count of verses everywhere is done systematically, and in both places the number is the same as above, with a few changes in words. Out of the above elegies, the first three were published in Qamar Mazmun, and have also been included here.

Deh Majlis Volume II, Handwritten Format: 23×15

Written in the Format 23x15, the second copy of '*Deh Majlis*' has the same style as the first copy but is written with more care. It is in Persian script and was written by high-quality writers. The purpose behind its compilation is written in the following words;

> *This book of elegies is written by His Excellency the King... all these were composed in the beginning of 1284 A.H. and it was named by the King as Deh Majlis in 1289 A.H.*
> (Translated From Persian)

On the last page (page 366), the year and the name of the supervisor is different:

> *Deh Majlis is completed in 1289 A.H. under the aegis of Raees ud Daulah.*

In this collection the elegies are in the following order:

	Elegy Heading	Topic	Year	Verses
	The first line of Mustafa's Diwan is Shere Khuda	About Hazrat Ali	1284	69
	May Allah never estrange any friend	About Hazrat Imam Hussain	1285	103
	The story of martyrs pierces my heart	Martyr of Imam Hussain	1286	100
	Ali's head got a taste of the sword	Hazrat Ali	1286	101
	The new moon is camouflaged with sorrow	Hazrat Abbas	1287	10
	Huda has the same name of Allah	Hazrat Ali	1287	84
	Ask the ironsmith the sharpness of the strong head	Hazrat Ali Akbar	1288	123
	God give me the taste and craziness	Hazrat Ali	1288	122
	Qasim! ...	Hazrat Qasim	Muharram 1289	98
	How the heart is relieved of tragedy	Hazrat Imam Hussain	1289	56

In *Tosha e Akhrat*, the arrangement of the above elegies is like this: 8, 51, 59, 9, 30, 10, 38, 11, 27, and 52. The number of verses is the same, only there are changes in words in some places. The third elegy, '*The new moon is camouflaged with sorrow*', was issued as a booklet with the support of *Raees ud Daulah* Bahadur on 25 Zilhij 1287 A.H. In the same way, the 7th and 9th elegies were issued in the form of a booklet in the same year that they were compiled. At that time, the 7th Elegy had only 50 verses.

Deh Majlis, Volume III, Handwritten Format: 24×16

In this beautifully written copy in the format of 24x16, on every page there were three verses (bund), and on some pages there were two verses. The number of pages is not continuous, the numbers have been missed in some places. The verses are counted in every elegy. The last elegy is written in a two-column style with 11 lines. In some elegies, an explanation is given in between the lines or in the margin. In the last elegy there are different headings, and all are given in red ink. In the beginning there is a list of elegies, and the following sentence is written:

'Completed today: 25 Zilhij *1293 A.H.'*

	Elegy Heading	Topic	Verses
	Better than any thought is the memory of Uqba	About arrest of The family	101
	The tragedy of Hussain is not related to anything	About Hazrat Muslim	105
	The mention of the plight of Hussain Ibn Ali brings sorrow	Hazrat Hur	86
	The daughter of Ali was brought before Umar	Hazrat Imam Zainul Abdin	114
	Accepting Mustafa is mandatory after Khuda	Hazrat Imam Hasan	85
	All the seven skies are obedient to the Almighty	Hazrat Ali	96
	Ahmed has control over Jibreel	Hazrat Abbas	100
	When the family came to the prison bare headed	Arrest of family	50
	My pen is inscribing a Miracle	Prophet Md.	98
	When *Qaaf* (mountain) was conquered then there was brightness	Hazrat Imam Md. Baqar	134

In *Tosha e Akhrat*, the arrangement is different, which means that instead of the arrangement shown above, these elegies are given in this order: 65, 22, 23, 14, 13, 12, 43, 66, 1, and 15. The number of verses (bund) is the same as in the handwritten copy, though there are slight changes in words. The third, fourth, and seventh elegies were published in the form of a separate booklet with the support of Raees ud Daulah Bahadur by Matbaey Sultani, Calcutta in 1295 A.H. The date-wise name (*Tarikhi naam*) was *Nazm Tarikhi* (1295 A.H.). This elegy was also published in the form of a booklet by Matbaey Sultani, Calcutta with the support of *Raees ud Daulah* Bahadur in *Ramadhan* 1295 A.H. On the title page, the date wise name is given.[569]

Deh Majlis – Volume IV- Handwritten-Format 27×18
Matbaey Sultani, *Calcutta in Jamadiul Sani in 1290.*
Pages 352.

Like the above mentioned three copies (volumes), its name is also given as "*Deh Majlis*" but it neither has ten elegies nor is much attention given to its writing. The introduction, subject matter, and year of its composition are also not given. On every page there are usually three verses (*bund*). In the beginning, there is a list of the elegies of this collection, and on page 106 this sentence is written:

By the order of his Excellency it is being put into writing by Md. Amir *bin Jawahar 27 Ramadhan 1289 A.H.*

	Elegy Heading	Topic	Verses
	Fourteen selves are the Saviour of the hardships of the world	Hazrat Imam Hussain	100
	The Sun should not be without shine in the sky	About Hazrat Imam Hussain	100
	Yadullah is the shatterer of Khyber gate	Hazrat Ali	116

569. This booklet was seen only in the library of Riyasat Mehmoodabad.

	Hussain Ibn Ali is the healer of all pain	Hazrat Ali Akbar	116
	The Face of Hussain is the reflection of the Prophet	Hazrat Imam Hassian	89
	Amirul Momineen is Shah Mukkaram, his name is Maula	Hazrat Ali	124
	This composition be accepted....	Janab Aun o Md.	117
	When the news of Martyr of Husain came	Events of Karbala	55
	Pretty eyes, great height, handsome body	Hazrat Imam Jafar e Sadiq	37
	Truly Hussain is the image of Mustafa	Arrest of the family	81

In *Tosha e Akhrat*, the arrangement of the above 11 elegies is given as 56, 53, 6, 42, 58, 7, 25, 60, 16, 63 and 57. The fifth elegy was published from Matbaey Sultani, Calcutta. An incomplete copy of the third elegy, like the other booklets, is in the format of 24x16. As the title page is missing, its exact date of publication is not known.[570]

Printed Elegies in the form of a Booklet

The handwritten copies of the four aforementioned collections of 41 elegies are part of the *Tosha e Akhrat.*

A	**First line (*misra*) of the Elegy Heading**	**Topic**	**Verses**	**As in TA[571]**
	In the world the birds are flying ...	Hazrat Ali	36	3
	Shabbir does good even to the evil	Ali Akbar	31	35

570. Proprietor of the Copy: Dr. Khalilur Rehman, Department of Urdu, Aligarh Muslim University, Aligarh.

571. *Tosha e Akhrat* - Md. Wajid Ali Shah Akhtar. Matbaey Sultani. Calcutta.1299 A.H.

	The sword of Asadullah is raised	Hazrat Imam Hussain	49	49
	Friends! let me weep today	Arrest of family	42	61
	The darling Prophet went to Heaven	Hazrat Imam Hassian	44	50
	In this world no brothers are separated	Janab Abbas	56	68
	The heart is devastated	Janab Qasim	50	26
	I am sacrificed at the altar of pious Hussain	Hazrat Ali Akbar	54	36
	Yadullah is the owner of the Sun	Hazrat Ali	43	4
	Sons of Muslim are amidst devastation	Sons of Muslim	63	47
	Strange tide of sorrow surrounds me	Janab Ali Asghar	152	46
	Friends this is month of Muharram	Janab Ali Asghar	43	45
	There is autumn in the garden of Mustafa today	Janab Abdullah Ibn Hasan	44	48
	The status of Shabbir is higher than the Sun	Janab Aun o Md.	54	24
	Family of Prophet bestows blessings	Arrest of Family	32	64
	In the garden of this world Murtuza is like an injured bird	Hazrat Ali	44	5
	The flowers and petals are pierced with tragedy	Hazrat Abbas	24	29

	Fatima is the healer of all sorrow	Janab Fatima Zehra	59	2
	Murtuza's darling is excellent and superb	Janab Ali Akbar	40	27

All the aforementioned handwritten booklets of *Deh Majlis* had a printed title page, and on every page, there were three verses (*bund*). In these booklets there is neither any printed title page nor is the name of the author, publisher, or year of publication given. Every booklet starts with a blank page of the format of 27×21, and on every page there are two verses. The first four lines (*misras*) are written in the slanting square, and then in one line there is a couplet (*bait*) in two sockets. Below it there is another verse presented in the same way. The writing is in bold letters and the printing is elegant. Perhaps these copies were the first copies of Matbaey Sultani, Calcutta. On the first page of this collection there are two big and small seals of the royal library. In places there are changes and deletions in the King's hand. In *Tosha e Akhrat* these corrections have been taken care of. The first three elegies from the above list, and the 5th, 6th, and the 19th, were first published in *Kulliyat e Soom*, then they were released in the form of booklet, and then they were included in *Tosha e Akhrat.*

By including all the elegies of the "five, four books" mentioned in the list of *Bani*, there are nine elegies which are found nowhere except in *Tosha e Akhrat.* These are as follows:

A	**First line (*misra*) of the Elegy Heading**	**Topic**	**Verses**	**As in TA**[572]
	The tearful eye is gotten from the cloud	Hazrat Imam Musiey Kazim	172	17
	The entire world is with Imam Raza	Hazrat Imam Raza	93	18

572. *Ibid.*

	O! The sorrowful fate write the plight of ninth Imam	Hazrat Imam Md. Taqi	91	9
	Ali Naqi the 10th. Imam is like full Moon	Hazrat Imam Ali Naqi	59	20
	Rise me above with Hasan Askari	Hazrat Imam Hasan Askari	78	21
	Why is the sky so melancholy	Janab Ali Akbar	165	44
	The eyes of Shirin were liked	Arrest of Family	48	67
	Why is the moon lamenting	Arrest of Family	54	36
	After two hundred and fifty-five days of Hijrat	Birth of Imam Zamana	150	69

Of these elegies, the first one was perhaps composed in 1296 A.H. because it was in this year, in the month of Zilhij, that Matbaey Sultani, Calcutta published it in the form of a booklet in the five-lined style over 25 pages. On the ornamental title page, the name of the book is filled with the drawing of a flower.[573] Other elegies were likely composed to complete the collection because the elegists do not usually compose elegies about the above-mentioned spiritual leaders or Imams as given in the previous Table. How many more collections in addition to those from *Tosha e Akhrat* were published in the form of booklets is not known.

Tosha e Akhrat (Printed)

Written: 1267–99 A.H., Language: Urdu, Genre: Collection of Elegies, Format: 30×20, Pages: 743, Written in Boxes. Antique Style.
Printed: 1299 A.H.
Printed by Matbaey Sultani, Calcutta with the support of Raees ud Daulah

573. This booklet was seen only in the library of Mahmudabad estate. (Riyasat).

In the middle is the name of the book, and in the last line is the name of the publisher and the supervisor. Before the name of the book, in light words over four lines, it is written the *Collection of Elegies*, and the name of the author along with his title and the date of publication is given. From page 2 up to the last page, every page is divided into four portions. In every portion the initial verses of sixtains are given in a slanting style, and the couplet (*bait*) is written in the old style. The counting of verses (bunds) is continuous, and the words are written either in the margins or between the lines. The printing is as per the standard of Matbaey Sultani. By the watermark on the paper, it appears that it is the bond paper of 1881. On pages 1023 to 1032, there is an elegy of *Hazrat Ali Asghar* which is written in the style of a *masnavi* in a 15-lined format.

In *Tosha e Akhrat*, on pages 2 and 3, instead of a list "*izhar o sabab kaifiyat Ijtima Marsia ha*" is written in eight verses of poetry. It goes like this:

After the Hamd is the Naat

....

Wajid Ali says loss to enemy
His pen name is Akhtar and his heart is sad
In Calcutta there is a place, Metiaburj
(here) For 26 years there is a reciter of Imam's name
One less than seven elegies were there
These are collected with much effort
And there was an arrangement of Elegies
There is one about Ahmed Mursal (Prophet PBUH)
The second one is for Sayyeda
How she is still restless in her grave
Ten are about Hazrat Mushkilkusha
The other one is about the great Hasan
There is one about Zain ul Aba
Another one laments about Baqar

There is one for Sadiq and one for Kazim
One is regarding the sufferings of Imam Zamin wa Samin
One is about Taqi, one about Naqi
And one for Hasan Askari
One is about the tragedy of Muslims
Again one for the tragedy of Hur
Two about Zainab's dear ones
May Allah *gives reward in return*

Weepingly two were composed for Qasim
About Abbas there are seven
About Akbar there are ten
Two about six-monthly Asghar
One is for the dear of Muslims
And one for Ibn Hasan
Whose name was Abdullah the pride
In ten is given the martyrdom of (Hussain)
Hussain the heart of Fatima
In two is written the tale of messenger of Sughra
In six there is relating of arrest of the family
The devastation of the family of Prophet
In one there is about Shirin
In another it is about the tragedy of Hind
May the Shah have mercy on us
No other sorrow but this, no other mourning but this

Akhtar looks for solution from Ali
Ahmed! I am looted in Hind I cry for help
The family of Prophet is here
This name (Tosha e Akhrat) is my last treasure
Written in 1298 A.H.
And presented on Panchshamba

In this poetic introduction it is only explained how many elegies were composed and in whose service. If a list is made of the above numbers, then it will be as per the arrangement of elegies in *Tosha e Akhrat*. There are 68 elegies in sixtains, one in masnavi, and the count of verses including the poetic introduction must be 5,650. The *Masnavi* has 152 verses.

Riyaz ul Uqba

Written: 1267–99 A.H., Language: Urdu, Genre: Collection of Elegies, Printing: 1300 A.H., Format: 30×20, Pages: 283, Boxed Type-Setting Printed: At Matbaey Sultani (Calcutta) with the support of Raeesud Daulah Zevar

After the printed title page there is a list of 27 pages. Thereafter, the series of elegies start. This book is printed in the style of *Tosha e Akhrat*.[574] The difference is that in *Tosha e Akhrat* there were all the elegies of Wajid Ali Shah, while in *Riyaz ul Uqba* there are selected ones. In *Tosha e Akhrat*, other than the 14 *Masoomeens*, there are elegies regarding some of the Martyrs of Karbala. In *Riyaz ul Uqba*, one elegy for each is taken to reduce the bulk. The number of verses (*bunds*) is the same as *Tosha e Akhrat*. 26 elegies out of 69 were selected and hence, it reduced the size to one third.

Only one elegy, '*Which moon rose in Medina*', which contains 141 verses (*bunds*) about Imam Hussain, was not in *Tosha e Akhrat*, and is found in *Riyaz ul Uqba*. It is quite possible that this was composed between the compilation of *Tosha e Akhrat* and *Riyaz ul Uqba*. Other than *Tosha e Akhrat* and *Riyaz ul Uqba*, the King's elegies were published by other publishers, but they were not new. It is the selected part of both these collections which is published with a new name. These new collections have not added to the compositions of the King, in fact they have caused confusion in the minds of commentators.[575] As compared to *Kulliyat e* Akhtari, there must have been

574. One copy of *Riyaz ul Uqba* is found in Safi Darul Mutaleya.

575. Heading "Books which are wrongly associated" (With the King) can be seen in Chapter 3.

a higher expense in the printing of *Tosha e Akhrat* because this '*kulliyat*' is longer, and the times had changed. The financial condition of the King was also not as promising, perhaps that is why these were selected, as these books were distributed free of cost.

Riyaz ul Quloob (Manuscript)

Written: 1298–99 A.H., Language: Urdu, Genre: Religious Tale,
Printing: 1300 A.H., Format: 33×21, Pages: 167, 15-lined,
Manuscript: Proprietor Library Nawab Salar Jung Museum, Hyderabad-Deccan
Start page 2, end page 334

In the name of Allah *creator of all beings*
Under the favour of the Last Prophet Mustafa
Under the kindness of Shah Ali the duldul rider
The twelve Imams favour me
I am relating a new story
People will remember it
This tale will be memorable
By God's grace it will reach its end.

The manuscript starts from page 2. The first page which was probably blank has been pasted. Up to page 88, on about 44 pages there are gold plated ornamental margins. After this there are no patterns in the margins. In places there are drawings of flowers, leaves, and birds.[576] The main book starts from page 323, and up to the last page 334, as an addendum, there is a copy of the writing containing the dates of his dethronement, his journey to Calcutta, details of his children, a list of his wives like that in *Bani*, and a complaint

576. The detailed list of Urdu books is on page 528 in the manuscript at the Library of Nawab Salar Jung Museum. The compiler of the list in this article writes the same thing. (*Naya Daur* – Monthly – Lucknow -May 1959, page 4). But for the secrets behind these enameled works, see Chapter 5 of this book.

dated 15 May 1878, addressed to the English Officers. The book is written in Persian script, while the addendum is in running hand (*zanjeera*). Ink of many colours has been used in the book. For the elegant writing and other niceties, it is worth displaying this manuscript in an exhibition. The adMirers and connoisseurs of the library did exactly the same. Due to the brittleness of the paper, it could be preserved better with the help of gum, but perhaps this was likely not done as it was feared that it would lose its shine and lustre. The printing of the manuscript was donc around 1300 A.H. or may be after that. On page 323 of the manuscript at the margin there is a couplet:

Three heirs went to Heaven One of them was very feeble

This couplet is from *masnavi Sabatul Quloob*[577] which was started in 1300 A.H.[578]

Riyaz ul Quloob (Printed)

Written: 1298–99 A.H., Language: Urdu, Genre: Religious Tale,
Printing: 1302 A.H., Format: 31.5×20, Pages: 116, 21-lined,
Printed: Matbaey Sultani (Calcutta) with the support of Raees ud Daulah Zevar

The counting of pages starts from the printed title page, on which details of the book, compiler, publisher, supervisor (caretaker of a library), and the date of publication are given. In all four margins on pages 1, 2 and 3, there is a creeper design, and on page 2 there is also a picture of the ornamental plate of *Bismillah*. From page 3 up to the end (except page 25), the margins of every odd-numbered page (*taaq*) provide a brief account of the subject discussed in the text. Other than the introduction, which is written in poetic form, the continuity of lines is undisturbed throughout the book. To highlight the headings, bold words are written. To show the lines of the couplet separately, cubicles with flower pattern is used. After the end of the

577. *Sabatul Quloob* (Handwritten). Volume 1. Md. Wajid Ali Shah Akhtar. 1304. 28.
578. *Ibid*, 13.

book on page 334, the heading "Important Information" is followed by the message below:

> *"Other than the Shia community, I don't allow members of any other community to peruse this book. This book is printed specially for* Shias. *No one should purchase it. This book, after being printed at the royal publication will be distributed free of cost... faqat."* [579]

Below this is the seal of the royal library, which is found in all the copies. No such announcement is found in the other books of Matbaey Sultani. There are many mistakes in the writing in *Riyaz ul Quloob.* But there was no corrigendum in any copy, nor were the mistakes corrected at the relevant place. In most of the copies of *Riyazul Quloob*, there are 224 pages, and thus it was inferred that the supplement which was found in the manuscript was missing in the printed copies.[580] However, this addendum is found in rare copies. The addendum is from pages 225–231 and on the last page, page 232, the above mentioned "Important Information" appears again.[581]

Mulla Md. Baqar Almajlisi Alsafhani (1037–1111 A.H.) wrote an Arabic book titled *Baharul Anwaar.* It had 25 Volumes, and he himself wrote its summary in Persian under the title *Hayatul Quloob* in three volumes for the Persian people. In *Hayatul Quloob*, there is an account of the life of the Prophets, events in the Quran, and the interpretation of '*Hadith*'. These books of *Mulla Majlisi* are regarded very trustworthy by the members of *Ithna Ashri. Riyazul Quloob* is the free translation of the early chapters of the First Volume. In the poetic introduction of 14 verses, the name of the book, its purpose, and its date of compilation, is given in the following words:

---

579. For the reason behind this announcement see *Guzishta Lucknow*; Maulvi Abdul Haleem Sharar. Naseem Book Depot. Lucknow. 87.
580. *Naya Daur* (Monthly, Lucknow). May 1959, 4.
581. The flawless copies without the addendum can be seen in the library of Salar Jung Museum (Hyderabad, Deccan) and in Ittehad Library (Calcutta).

One day it came to my mind
That the community should be benefitted
Hayat ul Quloob which is in Persian
If it comes in Urdu then it will be very good
Then I started the translation
I filled up my glass with good deeds
I gave it the name Riyazul Quloob
So that the Sun of Akhtar never sets
Now on twelve hundred there are ninety eight
Know you gentle man it is the hijri year
In this year I started the work
May Allah *enlightens my heart*

Riyazul Quloob is not the verbatim translation of *Hayatul Quloob*, but the translator has, in places, made deletions and additions and has given it the look of a different compilation. In the beginning, most of it is written in prose, while there are poetic translations of a few individual couplets or verses. On page 163 there is the *Qat'a* of Mir *Taqi Hawas*, and on pages 192–204 there is a newly composed elegy of 116 verses (bunds) by the translator. In the last verse (*maqta*), he prays for himself and for Queen Victoria. The first section of Chapter 5 is mostly in poetic form. After completing this Chapter, the compiler gave up the idea of translating in prose form, and whatever he had translated previously, he began to compose in poetic form instead. The poetic form of the translation comes before us as '*Sabatul Quloob.*' The first section of Chapter 5 and some more verses are taken from *Riyazul Quloob.*[582]

582. For example, some 88 verses from page 247–249 of Volume 1 of *Sabatul Quloob* (Handwritten), without some deletions or additions but with slight changes are extracted from page 211–14 of *Riyazul Quloob.*

Sabatul Quloob (Manuscript 1)

Written: 1300–03 A.H., Language: Urdu, Genre: Religious Epic (Masnavi), Printing: 1303–04 A.H., Format: 21.5×19.5, Pages: 520, 21-lined, Script: Arabic & Persian

Three handwritten copies of this *masnavi* were recovered. All three are incomplete, but very important. It appears that one is the starting one and the other is the concluding one.

From page 2 of Handwritten Copy 2, the following is extracted:

The starting Stanza:

The hearts and life of people
…………………
I come from the deviation path
I observe the prayers of Allah
My thanks be not denied
If I get pain Allah *is the healer*
He is incomparable
He has no parallel in either world
Those who are close to Him
They are in expectation of His rewards

This is Volume 1 of Sabatul Quloob
This is in Urdu language the good one
It is the work of three and a half years
The essays are good, it is pleasing
O! it is four plus thirteen hundred
In this hijri year this tale ends
I drank much blood (worked hard)
Only then I could weave these pearls
Perhaps this will be the means of my salvation

I am requesting the Almighty

(Concluding section, page 1,061, Handwritten Volume 1)

The Handwritten Copy 1 starts with the following couplet in the first line of page 2:

The divine blessings I have in my lap these are seven by your mercy

This is the first copy of the King's *masnavi,* which was made fair by different writers in the presence of the King. It has many pieces of evidence, some of which are presented here:

A. There is a couplet on page 63:

Prophet came to this world with sweet voice
O youth! accept this and remember it

In the first line the writer wrote '*aaey*' after the word '*khush.*' The King marked '*swad*' at the word '*khush*', corrected it and wrote '*awaz*' in the margin. This correction shows that the King noted the writing of the writer.

B. From page 344–364, from 534–538, and from 540–548, in total on 35 pages, on every first line of every page, the first words were written by the King's pen. Perhaps by this, the instruction is given that while making fair the copy of the manuscript, the copyist should begin the page with that particular line (*misra*).

C. In some places, inverted commas were given, but the space was left blank. This may be because at the time of making the fair copy, the copyist was either unable to read those words or some words were missing. There could be no person other than the King who could tell us about filling in the gaps. There are some more characteristics of this manuscript which are given below.

i. Three or more writers wrote different parts of this manuscript. The content which is on page 524 is missing on page 525, the page which is on page 524 and 525 is not on page 731.
ii. Two pages (443–444 and 457–458) have been changed for some reason. There is a line joining them.
iii. Pages 130–131, 142–143, 138–139, 532–533, and 614–615 are separated, but this has not caused any disturbance because on every page, the words which are given in its support are the words from where the left side of the page starts.
iv. The margin of five pages (pages 57–58, 59–60, 117–118, 303-304, and 379–380) of Manuscript 1 has been vertically cut from the side. In Manuscript 2, there are added verses in the margin.

The first page of the manuscript and the lower part of the last page are missing. Some other pages are torn. The numbering of pages is done by the copyist. There are two couplets in each line and on every page, there are 42 verses. The first or last couplet is written in the middle of the line to demarcate the sections. Arabic matter is written in Arabic script in red ink and the couplets in the heading are also in red. The meaning of difficult words is given between the lines or in the margin in light ink. Where the copyist has made small mistakes, they have been corrected neatly.

Sabatul Quloob (Manuscript 2)

Written: 1300 A.H., Language: Urdu, Genre: Religious Epic (Masnavi), Printing: 1303 A.H., Format: 31.5×20, Pages: 238 (Incomplete), 21-lined, Proprietor: Maulana Azad Library, Aligarh Muslim University, Aligarh

This manuscript was written by keeping the previously mentioned manuscript (Manuscript 1) in front. The copyist tried to keep the pages in line with the previous one. This conclusion is drawn by comparing both the copies with each other. Following is the evidence in support of this claim:

A. On page 3, both the manuscripts start with the same couplet, but in spite of the set up (*muster*), all the pages of the manuscript are not in consonance. This is because of the mistakes which are in the first copy, but are not in the second one, and also due to the deletions and additions which was done later on. Based on these mistakes, deletions, and additions, it is clear which copy is of earlier writing and which comes later. In the first copy there are mistakes in the set up.[583] Different writers have written it. There are also couplets in the margin.[584] The other copy is only in one hand.[585] There is no mistake in the set up and in the margin, there are no couplets that were not found in the margin of the previous copy.[586]

B. The previously mentioned copy was written in red ink. In this copy ink, red ink, indigo, gold water, and other colourful inks are also used. But in spite of this, there are some shortcomings which are not found in the previously mentioned copy. In the previous copy, to demarcate the sections, couplets were used which were written in the middle and the space on the side was left blank. Also, there were additions in the margin. In Manuscript 2 these additions have been collected, and to bring the pages in similarity and in consonance with the pages of Manuscript 1, the writer has not written one couplet in the heading but has written two couplets in one line. To highlight it, he has changed the colour of the ink. And where there was no need to

583. *Sabatul Quloob.* Volume 1: Manuscript 1; On Page 64 & 96 instead of 21 there are 22 lines.

584. There is a couplet in the margin Ibid at 264.

585. This is the handwriting of the writer who had written beginning and some other parts of Manuscript 1.

586. Both the couplets which are in the margin of both the copies were perhaps composed after the compilation of both the copies. (For example, on page 446 of both the copies there is an addition of three couplets). Those which are in the margin of Manuscript 1 and not in the margin of Manuscript 2 were included in the text of Manuscript 2.

include the additions, there the headings of Manuscript 2 are like the headings of Manuscript 1 (i.e. in the same line). If there was no condition to keep the pages of both manuscripts in consonance, then there would not have been any need to compress the matter in Manuscript 2. From the beginning up to the end, the heading couplets would have been written as one couplet in one line, but the copy would have extended and the pages would not have been in consonance.

C. In the content of the prose, if there was a deletion or addition then a clever writer would expand or compress the content to adjust the corrections.[587] But if such corrections appear in the poetry, then one will have to wait until there is room for expansion or compression.[588] This exercise in the above mentioned two manuscripts indicates which copy is the original and which came later: from pages 7–8, 14–54, 276–286, 290–302, 319–368, and 376–377, the pages of both the copies match. But in the middle pages, there are extension of lines in one copy or the other. Following are the examples of this:

a. In Manuscript 1 on page 6 there are two couplets in the margin. Without changing the set up (*muster*) to adjust them, there was need for a line. The writer, in order to adjust this, started compressing the content: In the Manuscript 1 on page 3 there was content in Arabic in two lines; he compressed it to one and a half line. In this way he gained half a line of space. Then on page 4, the Arabic content was on one and a half lines, but he wrote it in one line and in this way, he gained another half line. The last line of page 5 of Manuscript 2 was the first line of page 6 of Manuscript 1, but by including two

587. On page 243 of *Bani* for the addition of *Majmuaey Wajidia* see, Chapter 3 Section 2 of this book.

588. In *Kulliyat e* Akhtari this was the problem in which the empty space was filled with a flowery pattern.

couplets from the margin of page 6, the pages in both copies of the manuscripts at page 6 came in consonance.

b. A line was to be added on page 13 of Manuscript 2, for this the act of compression started with the headings: On pages 9 and 10 of Manuscript 1, the headings were written in between, in half lines, in good writing. There was no scope to compress them from pages 10–13. The writer compressed the same headings, which means that without leaving blank spaces, the headings were written with different ink. In this way, the additions on page 13 were compressed. In the half line it was written:

   This is the date of birth of the person This is engraved in it

   The line which reads as "*Waris e Taj o nageen 1274*" is not found in Manuscript 1. Perhaps this was done based on oral instructions which were also later deleted.[589]

c. In Manuscript 2 on page 287, the writer mistakenly left one couplet. When he realised this, he wrote that couplet in the margin, but it was not possible to change the lines. Thus, at the end of this page it became necessary to include the first couplet of page 288 of Manuscript 1. In the above two examples (a and b) it was necessary to compress, but here it became important to expand. Had the content of Manuscript 2 not been expanded, it would have continued in this way. On page 289 of Manuscript 1, the Arabic content was on one line. The writer wrote this content in Manuscript 2 in one and half lines, and in this way both the manuscripts became identical.

---

589. From the wordings "*Waaris e Taj o nageen*" (130+6+404+707) the figure 1247 is inferred (retrieved) In the manuscript 1274 is wrongly written. Had it been written 1247 then also it would have been against reality. The year of Wajid Ali Shah's birth is 1238 and perhaps because of this misstatement it was deleted.

d. On page 373 of Manuscript 2, there was only one line for the first couplet (*misra*): "*Sikander ye boley ho rehmat naseeb*". The space for the other line was empty. In Manuscript 2, the other line is also there: "*za sooey Khudawand dur o qareeb*". This was given in inverted commas, which indicates that it was noted both by the King and by the writer and for some reason Manuscript 2 was left incomplete. This claim is further confirmed by the fact that in the last part of Manuscript 2, space was left empty for the Arabic content and for other such text.[590] In the beginning part of all the left side pages, headings were written inside a circle. After page 79, the circles were empty, and from page 321 there were no circles. Other than the differences between the original and the copy, between the complete and incomplete, and differences in couplets and wording, there are two notable differences between Manuscript 1 and Manuscript 2. These are as follows:

A. In several margins of Manuscript 2, there are verses which are in the same place in Manuscript1, which also indicates that this addition was done after the compilation of both the copies. In Manuscript 2, these verses are present even today, but from Manuscript 1 they were either deleted, or the entire strip was separated. Had this act been done without the consent of the King, there would not have been another strip with the handwriting of the writer. On page 304 of Manuscript 2, in some places the removal of this content can be seen even today: "...this page is changed". In this margin there are no verses, but there are only one-word headings.

B. There is no seal on Manuscript 1. But it is more correct to say that there was a seal, but to destroy this sign, the first page and half of

590. See, *Sabatul Quloob,* Volume 1 (handwritten) Manuscript 2 page 351 and page 378 for full couplets *(misras)* and page 442 (at two places) for Arabic matter.

the last page were also destroyed.[591] On Manuscript 2 is the seal of "Amir Ali Khan Hilal." The presence of this seal is as mysterious as the missing seal of the royal library. In manuscripts, seals are usually given in one or two places, either in the beginning or at the end, or both. In this manuscript, the seal of 'Hilal' is in three places: on pages 1, 2, and 25. This seal is equal to the circle of rupees. Within the big circle, there are two small circles, which meet at a point and look like a crescent. In the middle of the crescent, "*1275* Mir *Ali Khan*" is written, and in the middle of the small circle the word 'Hilal' is written. If this is the seal of the pupil of Mir Ali Ausat Rashk, and of the supervisor of Matbaey Sultani 'Hilal', then it creates some doubt, as he had died before 1292 A.H. After the publication of *Sheva-e-Faiz* in 1277 A.H. his name is neither seen in the books of Matbaey Sultani nor in *Qata'ey Tarikh.* The seal of a deceased person on the book raises many questions. In this situation, the following are the only possibilities:

1. In *Bani* (written in 1291–1294 A.H.), the statement of Wajid Ali Shah is wrong. Hilal was alive in 1300 A.H.
2. It may be the seal of some another 'Hilal'. The pupil of Rashk and the master of Jalal is not Hilal.
3. The portion containing the seal of Hilal was composed before the death of Hilal.
4. Someone forged the seal of the deceased.

The circumstantial evidence and other indications point out the last possibility as the most trustworthy. It has now been proven that Manuscript 2 was written by keeping Manuscript 1 in front. The writing and arrangement

591. More manuscripts are found in the library of Wajid Ali Shah in which with the intention of destroying this seal, there are signs of destroying the manuscript with audacity. *Bani,* 222–34.

also prove that Manuscript 2 was written by the same writer who wrote parts of Manuscript 1, and he was aware of the mindset of the King. Otherwise, it would not have been necessary to take so much care to make the corrections with different coloured inks, and to make the pages identical. Before completing the manuscript, its owner passed away. Had this manuscript been included in the royal library in the lifetime of the King, then it is certain the seal would have been there. After the King's death, when everything was in disarray, and the English had started to interfere, the person who took the incomplete copy thought it would be convenient to own it by adding his own seal to confirm his ownership. Who knew that these manuscripts of historical importance, which were once jointly presented before the author's table, would be collected in one place after 80 years and a journey of hundreds of miles, and in a condition where in one version the page with the seals is missing and in the other, the seal that is there is not of the author or of the true owner. Manuscript 2 is incomplete after the following couplet on page 476:

He will come and Serve You you will get peace don't worry

Sabatul Quloob (Manuscript 3)

Written: 1301–03 A.H., Language: Urdu, Genre: Religious Epic (Masnavi), Printing: 1304 A.H., Format: 24.5×21, Pages: 191 (Incomplete upto the end), 15-lined
Script: Arabic and Zanjeera

The manuscript starts from page 543 and it ends at page 934. Following are the verses from the beginning and end:

Start of page 543:

I regret that it was the day of sacrifice
There was enthusiasm in the heart to be sacrificed
When Khalil reached the stone
By the order of Allah *the Almighty*

There he was made to lie down at the left side
He was shown what he had not seen

Final Verse: Page 924

The story is related this way
Qaroon used to make an elixir
He said he discovered it himself
benevolent! I got it myself
Musa was himself an elixir
He told him listen! You pious

The initial verses are similar to Manuscript 1 and 2 on page 341, and the verses of the last section are found on page 588 of Manuscript 1. The previous verses are related to the sixth section of Chapter 7, and the later verse is related to the eighth section of Chapter 13. The pages are so damaged that, for the sake of their safety, it is better not to tamper with them. The identification of the pages of this copy, along with the pages of Manuscript 1, turned out to be correct word by word. In Manuscript 1, for different traditions, in the margin words like "*az muk*Hali*f*", "*az muwaqif*", and "*az fareqain*" were written. In Manuscript 3 the same is done, but in Manuscript 2 this is not so. Manuscript 2 is incomplete from page 476, but the flaws in its writing occurred before that. Manuscript 2 is okay up to page 321, hence it appears that the beginning of Manuscript 2 form part of the beginning of Manuscript 3. After completing some portions of Manuscript 2, it is quite possible that the King thought of writing it in new style, and in this way the remaining part of the *masnavi* was written in the style of Manuscript 3.

From the viewpoint of writing and decoration, this copy is unique. On every page there is a double golden margin (*jadwal*). The counting of pages was done amidst the margins. The writing was done in red, indigo, light pink, saffron, yellow and many other colours. Between the lines there is a design of delicate, colourful creepers, leaves, flowers, and birds, and the enamel work is eye catching. On every right-side page, in the bouquet or the belly of a fish, lion, rhinoceros, elephant, crocodile, camel, or duck, there are indexes which point at the left side page. On every left side page, in the middle of the margin there is an 11cm space with sunflowers and shields, and in between is the heading of the article alongside a crown. On the crown there is an umbrella, and on the umbrella, a golden hawk is drawn with utmost expertise and neatness. Alas! Such a wonderful and elegant work was done on ordinary paper which could not bear the weight of the golden art. Between the pages, thin paper, like that in a photo album, is placed. This somehow secures the artifact, but partly due to the damp climate of Bengal and partly due to carelessness, all the pages have been destroyed. If more care is not taken, then the remaining book will be destroyed fully. The document can be preserved with the use of gum (*wasli*). But this dims the glow and luster of the enamel work.

Like *Riyazul Quloob*, the topic of this *masnavi* is an account of the Prophets and their Miracles. The difference is that in *Riyazul Quloob*, a summary of the beginning of Volume 1 of *Hayatul Quloob* is given in the form of prose, and Wajid Ali Shah translated the same book in poetic form in the *Sabatul Quloob.* With some changes and additions at places, he related his own tales. Often in the light of upcoming events, he wrote about the temporal nature of the world and its selfishness. Similar feelings are also composed in the form of poetry. In Volume 1of *Hayatul Quloob* there are 38 Chapters. In the last Chapter there is the tale of '*Haroot & Maroot.*' In *Sabatul Quloob* there are also 38 Chapters, and this Volume concludes where Volume 1 of *Hayatul Quloob* concluded.

Two characteristics of Wajid Ali Shah which are rarely seen in some of his compositions are in full swing in this *masnavi.* The first is that of composing a poem. In his other *masnavis*, the headings were in prose, while in this *masnavi* even the headings are in poetic form. The other characteristic is that of expressing the same subject in various ways and styles. In this *masnavi* there was much scope to do this. It was no less difficult to compose the first, second and third chapter in poetic style, moreover it was also difficult to give more importance to the traditions than to the headings. In prose, often the words "*therefore it is tradition, therefore it is mentioned...*" are repeated frequently, which becomes very boring. To avoid this boredom, the style the poet adopts can be appreciated only by one who has perused the *masnavi*. Readers who go through the headings cannot stop to appreciate the mental caliber of the poet. This is the longest *masnavi* in Urdu literature. For this reason, the number of verses is written with the initial couplcts of thc *masnavi*.

A selected portion of this *masnavi* is presented in the form of the following table for ease of reading. The author has mentioned only the initial verses of each chapter here, to give an idea of the subject matter it contains. Each chapter has various sections as shown below. Some proper and spiritual names are explained in the corresponding footnotes. (Translator).

Chapter	**Versified Heading**	**Number of verses in Sections**	**In chapters**[592]
	In the Glory of Allah the Almighty	90	1012
	Translation of the Preface	177	
	Up to here was the saying of Akhwand Sahab Akhtar! Now start your narrative		
	First praise your poetry After the praise of Prophet start the story	68	
	Now turn your pen in praise of God Pray that Khuda has mercy upon us	113	
	Now explain the reason of compilation Happily, merrily and with pleasure	30	

592. Counting of figures under the sections. The starting headings is not versified.

	Pedigree of Late Bakhshi ul Mulook Fatehud Daulah Bahadur Barq Master of Nazim About the army and Akhtar	442 92	
	This is the first Chapter Listen you envy of Nymph I have explained something here This is First section Listen You Beauty! This is all about the divine mission	253	1734
	There are many enemies of the Prophets You good soul! they are of many kinds	814	
	The Third Section starts from here Now the sun of narration is rising	667	
	Second chapter starts from here The Sun of divine revelation rises It is in the praise of Adam and Eve If you read it is the First section Second section starts from here The Sun of demand rises The Third Section starts from here The Sun of greatness rises Audience! Listen to the Fourth Section It is stated with assurance Dear! this is the Fifth Section It is about the generation of Adam Sixth Section starts from here Why not the Sun of Greatness rises? My Dear this is the Seventh Section Dear it is about the death of Adam	755 1151 889 1039 851 26 388	510
	Chapter Three starts from here The sun of bravery rises		572
	Chapter Four starts from here Sun of narration has risen Son I have written two sections here This is First section Listen you Clever! Dear this is Second Section It is about being divine	378 823	1201

	Fifth Chapter starts from here I am lighting the candles of delight This is First Section You Sweet Self It is the tale of Hud[593] and Semitic[594] tribe O! Cup Bearer quench my thirst with that red wine Then I will do something of Second Section	752 181	933
	I start Chapter Six from here So that the star of poem rises		514
	You Skillful this is the Seventh Chapter Everywhere there is name of Allah You Pious! Listen this is the First Section There is so much the praise Now I start the Second Section The sun of writing rises The Third section starts from here The star of friend of Allah has risen Fourth Section The Listeners! this is the Fifth Section It is all about wives and children The Sixth Section starts from here The sun of empire rises	409 857 414 142 624 345	2791
	Now the Eighth Chapter starts again Akhtar! the star of poetry is rising		870
	Friends now listen this is the Ninth Chapter If you see some fault then hide it		1153
	The tenth Chapter starts from here I am explaining all the *usul* and *furu* (roots and branches/tenets of Islam)		2893
	I started Eleventh Chapter from here The Sun of tale telling has risen		460
	The Twelfth Chapter starts from here The Sun of narration rises		236

593. Prophet Hudd sent to *Aad* tribe. 11th. Sura of Quran.

594. Ancient *Semitic* race as mentioned in Quran.

	Thirteenth Chapter starts from here		
	The Sun of dialogue has risen		
	I have written some sections here		
	Listen benevolent this is the First Section		
	Second Section starts from here	303	
	It starts with my details		
	The Third section starts from here	1073	
	It rises the sun of Prophethood		
	Fourth Section starts from here	1111	
	The star of my fortune rises		
	The Fifth Section starts here	259	
	The start of saraielies[595] rises		
	Now the Sixth Section starts		
	Here it is about the descending of Torait[596]		7627
	Now there is continuity of seventh Chapter	1135	
	It is the full tale of Haroon[597]		
	You the Envy of Nymph! This is the Eighth Chapter	393	
	Wrote about the slaughter of a cow	397	
	Now I am narrating the Ninth Section		
	The Ninth Section is revealed	1025	
	The Tenth Section starts from here		
	The Sun of teaching rises	978	
	O! Heart eleventh section starts		
	It is narration of the death of Musa[598]	337	

595. Sariel is an angel mainly from Judaic tradition. He is one of the holy angels. en.wikipedia.org

The Judaism is an Abrahamic monotheist ethnic religion that comprises the collective spiritual cultural and legal traditions of the Jewish people. www.bing.com Here the line with Urdu word *Sarielies* indicate the birth of Judaism. (Translator)

596. The Old Testament - Part of the Bible containing the scriptures of *Hebrew, Torah* and *Pentateuch*. Urdu – English Dictionary - 375 (Translator).

597. Haroon (a.s.) or Prophet Aroon, brother of Prophet Moses. *Id* at 1130.

598. The story of Prophet Musa (a.s.) (Moses) is a significant and inspiring narrative in Islamic tradition. Musa (a.s.) confronted the *Pharoah* along with his brother Aroon (Haroon) to release the Israelis, and when the *Pharoah* refused, he was drowned in the river. www.bing.com

	O! Heart the Fourteenth Chapter is manifested The Fourteen *Masoomeens* are benevolent		214
	Chapter Fifteen starts from here Now the star of Akhtar rises again		120
	The Sixteenth chapter starts from here Now the tales of Eliyas[599] are rising		393
	Son now I am writing the seventeenth Chapter It is about Zulkafl[600]		134
	Now the well written Chapter Eighteen Here there are tales of Luqman[601] and his relatives		811
	Nineteenth Chapter starts from here In it some other tales are included		445
	Starting the twentieth Chapter from here Tales of Dawood[602] are manifested here This comprises some sections Listen the Intelligent this is the First section The Second Chapter starts from here Now the Sun of tale telling rises The Third chapter starts from here And the Sun of narration rises	 483 488 53	1502
	The twenty First Chapter starts here The Sun of seriousness rises		265

599. Was he a Prophet of God who was sent by Allah to guide the Israelis? As per some Islamic traditions, Eliyas is said to be from the progeny of Aroon. www.bing.com

600. He is an Islamic Prophet although not much is known about him.

601. It is the 31st Sura of Quran and composed of 34 verses. It takes the title from sage *Luqman* and his advice to his sons from 12–19 Surahs. https://en.wikipedia.org/wiki/Luqman_(s%C5%ABrah)#

602. Also Called David, he is a prophet and messenger of God (Allah) in Islam. He was a righteous, divinely anointed monarch of the United Kingdom of Israel. *Ibid*

	The twenty-second Chapter starts Here there are tales of Suleiman[603] The First Section starts from here It is the rise of the narration of Suleiman The Second Section starts from here The Sun of narration rises The Third Section starts from here I have faith the Sun rises in the sky The Fourth Chapter starts from here And the Sun of sermon rises	394 260 302 300	1816
	Chapter Twenty-Three starts now And the Sun of stories is rising		125
	Chapter Twenty-Four starts The tales of Hanzala[604] are starting		318
	The twenty-fifth Chapter starts There are tales of people		106
	The twenty-sixth chapter starts The tales of Zakaria[605] and Yahya[606] are started		675
	By Allah's consent I will narrate O! Young this is the twenty-seventh Chapter		317

603. He is revered as a major Prophet by Muslims. He was the Third Ruler of Israelis and is known for his wisdom and intelligence. *Ibid.*

604. It is an Arabic/Quranic name which means 'take a bath with the help of angels'. It is also the name of a Prophet and of *Sahaba* of Prophet Muhmmad (PBUH). https://quranicnames.com/what-is-the-meaning-of-hanzala/#google_vignette

605. Or Prophet *Zachariah* is the name of a Prophet who is the father of Prophet *Yahya.* (Translator)

606. Name of a Prophet and son of Prophet *Zakaria.*

	This is the twenty-eighth Chapter In this there are tales of Eisaa[607] in abundance Dear there are many sections in this O Benevolent! listen this is First Section They are pardoned and are free Intelligent! Listen this is the Second Section Now son of a clever person read the Third Section Many tales are narrated here Son Section Fourth starts from here There is narration of the Divine food Now the Fifth Sections appears It will have narration of Divine revelations The Sixth chapter starts now The Sun of tales is rising	507 54 973 217 1583 314	4134
	The Twenty Ninth Chapter starts The Sun of humbleness starts		1101
	Now the Thirtieth Chapter starts The tale of Yunus (Prophet Jonah)[608]starts		722
	If you thank Almighty the more Remember this is the thirty-first Chapter		665
	Now the thirty-second Chapter is manifested It is narration of the companions of Ukhdood[609]		193
	The thirty-third chapter starts now There is tale of Jirjees. [610]		88

607. In Islam Jesus or ISA (a.s.) is believed to be penultimate prophet and messenger of Allah. He was sent to guide the children of Israel with a book called Injeel (Bible). https://en.wikipedia.org/wiki/Jesus_in_Islam

608. *Yusuf Ibn e Matta* is a prophet of Allah in Islam corresponding to Jonah, son of Amittai in the Hebrew Bible.

609. The tale of *Ashab e Ukhdood* unfolds in the Surah *Al-Buruj* in the 85th. Chapter of the Quran. The People of the Trench or *Ashabul Ukhdoon* left an indelible mark on the pages of Islamic history for their unwavering allegiance to Allah in the face of extreme persecution. (Alustadh; The story of Ashabul Akhdood)

610. Also known in English as St. George. (Oxford Urdu-EnglishDictionary). 417.

	Son I will now compose the thirty-fourth Chapter There is tale of Khalid[611] in detail		64
	Chapter thirty-five is discovered It is all about the Prophets		155
	The thirty-sixth chapter is "Salle Ala" It is all full of rare events		972
	The thirty-seventh Chapter starts now I am like cheerful candles amidst a night of celebration		413
	I am writing the thirty-eighth Chapter happily Now there is tale of Haroot & Maroot.[612]		

In *Sabatul Quloob* Volume I, out of an estimate of 43, 160 verses, only the first 28 couplets are on Page 2 of Manuscript 2. All the other verses are taken from Manuscript 1. In this count, those verses are not taken which are in the margin of Manuscript 2 and which were probably deleted with the consent of the author. Moreover, in this count even those verses are not taken which only for the taste of the tongue were included by the poet by referring to another poet.[613]

The end of Volume 1 of *Sabatul Quloob* indicates that the King, in three and a half years, from 1300 A.H. to the middle of 1303 A.H., had completed

611. Khalid was a 7th Century military commander. Though he initialy headed campaigns aginst Prophet Muhammad, later he embraced Islam and spent the rest of his life in the service of the Prophet. (Wikpedia)

612. Two angels who were suspended by their feet in a well in Babylon because they taught magic to man. Oxford Urdu-English Dictionary. 1130.

613. For example, from *Sabatul Quloob* (Handwritten) Volume 1 only the first couplet from the following verses given on page 238 are counted. The second one is not counted:
Someone has composed this unparallel line It is written on the top of the line Janab
Not every woman is a woman, nor every man is man Khuda has not made all the fingers equal

Volume 1 and had started the translation of Volume 2. He also planned to complete Volume 3.

This book has no more space
That all the narratives be blessed
In the book of Imamat friends!
I will explain[614] *all that*

But towards the end of 1304 A.H. when he suffered a deadly disease and became hopeless about life, he composed some verses and finished it there:

I drank so much blood
Only then I could weave these precious rubies
Perhaps this will achieve salvation for me
I am appealing before Allah

Sabatul Quloob (Volume 2)

Written: 1303–04 A.H., Language: Urdu, Genre: Religious Epic (Masnavi), Printing: 1304 A.H., Format: 25×22, Pages: 79 (Ending Incomplete) 15-lined
Script: Arabic and Zanjeera, Start page 3, end page 160

This is Volume 2 of Sabatul Quloob He knows the points of Al Quloob
This comprises some Chapters Listen! Arjumand this is Chapter One
Here it is mentioned the lineage of Shah The family is full of wonders
Especially there is mention of the forefathers There are many specialized sections.[615]

---

614. *Sabatul Quloob* (Handwritten) Volume 2, 13.

615. In *Hayatul Quloob,* Volume 2 page 2 this is explained below:
"Volume 2 is about the date of birth and death of Miracles and wonders, which are given in some chapters regarding the greatness and condition of the parents of Wajid Ali Shah. The first part is about his family..."

Listen friends! With the bag full of money
Then she ran towards Abdullah
She then happily greeted him
Asked from which tribe are you
How you are related to Arab tribes
I have not seen the beautiful face like yours
He said I am Abdullah[616]

The Second Volume of *Sabatul Quloob* starts from page 3. The initial pages are numbered in red ink. On the other pages whenever there is a change in important paras these figures are given. The writer of *Sabatul Quloob* Volume 3 also wrote this copy with precision. But here the enamel work, like that of manuscript 3, had not been completed, and he discontinued the work before it could be. The margin is also single. There were no signs of stitching or cutting. This shows that these parts (*juzu*) were kept in the same condition as they were in when returned by the writer. Like the first page, some more pages were possibly destroyed. Given the brittleness of the paper and the importance of the manuscript, the pages have been preserved with the help of '*wasli.*'

The First Volume of *Hayatul Quloob* was translated by the King in 1303 A.H., but he died at the start of 1305 A.H. Consequently, the work of composing Volume 2 of the *Sabatul Quloob* was presumably not done around 1304 A.H. The gold-plated copies of the Royal Library were not prepared from the manuscript of the King, but they were compiled with the first or second copies after he had revised them. Keeping in mind this process of working, it can be assumed that the translated manuscript and the first copy did exist but could not be recovered. If any such work was available, then the extent to which the King had completed the work could have been determined. In the copy of *Hayatul Quloob*, in places there are

616. *Hayatul Quloob*, page 114.

corrections made by the King's pen, and they are underlined with red ink. One paper, used as a bookmark, contained three different lines (*misras*) of *Sabatul Quloob*, and some more content is found between pages 112–113. One more bookmark is found between pages 256–257. Immediately after the first bookmark, on the 12th line of page 114, is the point up to which the copy of this manuscript is complete. Thus the second bookmark is certainly the point where the composition is completed.

This Volume of *Sabatul Quloob* comprises 1208 pages and 68 Chapters. Due to the long period of time, there are imprints of the bookmarks on the pages between which they were found. [617]

As with the First Volume, the poet of the Second Volume has regarded the *Hayatul Quloob* of *Mulla Baqar Majlisi* as the original, and has limited his work to its verbatim translation. In some places in the *Saaqi Nama*, he has made additions or deletions based on his own choice. The Arabic content has been left intact, and in some places, after it was copied, it was also translated. The verses of this Volume have been numbered according to the following headings:[618]

617. *Hayatul Quloob*, Volume 2. Publishers: Munshi Naval Kishore. Lucknow. Rectification by *Maulvi Syed Tasadduq Hussai Sahab Kazmi.* The year of Publication is not mentioned anywhere in the book.

618. The writing of the Masnavi is done in the prose style, hence from every page only those verses are taken which are complete. The counting is done from the verses of the heading up to the end of the chapter or sections. In the counting of the First Chapter, one couplet from Volume Two is also included. Verses of other poets which are taken to enrich the language are excluded from the counting.

	Poetic Heading	Sections	Chapters
1	This is Volume 2 of Sabatul Quloob They know the points of Al Quloob This comprises some Chapters Listen! Arjumand this is Chapter One As for the lineage of Hazrat this is the First Section Up till Day of Judgement its attachment will remain He was Zehra's son Now you eloquent speaker Listen to Section Two The divine light starts here And prayers before Allah The Third section starts from here It is about the forefathers The Fourth Section starts from here The Sun of the companions (of elephants) rises The Fifth Section starts from here Here there is mentioning of zamzam	20 1245 152 341 1115	
	No outsider to have right on the Prophet Now listen to Chapter Six systematically	92	
2	Audience! Listen to Chapter Two This is surely divine revelation		71
	Chapter Three starts from here The date of birth is revealed		1304
	The one who is supreme among all the Prophets His birth is explained systematically He is Syed peace be upon him Young man this is detail of the Miracles Have written all these Miracles which were witnessed at that time		Total verses of volume 2: 4,987

It could not be traced as to how many verses were before page 3. Keeping in mind the style of writing of manuscripts, it would not be wrong to imagine that page one was blank, and the text began on page two. In the 15-lined format, there are around 32 couplets. Hence no more than 16 verses from

Hamd, *Naat*, and *Manqibat* could have been destroyed. At the end of the work, it cannot be said how many verses were lost or could not be written. In Volume 1, one Chapter is reserved for each Prophet, in which there are different sections for the narration of their birth, death, Miracles, and other events. The longest chapter is for *Hazrat Musa*, in which there are 11 sections and 7,627 verses. Here, the entire Volume is dedicated to the Last Prophet, and the details of his birth continue beyond 5,000 verses. This overwhelming introduction indicates that only this narration would have been strangely voluminous. The pen which started with imaginary stories, travelled through different genres of literature for a period of 50 years, and ultimately reached a point where the following couplet explains his work in the most suitable manner:

Now I am characterizing the Last Prophet (PBUH)
Thank Allah *this end is befitting (Shibli)*

Books Which Could Not Be Recovered

In the following pages, only those compositions of Wajid Ali Shah are discussed which were available in various libraries and were within the reach of those with refined taste. Other than these books, the names of other books were also found in some discussions, but it is difficult to say whether these were fully destroyed or if they still exist somewhere. Such books can be divided into the following categories:

A. Books where the topics are connected to their names or with some remote evidence. As this is based on imagination or probability, there is the possibility of some incorrect conclusions.
B. Books which were mentioned in the discussions of commentators. There is hardly any chance of mistakes in such books.

The following books fall under Category A:

1. *Maqtal e Motabir*

Wazir ul Sultan writes about this book: '*Complete narration of Nohas and Salaams and an effective statement regarding maqtal e motabir.*'[619] *Kulliyat e Iman* was pulished much before the compilation of the *Wazir Nama* and the *salaams* and *nohas* which were not in the First Edition were included in the Second Edition.[620] May be this added composition was known by this name at the time of the publication of the *Wazir Nama.* If this assumption is correct, then like *Gulzar e Hussaini* and *Kashkol* Akhtari, only the name is new and the composition behind it first appeared in *Mulk e Akhtar* and then in the Second Edition of *Kulliyat e Imaan*. The King himself does not mention this name, which indicates that up to the time of the writing of *Bani* the name was different.

2. *Daftar e Pareshan*

3. *Daftar e Humayun*

Regarding the first of the above mentioned two books, *Wazirul Sultan* Bahadur writes that it is about the miseries of *Imam Hamam Alaeissalam.*[621] Maybe this statement is correct or maybe it is wrong. As mentioned earlier in this chapter, it is quite possible that both of these names are of collections which are part of *Malazul Kalmat* and *Kulliyat e* Akhtari.

619. *Wazir Nama.* Wazir ul Sultan Md. Amir Ali Khan Amir. Publication Nizami. Lucknow. 1293. 317–18.

620. See discussion under the heading '*Imaan' Supra.*

621. *Supra Note* 618 at 317.

4. *Tajjali e Ishq*

5. *Mahinama*

6. *Muraqqaey Farrukh*

These three names are found in the list of *Bani*, but the books are not available.

The following books come under Category B:

7. *Dastoor e Wajidia*

In *Bani*, this book has the same name, but in the *Wazir Nama* it is likely named *Dastoor e Wajidia*, in which the full list and some notable extracts are presented.[622] The book is in Persian, and was likely compiled a little before or after 1265 A.H. It has 66 sections related to the administration of the country and the strong orders which were made mandatory for the ministers, workers and subjects.

8. *Tarikh e Khaas*

9. *Tarikh e Mashghala*

10. *Tarikh e Deher*

All three of these names are found in the list of *Bani.* All books with the word '*Tarikh*' were handwritten and used the collection of Urdu letters which were compiled in the year 1276 A.H. By this calculation, these three books should have been handwritten, and must be collections of letters. Regarding *Tarikh e Deher*, it can be assumed that it must be the collection of those letters which were sent by the King to *Malka e Deher Nawab* Navrozi Begum. Regarding *Tarikh-e-Mumtaz* and *Tarikh e* Ghazala, we have seen that these are letters by the King, and as they were addressed to *Mumtaz Begum* and Malka Ghazala, they were named *Tarikh-e-Mumtaz* and *Tarikh e* Ghazala. Regarding *Tarikh Firaq*, it has already been mentioned that Malka Deher

---

622. *Ibid*, 132–52.

had written the letters to which the King had responded, and thus there can be no better name for such a collection of letters than *Tarikh e Deher*. The first two books were probably a collection of the letters from Seemtan Begum. The information given in *Tarikh Firaq* and the Ghazals of *Sheva-e-Faiz* proves that no more letters were written by anyone else, and that no more responses was given by the King to anyone else as much as to Seemtan Begum. During those days, she was the highest on his radar. *Sheva-e-Faiz* begins with the name of this *Begum.* In sum, it can be said that at least one of the above two books was related to Seemtan Begum.

11. *Mujahida e* Akhtari

Mirza *Hatim Ali Meher's Qata e Tarikh* goes like this:

This is the magazine of the army of the King
Which mentions the discipline of the regiments
Meher pray before Huzoor e Mualla
Name of the Tarikh is Mujahida e Akhtari 1211 + 58 = 1269

This indicates that in 1269 A.H. the King had composed a magazine, the original name of which must have been something else, though *Meher* suggested *Mujahida e Tarikh*[623]. At the beginning of his rule, the King was very much interested in the regulation of the army.[624] For this purpose, he himself wrote their code and regulations in Persian.[625] This style of working

623. *Almas* Darakhshan.- Mirza Hatim Ali Beg Meher - Matbaey Elahi. Agra. 1895. 469.

624. *Tawarikh e Nadirul Asar.* Munshi Naval Kishore. Publication Munshi Naval Kishore. Lucknow. 1863. 125–26.

625. In *Sabatul Quloob* (Handwritten). Volume One, page 26 he writes:
... Zaban e digar mei toh thhi aarsi
He used to teach regulations in Persian
And in *Ishq Nama* (poetic) in *Daastan* 63 where the terminology relates to warfare the following couplet is found.
Ye 'qeh qeh' nahin Sheesha e Badaah ki
The regulations are in Persian

with army regulations could not have continued beyond 1263–64 A.H., but the terminology which was used to teach the regulations perhaps did continue. Most probably, in 1269 A.H. the King compiled them in the form of a magazine. After the compilation and translation of Irshad Khaqani, we do not have any information about the preoccupations of the King, hence it is not surprising that he had time to compose the magazine.

12. *Risala e Mausiqi*

One more *Qataey Tarikh* is found in the *Gulistan e Sukhan* of *Asir*, titled *Tarikh e Risla e Mausiqi Tasnif Hazrat Sultan Alam.*[626] The Book *Sautul Mubarak* was published before the writing of this magazine. Hence the anonymous magazine made from this *Tarikh* is definitely not *Saut ul Mubarak. Munshi Naval Kishore* perhaps addressed this magazine as *Risala e Mausiqi* and he also mentioned that it was published by Matbaey Sultani.[627]

13. *Hidayatul Sultan*

A 58-page Persian book titled *Shrah Hidayat e Sultani* was published by Matbaey Sultani, Lucknow, which is now unavailable. *Ramooz e Tadqeeqat* was its historical name. This book is the writing of *Munshi* Amir *Minai*, which is explained in some of the compositions of the King. Its perusal reveals that his book was in Arabic and contains advice and instructions. In his explanation Amir displays the richness of the language, and at the end he wishes:

> *"O My beloved King! Kindly accept the services of this humble slave."* (Translated from Persian)

626. *Gulistan e Sukhan/Author Riyaz.* Munshi Muzaffar Ali Khan Asir. Matbaey Sultani. Lucknow. 1271. 535

627. *Tawarikh e Nadirul Asar.* Munshi Naval Kishore. Publication: Munshi Naval Kishore. Lucknow. 1863. 127.

In two other books titled *Comentary: Nasaah e Akhtar* and *Commentary: Sahifaey Sultania*, the commentators wrote about the King's writing. The titles of these books have the orginal name of the King's books. Thus, in the title *Sharah Hidayatul Sultan*, the word '*Hidayatul Sultan*' must be the original name of the book. The compilation of *Hidayatul Sultan* must have been before 1268 A.H.

Books which are wrongly associated:

In the present times, due to the ignorance of commentators and the carelessness of pubishers many books are associated with Wajid Ali Shah which were neither composed by him, nor were they known by the titles which are commonly circulated. Thus, when the original writings of Wajid Ali Shah are listed, such a practice will not serve any purpose except making unnecessary additions. Following is the list of such books, which can be divided into two categories:

Books which are a selection of compositions or parts of them. These are as follows:

1. *Qasaid Mubarak*

There is the text by the King with the same name, and it is entered in the *Wazir Nama* with this name. But in the *Wazir Nama*, *Kulliyat e* Akhtari and *Kulliyat e Soom* are not discussed with this name because for both part (*juzu*) and whole (*kul*) only one name should be used. In the *Wazir Nama*, the name of a part is entered by mistake.[628]

2. *Masnavi Ganna*

This masnavi, comprising 200 verses, is part of *Kulliyat e Soom* and *Kulliyat e* Akhtari. The writer has not given this *masnavi* a separate identity because *masnavis* of this size or even longer than this are part of *Kulliyat Sheva-e-Faiz.*

628. For further details see Chapter 3 of this book.

3. *Daftar e Gham wa Behre Alam*[629]

This book is a collection of 24 elegies (*marsias*) spread over 180 pages. 23 *marsias* are taken from *Tosha e Akhrat*, and one is taken from *Riyaz ul Uqba*. The publisher has only slected elegies. The number of '*bunds*' is the same as it was in the original collections, and the headings and setting of the elegies is as per *Tosha e Akhrat*. The year of publication is not given, but on the title page with Wajid Ali Shah's name, the words '*Ali* Allah *Muqamahu*' are written. On the last page the word 'late' with the name of Mufti Mir Abbas Sahab indicates that it was published after the death of Mufti Sahab in 1306 A.H. It seems that the commentator is unaware of the original collection of elegies but is aware of the present collection. Sometimes he counts *Daftar e Gham* and *Behre Alam* jointly, and sometimes separately.[630]

4. *Tarikh Pari Khana*

In 1914, while translating *Ishq Nama* (Persian), Mirza Fida Ali Khanjar likely referred to it as '*Tarikh Pari Khana.*'[631] Thereafter, this title gathered so much popularity that even after correction the common people were not ready to address the book as *Ishq Nama*; they were adamant in calling it *Tarikh Pari Khana* or only *Pari Khana.*[632] *Khanjar* named his translation *Mahal Khana e Shahi*, but did not use it in the writing. In the modern translation, there is some innovation, and the name given is *Pari Khana.* Five Editions by *Khanjar*[633] and two editions by a new translator, *Tehseen* Sarwari, were published within a span of 50 years. The abundance of these publications shows how a baseless name misguided the public. The same thing happened with *Ishq Nama* (Persian) and *Ishq Nama* (Poetic). *Khanjar* did not name the poetic form of the book *Pari Khana*. When the extracts from *Masnavi*

---

629. *Aab e Baqa.* Khwaja Abdul Rauf Ishrat. Naami Press. Lucknow. 1918. 161.

630. *Ibid.*

631. *Mahal Khana e Shahi,* Mirza Fida Ali Khanjar. Nami Press. Lucknow. 1934. 3.

632. *Hamari Zaban* (Weekly, Aligarh). Issue 8.12.1965, 9.

633. *Hamari Zaban* (Weekly, Aligarh). Issue 15.02.1966, 8.

Ishq Nama reached the readers, then they did not hesitate to refer to it as *Tarikh Pari Khana (Poetic)*.[634]

5. *Khaqan* Sarwar

This 32-page short book is a selection from *Masnavi Ishq Nama*, which instead of being an expression of the original *masnavi*, is in fact a reflection of the bad taste and commercial-mindedness of the compiler. *Ishq Nama* is one of the best compositions of Wajid Ali Shah. Publishers have wanted it for a long time, but to date, no one has been able to publish it. The compiler of *Khaqan* Sarwar was a bookseller. He managed to acquire some initial pages of the *masnavi* from somewhere, and he copyrighted them in his own name under the title of '*Intekhab*'. Those who were aware of the name of the *masnavi* or who knew the last verses could say who the *masnavi* belonged to. But the compiler neither met those who were aware of it,[635] nor he could recover the last verses. He also did not admit his own limited knowledge of them. The added verses could fulfill this need. Even the most unsuitable addition would have been better, but the abrupt verses of the compiler fall below that standard too. They could be identified easily. For instance, it goes like this:

---

634. *Hamari Zaban* (Weekly, Aligarh). Issue 8.12.1965 and *Naya Daur* (Monthly, Lucknow). Issue August 1959, 71.

635. In the beginning of the twentieth century when *Khanjar* named *Ishq Nama* as '*Pari Khana*', Aasi wrote '*Khaqan* Sarwar' and Khwaja Ishrat wrote it as 'Sarwar *Khaqani*' and a fourth person *Fazil* regarded it as self-written biography (which is not the title but a condition) and it shows the ignorance of the writers regarding its original name. Maulvi Najmul Ghani Khan who wrote many verses of this *masnavi* was also unware of its original name. For the misstatement of *Khanjar* and *Aasi* see *Mahal Khana e Shahi* and *Khaqan* Sarwar and for Khwaja Ishrat, Fazil Lakhnavi and Maulvi Najmul Ghani Khan see *Aab e Baqa* (p.166) Magazine '*Zamana*' (Monthly, Kanpur) July 1910 (p.16) and *Tarikh e Avadh* Volume 5, 47.

Short expression breached the arrogance
Masnavi was named as Khaqan Sarwar
What to say about my condition
It was the twenty second year (of my life)

The verses before and after this are the verses of *Daastan* 17 of *Ishq Nama.* The compiler regarded it as the first *Daastan*, though no *Daastan* is in its original condition. This misunderstanding is further confirmed not by the above added verses, but by the *Qata e Tarikh*, which is found at the end of the book, and which is apparently associated with Hakim Zamin Ali Jalal:

The masnavi which is Khaqan Sarwar
Its composer is a poet like Akhtar
Aasi has selected it
So that more people may like it
Jalal *write the year of its printing*
You write it as Sarwar *Afzai Khaqan* (Is it 1317?)

The suitability of the date and the expulsion of meaning and numbers are all beyond comprehension. It is quite possible that, like the title and added verses, this *Qata'a* is also the composition of Aasi Sahab. Hence, how can it be connected with Jalal?

6. *Sarmaya e Imaan*

One of the daughters of Wajid Ali Shah published a selection of his elegies under the title *Kalam ul Mulook*, which was regarded as *Sarmayeay Imaan*. Ignorant people consider this to have been written by Wajid Ali Shah, while all its portions have been published by Matbaey Sultani.

Books which are not the writings of Wajid Ali Shah

1. *Tazkiraey Akhtar*

In the beginning, based on the reference of *Garsaan wa Taasi,*[636] *Dr. Syed Abdullah*[637] regarded *Tazkiraey Akhtar* as the writing of Wajid Ali Shah. In fact, this is the writing of *Qazi Md. Sadiq Khan Akhtar* and its correct name is '*Tazkiraey Aftab Alam Taab*'.[638]

2. Sarwar ***Sultani***

In the year 1264 a.h., Wajid Ali Shah received the rhythmic translation of Twakkul Beg Hussaini's book '*Shamsheer Khani*' by Mirza Rajab Ali Beg Suroor in Urdu.[639] This book has been published many times by Matbaey Sultani and other publishers. The publisher of *Masnavi Huzn* Akhtari, Mehbub Ali Sahab, has associated this with Wajid Ali Shah.[640]

Unfamiliar compositions

Some of Wajid Ali Shah's compositions were unpublished and also unknown. If one examines such writings, then there is a possibility that they are unreliable. The reason for this is that these compositions were found in old, handwritten diaries (*bayaz*). These compositions should have been in his authorised collections but may be due to lack of care taken by the King they were not found in the authentic collections of the poet. Hence, it cannot be said with full authority that it is the writing of the King. Among these unfamiliar compostions are also those which were apparently very popular

---

636. *Khutbaat e Garsaan wa Taasi.* Maulvi Abdul Haque (Compiler) Anjuman Taraqqi Urdu. Aurangabad. 1935. 101–02.

637. *Shoarraey Urdu Ke Tazkirey.* Dr. Syed Abdulah Maktabaey Jadid. Lahore. 1952. 4

638. *Sukhan Shooara.* Maulvi Abdul Ghafoor Nassakh. Munshi Naval Kishore, Lucknow. 1874. 16.

639. *Sarwar Sultani.* Mirza Rajab Ali Beg Suroor. Matbaey Masihae. Lucknow. 1268. 4–5, 196.

640. *Huzn e Akhtar.* Md. Wajid Ali Shah Akhtar. Md. Ali (Compiler). Daeraey Adabia. Lucknow 1922. 147.

and famous, but an investigation reveals that these are actually distorted forms of the unfamiliar compositions. For instance, the following couplet is associated with Wajid Ali Shah:[641]

There was a time when pearls were crushed under my feet
I am the same with sunshine on my head and stones under my feet

When he was leaving for Calcutta, he went to *Dargah Hazrat Abbas* in the afternoon, where stones were spread over the road. When it became difficult for him to walk on that gravel, he expressed his inner feelings immediately, in the form of the above verses. But in this flow of language there could be some impurities. One of the poems of *Mulk e Akhtar* is in the same style (*zameen*), but neither this first couplet nor any other couplet with the same meaning is found there.[642] The writer has associated one more couplet with Wajid Ali Shah:

I glance at the doors and walls wistfully
Be happy countrymen I am now departing

This couplet is a reminder of his departure from Lucknow. But one is hesitant to call it a couplet. The last two lines (*misras*) of a pentagon (*mukhammas*) is not called a couplet (*sher*). As revealed from the pentagon, this is the addition (*tazmeen* of couplets) to the pentagon[643] *Mukhammas* is the composition of the King, but in his writings neither this *mukhammas* nor any other *salaam* or Ghazal in this style is seen. Among the music-lovers and writers, one more Ghazal is very popular. It goes like this:

---

641. Hunar*mandan e Avadh/Qadeem* Hunar. Syed Israr Hussain Khan Sarfraz Qaumi Press. Lucknow. 1936. 48.
642. *Mulk e Akhtar*. Md. Wajid Ali Shah Akhtar. Matbaey Sultani. Calcutta 1296. 128, 129.
643. *Majmuaey Hujuyat (*Handwritten). Maktoobaey Hatif-Lucknavi. 1913. (Safi). 26–27.

The wind moved in such a way that O God the drape (aanchal) fell down
She peeps from the Window after drawing aanchal[644]

This is not the king's composition. No other poem or Ghazal of this style is found in the collections (*Kulliyat*) of the King. Composed in pure Lucknavi style, this Ghazal is the creation of Wajid Ali Shah's son, Aasman Jah Anjum, and it is present in his published collections (*Diwan*). The correct couplet (*matla*) is like this:

Elahi! let some gust of wind dismantle the aanchal so that the face is shown
The Unkind peeps after covering the blinds with the aanchal[645]

The singers like the *matlas* used the verses, and they were not aware of the last couplet (*maqta*). There are many instances of changes and modifications in which people have willingly or mistakenly associated some unfamiliar compositions with Wajid Ali Shah. The above instances are enough by way of caution to show that this has happened and may happen again. To my knowledge, there are very limited compositions which are unfamiliar but trustworthy. The following are the examples of these:

1. *Majmuaey Hujuyat*

There is a handwritten magazine entitled *Majmuaey Hujuyat* which was also copied down from the handwritten diary of Nawab Zehra Begum, resident of Mansoor Nagar, Lucknow by Hatif Sahab on 21 May 1913. In this collection, there is satire about Nawab Ali Naqi Khan and his associates written by other poets, and three '*Munaqibs*' by Wajid Ali Shah. Following are the first and last couplets of Wajid Ali Shah's compositions:

---

644. *Adab Aur Tehzeeb.* Fursatullah Ansari. Azad Kitab Ghar. Delhi. 139.
645. *Daftar e Hasrat*, 85.

Pentagon (Mukhammas):

So much of gloom in the city By God mankind is sad
Trouble falls from the sky ....
Hussain! Come I shriek
(First bund)
Wajid Ali Shah *is a lover of Imam Akhtar of Hind is a slave of Panjtan*
Groundlessly he is blamed He does not need help from outsiders
Hussain! Come I shriek
(Tenth Bund)
Sixain (Mussaddas)
The cloud of sorrow and oppression envelopes my heart
The sky has struck a thunderbolt on my abode
The slaves of Dawar have attacked the nusairi
The accursed have destroyed my royals
Help of the oppressed is necessary, it is time to solve my problem
I am usurped in Hind I shriek for the King of Khurasan
(First Bund)
If the Moon of Fatima looks at me Akhtar
It will not be a surprise if Allah *becomes benevolent Akhtar*
My inauspicious star has vanished Akhtar
Why raising a hand Akhtar is not welcoming morning
Help of the oppressed is necessary it is time to solve my problem
I am usurped in Hind I shriek for the King of Khurasan
Pentagon (Mukhammas)
My morning comes after a weeping night
The day passes in extreme sorrow and melancholy
All the time I weep and shriek I look at the walls and doors wistfully
Adieu! my countrymen I depart! (First Bund)
Wajid Ali Shah*'S VERSE*
Akhtar bids adieu to the entire city Have no time to say more

Allah my countrymen be not devastated I look at the walls and doors wistfully
Adieu! my countrymen I depart! (Twelfth Bund)

There is no doubt in associating this composition with Wajid Ali Shah. First, this composition was recovered from the treasure of one of his wives.[646] Second, it was proved by the *munaqibs* (poem praising the Prophet's companions) of that period that Wajid Ali Shah composed such verses, but those *munaqibs* are not found in the collections of Wajid Ali Shah. Mushir mentions one of his *Munqibats*:

With strange sorrow all the masses wept With them wept the walls and doors
This noisy expression was on everyone's lips That Hussain Come for Help!
Munaqib that the King composed On reading that everyone wept
Someone was weeping in Karbala *I cannot tolerate this howl and cry*
Someone lamented in the mausoleum That Maula is amidst pain and sorrow
Take away the grief of Jaan e Alam For Sakina's sake help him[647]

Third, in the Library Jama Masjid, Bombay, there is a handwritten magazine titled *Ittla Nama* Amir *Ali Manzoom*, in which first the King's *Mukhammas* is given and a reply to it "which is very satirical." [648] The person who responded to it was named as *Mujtahid.* The first couplet (*matla*) and the last couplet (*maqta*) are as follows:

The person who heard this Munaqib Thought of respnding to it
Hussain come I shriek
Mujtahid saw in his dream Martyrs of Avadh are weeping

646. In 1964 some of the writings of Wajid Ali Shah were included in the Maulana Azad Library, Aligarh Muslim University, Aligarh on which the name of the same Begum was written.

647. *Masnavi Musheer* (Handwritten). Gauhar Ali Musheer. 1276. Khuda Bakhsh Library. 177.

648. *Urdu Khutoot.* Shamsul Reman. Kitabi Duniya. Delhi. 1947. 109–10.

They create pedomonium before Ali And they say raise your hands
Hussain come I shriek

Fourth, the poet has expressed his heartiest feelings that no other could express with so much expertise and purity. And perhaps this was the reason that a composition where there are so many painful and melancHolic expressions would not be suitably placed in a collection which is full of joyous and cheerful expressions. "Pearl below the feet' and 'stones below the feet" were expressions with morals and hence they were excluded from the Diwan.

2. *Marsia*

A handwritten Elegy was recovered from the library of Shehzada Jehan Qudr. On it is written "*Panjum Mahe Alam 1302.*" He is the same writer who scripted *Sabatul Quloob* and *Riyazul Quloob* in chain writing (*zanjeera*). He wrote this elegy in the same style. In the 100 *bunds* of this elegy, the first and last couplets are as follows:

First Couplet (*Matla*)
Voice from heaven gives me this grief
Today there is no smile on my lips, only grief
My heart is dedicated to grief…
There is no remedy for my grief and pain
There is restlessness in my heart
……………………

Last couplet (*Maqta*)
Be silent you sad Akhtar as Shimr is coming
He stabs the sword into the divine chest
He is showing bravery to the thirsty
This is the horse (duldul) of the helpless King
The Sun is eclipsed and moon is shrouded by the clouds.

No collection of elegies was found after 1300 A.H., hence there is a lesser chance that this elegy would have been a part of some collection. Among all the discovered compositions, this is the last elegy. Its association with the library of *Jahan Quder* and the script of the writer owes much to its authenticity.

3. *Marsia*

There is one more handwritten, 120 'bund' elegy found in the personal library of *Sarkar Amdatull Ulema*. The first and last verses of the elegy are as below:

My pen is the envy of the intelligent in the sky
In the field of eloquence my knowledge is supreme
In every matter the sky sacrifices its grandeur
Each of us is the friend of Isaa
*I send the ad*Mir*ation of flowers and garden to* Najaf
Abid (a.s.) then buried Sarwar*'s (a.s.) body*
It is heart rending so stop the pen (expression) Akhtar!
This is the time that you again request the master
Your fan is very restless these days
I am not convinced of the medicine of physicians
From your treasure give me health

This elegy is copied from a personal library in Hyderabad. Apart from the use of the word '*Akhtar*' in the last verse and a slight resemblance with the style of Wajid Ali Shah there is no other evidence to show that this elegy is the composition of the King. Considering the mention of trouble and ill health in the verses, and that this elegy is unpublished, it can be assumed that it was composed during the King's last prolonged illness.

The writings of bygone days – original, fake and artificial – are found in abundance, and one cannot expect that each and every word of such writings can be authenticated. But it cannot be denied that the more valuable and important a writing or composition is, the more strongly and deeply it will be investigated. The writer, publisher, seal, library, and comments are all secondary type of evidence. Based on the situation, these factors can be regarded as either weak or suitable, and the best measure is to discuss and consider the quality and attributes of the compositions of the original author, and then to look for these in the composition which is under consideration.

Section 4:

Salient Features of the Writings of Wajid Ali Shah

Objections regarding Writings: No one can defy the details of the writing skill and mental calibre of Wajid Ali Shah, as discussed in the previous pages. From the viewpoint of Wajid Ali Shah's impressive writing and compositions and his varied pastimes, it was unbelievable that a King who spent his time in such luxurious indulgences could be so efficient and skilled. Wajid Ali Shah's courtiers and some of the writers who were free of these luxurious indulgences and were concerned for their livelihood could not deliver even half of what the King did. It is both sad and surprising that the genius King faced the accusation that his compositions were in fact the creation of his associates or his opponents, who wrote either to please him or to blame him. In his own period, witnessing the downfall of literary ability, the King expressed faith in the talent and calibre of the forthcoming generations and very hopefully says:

I indicated the knowledge and education
So that the writer gets some appraisal
Otherwise where I am and where are such times
It is now Issa's religion and those times have vanished
Who will care for the art
No one will be concerned about Arabic or Urdu
It was up till us only
My own livelihood is also gone

But yes those who are to born new
Those who will rise anew
They will understand these times
They will understand this reality.[649]

These objections to the understanding of the situation forces one to conclude that the period of fairness is as far away today as it was a century ago. In a way, Wajid Ali Shah was lucky that during that period, even if no one was appreciative of his work, at least his work was not cruelly labelled as forged, fake, borrowed, or purchased. Today he is not only devoid of such appreciation but he cannot even protest. Writing a document himself and having it written by others, translating something himself and having it translated by others, and printing books himself and motivating others to have their compositions printed were services of knowledge and literature which he delivered as a duty. Perhaps he wished to see that coming generations would remember him for this invaluable service. But alas! Today, though there are memories of this fine gesture, these are being destroyed by the cruel hands of times. Most of these objections are creations of the present century by those who seek hollow reputations. The people who object have not seen the books but have only heard about them. However, they comment and object as if they have seen the compositions themselves. There is another category of people who object – people who are in some way acquainted with the books, but due to external evidence and their own mindset, they fail to be fair and neutral. The first group of people, who are dependent only on what they have heard, is irrelevant and can be ignored. The quality and attributes of the compositions form a silent response to the second group.

Hearsay:

The statement of the late *Maulvi Abdul Haque* represents the objections of the first category. He says:

649. *Sheva-e-Faiz.* Md. Wajid Ali Shah Akhtar. Publication Sultani. Calcutta. 1277. 143.

"It was a strange habit of Wajid Ali Shah *that he entered his library, tampered with some books, and randomly copied some things from the pages of different books. In this manner, from whatever book came his way, he copied something and would never consider the topic of the particular book, or that he had gathered extracts from books of various topics randomly. In fact, the King's books were written in this way, and he and his courtiers regarded this as a work of high standard. To write an explanation of such odd books was the job of the late Munshi."* [650] It is enough to say that this narration is connected with the early fame of *Maulvi Abdul Haque Sahab* and upon the death of Amir *Minai*, he scribbled this merely as a short note, hence it is worth ignoring. In the evaluation of Maulvi Sahab himself, he was not convinced about it. He writes:

"There are two articles which were published by the late Sheikh Chand, who without consulting me had included them in the book. One is regarding Munshi Amir *Minai, who died in Hyderabad. On the day of his death I wrote this article and had it published in the magazine Afsar. It is a light hearted article in which there is neither a full characterisation, nor is there a complete discussion on his compositions. At the time of the publication of new editions*[651] *I was in Eastern Pakistan, from where I again wrote to the late Qazi Ahmed Mian Akhtar Juna Garhi that these two articles be excluded from the magazine, but at the time of writing, he forgot to do it."* [652]

Due to the ignorance of these people, an irresponsible point was circulated for about 61 years. At different periods, various publications printed various editions, and no one could find the facts, and Maulvi Sahab could not

650. *Chand Humasar.* Publication Latifi Press, Delhi. Article "Amir Minai" (Published 1900), 2.

651. *Chand Humasar.* Pakistani Edition of 1953. (Publication Fourth- "*Baad Nazr Saani wa Izafa*". Publication Anjuman Taraqqi Urdu.

652. *Chand Humasar.* Pakistani Edition of 1953. (Publication Fourth- "*Baad Nazr Saani wa Izafa*". Publication Anjuman Taraqqi Urdu. The 1961 Pakistani Edition (With Changes?) Extract from the Preface by the author. This change was made after opposition of the article in Pakistan.

compensate for his mistake.[653] It is true that Maulvi Sahab did not admit that his claim was baseless in the above extract, but nothing more could be done by a person of his stature. The above claim cannot be applied to a single book by Wajid Ali Shah. It can however be applied to *Majmuaey Wajidia*, but there is a statement by the King that this is a collection of documents from his education, compiled in the form of a book. This book was published in 1266 A.H., and Amir Minai had no connection to the King until 1268 A.H.[654]

The second objection is no less harmful than that of Maulvi Abdul Haque. But that was a result of Wajid Ali Shah's foolish friendship with Amir Minai. This statement is in favour of the King. The statement says:

> "Learned authors (*Nisar Ahmed Farooqui*) and erudite Editors (*Md. Tufail*, Editor, *Nuqoosh*) should know that the autobiography (Explanation of the *Ishq Nama*) which was compiled regarding Wajid Ali Shah does not exist in the world. The intention of the English was to open a front of opposition against the learned Wajid Ali Shah, which they did by taking the seal of the King and linking certain writings with him."[655]

There are anonymous books which were once considered useless and 'purchased' and were thought to be the compilations of Wajid Ali Shah. Here, these are rejected as his writing. Such baseless objections can only be responded to in this manner. Of what has so far been written about Wajid Ali Shah and his luxurious indulgences, the major part was written by the bold pen of the King himself, and if one excludes this, then what remains is not enough to raise an eyebrow at his so-called lavish lifestyle.

---

653. Anjuman Taraqqi Urdu Hind published this book with the article: "Amir *Minai*" in 1966 which is included in the syllabi of many courses. Its July 1960 Edition was regarded the fifth Edition. It is not known as to how many editions have come out so far and how many students are benefitting from it.

654. *Sharah Hidayatul Sultan.* Munshi Amir Ahmed Amir Minai. Matbaey Sultani. Lucknow. 1268. 56–57.

655. *Abul Hasan Hasni Jafri*; Editor Magazine *Payam e Amal* (Lahore) in his editorial. Issue October 3, 1964.

His autobiography and his writings are examples of his bold etiquette, diverse persona and knowledgeable engagements. If by his writings his luxurious indulgences are revealed, then he must be upright in his admissions. This is only one side of a person's life; being unaware of or disregarding the other side, not caring to know the reality, or intentionally creating misunderstandings after learning the reality is the proof of parochial-mindedness and prejudice. Whenever one is reminded of the luxurious indulgences of the great King, and that his days and night were spent in opulence, these books and writings would vehemently contradict these misconceptions and reveal that such a person is prejudiced, uninformed, and does not want to highlight that he misread historical facts. The English used various means to give Wajid Ali Shah a bad name, and if they made use of some forged books to achieve this, then so far no such book has been discovered. The books which are associated with Wajid Ali Shah are his original writings, most of which are found in the list in *Bani*. In addition to this list and the seal of Matbaey Sultani, this fact is further authenticated by the *Qata'at e Tarikh*, which was written not by enemies, but by friends.

Baseless Findings

In educational circles, the objections that cause misunderstandings are more dangerous and harmful, though they had marginal importance in the comments of contemporaries. Their argument on the first sight appears to be reasonable until one sees the mind which was behind it. *Masnavi Ishq Nama* is often regarded as the composition of *Asir*. The idea behind this was that *Asir* was a better poet than Wajid Ali Shah and *Masnavi Ishq Nama* is a good *masnavi*, hence it is not Wajid Ali Shah's creation. The claim is that *Asir* composed it and gifted it to Wajid Ali Shah. This apparently simple narration is presented in a manner which seemingly meets all the requirements of research. But is it actually true? Wajid Ali Shah, *Asir*, Amir, *Qalaq*, Barq and the witnesses of their calibre and talent are all in eternal sleep. The proof and explanation of what they did and what they said falls on the shoulders of the present generation, who should remind others of the facts of past generations and should reach a reasonable conclusion. Those who blamed Wajid Ali Shah were unmindful of this great responsibility. For instance, in a self-written narration of *Asir* one could realise only this much:

> *"I was hopeless about this world, was not interested in magnificence and glory. Suddenly a special person came and took me to Diwan Khas, where Hazrat Sultan Alam Md.* Wajid Ali Shah *Akhtar was adorning the place... He greeted my humble self, gave me a place of honour to sit. He gifted me such a book which was a selected one. As per his order, I composed it. He was pleased to hear it, and I was also interested in his delight."*[656]

"Though *Asir* did not disclose the name of the book, it is believed that it was the *Tarikh Pari Khana*. Based on his wishes, it was composed in Urdu and was given the name of *Pari Khana Poetic.* It cannot be said with confidence who composed it, but it reflects the style of *Asir*. It has no small connection with Wajid Ali Shah's poetic calibre."[657] Wajid Ali Shah's poetic skill is indicated by addressing the *Ishq Nama* as *Pari Khana.*[658] *Asir's* familiarity with *masnavis* will be described soon. Right now, it is important to point out the reality that the above narration depends upon the poetic calibre of the writer. In the year 1959, the *Ishq Nama* had no connection with Wajid Ali Shah's poetic talents. However, for 15–20 years he presented the verses of the *Ishq Nama* in the following words:

> "*Sultan Alam* himself writes (page 203–210) that he had composed it in the form of a poem (page 213) ... In *Pari Khana* he himself writes (page 239) that *Jaan e Alam* composed the *Pari Khana* Poetic, (page 243)"[659]

---

656. *Aab e Baqa.* Khwaja Abdul Rauf Ishrat. Naami Press. Lucknow. 1918. 29.
657. *Naya Daur* (Monthly, Lucknow). August 1959, 71.
658. For the suitability of the name *Ishq Nama* see Chapter 1 & 3 of this book.
659. *Begmat e Avadh.* Sheikh Tassaduq Husain. Kitab Nagar Lucknow. 1956. This book is the collection of those articles which were published in various magazines, and which was published in the form of a book in 1956.

Maulvi Najmul Ghani Khan also had a taste for poetry,[660] and the copying of the *Ishq Nama* is proof that whether or not he read any other masnavis, he perused this *masnavi* or some of its verses. Despite this he opines:

> *"He* (Wajid Ali Shah)*, while relaxing in luxury and comfort, talks about love and romance composed randomly."*[661]

The first person who objects says that it is like the 'style of Asir', and the second person comments that Wajid Ali Shah 'composed randomly.' I do not agree with the opinion of people who perused the compositions of the poets of Lucknow School, but when there is a comparison between the works of Wajid Ali Shah and *Asir* in the eye of a distinguished person, the following paragraph is the best description to refer to:

> *"Whenever I compare the compositions of* Wajid Ali Shah *with that of Asir,* Barq*, Amanat, Qalaq, Beher, or Seher who were his court poets, I am convinced that his work was no less impressive than their's, but in fact compared to Amanat his excellence and supremacy is well established."*[662]

The narrative of *Asir* regarding Wajid Ali Shah's style of composition is also very interesting.[663] It is not limited to the narrative of *Asir*; in fact, there is no shortage of contradictory and differing opinions. Everyone has their own opinion which is guided by situation and personal motivation. The opinion of the compiler of the book *Hamari Shayari*, his understanding, poetic taste, fair evaluation of literary work and his fondness for Wajid Ali Shah are quite well known. But despite this he says:

> *"Some portions of the Ishq Nama are so poetic that one doubts whether it is the composition of* Wajid Ali Shah*."*[664]

660. Maulvi Najmul Ghani Khan is the compiler of a book like *"Behrul Fasahat."*
661. *Tarikh e Avadh*, Maulvi Md. Najmul Ghani Khan. Munshi Naval Kishore Publication. Lucknow. 1919. Volume 5, 111.
662. *Lucknow Ka Dabistan e Shayeri*. Dr. Abullais Siddiqui. Gilani Press. Lahore. 1955. 72.
663. *Durrul Taj*. Md. Muzzaffar Ali Khan Asir. Sultani Publication. Lucknow. 1270. 72, 112.
664. *Hamari Zaban* (Weekly) Issue 22.9.1965, 10.

He is also hesistant to associate the *Ishq Nama* with Wajid Ali Shah: *Asir* in his masnavi *Maaruj Fazail* writes;

That Wajid Ali Shah *Sahab ruler under whom the empire flourishes*
Greeted my humble self Made me sit near him mannerfully
Gifted me such a book which was like a beautiful flower
I composed it he was pleased I too wished his delight

These verses show that *Asir* composed a book on Wajid Ali Shah's orders, and perhaps this was the *Ishq Nama.*[665] The narration of *Asir* is in both prose and poetry. But the manner of drawing conclusions from this reveals the personality of a person. Some want a sensational discovery, some want appreciation for their understanding, while some want to defend Asir. But there is no proper way to defend him:

> *"If the masnavi Ishq Nama is composed by Asir even then* Wajid Ali Shah *will be regarded its author because he had composed the Persian Ishq Nama, hence it will not be correct to call Asir as its author."*[666]

Both critics examine the important and valuable parts of the composition, but their standard of poetic comprehension is not satisfactory. Too much brightness blurs the vision. It is important that if other verified sources are not available, then the less important parts of the *masnavi* should also be considered, and one should question whether ustad *Asir* would stoop to such a low standard of composition?

The Reality: Like the narrative above, *Asir* has given another statement also which is in the form of a poem, as follows:

When something remained Opportunity to enhance the luck was born
A staff came from the state He brought something with him

665. *Hamari Zaban* (Weekly) Issue, 15.1.1966, 4.
666. *Hamari Zaban* (Weekly, Aligarh) Issue 15.1.1966, 4.

It is prose and the order was given The poem should be very eloquent
The joy will continue Don't worry you will be called
Quickly compose the rhyme Don't be restless the idea will come
I kept that thing on my head often on my eyes and heart
Hope is manifested on face The morning of troublesome night dawned
My heart got some satisfaction and I started composing
I composed a poem of that My zeal was full [667]

The prominent difference between the narratives above is that in the first, it is stated that the King himself gave him the prose book in *Diwan e Khas*, and in the second it is written that it was delivered by the household staff. If the item delivered by the staff was the *Ishq Nama*, the poetic translation of which the King wanted be associated with, then *Asir* could not have had the courage or permission to discuss it, and several people had been included in this deal. It would have been better if *Asir* had disclosed its name. But as he did not disclose it, ignoring the eyewitnesses, logical evidence, and truthful tradition based on unlikely assumptions is neither wise nor acceptable. Then, why not include the other *masnavis* in this suspicion? When there are differences in the narratives of *Asir*, and if, in our view, every narrative is truthful, then for every narration one *masnavi* would be removed from Wajid Ali Shah's treasure. Many of Wajid Ali Shah's *masnavis* have been converted from prose to poetry. Why limit the area of investigation?

There is one more tradition which supports the association of the *Ishq Nama* with *Asir*. In many places, *Asir* bragged about his work, but he did not mention the title. This folly of *Asir* was corrected by his follower *Aftabud Daulah* Qalq. But Qalq*'s* story is only hearsay; though Qalq is the storyteller, the narration was made not by him but by *Faazil Lucknavi*, and that even after Qalq*'s* death:

"Wajid Ali Shah *asked Asir to compose a masnavi Ishq Nama, and had the illustrated version written by other writers. The pages on which there were*

667. *Supra Note* 662 at 266–67.

> *illustrations and pictures had some space left for couplets. The King said that it should be filled with couplets. Asir said that all the events had been covered and it would not be easy to fill the empty space, but the King insisted that it should be done before him. Then Asir mannerfully said that sitting in the courtier's dress and composing will not be an easy task, and if I am allowed I can sit in another room to compose. This request was accepted, the binding was opened, and the tales were distributed among the various writers. Asir started composing couplets for different tales and the writers started their work. During this exercise the King visited the room and enquired as to what was the progress. The King was pleased to hear the couplets and expressed his appreciation, and was proud of the fact that such genius poet was in his court."*[668]

No one can understand the meaning and context of this narration, as the writer *Faazil* was himself unable to comprehend it. In the same issue, after a few pages he writes:

> *"The fact is that at the age of 10 or 12, a graceful maid had spoiled the habits of* Wajid Ali Shah. *This was admitted by the King in his poetic biography."*[669]

The name of this autobiography is not given, but if it is not the *Ishq Nama*, then what biography would it be? And if it is the *Ishq Nama*, then what is the *Ishq Nama* that *Asir* had composed?

Janab Faazil, using Qalq as a reference, associates this biography with Asir in an organized manner. It is then incumbent upon Qalq to clarify the subject matter of the *Ishq Nama.* But Qalq was helpless, and an answer was impatiently expected. It may be that he discussed this with *Faazil Sahab*, but if there was any mention of the biography, then it is unclear why *Faazil* made this mistake. For the sake of argument, even if one accepts that by *Ishq Nama* he means the same biography which I associate with Wajid Ali Shah, a question remains unanswered: if a book was presented in the court with so much preparation, in which changes were made by *Asir*, and which was

---

668. *Zamana* (Monthly, Kanpur). Issue July 1910, 3.

669. *Zamana* (Monthly, Kanpur). Issue July 1910, 16.

copied by the writers, then how was it left unmentioned by *Asir*? This is also not mentioned by any other person. Above all, Wajid Ali Shah, who was competent enough to criticise and pass strictures, did not even approve that his master (*ustad*) should add words in his compositions at the time of their correction. How then would he have accepted a *masnavi* with thousands of verses so gladly and wholeheartedly, and with the accolades mentioned by Qalq. Then, the claim by Sharar[670] and other well-informed people[671] that Wajid Ali Shah's compositions are his own would appear to be hollow and far from reality.

In this context, the statement of Mohsin Ali Mohsin Sahab Tazkira Sarapa Sukhan in support of Qalq needs attention. In his commentary *Mohsin* mentioned *Asir* in five places, and each time he wrote "*Masahib Khas Sultan Alam*" (Special companion of *Sultan Alam*) with the titles. But the mention of his writings is not the same as shown here:

"*Sahab Diwan Farsi wa Rekhta*, the *Ishq Nama* (page 127), one Farsi *Diwan*, and two *Hindi* Diwans are associated with him (page 273). *Sahab Diwan Shagird Rashid Mian* MuShafi (page 332) ... *Sahab Diwan Shagird* MuShafi (page 358), *Sahab Diwan Hindi* and *Persian* (page 363)."[672]

In these narrations, he only mentions the *Ishq Nama* as the work of *Asir* once. The contradiction in these statements is proof of the fact that whatever Mohsin wrote were only comment and observations and there was no intention to correct. Perhaps the compiler did not peruse the entire collection, in which case one cannot be convinced that by *Ishq Nama* he meant the same *masnavi* which is the subject of the present argument. Like Qalq, he has only mentioned the name, which is not decisive proof.

The statements of *Asir*, Qalq, and *Mohsin* are not wrong, but the justifications made based on such weak narrations are wrong. *Asir's masnavi*

---

670. *Jaan e Alam.* Maulvi Abdul Haleem Sharar. Adaraey Faroghe Urdu. Lahore. 1951. 81.
671. Compilers of *Wazir Nama* and *Boostan e Avadh.*
672. *Sarapa Sukhan.* Syed Mohsin Ali Mohsin. Pubication Munshi Naval Kishore. Lucknow. 1874. (1277)

must be searched for in *Asir's* collections. After doing this, we will have two options before us: one option is a composition with *Ishq Nama* as its title and the other is a composition which has no name or title whatsoever (*Gumnam*).Those who opt for the *Ishq Nama* remember it by that name, but those who dither with the unnamed book would not hesitate to associate any book which comes their way with it. Many people followed this path. But I move ahead and look for more options.

In his commentary, Amir *Minai* mentions a romantic *masnavi* by *Asir* titled "*Durrul Taj*".[673] *Asir* completed this masnavi in 1268 A.H.[674] and Matbaey Sultani published it in 1270 A.H. The *masnavi* was composed on Wajid Ali Shah's wishes.[675] The book is rare but not nonexisting. In the beginning of this *masnavi*, *Asir* (under the title 'Dar sabab Taalif kitab Guyad') explains his romantic indulgences in around 6 pages and promised to compose his romantic biography.

In short I strongly resolve
I will compose a real story
The tale which be known to the world
My lovers be in isolation
Whosoevr hears this becomes awestruck
The garden of the world becomes colourful[676]

Hence, with "*Dar byan ishq Guyad*"[677] ('I am narrating about love') and "*Dariban e Maashooq Guyad*"[678] (I am narrating about my beloved), he

673. *Intekhab e Yaadgar.* Munshi Amir Ahmed Amir Minai. Tajul Mutabey. 1297. 14.
674. *Tarikh bhi hai isi mein paida Hai Khamshi Aey Asir Zeba.* (*Date is given in this ---- Silence is suitable Asir*) 1268. *Durrul Taj.* 242.
675. *Diwan e Asir.* Md. Muzzaffar Ali Khan Asir. Publication Munshir Naval Kishore. Lucknow. 1286. 501.
676. *Durrul Taj.* Md. Muzaffar Ali Khan Asir. Matbaey Sultani. Lucknow. 1270. 31.
677. *Ibid,* 31–36.
678. *Ibid,* 36–40.

proceeds to repeat words like '*Ishq*', '*Aashiqan*', '*Aashiq*', and '*Maashooq*'. In various places in the *masnavi* there are narrations which can be illustrated. It is not a continuous story and there is an attempt to streamline different events into one. At the end, he writes in clear words:

I am writing ishq nama from here
The reins of the pen is pulled[679]
Name of the masnavi is Durrul Taj:
Poetry is raised to higher pedestal
The suitable name is Durrul Taj[680]

The same name is printed on the title page. But those who composed the *Qata'at e Tarikh* did not bother about this name. They composed *Qata'as* with the word *Ishq Nama*. There are two *Qata'as*. Maqbool ud Daulah Qubool writes in his *Qata'as*:

The King has himself composed ishq
One who is himself the crush of the world
When the purpose of this epic is achieved
Then the critics appreciated it
Know the year of its publication from Qubool
About the one who is the pride and honour of the world (1270)
(Translated from Persian)
The second Qata'a is of Amir Ali Khan Hilal*:*
When I started deciphering its date
This humble Hilal *remained secluded*
A verse came to my mind like a precious pearl
The love tale which was in the King's heart (1270)
(Translated from Persian)

679. *Ibid*, 191.
680. *Ibid*, 240.

The narrations of Qalq and *Mohsin* are well justified by this *masnavi* and its *Qata'at e Tarikh*. Qalq has claimed there is a *masnavi* named *Ishq Nama* written by *Asir*. Nowhere in his statement does he say that the masnavi was later owned by Wajid Ali Shah. It would not be a surprise if there was a mistake in his statement and its understanding by *Faazil*. I find contradictions in *Faazil's* statement because I am looking for proof of my original thinking. There is a possibility that both the statements are correct and there is some fault in their expression which gives rise to misunderstandings. *Mohsin's* statement, which is probably from the same period as that *masnavi*, is perhaps based on hearsay. He only heard about the popularity of the *masnavi*, he did not see it himself and just stated whatever he heard. In the commentary, the mention of the popular name without the real name is for this reason only. *Asir's* unknown narratives are also not beyond his masnavi *Durrul Taj*. On the King's invitation, he visited the court, and the affectionate behaviour of the King is mentioned by him in the *masnavi*.

A. *On hearing the abject condition One day the King ordered*
Bring him who is that heartbroken I want to hear his couplets
On hearing this I was happy my heart was more happy than myself
When Imdad Hussain Khan heard this Then he conveyed to me quickly
A special messenger came to me Tomorrow you are requisitioned
What to express my happiness at that moment My heart is overwhelmed [681]
B. *How to express the affection He started reciting my couplets*
And ordered me to sit I paid salaam thrice and sat[682]
C. *Gave me the place nearby I enjoyed this nearness*
Some couplets which I had composed my thoughts which were expressed
I was so much impressed I read out slowly slowly
Allah*! What good conduct Thy self appreciated repeatedly*

681. *Ibid*, 62.
682. *Ibid*, 68.

The appreciation of the pomp and splendour with which the King had asked *Asir* to incorporate into his poems was explained by *Asir* in his own masnavi:

He said this much only you could compose such couplets
You are known for your goodness I want praise for majesty and grandeur
I said okay again when my impatience brings me here
I will recite some new couplets I will bring some other gift[683]

But the narration of stories and dance dramas towards the end of the *masnavi*,[684] which is unnecessarily strange, shows no indication of how *Asir* came to know of those events, other than the staff delivering the one 'thing'. During the initial years of their association (*masahibat*), he composed his work based on the wishes of the King, and often he composed voluntarily just to please the King. Later, during the early years of Amjad Ali Shah and Wajid Ali Shah's reign, he became the object of their anger and displeasure and spent some years in prison.[685] During this period of abject misery, the King again favoured him and asked him to write. The King made a wish to complete the unfinished part and thus as it relates to *Asir's* hard times hence it is obscure and inconsistent. And to highlight the defects in this part of the masnavi, we cannot disregard *Asir's* humbleness:

> *"I, as per his order, composed it. He was very pleased to hear this; his happiness delighted me."*[686]

From '*Bismillah*' upto '*Kar Khatima*', the basic work of the *masnavi Ishq Nama* was completed by 1266 A.H. It is quite possible that someone made corrections to it, and that additions were made up to 1270 A.H.[687] But the

683. *Ibid*, 89–90.
684. *Ibid*, 182–238.
685. *Ibid*, 125–227.
686. *Aab e Baqa*. Khwaja Abdul Rauf Ishrat. Naami Press. Lucknow. 1918. 29.
687. *Hamari Zaban* (Weekly, Aligarh). Issue 15th. January 1966, 4.

Ishq Nama is not the name of the corrections or additions, it is the name of the *masnavi* and in absence of any proper evidence, cannot one say that it is not the composition of Wajid Ali Shah.

Arguments regarding the characteristics of the Composition

After identifying the motives behind the objections and replying to them negatively, it is not necessary to also respond positively. It is the duty of the complainant to prove the charge, and not of the accused to clarify his case. But due to quality and attributes of the composition, an evaluating eye could fall prey to some suspicion. Hence, evidence that has not previously been presented is discussed here to prove that the compositions of Wajid Ali Shah are original.

Just like fragrance of the flower is fused in the flower
Similarly I am engrossed in my writing
Anyone who wants to see me
Must see me in my compositions
(Translated from Persian)

There is no better way to identify the compostion or poetry of a poet than to look for the attributes of which one is aware or may become aware after going through the work. If the speaker is behind the bar or hidden, then the best way to identify him is by his voice, but if death has silenced him, then it is the writing which reveals his identity. To start with, the attributes of Wajid Ali Shah's work will form the basis of the comparison between his work and the work of others, and certain principles will be laid down to identify the salient features of his writing. In this way whenever there is even the strongest evidence to show that the *Ishq Nama* or any other composition is not the work of Wajid Ali Shah, until and unless such principles indicating the salient features of his work are rebutted, any objection will not be considered valid. Based on these inferred principles, I now examine the *masnavi Ishq Nama* to judge whether my conclusions are wrong, or those who claim *Ishq Nama* to be the work of another poet are at fault.

1. The manuscript[688] of the *masnavi Ishq Nama* is in Wajid Ali Shah's handwriting.

Before associating the manuscript with Wajid Ali Shah, it is important to prove that it is a manuscript. On manuscripts it is not written that it is a manuscript. This is determined with the help of features and signs. When the writer sits down to write something, the original book is kept before him. He knows what to write and within how much space. The nature of their mistakes can be identified by the Corrigendum of the original book. When a poet or writer composes something, he is unaware as to what he will write next. He thus keeps changing the narrative based on his thoughts and speed of his pen. If he writes something and then needs to make a change, he changes or deletes the content on the paper. A writer usually does not look back, and if he wants to make corrections, this is done differently. The basic difference between "*Naql Seena Bars Safina*" and *Naqal Safina Bar Safina*" provides valuable knowledge. A writer with a poetic mind who has limited knowledge, or who is motivated by copying down from a handwritten or printed *masnavi*, then it is possible that he may make innumerable mistakes, but it is not possible that he would make the same mistakes as are made by a poet in his writing. A poet not only has a poetic mind but also an aesthetic sense, and the changes made by him are based on the topic, poetic composition, and characteristic features of the work. These points are to be kept in mind while perusing the mistakes and their corrections in the manuscript of the *Ishq Nama*.[689]

---

688. By manuscript is meant the handwritten manuscript of Anjuman Taraqqi Urdu Hind, Aligarh.

689. *Maulvi Abdul Haque* in whose times this manuscript was moved from the collection of Hasrat Mohani to the library of Anjuman, and Prof. Masood Hasan Rizvi who has seen

To put it concisely, a poet or writer can make many mistakes when their pen moves impulsively, and their thoughts start pouring naturally and spontaneously. In this condition, the psychology and emotions of the writer take over his educational competency. Insightful people who have perused the work of celebrities, examiners at universities who examine the work of high-class students, and editors of newspapers who correspond with writers know very well that no writing is free of mistakes.[690] The deeper the concentration, the faster the pen, and the more varied the mistakes. If the writer's head is in the sky and their pen touches the paper, then the word '*shah*' could be written as '*Sah*' or the word '*Ali*' as '*ali*' (with alif). Or instead of Wajid Ali Shah, the name could accidentally be written as 'Amjad Ali Shah', '*Ali Shah*', or '*Md.* Wajid Ali Shah', and the mind is so deeply engrossed that it feels that whatever was written has been written correctly. In poetry there is one more hardship, which is taking care of rhymes, repetition of words (*radif*), poetic metre, and artistic points. If the work is done on lined paper, then taking care while writing lines (*misra*) on one above the other becomes challenging. If the writer is fast, then the pen may be a hurdle. Cleaning the strands of the pen and fingerprints on the paper while wiping the ink from the nib becomes obvious. Peruse the *Ishq Nama* from start to finish; there will hardly be any pages on which there are no such aesthetic mistakes. The places where corrections were not made are much more in number than the places where corrections were done. Explaining all of them is not possible. Only a few examples are being cited here:

---

this copy (See, *Hamari Zaban* – Issue 15.1.1966) must be aware of these adornments. Either these learned people gave no importance to these adornments, or they were unabe to understand their importance. It is not possible for the writer of this book that after the investigations of these learned people, presenting his writings in a light manner regard this copy as manuscript.

690. In support of this claims work of many distinguished writers can be presented but it will not be improper if name of Hali is quoted here who in *Muqadamae Sher or Shayari* wrote 'member' instead of 'menbar'(with noon alphabet) and all his life he kept blessing the writer that he drew his attention towards it. (See, *Muqadamae Sher or Shayari*, 37).

A. THE FLAWS OF WRITING

All the mistakes in the manuscript can be regarded as flaws of writing, but here only mistakes which are due to the excess of words or in distorted form are presented:

1. Headings

> "The 73rd tale about that lady who is like the 'Hoors' and resembled the full moon."
> (Translated from Persian)

On page 261, the intention was to write "*awurda bood*" in the heading. These words are in the middle. Then it came to mind that two words, "*Badr kardansh*", should be added. This addition filled the space on the left of the page, but the space at the right looked odd. To create balance, a flower was drawn on the left and a whole creeper was drawn on the right. In other headings it was taken care that if in one line only one or two words were to be written, then they should be in the middle of the line. Where this could not be done, a drawing was made in the above manner to remove the imbalance. Had this been written by a professional writer, he would have known how the space was to be used based on the measure of the lines before copying the words.

2. Words

The writer made spelling mistakes. One word is written correctly in some places and incorrectly in others.

Words	Wrongly Written	Correctly Written
Gulzar	Page 181 with 'zaal'	Page 181 - has done this in the couplets
Sarguzasht	Page 216 with 'zey'	Page 216 corrected this
Beher	Page 360 with 'hay'	The spelling is corrected
Umrao Begum	Page 367 with 'ain'	Page 359 (or the heading of *Daastan* 52)

Mulazim	Page 359 with'zaal'	Page 360 corrected with 'zey'
Nazr	Page 373 with 'zoey'	(Misra: *kare nazr rizwan agar har behesht*)
Chausar	Page 381 with 'swad'	(Misra: *kahin koi Chausar laga khelne*)

3. Dots (Nuqta)

It is possible to read words incorrectly due to the absence of '*nuqtas*' or an irregular 'shosha' (upward serif). The writer corrected this in some places and left it unattended in others. For instance, on page 284 the words should be:

> *"Sukhan mukhtasar thhi jo baqi* ***hayat*** *– Khuda ne mujhe iss se bakhshi* ***nijat."***
> ***(I say because the life is short – Khuda has awarded salvation to me from it [life])***

Instead, they are:

> *"Sukhan mukhtasar thhi jo baqi* ***Janab*** *– Khuda ne mujhe iss se bakhshi* ***Sahab"***
> ***(I say Gentleman the life is short – Khuda has given me a companion)***

Here the words '*hayat*' and '*nijat*' are rhymes but are read as '*janab*' and '*sahab*'. In the manuscript there is no difference between '*yayay maroof*' and '*yayay majhool*' (i.e. big and small '*yay*'). The dots or '*nuqtas*' are intentionally not provided or are written on the top instead of the bottom and vice versa.

4. Pages

Pages were counted by the writer using his own pen, and there are numerous mistakes.

5. Lines (Misras)

Some of the *misras* were imbalanced due to either an increase or shortage of words or because the meaning of some improper words was obscured. The mistakes are very apparent:

Page 144 - Pari *khana mein* ***go*** *bada (jo) zabt thha*
Page 189 – *Sar uske thhey goya ke they (ke) deepak* ***ke*** *sar (ka)*
Page 294 – *ke aatish mein angushtari usski* ***jale*** *(jali)*
Page 215 – ***Khudai*** *ki qasam befawa mein nahin* ***(****Khuda****)***
Page 210 – *Magar mujh ko walid* **ko** *andesha thha (ka insead of second ko)*
Page 295 – *Dikhaey jo* **ussko** *dagey badan ('uss mei ko' instead of ussko)*
Page 313 – *Kahun kya ke* ***jab*** *mai juda ek lutf (sab instead of jab)*
Page 399 – ***Khata*** *hogi mujh par sitam dhaaegi (khafa instead of khata)*

6. Flaw in Writing

There are many such mistakes in the writing, but it is better to give attention to these. For instance, in the heading of *Daastan* 129, first '*Begum Hazrat*' is written, but in the same heading when the name is written again, it is written as '*Hazrat Mahal*' (page 509). It is possible for a stranger to regard both of these as the same. But in both the *Ishq Nama* and *Daastan*, the verses indicate that these are two different people, and in Daastan 129 there only *Begum Hazrat* is mentioned.

7. Phonic Mistakes (Sauti)

Some examples of incorrect writing reveal another possibility. Though these appear to be spelling mistakes, but the similarity of sound is seen in a different form:

Page 300 – *Wo Darulka mere makanon ka thha*
safa baksh in boostanon ka thha

In place of '*Darulka*' the word '*Darogah*' is written. The writer was misled due to the sound – in 'darogah', from the word 'ghain' 'noon gaf' and from 'gaf' the sound of 'kaaf' is inferred.[691] There are more such examples in the manuscript:

691. In the manuscript the alphabets *'kaaf'* and *'gaaf'* are written similarly.

Page 379 – *Nai* ***Daastan*** *Sunaney laga – Dastanein*
Page 400 – *Koi Badakash aur* ***muja*** *nahin – mujh sa*
Page 435 – *Kiya muntakhib Taefay* ***Maine*** *chand – Mai ne*
Page 481 – *Safar hai* ***rahe*** *aashiqi mein sitam – Rahe Ishq*

8. Fingerprints

The writer wrote the manuscript in the well-established Arabic script, and over 382 pages the fingerprint impressions in a few places are not surprising. If these impressions are found continuously however – in at least 25 places – then it will be considered a habit of the writer. These light or deep impressions are found on the following pages of the *Ishq Nama masnavi*:

139, 153, 233, 240, 256, 258, 263, 277, 288, 289, 296, 334, 335, 372, 393, 401, 405, 406, 408, 416, 430, 434, 461, 463, 466.

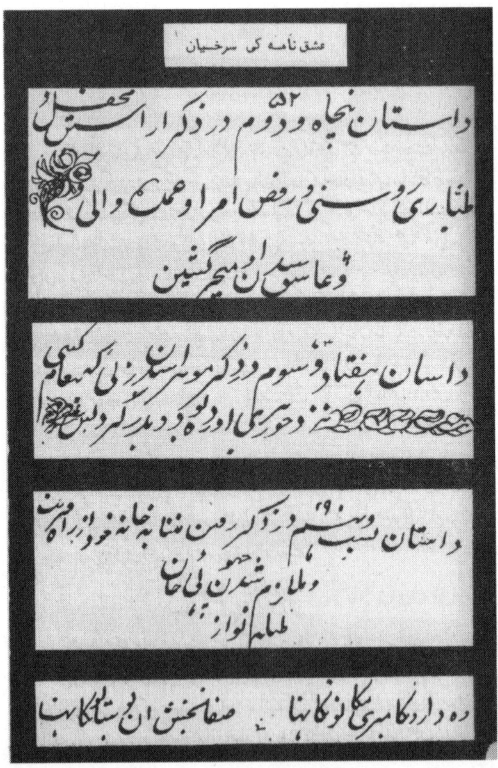

Image A: Headings of *Ishq Nama*

9. Corrections of Writings

It was a common practice with writers that if one word was written incorrectly, then they remove and rewrite it. Other writers scribble the correct word over the wrongly written word, or they remove the wrong word with their pen and write the correct word at the side or on top of it. The writer of the *Ishq Nama* was not interested in correcting the words. If a word was wrong, then it was left like that. Corrections were made only at places where they would not ruin the appearance of the page, or where the correction of the meaning was thought necessary. Instances of scribbling one word over another are rarely found. For any change, the corrected word was written in the margin, and the incorrect word was lightly marked. The word which was deleted was marked with the Urdu words '*la la la*' (page 358), the words '*badal*', '*galat*' or '*sahih*' were written, (page 225, 301, 305), or only two *zabars*[692] were made on top of it (page 251, 371). In places where, by mistake, a '*markaz*'[693] was written instead of a dot, the upper part was scratched with the nib of the pen until only dot was left (page 387), or verbal advice, such as '*Hua bar har do misra sahih*' (page 489), '*shaban mein sahih*' (page 509) or '*jama sahih*' (page 454), was written. The *misras* or couplets which were changed were written in the margin, and despite so many mistakes, the neatness is commendable. On a cursory look it is difficult to regard it as a manuscript.

DECORATIVE DESIGNS

Just like the incorrect pronunciation of couplets sounds bad to the ears, disproportionate decorative designs appear ugly to eyes which have a taste for art. The art of writing is a kind of painting, and the writer of the manuscript has shown aesthetic taste by filling the gaps and empty spaces with

---

692. Vowel sound 'e' as in 'herd' denoted by the symbol ´. Oxford Urdu-English Dictionary. 668. (Translator).

693. Upper stroke of letters 'kaaf', 'gaaf'. Oxford Urdu-English Dictionary. P. 998. (Translator).

attractive drawings, and the corrections do not look like ugly blots. Even if the decoration was only to fill the empty spaces, it was still not the job of a copier or writer. In a manuscript, decorations were often used to remove the written words. Every written word has a different form and shape, and its dots, curves, and circles cannot easily be converted into any intended design or shape. They can only be converted into some special designs, and an in-depth study as to why a writer chose a particular shape would provide deep insight into their wisdom and taste. It is unusual for a copier to possess the standard or aesthetic skill needed to conceal a mistake or flaw. The following document is presented as an example:

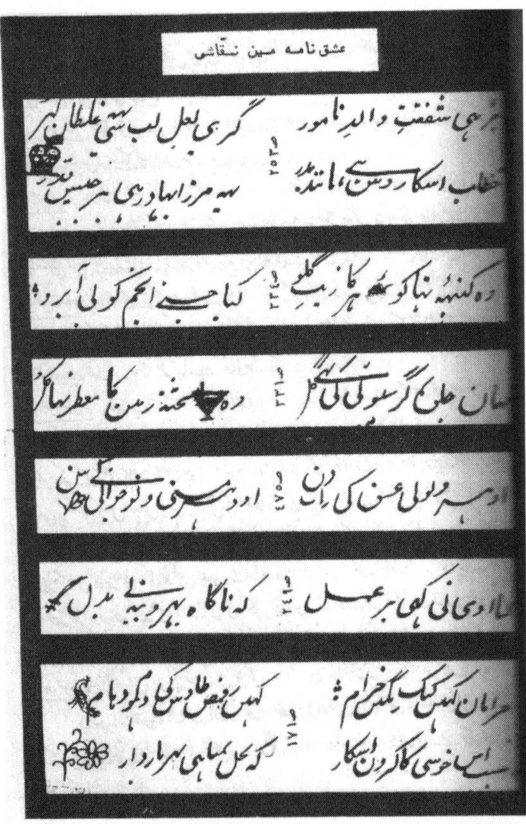

IMAGE B- Painting in the *Ishq Nama* to hide a mistake. Note the drawing of a crown, goblet, sword, peacock and flower.

1. Page 171:

   Somewhere the partridge is moving somewhere the peacock dance spreads commotion

   The last line ended before the limit, and so something, like a flower, could be drawn there to fill the gap. Here, the scene of a dancing peacock is drawn.[694] (see Image B – Second line from below)
2. Page 249:

   Man followed the saying suddenly the impostor attacked

   Here too there was empty space. As the poet has written about an attack by an impostor with a sword in his hand, in the empty space a sword is drawn. (Image B – Third line from below).
3. Page 253:

   His luck is shining like moon This is Mirza *Birjis Quder* Bahadur *Sallamahu*

   In the second line, a blessing ('*sallamahu*') is not part of the *misra*, and the writer realised his mistake after writing.There are mentions of other princes and princesses in the manuscript, but nowhere does the word '*sallamahu*' appear. The mistake could be corrected by inserting '*la*' or '*ghain*', or with two *zabars*, but that would have spoiled the affection with which the word (*sallamahu*) was inserted. Therefore, the writer connected the points of '*sa*' and '*lam*' in the form of a circle, and gave it the shape of a crown. The crown has an association with 'Prince', which was expressed in the word '*sallamahu*', and then it was artistically transformed into the shape of a crown. (Image B – Second line from top).

694. Strangely enough, the approach used by the King is seen even today. In this era of internet and smartphones, Android phones use the same approach - in WhatsApp, if someone writes the word 'like', an emoji of a heart appears. (Translator).

4. Page 231:

   Where the white rose was blooming that piece of land was full of fragrance

   The word *thha* (was) appears twice in the *misra* (second line). To delete one of these, the shape of a goblet is drawn, as flowers are often compared to goblets. (Image B – Fourth line from below).

5. Page 334:

   That necklace was adorning the neck which insulted Anjum

   In this line, the letter 'ei' in the word '*koi*' was thought to be unnecessary, hence the points were connected, transforming it into the shape of an apple. Perhaps the idea of an 'apple' was evoked by the word *zeb* (suitability) and *kantha* (necklace). The King thought like this and hence made image of an 'apple' though not visible in the image. (Image B – Third line from top).

6. Page 475:

   This side the enthusiasm of romance day and night On the other side lethargy of youth

   In this line, to change the word 'sin' to '*din*' (day), the curves of '*seen*' were joined, and the '*noon*' and '*dal*' was converted into a leaf shape (Image B – Third line from below).

7. Page 171 –

   I will express the reason of this joy The seed of my wish is laden with fruit

   In the second line, there was empty space. Drawing only one flower could cover the gap, but to show the idea of 'laden with fruit', a branch full of flowers was drawn. (Image B – First line from below) Writing the original statement and unconsciously making mistakes but then giving so much attention to correcting the mistake, are two conflicting mindsets, but it is not that these cannot both be present. Even a prolific poet does not have such a strong memory that he can just pick up a pen and write spontaneously. This requires concentration, and in this condition his impatient fingers move aimlessly on the paper. What the writer of *Ishq Nama* actually scribbled or wrote carelessly and at how many places is not known. But whatever could be seen in the documents is not meaningless and is comprehensible.

They are given as much attention as is usually given in a thoughtful moment. And that is why they are neither so good nor in abundance.[695]

POETIC AND AESTHETIC INTRICACIES

The dancing peacock, sword, goblet, necklace, leaf, and the laden branch reveal the meaning of the drawings, and at the same time indicate that the writer visualized whatever he wrote and felt it with his eye of imagination. Then, if he comes across a flaw, he corrects it with such mastery which cannot be the job of a writer. For instance, in *Daastan* 90, there is mention of visiting a prostitute's house. The king is sitting on a chair in the dress of a soldier, the prostitute has a crush on him, and she does everything to please him. The scene is sketched in the following couplet:

1. Page 345:

   She is standing with heart in her hand often with Khaasdan[696] *and often with Paandan*[697]

---

695. *Anis* has discussed this condition.
Pen retreated after giving a dot on the nail
When no other resemblance could be imagined of the beauty spots on the face of the king.
This could be a reason for the fingerprints of Wajid Ali Shah on the royal writings.

696. A utensil usually made of silver, used to serve *'paan'* to guests. (Translator)

697. An ornamental utensil with a lid made of silver or any other metal containing all the ingredients like *kattha, lime supari,* and beetle leaves to instantly prepare *'paan.'* (Translator).

Khasdan and *Paandan* are words with a similar meaning, but 'standing with a '*paandan*' is not romantic. One sits, not stands, with a *paandan*. It is better that he realised this at once, and at the same place drew a perfume bottle (*itrdaan*). This was corrected at the right time because a spelling mistake in a '*radif*' or rhyme could be ignored, saying that the mind of the poet was diverted, but a flaw in this poetic elegance would have been unpardonable.

a. From Correct to Aesthetic

The difference between the poet and the writer starts from this aesthetic sense. This is the argument regarding authenticity of *Ishq Nama* as the work of the King. Thus, by way of argument it is being said here that when a common writer writes or copies something then there is a difference in the aesthetic style whereas the content of the text and the margin show copier's style which may not be so eloquent or aesthetic. But in this case because the manuscript is in the King's hand and the text and the margin show the same handwriting and eloquent style hence the examples below further prove that 'Ishq Nama' is the original work of Wajid Ali Shah. Some examples of correcting an expression to make it more eloquent are as follows:

1. Page 187:

   My name was on the tongue every moment
   The string of tears rolled down many times

   The corrected word in the margin is '*Jhari*' instead of '*lari*'.
2. Page 200:

   The Sun in front of whose brightness
   The 'toor' of beauties was concealed like a star

   The corrected word in the margin is 'Noor' instead of '*toor*'.

3. Page 324:

   At end (anjaam) this was recovered
   That he interfered in every work

   The corrected word in the margin is '*inaam*' instead of '*anjaam.*'

b. Rectification of Composition

When an event is related, care is taken that no detail is left out which may cause discontinuity. It is also necessary that the composition be compact, and the lines and couplets are merged into each other. Generally speaking, at the time of composition, the poet can make a mistake, but its correction is also the poet's job. In the manuscript there are several instances of this which are presented as follows:

1. Page 202:

   When half of the month of Shaban passed
   It was the time of the birth of the King of mankind (Shah e Anam)
   The forts were adorned exquisitely
   And in the same way the garden of heaven was adorned

   The poet forgot to mention where the celebration was held. He added another couplet between these couplets:

   The gathering was organized in the fort of the King
   All the preparations were alluring and fascinating

   In another place, the couplet was correct, but the musical composition was not satisfactory:

2. Page 151:

   She was a beauty with fair complexion
   The human wisdom was nonplussed
   Her height and walk created havoc
   The killer (qayamat) herself came forward

At the time of composition, there is chance of a word falling from the poetic metre. There could be flaws such as excessive words (*Taa'qeed*), or that something is said in two ways. The poet, by adopting a more eloquent style, proves his supremacy over the writer:

3. Page 204:

I was surprised at the décor of the court
I remained stood by the wall

The second line was written as '*Khare lag gaye reh ke deewar se*', but the correct form is '*Khare reh gay lag ke deewar se*'

4. Page 311:

There was an urge to see the beauty of Yusuf
She reached the place after dithering

The second line was written as '*lab e chah phahunchi wo gum karda rah*', but the correct form is '*lab e chah pahunchi wo gum kar ke rah*'. In the manuscript there are many instances of writing incorrect rhymes or '*radif*' or of repeating rhymes. These are:

5. Page 195:

In the plant of my wish fruit has come
Then she was made Nawab Izzat Mahal

The first line was written as '*Nihal e tamanna mein aya samar*', but the correct form is '*Nihal tamanna mein aya jo phal*'

6. Page 200:

The value of the beloved was increased
She was fairy and got the title of 'Amir'

The first line was written as '*Badhi qadr e mashooqaey dil pasand*', but the correct form is '*Badhi qadr e mashooqaey dil pazeer*'.

7. Page 157:

When he saw the shining belly
Then the Mirror *maker became unconscious*

The second line was written as '*Toh aina saazon ko hairan hua*', but the correct form is '*Toh aina saazon ko sakta hua*'.

8. Page 333:

The fear of heart caused commotion
With uncovering shame disappeared

The second line was written as '*Hui behijabi se kafoor shama*', but the correct form is '*Hui behijabi se kafoor sharm*'.

9. Page 276:

How to conceal my sad story
How fire can be hidden under trash

The first line was written as '*Chhupaun mei ghamnak ahwal kya*', but the correct form is '*Chupaun mein ahwal e ghamnak kya*'.

10. Page 261:

I wanted that the world be free of rubbish
The flame which has blown be buried under the earth

The first line was written as '*Ye chaha ke khas kum jahan pak shud*', but the correct form is '*Ye chaha ke khas kum jahan pak ho*'.

11. Page 146:

Very clear hearted and good natured Amin
If name is asked it is Md. Amin

In the first line, the name 'Amin' should have been 'Hussain'. *Hussain*

12. Page 229:

The warmth of luxury continued all the time
I was with her all the time

The second line was written as '*Unhin se raha rabt aathon peher*', but the correct form is '*unhein se raha rabt sham o seher*'.

13. Page 287:

The same narration was all the time
The same anxiety all the time

The second line was written as '*Yehi fikr rehti thhi sham o seher*', but the correct form is '*Yehi fikr rehti thhi aathon peher*'.

14. Page 269:

These affections, this intimacy
This was the companionship, this was the unity

The first line of the above couplet was written as '*Yehi sohbtein thhein yehi irtibat*', but the correct form is '*Yehi sohbtein thhein yehi ikhtilat*'.

These mistakes are often made when there is more concentration on a single point, as found on pages 146, 229, 287, and 269 above. Often the poet is involved in some wordly indulgence, as seen on pages 195, 157, and 333 above. Often the Urdu or Persian construction of the line (*misra*) demands something as per the suitability or spirit of the particular language as in the examples from Pages 195 and 276 above. Sometimes, the real rhyme demands something else, as in the examples from pages 195 and 200 above. The writer has corrected his mistakes, but the change of the '*radif*' and rhyme could not be corrected in the manuscript. For instance:

15. Page 159:

He got me near Firoz
With much sorrow and hopelessness

This is a narration by the King of bringing '*Manna*' (a pronoun to replace 'usse' in the couplet). The word should have been '*usse*' and not '*mujhe*'. Similarly, in some places, rhymes can be indicated, but in the manuscript, there are places where the lines are incomplete, and it is difficult to guess what the poet wanted to say. For instance:

16. Page 385:

When you sing then the garland may come
You sing then it is like the colourful peacock

The second line was written as "*Jo nachen toh taus e rangeen ada*", but the correct form is "*Jo nachein toh taus rangeen banein*". Here there is a rhyme but no radif.

In light of the above evidence, if there is no hesitation to accept the manuscript as manuscript, then two possible problems are seen. The manuscript does not belong to a person who cannot make such mistakes, but it belongs to him who naturally makes such mistakes. Writing 'Birjees Quder' as the word '*Sallamahu*' is a mistake which is not expected from *Asir*, but it can be expected from Wajid Ali Shah. Only this evidence can be decisive. And if this evidence is supported by other evidence, then the decision cannot be disputed. It is important to explain this fact further:

1. Birjees Quder

In *Huzn* Akhtari, Sheva-e-Faiz, *Bani*, and in several other places, Wajid Ali Shah has addressed the fighters of 1857 as 'rogues and troublemakers' but he never uttered a word about the revolutionary Prince (*Shehzada*). His lawyer Maulvi Masihuddin Khan addressd him as 'illegitimate',[698] and because of this indiscreet and injudicious act, he was removed from his position.[699] *Huzn e* Akhtari is related to that period.[700] Immediately after *Huzn e* Akhtari, Birjees Quder's name again appears in Qamar Mazmun:

I am Akhtar and my sons are Kaukub and Birjees
The 'takhallus' of my family is bright like the Sun and the moon.

---

698. Dad, 161–62.

699. *Safeer e Avadh.* Maulvi Md. Masihuddin Khan- Al Naazir Pres. Lucknow. 1929. 128.

700. *Huzn e* Akhtari. Md. Wajid Ali Shah Akhtar. Matbaey Sultani. Calcutta. 1276. (National Library, Calcutta). 81–82.

How could a boy of 14 or 15 compose poems, and if he did, how could *Akhtar* come to know about it? Birjees Quder was in Nepal. The King in Metiaburj, Aasman Jah Anjum, and Jahan Quder Nayyer were the same age as Birjees Quder and were with the King, but only name that was famous was chosen. When the complaints against the English were written in *Mulk e Akhtar*, Birjees Quder was again mentioned:

"I have left my son Birjees Quder *there, leaving aside my love for him."*[701]

And when in the Appendix of *Riyaz ul Quloob* these complaints were explained with more intensity, this name was added:[702]

This Prince is residing in Nepal
May Rabb e Karim Take care of him[703]

These lucid narrations from the *Ishq Nama* to the *Riyaz ul Quloob*, spread over 35 years were in addition to those events and references which were related to the Prince in exile. In these narrations, there could be mistakes regarding opinions, events, and political facts. Thus, it is expected for a father who is so engrossed in his affection for his son to also make some mistakes in his writing.

2. Painting

Making artful and floral designs is indicative of fine gestures to cover mistakes, was a characteristic feature of Wajid Ali Shah's writing. He was such a genius in painting that had he not been the King, then he would have earned a

701. *Mulk e Akhtar*, Md. Wajid Ali Shah Akhtar. Matbaey Sultani, Calcutta 1296. 202.
702. *Riyazul Quloob*. Md. Wajid Ali Shah Akhtar. Matbaey Sultani. Calcutta. 1302. (Ittihadiya Library).
703. *Riyaz ul Quloob* (Handwritten). Md. Wajid Ali Shah Akhtar. (Library Salaar Jung Museum) 324.

livelihood adopting this profession.[704] Whenever he wanted to express secret intentions to his uninvited Begmats, he resorted to the art of painting.[705] In corrections, taking care of eloquence and the decency as to which word was to be marked as 'wrong' and which word should be deleted were the hallmarks of Wajid Ali Shah's original thinking. The '*ayats*' of the Holy Quran could not be deleted, as that would have been a sacrilegious act, nor could they be rendered wrong as that would have been violated reality, but in the matter of writing and compilation such changes were expected. The way Wajid Ali Shah overcame such situations reflects his special personality.[706] There is hardly any parallel to the symbolic indications of designs uniquely presented by royal successors.[707]

3. Music

The mastery which Wajid Ali Shah enjoyed over music needs no introduction. The person who taps his thumb to tunes even while sleeping[708] is not beyond expectation that in sheer indulgence he writes '*darulka*' instead of '*daroga.*' In Indian songs, there is no sound of '*ghain*'. To lessen the strangeness of '*ghain*' and to bring out a sweet tone, *ghain* is substituted with *noon* or *gaaf*, or sometimes only by '*gaaf*'. Like the musician, when the prosody writer streamlines his composition, instead of '*rahe ishq*' he pronounces '*raheyishq*', and '*mujh sa*' is pronounced as '*mujsa*', because this is this style which is required by metrical analysis (*Taqtee*). In light of the evidence regarding the prosodic style, poetic bent, and prolific approach of Wajid Ali Shah, who

---

704. Arun, 136.

705. *Tarikh e Firaq*. Md. Wajid Ali Shah Akhtar. 1276. (Khuda Baksh Library). 123, 152, 238, 256–57.

706. *Mubahisey Bainul Nafs wal Aql-Copy 1*. Md. Wajid Ali Shah Akhtar. Calcutta. 1290. 54 & 73.

707. For further details see the mention of handwriting in the section relating to Wajid Ali Shah's cultural contributions in Chapter 4 of this book.

708. *Urdu Adab ke Aath Saal- Ishrat Rehmani. Kitab Manzil Lahore. 145. Al Manazar*, (Monthly), January 1930, 36.

can say that he was not a prosody writer, or that with such a preoccupation of mind, he would not make such mistakes?

4. Spelling

Spelling mistakes are usually made due to similarities in pronounciation and sound. There are abundant spelling mistakes in the writings of Wajid Ali Shah. If such mistakes were not corrected then and there, or if the same word was repeated with the incorrect spelling, then it could be assumed that the writer was not aware of the correct spelling. But when this is not the case, then such thinking shows ignorance regarding the real reason behind the mistake. Other than the *Ishq Nama*, the same mistakes are seen in all the writings of Wajid Ali Shah, and in those that are associated with him. Instances of such phonetic spelling mistakes are presented here:

- '*aaza*' is written with '*zoey*' instead of '*ain*' (Page 455. Qamar Mazmun)
  (Handwritten Manuscript)
- '*sala*' is witten with '*alif*' instead of small '*hey*'. (On the flyleaf of '*Khwab Mubarak*' *Bahar Ajam* (Handwritten). Volume 3.)
- '*Nazar*' is written with'zoey' instead of '*zey*' (Manuscript of *Raazi Nama Mussadiqa Maulvi Md. Haider Sahab*)
- '*Ibtida*' is written as '*Iptida*' (*Bani* [Handwritten Manuscript] Page 249.)
- '*Majmei*' is written instead of '*majma*'. (*Bani*, Page 55. ['*dehnaym baien goomta hua majmein ki taraf... daudta hua.*'])

5. Fingerprints

In the above-mentioned *Raazi Nama* and *Bani*, some fingerprints are also found. This indicates another habit of the writer – embracing the pen when it does not work smoothly. Though these fingerprints are very light, if one had the fingerprints of all ten of Wajid Ali Shah's fingers,[709] this hypothetical evidence would be irrefutable that the manuscript of the *Ishq Nama* is the writing of Wajid Ali Shah. Such fingerprints are also found in other books written by Wajid Ali Shah. For instance, in:

1. *Sabatul Quloob* Volume 1 Writing 1, page 246.
2. *Masnavi* Mushir (Handwritten).
3. *Tarikh e Jamshedi* (Handwritten).
4. Qamar Mazmun.

6. Mistake of the Pen

Examples of the incorrect or extra words, or the changing of a '*radif*' or rhyme amidst intense preoccupation or concentration are found in *Bani*[710] and Qamar Mazmun. These mistakes were probably corrected by the copier (writer) who copied the original writing. But such mistakes, which were not of writing, were found in the printed books. For example:

Munnawwar Begum is illuminated in the moonlight
Munnawar Begum is the valley of 'Toor' mountain.

In the first verse (*matla*), the rhyme is '*roshan, daaman*' and from the second verse upto the last verse (*maqta*), the rhymes are '*khanjar*', '*haider*', '*safdar*', and '*akhtar*'. In the 12 verses of the Ghazal, only the first verse '*matla*' is different. Another example is:

Shaida Begum *I am restless in your separation*
I am without food and water and thirsty Shaida Begum

709. Such fingerprints of people who were recepients of a pension from the government are well secured. But even if the government gathered the fingerprints of Wajid Ali Shah, then to date, even after many attempts, these could not be procured.

710. *Bani* (Handwritten manuscript). 248. He wanted to write the last verse (*maqta*), but he wrote the first one (*matla*) and then corrected it.

Allow me to meet you in isolation
Shaida Begum *I am indulged in the kiss*[711]

In this Ghazal only the rhyme of the third couplet is different. Ulema e Danishmand Aur Khush navees Jawahar Raqam was employed for making these manuscripts fair.[712] But he was likely only authorised to correct superficial mistakes but had no right to correct a line or couplet of the poem. This is the reason that the King transformed the word '*Sallamahu*' into an image of a crown. It would have been objectionable if a common writer had done it because the other princes' names were not written with this suffix.

In this regard, there is an interesting story. Wajid Ali Shah composed some verses in appreciation of *Wazirul Sultan* Bahadur. This line '*manam misle fawwara dar neher*' was in his praise. As there was an element of reproach in it, it irked *Wazir Sultan*,[713] but he could not prevent it from being published.[714] The continuous changes of published pages, corrections of words in the same places, or the corrigendum, do not indicate negligence by the publisher or writer, but the carelessness and arrogance of the author, who did not concede to the fact that his contemporaries had pointed out flaws in their poetic composition. He had the printed one corrected whenever he liked, and it was often left to the honesty of future generations that they read the verses as they find them in print:

Everyone sees the open vessel
When it is presented before someone

Or if they have any understanding, then they could interchange the rhymes themselves. For these reasons, although the *Ishq Nama*, is a manuscript, it is

711. *Sheva-e-Faiz.* Md. Wajid Ali Shah Akhtar. Publication Sultani. Calcutta 1277. 233–34.
712. *Asadul Akhbar* (Agra) Issue 118. 1265.
713. *Al Manazir* (Monthly, Lucknow). January Issue, 1930, 42.
714. *Mubahisey Bainul Nafs wal Aql-Copy 1.* Md. Wajid Ali Shah Akhtar. Calcutta 1290. 47.

unbelievably vivid and fair. But this is not limited to this manuscript; all the manuscripts of Wajid Ali Shah are like this. Some changes were made in the published copy, and these changes may have been made by Wajid Ali Shah or his master Barq. But in this manuscript, there is not a single impression from Barq, *Asir*, or any stranger.

THE STIMULANT EMOTIONS

There are always some stimulating emotions behind every literary creation, big or small. Wajid Ali Shah's work is not an exception. The only thing required is that these creations be studied with the same depth, farsightedness, and purity with which they were penned. If there is any doubt regarding their sincerity, the writer's biography should be examined to look for any contradictory elements. Perusing the works of Wajid Ali Shah, or even their associates lists, would confirm that there are two emotions which dominate his work intensely: *firstly*, divine love (religious) (*Ishq Haqiqi*), and *secondly*, mundane love (*Ishq majazi*). His divine love is represented by his creation of the *Masnavi Sabatul Quloob.* His mundane love is represented by the *Ishq Nama*. These two feelings dominated Wajid Ali Shah's entire life. There was no clash between the two. It was necessary that during his youth, there was indulgence and romance. When youth vanishes, it leaves some footprints behind, and over time there must be some bent towards religion.

During youth there are many conflicting thoughts:

Allah*! Have mercy, forgive me*[715]

During old age there must be some reminiscence of youth:

You the Singer! I fall on your feet
Hear the noise of 'chham chham'[716]

715. *Ishq Nama* (Poetic) - (Manuscript). Md. Wajid Ali Shah Akhtar. *Daastan* 73.

716. *Sabatul Quloob* (Handwritten). Md. Wajid Ali Shah Akhtar. 1304. Volume 1, 663.

For a satisfactory life both these emotions are necessary.

The *Masnavi Ishq Nama* was the composition of his youth. In the *masnavi*, the poet regards the bartender (*saqi*) as the source of all forthcoming events. At the same time, he also expresses his feelings with great eloquence. To understand the inspiration behind it, two '*Saqi Namas*' are presented here:

Bartender who does not have the goblet
His house in the world is without lamp
Strange is the value of the decanter of the bar
This is the bright candle of the house
The moon is lighted with the wine
Without it there is no brightness in the house
Every drunkard says like this
That every glass shines like a lantern
This is the brightness around me
The pitcher is not less than lotus in the night
When night falls while I think over
I write in this light[717]

In the other *Saqi Nama*, he relates about his marriage with *Sikandar Mahal Saheba.* With the reference of *Sikander* the feelings of the King himself are expressed:

Come! Let's go and roam about in the garden
See the flowers of Lala and Yasmin
Sorrow and happiness are all transitory
The life spent in love is worthwhile
Neither Kings nor officers endured
Death concludes every story
Those who want this world get trapped in it

717. *Supra Note* 714. Dastan 123.

I have no spare time
Sitting on the seat of ruling (is strange)
There is another empire which comes
From the beginning I am the King of the empire of love
Congratulations to myself I wear the crown of romance
In the empire of love
Sikandar Mahal came under my orders submission

The above two verses are by a person who would soon be dethroned and is aware of it. He wants to do something which would be everlasting. It would have been very difficult for an outsider to have composed it, and with such a deep touch of reality. The collection of letters was compiled with this purpose in mind and in the prefaces of *Tarikh e Firaq*, the reason is given that people should recognize the 'King of the empire of love.' The *Ishq Nama* is the first step in this kind of introduction. As the *Ishq Nama* was in Persian, it was not necessary that it should be composed (in Urdu), or that the King should himself compose it. But this thought reflects ignorance of a strange quality of the King. In any work of Wajid Ali Shah that contains both poetry and prose, the prose precede the poetry, and while the prose could be the writing of any other person, the poetry is the work of the King. He wrote the book Irshad Khaqani, and this was then translated. When he had time, he composed it into a poem.[718] When he had a dream, he put it into writing and did not wish to write it as a poem, but if he could find time, he did it.[719] When he received the letters from the 'Begmats', they were useless after reading, but he composed them.[720] In the marriage of his children, the invitations were to be sent by others, but he himself composed them.[721]

718. See the details of *Sheva-e-Faiz* in this Chapter.

719. See the details of Qamar Mazmun in this Chapter.

720. *Sheva-e-Faiz*, 58–90.

721. Qamar Mazmun. Md. Wajid Ali Shah Akhtar. Matbaey Sultani. Calcutta. 1281. 16–21 & 66–70

Maulvi Amir took the responsibility to make them understand, but using the same poem.[722] Taslim and Mayil applied for employment by writing poetry.[723] *Meher* wrote a horoscope, but in a poem.[724] All this indicates that Wajid Ali Shah liked everything to be in poetry. He read it attentively, and he himself composed it. Consequently, there is no reason that, when *Ishq Nama* was to be composed, he would have asked another person to do it for him, as it was in a form and topic of his choice.

In the context of form and topic, and divine and mundane love, it is interesting to note that Wajid Ali Shah was caught in an emotional dilemma. In 1264 A.H. he was busy with the compilation of the Persian *Ishq Nama.* While this book was yet to be completed, he fell ill and the whole year passed in the illness. During his illness, he repented his sins and started the poetic translation of *Hamlaey Haidari* as a pastime. But with the speed of his work and his health, the old thoughts again engulfed him. In the last *Daastans* of the Persian *Ishq Nama*, he related his own illness and about the deaths of others, and then he started composing this *Ishq Nama.* He found the courage to compose while he was working on *Hamlaey Haidari*, but *Hamlaey Haidari* was left incomplete, and his entire attention centred on the poetic *Ishq Nama.* The same thing happened when he wrote the *Sabatul Quloob.* The translation of *Hayatul Quloob* was underway in the same form as the *Sabatul Quloob*, in prose. But then his previous habits again took dominance. *Riyazul Quloob* was left incomplete and whatever he wrote was restarted in the form of poetry.[725]

Apart from the liking for poetic composition the King, in the matter of the *Ishq Nama*, was inclined towards sex rather than religion. In the writing of the *Sabatul Quloob*, he focused instead on religion. This change was due

722. *Urdu Khutoot.* Shamsul Rehman. Kitabi Duniya. Delhi. 1947.109–110.

723. *Aab e Baqa.* Khwaja Abdul Rauf Ishrat. Naami Press. Lucknow. 1918. 162. *Supra Note* 720 at 44–46.

724. *Almas* Darakhshan. Mirza Hatim Ali Beg Meher. Matbaey Elahi. Agra. 1895. 448–51.

725. See the details of the books *Ishq Nama, Haibatey Haidari, Riyazul Quloob* and *Sabatul Quloob* in this Chapter.

to his age. The writer of the *Ishq Nama* was a youth of 26. When he picked up a pen to write the *Hayatul Quloob*, he was an old man of 62:

The discernment which I have for truthfulness
I have a liking for reading Elegies
I am fed up of imaginary tales and Ghazals
It was amusing up to youth time
*I am only an ad*Mirer *of Prophet's family*
*This ad*Mir*ation diffuses every sorrow*
I don't feel like going anywhere
Nor do I want to meet the sweethearts of this world
Neither they are interested nor am I yearning
Neither they are robust nor am I a muscle man[726]

But the old man had the courage of a youth, and in Chapter Five of this book, when the matter reached "*Qissa Hudd Aur Qaum Aad*", the evil deeds of that community reminded him that in the followers of Adam & Eve, Yusuf & Zulaikha, Sulaiman, Bilquis & Ibrahim, and Musa & Issa, there is no shortage of tales that would be better expressed in poetry than in prose. He completed *Riyazul Quloob* while describing the '*Aad*'[727] community, and he built up his courage and became engrossed in work which would become the certificate of his natural inclination, scholarly abilities, and religious allegiance.

The '*Shah Nama*' of *Firdausi*, the '*Khawar Nama*' of Rustami, and the '*Safar Nama*' of Taslim[728] are the longest *masnavis* in Persian and Urdu literature and were composed to receive honour and rewards from the rulers of the time. In this context, feelings of patriotism and fame were active in

726. *Riyazul Quloob*. Md. Wajid Ali Shah Akhtar. Matbaey Sultani. Calcutta. 1302. (Ittihadiya Library). 212.

727. Ancient Semitic race mentioned in the Quran. (Translator)

728. *Tawarikh Badiy*. Munshi Amirulah Tasleem. 1303. (Raza Library). *Tawarikh e Kaamil*. Munshi Amirulah Tasleem. 1308. (Raza Library). *Safar Nama Khusravi*. Munshi Amirullah Tasleem. 1312. (Raza Library) are collecitvley the poetic history of the empire of Rampur.

the minds of the authors. The following questions require attention: what was the wish of Wajid Ali Shah? What did he expect in return? Which emotions encouraged him to have the patience to undertake the challenge of composing 48,000 verses? In the *masnavi Sabatul Quloob* itself, the King replies to these queries, as seen in the following extracts:

A. *I drank the blood of my heart*
Then I was able to get this Kalam e Khuda
It was not composed so far
By any eloquent poet
No ascetic thought of this
To compose the word of Allah
My friend! In the Hadith of Mufazzal Nasikh
He composed such inattractive verses
Poetry, Hadith and composition
Wassalam it's all in prose (*Sabatul Quloob*, Volume 1, 140).
Hence I shouldered this burden
No comparison between a dust particle and the Sun

B. *Akhtar! you did not have the guts*
To compose about Khuda
But this is the Miracle *of the Qurān*
This is by grace of the eloquent speaker Prophet
That an unwise like me translated it
I wrote in poetic form by the grace of Allah
Allah*! The forgiver forgive me.*
If some mistake is committed by my pen (*Sabatul Quloob*, Volume 1, 257).

C. *Khuda! For the sake of Muhammad*
Absolve me from this melancholy
Don't agitate the ranks of Muslims
Don't let enemies rejoice at Akhtar (page 458)

D. *I am the darling of friend of Khuda*
Good or bad but I am fine
*My own ad*Mir*ation is abominable*
*Note this I am his ad*Mirer
Only Ali can identify Ali
....
I am a brute of the wilderness of lion
There is sign of that name in me
I am Wajid Ali hence I got 'Ali' (a.s.)
Nothing else is so apparent
I am not afraid of enemy's jealousy
Every time Safdar saves me (page 817)

E. *Forgive my follies this moment*
I am unable to forget the charm of the singer
The pious heart is lost
The imprint of devotion has disappeared
The heart of the lover beats fast
Even the simple heart becomes lively
I am fortunate in this world
Only I am the divine speaker
The expression is adorned by my words
My thinking is decked up,
verses should dominate the arrogance
Don't bother if the goblet is empty
On every verse the beauty will fall
This is true don't regard it as boasting
I am the writer of Almighty's composition
Listen! I am the beloved compiler of Almighty (page 869)

F. *The judges are people of high level*
The eloquent reciters mention the King of Kings

I am the servant of the elderly
I am dust, though I am addressed as star (page 1017)

The above verses show that, though he was working continuously for a long period, was conscious of his endeavours, he was not bothered about appreciation by the world. He often boasted that he was the composer of the Almighty, and if he wished for anything in return then it was that his sins be forgiven and the Islamic community be acclaimed. When, due to his deadly disease, he lost all hope of surviving, he regarded these services as his salvation treasure and concluded this *masnavi* with a prayer. Those who have perused the long *masnavis* of Urdu know that at such points, the poet mentions his efforts with pride and glory. No such similarity is found at the end of *Sabatul Quloob.* Modesty in arrogance and meekness in humility are hallmarks of Wajid Ali Shah's compositions. Whenever he depicts pride in his work, he takes care that his narration should not be taken as arrogance and haughtiness. To forget the bitter experiences of life, people have tried to find solace in religion and opulence. Wajid Ali Shah too submitted to the current which flowed between the two. Among the works of Wajid Ali Shah, the ferries which were away from this flow could be an object of suspicion, but to reject the existence of those which do exist within this flow is equal to refuting the very existence of the flow.[729]

ALTERATION, CHANGE AND VARIEGATION

In a letter to Shaida Begum, Wajid Ali Shah reminds her of one of his habits of which people were aware:

> *"Darling you have complained that in reply to your two letters I send one letter then listen dear it is one and the same thing. I hate useless talks, and I am in the habit of talking straightforwardly. I cannot be superficial, and I*

729. All the three factors namely, religion, sexology and emperorship are reflected in *'Tamghaey Wajidi'* and in the poetic dream of 'Qamar Mazmun.' The relation of crown or medal (*tamgha*) is with consciousness while the connection of dream is with unconsciousness.

am afraid of too much attachment. I am not like you that I should write in a futile manner, write the same thing twice. By the Almighty's grace you are well aware of my temperament. Sad that you are sarcastic towards me for being careless, see what misery I am in..." [730]

People who were familiar with Wajid Ali Shah's personality mentioned that according to *Gumbas*, Wajid Ali Shah took care of the pigeons himself, and that every day about 56 eggs from these pigeons were presented to him, on which he, without any hesitation, wrote the date in Persian with his pen in different words. In the view of his associates, this proficiency was praiseworthy and the ridiculous narrative of *Gumbas* was only clerical.[731] May be the statements of his associates were exaggerated, but they were not fabricated. Had his associates not been aware of this quality of the King, then in all the publications of his writings, there would not have been drawings of creepers with a different design on every page. If a fish is drawn, then it must be of varied design. If the writer sits down to write, then instead of using the better option of Arabic script he would switch to chain writing (*zanjeera*), where the ink in eight or nine colours would be used. From the days of his reign up to his days of his exile, we see one and the same Wajid Ali Shah – a hater of monotony and repetitiveness, and a lover of innovation and novelty. Neither a fairy-faced (*Pari chehra*) woman nor a single genre of poetry could hold his attention for long. He was tired of his writing, which was always the same, and he disliked rule that one must write from right to left and top to bottom, that one must always compose in the same poet metre, and that words in the dictionary must be arranged alphabetically. He wanted to create diversions from the straight path, but innovation and artifice also have limits. Too much novelty becomes ridiculous. The writers of the dictionary have given a name to every letter of the alphabet, and they are always linked to a word with the same name. Wajid Ali Shah also wanted

730. *Adab Ka Maqsad* (Dr. Syed Noorul Hasan Hashmi-Hindustan Kitab Ghar. Lucknow. 1956) with reference to *Tarikhe Mazzhab* 191.

731. *Gumbas*, 55.

this style, but he gave these letters new names. Two examples of the Urdu alphabet '*ray*'[732] and '*seen*'[733] are given new names different from the popular ones. Similarly, though Wajid Ali Shah did follow certain established systems regarding some letters [734] he also took diversions. Those who are unaware of his style can criticize him easily:

"*Ekhattar...* should remember that it is '*kaaf*', which is from pure Hindi alphabets, in which the sound of '*ha*' is collective. In the Urdu way of writing, it is written as '*do chashmi hay*', thus it is not Arabic '*kaaf*' but Hindi '*kaaf*'.[732] But whether Wajid Ali Shah was aware or unaware of the Hindi '*kaaf*', or '*do chashmi hay*' can be identified by referring to *Sautul Mubarak* and *Malazul Kalmat.* However when the writer uses the printed version of the alphabet, and the reader depends only on the word form, then differences or misunderstandings are bound to take place."

Like the letters of the alphabet, the names of months, details of titles, and the reasons behind an event cannot be innumerable. But in the collection of his letters, the innovative pen of Wajid Ali Shah not only brings out new styles in *hamd*, *naat manqibat* and the headlines, but he looks for a justification for every collection.[733] In the collection of elegies, elegies which were about one person were arranged systematically. What would have been wrong if all of these were given one heading? But if there were 10 elegies, then there were 10 headings, and all of them were different.[734]

This state of alteration, change, and variegation did not apply only to the writings which were written during one period. It is likely that every narration that he had written, and which came to his perusal again, underwent a change. Even small changes, variations which cannot even be called corrections, can

---

732. *Tarikh e Avadh*, Volume 4, 111–12. Wajid Ali Shah in '*Najo*' refers to '*kaaf*' of '*ekhattar*' as the '*kaaf*' of Arabic. *Maulvi Abdul Ghani Khan* objects to this.

733. Some extracts from the collection of letters, *hamd* and the reasons of compilation are presented in the explanations of *Tarikh Firaq, Tarikh e* Noor, *Tarikh e Badr* and *Tarikh e Jamshedi.*

734. See the elegies regarding *Janab Ali Akbar, Janab* Imam Hussain and *Hazrat Ali* in *Tosha e Akhrat.* Md. Wajid Ali Shah Akhtar. Publication Sultani. Calcutta. 1299.

be seen in the new and old writings. *Sukhan Ashraf* and *Diwan Mubarak* were attended twice. The Ghazals which were in the original *Diwan* are not the same in *Kulliyat e* Akhtari, and those found in *Kulliyat* Akhtari are not the same in Nazm Namvar.

The manuscript of the Persian *Ishq Nama* was written earlier. The *masnavi* was composed by keeping this copy in front, and a person with a tendency to innovate was bound to make changes. Details about some important changes were already given in the explanation of the *Ishq Nama.* In these changes, the personal knowledge of the composer is seen at every step. But apart from the change in the content, the change in the headlines can prove decisive. The headlines, both in the prose and the poetry, are in Persian. There was no need to change them, but changes were made.

These changes in the usage and meaning of forms was the job of the person who, like the printing style, thought it insulting to copy down the narrative in the same words. No associate would dare make such change in the composition of the King.

4. Bent Towards Persian

Sharar writes about Wajid Ali Shah:

> *"His status in Persian was slightly below Abul Fazal. When he started writing, he wrote within moments two to four stanzas (bund) in prose which would remind of the mastery of the famous prose writers of Persian."*[735]

Apart from this commendation by Sharar, the examples of prose and poetry do not deserve such appreciation. Compared to his Urdu compositions, they are very limited. Until and unless it is well assured that the initial examples of Persian authorship in the *Ishq Nama* and *Majmuaey Wajidia* and the last examples in *Mulk e Akhtar* and *Malazul Kalmat* are

735. *Jaan e Alam.* Maulvi Abdul Haleem Sharar. Adaraey Faroghe Urdu. Lahore. 1951. 78.

real, it will not be possible to either confirm or rebut the arguments of Sharar or his contemporary historians.[736] But Sharar also discusses the impromptu writing of the King, which points at his natural and original inclination, and there are many ways to verify this.

Abundant use of unfamiliar words and Persian structures in Urdu is present in the compositions of the writers of that period. There is one more flaw in the writing of Wajid Ali Shah, that while writing in Urdu he would abruptly switch to Persian:

a. *"Including this one, six of your letters have been received. I even have the dates. See how the times have changed. I have respectfully received 1,000 rupees for an Eid dress on behalf of Zulfiquar ud Daulah... I will send its receipt."*[737]

b. *Lift with care. Beware! There must not be lavishness... written in the hand of Jaan e Alam..."*[738]

c. *The reality is that Prophet Anam*
Name of only Khuda is better than yours
O! The advocate of Day of Judgment Help me
O! The commanders of prophethood help me
O! The medicine for all the sick ones
O! The consoler of sinful acts
I am sacrificed on you
I am a humble servant of yours
There is sorrow in my heart and your love in my mind[739]

---

736. Like Durga Prasad Sahab in *Boostan e Avadh* (Kunwar Durga Prasad Sandelvi - Matbaey Ahmedi, Lucknow.1892). 173–74.

737. *Tarikh e* Ghazala. Md. Wajid Ali Shah Akhtar. (Compiler: Wasi Bilgrami) Publication Mufeed e Aam. Agra. 1914. (Azad) 26.

738. *Tarikh-e-Mumtaz*. Md. Wajid Ali Shah Akhtar (Compiler: Dr. Md. Baqar). Urdu Markaz. Lahore. 1952(Azad). 49. On page 55–56 there is one more such example.

739. *Behre Ulfat*. Md. Wajid Ali Shah Akhtar. Matbaey Sultani Lucknow. (Khuda Baksh, Raza) 12.

In these examples it is evident in the original that the writer unintentionally uses Persian in a manner which is applicable to both in Persian and Urdu. The style of changing direction of the pen (nib) at the natural inclination of the writer and the temperament hardly change. Habits become part of the disposition. In the beginning, one or two verses were in Persian. In *Sabatul Quloob* many verses are continuously in Persian[740] but there too there is one line (*misra*) in Urdu and another in Persian. In the *Ishq Nama* the natural compliance of the writer with the Persian language is manifested in places. For instance:

- *I wanted that the world must be purged of rubble*
- *The lost one reached the desired place*
- *He got a new evidence*

Such examples are seen in abundance. In three *Dastans* there are complete couplets in Persian:

She was so sick that she passed away
She left the world as she suffered with lung infection
My heart sighs in her bereavement
It is said the world is purged of rubble (Dastan 20)
The four brothers who came before Huzoor
Rejoiced at the mercy they got
Such mercy was their life. (Dastan 72)
....
O! What is the use of such things
The disease worsens and medicine is futile
During Spring have the free will
Stay at banks, don't go into the stream[741]

740. *Sabatul Quloob* (Handwritten) Volume 1. 1043–44.

741. This couplet is also found in the Dastan of the *Ishq Nama* (Persian).

This amalgamation of Persian and Urdu is found in all the long *masnavis* of Wajid Ali Shah. It is explified by the following:

Those who are pious become obvious
Allah *showers his blessings on them*
(*Afsanaey Ishq*, page 12)

Saints are not Khuda
But they are not different or away from Khuda
(Daryaey Taa'shuqq, page 16)

Where are you the moon faced
Reveal before me whatever you have
(*Haibat e Haidari*, page 34)

Khuda ! Have mercy on me
Bless me Allah *with life*
(*Huzn e* Akhtari, page 151)

In such poetry, it is futile to look for some commendable construction because these are composed spontaneously, and often a maxim or phrase is also considered. This amalgamation of two languages has been discussed to indicate that a practice which was rarely used by others was part of the regular style of Wajid Ali Shah.

5. Frankness

People write for others, and every responsible and popular writer not only expresses his own thoughs and ideas but thinks it necessary to respect the feeling of his readers. Though Wajid Ali Shah wrote plentifully, sadly the abscence of consideration in his writings for what to write and what not to write created distance between him and his readers and deprived him of their positive reception. At the same time, it put a weapon in the hands of his biggest critics, who envied his popularity.[742] For Wajid Ali Shah, forthrightness was important.[743] He also advised others regarding this:

> *"I agree that mash*Allah *since you attained maturity and expressed the events of my life and your affection for me then (I say) that it must be put in writing in a fine manner and must be related with truthfulness and without any poetic exaggeration."*[744]

But this advice was neither followed by him nor by others. *Sawaneh Salateen e Avadh* is the most authentic book on this topic, but when its compiler presented his manuscript, he was very disappointed.[745] For writing and publication there was King's own publication house, but the other printers in Lucknow had to close their presses because they published a book which was not liked by the King.[746] If the king lost a case and a lawyer informed him of it, then his frankness was acceptable:

> *"Wazir ul Sultan you have not been to a respectable court, hence you are not aware of the etiquette. Kings are unfamiliar with words like defeat and hopelessness."* [747]

Being aware of this strange kind of frankness of the Kings, one should not be surprised to see such narratives in the writing of Wajid Ali Shah. This could be exasperating for his family members, for those who had faith in him, for religious people, and for his countrymen. It was not possible for people to stop the forthright pen of a sovereign King, but it was possible to

742. See the statements of writers in Gumbas, 76, Tarikhe Avadh Volume 5, 100.

743. *Riyazul Quloob.* Md. Wajid Ali Shah Akhtar. Matbaey Sultani. Calcutta.1302. (Ittihadiya Library). 212.

744. *Tarikh-e-Mumtaz.* Md. Wajid Ali Shah Akhtar (Compiler: Dr. Md. Baqar). Urdu Markaz. Lahore. 1952(Azad). 56.

745. *Qaiser ul Tawarikh.* Syed Kamaluddin Haideralias Mir Zaair. Publication: Munshi Nawal Kishore. Lucknow 3rd. Edn. 1907. Volume 1, 16.

746. Aspar Nagar, page "dal."

747. *Jaan e Alam.* Maulvi Abdul Haleem Sharar. Adaraey Faroghe Urdu. Lahore. 1951. 33.

prevent the ill effects caused by it. In the present times, if a book is seized then it becomes difficult to find, though people could have purchased it freely at the time of publication. The books of Matbaey Sultani were gifted to special people, and these must have been listed. It was not difficult to look for such books and destroy them. For unpleasant portions it was not necessary to destroy the whole book. This could be done by separating some of the pages, and this could be done even by people who often handled the book. *Majmuaey Wajidia* is in very few libraries. *Malazul Kalmat* is also not found in most libraries, and wherever it is found it was without the Appendix. In *Riyazul Quloob* it was as if there was no Appendix. What could be said of the *masnavi Ishq Nama*? It was not possible for a publisher to publish this book (*Ishq Nama*) and be guilty of violating law. We can comment on this book only on the basis of a particular viewpoint.

There are 53 verses in "*Dastan Shust wa Shashum*" in the *masnavi Ishq Nama*, entitled "*Dar zikr Awurdan Masahiban Khas Ba Mazhab Ithna Ashriya*". There were four parts collectively, and in two of these there is malediction (*tabarra*), name by name. In the copy in Mehmudabad, these two couplets were printed, but were later deleted. These are still present in the copy of Anjuman. Had this been the translation of the Persian *Ishq Nama* then there would be no '*Tabarra*' in it. Hence, if it is not there, then how is it found in the present copy? If *Asir* did this to please the King, then it was unbecoming of him as the King's associate (*Masahib*).

6. Dramatic Style & Dialogue Mannerism

Often a person's innate weakness comes as a blessing for him.[748] Because of Wajid Ali Shah's deafness, his other talents were revealed. Thus, he started

748. On the deafness of Wajid Ali Shah and for the conclusions resulting from it, in the forthcoming pages, under the headings "Wajid Ali Shah ki Saqafati Khidmat", "Wajid Ali Shah ba haisiyat Shayir" and "Wajid Ali Shah ba haisiyat adeeb" there is detailed a discussion about it. Regarding dialogue style, it would not be out of place to mention that in the letters of Mirza Ghalib, this same style became obvious when, due to old age, he had become hard of hearing.

highlighting those portions of literature and poetry which were not attended to by other poets. Consciously, his tendency towards playwriting was in fact an improved form of this desire to see the '*nakhl*' (tree) as a '*bardar*' (laden with fruit), and the '*taoos*' (peacock) as '*raqsan*' (dancing). For this emotion, in poetry and literature it is not only necessary that the couplet be an emobodiment of poetic beauty, but if the need arises then it should be possible to show it in pictorial form. In the prose and poetry of Wajid Ali Shah, and especially in his *masnavis*, this condition is in superlative form, and the *Ishq Nama* is the magnum opus of his talent. He not only composed the dialogues, but he dramatically brought them to life. Whether it is poetry or prose, *masnavi* or letters, his dialogue is the reflection of his personality; it is not the style suggested by others.

Sabatul Quloob

Like the *Ishq Nama* (Poetic), there are strong chances of doubting the *masnavi Sabatul Quloob*. There are many reasons behind this misunderstanding: *first*, the extraordinary length of the *masnavi*, *second*, in one of its copies the seal of Amir Ali Khan Hilal appears, and *third*, the statement by Wajid Ali Shah that he wrote it at the age of 53. As for the length of the *masnavi*, it comes to mind that a '*rangeela piya*' like Wajid Ali Shah cannot linger over a book on a scholarly and dry subject for a long period. The seal indicates that the book was written in the lifetime of Hilal and was written by this "*qadeem khan*Azad." This raises the question of whether Wajid Ali Shah was aware of his age. But this kind of suspicion regarding a person whose entire life was dedicated to the work of writing and composing would be very unfair. Even stronger evidence cannot rebut the qualities of his writing which have been discussed already, and which are spread over the pages of this *masnavi*. Those who want to know the reality can satisfy themselves by perusing the *masnavi* itself. I present here some more irrefutable evidence so that no doubt remains:

1. Had *Sabatul Quloob* been a 'purchased' work, then in *Bani*, where the death of Hilal is mentioned, there would have been mention of

the completed or ongoing work on the *masnavi*. Such an important work would not have been overlooked. But there is no mention of it in the list of *Bani* because not even an idea of this writing existed at that time.

Below sketch from *Sabatul Quloob*:

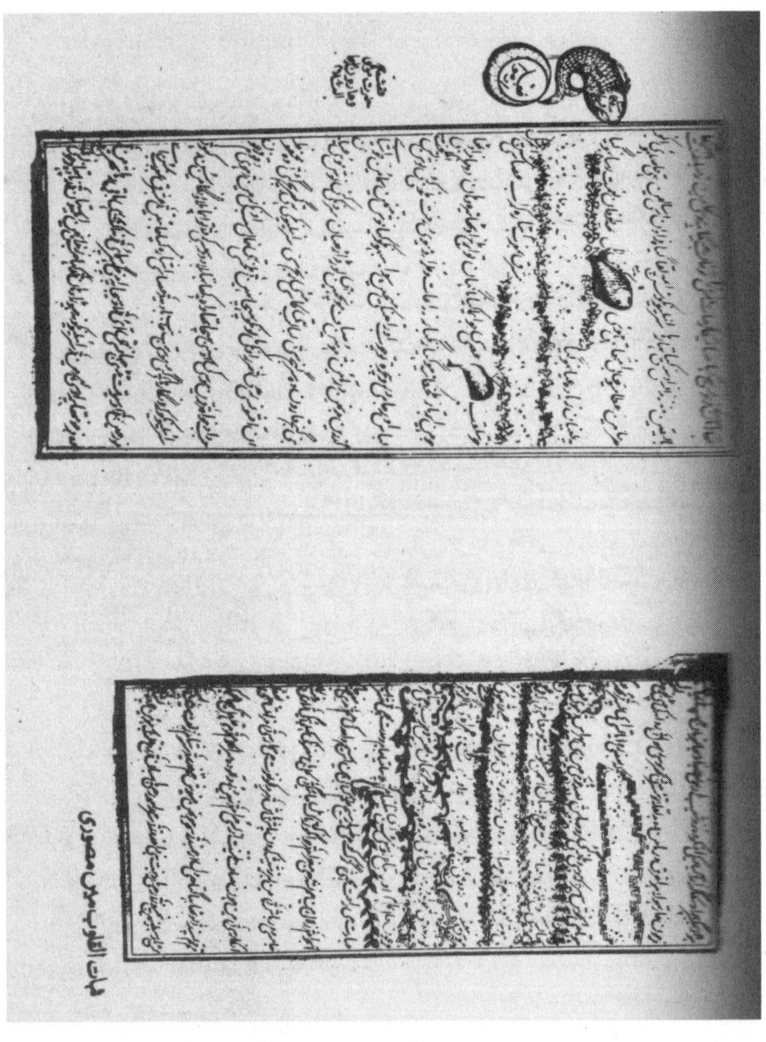

Painting in *Sabatul Quloob*: Note image of fish, zanjeera style typical of the King's writing

2. *Riyazul Quloob* was written first, and the idea of writing *Sabatul Quloob* resulted from this. The fact that *Riyazul Quloob* was incomplete and imperfect, and the presence of verses from *Riyazul Quloob* in *Sabatul Quloob* is enough to decide on the order of the writing of these books. There is no mention of *Riyazul Quloob* in the list of *Bani*, as both of these works came later.
3. The first volume of the printed copy of *Hayatul Quloob*, which was kept in front at the time of making its poetic translation, must be in the royal library. Its second volume is available, on which corrections were made by Wajid Ali Shah's pen.
4. The compilation of *Sabatul Quloob* Volume 1, Manuscript 1 was under the supervision of Wajid Ali Shah.
5. In the verses of *Saqi Namas*, the humbleness, humility, arrogance, awareness, and personal impressions of Wajid Ali Shah could not have been composed by any other person first and then relate it to the King. The following will explain this:

This humble Akhtar now narrates
Listen with your heart to the composition of a saint (durvesh)[749]
Friend! translate the Hadith (sayings of Prophet)
Don't be so impertinent in public[750]
From Huma I became a black crow
Black crow is in my contemplation[751]
Who is the poet the speechless Akhtar
Whose Urdu narration is distorted
Who does not have the ability to compose
'Faulun' (metrical unit) is beyond his reach [752]

---

749. *Sabatul Quloob* (Handwritten), Md. Wajid Ali Shah Akhtar. 1304. Volume I, 31.
750. *Ibid*, Volume 1, 681.
751. *Ibid*, 972.
752. *Ibid*, Volume 2, 119.

Prove that you are Haideri
Neither Akhtar nor this empire will survive.[753]

6. The '*Darogah*' of the royal library, Atarud Daulah Md. Ali Mohsin, said while composing *Diwan 'Mazaq Muhabbbat'*:

   When she gives love then the wish of the beggar is fulfilled
   Dust particle (a humble self) is honoured by the Sun
   The beggar was commanded to be present by Huzoor
   A drop was honoured by the flow of light
   The moon of virtuosity shows its lustre
   In every city there is impact of my King
   He is benevolent, Generous, Affectionate
   All his quality is God given
   There is knowledge in the depth of every composition
   He is the interpreter, aware of Hadith and the limit of knowledge
   The Creator has made him the emperor of poetry in the country
   The poets of the country are convinced of him
   Poetry which is full of meaning
   Prose which became the (wealth) of the native speakers
   The King of Excellence has let lose the stream
   His Excellency has written many books
   He is busy in the recital of Khuda & Muhammad
   With little effort he wrote endlessly
   The entire masses are convinced of the truthful King
   Though he spoiled the temporal but he built his next world. [754]

   The *Diwan Atarad* was completed in 1301 A.H. and was published in 1302 A.H. This was the time when work on Volume 1 of *Sabatul Quloob* had started, and other than the '*darogah*' (librarian) of the

753. *Ibid*, Volume 1, 121.

754. *Mazaaq e Muhabbat*. Md. Ali Khan Mohsin. Publication: Munshi Naval Kishore. Lucknow. 1885. 269–70.

library, very few people knew what the King had done or was busy with. The narration of Mohsin regarding the interpretation by the King, the awareness of *Hadith*, and his prolific writing is not an exaggeration, but it is the statement of truth, the proof of which is this *masnavi* itself. The *Sabatul Quloob* was started in 1300 A.H.:

Son! In the thirteen hundredth year my age is 53 years

When, after composing 14,000 couplets, he reached Chapter Seven, the year had not changed.[755]

You young one! Twenty and eight years have passed
Year thirteen hundred also surfaces

In translating the *Hadith* and interpretation (*Tafseer*), composing so many verses is not an easy task. In the last couplet, his stay of 28 years in Metiaburj is mentioned.[756] 1272 A.H. was the year he was exiled, but in the previously mentioned couplet, his age is given incorrectly. He was born in 1238 A.H., and in 1300 A.H. he should have been 62. Mistakes regarding his age are often seen in his writings. Wherever he made such mistakes, the given age was less than his real age.[757]

7. In the following generation of Atar ud Daulah, there is a mention of an anonymous storyteller (*raavi*) who knew that important work was being done, but he could not grasp the nature of the work:

"During the last years King was translating the Persian prose book "Mehboobul Quloob" in Urdu poetry, and in the evening up to ten o'clock at night he did the work without a break. The King's eyes were on the original book and then continuously on the page on which he

755. *Supra Note* 752 at Volume 1, 13–343.
756. In *Bani* (Handwritten) on page 219 their period of stay in Metiaburj is given as twenty years which is correct. Here the mentioning of Metiaburj is also found in the forthcoming veres.
757. For example, see *Bani*, 240–41.

> *was writing. and the pen did not stop at all. It could not be seen that he even broods while composing. He read the Persian and then he started writing the translated verses. The onlookers could perceive that he was copying the book. Perhaps this book could not be completed as he passed away. After his death the government staff who took away his other belongings also took this manuscript, and after that nobody knew what happened to it."*[758]

Despite the partial details, and the lack of knowledge about its correct name, it's the translation of the book which shows that the statement is based on reality. The narrator was not a close confidant of the King, and could not find out that one volume of the book had been completed and had reached the stage of becoming an incomplete and imperfect gilded copy.

SECTION 5

WRITING STYLE OF WAJID ALI SHAH

Importance of Writing

For authors, it is difficult to express their thoughts to other people without the medium of a pen. I have no hesitation in admitting that Mir Anis composed his verses in solitude, and when he came out of seclusion, he dictated the stanzas to reduce them to writing. When Wajid Ali Shah moved from Sultan Khana to Imambarah, he asked the writers to write the elegy and the '*salaam*' simultaneously, which he had to recite in the '*majlis.*' For a prolific writer

---

758. *Al Nazir* (Monthly, Lucknow) Issue January 1930, page 42, Article "Sultan e Alam Wajid Ali Shah". Up till that period many of the associates of the King were alive; the essay writer Late Israr Hussain has mentioned the story related by any one of these. He recovered the second manuscript of Sabatul Quloob Volume 1 and after completing a book "Hunar*mandan e Avadh", he* began writing another book "*Hayat e* Wajid Ali Shah", but before he could complete it, he passed away and the manuscript which he had gathered with so much labour was lost. Manuscript 2 is recovered from his house. On it is his starting signatures dated Novrmber 11, 1939 and the last one is dated January 3, 1940.

with a good memory, this was an easy thing. But it is very strange to think that this was regular practice, and that poets behaved like blind or uninformed men. This is especially so when we know that the poet was not incompetent in writing, nor he was so lazy that he would avoid the labour of writing. In matters of writing and composition, in addition to poetry there is also the work of prose, and despite the fact that there are instances in history where due to some accident, the writer lost his vision or his hands were chopped off, the poet took the support of writer, which could not have been done without reducing the matter into writing, nor could it have reached us. The 'speedy' and 'wistful' pen of Wajid Ali Shah often displayed its creativity:

If my writing is a boat
Then my pen is like the pole of the ferryman[759]
The beauty of my pen is the composition of Khuda
The mastery of my pen is the message of Khuda
It is the shield of black ink
I have no urge for fame[760]

It is quite possible that out of his writings and compilations, much was dictated, and that which was written by him was destroyed. However, the remaining treasure invites the enlightened to learn something from it. In various fields of knowledge, if it is possible to differentiate between the original and the forged, then by looking at it the experts can also say handwriting belongs to the author, or to someone else, and the writing also speaks of the psyche of the writer. Wajid Ali Shah's handwriting is not only a centre of attraction for such experts, but it is also useful for those who had so far regarded the work of Wajid Ali Shah on rational grounds as his own handwriting.

759. *Ishq Nama* (Poetry), (Handwritten). 16.
760. *Sabatul Quloob* (Handwritten) Volume 1. 856.

Explanation Regarding Special Signatures

In the details of the manuscripts, such rational grounds were used to prove that a particular work was handwritten by Wajid Ali Shah. With mutual comparison of the writing, there could be some doubt that it is not the writing of Wajid Ali Shah. This doubt can be transformed into certainty when people compare the writing to that on page 94 of the book *Lucknow Ka Shahi Stage* because there is no relevance and suitability between this book and the writing of this thesis. Before giving a reply, suppose the statement given in this thesis is wrong and the photocopy of the book is correct, though the owner of the book has not given any reliable evidence in support of his claim. At most, the narrative given by Sharar in the margin of page 92–93 could be seen as supporting evidence:

> *"I stayed in Calcutta in October or November 1941 for about nine days. At that time the first part of the original memorandum was present anywhere in these two places which I copied down... The replies of Wajid Ali Shah are written under the title "Explanation Regarding Special Signatures" in his own hand. Had I got the entire memorandum then the name of the real presenter could be discerned."*

The detail of the memorandum which is written on page 93–94 of the book is the same as that found in the document 'Dal' below.

The book *Bani* (Manuscript) has 80 or 81 pages, and as stated in the above extract, the memorandum is incomplete because the later pages are blank and torn. This is not the original memorandum, it is a copy. In the manuscript of *Bani*, there are more such narratives which are made fair by the copier. At the time of the publication of *Bani*, some works were published while others were destroyed. The detail of this memorandum is in the deleted part.[761] The similarity found in the attested writing of both the document and the book is that both statements start with "*Explanation of special signature*" and these are

761. See detail of the book *Bani* (Manuscript).

two different orders written in two different applications. In the document '*dal*', the memorandum and the order are written in one hand and in one ink. In the attested document there is only an order, not a memorandum.

Apart from the differences in the writing the other difference is that the document numbered '*dal*' is in Urdu and the script is in Persian, while the attested document uses a combined script with Urdu and Persian. Obviously out of these two docuements only one, not both, could be that of Wajid Ali Shah. There is some oversight by the aforementioned person because he does not remember that 16 years ago, in which month and where he had seen the writing and so could not have remembered the structure of the writing, which is even more difficult. Apparently, the cause of this misunderstanding are the words "*Explanation of special signature*", which was used to differentiate the two writings. Now considering that the writing which the aforementioned person saw in Calcutta is not the one shown in Image Y, we now proceed to discuss the meaning of the three terms which were at the beginning of both documents.

When an application is presented in a government office, the officer passes his order either orally or in writing, which is called 'order' or 'noting.' This order is usually a few sentences, at the end of which there is either a signature or initial and the date. The staff of the office can usually identify an officer by looking at their writing or the working style. But if the need arises, and copies of such applications are sent to various offices and the same statement is entered without any explanation, it will be difficult for others to identify it. Because of this, the tradition of using a seal was adopted. During the royal period, applications were also presented. The King, or the ministers or office bearers passed orders on some of these, and even though they had signatures or seals, it was difficult to get these signatures and seals on the copies of such orders. Had there not been any means to safeguard from this misunderstanding, then there would have been many difficulties. The King, while writing an order, sometimes wrote '*ba qalam khas*', or '*ba dast e khas*', or '*ba daskhat e khas*'. Had the copier copied it identically, there would have been doubt over whether the writing was of

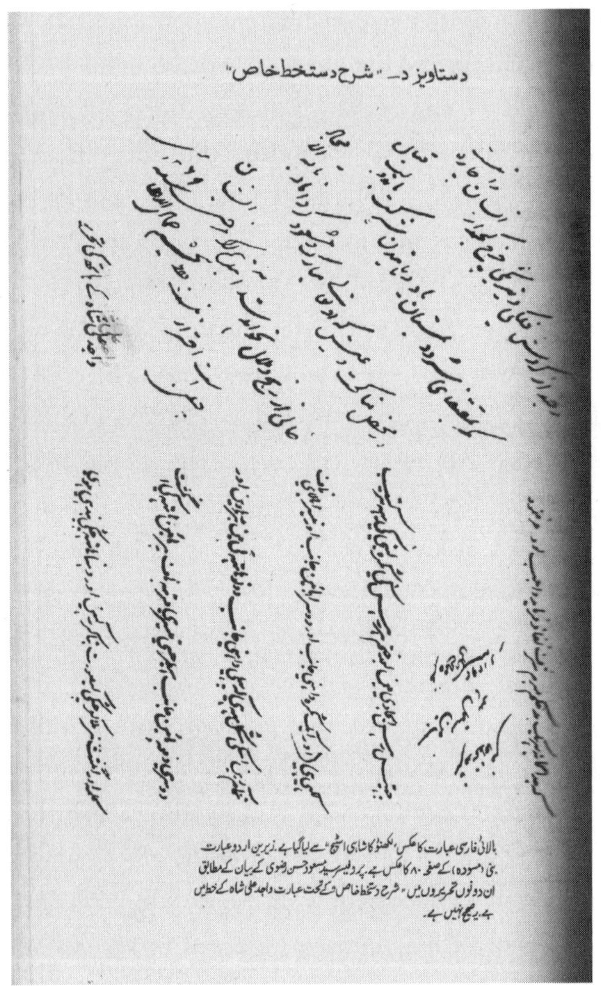

دستاویز د۔ "شرح دستخط خاص"

بالائی فارسی عبارت کا عکس، "لکھنؤ کا شاہی اسٹیج" سے لیا گیا ہے۔ زیریں اردو عبارت
بی (مسودہ) کے صفحہ ۸۰ کا عکس ہے۔ پروفیسر سید مسعود حسن رضوی کے بیان کے مطابق
ان دونوں تحریروں میں "شرح دستخط خاص" کے تحت عبارت واجد علی شاہ کے خط میں
ہے۔ یہ صحیح نہیں ہے۔

IMAGE Y: Document 'Dal': Special Signature of the King

the King.[762] The safe way to avoid such misunderstandings was to add the word '*Sharah*' (Explanation) in the beginning, and if nothing is written then

762. The seller of *Sabatul Quloob* Copy 2 became doubtful by seeing the words *"Afi ana"* with the King's name that the writing was of the King and he expressed this doubt on the fly leaf of the book. But in other copies of *Sabatul Quloob* and in the collection of letters this same thing is written. And this is the copy of the original.

"*Sharh b daskhat e khas*" (Explanation of special signature) or '*ba saad e khas muzzaiyan shud*' should be written. In such clerical sentences the word '*khas*' (special) was reserved for the King only. It was not used for ministers or for other officers.[763]

The custom in the court of Avadh was not different from that of other courts. The people who perused the papers of *Darul* Insha would frequently come across such sentences and would understand them easily. For example, in Rampur there is a collection of memorandums which was presented to Nawab Kalb Ali Khan by Amir Minai and Asir in which there are orders by Wajid Ali Shah, his ministers, and other office bearers. The wording "*Sharah b daskhat e khas*" (Explanation of special signature) is only at the top of those orders which are given by the King. In the orders of others, the words "*sharah dastakhat nawab*" or only "*Sharah dastakhat*" is written. A similar collection is in Lucknow University which is probably of '*Baitul Ijra.*' There also the same trend is followed, where applications and orders are saved in '*Baitul Ijra*'. For the staff perhaps the copies are prepared in the form of a register. This collection is of the same style. In Calcutta Munshi Al Sultan Mehmudud Daulah Bahadur collected only his memorandum for his memory. In the book containing this collection, the word '*Sharah b daskhat e khas*' is written on the head of every memorandum. These collections were compiled by different people during different periods, and their copying is evident from their appearance and the heading which is entered in the beginning. The handwriting of each of these is different but in every collection the ink of the application and "*Sharah dastakhat*" is the same. An innovative person like Wajid Ali Shah, who did not write his name in his letters in a regular manner, could not bear to write the same monotonous words without any innovation and novelty. In the headings of *Mulk e Akhtar*,

763. Some parts of the thesis of *Dr.* Momin *Moiuddin* are published in "*IndoIranica*" (English Trimonthly, Calcutta) Volume 18, Issue No. 2, 3 & 4, which is related to this topic. The aforementioned has been awarded the degree of Doctorate from Edinburgh. On inquiry he confirmed the opinion of the author of this book.

these three words, with some changes, are written to bring some novelty.[764] In the printed headings this was not the trend, and it was his innovation to divert from the common path. Hence, whenever these three words are seen in manuscripts and documents, that writing cannot be of Wajid Ali Shah. In this way the writings which were verified in "*Lucknow Ka Shahi Stage*" were not of Wajid Ali Shah.

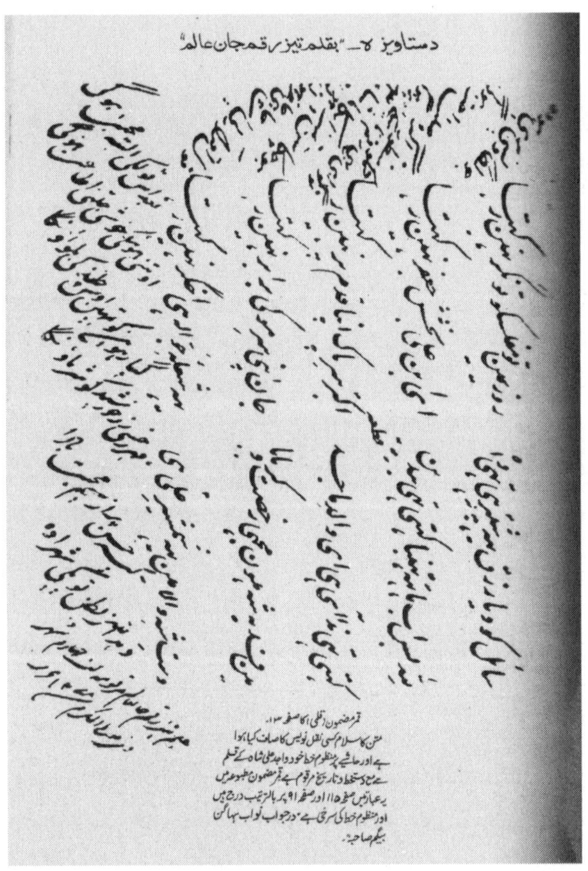

'HAY': "*Ba qalam e tez raqam Jaan e Alam*" *meaning in the speedy hand of Jaan e Alam (From Qmar Mazmun (Handwritten))*

764. *Mulk e Akhtar.* Md. Wajid Ali Shah Akhtar. Matbaey Sultani, Calcutta 1296. 39, 147–49, 152–53, 160, 201.

Attested Writings

The writings of Wajid Ali Shah must not be looked for in *Darul* Insha or *Baitul Ijra*, but in those papers which were around him. The attachment and spontaneity which will be found in these papers will not exist in formal documents which were written out of duty.

The books which were in his study and the books which were written by him fall under such papers. The writings of Wajid Ali Shah on these papers is not a matter of surprise. In fact, their absence from such papers is surprising. When a person draws a line or notes something in the margin while reading a book, no signature is added. Only one of Wajid Ali Shah's writings has been recovered which has his signature along with a date. (The document '*hay*'). All other writings are verified by knowledgeable people or by circumstantial evidence. The following will explain this:

1. In 1959 in Patna, there was an Exhibition of Rareties in which there was displayed an Order with the title '*Ba Khat o Ibarat Wajid Ali Shah.*' (In the handwriting of Wajid Ali Shah). The good services of *Wazirul Sultan* Bahadur were reduced to a certificate by Wajid Ali Shah himself.[765] Perhaps this was that Order, and it was verified by the late *Wazirul Sultan* Bahadur.
2. During the last phase of the King's life, the government was considering giving the Wajid Ali Shah's heirs an allowance from the English treasury instead of the royal treasury. This was not approved by the King, and to stop this an agreement was prepared. The manuscript of this agreement was written by the King himself. There was an attempt to destroy the agreement by burning it. A photocopy of it is in the royal library. This was verified by *Shamsul Ulema Maulvi Md. Haider Sahab*, who was the manager of Shahi Imambarah.[766]

765. List of the Exhibits. *Idara Tehqeeqat Urdu.* 67. 190.

766. *Zamana* (Monthly, Kanpur). Issue: March 1911, 235. The narration of *Nazm Taba Tabai.*

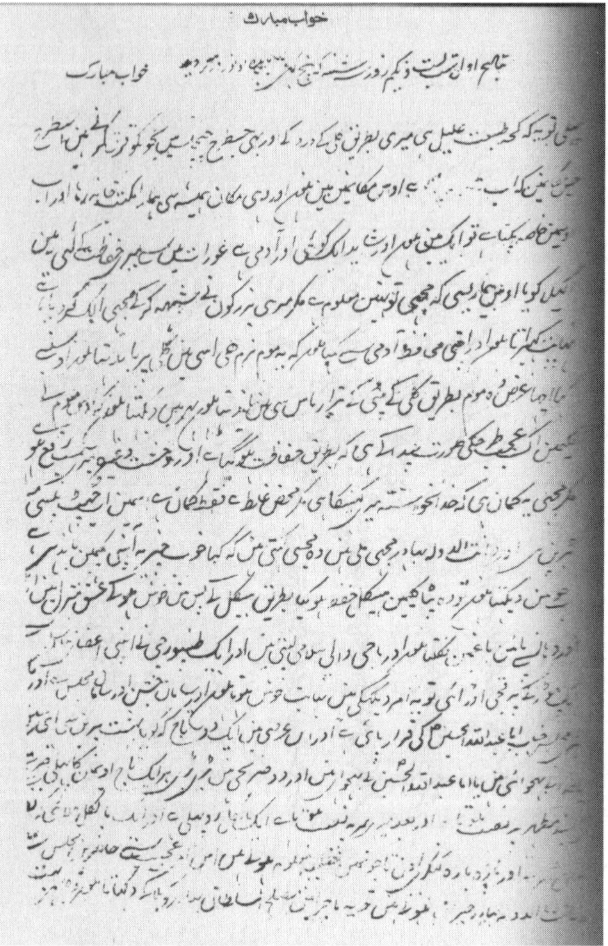
خواب مبارک

KHWAB MUBARAK – (THE FAMOUS DREAM)

3. *Raja Sir Ali* Md. Khan Bahadur (Mehmudabad) had the honour of becoming the King's pupil, and he verified that the King used to give feedback on his compositions.[767]
4. Mushir had composed a *masnavi* on Wajid Ali Shah's wishes, and on its gold-plated copy, the corrections were made by the King's

767. These writings are with the successors of the last Raja. The thesis writer could not get access to it.

pen. The King has described him as his pupil,[768] and Mushir also acknowledged being his pupil in his *masnavi*.[769] The scribbling of a pen on the precious copy of the royal library cannot be the work of anyone else but the person who had ownership over the work and so the right to make corrections.

Summary of The Dream

He writes that in his dream he sees himself confined in a house like children who were confined when they suffereed small pox. In this house good food was prepared for him, and some men and women were there at his service. He says he did not know which disease he had, but that the elders confined him under some suspicion. Then he told his caretakers that he was given some wax to wear around his neck, which he wore with a heavy heart. Then gradually, he realised that the wax had taken on the strange shape of an iron collar, which was appreciated by people like Dayan ud Daulah Bhadur. Then he moved towards the garden, where he saw some muisicians, which pleased him. There was a celebration, but a *majlis* (congregation) was also organized. The *majlis* was in the name of Janab Aba Abdullah Hussain (a.s.), and people said that a crown and two Zarih Mubarak were either sent by Allah or by Hussain from Heaven. The crown was first kept on the Zarih Mubarak, then it was put on his head. One of the Zarih Mubarak was of silver and the other was of gold, and and they had a strange glow around them. This incident amazed everyone in the *majlis*, including Dayan ud Daulah Bahadur. Then he called Maslah ul Sultan Bahadur, and showed him this entire event, which gladdened him as well. This indicated, that as he had presented a Crown on the *taboot* (coffin) of Janab Amirul Momineen, this was the reward. Then the *majlis* started, with everyone in attendance, and he felt that Janab Fatima (a.s.) and Imam Hussain (a.s.) were also present at the *majlis*. Then

768. *Bani,* 245.

769. *Masnavi Musheer* (Handwritten) Gauhar Ali Musheer 1276 (Khuda Bakhsh Library). 18.

he started reciting a dirge (Marsia Khwani) before the Zarih Mubarak. Then also he felt that Janab Fatima and Janab Imam Hasan (a.s.) were there, and they were weeping, and he also wept. Then he felt as if Janab Fatima asked Imam Hussian, 'Do you see how people are weeping for you?. Then suddenly, he heard a voice near him which said "Amma I am in shock , cannot forget my son Akbar I cannot see who else is wailing." Hearing this, all the people started weeping intensely and there was so much commotion that it broke his sleep, and he woke up. (21 day of Navroz, Wednesday)

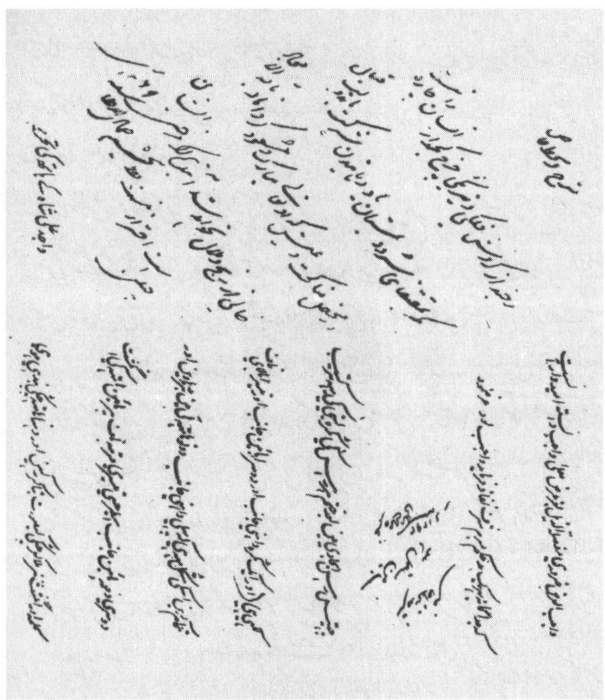

SPECIAL SIGNATURE – In the Hand of the King

5. Four bulky volumes of the dictionary of *Bahar e Ajam*, on the wish of *Fatehud Daulah* Bahadur, were beautifully written by Mir *Hamid Ali* in 1265 A.H.[770] On these books, the 1280 A.H. seal of Wajid Ali Shah

770. The writings on the volumes of *Bahar Ajam* given in this Chapter.

is given, and in places the King has made notations in the margin, indicating where he agreed or disagreed with the dictionary writer. Writing in the margins of the books, which were the property of the royal library, could be done only by a person who had the power and the aesthetic taste to do it. *Bahar e Ajam* was under the King's study for a considerably long period, and in *Mulk e Akhtar* and *Malazul Kalmat* the King made reference to the dictionary. On the flyleaf of the third volume of this book, a dream had been put into writing, probably immediately after it occurred, and which has been included in the Qamar Mazmun.

Some Examples

In the previous pages, many writings were associated with Wajid Ali Shah and in many places, examples were also presented. There are differences between these writings, but this should not be a cause for doubt. Experts opine that even two original signatures may not be identical, least of all in writing from different periods. The '*Safarnama*' of Nijat Hussain Azim Aabadi, the '*bayaz*' of Wazirul Sultan Bahadur, the Mahtab ud Daulah Darakhshan, and the manuscripts of the *masnavis* of Agha Hujjoo Ashraf were written by the authors at different periods of their careers, and in all of these, there is neither similar handwriting nor is any of them is free from mistakes.[771] Despite this, the writings are by these authors. In view of the possibility of such differences, some points are presented here. However, academics will note that these cannot be applied to every piece of writing:

A. The writing done using calligraphy (*kitabat*) is different from normal writing. One is called '*Mashaqqi*' (a small plank for practising

771. The copies of writings of the Chief founder of *Shanti Niketan (Vishwa Bharti University)* Rabindra Nath Tagore are also of great interest through they are in different languages and are often published in various newspapers and magazines. The manuscripts of the poems of Tagore need special attention as to cover the mistakes of the pen he invented a new art.

calligraphy), and the other is called '*Tabai*' (natural, inborn). One who is aware of calligraphy can, based on need, write in '*mashaqqi*' or in '*tabai.*' Writers often did this.

B. There can be differences in '*tabai*' writing. Sometimes a person writes attentively, sometimes carelessly, and often out of need, scribbles are made. In this way, even writing done in one sitting can show significant differences. Students writing in examinations write very carefully, but if the speed of their thoughts surpasses the speed of their pen, then as they continue theor writing becomes messier. If the beginning and end of an examination copy is compared, then it would never have the same handwriting.

C. Innovative people often try to decorate their writing. In this exercise, the form of the '*tabai*' style is lost and becomes difficult to identify.

In addition to the reasons mentioned above, differences in the pen, ink, posture, weather, and age can cause prominent differences in handwriting.[772] By way of proof, I am presenting writings which were written in the same period and in same conditions, but can be regarded as the writing of one person is only possible if we admit that there can be differences in the handwriting of the same person.

In the documents '*Alif*', (the list of *Bani*), '*bay*' (the headings of the *Ishq Nama*), '*jay*' (designs in the *Ishq Nama*), and '*hay*' (*ba qalam tez raqam Jaane Alam*) (By the fast-moving pen of Jaan e Alam.') the '*tabai*' writing of Wajid Ali Shah was presented. In these there are also prominent glimpses of '*mashaqqi*' writing. The document '*wow*' gives a mixed picture of both of these handwriting styles. The writer formally started writing this Ghazal in '*mashaqqi*' writing, but after some verses the handwriting began to distort,

772. On Sir Syed Day an Exhition was held in the Maulana Azad Library of Aligrh Muslim University where the manuscripts and books of Wajid Ali Shah's contemporary Sir Syed Ahmed Khan Ghafarla were displayed. The differences that can happen in a person's writing over a period of 50 or 60 years was indicated in this exhibition. As was the custom of that time, like Wajid Ali Shah, Sir Syed was aware of good handwriting.

Document '*WOW*'
Manuscript 'Qamar Mazmun' pp. 284–85.

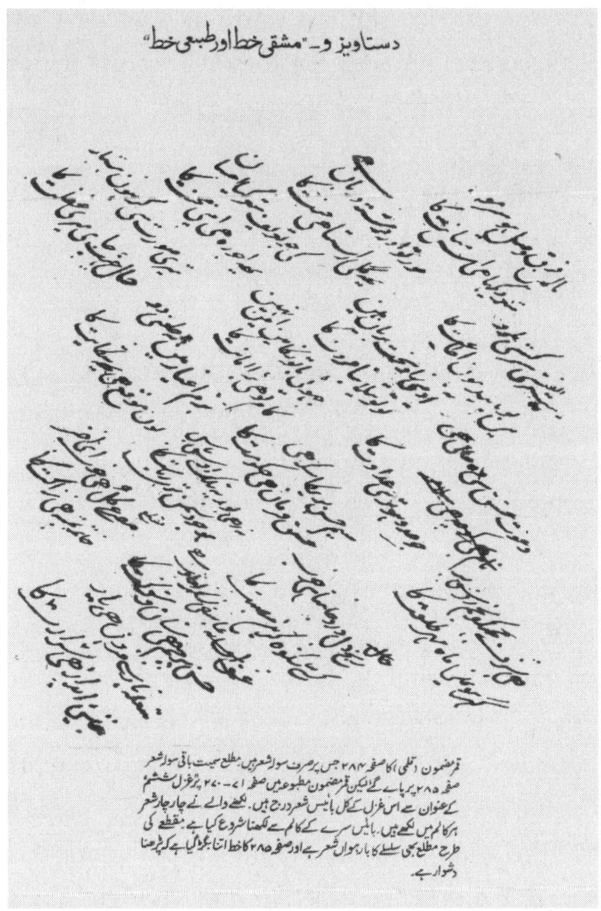

دستاویز و۔ "مشقی خط اور طبعی خط"

قمرمضمون (قلمی) کا صفحہ ۲۸۴ جس پر صرف سولہ شعر ہیں۔ مطلع سمیت باقی سولہ شعر
صفحہ ۲۸۵ پر پائے گئے لیکن قمرمضمون مطبوعہ میں صفحہ ۱۷-۲۷۰ پر غزل ششم
کے عنوان سے اس غزل کے کل بائیس شعر درج ہیں۔ لکھنے والے نے چار چار شعر
ہر کالم میں لکھے ہیں۔ بائیں سرے کے کالم سے لکھنا شروع کیا ہے۔ مقطع کی
طرح مطلع بھی سلسلے کا بارہواں شعر ہے اور صفحہ ۲۸۵ کا خط اتنا بگڑ گیا ہے کہ پڑھنا
دشوار ہے۔

DOCUMENT 'WOW': *Qamar Mazmun* (Manuscript) pp. 284–85. Original writing.

and mistakes were made. By the end of the document, the writing was so distorted that there was no resemblance between the first and the last verses. The reason for this is the high speed with which is was written. Wajid Ali Shah himself is proud of his speed:

It is very difficult to compose Ghazals *in such a hurry,*
Who in this world is like you Akhtar! [773]

Even others thought that this was worth mentioning. Other than the narrations of Sharar and[774] *Naubat Rai Nazar*,[775] note the narration of *Asir*:

He composes a hundred verses in a fleet
Have not seen such a fast orator
There is no one in his competition
Allah*! what a speed of creativity!*[776]

The oratorship in long '*behers*' and awkward meters are a great feature and show the skill of his expression. But alongside these qualities, there are also certain shortcomings, one of which is terrible handwriting. A glimpse of this is presented in the Ghazals in the document '*dal*' above.

Qamar Mazmun Manuscript pp. 196/197

The writer started writing the Ghazal '*be ziya gushta aftab imshab*' in ordinary Persian script, but when he switched to a new column, there was change in his handwriting. As '*maqta*' was reached, the handwriting changed a lot. To adorn the words, the '*markaz*' (the upper stroke of the letters '*kaaf*' and '*gaaf*') and the '*kishish*' (the flourishing stroke forming the initial part of the letter '*kaaf*' and the curve of letters like '*sheen*' and '*fay*') were made slim or in a curved style. The date and details of the '*mushaira*' for which

773. Nazm Namvar. Md. Wajid Ali Shah Akhtar. Matbaey Sultani. Calcutta. 1287. (Raza, Ittihadiya, Khuda Baksh) 172.
774. *Huzn e Akhtar.* Md. Wajid Ali Shah Akhtar. Md. Ali (Compiler), Daeraey Adabia. Lucknow 1922.
775. *Shams Bangala.* (Magazine, Calcutta). February Issue. 1908. 1.
776. *Durrul Taj.* Md. Muzaffar Ali Khan Asir. Matbaey Sultani. Lucknow. 1270. 117.

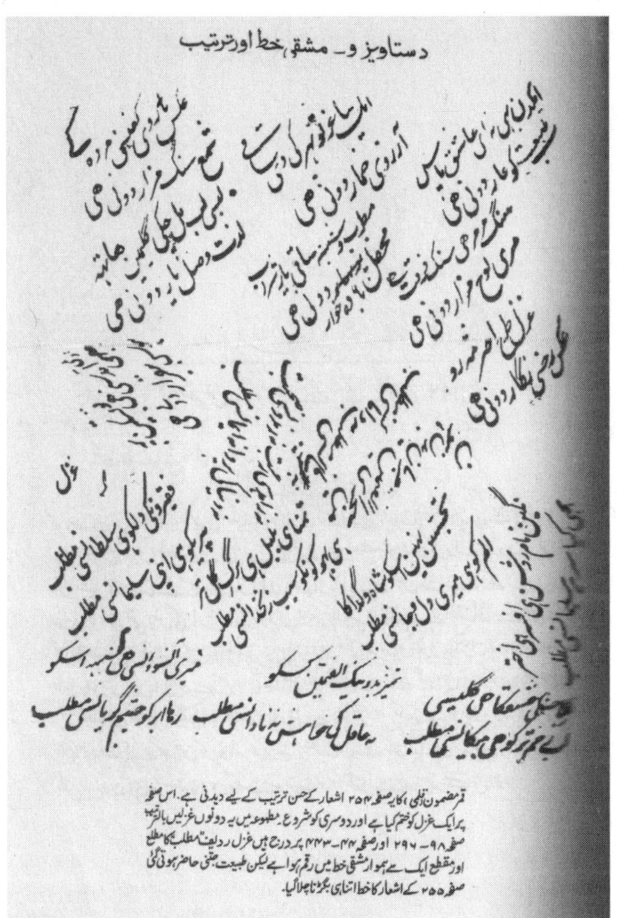

دستاویز و- مشق خط اور ترتیب

قمر مضمون (قلمی) کا یہ صفحہ ۲۵۴ اشعار کے حسن ترتیب کے لیے دیدنی ہے۔ اس صفحہ
پر ایک غزل کو ختم کیا ہے اور دوسری کو شروع۔ مطبوعہ میں یہ دونوں غزلیں بالترتیب
صفحہ ۹۸-۲۹۶ اور صفحہ ۴۴-۴۴۳ پر درج ہیں غزل ردیف "مطلب" کا مطلع
اور مقطع ایک سے ہموار مشقی خط میں رقم ہوا ہے لیکن طبیعت جتنی حاضر ہوتی گئی
صفحہ ۲۵۵ کے اشعار کا خط اتنا ہی بگڑتا چلا گیا۔

DOCUMENT 'WOW'- From Qamar Mazmun (Handwritten). The special style of setting the Ghazal is worth noting.

this Ghazal was composed was written carelessly at the top of the page. In '*Gulzar e Hussaini*', '*Bani*', and '*Mulk e Akhtar*', a few titles, some advice, and index words (seen in the documents '*alif*' and '*bay*') were similarly written in a careless manner. In the aforementioned Ghazal the last line (maqta) was written in a special style, and the style of the word '*Akhtar*' is also seen in other Ghazals, some of which were written either in a hurry, others with patience. See the document '*hay*', in which this signature closely resembles the signature of document 'Zay'.

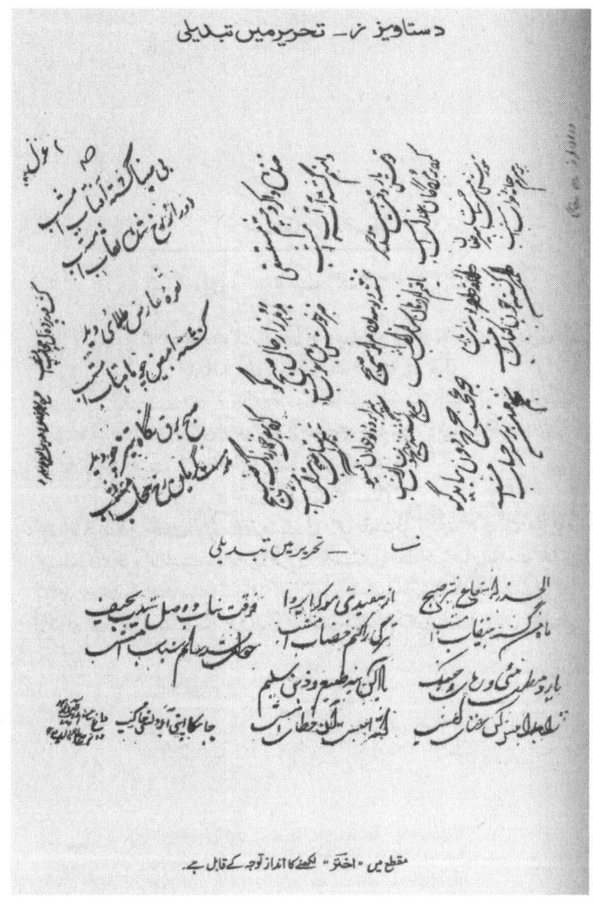

DOCUMENT 'ZAY': Style of Writing the Name '*Akhtar*' in Maqta is worth noting.

Qamar Mazmun Manuscript pp. 232/233

The flaws and good qualities that are seen in the document '*zay*' were clarified and made beautiful in the Ghazal "*Kya bayan hogi zabanon se tabahi hijr ki*", found in this document. The style of decorating the verses is also attractive. Whenever there was mistake, it was removed and rewritten.

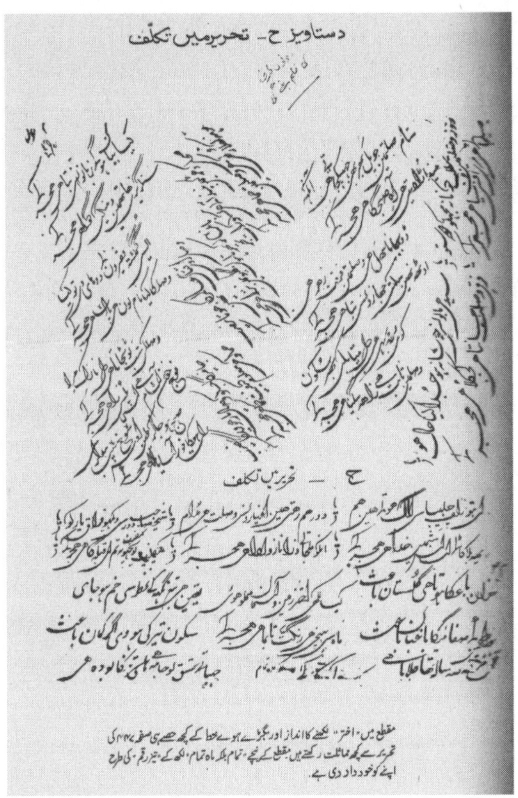

دستاویز ح۔ تحریر میں تکلف

ح — تحریر میں تکلف

مقطع میں "اختر" لکھنے کا انداز اور بگڑے ہوئے خط کے کچھ حصے ہی صفحہ ۲۴۷ کی تحریر سے کچھ مماثلت رکھتے ہیں۔ مقطع کے نیچے "تمام بلکہ ماہ تمام" لکھ کے "تیز رقم" کی طرح اپنے کو خود داد دی ہے۔

DOCUMENT 'HAY': Formal writing

But in one place a word was struck out, and the word '*kaifiyat*' was written again. After the '*maqta*', the formal writing of the words "*tamam balkey maah tamam*" indicates the freshness, humour and innovative style of the writer. In the Ghazal "*gulistan baiss aur baghban baiss*" which starts on the same page, initially the same formal style of writing is used, but could not be continued as it needed so much attention. Hence, it was written in ordinary '*tabai*' style.

Document 'toey'

Sabatul Quloob, Volume 1, Indications (Index) of Copy 'Avadh'

In some places in *Sabatul Quloob*, to provide instructions for the writer who was decorating the copy, a few words of the first couplet are written, and indicate the same flowing style which was found in the document '*zay*'. But on page 63, where the word '*khush*' is written, the symbol '*swad*' was made and the word '*awaz*' is written in the margin in a decorative style. Had this been the work of a writer or of any other person, then the additional word '*awaaz*' would have been written as quick scribbles as was seen on the pages of printed books. This was written by the King two or three years before his death. After this, these indications of his writing were not found anywhere else except in the words written in the published copy of *Hayatul Quloob.*

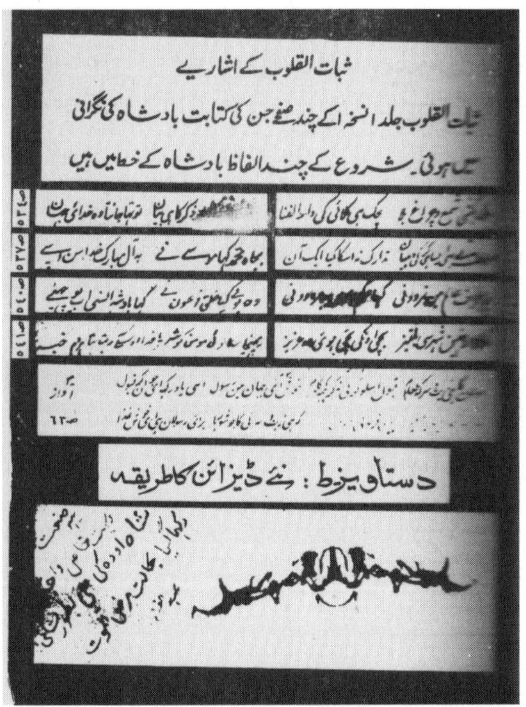

ثبات القلوب کے اشاریے

ثبات القلوب جلد ۱ نسخہ ۱ کے چند صفحے جن کی کتابت بادشاہ کی نگرانی میں ہوئی۔ شروع کے چند الفاظ بادشاہ کے خط میں ہیں

دستاویز ط : نئے ڈیزائن کا طریقہ

DOCUMENT 'TOEY': Indices of Sabatul Quloob – Last writing of the King written on his death bed.

The Style of New Design:[777]

777. *Jaan e Alam.* Maulvi Abdul Haleem Sharar- Adaraey Faroghe Urdu. Lahore. 1951. 40.

Wajid Ali Shah's passion for experimenting with handwriting is evident not only from the pages of the Qamar Mazmun but can further be corroborated by the proof given by his royal associates. Sharar, while explaining the innovativeness of the King, writes:

> *"While he was to write in his own hand a nice or proposed title on the paper, and before the ink was dried, he bent it in from the middle and pressed it hard. After this, when he lifted the pen a new shape which contained the curves of a word was created, by keeping this in front he used to have gardens or buildings constructed which came out as the novel thing."*[778]

Buildings which existed until the Second World War provided clear proof for the above statement, but as the saying goes: '*navishta ba mand sia bar sufaid*'.[779] Only one writing remains which displays this art. It is difficult to find out what was written in this document because the words are written in a distorted form, and the ink has distorted the shape of the letters. But the design exists, and it is eye catching and gorgeous. This was verified by the painter of Wajid Ali Shah's court (*Darbar e Wajidi*), the late *Abdul Ghani*. *Abdul Ghani* was a resident of Azimabad, but he later settled in Metiaburj. As apparent from his narrative he secured the writing of his benefactor which was written on his death bed. In this document, on the upper left corner, the fingerprint beside '*tay*', the last letter of the word '*sanat*' needs attention.

778. *Ibid.*

779. Like written on white paper in black, means very clear and obvious.

FOUR

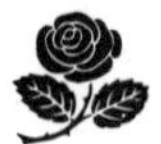

Cultural Contributions of Wajid Ali Shah

NATURE OF CONTRIBUTIONS

The civilization of a country is the reflection of the collective efforts of its people. The life of a person is not long enough, nor are his resources so exhaustive, that he should embrace all the fine arts. It is also not necessary that the efforts put in be revolutionary and record forming. Based on his competency and preferences, a person makes changes in the established traditions of fine arts. If such changes conform to the demand of the time, they become popular and a part of the culture, but if such changes are contrary to the spirit and demand of the time, then they die out and remain imperceptible. In the cultural ethos of India and in the particular culture of Lucknow, the efforts of Wajid Ali Shah were absorbed like rivulets running down and assimilating in the river. Wajid Ali Shah was not the ruler of a huge empire, nor did his regime extend over so long a period that it became the subject of immense inheritance. However, he was apprehensive about the future of the culture which he himself had inherited and had the urge to preserve it. Hence, he continuously worked towards this preservation,[1] and made some progress in this regard. He worked towards the goal that the artisans and intellectuals should not feel inferior. Royal accolades were not enough to keep the oriental culture vibrant and permanent. It also required royal sponsorship and support. Wajid Ali Shah was quite mindful of this sponsorship. Wherever Wajid Ali Shah's cultural ethos deviated from the ancient culture of India, it was in an effort to preserve his uniqueness.

The cultural philosophy of Wajid Ali Shah was not like the light of stars falling from the sky but was down to earth; he tried to modify and transform the existing saplings of cultural ethos. His innovative efforts spread from ancient religious dances to *kathak*, from ancient *ragas* and songs to present-day *thumri*, from ancient mushairas (that were of the typical form and were only verbal) to exemplary or allegorical mushaira (in which the compositions of famous poets were recited by a person while being dressed up like that poet), from established archaic poetry to free poetry. This all happened under the guidance and sponsorship of this great ruler. Despite limited resources, the fine arts of painting, calligraphy, gardening, and architecture were preserved and flourished under him.

THE INFLUENCE OF ENGLISH

Common English people did not value Indian art and culture. Wajid Ali Shah and the two rulers before him had no liking for Western culture. However, Wajid Ali Shah deviated from the earlier rulers in that he accepted the good points from Western culture and preferred to adopt and assimilate them into the Indian ethos. This indicates his open-mindedness and non-communal approach. These ideas have manifested in the following practices:

---

1. The following couplets are given at page 142 of *Sheva-e-Faiz Otherwise where I am and where are such times*

It is now Issa's religion and those times have vanished Who will care for the art

No one will be concerned about Arabic or Urdu

1. At present we see that the Government displays products of Indian culture with great pride in the International Exhibitions. This good practice started in the international fair in 1851 at the initiative taken up by Wajid Ali Shah.[2]
2. At present the army practice is done in the English style, and for this the English terminology is translated into Hindi. Wajid Ali Shah introduced this English style into his own army, alongside new ideas as expressed below:

People are being employed
They are selected from various walks
When several youth were assembled
The regiment was ready
The exercise was new, the language was new
The groups were formed
They work so swiftly
We lag behind the fair (English)
Such innovations were made in the exercise
The boss will come and see
There were mounted soldiers in groups
The horses were worth seeing[3]

The terminology was in Persian, which was the official language at that time. Note the terminology of today and that of a hundred years ago:[4]

---

2. *Safeer e Avadh*. Maulvi Md. Masihuddin Khan. Al Nazir Press. Lucknow. 1929. 91.
3. *Riyazul Seher*. Sheikh Aman Ali Seher. Karnama Publication. Lucknow. 1291. (1291 denotes the Islamic Year Hijri corresponding to 19th Century of that time). 191.
4. *Guzashtaey Lucknow*. Maulvi Abdul Haleem Sharar. Naseem Book Depot. Lucknow. 66.

Persian	Hindi	English
Raast ru	*Daahne Ghoom*	Right Wheel
Dast chip bgard	*Bayein Murr*	Left Turn
Pass biya	*Peechey Murr*	About Turn

The present government has formed an army and police force consisting of women, but the orthodox section of the society still regards it as objectionable. But about a century ago, in the backward society of yesteryear, Wajid Ali Shah formed a regiment of women and made it the "envy of the English army",[5] though it is often associated with his bent for feminism. This small regiment was formed for the security of the palace. The expertise of these women in the military arts is evident: in 1858, when the English army entered *Sikander Bagh*, it was this regiment and its valour which caught the eye of the English. Their sex was revealed only at the end, after they put up a brave fight against the English soldiers.[6]

Some time ago, it was considered a matter of pride and courage when high-achieving Indians were endowed with English titles. During the reign of Wajid Ali Shah, English men were endowed with 'Hindustani' titles; the certificate of "*Maalijudd Daulah Haaziqul Mulk* Dr. Joseph Bhadur Hikmat e Jung" is still displayed in the Edinburgh Museum.[7]

It was not difficult for Wajid Ali Shah to adopt the foreign culture and lose his identity, like Nasiruddin Shah did before him.[8] But the way Wajid Ali Shah assimilated the influence of the English indicates that he wanted

5. Bhatnagar G.D.; Administration of Oudh Under Wajid Ali Shah. Thesis For Ph. D. of Lucknow University.Tagore Library. Badshah Bagh. Lucknow. 9.

6. Sen. S.N.; Eighteen Fifty Seven. Delhi. 1959. Citing Gordon Alexander. Forbes & Mitchell. 242.

7. Fayrer Sir Joseph; Collections of My Life. London. 1900.106.

8. For details see Knighton's book entitled *Private Life of an Eastern King*. Knighton W.; the Private Life of An Eastern King. London. 1921. (Edited by S.B. Smith).

to add a new dimension to his own culture. Had he known the English language, and had the English been sincere and affectionate,[9] Wajid Ali Shah would have been more successful in his efforts, which, instead of becoming an object of criticism, would have been enriching and valuable.

THE PATRONAGE OF FINE ARTS

Cultural richness can be seen as a benchmark of a nation's civilization, as it is this richness which differentiates a cultured nation from an uncultured nation. Before Wajid Ali Shah's reign, the progress of art and culture did not meet this standard. The previous Kings, namely Muhammad Ali Shah and Amjad Ali Shah, were mainly interested in religious affairs. Hence, the publication of religious books and the establishment of 'madrasas' was their first priority. Their decade long reign is marked by such achievements.

Wajid Ali Shah, apart from religious affairs, showed special interest in various fine arts. Thus, arts which had until now continued only as weak traditions, reached the zenith of popularity and progress under Wajid Ali Shah's royal patronage. Coordination and benefaction between a ruler and his subjects is essential for the proliferation of fine arts. This was absent during the reign of previous Kings, though the seeds of such patronage were sown during the period of Asaf ud Daulah and Nasiruddin Haider. Wajid Ali Shah's innovative nature and sponsorship provided great opportunities to the intellectuals and the competent to nurture their abilities. His work to inspire, enthuse, and support the intellectuals is the supreme cultural contribution of a great King. It is not necessary for Kings to know and learn the arts which they are inspiring and sponsoring; such abilities require thoughtfulness and rigorous practice, which can distract from administrative affairs. Whether or not Wajid Ali Shah was ignorant of administrative matters is a different

9. Wajid Ali Shah wanted to have the administration of some of his districts on English pattern but this was disapproved by the government and he was told that if so then why he does not hand over the empire to the English. *Supra Note* 5. 59–63.

historical question. The reviews of his contemporaries[10] show that it is because of his bent towards such intellectual pursuits, that people held him responsible for the unsatisfactory condition of his empire. Wajid Ali Shah paid a high price for his name and fame in the field of art and culture.

Good administration is the duty of Kings, but it is also an equally important duty to promote the culture and commerce of their country, and to inspire and encourage their artisans. Not all the Kings of the world conquered forts and seized territories. Each led their administration according to their preferences; and among them there were some who pursued more destructive goals. While highlighting the weaknesses of Wajid Ali Shah, it will not be beyond the historical vision if one admits that though not so proficient in administration, but he was very dynamic in patronising the cultural activities of his countrymen. The English presented a dismal picture of the great King in order to gain a political advantage:

"The King was such an imposter that he changed his clothing often, like the Pukhraj Pari and Neelam Pari and entered the '*Akhara*' (Wrestler's ring). He often showed familiarity with '*sitar*' was very comfortable with musical instruments as if the sitar and the drum were his friends. He even defied the babbler consequently whosoever was in such Lanka was an expert."[11]

But such a statement presents a prejudiced historical viewpoint, revealing an ignorance of reality. *Asir* was not considered Wajid Ali Shah's '*masahib*',

10. A. "Sahab Zaidatul Akhbar opines in this Chapter (Chapter regarding translation of *Hamla e Haidari)* that it is the job of the Kings to remain engaged in the administration of the state and not in poetic affairs. If *Hazrat Sultani* entrusts this work to *Malakul SHoora Qazi Md. Sadiq Khan Akhtar* then the translation job will be done nicely, and if he himself is engaged in the administrative affairs, then the administration will run smoothly." Maa'sir-(Monthly, Patna) Issue December 1942. Referred by Asadul Akhbar (Agra), 118.

B. "There is no dearth of anything under Khuda...animals, museum, the reality of dedication was revealed after witnessing the *Sultani* architecture... *Subhan*Allah... excellent... it reveals much caliber... I wish this much attention was also paid to the administrative affairs." *Avadh Punch*... (Lucknow). Volume 1, Issue Dated May 6, 1882. 2.

11. *Tarikh e Avadh*, Volume 5, 243.

but his master.[12] We cannot disregard the narrative of Asir, who says that often, when the King went to the courtyard, he would be dressed like a '*pari*', and that when he became a '*masahib*',[13] he began to play the drum. First, he learned the art of playing the sitar and was then engaged as an assistant.[14]

In response to the unjustified statement in the extract above, some sympathisers praised him profusely:

> "...the head of the. congregation of the honourable court of Avadh identified and honoured intellectuals with prestigious posts..."[15]

In support of this statement, it is shown from the statement of Wajid Ali Shah himself[16] that he would easily reward anyone who praised him. But the one who is generous gives to the needy voluntarily and abundantly Wajid Ali Shah was not such a givers. During his reign there was not a single instance where the deserving were devoid of their reward, but there were also no instances where the deserving were given what was their right. The previous narrative reflects upon Wajid Ali Shah's temperament, while the latter resembles the characteristic feature of oriental courtyards, in that the less is said, the better. Not everyone knows the art of pleasing the courtiers, nor does every artist accept it. In the court of Wajid Ali Shah, those who were honoured were mostly people who were well-versed in the art for which they were honoured. Those devoid of rewards were those who did not deserve them. Instead of providing a list of those who were honoured and rewarded by Wajid Ali Shah, it will not be out of place to mention an event.

12. *Tarikh e Avadh.* Volume 5. 110.

13. *Mazaq e Muhabbat.* Md. Ali Khan Mohsin-Munshi I. Naval Kishore Publication, Lucknow. 1885. 317.

14. *Mara'tul Awza* (Handwritten), 73.

15. *Mazaq e Muhabbat.* Md. Ali Khan Mohsin-Munshi I. Naval Kishore Publication, Lucknow. 1885. 317.

16 *Tarikh-e-Mumtaz.* MWASA (Compiler: Dr. Md. Baqar). Urdu Markaz Lahore. 1952 (Azad) 53, 56.

Anis[17] is to Lucknow what Ghalib is to Delhi. He, being devoid of any title or honour, was a stain on the Wajid Ali Shah's reputation as a connoisseur. *Anis* himself was pained by this:

When I will desert this place and go to the Other World
I reached there when customers left the market

But he was a master, he displayed his art but did not sell it. Wajid Ali Shah tried connecting with him. He invited him to write a poetic account of Avadh, for which he was offered an abode in Qaiser Bagh. It was thought that even if *Anis* did not want to compose in appreciation of the King, he would at least write this account. However, *Anis* did not agree to this either.[18] He composed blessings, and received the status of an elegy writer, but not of a genius.[19] In this regard, Mirza Ghalib was more liberal than *Anis*. He wrote his appreciation (*Qaseeda*) from Delhi, and payment was fixed for him. Had Wajid Ali Shah been on the throne for longer, it would not have been surprising if Ghalib had landed in Lucknow.

Wajid Ali Shah mentions that 1,700 poets and 500 physicians were associated with him.[20] While relating the prosperity during his reign, he

---

17. *Meer Babbar Ali Anis* (1803–1874) is one of the glittering stars of Urdu poetry. He was master of *marsia* or elegy and specialist of Rubai or four-line poetry. He adorned the court of Kings of Avadh including that of Wajid Ali Shah. He took Urdu poetry to unprecedented heights hence is an immortal poet.

18. *Waqiyat e Anis,* Mir Mehndi Hasan Ahsan Lucknavi- Muta Bae ahsal Matabae Lucknow, 1905. 82, 83.

19. Value of a thing after its fall. Same Anis who lamented for not getting proper recognition got new sting after the dethroning of Wajid Ali Shah and the fall of Qaiser Bagh:
The threshold from where thousands were enriched The house is destroyed the abode devastated Neither the residents are left nor the house is spared The earth is overturned the times changed
O my detiny! The sky struck the lightning Over the grain which was of my share
I accepted with patience in the reign of Alam Any iota of grain which I got as a pearl
Beware that You Are Not left behind Anis! Get up the Clan is moving

20. *Huzn e* Akhtari, MWASAA. 1306 (Raza Library, Rampur). 71.

mentions with pride that, during this period, some 8,000 people came to reside in Lucknow.[21] The lowest estimate of the annual income of the royal treasury is stated to be one crore and twelve lakh rupees.[22] The Resident says that all this money was spent, and the empire was almost bankrupt.[23] The extravagant spending from the King's treasury was on dance and music. Contemporary historians state that, to present the imaginary stories as real, astronomers, fortune tellers, poets, and writers were employed in great numbers so that in the dance dramas, they could be present to train the characters to be more realistic.[24] For the construction and decoration of the stage, similar workers were employed in abundance. There was not much expenditure on the affairs of the government, and the above narrations explain the superfluous expenses which were incurred in promoting the fine arts in Lucknow. Thus, the employment of 1,700 intellectuals and artisans is not in itself surprising. The surprising part is that even after his dethronement, while he was in exile, the same trend continued. Tens of thousands of have-nots got shelter in the name of artisans who proliferated their talents and were benefitted thereby.[25] After he lost his throne, it was very easy for the King to keep away from such alimonies, stipends and charities. But other than a few exceptions where there were refusals, there were also instances where maintenance of the needful was given preference over the maintenance of his own self and children.[26]

---

21. *Jawab e Blue Book*. MWASA. (Published from Under Beni Prasad Nawaz Ganj, Lucknow. 88.

22. *Mara'tul Awza* (Handwritten), 10.

23. *Supra Note* 5. 142.

24. *Asrar e Wajidi* (Handwritten), Munshi Zhairuddin Bilgram 1266–78 A.H. (Tagore). 141.

25. *Adeeb Urdu* (Monthly, Lucknow) Issue January 1922, 25.

26. *Malazul Kalmat*, Mwasa M. Sultani Publication- Calcutta-1297 (Avadh, Azad). 712. It is expressed as follows:
But Your men are also your obligation
There will be no peace without feeding them It is not that only your children should get
And others go bare handed hopeless from Akhtar.

INNOVATION

Before discussing Wajid Ali Shah's interest and skill in knowledge and fine arts, it is necessary to mention his most important attribute: Historians regard this to be his innovative and ground-breaking approach. The compiler of *Aftab e Avadh* writes:

> "*Hazrat Padshah* had an innovative temperament which is manifested in his garments, buildings and their decoration which is worth seeing." [27]

The innovative nature of the King was not limited to the fields mentioned in the above extract. In fact, from the use of novel words and terminology, to the delicacies of the fine arts, from dresses to luxury items, everywhere the King was either a pioneer of novel things or was innovative in his approach to them. This sent a message to those who wanted to please him that anything they want to present before him must have a touch of novelty. It is matter of disappointment that some innovations were meaningless and not very beneficial, and died out over the course of time. Very few creations survived the test of time, and it is difficult to say which of them originated during his period. The initial forms of '*kathak*', '*thumri*', '*elegy*', and dance drama must have originated before his time as it seems impractical that these arts originated and became popular within only a short, 10-year period. Not only were these new and rudimentary practices improved and developed under his guidance, but the masters and experts of many fine arts were born during his time. Art cannot progress without innovation, and an artist cannot survive without inspiration. Wajid Ali Shah imbibed these qualities in abundance, and hence there is no doubt that *Nazm*, for the appreciation of his work, selected him as a person who was a patron of art and literature, and was himself experimenting in the fields of prosody and poetry.[28]

---

27. *Aftab Avadh* (Handwritten), 1874–75, Mirza Md. Taqi, Tagore Library, Badshah Bagh Lucknow. 152.

28. *Nazm Taba Tabai.* In verse (band) 13 & 14 Maulvi Syed Ali Haider, Publication Azam Jahi, Hyderabad. 216–20. Nazm says:

Following are the characteristic features of the King's innovations:

1. From 1267 A.H., the King added the words '*Akhtar Nagar*' to his coins.[29] The inhabitants of Lucknow also started calling Avadh by this name.[30] Akhtar Nagar is the old name of the state of Avadh, and is probably associated with Meerza Roshan Akhtar, who is known by the name Md. Shah Ranageley.[31] The King coined this name in context of his 'takkhallus' (pen name).
2. Wajid Ali Shah declared 13 Zeeqad 1269 A.H. as the first *Wajidi* month of a new era (year). The names of its twelve months are: 'Wajidi', 'Muhammadi', 'Akhtari', 'Sikandari', 'Sulaimani', 'Nabini', Imami', 'Sanobar', 'Maratib', 'Mansoori', and 'Hussaini'.[32] It is quite possible that in state offices, these new months were followed, but this is not mentioned by contemporary historians, or in the coins of Wajid Ali Shah.
3. Wajid Ali Shah's courtiers used to wear a cap that he granted them. The King called these hats '*alam pasand*', and commoners called them '*jhoola*'. The cap had golden embroidery, which was raised to a round circle above the forehead, and a cotton '*jhoola*' that hung down to the neck. The name of the cap is likely drawn from this design.[33] When discussing the courtesans, Nawab Gaus Md. Khan writes:

"If no body appreciates it—go to Hazrat Akhtar- This which you have written an album of comparison with and without rhyming words.... Don't be disheartened, if there are lakhs of ignorant, one who is of discerning intellect excels them all.

29. Dayal P, Catalogueof the Coins of the Kingsof Oudh, Allahabad. (1939). page (Jeem).

30. *Nazm Taba Tabai* page, 215:

"Ilahi *again Akhtar Nagar be inhabited- again the royal gives appearance here- so that its devastation disappears and the presence of Akhtar makes it happier. The bride of "chauthi" is looted*"
Shair Lucknavi (Handwritten Bayaz)

31. *Tarikh e Iqtidaria* (Handwritten) Volume 1, page 9. *Israr e Wajidi* (Handwritten) 486.

32. Lucknow Ka Shahi Stage, Prof. Syed Masood Hasan Rizvi, Kitab Nagar, Lucknow. (1957). 181–82 referred by 'Zohdatul Kwaif.'

33. *Jaan e Alam*. Maulvi Abdul Haleem Sharar. Idara e Farogh e Urdu. Lahore. 1951. 26.

"in the cap and dress of the courtiers, a sort of solemn grandeur was noted."[34]

This special grandeur was the result of the King's novel choice.[35]

4. The commentators have given the names of dresses created by Wajid Ali Shah: '*Qubaey* Noor',[36] '*Jaamaey Husn*',[37] and '*Jaamaey Fanoos Roshan*'.[38] The context in which they are described indicates that these are male garments, but there are no further details.
5. Certain terminology is also associated with Wajid Ali Shah. For example, 'wine' was called '*aab e haram*' (forbidden water), blankets were called '*Shab Khwabi*' (night comfort), sandals were called '*aaram paaeey* (foot comfort), hookah was '*labey maashuq*' (lips of the beloved), edible tobacco was '*khush talab*' (gentle need), the head pillow was '*aaram sar*' (head comfort), and the side pillow was '*aaram pehlu*' (side comfort).[39] However Wajid Ali Shah himself did not follow this terminology strictly.

MUSIC

Music is related to sound, and some authorities claim[40] that the King was hard of hearing. In such a situation, understanding the intricacies of music is a strange fact, and it is possible that there are contradictory accounts. At present, keeping aside this controversy, it is relevant that Bethune, a veteran

34. Sairul Mohtasham. Nawab Ghous Md. Khan-Sarkar Gulshanabd Publication. Jawrah. 431.
35. *Mara'tul Awza* (Handwritten). Lalji Wald Seetal Prasad. Raza Library, Rampur. 94 & 109.
36. *Aaien Akhtar*, Ghulam Haider Saghir Lucknavi. Avadh Press Lucknow. Second Edition. 1912. 31.
37. From page 86 of *Bani* it looks as if this was the dress of dance drama. (*Rahas*). On page 259 of 'Nataijul Zehan' it is mentioned as a muffler (*guluband*).
38. The luster of the holy body is reflected thru the dress - The name of this dress is 'Jamaey Fanoos Roshan.' *Diwan e* Barq- Md. Raza Khan Barq. Sultani Publication. Lucknow.
39. *Qadeem* Hunar, 36–37.
40. *Khushmarkaey Zeba.* Saadat Khan Nasir. Khuda Baksh Oriental Library, Patna. 16200 pg.

of western music, was also hard of hearing.[41] Like Bethune, the Wajid Ali Shah's services in this field were more concerned with teaching and training than with hearing and singing.

The indulgence of Wajid Ali Shah in the histrionic arts,[42] in making music the means of various movements of dance,[43] and his excellence in instruments which lacked the delicacies of the flute – like the '*sitar*', 'drum', '*taasha*'[44] (semi-spherical drum), which is, '*sarangi*' (an Indian stringed instrument), and '*pukhawaj*' (a kind of drum, timbrel) – was perhaps because of this shortcoming. As the common belief goes, if ears cannot understand the pleasure of a thing, the eyes become more competent in understanding its intricacies.

After analysing Wajid Ali Shah's verbal expressions and practices, authorities conclude that his indulgence in the fine arts was not cursory or only to placate his interests.[45] He was an ardent lover of art, approached it with full dedication, and presented such a high standard that even the work of experts could not satisfy his taste and high criteria. According to Sharar, the mastery of an art could be judged by whether the artist was employed by the King.[46] This standard for appraising an art – based on the King's patronisation, his indulgence in the art as a pupil, and his assembly of masters – became a reason for the development of new trends in Indian music. Thus, unprecedented popularity was achieved by '*thumri*' as a style of song, by '*sitar*' as a musical instrument, and by '*kathak*' as a dance.

---

41. Note the biography of Bethune in Encyclopedia Britannica. Apart from this, the inventor of gramophone, telephone and of several devices related to voice, Addison was also hard of hearing. From scientific viewpoint snake is also known to be deaf but his movement on the sound of flute is a common experience.

42. According to American Association of Community the term denotes any dramatic representation of a scene, mainly over emotional acting. (Translator).

43. Detail on other pages regarding the dance.

44. *Al Nazir*, (Monthly, Lucknow) Issue January 1930, 37–38.

45. Urdu Adab ke Aath Saal page, (Thesis of Dr. Abul Lais Siddiqui), Lucknow Ka Shahi Stage. 143–44.

46. *Jaan e Alam Ki Shayari.* Mukhzin. Delhi. Ishrat Lucknavi's Essay. October 1908. 68.

The establishment of a college of music, the rewarding of artists and musicians by the King, and his interaction and cooperation with the band of great intellectuals is widely acclaimed. We are often reminded that:

> "From Akbar up to Wajid Ali Shah no one bothered to establish a musical institution or to patronise its compilation or propagation."[47]

However, it would be fitting to say that very few know that Wajid Ali Shah pioneered the elements that are now regarded as the remarkable achievements in the field of art by the present-day (2025) government.

Alas, he was defamed, was not appreciated for his invaluable services. The '*Pari Khana*'[48] that he established, which was later renamed as '*Rahas Manzil*', gave unquestioned services in Lucknow and Calcutta. This was like the institution that was established for the patronisation of music, but it took the art into the common parlance and popularised it. It achieved very high standards, which can be regarded as the highest accomplishments of any such institution. Its first student was Wajid Ali Shah himself. He became a teacher there during his residence in Metiaburj, wrote books on the subject of teaching and learning, awarded prestigious titles to the masters, and gave grants which absolved them from the worry of income for generations to come.[49] He inspired his pupils to remain dedicated towards their art, and towards sheer enjoyment.[50]

---

47. *Adab Aur Tehzeeb*. Fursatullah Ansari Azad. Kitab Ghar Delhi. 92.

48. In both prose and in poetry Wajid Ali Shah regards it as an educational house (Taleem Khana). Note the headlines of *Ishq Nama* (poetry) 'Dastan 21' as follows:
He got place in 'Taleem Khana'
As usual there was only singing (Dastan 71) One day I was in the 'Taleem Khana'
There something strange happened (Dastan 92) He got a place in Taleem Khana
That he receives the training of dance and singing (Dastan 121).

49. *Muraqqaey Khusravi* (Handwritten). Syed Md. Azmat Ali AlviNaami Kakori. 1286. Tagore Library, Badhshah Bagh. Lucknow. 169 & 189.

50. *Bani*. MWASA. Sultani Publication. Calcutta, 1877. (Khuda Baksh, Avadh). 323.

He also did everything possible to promote the pious art associated with *Mahadev* and *Parbati.* It was neither within his control, nor within the control of the present government, to regain the prestige of the art, which had moved from the holy altars of the temples to the luxurious rooms of the opulent, and to make society accept it's the grandeur and greatness.[51]

There is not much difference between Wajid Ali Shah and any present-day government regarding their style of working in the field of art and culture. The main difference is on the grounds of antiquity and modernity, and collective efforts as in a democracy versus individuality. Wajid Ali Shah produced commendable results in a short amount of time, because of the personal attention he gave. The efforts of the government, however, could not revive classical music in a meaningful manner. The success of Wajid Ali Shah and the defamation of '*Pari Khana*', was perhaps because his style of working was passionate, and his attention was centred on limited fields of music.

The planning of the present government is based on established grounds, and it aims to achieve high standards. Considering his age, and that at the time his contributions were at a rudimentary stage, it is futile to expect that Wajid Ali Shah's start would have been more promising and far-reaching. His passion for music developed gradually; he felt that music is an art, that it is not merely a thing of momentary joy, but can achieve spiritual bliss. "*Dukhaiyya, sikhayya, prakhiyya*" is the age-old idiom about music. No artist can reach their pinnacle without passing through these difficult stages. Wajid Ali Shah passed the stage of '*dukhaiyya*' stealthily, as it was during the prime time of his youth.[52] Then came the time when he witnessed the expertise of *Qutub Ali Khan*, and then learned from the masters of music, practising the art of '*tabla*' and '*sitar*' with full fervour.[53] This indulgence in

---

51.

52. *Sautul Mubarak.* Md. Wajid Ali Shah Akhtar. Publication Sultani. Lucknow. 1269. (Raza Library, Rampur) 4 & 5.

53. *Mahal Khana e Shahi.* Mirza Fida Ali Khanjar. Nami Press. Lucknow. (1934). 40–49.

the attainment of knowledge and art would have been commendable had he not become addicted to women, which after *Mahadev* and *Parbati*, added a sexist dimension to his music.

The merging of music with the killing beauty and voices of the fair sex presented a deadly combination. Wajid Ali Shah was already a victim of this addiction, and with his indulgence and mastery over music, his urge to gather women with a talent for singing gained momentum. He also desired the women who were already present to master the art of music and singing.[54] No educational institution with good intentions is founded in this fashion, nor were such women found in decent families. Only women with a lust for money and ambitions to rise in life entered this arena. Thus, only poor women, or those who were professional singers, came forward. Musical institutions try to avoid such people, but '*Pari Khana*' was founded in this way. The instructors in this field were those who worked for a daily wage. Wajid Ali Shah left no stone unturned to make this institution prominent. A building was specially constructed for it, and had guards to ensure that only masters and professionals in the field could enter. The King entrusted this work to Nawab Khas Mahal.[55] There were no restrictions on admission into the institution. Every girl who wished to attend was accepted.[56] It is likely that boys were also admitted; the ones who were mentioned as its beneficiaries[57] had no other means to receive education.

All the instructors and beneficiaries were rewarded. The intellectuals were also aware of their mastery, and said "Certain things were mastered by the prostitutes within a short period of time, those who were crude singers and could not imagine the intricacies of the art were made proficient and raised to the position of singers."[58] However, this did not change the mentality of

54. *Id.* 47–49.

55. *Id.* 52.

56. *Id.* 53.

57. *Fasanaey Ibrat*; Mirza Rajab Ali Beg Suroor. Publication: Nujumul Uloom Karnama. Lucknow. 1884. 86.

58. *Id.* 89.

certain people. Ultimately, the patron cannot be blamed for this, but the people who benefitted from it. Though there was enlightenment, and the society was known to be advanced, even today the people who enter the world of music and singing are not respected as they should be.[59]

In music, Wajid Ali Shah is regarded as a pioneer.[60] The height of art and talent that was achieved by the King could not be reached by many. Sarwar, who was himself very talented, writes about Wajid Ali Shah:

> "In the art of music even those who were proficient became speechless before Hazrat (The King). His vision was great and defied every other, he innovated, his tones ascended and descended Miraculously, every tune showed originality with innovation and novel style, other visionaries could not reach his standard. He shows strange delicacies in the '*tappa*', '*thumri*', 'Ghazal' and '*daadra*' when he sings. His every sentence is piercing, it bruises the heart, the commentators are unable to feel it, his tone and voice is god-gifted, it humbles others."[61]

Wajid Ali Shah learned the various genres of music from masters in the field. In '*sitar*' he was the pupil of Quli Qutub Shah.[62] After he was crowned, he gave him the title of "*Qutubud Dulah Muftahul Mulk Masahib e Khas Md. Quli Qutub Ali Khan* Bahadur *Samsamam Jung.*"[63] Chhotey Khan was proficient in the '*tabla*' and trained the King. He was given the title of "*Anisud Daulah Monisulmulk Masahib e Khas Khan*Azad *Khan* Bahadur *Dilawar Jung.*"[64]

Ghulam Ali Khan Farrukhabadi was a familial master, and the King learned to sing from him.[65] In addition to the titles he had received from his family, the King also gave him the title of "*Gulam Ali Khan Najeebud*

60. Durrul Taj; Md. Muzzaffar Ali Khan Asir. Sultani Publication. Lucknow. 1270. 122. Iss Bazaar Mein, 150.
61. Supra Note 57. 84–85.
62. *Mahal Khana e Shahi,* Mirza Fida Ali Khanjar. Nami Press. Lucknow. (1934). 40–41.
63. *Asrar e Wajidi* (Handwritten), 306.
64. *Mahal Khana e Shahi.* Mirza Fida Ali Khanjar. Nami Press. Lucknow. (1934). 51.
65. *Id.* 48–49.

Daulah Muntakhibul Mulk Masahib e Khaas, Hazrat Gulam Ali Khan Bahadur *Tahawwur e Jung.*"[66]

Famous rebec players, flute players, guitar players (sarod), and drummers gathered in Lucknow at that time. This included Gayan Khan, Bahadur Khan, Saar Khan, Gulam Hussain Khan, Rahim Sen, Bakhshu, as well as the distinguished masters from the family of Tan Sen: Pyar Khan, Jafar Khan, Haider Khan, Basit Khan, and Md. Khan.[67] It is this generation of masters that is today regarded as the backbone of Indian music. Until Wajid Ali Shah was dethroned, none of them thought of moving out of his group. But the moment Wajid Ali Shah went to Calcutta, they dispersed. Chhotey Khan, Gulam Hussain, and a few others accompanied him to Calcutta.[68] Some turned towards Kanpur, and some, in search of a livelihood, moved to Gwalior, Bhopal, or the Deccan.[69] "Jaadi" and "Jhuman" prostitutes, who adorned the '*Shabistan e Aish*' of *Nawab Kalbe Ali Khan*,[70] became court dancers during Wajid Ali Shah's time.[71] If one researches other kingdoms, it may be revealed that those who were once the jewel of Qaiser Bagh later illuminated the gatherings in such kingdoms.

The Wajid Ali Shah of Metiaburj, who was in exile, was not the same young and energetic Wajid Ali Shah who had the competency and capability to spend lakhs and lakhs on patronising institutions. But his fervour and enthusiasm for music, which formed remarkable records in Lucknow, was unabated, and he worked on the renewal of such institutions in Calcutta. Previous bitter experiences showed him that, due to the untrustworthiness of '*dhaarris*'[72] and the guile of young prostitutes ('*nauchis*'),[73] the pupils

66. *Asrar e Wajidi* (Handwritten). 306.

67. *Murraqaey Khusravi* (Handwritten). 236. *Qadeem* Hunar, 61.

68. *Bani*, 309. Avadh Pension Papers, 20–21.

69. For details see *Aaj kal*, (Monthly, Delhi). Music Numbers (August 1956).

70. *Akhbarul Sanadid*, Moulvi Md. Najmul Ghani. 1900. 677.

71. *Durrul Taj*. Md. Muzzaffar Ali Khan Asir. Sultani Publication. Lucknow. 1270. 235.

72. Caste of Muslim musicians.

73. Young prostitutes.

developed the same temperament as the masters,[74] and ultimately the institution gained a bad reputation. With maturity and a calm mind, he was competent enough to spend his time on creative things.[75] He took the institution under his control, and enrolled girls from decent families. He separated the work of teaching from the use of instruments, as he thought that this awakens the urge for pleasure, but does not satisfy the learning of art. He explains the style of working that he adopted in the following words:

> "When the third year is completed then my fragile self becomes busy with the job of teaching with full dedication, now by Allah's grace awareness and understanding of the new tunes becomes matured, to make them dancing, singing, teaching the meaning and the gesticulation, picking the pieces from leg, dance as per quaver, are all instructed by me. No instrument player, singing dancer or performer had any interference or participation in it, all the time I am their only companion and hardly asked any musician to play the music. After two three months 'dharpad' on snap of fingers. 'chatrang', 'tarvat', 'tarana', 'dhammal rupak', 'teora chautala', 'dheema tatala', 'Kabir ki chabb', 'baram lachmi', 'sol faakhta', 'chabb tala', 'chachar', 'Ghazal', 'addhha', 'khayal', 'thumri'[76], are sung. They work on 'tambur'[77] without 'tamboora' also they can sing, they take out the pieces from 'jawahar lachchey ke chuon', I have instructed them some two three hundred such things and keep on instructing."[78]

How much vision Wajid Ali Shah had in matters of instruction and teaching, and how deeply he was involved, is evident from the following narrative: "Within a period of three years on a slow tune (*tataley*), some fifty-two types of melodies (*lay*) were taught to *Ali Khan Pukhawji* along with '*sahibat e jalsa.*'"[79]

---

74. *Bani.* MWASA. Sultani Publication. Calcutta. 1877. (Khuda Baksh, Avadh). 323.
75. *Mulk Akhtar.* Sultani Publication Calcutta. 1296. 57–58.
77. A kind of drum.
78. *Bani.* MWASA. Sultani Publication. Calcutta. 1877. (Khuda Baksh, Avadh). 321–22.
79. *Id.* 312.

Moreover: "So much labour was expended on the occupants of Radha Manzil and Sultan Khana, that the morning meal was taken in the evening and the evening meal was taken in the morning."[80]

As so much labour was done for such decent ladies, their reputation was saved, as they were prevented from resorting to prostitution. Strangely enough, they could not propagate their art by living only within the four walls of the house. It died with them, and the debate over the institution, which had been the subject of discussion in some specific circles, also ended.

In 1292 A.H., there were around 216 pupils in the institution, of which about 43 were under Wajid Ali Shah's supervision.[81]

The expenditure is stated to have been about 8,598 rupees monthly for the students, and 3,261 rupees monthly for the teachers.

Out of these teachers, 15 were singers, 2 were drummers, 23 were tabla players, 46 were sarangi players, 22 were cymbal players, and one was a piper. There is also a mention of some other artists.[82] These artists were the subordinates of the King, and some of them were his pupils. This included Pir Khan Mughni, [83] Ali Baksh Khan Mughni,[84] Taj Khan Mughni,[85] Nisar Ali Khan Pakhawji,[86] Inayat Hussain Khan Mughni,[87] Khwaja Buksh (a *Tabla* player),[88] and Ghulam Md. Khan[89] ('*qanoon nawaz*').[90] Four types of '*raginis*',[91] ('*jogia*', '*kantar*', '*juhi*' and '*Badshah pasand*'), were reportedly

80. *Id* 323. Alas so much of labour was done with such

81. *Id* 331.

82. *Id* 332.

83. *Id* 311.

84. *Id* 312.

85. *Id* 317.

86. *Id* 312.

87. *Id* 320.

88. *Id* 315.

89. *Id* 318.

90. A kind of dulcimer, musical instrument with strings manually struck by hammers.

91. Female counterpart of 'ragas'. These are designated male in the classical music of the Indian sub-continent. Modification of the musical mode called 'raga'. Oxford Urdu-English Lughat. 638.

invented by the King.[92] But in the narrations of Wajid Ali Shah himself, he mentions only '*ragini*' *and* '*Sultani*', which is in '*dharpad*'.[93]

DANCE

The invention of '*thumri*' is associated with Wajid Ali Shah.[94] But '*thumri*' is also mentioned in books found from before his time. [95] He himself mentions that during his separation from his beloved, he started compiling '*thumris*'.[96] Of these, one of his favourites was "*Sun o Guiyan Saiyyan Hai Rahu des.*"[97] The reason for this misunderstanding is that '*thumri*' is a style which is collectively found in both music and in dance.[98] Wajid Ali Shah heard this from one of his beloveds, and liked it.[99] In line with his innovative nature, the form he developed, as the name implies, is closer to dance.[100] This special style of the Lucknow school is dominated by his likings. In '*dharpad*' and '*khayal*,' there was no scope for innovation, but Wajid Ali Shah wanted to not only hear, but also visualise it. Under his patronage, not only '*thumri*', which is called the 'Ghazal' of classical music,[101] but also dance was performed, within the fine genre of Persian poetry, namely 'Ghazal.'[102] Ultimately, this mode was developed at such a pace that the tradition of '*kathak*', in the ancient religious ballet of Mathura and Vrindavan, followed this new version.

---

92. Qadeem Hunar, /Hunarmandaan e Avadh- Syed Israr Hussain Khan. Sarfraz Qaumi Press. Lucknow. 1936. 56.

93. *Najo*. MWASA. Sultani Publication. Calcutta. 1286. (Avadh). 44.

94. *Aaj Kal* (Monthly, Delhi) Musical Number Issue, August 1956, 23.

95. *Risala dar Mausiqi,* (Handwritten). Tohfatul Hind wa Naghmat Asafi, 64.

96. In the same period I compiled many *'thumris'*. Ishq Nama (Poetry, Handwritten) Dastan-15.

97. *Mahal Khana e Shahi.* Mirza Fida Ali Khanjar. Nami Press. Lucknow. (1934). 30.

98. *Marg* (English Tri monthly, Bombay) September Issue, 1949, 41.

99. *Supra Note* 97 at 30.

100. *Marg* (English Tri monthly, Bombay) September Issue, 1949, 10.

101. *Aaj Kal* (Monthly, Delhi) Musical Number Issue, August 1956, 23.

102. *Marg* (English Tri monthly, Bombay) September Issue, 1949, 11–12.

The word '*kathak*' comes from the word '*katha*' which means tale, story, or event, and '*kathak*' denotes the person who performs it.[103] '*Kathak*' became the medium of expression, used for displaying and presenting events related to idols, deities, and national heroes. The style which became popular over the centuries, as it expressed contradictory emotions, was the drama of Krishna and Radha. This religious ballet of the medieval period would have lost its significance had the patronage of two Kings not given it the status of a secular art. Akbar the great appreciated its artistic value and brought it out of anonymity, giving it the colour of Islamic style and temperament. After Akbar, it became an extravaganza, full of luxury and opulence,[104] and was later liberated by Wajid Ali Shah, further giving it a place of pride in within Indian dance.

Contemporary writers never mentioned that Wajid Ali Shah used to dance. The narration of some writers of the twentieth century, who say that Wajid Ali Shah never danced in any period of time,[105] is as ridiculous as the common belief that Wajid Ali Shah danced on the streets of Lucknow during the festival of Holi. Art is neither Hindu nor Muslim, and an artist is neither low nor deplorable. The days are gone when one used to say:

> "Singing, dancing is appalling (*laa'nat* hai). Hazrat Wajid Ali Shah was a King, but people are sarcastic about him too."[106]

Wajid Ali Shah danced, he mentions this himself.[107] He was an inventor of this art. This is evident from the photographs and narrations which are found in abundance in *Bani*. He was a master of this art, as is confirmed by

103. *Marg* (English Tri monthly, Bombay) September Issue, 1949, 11–12.

104. *Marg* (English Tri monthly, Bombay) September Issue, 1949, 2–3. (Institution of Mulkraj Anand)

105. *Jaan e Alam Ki Shayari.* Mukhzin. Delhi. Ishrat Lucknavi's Essay. October 1908. 67.

106. *Gunchaey Raag*, Md. Mardaan Ali KhanRana. Munshi Naval Kishore Publication. Lucknow. 1863. 138.

107. *Sheva-e-Faiz*, 181.

the fact that Badshah Pasand Lucknavi,[108] Qaim Khan, Qalander Bakhsh, Haider Ali, Md. Hussain Bishan, and Gulam Abbas were his pupils.[109] He had an aesthetic interest in his art, and what better way to prove this, than the fact that in *Bani*, the illustration of various 'quavers'[110] use male images, and there is no mention of the female figure. But when the same 'quavers' were repeated in other places, the male images were replaced by female ones, where the chest was replaced by breasts and nipples.[111]

In the art of dance, Thakur Prasad is mentioned as his master.[112] But for some unknown reason, Wajid Ali Shah did not mention the name of his master, nor did he mention '*kathak*'. Thakur Prasad was the son of Prakash Kathak.[113] Like Wajid Ali Shah, both of them brought out magazines on the art of 'dance', and Prakash Kathak mentions Wajid Ali Shah's 'quavers' in his book.[114] Kalka and Bindadin were the sons of Thakur Prasad. [115] Creating beauty, exquisiteness, elegance, and fine sex appeal in the Kathak of Lucknow School, the contribution of Thakur Prasad, Wajid Ali Shah, Prakash Kahak, Kalka and Bindadin is especially mentionable.[116] Commentators have collectively mentioned their contributions; they regard the work of Prakash Kathak as excellent poetry (*Sehr e Halal*),[117] and the grandeur of Wajid Ali Shah as the flag-bearer of this art.[118]

---

108. *Gunchaey Raag*, Md. Mardaan Ali KhanRana. Munshi Naval Kishore Publication. Lucknow. 1863. 140.

109. *Bani*, MWASA- Sultani Publication. Calcutta. 1877. (Khuda Baksh, Avadh). 309–20.

110. A tune, a musical mode. 901. Lughat.

111. See, Naghmatul Hind, Sarmayeay Ishrat Aur Ghunchaey Raag.

112. *Marg* (English Tri monthly, Bombay) September Issue, 1949, 10.

113. *Ibid.*

114. *Ibid*, and in *Naghmatul Hind* (Part one) on page 360 name of Prakash Kathak's book is mentioned as "Pothi Prakash."

115. *Marg* (English Tri monthly, Bombay) September Issue, 1949, 10.

116. *Ibid.* 11.

117. *Muraaqaey Khusravi* (Handwritten) 227. "Among the dancers the dance of Prakash Kathak is unimaginable."

118. *Gunchaey Raag*. Md. Mardaan Ali KhanRana. Munshi Naval Kishore Publication.

In '*Shastras*', three kinds of dances have been mentioned: '*narat*', '*nritya*', and '*naatia*.' In '*narat*', the movements of the body, due to their fineness, are very eye-catching, though there is no specific purpose behind them. But in '*nritya*', the movements are meaningful and the gestures indicate an event. In '*naatia*', dramatic effect and narration is created.[119] '*Kathak*' is the amalgamation of these three types, though it is dominated by '*nritya*'. This dance is performed solo. There was no shortage of dancers in his court, nor was there a lack of innovation. He established group dances with various versions, including those that depicted both vocal and visual charm. In '*Sautul Mubarak*', there are 32 named versions of this attractive setting[120] Note the narrative of a commentator regarding the charm of this dance:

> "There is always attraction in this concert, soul of *Md. Shah* is restless. There are unique quavers in the dance which please everyone, the song is of a new style... suddenly fate favoured the men and women, another concert was arranged. God's glory is great, what a creative mind, one name but the work is different, such a heart-winning song and the dance style is unique. The famous dance has a few styles, but this invented one is different which is remembered by him. Names are so charming that they please beyond expression. The name of one is '*Rahas Naiyya*', it is a humble specimen of the ingenuity of the pioneer. Some ten to twenty prostitutes formed the shape of a boat, some fairy-born foolish ones joined them, dancing... then another group came who had different names and different jobs, when this concert was over then there was the scene of garden and desert, *Seemtan* Queen entered the arena."[121]

From an artistic point of view, this dance is ordinary, and as is obvious from the above extract, these dances were used at the beginning of the

---

Lucknow. 1863. 127; "The King of Avadh was so proficient in dance movements that the Kathak was convinced beyond limits of his excellence."

119. *Marg* (English Tri monthly, Bombay) September Issue, 1957, 16.

120. *Sautul Mubarak.* Md. Wajid Ali Shah Akhtar. Matbaey Sultani. Lucknow. 1269. Raza Library, Rampur. 108–62.

121. *Fasanaey Ibrat*, Mirza Rajab Ali Beg Suroor Publication Najmul Uloom Karnama. Lucknow 1884. 82–89.

concert to attract the crowd. Wajid Ali Shah has named both the dance and the concert '*rahas*'. Whether the inclusion of dance spoiled the show, or it made it more entertaining is a different question. Though previously it was done at the initial stage, in present-day movies these can be included in the beginning, middle, or end of the film, and add amusement to the show.

RAHAS (DANCE DRAMA)

There is difference of opinion in matters of the pronunciation, meaning, gender, and nature of the word '*rahas*'. The introduction of this debate later in the chapter will explain the misunderstanding. Wajid Ali Shah coined the word '*rahas*' himself.[122] Some misunderstandings can be resolved with the comments of contemporary historians and of Wajid Ali Shah. Right now, in light of these comments, some forms of Wajid Ali Shahi '*rahas*' are presented. Wajid Ali Shah was likely aware of terms like 'drama', 'stage', and theatre'. From 1837 to 1847 (from the age of 15 to 25), he visited Kanpur many times, where English theatre companies had already been established, and were in operation.[123] But from Lucknow to Calcutta, there was nothing in those '*rahas*' which related to the English theatres. Just like a plant grows from a sapling, similarly Wajid Ali Shah's interests grew gradually, and were revealed in the form of the rahas '*Daryaey Taa'shuq*' and '*Afsanaey Ishq*'. For

122. There are multiple opinions regarding the dictum of the word 'rahas'. Thus in 'Firangey Asifia' the appreciation of 'rahas' is given with reference to Wajid Ali Shah and its pronunciation is also mentioned. The historians of Wajid Ali Shah period they write it as (Israr e Wajidi, 141) (Example: 'the concert and pleasure of Rahas Manzil all the time, which is adorned better than Qaiser Bagh' the latter one is changed form of 'ras'. In the beginning Wajid Ali Shah also wrote it as 'raas' (Persian Ishq Nama) but then he composed 'rahas' (He says ' I wished that today I should compose 'rahas"- - Ishq Nama (Poetry) and then he clarified its pronunciation in Sautul Mubarak.: "......the word 'rahas' is masculine gender. By way of proof the narration of Wajid Ali Shah needs attention- "First Rahas" (pehla) "Second Rahas" (Doosra). (Bani 70–72).

123. Roberts Emma; *Scenes and Characteristics of Hindustan.* London. 1837. Volume 1, 44–45.

further betterment of this art, he first focused his attention on music, until dance exposed more possibilities. The drama of Krishna and Radha came his way, and once he was satisfied with this, he started work on the practical play of the *Dastan Masnavis.* He fulfilled this with such perfection, the expenses of which were not within the competency of any trading company.[124] Wajid Ali Shah and his contemporaries used the term '*rahas*' for both the staging of the story of Krishna and Radha through dance, and the performance of the '*masnavis*'.

However, a name cannot change the nature of a thing, though it becomes a hurdle for understanding. Perhaps it can be called the humbleness of Wajid Ali Shah that he did not give different names to different things. Ballet, Cabaret, or drama do not have proper translations even today, and if someone from the Lucknow of Wajid Ali Shah watches this in a film, then he may call it a '*rahas*'. Today, there is hesitation to refer to Wajid Ali Shahi '*rahas*' as drama, but the educated English did not hesitate to call them comedy. Their rebellious attitude is evident from the statement that 'people go to watch the silly comedies out of the King's force and fear.'[125] Comedy is an offspring of drama, which for convenience is called '*Tarbia.*' (Comedy).

Like the '*rahas*' of Wajid Ali Shah, the Shahi Stage travelled swiftly from the seat (*masnad*) of the concert to the platform of the garden, and from the platform of the garden to the surrounding palaces. Here, the application of the word 'stage' is thought to be improper; this idea is not wrong. Stage presupposes a screen, and the dramas of Wajid Ali Shah were shown on a screen which, in today's parlance, could be equated to the three-dimensional panoramic screen. With the progress of film and technology, we could attain this expertise after a century, so that the plays written by Shakespeare in absence of technology were shown on lifeless screens. With lakhs of rupees and the help of thousands of men, these are filmed and exhibited in various

124. In 'Lucknow Ka Shahi Stage' these stages are covered in a perfect and correlated manner. Debating this is futile.

125. Colonel Solomon Resident. Volume 1, 178.

cities, and yet the moviegoers see only the shadows of reality. The reality is seen only by the film crew and the visiting crowds. Apart from the argument of drama and stage, Wajid Ali Shah can be compared to a writer, director, and producer – he wrote the dramas, created the stage, and made arrangements to film it. Visitors were invited to see the realisation of the play. Film is produced and then destroyed, and there would be no blame on the creativity of the maker, nor could the visitors delete the scenes they had witnessed. The people who wrote about Wajid Ali Shahi '*rahas*'[126] are those who figuratively saw the making of a film. The only difference is that during those days, it was not possible to make a film, or we would have also witnessed the scenes which they had seen. This would have made it possible to understand how, a century ago, people were made to believe Miraculous scenes which today would be disregarded as just a camera trick.[127] The sets of Wajid Ali Shah are called '*rahas ke makanat aur parikhana juda juda.*'[128] This terminology is not enough to evoke the imagination of a 'stage', but if these stages are not called '*pari khanas*', then there is no word in Urdu which could reflect this imagination. There is scepticism towards calling Wajid Ali Shah the first Urdu playwright. This may be possible, but he was never seen from this angle. Nobody bothered to credit Wajid Ali Shah as the first dramatist of Urdu literature but it is this image of him which is mostly remembered even today. He did not want to present his creations on artificial and inanimate screens, he wanted even the visitors to believe with full force that whatever occurred, occurred with music, impression, and colour.

---

126. Tarikh e Iqtidaria, Aftab e Avadh, Murraqaey Khusravi, Israr e Wajidi etc. depict the actual plight.

127. On page 130–138 of 'Lucknow Ka Shahi Stage' there is explanation of only one 'rahas' which is an extract from a book. If only this narration is believed then showing the real fight scene in open field, fort made up of paper, flowing of blood with the strike of sword, are all different from the stage which one can imagine during the period of Hindustan at that time. Even today's developed stage is unable to show these Miracles.

128. *Murraqaey Khusravi*, (Handwritten) Alif. 206.

Wajid Ali Shah was not interested in the nomadic drama style being staged, otherwise in Metiaburj, where he was not financially able to form them, he would, like the '*rahas*' of Krishna and Radha, have shown interest in producing '*rahas*' of the *masnavis*. The impressive drama of Krishna and Radha does not need a screen. It is a romantic and spiritual presentation, and romance equally impacts and satisfies the educated and the ignorant, the prince and the pauper, the urban and the rural, the artist and the actor. During his 31-year stay in Calcutta, he prepared only this rahas, and the first troupe which he trained was related to Radha. Among the occupants of Radha *Manzil* there were eighteen 'names' (ism), and its training started in 1278–1279 A.H. The second troupe was prepared in 1285 A.H. In this troupe, called '*Sarda Manzil walian*', there were fifteen 'names' (ism), and their job was also to present the drama of Krishna and Radha.[129] For an innovative and novel thinker like Wajid Ali Shah, his preference for the same drama was not without any solid reason – he had a strong liking for this drama. Among his *rahas*, this drama has a basic importance. It was also a basic part of *thumri* and *kathak*, and for presenting this there was no material which he would not provide, even during periods of paucity. One troupe after another, and then again a third '*Sultan Khane Walian*'[130] was prepared, as although the drama could not be changed, its actors could. From Lucknow to Calcutta, the mysterious silence of contemporary historians is because they had no interest in this drama. However, Wajid Ali Shah was an artist, and this drama has given a shine and glow to Indian fine arts that can be understood only by an artist.

This period of Metiaburj also dispels some other misunderstandings. On the whole, it is wrong to consider Wajid Ali Shah's singing and dancing to be a '*rahas*'. '*Rahas*' was easier than singing and dancing. This can be verified by the following narration of Wajid Ali Shah himself:

129. *Bani*, MWASA- Sultani Publication. Calcutta. 1877. (Khuda Baksh, Avadh). 310–312.
130. *Id.*

> "*Rahas* is not related to them (Chhote jalse walion), their only job is to sing and dance...[131] I did not ask them (Khas jalse walion)[132] to do *rahas*. They will make this work very easy."[133]

Both the '*jalsas*' (groups) were trained in dancing and singing for five and three years respectively. They were not given the job of '*rahas*'. The standard of singing and dancing was so high, that the end result would have been so fine, were such super excellent artists to participate. Of the various forms of '*rahas*' or '*kaam*', two group dances and one in the form of a Krishna and Radha drama are found in *Bani* itself.[134] The third form is the rahas of *Dastan Masnavi*, in which all the preparations were improved, and which was presented in Lucknow in the most befitting manner.

Wajid Ali Shah often participated in the '*rahas*' of Lucknow himself. This was in line with his age and the fondness for the idea that someone who is instructing must also demonstrate the actions himself. A commentator has narrated as below regarding *Afsanaey Ishq* and dual acting:

> "...In short the detailed narration of this story and all the minor items were prepared on his (Hazrat's) instruction, the artificial was also shown as real, forests and mountains, magical hunter lands, 'djinns and fairies, a pair of parrots, 'Fakir bayaban, saara paristan' (pauper in the deserted land, the whole of fairyland); everything was presented, everything was displayed clearly. Hazrat first played the Moon (*Badruldaja*), then a boy, and sought the blessings of the beggar. Then, after the ritual of '*chhati chilla*,' took the form of the moon quite true to the story."[135]

The abode of players, their dress, the decor, and the magic tricks performed in the '*rahas*' were not at all surprising, at that time such innovations were unseen. Today, even those from rural areas, who have seen the people working in a studio, know that the deceitfulness and trickery is but the creation of wisdom and money.

---

131. *Id.* 318.

133. *Id.* 324.

134. *Id.* 69–124.

135. *Murraqaey Khusravi,* (Handwritten), 205 'bay'.

ARCHITECTURE

Before making '*Fakir bayaban, saara paristan*', Wajid Ali Shah had presented evidence of his 'clarity, purity, and innovation'[136] while he was still a prince, when he had Huzoor Bagh constructed.[137] The three buildings of Huzoor Bagh, namely Shenshah Manzil, Khas Makan, and Falak Seer, were each constructed for different weather. As there are no reminiscences of these constructions, it is futile to guess as to how Shenshah Manzil was kept warm during the winter, and how Khas Makan was kept cool and airy during the summer. Such craftsmanship was nothing strange or special in the residences of the rich of that time. The example of wonderful work and innovation was a part of the Huzoor Bagh named Goshaey Aafiyat, which is described by the following words:

> "Of all the lofty trees the tree of mulberry is so big that I have not seen such a big tree before. Below it, a marble platform is built so that during the monsoons, it can be used for sitting. Every Friday, underneath it there is gathering of fairies and singers. Sweet singing birds and peacock sit on the tree, here hunting is forbidden and hence the name 'Goshaey Afiyat.'"

From the suffocating enclosures to the special picture galleries of *rahas* are compared to the different forms of arena. The platform built in *the Goshaey Afiat* as per the demand and suitability of the occasion was the first stage of Wajid Ali Shah's innovative and amazing temperament. His fondness for presenting the '*rahas*' with the background of nature continued to progress with the passing of time, and he established various picture galleries as per the requirement and suitability of the work:

---

136. *Mehel Khnaey Shahi*. Mirza Fida Ali Khanjar. Nami Press. Lucknow. 1934. 94.

137. On page 149 of Tawarikh e Nadirul Asar the name of this garden is given as 'Hazrat Bagh' but Wajid Ali Shah himself writes it as 'Huzoor Bagh.' The couplet of Dastan 88 of *Ishq Nama Manzoom* (Handwritten) draws attention:
Strange garden from where autumn is away Which gained the title of 'Huzoor.'

> "Concerts of (*Rahas Afsanaey Ishq*) were held in Qaiser Bagh and *Shah Manzil*, houses were built, '*Parikhanas*' were constructed separately, from the ingenious and inventive mind strange creations resulted and then the palaces and mansions were named accordingly."[138]

The use of words like *ajeeb* (strange) to describe the conditions and '*Inder asan*'[139] and '*Rahas Manzil*'[140] indicate that these buildings were constructed for purposes other than living. Contemporary commentators were not aware of these purposes and hence started describing these creations as '*ajeeb*' or '*ajab*'. During the revolutionary period of 1857–1858, these buildings were destroyed. The later commentator Sharar was so impressed by these '*ajab*' and '*ajeeb*' creations that he drew a parallel between Wajid Ali Shah and Shahjahan.[141] Wajid Ali Shah's interest in architecture, like the interest of any other art director, arose from the need to construct novel and unique state-of the-art stages, in which there was more emphasis on the decor and elegance than on stability and permanence. Wajid Ali Shah was successful in his mission, which is evident from the comments given in appreciation of these structures. However, these structures lacked permanence. This is verified by the fact that the tomb of Saa'dat Ali Khan and his which was adjacent to these buildings,[142] stands tall even today, while there is no sign Begum, of his picture galleries.

Another reason for his architectural interest was he wished to leave behind formidable footprints and memoirs, and hoped that this exercise of beautification and adornment would uplift and benefit the common man.[143] The symbol of this stimulating passion of Wajid Ali Shah is 'Qaiser

138. *Murraqaey Khusravi* (Handwritten), 206 'alif'.
139. *Israr e Wajidi* (Handwritten), 307.
140. *Murraqaey Khusravi* (Handwritten), 208 'alif'.
141. *Guzishta Lucknow*. Maulvi Abdul Haleem Sharar. Naseem Book Depot. Lucknow. 82–3.
142. *Tarikh* Anjuman *e Hind Avadh*. Khan Bahadur Sheikh Siddiq Ahmed. Naval Kishore Press Lucknow. 1937. Volume 1, 57.
143. *Wazir Nama,* Wazirul Sultan Md. Amir Ali Khan Amir. Nizami Publication. Kanpur. 1293. 158.

Bagh', which he wanted to develop as the eighth wonder of the world.[144] However, if only the size and cost of a building used as a measuring scale, then speciality of this building is not more than the fact that none of the forefathers of Wajid Ali Shah had built such an edifice.[145] According to a study, some 30 crores (300 million rupees) were spent in the construction and decoration of this building, and according to another study, some 80 lakhs were spent. I It was built in a period of three years, from 1848–1850.[146] Royal associates and tourists were of the same opinion regarding the grandeur of this building.[147] But this appreciation was like the appreciation of a cover more than the book, or of a frame more than its portrait. The formidable structure of Qaiser Bagh is an indicator of the harm caused to Indian architecture by the imitation of western work in the 19th century.[148] This manifested, not only in its name, but also in the items of luxury and decor in which '*pardaey Suqarlati, wa makhmaley kashani wa attlas angrezi wa gorant Fransisi*'[149] were perhaps waiting for the horrifying moments of 1858, when the magnificence and grandeur of Qaiser Bagh would wallow in the blood-drenched[150] fields.

After the devastation of Lucknow, Wajid Ali Shah moved to Calcutta, where again he felt a need[151] to rebuild the structures, to house his people. The Wajid Ali Shah of Calcutta was not the same Wajid Ali Shah who had the courage and competency to spend lavishly on his people. The cost of

144. Qidwai, 58–9.

145. Hilton E.H. The *Tourist's Guide to Lucknow*, 1913, 69.

146. *Tawarikh e Nadirul Asar*. Publication Munshi Naval Kishore. Lucknow 1863. 148.

147. *See* Sairul Mohtashim, 399–409, and Nasr Murassa of Amir Minai (Handwritten).

148. Journal of U.P. Historical Society – Volume 9. Issue Dated July 1936.

149. *Sairul Mohtashum*. Nawab Ghous Md. Khan. Publication Sarkar Gulshaabad.Jawrah. 406.

150. *History of Asafuddaulah*. W. Hoey. Oudh Government Press. 1885. 143.

151. *There are rented houses and me*
These are English Gods and me. Sheva-e-Faiz, Md. Wajid Ali Shah Akhtar, Sultani Publication. Calcutta. Tagore. Library Badshah Bagh , Lucknow./ Khuda Baksh Oriental Library Patna. 312.

18 palaces was met by selling the precious treasure which had been saved by the English officers from being plundered and sent to Calcutta.[152] The value of this treasure is estimated to be 25 lakh[153] (2.5 million) rupees, but it was not valuable enough to construct buildings in Calcutta with enough grandeur and stateliness to be on par with the buildings of Qaiser Bagh in Lucknow. Instead of the shine and lustre of gold and silver, the design of these buildings left the foreigners in awe and reverence.[154] They regarded the King as a master of drawing and decor.[155] Another commentator, who had not been very happy with the King, was convinced of his fineness and subtlety and says:

> "I took many excursions. I saw such buildings that I was convinced of paradise, that of course, there is the existence of paradise...there is no dearth of anything before Allah...everything was positioned at the right place, in short the best appreciation is that there cannot be further appreciation.... but alas!..." [156]

During those days, there was no such building in Calcutta which depicted the '*Lucknavi*' taste. During some special occasions, commoners were allowed to visit the royal buildings,[157] while in Lucknow the King did not like it if even limited people visited Qaiser Bagh, and said that "my house is not a place of amusement."[158] The residence of Wajid Ali Shah, which is known as Sultan

---

152. Raja Burdwan Kothi is taken on rent for five hundred. *Sheva-e-Faiz*, 8.
153. *Aftab e Avadh* (Handwritten), 155–56.
154. *Wazir Nama,* Wazirul Sultan Md. Amir Ali Khan Amir. Nizami Publication. Kanpur. 1293. 159.
155. *Jane Alam*; Maulvi Abdul Haleem Sharar. *Idara Farogh e Urdu,* Lahore. 1951. 39.
156. *Avadh Panch*. (Lucknow). Issue Dated May 6th. 1886, 2.
157. Gupta N.N. *Reflections & Reminiscences*, Bombay. 1947. 34. / Guzishta Lucknow 87–88. Adeeb Urdu (Lucknow) Issue Dated January 1, 1922, 22.
158. *Tarikh e Avadh,* Maulvi Md. Najmul Ghani Khan. Munshi Naval Kishore Publication. Lucknow. 1919. Volume 5, 182.

Khana, was the building of the Maharaja of Burdwan.[159] When it was made to be a permanent residence, it was extended, and the difference between the original building and the renovated building is quite noticeable.[160] The tall, gothic columns, higher platforms, spacious balconies, venetian blinds, which were the common feature of the western-style buildings of Calcutta and Lucknow, the lower seating (*nichli kursi*), Wajid Ali Shahi architecture, beautifully carved niches, open corridors and verandas remind one of the style of architecture which was a characteristic feature of Avadh. A glimpse of this is seen in the royal buildings of Hussainabad, Badshah Bagh, and Qaiser Bagh.

During his exile, he attempted to refresh his memories of foregone days, and so not was the interior design repeated, but even names like Asad Manzil, Rahas Manzil, Jahan Numa, Sibtainabad, with which his fond memories of the past were associated, we reused. Wajid Ali Shah especially missed '*Rahas Manzil*' – this was the picture gallery where he organised the royal concerts of '*rahas*'.[161] In the *Ishq Nama*, only the name of the building is mentioned.[162]

The following sketch by *Qalaq* is worth noticing:

The concerts of Rahas Manzil, the continuous amusement
The decor of which surpasses paradise
Every envy of the moon is lost in its beauty

---

159. *Sheva-e-Faiz,* 8: The King says: 'Raja Burdwan ki Kothi- paanch sow ki kiraey par li hai'.

160. For the location and situation of the royal buildings see the map "Plan of the City of Calcutta" by Surveyor General of India, Third Edition. This map shows the location and area of the mansions and gardens. The camera photographs of some of the buildings were taken after the death of the King towards the end of the nineteenth century. Due to passage of time these photographs have lost their imprints and it is difficult to get their copy. In the opinion of the author there are no other pictures of 'Shah Manzil', 'Rahas Manzil', and 'Murassa Manzil' etc. anywhere else.

161. *Tarikh e* Ghazala. Md. Wajid Ali Shah Akhtar. Compiler Wasi Bilgrami Mufid e Aam Publication, Agra. 1914. (Azad). 23.

162. See the translation of Ishq Nama, Mehel Khanaey Shahi, 108. Or Pari Khana, 151. Perhaps *'Raas Manzil'* is its original name. In discussions wherever there is mention of the word *'rahas manzilein'* there it denotes not any particular building but the picture galleries.

The day is spent in dancing and singing
This luxurious drink made me senseless
I forgot all the worries of the world
The groups of flowers came
They were busy in strolling in the garden
The glow, the scent and the youth
Like the newlywed bride
They came like the peacock of heaven
They showed new style in every step
Each of them were playful
Some exhibited the beauty stance
Some had the cloth (aanchal) fallen on shoulders
Some turned their legging under the waist
Faces and dresses were luminous
They were cleverer (faster) than the lightning[163]

There is no such powerful narration regarding the '*rahas*' of Calcutta but somehow some lines as below were composed regarding it which are to some extent satisfactory. Like the '*Rahas Manzil*' of Lucknow, the '*Rahas Manzil*' of Calcutta too was reserved for the royal *rahas.* The poet explains:

'*Rahas Manzil*' is the playground of fairies
The room strangely becomes Solomonic
Darakhshan! the year of construction is revealed
The house becomes concert of royal (Khaqani)[164]
111 353 762 53 15 1294 h (Islamic year reiterated in poetry).

This building was part of the 'Shah Manzil'. This name denotes the continuance of all the buildings which were spread between the Hooghly

163. Safar Aashob, Khwaja Arshad Ali Khan Qalq. Karnama Publication Lucknow. 1289. band (stanza) 93, 94, 95.
164. *Bani*, 383.

river and the Shah Raah.[165] Rahas Manzil was situated at the bank of the river, and was adjacent to the Sultan Khana.[166] When the doors between Sultan Khana and Rahas Manzil were closed, the two buildings were separated, but otherwise, it was considered part of Sultan Khana.[167] Rahas Manzil was a single floored building. Its inner portion was very spacious, but it was surrounded by high walls, which made it unsuitable for residential purposes.[168] During the Second World War, the foundation of this building was laid. Its beauty fascinated the New Theatre group, and old traditions of stage construction were renewed. Some shots for the silent film '*Turki* Hoor' were filmed here, but this had been when the building was about to collapse, and the film company had modified it for their own use.[169]

GARDENING

Three gardens of Lucknow, namely *Huzoor Bagh*, *Sikandar Bagh*, and Qaiser Bagh, are closely associated with Wajid Ali Shah. The foundations of *Huzoor Bagh* were laid while he was a prince, and the formation of 'Wajid Ali Shahi Rahas' and 'Jogiana fairs' took place in the romantic ambience of this garden. Other than the traditional creepers, flowers, and plants, further details are found in the '*Ishq Nama*' as follows:

> "In the newly formed parterre of this garden, there were thousands of strange plants, each different from the others."[170]

165. The statement on oath given by Nawab Sarwar Jigar Begum D/o Mirza Jahan Quder) in Calcutta High Court Appeal No. 221/1900. Printed record of case *Faridun Jah v. Nawab* Sarwar *Jigar Begum* 121.

166. Ibid. Statement on oath of Mirza Md. Muqeem S/o of Asman Jah at page 99.

167. Ibid. Statement on oath of Eidi Begum Mamtua Wajid Ali Shah)

168. Ibid. Statement on oath of Nobin Chand Boral, Attorney, Calcutta High Court.

169. A man named Wazir worked in the shooting of this film. At present there is shed of Jute Mill and the area is known as 'Aahni Phatak.'

170. *Mahal Khana e Shahi*. Mirza Fide Ali Khanjar. Nami Press. Lucknow. 1934. 17.

These rare plants were not meant only for amusement, but growing and taking care of them depicted a special kind of taste. Both favourable and unfavourable commentators have agreed that Wajid Ali Shah had a special taste for natural history and had an immense liking for the study of nature. This passion for nature gave way to the formation of gardens, which paved the way for his collection of different species of birds, water animals, and other living creatures. From one viewpoint, this passion may be evaluated as a pastime, and as a show of pomp as is commonly found among the rich. But those who studied the nature of Wajid Ali Shah closely would realise that, for a fickle minded person like him, even the prettiest and the most charming birds and flowers could not have a lasting impact. Allah had gifted him with a mind which sought the best and had created an unending variety of plants and animals to satisfy his need for these newer and better things, providing rich resources to satisfy him.

Huzoor Bagh was devastated in the First World War, but *Sikander Bagh and* Qaiser Bagh exist even today, though in dilapidated condition. *Sikander Bagh* was also built while he was a prince, and about five lakhs were spent in its construction.[171] The English established a horticulture institution there, after the land has been reddened with the blood of 2,000 freedom fighters.[172] At Qaiser Bagh, which achieved fame due to the music and songs of the rebec, the call of peacocks and the rattling of swords were symbols of a charming amalgamation of old traditions and innovative trends.

Lala Devidayal regards the art of nurturing a garden to be exemplary, and says:

> "A square piece of land measuring 5 acres is divided into four parts, and each part is again divided into four parts where each parterre measures forty metres (gaz), some named as *Asad Chaman, Mahi Chaman*... in fact there were different types of parterres... from a distance they appear as if a lion or bear is sitting or the peacock is standing with its wings spread or the falcon

171. *Id.* 108.

172. *Eighteen Fifty Seven*. Sen S.N., Delhi. 1959. 228.

is preening itself. Among these there was a rivulet flowing, which quenches the thirst of the parterres. It also has taps with different shapes, like water is flowing from the beak of the peacock, or the puppets are gargling water from their mouth, often from the bellies of deers or from the udders of cows water is oozing out, the borders of the rivulet are of marble, leaving aside the middle of the tank at the sides there is a grape creeper measuring a span, and on both the sides there are creepers and leaves made up of black stone and *Sang e eesa* (Isaac Stone) and Saang e Musa (Musa Stone). There are many fountains in the middle of the tank in which there are chandeliers with candle stands so that if these are lit up in the night then the beauty of the fountains is enhanced. In fact, no parterre is without charm, there are platforms of marble on which a stag is erected whose eyes are of garnet, face is of emerald, and legs are of black stone. On some platform a deer is standing who has protruding horns, somewhere the cow is feeding the calf, at one place there is a peacock which appears natural. Thus the decoration is made tastefully, at the corners of the parterres there were walls of cages (*qafas*) made up of gold and silver wires, in which many small creatures were released and whenever the fragrance of flowers touched the enclosures, the creatures chirped with joy. In the same garden was the enclosure '*Barah dari*' which has now been brought to *Banarasi Bagh*, the King purchased it from a Kabul merchant for one lakh rupees."[173]

Witnessing the present state of Qaiser Bagh, references to its glorious past seem to be an exaggeration, but in the above extract there is no description which seems unbelievable or unreal. In the Banarasi Bagh of Lucknow, the Mughal Garden of Delhi, Kamla Nehru Park of Bombay, and Vrindaban Garden of Mysore, people in search of innovation and beauty have gathered unique items which were once found in Qaiser Bagh, and had been the centre of attraction.

After the devastation of Lucknow, the gardens were rebuilt in Calcutta. The names Bagh Dil Kusha and Badshah Bagh depict the same connection was seen in the case of the buildings. It was not possible for the deposed king, who was so fond of having meaningful and significant names, to rebuild

173. *Phal.* Lala Devidayal. Imperial Book Depot, Delhi. 1908. 34–39.

the gardens which had been built when he had royal rights over the land. The gardens were built with the same expertise which was the characteristic feature of the buildings in Calcutta. This is explained in the following words:

> "Garden and parterres were built with such figurative and geometrical shapes that the onlooker was aghast at the expediency of the King."[174]

The road which connects Calcutta to Metiaburj is, even today, known as Garden Reach Road. Today, there may not be a single tree remaining that had seen the grandeur of Wajid Ali Shah's reign.

The commercial progress of Calcutta has bulldozed many precious memories of the past, and the day is not far away when the last milestone of the golden period – the name of the road[175] – will also be replaced[176]

NATURAL HISTORY

Kings have often shown interest in bull fights (and other animals) for their entertainment, but there are few Kings who took care of living creatures and were affectionate and kind towards them. Wajid Ali Shah is considered one such King. During his period, animal fights were organised to entertain some English guests.[177] Instead of bloodshed, Wajid Ali Shah's parks had shows where a pigeon and a cat were kept in one cage and the pigeon, instead of escaping, would ride on the cat's back,[178] or where men weighing four or five maunds (approximately 300–400kgs) sat on the back of a tortoise, and

174. *Guzishta Lucknow*. Maulvi Abdul Haleem Sharar. Naseem Book Depot. Lucknow. 82.

175. In the beginning of this century there was some diversion in the road due to the construction of King George Docks hence the word 'circular' was prefixed. After Independence there was a change of about one and a half or two miles but however the old name is retained.

176. The translator feels proud to mention here that the name has been changed for a better cause as it is now named as Wajid Ali Shah ROAD.

177. *Recollections of My Life*. Sir Joseph Fayrer. London. 1900. 92.

178. *Reflections and Reminiscences*. Gupta N.N. Bombay. 1947. 35.

people enjoyed its slow crawling.[179]

The king was personally interested in birds, and in his aviary there were hardly any species of birds which were not found.[180] The King gave special attention to the safety of the pigeons, and the citing of date-wise collection of the eggs of pigeons was though done in a negative manner.[181] The art of breeding new species of pigeons would not have been possible without proper care and maintenance of both the birds and those caring for them.[182] Pigeon-flying was not only a pasttime, but was a subject of study and art.[183]

The King not only studied the pigeons, he spent good amount of his wealth and time in studying the behavioural characteristics of the various rare animals of his "Live Natural History Museum."[184] The results of such studies may have been documented in the *Mahi Nama*, which is unavailable now, or in *Bani* in the form of titles, which are not comprehensible. For instance, In the second section of the third chapter, 43 different animals and trees are given hundreds of 'titles' (*Khitab*). (*Hawalaey Qalam Istigasa raqam.*)[185] Out of these varieties 46 titles are given to a special kind of nightingale (bulbul). Thus, from this list of 46 titles the titles "Shab Sada, Tasbih Go, Zevar e Gul or Mukhzanul Aswat" appear to be the proper noun of some of the nightingales. But this could also be the noun for all the nightingales of the same species. 32 titles for pigeons and 29 titles for fish are found though these are the differentiating names for different species of pigeons and fish. This is because naming the white Shirazi pigeon as '*baad e Saba*' and the yellow Shirazi pigeon as '*Hina Rekhta*' or calling the '*rohu* fish' as '*Shah Pasand*' and '*kuwa* fish' as '*Zaag Samandri*' is evident from clarification here – I'm

179. *Jaan e Alam.* Maulvi Abdul Haleem Sharar. Idara Farogh e Urdu. Lahore. 1951. 47.

180. *Supra Note* 177. 94.

181. *Mutinies in Oudh*. Gubbins M.R. London. 1859. 55.

182. *Supra Note* 177. 92.

183. The book titled *Muljaey Kabutar* (Handwritten) was written because of Wajid Ali Shah by *Muqarrab Sultani Monisudd Daulah.*

184. *Supra Note* 174. 85.

185. Bani, Md. Wajid Al Shah AkhtarSultani Publication. Calcutta. 1877. 345–60.

not sure how the first part the documents of the writer himself.[186] Perhaps the species '*Khanazaad*' among the eight kinds of Persian Bulbul, and the species '*Musahiba*' among the eight kinds of *mynahs* are those which are most commonly found, but for the remaining seven titles, it is clear as to what species they refer to. The same is true about the 333 kinds of trees which are described in the book. Wajid Ali Shah named thousands of animals,[187] but their connotation and suitability is revealed only when the specific item is presented before one's eyes.[188] In Urdu, '*Lal*', '*neel kanth*', '*chhoi mui*', and '*Suraj Mukhi*' have the same connotations and it cannot be said that the person who chose such names did it without any observation or relevance. In biology, botany, and geology (*jamadat*), the scientific names also have certain connotations, but only students of these disciplines can explain them. His study and observations can be explained by only those who were aware of his nature and temperament. People with direct knowledge consider this attempt to be an indicator of a special kind of psychological state, and say that 'because he could not distribute and award wealth and land, hence he satisfied his ego by awarding titles' and 'this passion of Wajid Ali Shah reached its peak of obsession.'[189] The names given by Wajid Ali Shah are not the names of individual animals, but the names of different species. At the beginning, he proudly writes that only his thoughts are behind these names, and of no one else's.[190] There were many people who also desired titles, they even suggested titles to him, but they did not receive this blessing.[191] The habit of associating every good or bad point with the companions (*Masahib*) of Wajid Ali Shah continued when translating his passion and likings, but

186. *Id.* 353 & 354–55.

187. *Supra Note* 179. 39.

188. *Adeeb Urdu* (Magazine, Lucknow). Issue January, 1922, 24.

189. Urdu Adab ke Aath Saal. 160–61. Thesis of Dr. Abullaiss Siddiqi.

190. *Supra Note* 185. 345.

191. Qaiser Shah e Avadh; Munshi Md. Qudratullah Qudrat. Publication Aftab Qudrat. Agra. 1864. 14.

this was done by way of sarcasm:

> "Achieving knowledge, even though in unfavourable conditions, is always appreciated. '*Aala Hazrat*' is surrounded by such people who are always careful to see that there comes no hindrance in his observations of nature. I don't know whether such persons were the members of the Scientific Society which was recently founded by a learned cleric (Maulvi) of Ghazipur whose patron and president is Duke of Argyll, and whose books are related to him,[192] but the enthusiasm with which they remain associated with the natural history of the King within the precincts of Garden Reach demand that they deserve an honour which this Society is authorised to give. Presenting a pair of peacocks in the service of '*Aala Hazrat*,' costing thirty thousand rupees, or presenting before him a cage costing fifty thousand rupees, was not a difficult task for them. Getting it approved by the King, even an ordinary animal or bird having a distinguishing and extraordinary mark on it was enough to get it approved and accepted by the King, and in this thousands of rupees from the state treasury were filched."[193]

The writer opines that even in exile, the King's passion for collecting living beings from different countries continued unabated, and for this he spent every last penny from his treasury, and even sold the silver leg of his bed to meet such expenses.[194] His companions were responsible only for taking hundred rupees instead of one. Interests created by external factors and favourable situations do not last for long. The proof of a Wajid Ali Shah's bent for nature was revealed when he declared a graveyard as a sanctuary. The nature of his interest kept on changing with changing times and conditions. Often, the animals were shown in stone, often they were depicted in the curves of the boundaries, and often a tasteful artist drew them on canvas.

---

192. Perhaps by this it is meant the Society founded by Sir Syed Ahmed Khan which was later again formed by late Sir Syed Ahmed in Aligarh. See *Hayat e Javed*, (Khwaja Altaf Hussain Hali. Punjab Academy. Lahore. 1957). 175–79.

193. Knighton W; *The Private Life of an Eastern King. London.* 1921. 206–7. With reference to the Newspaper *Harkaru* (Calcutta, May 1864).

194. *Id.* 208–10.

Throughout his life, there is not a single event where hunting an animal is reported. Friends of speechless animals do not need any motivation, appreciation or advice from others. It is for his own interest and attachment that he paid the demanded price, and in this way, he inspired others and even benefitted them.

Wajid Ali Shah was interested in all living creatures, but his deeper interest in birds was perhaps because he also loved music, and the singing birds are gifted with naturally sweet voices.[195] The main requirement was that these cute musicians of nature be kept in suitable surroundings, and even though they were caged, they should not feel suffocated. Wajid Ali Shah did not fail in his hospitality towards these guests:

> "The King the building Noor *Manzil* constructured some two hundred metres (gaz) away from the banks of Bhagirathi River with special arrangement. There was a pond adjacent to it surrounded by concrete staircases. Across the pond near Noor *Manzil* there was an enclosure where a lion lived around the pond and the building across the compound an iron gate was erected. On the other side of the compound there was a delicate and beautiful bungalow, in the compound there was many types of animals and birds which were brought from all over the world, where the deer and chinkaras could be seen galloping, cranes, geese, herons and peacock roamed around or they were seen even standing on one leg near the pond for hours, within the enclosures wild animals were kept. [196] There were also cheetahs and lynx who instead of being caged were chained and who kept lying on the bed.[197] In *Sultan Khana* big houses were built covered with iron nets and were called '*kunj.*' Many types of singing birds were let loose in it, who flew with full freedom, laid their eggs, and the eggs were hatched because

195. *Sautul Mubarak.* Md. Wajid Ali Shah Akhtar. Sultani Publication. Lucknow.1269. Raza Library Rampur. 15–16, 52–53.

196. *Jaan e Alam.* Maulvi Abdul Haleem Sharar. Idara Farogh e Urdu. Lahore. 46.

197. *Id.*50. Also in *Sairul Mohtasham* (Nawab Ghous Md. Khan. Publication Sarkar Gulshanabad Jawrah). 429. "...And some lions were so domesticated that they were tied with chain and lay out of the cage, while some were without chain but they were never so ferocious so as to attack or harm anyone."

> there were also nests for this purpose.[198] There were so many singing birds and other birds that when in the morning there was a gathering of some two to three hundred bird breeders there for cleaning the cage and feeding the birds with dough then it gave the look of a fair.[199] This creature (bulbul) is like a musical instrument (mouth organ) which keeps on playing and such tunes come out of it which cannot be expected from an instrument the moment the door of its cage is opened and it was kept in the middle of the parterre then at that moment its jubilant chirping and singing with overjoy was a scene worth seeing and hearing."[200]

Wajid Ali Shah's attachment to snakes and fish cannot match his deep interest in koels, black songbirds (shaama) cuckoos, nightingales or peacocks. But for eyes which were always in quest of splendour and beauty, even such creations of Allah were not worthless. Feeding the fish with his own hand was routine,[201] and in *Mulk Akhtar* a short code of conduct for the fish farmer was included with this purpose. Tanks with special arrangements for colourful fish were constructed.[202] Big fish were kept in streams or ponds and a ring-shaped ornament was put in the septum of the fish to identify them. The construction of artificial mountains and waterfalls was also regarded as Wajid Ali Shah's invention for rearing snakes, and it is said that foreign tourists watched with surprise as the snakes chased frogs, and would to save this as pictures or in writing.[203]

During his times, it was not a common practice to collect such a variety of animals, nor were they reared in such a way. In present zoos, care is taken regarding the number of animals and their exhibition, and in this regard Wajid Ali Shah's customs were a link between the past and the present.

---

198. *Supra Note* 196. 51.

199. *Id.* 51–52.

200. *Id* 52.

201. *Id* 53.

202.

203. *Id* 40–41.

PAINTING

We know about the painting calibre of Wajid Ali Shah when *Ishq Nama* was scripted. Surely his talent came to the forefront when he was attracted to other fine arts and natural history. This is because painting for its raw material and stimulants looks to the same attention which is required to instil liveliness and splendour in other fine arts, especially dance. People with taste, search tunes for music, impact for poetry, contour for dances and sketches for painting. Wajid Ali Shah's attachment to the first three fine arts had been established from the period of his princeship, and painting came later. By looking at the casual sketches of the *Ishq Nama*, it is difficult to form an opinion regarding the King's expertise in painting. However, on the basis of some narrations, it can be said that Wajid Ali Shah was well versed in this art, and while his associates appreciated him for his excellence in other area, they also considered him a master of the art of painting.[204] Appreciation of his mastery is shown in a letter, using the following words:

> "...suddenly a picturesque page appeared...love to the King of land and sea who drew the image of land and water on paper. Though you have written that it is *Sunderban*...you made sketch of *Raapti* but it appeared to me as *Kausar* and *Tasneem*, the tree appears to be the envy of Juniper and *saro* (tree)...the black sketch stings the heart and the image of the fish is the decorum of the sky and earth...and the image of the boat is made so swiftly...many times it came to my mind that I call the writer *Raqam Khan* and *Behzad Raqam Khan* and show him and ask him to swear...Dear you are the master in every art, a great inventor and highly commendable...but from whom should I learn painting so that I send the reply in sketches."[205]

The above statement is very valuable because other than this, there are no pictures or narrations which explain that he was excellent in all sorts of

---

204. Ruqa't e Begum, 27. *See* the narration of Shaida Begum in the letter where she praises the King in these words 'He was moon of the Cannan in beauty, Mani in sketches, unparalleled in giving alms, *Khaqani* in versification.'

205. *Tarikh e Firaq* (Handwritten), 255–58.

painting. Maybe the book titled *Murraqaey Farrukh*[206] is a collection of the pictures made by the King. Another available collection of pictures of the lithography in *Bani*[207] is apparently associated with the King, because *Bani* was compiled by him. But there is nothing in those pictures which indicates that they were the work of an expert artist.

Some ornamental and painted manuscripts from '*Kutub Khanaey Wajidi*' can be presented to show the expertise and mastery of painters and artists of the royal court. Their delicate and fine sketches are the life savings of brilliant artists. The paintings of *Riyazul Quloob*, and of Volume 1 & 2 of *Sabatul Quloob* in particular can be regarded as a milestone in their art, because in these three manuscripts the painter has presented such an exemplary fine art, which is not found in any other manuscript. For instance, while turning the pages of *Sabatul Quloob*, which is the last complete example of this fine art, one will find pictures of delicate creepers on every page, as well as images of snakes, cobras, birds, butterflies, and colourful fish in the margins. From this incongruous painting, which was not done systematically, one may infer that it was made to adorn the manuscript, in which regard is given to the King's taste. Apparently, this is true, and other people have interpreted it in the same way. But if one concentrates on the symbolism of this painting, then one may discover that the painter has presented a high standard for covering errors with images which the King, some thirty years ago, had presented by making a crown on the word *Sallamahu.*[208]

These sketches are not lifeless, but they are artistic metaphors; birds are flying, cobras are swallowing, fish are swimming, and creepers are growing. Where the writer had written some words incorrectly, the painter made partridges, quails, peacocks, storks, butterflies, petals, or leaves.[209] The combined connotation of these things is 'flying', and the places at which they

206. *Bani*; Md. Wajid Ali Shah Akhtar. Publication Sultani Calcutta. 1877. 242.

207. *Id* 42–57 & 64–68.

208.

209. *Sabatul Quloob* (Handwritten), Volume 2, 22, 27, 35, 60, 69, 82, 126.

are drawn denote 'flying'. If the writer incorrectly writes the word '*raheem*', then adding partridge cannot delete the '*meem*', and so at such places, the painter has drawn a stork or heron. Similarly, if a collection of words or an entire line is wrong, then it cannot be corrected by drawing birds. Instead, at such places, the painter has drawn snakes, cobras, mountainous ranges or beehives.[210] The last two words are probably used by the painter for covering, as these two denote a source of wealth or blessings. Where the writer forgets to write something, entire lines (*misras*) are written in the margin, within the body of a fish.[211] The added verses of the King, or the margins of the dictionary, are surrounded by images of creepers.[212] This art had no name during the painter's time because it was connected with commercial art, and commercial art has gained significance only in the present century. Its initial footprints were found in the previous century, and in Urdu literature it was presented by Wajid Ali Shah himself.

CALLIGRAPHY

Wajid Ali Shah can be held responsible for the abundance of errors in the gold-plated manuscript of *Sabatul Quloob*, and for their attractive corrections, because its special writing and corrections were made to satisfy his taste, and its compilers were his own disciples and trainees. We have seen before that Wajid Ali Shah was tired of the monotonous Persian script, and if he came across something novel while writing, then he wanted to transform it into an art. We have also seen that Copy 2 of Voume 1 of *Sabatul Quloob* was being written in Persian script, but for some unknown reason it was switched to the '*zanjeera*' style. Towards the end of his life, even ordinary work was done in the same script. The change in script was due to a change in Wajid Ali Shah's temperament, and the script, which, in the absence of any popular script, was named '*zanjeera*,' was his own invention. In the art of good handwriting,

210. *Sabatul Quloob* (Handwritten), Volume 2, 22,27, 35, 60, 69, 82, 126.

211. *Sabatul Quloob* (Handwritten), Volume 2, 26, 27, 36, 43, 47, 48, 49, 67, 75 etc.

212. *Sabatul Quloob* (Handwritten), Volume 2, 5,19, 21, 25, 62, 74 etc.

the training for correction of words was done by connecting many words together. Wajid Ali Shah must have come across such an exercise. During that period, the tendency was to practice on a board or slate; it was a trend to write many words together[213], and in his writing such style is obvious.[214]

Writing the '*zanjeera*' script in continuation, while taking care of the normal standard (kursi), was not an easy task, and the writer of *Sabatul Quloob* did not strictly take care of this. He wrote thousands of lines in this way, and if reading them was such a difficult task, then surely writing them would have been much time-consuming. This can be imagined by one who has written like this. It is not surprising then, that he made innumerable mistakes, and Wajid Ali Shah himself appointed a painter to correct them.[215]

Sabatul Quloob (Handwritten), Volume 2,

Illustration of Zanjeera: Writing From Sabatul Quloob Given Here – Page 504 of Urdu Book.

The innovation or invention of the '*zanjeera*' script, whether good or bad, can be attributed to Wajid Ali Shah. Wajid Ali Shah desired that his books be handwritten, and whatever is written must be written with strict formality.[216] This passion supported the art of calligraphy at a time when there was a day to day increase in the number of presses; the demand for the writers was

213. There is ample proof of this in the headlines of *Ishq Nama* (Manuscript). See page 397 of *Ishq Nama.*

214. In the manuscripts of *Bani* and Qamar Mazmun and in the copies of *Khwab Mubarak* even those words are written together which should have been written separately like *'Maine'* instead of *'Mai ne.'*

215. In the 158 pages of *Sabatul Quloob* (Handwritten), Volume 2, there are only four places (pp. 113, 139, 156 & 157) where the correction is done in the old style of scratching.

216. *Tarikh e* Ghazala, Md. Wajid Ali Shah Akhtar (Compiler Wasi Bilgrami) Publication *Mufeed e Aam.* Agra. 1914. 41. *Tarikh-e-Mumtaz,* Md. Wajid Ali Shah Akhtar. (Compiler. Dr. Md. Baqar) Urdu Markaz. Lahore. 1952. 56–59.

increasing, while the number of calligraphers was falling. During the royal period, Mirza Khush Raqam was employed to correct the manuscripts for 50 rupees per month. Munshi Naval Kishore wanted to employ him at the same rate to write his title page, but Mirza Khush Raqam did not agree. He said that "I don't want to earn my livelihood by filling up pages like ordinary writers, there must be difference between writers and calligraphers"[217] (*khush navees*). Like Mirza Khush Raqam, there were many graceful calligraphers who were associated with the state for writing letters, (qata'as) and plaques, correcting manuscripts, compiling handwritten documents, or for correcting printed books. In 1292 A.H., Wajid Ali Shah declared Raeesud Daulah Ali Hasan Bahadur as the officer of other calligraphers, and also mentioned the names of Jaleesud Daulah, Rafatud Daulah, Zarghamud Daulah, Tarsiud Daulah and four other titled calligraphers holding official posts.[218] This narrative indicates that, other than these five calligraphers, there were other calligraphers who sustained the tradition with honour. This perhaps cannot be revived.

Matbaey Sultani

In the cultural life of a country and community, two institutions have special importance: the press and the libraries. The development of knowledge and literature depends on these institutions. Wajid Ali Shah got these two institutions when he was coronated, and they were snatched away from him when he was dethroned. Had he not known the importance of the contribution of these institutions, he would not have thought of establishing them in Calcutta. The institutions of Calcutta were an indicator of his love for knowledge, and the survival of at least one institution – the library – would not have been difficult, had they not been victim of the same oppressive actions after his death due to which Qaiser Bagh and *Shah Manzil* were devastated and fell into oblivion.

217. *Begmat Shahan e Avadh*. Khwaja Abdul Rauf Ishrat. Hamidia Press. Delhi. 126.
218. *Bani*. Md. Wajid Ali Shah Akhtar. Publication Sultani Calcutta. 1877. 341–42.

Matbaey Sultani was established by Ghaziuddin Haider; I its old name is *Sultanul Mutabay*. In the beginning it was maintained by the English,[219] and its first publications were in iron printing.[220] Letho printing started in 1830,[221] and up to the period of Amjad Ali Shah both type of books were printed. After the coronation of Wajid Ali Shah, we find only the Letho printed books, and no English name is found among its supervisors. In terms of printing quality, the books printed by Matbaey Sultani were distinct, and apart from the compilations of Wajid Ali Shah, they published books by Fatehud Daulah Barq and Maqbool ud Daulah Qubool, the Diwans of Tadbirud Daulah, and the elegies of Qubool and Asir, Sarwar e Sultani of Rajab Ali Suroor, Jawahar Ubqaria of Mufti Mir Abbas Sahab, Taqwiyatul Soora of Sheikh Imamuddin Talib, Tehqiqulawzan of Abdul Ahad Rabit, Mukhzanul Fawaied of Maulvi Md. Faiq, Taqweem Sultani of Mir Zair, and innumerable others. On some books of Matbaey Sultani is written "*Matbaey Kasirul Munafaal masmasi ba Sultanul Mutabay*", but there is no source which indicates that these books were published for sale. In the books published by Matbaey Sultani, it is clearly written that they were meant to be distributed freely. During the fall of the empire, when this was the style, it would not be wrong to say that Matbaey Sultani was the Publication Bureau of the State, and that the books published by it were for the general public.

In Lucknow, this publication house was situated on the banks of the River Gomti in Kothi Kalanand, which until a few years ago, Lucknow people called Kalan Kothi Ghat. In 1272 A.H. (1856), when English rulers bulldozed Kothi Kalan,[222] Wajid Ali Shah thought of another '*Matba*' for the publication of his books. *Huzn e* Akhtari, published by Matbaey Sultani in Mochi Khola, Calcutta, was its first book which, in Shabaan 1276 A.H., broke the news of its

219. *The Raj Herald* (Monthly, Lucknow), Issue November 1934, 80.

220. Sprenger A.; *Catalogue of the Arabic, Persian and Hindustany Manuscripts of the Libraries of the King of Oudh.*Calcutta. 1854. 5.

221. *Id.* Page 'wow.'

222. *Jawab e Blue Book*. Md. Wajid Ali Shah Akhtar. (Printed at MohAllah Nawaz Ganj under Beni Prasad). 89.

reestablishment. *Riyazul Quloob*, published in *Shawwal* 1302 A.H., is the last book, and was found among other books published by the company. *Badshah Nama*, *Ishraq* Akhtari, *Mufidul Zahan* and some other books by learned people were published by this '*Matba*'. The King took a personal interest in the printing of books like *Mulk Akhtar*, *Mubhaisaey Bainul Nafs wa Aql* and *Riyazul Quloob*.[223] Perhaps it was the result of this personal interest that, while a Corrigendum was attached to the books published in Lucknow, the inner pages were not changed. In the books printed in Calcutta from the time of *Huzn e* Akhtari, such mistakes were corrected at the particular place, and often the printed parts were also replaced.[224] In printed books, the trend of leaving some blank space for some hand written matter was found both in Lucknow and in Calcutta. Instead of title page, in the style of handwritten books, the writing up to the publication of Qamar Mazmun was found.

In the books published in Calcutta after Qamar Mazmun, the title pages are printed and in some, the date of publication is also given. In *Najo* and *Sahifaey Sultania*, a list was published. In *Najo*, the presence of the word '*lumber*' makes it clear that English printing influenced Matbaey Sultani. [225]

Kutub Khanaey Sultani[226]

The reality is that Wajid Ali Shah was not very fond of printed books. Books were printed for others. For his own library, the printed books of others could find a place after being wrapped in golden covers, alongside fine-cut handwritten books. This valuable and expensive passion of Wajid Ali Shah was nurtured in his ancestral library, which had been maintained by his

223.

224. *See, Kulliyat e Akhtar*; (Md. Wajid Ali Shah Akhtar. Publication Sultani. Calcutta. 1278), Nazm Namvar (Md. Wajid Ali Shah Akhtar. Publication Sultani. Calcutta. 1287) and details of *Najo* (Md. Wajid Ali Shah Akhtar. Publication Sultani. Calcutta. 1286).

225. From the waste of Matbaey Sultani the few pages which were luckily discovered it can be imagined that the work of correction was done with so much of concentration and dedication.

226. On page 25 of *Qaiserul Tawrikh*, Volume 2, the library is addressed with this name.

227.

ancestors since the times of Shuja ud Daulah. For this library, the books of Hafiz Rehmat Khan and other learned families, which had been scattered across various royal houses of Lucknow, were acquired.[228] In the action by British Parliament, the King's lawyer declared the number of books to be two lakh.[229] During his twenty-two-month stay, Springer studied some ten thousand copies; their importance is evident from the incomplete list which has been published. It is not known if Wajid Ali Shah made additions to this treasure, but the care with which he treated it has been lauded by Springer.[230] Wajid Ali Shah's attachment to handwritten books is evident from the gifts containing precious manuscripts, presented to him by Governor-General Lord Hardinge in 1847.[231]

After the fall of the empire, there are stories regarding the selling of elephants, horses, arms, and other precious items, but there is no such mention of selling books. In 1856, the library was destroyed:

> "It was done by Major Karnegi Sahab (City Magistrate, Lucknow). One day the entire library, which was settled in the alMirahs of *Farah Baksh*, was thrown out. The new Commissioner Chief said, 'now you settle them', he was told that the entire staff had been dismissed, and those who were getting a one thousand rupee monthly salary had been removed. He said Karnegi Sahab should not have been so cruel." [232]

The ups and downs in the actions taken by officers were revealed when they acted passionately. New officers in Lucknow were not unaware of the importance of books. In November 1847, Lord Hardinge's Foreign Secretary

---

228. Sprenger a.; *Catalogue of Arabic, Persian and HindustanyManuscripts of the Libraries of the King of Oudh.* Calcutta. 1854. , Pages 'jeem', 'daal'.
229. *Safeer e Avadh*; Maulvi Masihuddin Khan. Al Nazir Press. Lucknow. 1929. 187.
230. *Supra Note* 228. Page 'ha.'
231. *Aien Akhtar*; Ghulam Haider Saghir Lucknavi. Avadh Press Lucknow. Second. Ed. 1912. 35.
232. *Qaiserul Twarikh*. Syed Kamaluddin Haider Alias Meer Zair.Publication Munshi Naval Kishore Lucknow. Third. Ed. 1907. Volume 2, 182.

and the compiler of *Tarikh e Hindustan*, Sir H. M. Elliot, had visited the library. They 'selected some historical books' and left.[233] In December 1847, Springer was appointed to make a detailed survey of the library. His report was published in 1854.[234] From February to August 1856, many things were sold, and there was constant pressure on the King's servants to hand over the library.[235] Wajid Ali Shah's servants did not hand over the library,[236] and reported to the King that the library was taken out of their custody under the pretext of security.[237] The wise and the loyal did not react positively, as they knew that after gaining possession of the library, Karnegi Sahab would act arbitrarily. It was feared that the truth would be buried and would not be easy to differentiate. After the downfall of the empire, 'the plundering wicked'[238] must have scattered these pages, which, though not relevant in those days, would still have fetched a high price if found.

In 1275 A.H., when his biographer asked him for some books, he had nothing.[239] With Sheva-e-Faiz and the collection of letters, he re-established the library. Like in Lucknow, the library of Calcutta was distributed over various royal buildings. The name of the building was written on the binding or the pages of the book when they were built, and all the books were collected in Imambarah Sibtainabad Mubarak.[240] Though there is nothing significant

233. *Qaiserul Tawarikh*, 5. "Whenever this Sahab visited a city many types of historical books were presented to him out of flattery or they were purchased and the stolen books of the royal library which were considered rare at that time were gifted to him." For further details see; *Tarikh e Avadh*. (Volume 5, Reprint, Maulvi Md. Najmul Ghani Khan. Publication Munshi Naval Kishore. Lucknow. 1919). 156.

234. *Supra Note* 228. Page, 'alif', 'jeem'.

235. *Safeer e Avadh*. Maulvi Masihuddin Khan. Al Nazir Press. Lucknow. 1929. 187–95.

236. See the protesting Circular at Rizvi, Volume 1, Plate 9.

237. *Safeer e Avadh*. Maulvi Masihuddin Khan. Al Nazir Press. Lucknow. 1929. 198.

238. Bani, 243. *Safeer e Avadh*; Maulvi Masihuddin Khan. Al Nazir Press. Lucknow. 1929. 187.

239. *Boostan e Avadh*; Kunwar Durga Prasad Sandelvi. Publication Ahmedi. Lucknow. 1892. 184–85.

240. Its written *'Pari Manzil'* in Nazm Namvar (property of Palace Library Murshidabad) and in the same book '*Hashmat Manzil is* written which is the property of Khuda Baksh Library Patna. Similarly in other copies too names of royal buildings of Metiaburj is written.

in these books, their existence is important as they are mentioned in the list of *Bani.* These books, instead of being at Imambarah Sibtainabad Mubarak, are found in various libraries of Hindustan and foreign countries.

An image of a crown and a fish was changed on the books of Calcutta, and in the place of year 1263 A.H., 1280 A.H. is written. This is likely the year of the library in Calcutta was re-established. On the books found in Calcutta, there was one more big seal which, because of a hazy print, is inferred to be the seal of the King. This seal was the seal of King's brother-in-law, Zulfiquarud Daulah Bahadur,[241] who was the maternal grandson of Mir Inshallah Khan Insha. He accompanied the King from Lucknow to Calcutta, and to Fort William, until the end.[242] Perhaps it was to acknowledge of loyalty, that his name is included in the seal. On November 22, 1893, this long-term loyal supporter of Wajid Ali Shah died in Calcutta, at the age of 85.[243] A few years before his death, he had lost his vision[244] and the culture which he had witnessed growing would also soon vanish.

Lucknow Model

Machi Gola or fish market – which, due to widespread use of the word was transformed into '*mochi khola*' – was a colony of fishermen. In 1856, when Wajid Ali Shah reached Calcutta, he found himself in this strange place. He recollects it in the following words:

The moment I reached Calcutta
The leaves of the garden (as if) started devouring (me)
Day and night rain, echo of lightning
Gathering of thunder, force of wind

---

241. On page 23 of *Mahal Khanaey Shahi* Wajid Ali Shah has regarded Nishat Maha'sl alias, Nanhi Begum, as the granddaughter of Insha. Zulfiqur ud Daulah was her brother. (See *Huzn e* Akhtari; Md. Wajid Ali Shah Akhtar. Publication Sultani, Calcutta. 1276). 43–44.

242. *Oudh Pension Papers*. Printed by B.S. Press Calcutta. 1913. 19.

243. Report of Anjuman Muhammadi, (Star Press, Calcutta) 1907–1912. 3.

244. *Supra Note* 243. 19.

People of this place are dishonest
They have no identity other than non belief (kufr)
Women are shameless and men are feminist
They remain unaffected even if a head rolls down
Meat, clarified butter, oil, water all are bad
One does not care for another
This is a piece of hell
On which Calcutta is built
What to say nothing is useful
Stones are cheap and flour is expensive
They carry net on their shoulder
They know the techniques to trap
I suffered so much at this place
My end seems near[245]

Wajid Ali Shah spent almost 35 years of his life in formal opulence, and so regarding this 'hellish piece of land' as his homeland was a matter of great courage for him. Either out of need, attachment, or for the sake of supporting oppressed and browbeaten men, women, and children:

> "The King not only assigned work to one based on his ability, but those who were ignorant and unskilled were also not devoid of his kindness. For instance, hundreds of women and children were kept for picking up dry leaves from the garden.... he provided for their food. The skilled people, who were the victims of western prosperity and were dying of hunger, were given a helping hand." [246]

Wajid Ali Shah started transforming the forest into a parterre and "gradually, near Calcutta, a second Lucknow bloomed, the population of which was more than 40,000."[247]

245. Sheva-e-Faiz. Md. Wajid Ali Shah Akhtar. Publication Sultani. Calcutta. 1277. 8–9.
246. *Adeeb Urdu* (Magazine, Lucknow). Issue January 1922, 21 & 25.
247. *Guzishta Lucknow*; Maulvi Abdul Haleem Sharar. Naseem Book Depot. Lucknow. 86.

All the houses gained a royal look.
This was a forest which is turned into a garden
There is prosperity and the royal court is alive
There is a garden where there was no flower.[248]

Sharar, who is the prime historian of this new Lucknow, gives an eyewitness account:

> "Those days Lucknow was not Lucknow, Metiaburj was turned into Lucknow, the same hustle and bustle, the same language, the same poetry, the same jokes, the same learned and pious people, the same rich group. The common people, the shop keepers and bankers; all were of Lucknow and there was not a single thing of Lucknow which was not found in its original form here." [249]

Sharar does not mention the bankers (mahajan) of this newly inhabited Lucknow. This matter is dealt with in detail in *Afsanaey Lucknow* by Sharaf, and in the Avadh Pension Papers, which also state that Billo 'mehetrani', Karim Baksh Barber, and the messenger Radhey all came from Lucknow.[250]

In the intellectual and cultural life of Calcutta, this small habitat of people from Lucknow was a pleasant addition. It was the first opportunity for the people of Calcutta to see and benefit from the representation of Lucknow culture in '*mushairas*', congregations, assemblies, and meetings. It was easy for Nassakh to criticize *Anis* and Dabir from home, but when he was caught in the gathering of '*Anisis*' and 'Dabir*s*', it became difficult for him to save his pen name (*takkhallus*).[251] *Nazm* has related more glimpses of contemporary rivalries, and has referred to the Daag's observation that

248. Afsanaey Lucknow (Handwritten). Syed Jalaluddin Haider Alias Agha Hajju Sharif. 1290). 278.

249. *Supra Note* 247. 86–87.

250. *Oudh Pension Papers*, 23–31.

251. Raees Ahmed Jafri. Wajid Ali Shah *Aur unka Ahad,* Kitab Manzil. Lucknow. 1958. 78–79. Referred to by Nazm Tabatbai.

the amusement which he experienced in the '*muhshairas*' of Metiaburj was not experienced in Lucknow.[252]

The gifts from the people of Lucknow to Bengal in religion and music is evident from the popularity of '*thumri*' and the observations of 'Azad*ari*', which was typical of Lucknow, and which is still prevalent in Calcutta. The tradition of '*khutba*' after '*namaz*', and the propagation and professing of the Shia beliefs of Lucknow, has its roots in Lucknow traditions.[253] Until the discussion of congregations by Afsos, there is no mention of the processions of '*zarih*' and '*zuljinah*' in Calcutta. But until the end of Wajid Ali Shah's reign, these processions increased in such a number that there were discussions to restrict them.[254]

The intellectuals of Metiaburj were mindful of the work of composition and compilation, but were devoid of the economic and mental peace which is so important for such work. By way of tradition and inclination, whatever was written by them was destroyed.

Among the memoires of that period, *Nadiratul Saaqib* by Maharaj Jai Gopal Saaqib, *Afsaanaey Lucknow* by Agha Haju Sharaf, and *Alhasanul Matin* by Abbas Mirza are regarded as unforgettable.

The first of these books is in Persian, and the compiler, after explaining the toughest rhetoric and ingenious language, presented 68 examples of different styles of elegant poetry about Wajid Ali Shah. It relates the devastation of Lucknow and the habitation of Calcutta in poetic form in Urdu. The last of these books is in Arabic, and is an account of the history of Avadh, from Burhan ul Mulk to Wajid Ali Shah, spread over hundreds of pages. Based on these books,[255] the gifts and donations by Sultania, and the compositions of

---

252. Adeeb (Magazine Allahabad. Issue 14.10.1910, 159.

253. *Tarikh e Abbas*; Maulvi Mirza Md. Hadi Sahab Aziz Lucknavi. Nizami Press. Lucknow. 105, 113.

254. *Statesman* (Newspaper, Calcutta). Issue 31.10.1886. (Editorial)

255. I had an opportunity to visit the library of Sir Meerza Jahan Quder. In the damp climate of Bengal about five or six alMirahs were left unopened for about sixty years and the handwritten and printed books were not strong enough to carry or to be read. Some of

Wajid Ali Shah, it is evident that the people of Metiaburj struggled to keep the eastern fine arts alive. Neighbouring them were the headquarters of the English. Due to the presence of the English, a school by the name 'King of Oudh's School' was founded, and place under the supervision of English teachers whose patron was the King himself. But neither the King nor his fellow men were happy with the English style of teaching.[256] For the education of their children, on 26 February 1887 the Hindus and Muslims of Metiaburj jointly established a madrasa by the name of 'Madrasaey Qaiserya'. There, apart from English, were arrangements for the teaching of Arabic, Persian, and Bengali.[257] Wajid Ali Shah was happy with this madrasa and wanted to reserve a large amount for its maintenance.[258] But the same year, the fate of the madrasa was sealed by the King's death on 21 September.

It was impossible to imagine Wajid Ali Shah's Metiaburj without Wajid Ali Shah. Hunar had foretold this in his *Qata'a*:

Hazrat Sultan Alam went to reside underground
These were the last changes of time in Metiaburj
People with the funeral procession beat their chest and head
Every mourner in Metiaburj *had his head rolled on the ground*
It was the love of heaven which brought them here
Otherwise who had his belongings in Metiaburj
The one who maintained the people of Lucknow
Who is such a lion hearted in Metiaburj
See in four days it will be a bounded place

---

the books of this library which were about Metiaburj were gifted to Maulana Syed Ahmed Ali Sahab "Sher e Punjab" but now they are lost.

256. *Statesman* (Newspaper, Calcutta) Issue May 6, 1886 (Editorial).

257. The printed advertisement of the Madrasa. This place at that time was known as 'burji' and is now known as Naya Imambarah. Copy of the advertisement is presented on page 517 of this book.

258. *Hamari Zaban.* (Weekly, Aligarh) Issue, 1.2.1966. Page 2. Referred to by Madrasa Report 1890.

Now what the intellectuals will do in Metiaburj
There will be no pile of flowers even for name sake
But there will be piles of dry leaves in Metiaburj
The line showing the year gives the news
Dust will fly all over Metiburj

2 247 204 56 621 451 205 100 1887 (The cumulation of these figures show the date 1887 as per the Urdu poetic genre "Tarikh")

Only Hunar knew how swiftly the government would disperse the kingdom that the King built during the 31 years of his stay in Metiaburj. Within three days of his demise, an Act comprising three sections was passed.[259] It stated that the Governor-General in Council would have the

259. The King of Oudh's Estate Act 1887. Act No. XIX of 1887. Passed by the Governor General of India in Council. (Received the assent of the Governor General on the 23rd September, 1887).

An Act to provide for the Administration of the Estate of His late Majesty the King of Oudh. WHEREAS His late Majesty Wajid Ali Shah, Kind of Oudh, was during his lifetime exempt from the jurisdiction of the Civil Courts, and it is expedient to make provision for the administration of his estate otherwise than under the authority of those Courts; It is hereby enacted as follows:

Administration of the estate of the late king of Oudh by the Governor General in Council. (1) The Governor General in Council shall have exclusive authority to act in the administration of the property of whatever nature left by His late Majesty the King of Oudh in regard to the settlement and satisfaction of claims against the estate of His Late Majesty, and may make distribution of the remaining property or the proceeds thereof in such manner as he deems fit among the family and dependents of His late Majesty. (2) No act of the Governor General in Council in connection with the administration to or distribution of the property left by His late Majesty shall be liable to be questioned in any Court.

Indemnity to Agent to the Governor General – The Agent to the Governor General with His late Majesty, and all persons acting under his order, are hereby indemnified and discharged from liability in respect of all acts done by him or them since the twentieth day or September, 1887, in connection with the preservation and administration of the estate of His late Majesty, and no suit or other proceeding shall be instituted in any Court against him or them, or against the Secretary of State for India in Council, in respect of those acts or any of them.

Effect of Act – This Act shall take effect notwithstanding any testamentary or other disposition

sole right to the King's property, and he would have the right to expend it. Whether there was a will or an heir was to be decided by the officers, and there would be no right to challenge such orders in a court of law. [260] As per the orders of the Governor-General Lord Dufferin, in place of the King's one lakh per month pension, 36,381 rupees were allocated for an allowance for survivors and 'old associates' of the King.[261] The share of each associate was not more than 2,766 rupees.[262] His personal belongings were also auctioned.

> "Had the buildings and houses been distributed in the same condition then perhaps they could last, but the English regarded it fair to sell off all the buildings and belongings and distribute the money among the inheritors. Consequently, all the buildings were dug up, gardens and parterres were desolated, in sum no reminiscence of the times of Wajid Ali Shah were saved."[263]

---

which may have been made by His late Majesty, and notwithstanding any proceedings which may have been or may be instituted before any Civil Court for administering his estate or collecting the debts due to it, and any person who under any probate howsoever, has received or realised any portion of the estate of His late Majesty shall be bound to account therefor to such officer as the Governor General in Council may appoint in this behalf.
INSERTED HERE BY THE TRANSLATOR

260. The entire Act has been published in *Statesman* (Newspaper, Calcutta) dated 24.9.1887. It is also given in *Oudh Pension Papers*.

261. As per *Avadh Pension Papers* on page 18 by 'old associates' means about those hundred and twenty three (123) persons who were with Wajid Ali Shah since the royal period. This is the exact amount which was to be distributed among 'old associates' mentioned on page 18, for his children mentioned on page 46 and for 'Begmats' mentioned on page 132.

262. *Oudh Pension Papers*, 18.

263. *Jaane Alam,* page 192. *'Chatkal'*, (Jute Mill), *'Battikal'* (Electric Supply Company) *'Rangkal'* (Shipbuilding Yard) and most of the land at the bank of the river where today there are a number of factories are in fact on the land on which once there were royal buildings.

264. One verse (bundd) of Safi Lucknavi's poem *"Zamimaey Lakht e Jigar"* is as follows:
Previously the Metiaburj was worth seeing Which was the permanent abode of Hazrat Wajid Ali Shah It was so adorned when he was alive Later after him the condition was totally different
Among the buildings only Sultan Khana is left He left for heaven and only the story remains Other than Sultan Khana two other buildings Qasrul Baiza and Sibtainabad Mubarak were

The above narration is of those days when some ruins of the Sultan Khana were left.[264] Now even those are destroyed. Only the traces of the mosque of *Sultan Khana* can be found. These were saved for the sanctity of the mosque and remind one that:

Allah's name will last

---

two royal buildings which survive even today. But both of these are Imambarah*s* and there were many changes in the construction. From page four of the printed *'Wakf Nama'* it appears that at the time of bidding there was no respect for the first Imambarah of Metiaburj. It was purchased by King's daughter in law Nawab Nadir Begum which was transformed into wakf in 1917 and it was given the name of *'Qasrul Buka'* but the people of Metiaburj even today recall it with its royal name.

FIVE

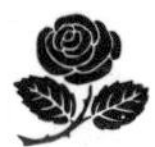

Prose Writing of Wajid Ali Shah

KING AS A PROSE WRITER

Other than the letters and the book *Bani*, there is no composition of Wajid Ali Shah in Urdu prose which is worth mentioning. Those were the formative years of Urdu prose. For learned conversations there was no such talent, strength, or generality in the language which could easily express all shades of thoughts. Wajid Ali Shah was mentally and geographically far away from what was being done by Sir Syed and his contemporary writers in North India.

For music, and for educational and religious discussions, he preferred Persian; for his collection of songs (*geet*), he wrote the Preface in Persian. Thus, in his own way he was struggling for the proliferation of Arabic and Persian. At the same time, he was not unmindful of the progress of Urdu – in his opinion, those matters which were to be taken to the common man should be taken in their language only. The Urdu translations of '*Majmuaey Wajidia*' and *Jawab e Blue* book had already been published. The Urdu translations of *Mafateh Khaqani* or *Namaz and Adiya*, which were compiled based on his wishes, still exist today, and explain his attachment to the Urdu language. In *Mulk Akhtar*, both Urdu and Persian prose are found, and care is taken that whatever is written in Persian is meant for those who are well-versed in Persian, and the letters which are written in Urdu are meant for those ignorant people who could at least read those.

A successful writer, who takes care of the taste and talent of their readers, reaches them. What he writes, why he writes, and how he writes depends on his own psyche – whatever he writes does not come from above. The daily annoyances of life, and his own observations and experiences, provide the material to write, and it is these annoyances, experiences, and observations which are consistently, effectively, and fruitfully expressed by his pen. By the time he wrote *Bani*, Wajid Ali Shah had realized that the Persian era was over. It was futile to write language with rhyming words. Now, whatever was to be expressed would be done in a plausible and simple manner. In the Preface of *Bani* he provides an explanation for this:

> The books Najo and Dulhan are distributed, ...but in those books there is no extravaganza....no recreation in the garden...no impact of love and romance, ..Some people regard it as saltless (tasteless) food, as a babble of the writer...but its study will give amusement ...it is in new shade...the tale is like a fresh flower....the decision lies with the intelligent, I am in the company of Bengalis. Rhymed language was not given so much importance but no meaning was overlooked and it was accepted that meaning should not suffer and the construction of language should not be doubted by anyone.[1]

The storyteller through his tales and the essayist through his essays profess their knowledge. The first Urdu dramatist was fond of using a dramatic style of writing. Wajid Ali Shah was gifted with strong imagination and his stories were the written form of his thoughts and knowledge. Wajid Ali Shah mentions the writers in the beginning of these stories, and talks about

---

1. *Bani,* - MWASA- Sultani Publication. Calcutta, 1877. (Khuda Baksh, Avadh). 2–3.

the people connected to this profession.[2] At the same time, he has written many stories which are more concerned with audibility than with visuals,[3] which reflect the writer's personality. For example, in his analogical mushaira (*tamseeli*),[4] at most the writer had seen street jesters reciting the verses of the Jurrat[5], who was blind. Then, with the help of his Begums and other associates, he organized another mushaira[6] and wrote the introduction. He did this work so expertly that the original story became a laughing stock in the new mushaira.[7] Had the entire story been played by the street jesters, there would not have been any mention of the King or his Begums, and so there would not have been as much elegance. At most, the original stories of the jesters reflect their inspiration (*muharrekat*). Wajid Ali Shah's thoughts regarding 'politics',[8] religion',[9] 'sociology',[10] and 'sexology'[11] are expressed in *Bani* along with the names of such stories. The success of the 'tamseeli mushaira' at that time was not very big but it inspired intellectuals.

The common way to narrate a story was to write whatever was observed. But in this narration, Wajid Ali Shah introduced a conversational style which is a salient feature of drama. This is clear from the following extract:

> Some persons became famous poets, who is this? This is Mian Nasikh,[12] who is this? This is Aatish[13], who is this third one ? This is Mir Insha. Who

---

2. *Ibid*, 124–26.
3. *Ibid*, 222–23.
4. A gathering of artists where they dress up like some famous character and give a dramatic presentation. (Translator)
5. *Bani,* 232–33.
6. *Ibid*, 230–48.
7. *Urdu Adab Ke Aath Saal,* 164–65. (Thesis of Dr. Abullais Siddiqui)
8. *Bani,* 190, 267.
9. *Ibid*, 75, 198, 268–70.
10. *Ibid*, 2–3. 187–89, 52–54.
11. *Ibid*, 273–85.
12. *Ibid*, 230–32.
13. *Ibid*, 323, 319.

> is this? This is Mian Sagir, ...this is Hazeen, this is Hilal, this is Nizami, this is Jaami..this is Zafar Shah Delhi , this is Akhtar Shah Avadh, this is Sauda, this is Rund, this is Zaibun Nissa Mukhfi, this is Sadar Mahal Sadar, this is Malkaey Mukhdarey Uzma, Alam Ara Begum Alim, this is the blind Mian Jurrat, each one of them recites one line (matla) or Bait, read all their compositions, and applaud them.

In this dramatic mode, there was no need for rhyming. It was written in such a realistic way that even a child could understand. And other than a few words of Arabic and Persian which appeared occasionally, there were no statements which could not be understood by people with only a common understanding. In some places, Wajid Ali Shah wrote the feminine plural as '*kurtiyan, saktiyan*,' which was obsolete by that time.[14] To avoid monotony and common style such puerile expressions are seen in other writings of Wajid Ali Shah. On the whole, the language of *Bani* is more realistic than that found in other writings of that time.

DISTINGUISHING FEATURE

Bani's topic and its unique style of writing is enough to give Wajid Ali Shah a place of distinction in the history of Urdu prose. But much before the writing of *Bani* Wajid Ali Shah wrote letters, which are a much more valuable and worthy treasure. They are not merely letters, but the letters of a King and a writer, and hence they hold a distinctive grandeur. In Urdu prose, every letter is not an example of literature, nor is every letter-writer an author. But when letter-writing is considered an important genre, and acknowledged as a permanent art, then the contribution of the literature which influenced and promoted the genre cannot be forgotten. While reviewing the prose writing of Wajid Ali Shah, the abundance and variety of his letters attracts attention. The collection of these letters has been discussed in detail in Chapter 3. A literary analysis of those letters is explained here. As some say, "these

14. *Ibid*, 323, 319.

letters are not written, but are woven like silk."[15] Those who understand the importance of the letters would agree with this statement, which presents their characteristic features – artificiality and literary formality. Letters, and especially most of the letters written by Wajid Ali Shah, enjoy higher status, surpassing any other writing in the same category, and have historic importance as they were written in a period when such examples of Urdu prose were rarely common.

REASON FOR INDIVIDUALITY

In the view of contemporary writers, there are two reasons for Wajid Ali Shah's individuality: firstly, the dialogue style, and secondly, its simplicity and plausibility. The dialogue style is a distinctive feature of his dramatic way of expression. In terms of cultural contributions, he had a natural inclination towards dance and music. He presented his religious thoughts as a debate between his psyche and wisdom. This dialogue style came naturally in letter, as their subject matter was a conversation between a lover and his beloved; in the imagination of a lover, the beloved is the sole audience throughout.[16] The simplicity and plausibility in the style of the letters is both natural and spontaneous because of this dialogue. For informality and spontaneity in conversation, it is necessary that if one resides in the heart (*dilnashin*), then the language should be plain and easy to understand.

Wajid Ali Shah was not attracted to Urdu prose writing, and had necessity not forced him, he would not have written a single letter in Urdu. It is said that necessity is the mother of invention. This necessity was behind Wajid Ali Shah's Urdu letter writing, and when there was no further need, his passion died naturally. To understand the nature of such need, it is important to keep in mind the literary ingenuity of Wajid Ali Shah and

---

15. Classical Adab, Khwaja Ahmed Farooqui-Azad Kitab Ghar Delhi. Publication Ibrahimia Hyderabad. 1957. 138.

16. You are with me when no one is there. (By Momin)

his contemporaries. The contemporary writers of the time wrote letters to the famous folk, all of those addresses were males. On the contrary, all the letters recovered from Wajid Ali Shah's collection are addressed to women, all of whom were allegedly writers or poets, but were also uneducated and came from poor or middle-class families. In such a situation, had the letters been written in Persian or even in advanced Urdu, then they would not have been understood. The Ghazals which were sent by the King, and the ways in which they were addressed, was more to satisfy his own passion for writing than to please the recipients. It was not necessary that such compositions be written in everyday language. This is because such complimentary sentences are meant for pleasing oneself and others, and are not to be followed literally.

The style in which the subject matter was presented to the reader should also be noted.

If, after reading the formal and decorative language of the address, it was known that the reader could understand such language, then the same formality would have been used for the body of the letter. But the writer had to consider the competence of the reader, otherwise writing formal compositions would kill the meaning of the letter. Wajid Ali Shah's diversion from formal composition reveals the real reason he wrote letters. This communication style marks the big difference between Wajid Ali Shah and writers at the time. However, it would be easy for anyone who is ignorant of this point to consider Suroor or Ghalib as Wajid Ali Shah's literary inspiration.

FIRST LETTER

Among the letters of Wajid Ali Shah, the one dated 'Second Zeqqad 1272' A.H. (5 July 1856) is the first written in Urdu prose. Earlier letters were written only in poetry. Considering every word, from the address to the signature, there is no[17] trace of Suroor or Ghalib's influence, though it has features

17. Letter is found in Chapter Three.

like literary taste, affection, brevity, and purity. In the coming three years, he wrote innumerable letters. While it is true that the style of the first letter could not be sustained for long, the change was felt only in the matter of the title and address, and the real content of the letter was written in the same informal and attractive language. "Writing letters requires more than pen and paper, they are written with blood."[18] A study and comparison of Wajid Ali Shah's letters shows that the paper is sprinkled and speckled with blood.

NUMBER OF LETTERS

Conversations between lovers are a special subject matter in letters containing Urdu poetry. In his personal life, Wajid Ali Shah is often seen as both a lover and the beloved. The enjoyment of love and romance in Lucknow continued without any letters or messengers. Though it was not easy for others to approach Wajid Ali Shah, but for Wajid Ali Shah there was no such hesitance to use the services of a messenger. But after his exile and house arrest, Wajid Ali Shah's condition was that of a forlorn lover. The urge for "Physical connection and spiritual embracing" showed him the path of "half meeting with the reader". Gradually, this tendency reached such great intensity that, during the initial days of his exile, other than letter writing, no other genre of composition or compilation is found. It is difficult to imagine the number of letters; Wajid Ali Shah became a prolific writer, and a life of exile and the isolation of house arrest left him with no other work. The first extract below is about exile:

There is abundance of snakes and the sound of rain
Noise of cricket, profusion of sea water
No one asks what you are doing 'Mian'?
O Youth! at least say do you suffer from a weak heart

---

18. *Classical Adab,* Khwaja Ahmed Farooqui-Azad Kitab Ghar Delhi. Publication Ibrahimia Hyderabad. 1957. 124.

Beloved! The whole day there are letters of beloved as my company
Or there is sound of lightning and the mercy of rains[19]

The second extract is about house arrest:

> O! Ghazala I cannot see any human as far as I can see... O! Ghazala there is a room with closed door as my residence, O! Ghazala the doors are closed O! Ghazala there is dreariness of solitude that for two years I have not seen the face of inmates of Mochi Khola O! Ghazala other than letter writing I have no other work..O! Ghazala I am your lover..O! Ghazala I write your name thousand times but still not satisfied...[20]

Among Wajid Ali Shah's allegedly hundreds and thousands of wives, none can complain of not getting a response to their letters.

> Allah o Akbar... Jaa n e Alam! cannot imagine you sitting at one place for the last twenty months...not seeing the Sun and the moon, this is your courage, this is the magnanimity of Kings, there is too much of leisure, and the sufferings are hard, the high posts have everything high. Other than all the hardships, there is powerlessness, helplessness, the abundance of writing is also a headache, this discomfort and suffering is too much, there is no writer, but there is abundance of writing, you are attached with everyone, anyone who gets the reply late or is not responded is complaining...[21]

The King insisted that everyone send letters:

A. If you will hear more, nothing other than sorrow will come, Don't consider me among the living, I am dead, I will hardly survive for six months or a year, I hope so long I am alive I will keep sending letters.[22]

---

19. *Sheva-e-Faiz,* Md. Wajid Ali Shah Akhtar. Publication Sultani. Calcutta 1277. 320–21.
20. *Tarikh e* Ghazala, 24. Md. Wajid Ali Shah Akhtar. (Compiler Wasi Bilgrami) Publication Mufeed e Aam. Agra. 1914. (Azad). 24.
21. *Tarikh e Badr* (Handwritten) Md. Wajid Ali Shah Akhtar -1276 (IDAARA). 20–21.
22. *Adab Ka Maqsad,* 181. Dr, Syed Noorul Hasan Hashmi-Hindustan Kitab Ghar .Lucknow. 1956. 181.

B. O! Ghazala your letters come late, O! Ghazala is it not possible that you write and send letters to me every day?.[23] He wrote as many letters as he received from someone.

C. Darling (Jan e mann) By God (Khuda) there is no letter of yours to which I have not responded or I missed it, but what to do if some are plundered and lost by the plunderers on the way.[24]

D. ...You are a liar! You say that you write continuously but altogether three of your letters came while about thirty or forty letters of others came and I responded to them accordingly, your three letters came and I responded to all the three. ..I keep engaged, the moment I receive letter I experience life...[25]

The Ghazals of Sheva-e-Faiz were sent to the 'Begmats' at short intervals, along with the letters. Thus, about two hundred and fifty Ghazals are expected to be in the sealed envelopes. Hence, it can be said without exaggeration that there must be around two and a half thousand letters.

COLLECTION OF LETTERS

It is commonly said that from the treasures of lovers, nothing other than the 'letters of beauties' and 'the pictures of the idols' are recovered. If there were pictures in the collections of Wajid Ali Shah, these must be adorning various museums. God knows if these are the pictures of the Begums who were said to be associated with him, or if, like the letters, these too were something far from reality. There is, without exaggeration, mention of thousands of letters which were sent or received, but within these there is not a single letter –

23. *Tarikh e* Ghazala, Md. Wajid Ali Shah Akhtar. (Compiler Wasi Bilgrami) Publication Mufeed e Aam. Agra. 1914. (Azad). 25.

24. *Adab Ka Maqsad,* 181. Dr, Syed Noorul Hasan Hashmi-Hindustan Kitab Ghar. Lucknow. 1956. 189.

25. *Tarikh-e-Mumtaz,* Md. Wajid Ali Shah Akhtar. (Compiler; Dr. Md. Baqar). Urdu Markaz. Lahore. 1952 (Azad). 49.

forged or otherwise – which was sent to the King by any Begum, or by the King to any Begum individually.

Despite their distance from reality, all the letters found in his collections have a distinctive importance for both history and literature. A common feature of the recovered collections is that they are in Urdu, handwritten, and are private communications between husband and wife. Every collection contains the letters of a single individual. There are four collections of letters from 'Begmats'. The work of compiling of these letters started in Zilhij 1275 A.H., and the King himself wrote the preface. There are three collections of the King's letters. The order for their compilation was given in Zeeqad 1275[26] A.H. and its preface was written by the writers of the Begmats letters.

The King considered both of these collections as his own composition. In light of this, two attributes of Wajid Ali Shah are fixed: *firstly* a writer and *secondly*, a compiler. One might question why the collections are associated with him if the letters are not his. But one should consider that the compilation of both the collections was the King's innovation. If IntezamAllah Shahabi, Imtiaz Ali Khan and Md. Ali Arsh Malihabadi are regarded as compilers when they published these letters, then why would that person who first complied these letters – namely, the King – be denied the same right of compilation. It was not difficult for the King to collect the letters and then write a preface for them, like he did for the Ghazal*s*. However, the custom of romance (*Sheva e Aashiqui*) demanded that, like he collected the letters of the Begums, the Begums should also have the honour of collecting his letters. To review the letter-writing literature of the King, it is necessary to identify these two attributes of his personality; the qualities which are necessary for a writer need not be necessary for a compiler.

26. *Tarikh-e-Mumtaz,* 58. *Tarikh e* Ghazala, 41. *Tarikh e* Noor (Handwritten), 182.

LOGIC BEHIND COLLECTION

It has been stated that "Letters not only reflect the literature or art of writing, but by them the academic, literary, social and political dates can also be compiled"[27] and that "Letters are the essence of biography."[28] The aforementioned collections and prefaces reveal that the King has said the same. He made such statements at a time when the publication of such private letters was unheard of. Letters were written to friends and disclosed events from one's personal life, the concealment of which was dearer than its publication. The same correspondence becomes more respectable between husband and wife because thoughts which cannot be shared with friends can be shared between husband and wife. Publishing such letters was a courageous task, and by publishing the letters between him and his Begums, Wajid Ali Shah displayed this boldness.

There was a time when these letters were opened in an unauthorized manner. It displeased both the King and the Begum:

> You wrote that someone is groundlessly jealous of me...firstly the letter is first opened and then it reaches me, I was surprised because the Post people dare not do this and I don't expect this from my relatives. You find out on your own that who is this man who did this and revealed the secret matter.[29]

Then came a time when these letters were written with real gold water. The publication of *Nuqoosh e Zindan* (Sajjad Zaheer's letters to his wife), and *Zere lab* (Letters of Safia Akhtar addressed to her husband Jaan Nisar Akhtar) has been regarded as the 'new thing' by twentieth-century commentators.[30] In the nineteenth century, an orthodox section of Indian society often both

---

27. *Nuqoosh* (Lahore Makateeb Number) November 1957, 10.
28. *Urdu Khutoot,* Shamsul Rehman. Kitabi Duniya. Delhi. 1947. 11.
29. *Ruqa't e Begum e Avadh*- (Raza Library, Rampur). 104.
30. In the Makateeb Number of *Nuqoosh* by Dr. Syed Abdullah. (Nuqoosh, Lahore). November 1957, 37.

appreciated[31] and criticized [32] Wajid Ali Shah's boldness and frankness. Those were the days of secrecy, but later the formality disappeared, giving way to frankness. This is evident from the following words:

A. ...at some places in the letters of the King and Begums this wine overflows, there are talks about cohabitation and teasing of lovers.[33]

B. ...in these (in the letters of Sajjad Zaheer) there is no decorum or the style of eye communication.... at places the secured whispers have travelled from privacy to public.[34]

Wajid Ali Shah was not a Socialist leader, but expressing one's thoughts from inside the four walls of a prison was a tradition that he started. This is commendable in that even the progress of society to date has not moved past the point he had left a century ago.

USEFULNESS OF COLLECTIONS

Before Wajid Ali Shah's compilation of these collections, there were no such collections in the Urdu language. Hence, his work added a new chapter. However, their usefulness is doubtful; Matbaey Sultani did not publish them, nor there is any proof of these moving out of the royal library. However, circumstantial evidence shows that the abundance of these letters initiated the tradition of correspondence in some reserved circles of Lucknow and Calcutta. Nazm Tabatabai and Sharar Lucknavi explain that people were very fond of rich, rhyming language, and that Wajid Ali Shah himself had liked it both in writing and in speech.[35] If this is true, then a change must

31. *Kham Khanaey Javed,* Volume 1, 210. (no further citation found)

32. *Tarikh e Avadh,* Volume 5, 106–07.

33. *Classical Adab,* Khwaja Ahmed Farooqui-Azad Kitab Ghar Delhi. Publication Ibrahimia Hyderabad. 1957. 167.

34. Dr. Khwaja Ahmed Farooqui in the Khutoot Number of Aajkal, *Nuqoosh*, Lahore. November 1957.

35. *Zamana (*Monthly, Kanpur) Issue March, 1911, 234.

have happened because of the letters between the 'Begmats' and of the King, in which the style of writing is plain and informal. Sharar discusses a group of writers and poets who always tried to bring out new styles of writing:

> At this point distinguished poets were present as the inmates of harem were interested in the art of poetry and the place was always in search of youthful poets who could write colorful statement because every second or third day a composition of new style was taken before the King.[36]

They credited these letters for their elegant writing:

> In search of a romantic Persian writing in the palace (Baitul Ijra) I came across an interesting pastime of beauty and beloved... the letters sent by 'Begmats' to the King... these were kept securely in 'Baitul Ijra', these letters which were called 'Towudud Nama' were usually written in romantic manner and in colorful writing... they were numbered at hundred and fifty which I started reading... I was much amused... In every letter there was a unique innovation and freshness. Therefore the first lessons of my writing were these 'Towadud Namas' which both apparently and by way of language were very attractive.[37]

This narration of Sharar revealed that these letters are 'the last rings of the chain' the first of which is found in the above-mentioned collections. Like Sharar, innumerable people had a taste for elegant literature, and quenched their thirst from it. Though today the nature of this quest has changed, the fans of history, linguistics, and biography can gain so much from these letters which cannot be retrieved from other sources.

COLLECTIONS OF WAJID ALI SHAH

Letters reflect the writer's personality. Smart writers, with the help of words and styles, can make their personality mysterious, but their letters may still reveal the things which they are trying to conceal. Wajid Ali Shah's life was

36. *Guzishta Lucknow*; Maulvi Abdul Haleem Sharar. Naseem Book Depot. Lucknow. 91.
37. *Dilgudaz* (Magazine, Lucknow). Issue June 1933, 123.

like an open book, of which some special pages – including his letters – were presented to the public by the King himself. They reveal the domestic life of the writer, his wishes, annoyances, pastimes, gracefulness, mannerisms, and humanism. Born and brought up in sheer affluence, he was a lover of opulence and the ruler of the most fertile land of Hindustan. Although now, devoid of all his prosperity and authority, he was in exile, his associates still expected the same applause and appreciation which was once within his reach. To whom should he express his agony? To whom should he show his bruises? He wanted to forget the present bitterness and remember the sweet memories of the past, but queries like 'What happened in London? What is happening in Calcutta? What will happen in Lucknow?' refreshed the agonies in his heart, from which he tried to escape. To love and to be loved is a common feature in these letters. They are all love letters; none are examples of wrath or displeasure. But together with the grief for his beloved, the grief caused by the times and by imprisonment has become reproachful part of these letters. Truly speaking these imprints provide much material to study the mind of Wajid Ali Shah.

VARIEGATION IN STYLE

If we compare *Tarikh-e-Mumtaz*, *Tarikh e Mazzahab* and *Tarikh e* Ghazala, we will find a clear difference between *Tarikh-e-Mumtaz* and the last two letters. A formal style of address, rhyming sentences, clerical writing, and detailed narration are hallmarks of the letters of *Tarikh-e-Mumtaz.* In places, he uses common language, but instead of being spontaneous it is well decorated. There was plain and simple Urdu in the letter dated 2nd Zeeqad 1272 A.H. to Shaida Begum.[38] Three days after sending this letter, there was a drastic change:

> Afsar Farq Jaleel Mumtaz Jahan Nawab Aklil Mahal Saheba on behalf of Jaan e Alam should know you are the pride of lovers! Your picturesque

38. The letter given in Chapter Three of this book.

> letter is received during the height of wait which quenched the thirst of my heart. By Allah's grace up till the moment of writing this love letter everything is fine and there is all kind of blessing from Allah and on this eve of fourteenth, health and life is always expected from the creator of sky and land.[39]

But his change proved to be an echo. On the one hand, such formal letters were written to Mumtaz Jahan while on the other hand, the letters written to Shaida Begum appeared more like a conversation than a letter. After three years, no letters were received in the name of Shaida Begum, but the letter of *Tarikh e* Ghazala shows an improvement in the style which was started in the letters addressed to Shaida Begum. The first letter of *Tarikh e* Ghazala goes like this:

> Fairy like my dear Nawab Malka Ghazala Saheba! Allah o Akbar why you enquired about me:
> Don't enquire about my welfare, forget it,
> If I die in separation, let me die
> Though you loved me the most but you took care of me too late. I praise your ignorance, received your letter, was apprised of everything, and became sad to hear about your tragedy.[40]

His varied style across different collections of letters reveals his innovative nature and his command of language and expression.

At the same time, it also emphasises that the King liked to reply in a style that matched both taste and the academic abilities of the recipient. Mumtaz Jahan was not totally illiterate, and for this reason her letters were very formal. Nawab Khusro Begum had performed Hajj and pilgrimage, and

---

39. *Tarikh-e-Mumtaz,* Md. Wajid Ali Shah Akhtar. (Compiler: Dr. Md. Baqar). Urdu Markaz. Lahore. 1952 (Azad). 34.

40. *Tarikh e* Ghazala, Md. Wajid Ali Shah Akhtar (Compiler: Wasi Bilgrami). Publication Mufeed e Aam. Agra. 21.

in her opinion singing Ghazals was impermissible (*makruh*).[41] Poetic elegies were sent to her in letters.[42]

Aziz Lucknavi relates an event where a writer, expecting a tenancy, wrote the letter in a continuous style (called *mehmila*, a kind of letter writing in which the letter is written without a full stop). When the King passed an order, it was in the same style. By way of thanks, the learned man again presented a letter. *Manqoot* or *manqoota* is another style of letter writing in Urdu in which the sentences are separated by dots or full stops. One can say that; manqoot' is the opposite of *mehmila* style.

This sentence merely means that the King responded to the letters in the same style as it was sent by the writer. But this sentence will be very light devoid of technicality and the real style.[43] This incident not only shows his command over the language, but it also shows his natural inclination towards it. If all the letters written to the King by Sarwar,[44] Ashir, Tauqeer, Hunar, Hilal, Shafaq, Zaair, Shafi, Abad Ali, and the various writers who wrote on behalf of Begums could be produced, along with his replies, it would have revealed that these men, in a bid to gain an edge over each other, presented elegant writing in the style adopted by King. But Alas only the letters by Ashir are available. These show that the King responded in the same style.[45]

---

41. *Makrooh* is one of the five legal divine sanctioning in Islam (Translator). It means reprehensible, hateful not illegal but discouraged by Allah. The Oxford Dictionary of Islam (Edited by John. L. Esposito). 2022.

42. *Sheva-e-Faiz*, Md. Wajid Ali Shah Akhtar. Publication Sultani. Calcutta 1277. 206, 218, 234, 263.

43. *Tarikh e Abbas,* Maulvi Mirza Md.Hadi Sahab Aziz Lucknavi. Nizami Press, Luckow. 209–211.

44. *Ruqaat e Begmat e Avadh.* (Raza Library). 62.

45. See the letters written to Shaida Begum and those received in response to it in *Ruqa'at-e-Begmat.*

LETTER OR DIALOGUE

"For a good letter, formal dialogue is not necessary, only informal daily language is required."[46] After a certain limit, this dialogue changes into a formal and artificial conversational style." The dialogues of *Tarikh e Mazzahab* and *Tarikh e* Ghazala present a style which started in the form of whispering, and which gradually took on a dramatic form. Words were invented to express the particular thoughts, feelings, and emotions. Poetry and literature was made impactful with the help of phonetic compatibility. Please note the starting signs of this dialogue:

A. "Why dear now the feelings of my heart are disclosed before you, see darling now I cannot travel, there is no strength left in my heart, see when I meet you, when I will see you, I have composed this Ghazal at a very awkward time, your heart knows it very well, keep writing the letters sooner as this is the only source of comfort, this will pacify my heart, what to write more about myself, I am the same, yours (faqat)."

B. "This is the condition in London, brother wants that I should get the throne, son also wants it for himself, there is a fight between uncle and nephew, I am lying ill here, nobody takes care of me, God forbid if something happens there then the Company will not spare me, Khuda knows what will be my plight and what will be the misfortune, now they have really become enemy. O! my dear I regret that I could not see yours and your daughter's face. Secondly this Rashk e Mahal has complained against Aasman Jah that he wants my son to be snatched away from me. Every day I am bothered by lawyers and they ask for the custody of my son Rashke Mahal , no body listens to my pleas I cannot give my heart my son to anyone. If you will hear more you will only be displeased."[47]

---

46. Dr. Syed Abdul Nuqoosh (Lahore) November 1957. Makateeb Number, 21.

47. *Adab Ka Maqsad,* Dr, Syed Noorul Hasan Hashmi-Hindustan Kitab Ghar . Lucknow. 1956. 189.

C. 'My dear that one bed is mine, for you and for your daughter I don't care even for my own life, had I been powerful today I would have fulfilled the wishes of many, all the beggars of Lucknow would have been rich, but no one can fight with destiny, I leave it on will of Khuda, keep your heart happy by all means, the phrase goes that one should spread one's legs as per the size of the sheet. By Allah's grace I am still well off and will remain so, you don't worry."[48]

D. "You write that you cannot manufacture lie, be fair enough to say that did you send so many letters previously like you send it now, previously there were not so many."[49]

Apart from an initial formal sentence, the letters *of Tarikh e Mazzahab* (as in the extracts above) are written without any grammatical arrangements, and so there are twists in his expressions. In places, the sentences and thoughts are unrelated to each other. The letters of *Tarikh e* Ghazala are memoirs from the prison of Fort William. In prison, a person longs to talk. Hence, if a letter turns into dialogue, there should be no surprise. But his dialogue is written with concentration:

A. "O! Ghazala, you swear on my head keep your hand on my chest and see where I am. Cannot write, don't know under pain of separation what I am babbling, O! Ghazala this world is very bad, though I give away my life; the rivals are backbiting against me, O! Ghazala I have not embraced you for long, connect your mouth with mouth, O! Ghazala please open the door of Rahas Manzil, let's go to 'Zard Kothi', I feel suffocated, very nice 'blinds' of 'khas' are hanging in 'Zard Kothi' O! Ghazala such a nice couch and bed was there Oh! Ghazala for Khuda's sake say something, get 'khas' palanquin, get

48. *Ibid*, 183.
49. *Ibid*, 189.

on it and lets go up to your house, O! Allah I am fed up of your insensivity."[50]

B. "SubhanAllah what a path of love and affection that one is in prison suffering badly and you instead of asking about my welfare you write sarcastic sentences. What do you know in what misery I am, dear if you don't get maintenance then you leave me and look for some other place. O! Wow you came after everyone arrived and instead of being ashamed you keep insisting again and again, do whatever you want, how long you will remain pleased with the situation (Bakre ki maa kab tak khair manayegi) I wept looking at your writing : "I saw the love of Sahib...futile to write more—Ghazala is only expecting money."(couplet)

C. "...and in the thirteenth letter that you write about your father, mother and brother and keep bothering me then You Ghazala listen either from this ear or from that ear, if you really want to keep terms with me then give up this effort and recommendation for your parents and relatives I wonder from where you got father and from where came your brother ... there was no one during the ruling period..."[51]

D. "WAllah ! I regret will you make me sick? Swear on my head Beware ! Beware ! console me now consider this letter as if I am talking to you, I got so many rings made for you sweetheart. ...as per your wishes."[52]

The King had a special way of sarcasm:

E. "By Allah's consent (Inshallah) you will receive very beautiful silver bed for your maternity...dont' deliver before that...consider me, let the bed arrive."[53]

---

50. *Tarikh e* Ghazala, Md. Wajid Ali Shah Akhtar (Compiler Wasi Bilgrami). Publication Mufeed e Aam. Agra. 23.

51. *Ibid*, 34.

52. *Ibid*, 36.

53. Adab Ka Maqsad, Dr, Syed Noorul Hasan Hashmi-Hindustan Kitab Ghar .Lucknow. 1956. 173.

F. "Here everywhere there is grace of Allah, the kingship is devastated."[54]

G. "You gave birth to daughter, but the bed is arriving soon...I have passed many orders if there is delay from my side then curse (laanat) of Khuda be on me."[55]

H. "I got two lakh rupees from English government, I swear on my head, and I swear on your head I have send all to Lucknow walis."[56]

I. "Two lakh more were granted by Governor-General Bahadur (KhuldullahhMalka) hence from that three thousand were sent for your fast-breaking.(Faqa shikani)."[57]

In the love letters, had there been a bold expression of cohabitation, that would not have been surprising. However, I did not receive a single letter where the subject was vulgar. At most, it contained the following:

> After two years when you regained health and vigor, what to say what shameful thought came to my mind, with hopelessness and wistfully I clutched my heart. By the grace of God again the good news of the health of beloved came, O! the comfort of my heart! O! my soul! Without the experience of the beauty I am restless day and night, without that how can I be at rest.[58]

At the beginning and end of each letter he used formal expressions like 'the urge to meet', 'the wish to unite' and 'the wish to kiss'. This is why these letters were popularly called 'love letters.' The King remembered not only his children, but even his relatives and servants by name. His humbleness and modesty demonstrate that the relationship between the King and his

54. *Ibid*, 172.

55. *Ibid*, 180.

56. *Tarikh e* Ghazala, Md. Wajid Ali Shah Akhtar (Compiler Wasi Bilgrami.)Publication Mufeed e Aam. Agra. 23.

57. *Ibid*, 22.

58. *Ibid*, 28–29.

Begums was not only sexual, but that he cared for everyone attached to him. These small things contributed to the popularity and respect of the King.

COLLECTIONS OF BEGUMS

The following couplet about the romantic correspondence explains the attitude of the Begums and their letters:

> I will write though there is no reason
> I am a fan of your name

The difference is that in those letters, the expression of love is not only in name. In most of the letters, and especially in *Tarikh e Firaq*, there are fine examples of 'asking' or 'demanding.' If letter-writing becomes a daily practice, then there is repetition of expressions. If it is not wrong to think of letters as 'pictures', then though 'Begmats' sent a number of pictures which are very beautiful and attractive, most of these were pictures of worry and anxiety (*Janab Ishq Tarddud Manzil*), taken from different angles. Letters by the King, though less in number, were of average beauty and attraction, but are pictures which takes us to different places and the changing scenes keep our interest alive.

Some letters of the Begmats are pre-1857, though most are from after 1857. Within these two or three years, Lucknow experienced turmoil which is unparallel in the history of the city. It was possible for the Begums to write about their suffering to the mayor of the city, but the letters written after the turmoil use rhyming words and are written in a light mood, which indicates that for Begmats, perhaps it was an unimportant event. It was the same conspiracies within the palaces, the same mutual rivalry, and the same tug of war for power. The subtle minded King was perhaps not in search of such news, or even if he was curious, the strictness of the Fort may not have allowed the delivery of such letters. In the collection, there are letters which verify the narration given in the Preface, and because these were replies to the King's letters, they reveal many important facts about the King.

'BEGMATI' LANGUAGE

Commentators have indiscriminately regarded the letters of the 'Begmats' as a masterpiece of '*Begmati*' language. The following comments explain this:

A. "The letters found in it (in the office of Wajid Ali Shah Baitul Ijra) were all written by the writers of the Begmats and were elegantly written in colourful language."[59]

B. "The Urdu language of Lucknow is quite famous and the language of the Begmats of Avadh is unparalleled. Many wanted to hear but the wish could not be fulfilled. Particularly the Urdu language of the Begmats of Hazrat Shah e Avadh was superior to the language of all the Begmats. This is because Jaan e Alam Akhtar was himself a poet and the Begmats were also well read and poetesses."[60]

C. "Shaida and Hoor were poetesses, in their letter there was also some poetry along with prose."[61]

D. "Regarding Urdu language Lucknow has a place of distinction. The standard language of the city depended on two sections of the 'fair sex;' Begmats and sweepers. In search of some idiom the intellectuals gave attention to them... these letters are part of those rarities... their main attribute is that they are the language of the palaces, the pure idioms of daily life, purely of standard quality, and the style of expression is plain and attractive. As most of the related happenings are by the forlorn Begmats hence they are full of agony."[62]

E. "...(Tarikh e Badr) is a valuable addition of elegant writing coming out of the pen of a royal Begum. Apart from its rhyming expression, idioms, analogies, terminology and similes and simple wordings, each letter is a true and painful tale."[63]

---

59. Maulvi Abdul Haleem Sharar- *'Dilgudaz'* Issue June 1933, 123.
60. Md. Imtiaz Ali Khan in *Ruqa'ate Begmat,* 2.
61. Md. Najmul Ghani Khan, *Tarikh e Avadh,* Volume 5, 107.
62. Md. Abdul Shahid Khan Sherwani, *Begmat e Avadh Ke Khutoot,* 145–47.
63. Md. Ali Arsh Malihabadi, *Ruqa'at e Badr*, 1.

F. "Women are the greatest guards of language and the standard language of Urdu depends mainly on Begmats, and the Begmats of Wajid Ali Shah enjoy a special status in this respect. This is the reason that in their letter the attributes of sweetness of daily language, arrangement of words, spontaneity of idioms, and innovative style of expression is found in abundance."[64]

G. "The Begmati language of Lucknow is famous for its sweetness and heart ravishing quality. Quite obvious then that the language can be found in its best form in no other place than in the royal palaces. The letters of Begmats of Wajid Ali Shah are the best specimen of Urdu mualla."[65]

Like in the above narratives, much has been said in appreciation of 'Begmati' language but if one looks for a defined principle in respect of its style and attributes, which could be a distinguishing feature in the language of commoners or the elite class, then no such quality is discovered. The writers have given their opinion by going through the contents of the letters, and when these letters are studied, no worthwhile conclusion is drawn. They contain some very light words from Arabic and Persian, and adopt styles to fulfill the requirement of rhyming, and for flaunting the art of elegant writing. Is this Begmati language? In Wajid Ali Shah's letters, the verbs were in the feminine gender, and there was a soft touch to the tone and style. But in the Begmats' letters, only the verbs are feminine while the words and thoughts are masculine. At the most, it can be said that the letters by the male writers, which they write under the name of Begmati language, and the letters by the Begmats have the same literary importance. The difference lies in the fact that though the Begums are no more but today in films, dramas, and novels the so called 'Begmati language' continues. These letters are from

64. *Classical Adab,* Khwaja Ahmed Farooqui-Azad Kitab Ghar Delhi. Publication Ibrahimia Hyderabad. 1957. 125.

65. Raees Ahmed Jafri, Wajid Ali Shah *Aur Unka Ahad,* Kitab Manzil. Lucknow. 1958. 661.

the time when Begums were alive, and so the research scholars of Begmati language are the ones to decide whether those letters contained Begmati language. My investigation, while acknowledging the literary and linguistic importance of those letters and refuting any incorrect beliefs, does not allow me to go beyond this. I am handing over the job to those who are interested in investigating this matter.

CRITICS OF BEGMATI LANGUAGE

While detailing out collection of letters, it has been proved that the letters which are associated with Begmats were actually not written by them, but that someone else wrote for them. After perusing the collections and reaching the conclusion that Begmats were usually not literate, and that their delicate hands were unfit to lift a pen, this is not an unreasonable conclusion. But it is also not so unreasonable that, after cursorily going through some of the letters, one should claim that the Begmats were writers and poets. Their letters are the great specimen of *Begmati* language, and their language can be taken as exemplary. Thus, looking at their character, loose morals, fun-loving nature, and an urge to satisfy their desires, this is a logical conclusion which should have been anticipated much earlier, but alas it has not yet been done. There are three reasons for this: *firstly* the exaggerated narration in those letters, *secondly*, dispersing of the authorized collections, *thirdly* disregarding the internal and external evidence. The commitment, carelessness, and irresponsible behavior weaken the opinion given by such people.

ILLITERATE BEGMATS

The inability of Begmats to read or write the letters is evident from the following:

A. The narratives of Wajid Ali Shah himself, from which it can be inferred directly or indirectly that other people wrote the letters, and his entire appreciation was meant for them.

B. The admission by the Begmats that they are illiterate, that the letters sent in their names were read by others, and that they also depend on others to write the replies.

C. The internal evidence from the letters and clerical narratives, which include simple and tough words of Arabic and Persian origina.

D. The clear statements of the letter-writers, which prove that this was not a secret. Everyone who wrote the letters knew. Out of these statements, two are mentionable. Mushir's statement indicates that the 'Begmats' did not know what had been written in their behalf:

There is a pupil of mine the eloquent
His name is Mir *Wajid Ali*
Once when I was in some problem
I went to meet him one day
To get rid of his problem
He talked to me about Sultan Alam
Then he quickly gave a letter to me
And asked me to write its reply
I had no idea but I wrote
I wrote the reply instantly
When I gave the composed letter
Darogah sent it then and there
Then the moment I reached Sultan
Almighty showered some happiness on me
My problem was solved
I was granted thirty (rupees) monthly
When the letter reached its recipient
I was employed in her palace
I was given the charge of writing letter
King gave me under the (control of) Fairy (Beauty)
When I got this post

I wrote many prose and poetic letters.[66]

The narrative of Nazm Tabatabai refreshes the memory of Metiaburj, and incidentally also discloses what happened to the letters:

"One day Nawab Taban Mahal's plangquin carrier came to me and said that His Excellency has composed a Ghazal *for Taban Mahal (Huzoor) and that she wants that the* Ghazal *should be responded by me. At first I was surprised that what sort of wish is this? but then when I read the* Ghazal *then I could make out that it was in appreciation of Taban Mahal which said: "Taban Begum is pretty and graceful and she is shrewd." Seeing this the following came to my mind:*
Taban Begum is caught in the grip of musk
She is the victim of the deadly eyebrow
The entire Ghazal *was composed then and there and was presented before His Excellency. It was well appreciated. .... its copy must be in the office of Baitul Akhbar.... That office is devastated. It's not known as to during bidding the volume which contained the love letters reached which grocer's shop."*[67]

E. The narrative of an eyewitness, Sharar, that poets and writers used to crowd the residences of Begmats to write letters.[68] In his autobiography, Sharar instead of 'Inshapardaz Begmat'[69] wrote '*Begmat Inshapardaz*' and it seems that he tried to play some trick to give some hidden message. One wonders as to after giving a clear narrative, what was the need of this verbal jugglery.

F. During that period there was no trend for women's education. Reading the Holy Quran was equivalent to being educated.[70] But

66. *Masnavi* Mushir, (Handwritten), Gauhar Ali Mushir, 1276h. 17–18. (Intikhab).

67. *Zamana* (Monthly, Kanpur). Issue, March 1911, 235.

68. *Guzishta Lucknow*; Maulvi Abdul Haleem Sharar. Naseem Book Depot. Lucknow. 91

69. *Dilgudaz* (Monthly. Lucknow), Issue June 1933, 123.

70. In *Masnavi* Mushir (Handwritten) on page 58 Zeb Mahal 's writer Mushir writes about his mistress:

this type of education, though it gave the ability to read, provided no expertise in writing.[71] The King on his own made arrangements for the education of the Begmats:

Listen from there something new
There was a teacher named Hasan
Ghulam Raza Khan the confidant
Honorably became my employee
*There was order that fairies (*Begmats*) should read and write*
Begums *should take lesson from teacher*
A building was fixed for schooling
Strangely the luck favored education
All the Begums *became obedient*
Within some time they were educated
Everyone got as per her capacity
Received the lesson of Sharia
Beauties learned the manners up till coronation
This was their pastime up till coronation

But this is about those Begums who were associated with the King before his accession to the throne. Those Begums, about whose writing there is so much discussion, are those who appeared during the last phase of reign. Even if it were accepted that they were literate, expecting that level of writing from them is nothing but presumptuousness.

From the evidence mentioned above, three points are more or less found in every collection. If anyone who is aware of it still overlooks it, then there must be a strong reason for this.

During less than a year Quran was completed
It enhanced the honour. She was now known as literate.

71. *Tarikh e Jamshedi,* Md. Wajid Ali Shah Akhtar (Handwritten), 1276h. (Avadh) 40.

'Bayaz' of Ashir

The biggest proof of the Begmats being poets and writers is in fact its weakest point. Whether we address it as the collection known as '*Ruq'at e Begum*' compiled by Imtiaz Ali Khan, or whether we consider the various handwritten copies of these collections, it would not affect the correctness of our conclusion. Those who benefitted from handwritten copies of *Mukhzan e Israr e Sultani*, *Tohfaey Sultani* and *Ruqa'at-e-Begmat* did not realize that though they considered the handwritten copies as originals, and the books as printed copies, the reality could be just the reverse. Those 'dilapidated parts',[72] instead of a compiled collection, could be the manuscript of that person who wrote letters on behalf of the Begmats but did not destroy them, because letter writing was his profession.[73] By using such idiomatic narratives, he earned his livelihood.

Ruqa't e Begmat, from whom these handwritten copies are compiled, can serve as a test to decide the authenticity of handwritten copies. This copy is the property of *Raza Library Rampur.* On page 39 of this copy, one poetic letter under the title of '*Ruqa'a Nazm* Hoor *Begum*' goes as below:

Come! So that I can see you Perhaps in this way my agony will decrease

Someone on page forty has written the following sentence in pencil:

"There were no pages beyond this, the matter on page forty and forty nine have been combined."

This Miracle of combining the odds will be seen in all the handwritten copies which are made from this.[74] In complete printed copies, the content from page 41–48 is not given in the handwritten copies. The handwritten

72. *Ruqa't e Begmat,* Avadh (Raza Library)) 1.

73. *If someone is writing to her then she must ask me to write (the reply)*
In the morning I place the pen in my ear and go out (Ghalib*).*

74. *Ruqa'at-e-Begmat* (Handwritten) 81–84, *Tohfaey Sultani* (Handwritten) 96–100, *of 'Mukhzan e Israr e Sultani'* (Handwritten), 69–72.

copy of *Mukhzan e Israr e Sultani* entered the Asfia library in 1939.[75] The handwritten copy of *Tohfaey Sultani* in the hand of Hafiz Abdullah Rampuri was written in 1934.[76] Only the size, format, and paper of these handwritten copies are changed, the order of letters is the same, and they are likely written by the same writer.

Proving that the printed copy of *Ruqa'at-e-Begmat* was a copy of the original manuscript is not so easy, because the copy which is to be authenticated as original is unavailable. However, logical reasoning can guide us, and the compiler's claim that those 'dilapidated termite ridden parts' which were purchased as books from Lucknow in and around 1892[77] hold much importance.

The content of the letters reveals that they were sent from Lucknow to Calcutta, and if they were found in Lucknow then they must not be original letters. It is possible that these were individual copies of the letters which were recovered together, or it must be a collection which was prepared by an unknown person, who kept the original letters in front. If one looks carefully, it will be revealed that both these situations are possible, meaning that the first part or '*Qism Awwal*'[78] is the manuscript of the letters of Begums. The letters which were sent were copies, and the collection compiled by the King was created by keeping these letters before him. The second part, which is called by the compiler as '*Qism Doom*,'[79] was the collection of letters copied by the King. The compilation of this did not require any particular intention, its compilation was natural, and he did not do it willingly—he was bound to do it. He had to write replies to such letters. Had this been just a formality, then there would have been no need to keep copies, but the poetry and its elegant writing indicates that these were done with much effort. The receipt of

75. Letter of the Librarian No. 65–66/TA2864 dated 25th January 1966 in the name of the Author.

76. Handwritten list of the '*Urdu Makhtootat*', Raza Library, Rampur.

77. *Ruqa'at-e-Begmat,* Avadh (Raza) 1.

78. *Ibid,* 3–120.

79. *Ibid,* 102–20.

the letter was sent immediately, while for the reply some time was promised. The original letter was kept close to the Begmats' heart, and thus he took them down in his diary (*bayaz*). In the dilapidated pages which were found by Imtiaz Ali Khan, the questions and answers were written randomly. The compiler, when putting them in the form of a book, collected the 'questions' or king's letter in one place, regarding it as '*Qism Doom*' in the last, and the answers which should have been in Part One were kept in the first part, considering the name of the book. In this collection there are 20 letters of the King, and all their questions and answers are inside. There are 71 letters of Begmats, of which two are of Navrozi Begum.[80] These are not in reply to any letter. In '*Qism Doom*', among all the 20 letters, not a single letter addressed to Navrozi Begum is found.

According to the narration of the compiler, the dilapidated parts were termite ridden, and were dispersed and scattered. The truth of this statement is found in the fact that these could not be compiled correctly.[81] Had those parts been intact, then the questions and answers of every letter would have been found, but whatever is available now is enough to prove it was a manuscript.

After proving a manuscript to be a manuscript, the name of the writer with whom this diary (*bayaz*) should be associated must be investigated. Ashir's link with Navrozi Begum is proved by the evidence of *Tarikh e Firaq*. The same Ashir was linked with Shaida Begum before 1857 as is obvious from the following statement:

> "...your two letters came ...through Mushi Safdar. Ashir read them out, my soul was pleased very much..."[82]

---

80. In *Ruqa'at-e-Begmat* on page 89 & 98. For the last part of page 98 see the bookish detail *of Tarikh e Firaq* . MWASA-1276 (Kuda Baksh Library. Patna)

81. *Ibid.*

82. On page 19 of 'Begmat e Avadh Ke Khutoot' while copying this letter the compiler wrote such a sentence which indicates that Shaida Begum was ignorant and the letter was read out by Ashir. 22.

Ashir also used to read the letters of Nawab Munna Jaan Saheba as shown below:

> "...Your...respectable letter... came, it ignited the flame of love, your pupil Ashir read it out to me...heart became very sad."[83]

Farkhanda Mahal claimed that the following couplet is her composition, but:

> "*As I quote My life is ending, my heart goes out*
> *Someone inside is squeezing my heart.*"[84]

Tarikh e Firaq Navrozi Begum has associated this couplet with Ashir when she says:

> "Ashir*'s couplet is as per my plight:*
> *My life is ending, my heart goes out*
> *Someone inside is squeezing my heart.*"[85]

This couplet, in the beginning, was part of the poetic letter of Shaida Begum.[86] In the same book it is often written on behalf of Farkhanda Mahal[87] and Navrozi Begum *alias* Hoor.[88]

This confrontation, coincidence, plagiarism, prose and poetry, rhyming, addressing and style of writing is found everywhere, and is more than enough to regard Ashir as the writer of the *Ruqa'at-e-Begmat* of the illiterate Begums. In confirmation of the narratives of the commentators, printed statement of the Begums like "I have composed this Ghazal",[89] "I have composed this poetic

83. *Ibid*, 96.
84. *Ibid*, 67.
85. Tarikh e *Firaq* (Handwritten). Tarikh e *Firaq*. MWASA-1276 (Kuda Baksh Library. Patna).
86. *Ibid*, 7.
87. *Ibid*, 67.
88. *Ibid*, 89.
89. *Ibid*, 14, 15, 30, 59.

poem"[90], and "This letter is written by me"[91] is unacceptable evidence, because the faithful belief in it suits those who read these letters for leisure, and not those investigators who, on the basis of study and comparison, attempt to reach a certain conclusion. The aforementioned claims of the Begmats are astonishing, because making such claims without a solid ground is unnatural. Ashir was not gifted with extraordinary ingenuity, but in his enthusiasm to please the King, and like Insha who, in search of a new witticism every day had become crazy, similarly Ashir too in search of a new letter and a new style daily[92] was misled, which is a matter of disappointment. Anis learned from his own similes, Ghalib for his audience made changes in his own '*qasidas*', and Ashir too, if for his enticing style of expression, had used the letters as his practicing board,[93] then neither is this coincidence bad, nor can it be regarded as plagiarism. If Ashir is made the subject of investigation, then his services would be far superior to most of his contemporaries.

A TALE

For the utility of Wajid Ali Shah's collections, and for understanding the events from the beginning until now, the events can be presented in the form of a tale:

> Ashir is a professional letter writer. Shaida Begum, Navrozi Begum and Farkhanda Mahal are three illiterate Begums. To read the letters from the King and to give their reply they take the services of Ashir. Ashir goes to their residence, reads out the letter to them, and writes replies for them.[94] If it was difficult to write a reply immediately, then he either brings the original letter with him or he takes it down in his diary (*bayaz*). Later,

90. *Ibid*, 7.

91. *Ibid*, 63.

92. *Tarikh e Firaq* (Handwritten), 45–46.

93. See for example, the rhyming words like '*nazeer*', '*munir*', '*zameer*', '*zaheer*' first on page 19 of *Ruqa'at-e-Begmat* and then on page 71–72 of *Tarikh e Firaq* for the several rhyming statements.

94. *Tarikh e Firaq* (Handwritten), 145.

keeping it in front he writes replies. As in the reply some ornate expression is required, hence first he prepares a manuscript in his diary and then by keeping that manuscript before him he writes the reply. Quality of the letter remains consistent with its remuneration. In some replies there used to be prose, poem, Ghazal etc. and there used to be much stress on elegant writing[95] and in some only a few lines were scribbled.[96] Navrozi Begum keeps her letters secret from Shaida Begum and Shaida Begum kept her letters away from Farkhanda Mahal hence none of them knew as to what was written for each other. In such a situation it was quite possible for Ashir to write the words, and expressions which he first wrote for Shaida Begum could repeat them for Navrozi Begum and Farkhanda Mahal.[97] This he does when he wants to ignore something or looking at the excellence of expression it becomes impossible for him to write different from it or better than it. But this he does at long intervals because he is writing all the letters for such a person who expects a new letter every day and dislikes confrontation or coincidence. That person is not expecting a letter from the letter-writer but from his ignorant Begums, and expects it in 'first person', voicing the tales of separation and desertion and secretive talks.[98] The letter writer, by imagining himself in place of a *Begum*, writes what he thinks the best. If it comes to poetry and Ghazal*s* then he displays his art of writing. He does not keep his name (Takhaallus) in the last line (*maqta*) as the king is not interested in him. For instance, '*narration of that fairy face and then his own story (verse)*'...he wants to hear his love story from his Begum but if the language of the Begum is not plausible, for

95. In 1273 for Shaida Begum and in 1275 for Navrozi Begum the letters were written with much care. See the *Ruqa'at-e-Begmat* alongwith the details of *Tarikh e Firaq*.

96. In *Ruqa'at-e-Begmat* other than letters of Shaida Begum and Hoor *Begum* (real name Navrozi Begum) the letters of other Begmats is also in the same style.

97. In *Ruqa'at-e-Begmat*

Letter of Navrozi Begum written on page 98 is original. Some letters of Shaida Begum on page 45 &50 and the letter of *Muna Jaan Saheb is* extracted from page 96.

The starting address of Shaida Begum*'s* letter on page 52–53 are used in the letter of Navrozi Begum page 14–15 *Tarikhe Firaq* (Handwritten).

The starting addressing of letter of Farkhanda Mahal on page 66–68 are again seen in the letter of Navrozi Begum on page 36–37 , Tarikh e *Firaq* (Handwritten).

98. *Tarikh e Firaq* (Handwritten), 74–77.

> example '*Zaban e yaar man turki wa munn turki nami danam*' (my friend's language is turki which I don't know), then Ashir through his good services overcomes this flaw. Meanwhile during that period mutiny breaks. After 1857 when the devastated Begums return, he helps Navrozi Begum by all means (*damey darmey sukhane*). And in return of this help due to the tender age and inexperience of the *Begum*, he gets so much control that he makes recommendations for himself in the words of *Begum*, and as compensation he acquires the right to write his name in the end of the letter.[99]

This merry go round of life, which went from the King to the letter-writer to the *Begum*, back to the letter-writer and finally back to the King, continued for an unknown period of time. Ultimately it ended, but the diary in which Ashir used to write his manuscripts reached the hands of a copywriter in a dilapidated, scattered, condition.[100] He regarded it as an 'unexpected blessing', because he could reserve its right of publication (copyright) for himself, and thus could publish it. If one observes closely, it is not difficult to find out that it is not a collection of letters, but the diary of a letter-writer[101] who neither cares for it nor he is capable of doing it. If in any letter, the beginning or ending is missing, then without any hesitation he combines both, and if there is no date given then he easily adds a date. [102]

The letters were published, and they became the center of attraction for historians and commentators. The historian neither understands that there was no trend of education among the women of that period,[103] nor

99. In almost every letter of *Tarikh e Firaq* this happened.There is nothing as such in the letters of *Ruqa'at-e-*Begmats. Perhaps the reason was that there was no need to write such repeated words in the manuscript. May be by the way it was written in original letters. *Tarikh e Firaq* (Handwritten) is the copy of the original letters.

100. *Ruqa'at-e-Begmat,* 3.

101. In the Preface of *Ruqa'at e Begumat* the compiler assures that he has arranged the dilapidated papers with 'minute observation', 'deep study', 'with excellent use of time and hard work', 'and with 'endeavor and extreme diligence.'

102. For verifying evidence see the book detail of Tarikh e *Firaq*.

103. *Tarikh e Avadh,* Maulvi Md. Najmul Ghani Khan. Munshi Naval Kishore Publication. Lucknow. 1919. Volume 5, 47–109.

understands that the internal evidence of the letter contradicts his own claims. His intention was the creation of a romantic world. He ultimately succeeds in doing this by the collection of these letters. But through the immaturity of the historians, the seal of verification is given to it, and people who regard him as trustworthy do not bother to question him.[104] By the printing and rarity of *Ruqa'at-e-Begmat*, it is revealed that the common people and the elite were equally interested in it. Another person who was familiar with it perceived the golden quality of it after about thirty years, and instead of having it printed again and being accused of interfering with the copyright, as he was himself a writer he started copying down and compiling from the printed copy as per his needs. He provided the same book with different names to Asifia Library, Loharu Library, Library Habib Ganj, and Library Rampur. He must have gained as much profit through the right of publication and right of compilation which would have been gained by the first publisher. Being of a similar temperament, it was not a difficult task for him, and because name of the writer and date of publication is not given on the handwritten copies, it was possible that it could have been written by one person, and been associated with someone else's name. The manuscript, though compiled from the printed copy, but the intention behind was that it may be taken as being compiled from the 'dilapidated' papers. But the one who wrote it was so selfish that he did not bother for a complete printed copy, hence all the handwritten copies which were taken down and compiled from the incomplete printed copies carried the same mistakes as that of original one.

---

104. Maulvi Najmul Ghani Khan, the owner of *Tarikh e Avadh* does not even give the name of the 'collection'. (See Volume 5, 106–08.)But after him different people have mentioned the specimen of elegant writing of Shaida Begum *by* quoting some mentionable addresses like '(*Mehr peshani, chehra* Noor*ani, abru kamaan, teer e mishgan, ...pariyon mein* Sulaiman, *tum par* Allah *ki amaan...*). In *Tarikh e Firaq* (Handwritten) the prolonged addressing (Khitab) is worth mentioning because it is with these 'addresses' that Ashir has served Navrozi Begum.In *Ruqa'at-e-Begmat* his letter is in the name of Shaida Begum. See *Tarikh e Avadh,* Volume, 5, 107, 27.

When the copy of Imtiaz Ali Khan became rare, then after a long time, in 1366 A.H. (1978) another publisher thought of publishing another collection. But this 'different' collection is not the manuscript of Ashir. Its only quality is that one has come out from a private library, and another has come from a famous writer's pen that has made it worth publishing.[105] This collection was published, and incorrect ideas were further confirmed and verified. Serving the literature is a commendable job, and anyone who is associated with the job or is included by the way is praiseworthy. In this collection, like *Ruqa'at-e-Begmat*, there are also letters of the King, and it would have been proper had this collection been named *Shah e Avadh Ke Khutoot.* But Imtiaz Ali Khan did not want to call his collection *Ruqa'at e Wajid Ali Shah* instead of *Ruqa'at-e-Begmat* nor did Mufti Intezamullah Shahabi want to call his collection *Shah e Avadh Ke Khutoot* instead of *Begmat e Avadh Ke Khutoot.* The reason is that the charm and romance which is in the word '*Begum*' is not found in the word '*Shah.*' The short names of books as mentioned in the Introduction and Foreword attract and impress upon the minds, but even then, it was not successful.

The outcome of this tale is that often, baseless fame instills misunderstanding, and if this fame is connected with the names of Wajid Ali Shah and his Begmats then it becomes all the more necessary to be cautious. It is the beauty of this belief that Begmats are still being called writers and poets, and had there not been the self-compiled collections of Wajid Ali Shah in their original condition, then it would have become very difficult to dispel this misunderstanding. The 'dilapidated papers' of Imtiaz Ali Khan and the 'personal collection' of *Mufti Sahab* are out of my reach, but the collections of Wajid Ali Shah still adorn the trustworthy libraries. It will be our fault if, in our haste and selfishness, we do not gain anything out of it. The idea of the Begmats being writers and poets would have been in favour of the King because had they actually been writers and poets, it would have been possible

105. *Begmat e Avadh Ke Khutoot,* Munshi Intezamullah Shahabi. Farooqui Press. Delhi (1366 A.H.). 5–6.

to say that due to their affection and attachment with the King they were greatly benefitted. Alas except for a few this cannot be said.

KING AS A COMPILER

As a compiler, it was possible that the King, as in the compilation of *Ruqa't e Badr*, would have deleted those phrases which indicated that the Begmats were illiterate. However, he preferred not to delete anything. For instance, many times Ashir, for the sake of rhyming, referred to the King as '*Bilquis e Shayem.*' (*Bilquis* is a feminine name) The King did not like this terminology. He warned Navrozi Begum that this mistake should not be repeated. The *Begum* was very much afraid and resolved that it would not happen again, and instantly in all the letters where the objectionable word appeared, it was rewritten as '*Sikander Shayem*' (*Sikander* means lucky) and the letters were resent.[106] But in the collection, the original letters were included and even to date, the word '*Bilquis Shayem*' is mentioned.[107] After seeing this example of academic uprightness, we can believe that if some letters or statements were not included in the collection, this was due to a mistake and not done intentionally. It is also the demand of academic uprightness that the contemptible and disgraceful words or subjects which were included by Ashir to invoke emotions[108] or where Ashir or other writers[109] had included it to lengthen the letters, should have been deleted at the time of compilation. But the King did not do this, and included the writings in their original form.

Now the conclusion has been drawn that the letters, which were so far associated with the Begmats, were in fact not written by them. But does this conclusion take away the worth and importance of those letters? Doubtlessly, the answer is no. Though there was no '*Begmati language*' in those letters,

106. *Tarikh e Firaq* (Handwritten), 298–99.

107. *Ibid*, 273 & 282.

108. *Ibid*, 107 & 210.

109. Not the abundance of formal greetings in *Tarikh e Jamshedi* (Handwritten). Md.Wajid Ali Shah Akhtar. 1276h. (Avadh).

they are the letters of the Begmats and reflections of the '*Lucknavi language*' which gave birth to writers like Sarwar and poets like *Shauq*. No matter how impressive and beautiful one is, he or she cannot dominate the Mirror. The Mirror reflects something more. Hence, in the Mirror of those letters, other than the whispering talks of husband and wife, there will be seen the etiquette of the Lucknow nobility, their amity and companionship, their interests and pastimes. This importance of the letters is above the common mentality which traded in those letters, and the name '*Tarikh*' given to them by the first compiler was forgotten.

WAJID ALI SHAH'S POETRY

His Studentship

For the introduction of Urdu poets, it is necessary to trace their line of studentship. For Wajid Ali Shah 'Akhtar', this is all the more important; like other facets of his life, this aspect is also not without contradiction. As per the latest information, Wajid Ali Shah started composing verses under the guidance of *Aminud Daulah Imdad Hussain Khan*.[110] By way of proof, the '*Mahal Khana e Shahi*' was produced,[111] in which the names of the book *Meezan* (Altab?) and *Sharah Asbab* are mentioned[112] which are not poetry books. In another tradition, there is no mention of proof. Lala Sri Ram along with other commentators have regarded Muzaffar Ali Khan Asir as Wajid Ali Shah's *ustad*.[113] But neither Asir himself, nor his pupil Amir, and not

---

110. G.D. Bhatnagar, *Administration of Oudh Under* Wajid Ali Shah. Thesis for Ph.D. of Lucknow University. 2.

111. On page 125 of *Mahal Khana e Shahi* the word Master (Ustad) is written with *Aminud Daulah'* name.

112. *Mahal Khanaey Shahi,* Mirza Fida Ali Khanjar. Naami Press. Lucknow. 1934. 128.

113. Lala Sri Ram. *Khamkhanaey Javed* (5 Volumes) Mukhzan Press. Delhi. On page 299 Sri Ram has not given any proof but it is not difficult to look for one. During that period when the first volume of this comment was published in Magazine *Zamana,* Kanpur in the essay titled '*Hazrat Asir Maghfoor Luckhnavi*' by Janab Fazil Lucknavi who was the pupil of *Asir,* was published in many installments. In the debate of Ishq Nama there has been the mention

even Wajid Ali Shah have confirmed this. During the period when Wajid Ali Shah started showing interest in poetic composition, the congregations (*mehfil*) of Nasikh and Aatish were still in existence. If Aatish is regarded as Wajid Ali Shah's *ustad*, which is often said,[114] then it is possible because at that time Aatish was popular,[115] and *Asir* had not yet reached that height of popularity. When Wajid Ali Shah first summoned him it was to hear his composition or to present his own composition before him, and not to take lessons from him.[116] If such companionship is called '*Mashweraey Sukhan*', then other poets too attended such congregations.[117] Out of these poets no one was elevated beyond the status of 'distinguished companion' (*Masahib e Khas*) and this was the time when the King was very pleased with *Asir.*[118] The King, in the Preface of 'Irshad Khaqani' has mentioned only the name of Fateh ud Daulah Barq as the master of the art of prosody and rhyming and admitted his studentship.

After Irshad Khaqani the King has, at many places, regarded Barq as his *ustad*, and wherever his name is mentioned it is mentioned with reverence. In the following verses he expresses about him after twenty five years of his eternal separation:

Fatehudd Daulah was fairy-born (lovely)
He was my appreciator and my master

---

of a misunderstanding created by this essay. The second misunderstanding also is seemingly created by same Fazil Sahab. Because only he tried to verify it, without any proper proof or extract he writes "However he was the pupil of Asir which is also verified in the 'Qasaids' (Persian & Urdu)." See '*Zamana*' Kanpur Issue July, 1910, page 14. In the essay there is no reference of any 'Qaseeda' nor the writer of the Author came across any such 'qaseeda' in which Asir had mentioned about the studentship of the Wajid Ali Shah.

114. *Aab e Baqa*, Khwaja Abdul Rauf Ishrat. Naami Press. Lucknow 1918. 16–17.

115. Wajid Ali Shah's couplet indicates: *the compositions of all the foregoing poets is cancelled Those who are a bit intelligent purchase the 'Diwan' of Aatish.* (*Sukhan Ashraf*).

116. *Durrul Taj*, Md. Zafar Ali Khan Asir. Matbaey Sultani. Lucknow 1270h. 62–72.

117. *Durrul Taj*, 108–12, 129–32, 236.

118. Wajid Ali Shah got published Asir's '*Masnavi*' and '*Diwan*' during this period.

I learned the art of poetry from him
He was my closest friend
His pen name was 'Barq'
He was with me in the fort
This was the end, he pleased before leaving
He died with me in the prison
May Khuda give him place in heaven
'Hoors' *be by his side in the grave*[119]

The Diwans of both Barq in 1269 A.H. (1853) and of *Asir* in 1271 A.H. (1855) were published by Matbaey Sultani. The supervisor of the publication house, Amir Ali Khan Hilal, composed a '*tarikh*' (date-wise composition) for both of them. He regarded Barq as 'Ustad Shah e Hind'[120] and Asir as 'Dast e Badshah wa Zaban e Wazir'[121] because *Asir* was engaged as an assistant[122] which was not an ordinary post.

The mastery of Barq and the studentship of Wajid Ali Shah was as formal as the mastery of Wajid Ali Shah himself, and as that of other poets like Jahan Quder Nayyer,[123] Amirud Daulah Amir Hasan Khan Seher,[124] Maqbool ud Daulah Mehdi Ali Khan Qubool,[125] Aftabud Daulah Qalq,[126] Taa'sudd

---

119. *Sabatul Quloob* (Handwritten), Md. Wajid Ali Shah Akhtar. 1304, h. (Avadh) Volume 1, 13.

120. *Diwan e* Barq,Md. Raza Khan Barq. Matbaey Sultani. Lucknow. 1269h. 672.

121. *Riyaz Musannaf,* Md. Muzaffar Ali Khan Asir. Baksh Khan. Lucknow 1271. 536.

122. *Mara'tul Awza.* (Handwritten) Lalaji S/o Seetal Prasad. (Raza) 73.

123. *Kitabul Marasi,* Sir Mirza Jahan Quder Nayyer. Shamsul Mutaley. Hyderabad. 48, 104. Majmuaey Nazm, 32.

124. The descendants of Raja Sahab Mehmoodabad narrate that on the manuscripts of the late Raja the corrections are made by Wajid Ali Shah's pen. The Author could not get these manuscripts.

125. *Bani,* - MWASA- Sultani Publication. Calcutta, 1877. (Khuda Baksh, Avadh). 239.

126. *Tarikh e Adab Urdu,* Ram Babu Saxena (Translator. Mirza Md. Askari. Naval Kissore Press. Lucknow. 1937. 262–63.

Daulah Aish,[127] Gauhar Ali Mushir,[128] Imdad Ali Ashir,[129] Laaiqud Daulah Shahid,[130] Muzaffar Ali Hunar,[131] Md. Abbas Shaaz,[132] and other persons[133] of '*Saba Siyara*', royal associates,[134] and the princes. Had Barq perused the compositions of Wajid Ali Shah deeply, which was expected of his status, then it is unclear why there were such flaws in the 'Diwans' and '*Masnavis*' of Wajid Ali Shah, which were later, after gaining maturity, corrected by the King himself. For the external attributes of his poetry, it was not necessary that he should have been a poet of the category of Nasikh. The literary ambience of Lucknow impacted Mir and MuShafi, while Wajid Ali Shah was a follower of Nasikh and Aatish. Though the King was a pupil of Barq,[135] while mentioning the names of his prominent disciples like Afrad Ali Ausat Rashk, Zamin Ali Jalal, and Aman Ali Seher, Barq did not mention the King's name, which is regretful.[136] But perhaps this happened because the relationship of Wajid Ali Shah with Barq in the field of poetry was formal. He did not develop the traditions of Barq, at places he claims innovations.[137] However in the compositions of Wajid Ali Shah there are traces of his master and mannerisms, knowledge, modesty, grace, affection and humility are the virtues which are jointly shared by both the master and the pupil.[138] Half of

---

127. *Bani,* - MWASA- Sultani Publication. Calcutta, 1877. (Khuda Baksh, Avadh). 236.
128. *Ibid*, 245. On Masnavi Mushir, (Handwritten), Property, Khuda Baksh Library, Patna, the corrections made by the King can be seen.
129. *Tarikh e Firaq* (Handwritten), 29–30.
130. *Ibid*, 246.
131. *Ibid*, 246. *Yaadgar e Zaigham,* 383.
132. *Ibid*, 246–47.
133. Qamar Mazmun. Md. Wajid Ali Shah Akhtar. Matbaey Sultani. Calcutta.1281h. 472.
134. *Jaan e Alam,* Maulvi Abdul Haleem Sharar- Adaraey Faroghe Urdu. Lahore. 1951. 80–81
135. *Lucknow Ka Dabistan e Shayeri,* Dr. Abullais Siddiqui. Gilani Press. Lahore. 1955. 411.
136. *Ibid*, 414.
137. *Kulliyat e* Akhtari. Md. Wajid Ali Shah Akhtar. Matbaey Sultani. Calcutta. (Khuda Baksh Library, Patna, Salar Jung Museum Hyderabad, Raza Library, Rampur). 82 & 91.
138. On the blank title page of *Diwan e* Barq (Printed) (property Salar Jung Museum), by way of Preface some lines are saved in the pen of Barq. To understand the character of Barq

Wajid Ali Shah's life in spite of all its luxuries[139] and sufferings[140] was spent under the patronship of Barq, and other than art of poetry it is not surprising to say that he also learned the art of war from him.[141]

POETRY AND CRAFTSMANSHIP

One of the contemporary and native commentators has declared Wajid Ali Shah as without a master '*Bay-ustad.*' Perhaps this misunderstanding is created by the King himself as appears from the following verses:

I am not a pupil of anyone
From the beginning my temperament is poetic
My nature is preoccupied with
The spirit of love which is in my heart
Often just for fun
I compose some poetry[142]
Khuda is witness that I am adorned by the poets
I am ignorant and they are my learned poets[143]

Though this is correct, like the Preface of *Irshad e Khaqani*, the doubtful narration may lead to many misunderstandings. Out of unsuccessful lovers,

---

this Preface and Diwan is in addition to those discussions which are narrated by Wajid Ali Shah and others.

139. *Masnavi* Mushir (Handwritten), Gauhar Ali Mushir (Khuda Baksh) 1276h. 123.

140. *Huzn e* Akhtari, Md. Wajid Ali Shah Akhtar. 1306h. (Raza). 41–42.

141. Barq was a master of his time in fighting with dagger and in martial art and the regiment of '*Maimanaey Shahi*' and '*Fauj e Qaa'ani*' were entrusted to him. See, *Afzalul Tawarikh,* Munshi Ram Sahay Tamanna. Matbaey Tmannaey. Lucknow 1879. 136–48 & *Khamkhanaey Javed* Lala Sri Ram. (5 Volumes) Mukhzan Press. Delhi. 555.

142. *Daryaey Taa'shuqq.* Md. Waji Ali Shah Akhtar. Matbaey Sultani. Lucknow. (Avadh, Khuda Baksh) 11.

143. *Adab Ka Maqsad.* Dr. Syed Noorul Hasan Hashmi. Hindustan Kitab Ghar. Lucknow 1956. 176.

when Umraul Qais and Mir Taqi Mir had to face failure, they did not resort to composing by learning the art of poetry (*Funn e Sher goey*). But when Wajid Ali Shah came across such a challenging situation, then he decided to include it in his poetry. A poet has innate power over the arrangement and selection of his words and thoughts, like a weaver bird has the ability and skill to weave his nest. The master does not do more than correcting the language and the narration.[144] Wajid Ali Shah's narrative, that he was poetic minded and romantic from the beginning, is not wrong. His interest in fine arts, worshipping the beauty, the wish to love and to be loved, intensity of taste for aesthetics, to be influenced and to be influential are all the conditions which are found in a poet, and which had impacted his feelings from the beginning up to the end. For their expression, it was not necessary that there should be the ambience of Lucknow or that he should fall in love with some Moti Khanam. Natural feelings find a way to express themselves. For Wajid Ali Shah, Moti Khanam's love became an excuse.[145] It is a matter of regret that the plant which needed natural surroundings and indulgence, was given by the wise men the environment of a laboratory and watered with chemicals. Consequently the plant, instead of reaching its full growth, withered. Wajid Ali Shah's advice:

Good subject, new composition, proper couplet
Akhtar! While are composing a Ghazal *take care of all this.*

This is such advice which, not surprisingly, must have come from his '*ustad*' because these attributes are related to prosody and rhyming. Wajid Ali Shah received this art from Barq.[146] And if all these attributes are in a poet and the couplet is ineffective, then that couplet is not worthwhile. To

144. *Muqadamaey Sher o Shayari,* Khwaja Altaf Hussain Hali. Maktabaey Jaddi. Lahore. 1953. 180–81.

145. *Mahal Khana e Shahi,* Mirza Fida Ali Khanjar. Nami Press. Lucknow. (1934). 15–16.

146. Irshad Khaqani, Md. Wajid Ali Shah Akhtar. Lucknow. 1269. (National Library, Calcutta). 3–5.

inculcate aesthetic beauty in verses and the ability to compose swiftly are divine attributes; they are god-gifted and not 'acquired'. Wajid Ali Shah, for these virtues, was the pupil of Allah.

THE HEIGHT AND THE DEPTH

In Wajid Ali Shah's compositions, there are some couplets which fit the high standard of poetry. But he has made excuses for such couplets:

My heartache gave me shudders
My tears made my cheeks wet
Dear! out of helplessness
I picked up my pen to express my feelings
Due to intensity of sorrow I wrote frankly
Thus excuse my poetry here[147]

And where there is an abundance of good subjects, new poetry, and fine examples and metaphors, he has himself appreciated it:

Now act with the Hindi instrument in such a way
That it affects the heart
All the colors should be shown
The poetry creates such an ambience
Friends should have this voice on their tongue saying
Great Praise! Praise! And Praise![148]

These are two types of poetry, of which one is regarded by the King as 'poetry' (and in our view it is craftsmanship). The other type is poetry in our view, but to the poet these are ordinary things. This gives rise to a debate regarding which much has been written.[149] For us, it is not necessary to

147. Sheva-e-Faiz; Md. Wajid Ali Shah Akhtar. Publication Sultani. Calcutta 1277. 19.
148. *Ibid*, 142.
149. For these debates note *Hamari Shayari* and *Muqaddamaey Sher o Shayari.*

agree with the views of the poet. It is enough to know that nature has gifted Wajid Ali Shah with a poetic mind and heart, but at the same time such an environment is given in which it becomes necessary to acquire the art. The poet often composed such verses naturally which reflected his innate interests, and often, in a bid to achieve the applause of his fellows, he kept in mind the artistic points but forgot the real motive and purpose of the poetry.

For the Ghazal compositions of Mir it is said: 'when he reaches the height it is abundant and when he falls below then also it is profuse'.

Wajid Ali Shah's *masnavi* writing resembles that of Mir i.e. when he goes higher it has no limits but if he goes low (below norm) then too it has no end. This particular resemblance with that of Mir's Ghazal composition is found in all the masnavi,[150] of Wajid Ali Shah – and they are mostly 'imbalanced' (ghair mutvazun). For illustration, a verse (*sarapa*) is presented which describes an event the poet had witnessed, but while expressing this he is seen to switch between real poetry and artistic poetry:

When all the beauties gathered
This youth saw something
That one beauty came forward
She looked golden like colours of spring
Wow! Her age was eleven
Youth was approaching and the
Days of indulgence
From top to bottom she bloomed like a flower
Around her neck was the garland of 'juhi'
She was gorgeous, beautiful and attractive
Her walk was also killing
She had a gold collar of moon and stars
The chain of which hung on her back

150. The Urdu term denotes a long poem which relates a story, collection of events, some biography etc. The couplets run in thousands. (Translator).

There was a golden amulet on her braid
As if it came down from sky
There was a necklace of 'Nad e Ali'
Looking at it impatience grew
In gentle walk the hanging 'dupatta'
Shine of golden powder on forehead
The whiteness of teeth worth praising
The signs of youth were appearing
The chest which was shining and envying the moon
It was not for the 'mehram'
In one dress two pearls
In one branch two fruits
In one branch there were two apples
On the chest there were two moons[151]

This illustrative description of the female figure was probably prepared in reply to '*Bahar e Ishq*'. The fact is that Shauqq's *masnavi*, though being so indecent and short, based on some artistic features it is 'poetic'. Wajid Ali Shah's illustrative description, though cultured, was more poetic than necessary. In appreciation of breasts, Shauqq says this much:

Two breasts on chest precious
High, smooth, firm, hard and round.[152]

Wajid Ali Shah has used several examples and metaphors for one quality, and did not care that lengthy expressions inhibit high-flown language. Had he wished, he would have used the above mentioned couplet as the reply to Shauqq's couplet. But Shauqq was often unable to reply, and often Wajid

---

151. *Sheva-e-Faiz,* 178–79. Sheva-e-Faiz; Md. Wajid Ali Shah Akhtar. Publication Sultani. Calcutta1277. 178–79.

152. *Bahar e Ishq,* Hakim Tasauq Hussain Khan alias Nawab Mirza Shauqq. 1276. (Khuda Baksh). Heroine's figuring (*sarapa*) in the beginning of the *masnavi.*

Ali Shah also failed to respond. The measure of Wajid Ali Shah's height and depth can be made by perusing Shauqq's *masnavis.*

DEPTH AND GIRTH

The personality of a poet is the center of his poetic creations. The flow of thoughts and events, no matter where they originate from, come to the same point and settle in the same whirlpool. Once out of the whirlpool, things may not retain their original form. If this is true then it reveals the swiftness of the whirlpool and its individuality. An unknown number of events led to the creation of *Kulliyat e* Mir, but Mir absorbed all the events and when he returned it, they formed an eternal reality and the personality of Mir. Intellectuals have regarded this reality as the depth of the composition, and the 'girth' and reflection of personality as the colour (style) of the composition. It is a different thing that in any poetic creation, so much is universal that one cannot identify the personality of the poet. But the reflection of the creator is always Mirrored in its creation, and his success depends on how much he has assimilated his self into it.

In Wajid Ali Shah's compositions, the elements of depth and girth are few because there was a very intense desire in him to dominate his composition, and he always feared that his composition should not dominate him. Perhaps this urge for fame is found in every poet, other poets dominate their last lines (*maqta*), but most of Wajid Ali Shah's compositions are like *maqta. Maqta* is the legacy of Urdu and Persian poetry. A poet does not compose to write *maqta* or to gain fame. His nature incites him to say something, and he becomes bound to compose poetry. Wajid Ali Shah's starting verses, most of which are found in *Diwan e Som* (and some in *Sukhan Ashraf* and *Guldastaey Aashiqan*), were composed in this environment, and it can be easily seen that they were not composed to fulfill the requirement of some '*mushaira*' or '*radif*'. There is freshness, clarity and enthusiasm in these verses. The poet was not aware of the fact that he was a 'poet'. This feeling was born due to the acquisition of art, practice, and real or unreal applause, and the more intense this feeling became, the more the fine subject, smart composition, and the poetry of '*radif*' and '*qafia*' progressed.[153] This speed of progress was normal. First an inheritor, then the feeling of an oppressed King and the desire that '*kalamul muluk*' (King's composition) should be '*mulukul kalam*' (King of Composition) worked wonders. Instead of going to battle (*razm aarai*), in which there was lesser chance of fame and more danger of suicide, he started the development of congregations (*bazm arai*) for better time:

Good that aggrieved like me has the passion for poetry
By verses I will earn much name and fame[154]

Contemporary newspapers demanded that "It is the job of the kings to remain engaged in the administration of the country and not in poetry and verses...His Highness must give attention to the administrative affairs so that the country is well governed."[155]

This advice was better for those kings who were kings by nature, and the courtesans had made him a poet. This advice was of no use for him who was a poet by nature, and was made King by the environment. After ten years of kingship Wajid Ali Shah reached the point from where he had started:

Akhtar! I am not in need of worldly wealth
I want paper, ink and pen[156]

---

153. Nazm Namvar,Md. Wajid Ali Shah Akhtar. Matbaey Sultani. Calcutta. 1287. (Raza, Ittihadiya, Khuda Baksh) page 283. *Though so much time elapsed Akhtar but up till now – The young heart becomes impatient due to poetic expression.*

154. *Sukhan Ashraf,* Md. Wajid Ali Shah Akhtar. Matbaey Sultani, Lucknow. 13.

155. *Muasir* (Monthly, Patna) Issue December 1942, 23. Referring to Asadul Akhbar (Agra) Issue No. 118.

156. *Sheva-e-Faiz,* Md. Wajid Ali Shah Akhtar. Publication Sultani. Calcutta 1277. 412.

But during this temporary kingship and thereafter, Wajid Ali Shah was not free of the thought that he was a King, and that his words and actions must be different from the commoners. This feeling gave birth to *masnavis* like *Ishq Nama* and *Huzn e* Akhtari, in which he relates both the brighter and the darker side of the life of Kings in the form of a lesson-giving autobiography.

DELIBERATION AND ART

In poetry composition, taking care of the artistic points and attempting to reveal one's own personality indicate though that the poet has deliberated consciously. This 'deliberation' is not poetic but academic and superficial, in which the attention of the poet is not on verses but on his own self and in a style which is different from others. The feelings and thoughts which are retrieved from the deep study of human nature and the revelations of nature are finely expressed by the poet in this poetic style.

For a thinker it is not necessary that he himself must have experienced the events. If he is directly aware of those conditions, then through his poetic expertise he expresses those conditions. Not many poets would have even touched wine, but there is rarely a poet who has not composed at least one or two verses while intoxicated. Since the zenith of elegy composition, there are hardly any poets who have any knowledge of the events of Karbala. Among such poets was *Anis*, who brought before us those happenings as if we have not just heard, but have seen them. This attribute in poetry comes not from knowledge but from 'deliberation'. Both Anis and Wajid Ali Shah gained knowledge about the events of Karbala through traditions, but one thought of composing them and the other expunged those parts from such traditions, which due to distance in time and place, were incomprehensible for us. In their place, he entered those elements which in our opinion are the best examples of philanthropy and virtue, and ultimately, we started to feel their agonies in our heart, not only out of holy belief and reverence, but in reality.

There is a gap between a poet and a scholar, and this gap is covered with the help of 'deliberation.' This is an art, and Wajid Ali Shah was just a beginner in it, because he does not attempt it. The feelings and thoughts over the expression of which he has a control are his own feelings and thoughts. For expressing them, poetic ability is required and not 'deliberation'.[157]

Wajid Ali Shah was not accustomed to scholarly deliberation. In the verses, where there is mention of some inessential things (*Lazum e mala yalzum*)[158] or meaningless words,[159] this is more the creation of his extraordinary intelligence, wit and command over language than due to deliberation. He writes such matters easily.[160] Poetry in which deliberation is required in addition to wordplay was beyond his competence. Some opine that '*Taarikh* is not included in the art of poetry,'[161] but this was not the case during the *Wajidi* period and in his court. The royal associates displayed their expertise in this art. Due to demand of the art, the King often composed '*taarikh*'.[162] But this genre requires in depth, hard work; a person with command over the language could make use of the proper and appropriate words while retrieving the 'date' or *taarikh* from it, which is an uphill task. The King was not successful in this. Similarly, composing in the hardest 'meters' and in

157. *Kulliyat e* Akhtari ; *The new glass rolled down in the bar due to anxiety of wine*
With the goblet of old verses I created havoc
The flower is plucked before blooming
In the parterre of subject hastiness harms me

158. *See Imaan,* Md. Wajid Ali Shah Akhtar. Matbaey Sultani. Calcutta @ Editions; 1288 & 1301. 132. *Salam; titled: Jalaya Aatishe ghaize Shahe din ne bayaban ka (The anger of Shahe deen burned the forest)*

Nazm Namvar. 270. Ghazal titled: *lagaya daag rukhsaron ki zau ne maah e tabaan ko.* (*The glow of the cheeks maligned the moon)*

159. Ghazal of *Sheva-e-Faiz* page, 26. (Ghazal; *Dilawar Hardam Mukarram Raha*) Here the Takhallus is Mahir instead of Akhtar. Same Takhallus is used in one of the elegies of Toshaey Akhirat.

160. *Tarikh e Abbas,* 209–11.

161. *Urdu Makhtootat,* Asfia Library 620. (Under reference of *Nazm Taba Tabai).*

162. The Tarikhs of *Ishq Nama* , Farsi Aur Manzum or the tarikh on page 239 of *Imaan* (Second Edition).

rare rhymes was the trend of poetry in those days, but the King often kept away from such tough orthodox styles.[163]

FORM AND SUBJECT MATTER

Before criticizing the composition (*kalaam*) of a poet, it is as much necessary to understand his personality as it is necessary to know the purpose of the couplet before understanding the purpose of a Ghazal, *masnavi*, elegy or *qasida*.

When any couplet or poet comes as part of any genre, then he does not change, but looking only at the 'part' makes it difficult to guess about the 'whole', as much as it is difficult to determine the height of a hill by looking at a rock.

To have an insight into the persona of Wajid Ali Shah, an opinion was formed about him that he was a poet by going through his poetic treasure, his life, and the conditions which prevailed at that time. He, as a poet, did not disregard the element of appreciation in his poetry. He was not accustomed to deliberation, but at the same time he always wanted that his composition be different and distinct from others.[164] To have a distinct identity in poetry without deliberation, even at a time when poetry was trending, was possible only when one took a diversion from the common line, or produced a composition superior than those in the trending style. To change the form (*Hayiet*) is not within the control of an individual; however it is possible that a poet should not adopt whatever form the majority adopts. If he does adopt it then he should change the subject matter and the wording, which is different from the common style. In a conscious attempt to imitate and to innovate, a poet ignores the real demands of poetry and consequently his composition becomes inconsistent. This is the problem for a poet who is

163. *Akhtar for the sake of Asir I composed* Ghazal – *Unnecessarily such poetry surrounded me* (Couplet)

164. This characteristic of the King has been discussed in the foregoing pages under the topic of change and variegation.

caught in a struggle to achieve individuality in the field of poetry. The Wajid Ali Shah of Ghazal composition is the same Wajid Ali Shah for which the Lucknow school is ill-reputed. For Ghazal composition, 'depth of heart' is required, and 'heart melting' passion. Wajid Ali Shah's heart was unaware of this passion. For him, giving up the composition of Ghazal was impossible.[165] This is because in Urdu poetry, this is the starting point. But the common topic of a Ghazal is misfortune, sodomy, Sufism, free thinking, the state of being in love, and hard times. But Wajid Ali Shah, setting aside these orthodox subjects, started adorning his *Diwan* with tales of his Begmats, and in the poetry containing *radif* and *qafia* (rhyming), he disregarded the trending topics. This innovation is concerned with changing the subject matter in a familiar form.

Though elegy writing was a thing of Wajid Ali Shah's period and school, the toil and sweat of the elegists of Lucknow took it to the heights of fame[166] within the blink of eye,[167] which had not been possible even for a genius like Ghalib. Wajid Ali Shah did not have a hard-working temperament, hence instead of losing his prestige by joining the race of Anis and Dabir's trending poetry, he considered the form (genre) started by them and composed traditions (stories) which were not a thing of interest for the elegists. For composing 'traditions', '*masnavi*' and not sixain (*mussaddas*)[168] was the proper form. Wajid Ali Shah adopted this,[169] but he was not happy with this experiment. It was not possible for him to change the genre or subject of elegy and to give this up was not in his nature. Thus he remained within the same field and continued to experiment. For his own satisfaction, he

165. *Akhtar, I enjoy poetry composition- Will not give up this passion until my death.* (Couplet).

166. (Couplet) My appreciation is because of poetry – poetry I took you to the skies – Anis

167. Elegy of Zameer; *"kis* Noor *ki mehfil mein meri jalwagari hai"* was the year 1249 as indicated by him is the starting point of a new era.

168. It is a poem where there is a set of pair of three couplets together making a sixain. (Translator)

169. In *Tosha e Aakhirat* (page 1022) is a masnavi of 152 verses which is concerned with the martyrdom of Ali Asghar

came up with the idea of compiling a *Diwan* for his '*nohas*' and '*salaams*'. Taking diversion from elegy writing, he resorted to a style which was not in the contemplation of others.

Eulogy (*qasida nigari*) is not a genre for Kings because others eulogize them, and so, why should they eulogize others? The eulogies composed in the form of '*Manqibat*'[170] are a different genre of eulogy, and Wajid Ali Shah made an attempt in this field.[171] But soon there was a big revolution in his family – he was no longer the King, and was told that the eulogy of the Governor-General was a kind of begging, and there was no need to face humiliation.[172] However, when he was the King he carried on the legacy and the high standard of his ancestors, but when he became subservient then against this legacy he composed a eulogy of 49 verses for Lord Canning. Kingship or subservience does not change the nature of a poet. In *Huzn e* Akhtari instead of writing his appreciation for the ruler of the time, he appreciated Colonel Konia, and once again was reminded that he is also a poet.

Though *thumri*, *Dadrey* and *geet* are not genres of Urdu poetry, one cannot deny their importance as creative poetry nor can one deny the fact that Wajid Ali Shah himself raised the status of ordinary poetry to a superior poetry, and created fine songs for fine music:

> If in the *Antra* by someone there are some sentences, then in the *aasnai* there are twenty wordings, hundreds of complications thousands of errors were found in such poetry. The King can be credited with introducing prosody and rhyming in songs, composing in a specific format (*taqtee*) gave leverage to even ordinary singers and trained the common singers into masters; there are plenty of witnesses to prove this.[173]

---

170. A poem which is in praise and glory of companions of Prophet Muhammad (PBUH). (Translator)

171. See the beginning part of *Kulliyat eSom* and *Kulliyat e* Akhtari.

172. Qaiser ul Tawarikh-Syed Kamaluddin Haideralias Mir Zaair. Publication Munshi Nawal Kishore. Lucknow 3rd. Edn. 1907. Volume 2, 378.

173. *Fasanaey Ibrat*. Mirza Rajab Ali Beg Suroor. Publication Najmul Uloom Karnama. Lucknow. 1884. 85.

After Amir Khusro, in innovation of pure Hindustani poetry and reincarnation the fusion of *geet*, *sangeet* and *nritya* is found in the persona of Wajid Ali Shah and his passion to promote this poetry is rarely found in any of the Urdu or Persian poet. Wajid Ali Shah did mentionable experiment in the form, subject and language of poetry and in common style he composed better than the commoners.[174]

In the above mentioned genres of poetry Wajid Ali Shah displayed his artistic competence. However this competence could not appear in those genres of poetry which were not in line with his nature. He was not accustomed to deliberation; he gives importance to the superficial level of an event, and did not bother to go deep into it. He was conscious of his superiority and wanted to include achievements, and he had command over language and cared to describe everything in detail. For such a poet there was no better genre than '*masnavi*', because in it there was no restriction of '*radif*', no specification of subject, no need to deliberate, no complaint regarding its lengthiness and above all the school and the period to which he belonged was majorly busy in Ghazal composition and in elegy. Wajid Ali Shah gradually switched towards *masnavi*[175] and remained attached to it up till the end.[176] The regret is that he realized this quite late, and did not completely give up 'Ghazal' and 'elegy.'

LANGUAGE

Wajid Ali Shah's bent towards *masnavi* was like revolting against his own school, as he made innovations in both the subject matter and language. The change of subjects continued from the love stories to his autobiography, and then transformed to learned and religious discussions. However his language remained the same, and was free of the artificial and formal expression

---

174. See the composition of Wajid Ali Shah and others in *Dulhan, Najo and Bani.*

175. See the detail in *Afsanaey Ishq.*

176. After '*Guldastaey Aashiqaan*' and '*Sukhan Ashraf*' there is hardly any collection which does not have '*masnavi*' attached to it.

which are the hallmark of '*masnavis*' of the Lucknow school. People opine that Wajid Ali Shah drew inspiration from Shauqq regarding the passion to express his love stories,[177] and for this he also adopted the language and style of Shauqq.[178] But this description indicates an ignorance of the King's natural inclinations. However the question remains, from where did he draw inspiration for this style and language?

Wajid Ali Shah wrote his first *masnavi* in response to the *masnavi* '*Sehrul Bayan*' of Mir Hasan. Some of his verses were in the style of Mir Hasan's '*Sehrul Bayan*' – plain but impressive. We have not come across those verses, but both of these *masnavis* are available. While comparing these two *masnavis*, we should not forget that '*Sehrul Bayan*' is the masterpiece creation of an expert, *and* '*Afsanaey Ishq*' is the first work of an amateur poet. At that time, Gulzar Naseem[179] was popular and people were fond of artificiality and formal expression in poetry. In spite of this, Wajid Ali Shah protected his first composition from external factors. After *Afsanaey Ishq*, the two *masnavis* '*Daryaey Taa'shuqq*' and '*Behre Ulfat*' were composed consecutively. Regarding language, expression, the simplicity of daily life, and the art of composing, these *masnavis* were superior, but they contain more artificiality and formality. The metrical meter (*beher*) of *Daryaey Taashuqq*, which is in the style of *Gulzar Naseem*, is an indicator that the poet accepted these external factors, but he did not change his distinctive style.

There is a fusion of poetry and art in this *masnavi*. But the fusion of the vibrant and unique style of Sehrul Bayan and *Gulzar Naseem* is reflected in the masnavi *Behre Ulfat*, in which the poet used a different '*beher*' than the

177. *Alnaazir* (Monthly, Lucknow), Issue January 1930, 34.

178. *Tazkiraey* Shauqq, Ataullah Palvi. Savera Art Press. Lahore. 1956. 236–39.

179. Maarkaey Chakbast wa Sharar. Mirza Md. Shafi Shirazi. Publication Munshi Naval Kishore. Lucknow. 1942. 27. Gulzar e Naseem. (1254): "After the revision by Aatish this masnavi was recited in a Mushaira where the distinguished poets of Lucknow had gathered... so far the style of uniqueness in masnavi was associated with Mir Hasan but now there were discussions regarding Gulzar Naseem."

other *masnavis*, but drew inspiration from their language and narration. The *masnavi* '*Tilism e Ulfat*'[180] and the first *masnavi* of Shauqq '*Fareb e Ishq*'[181] came into being when the composition of *Daryaey Taashuq* was completed.

To trace the association of Qalq with Mir Hasan or *Shankar Naseem*,[182] and to connect Shauqq with Mir,[183] *Asar*,[184] and Momin[185] means shying away from reality, because the distinct style for which Qalq and Shauqq are well known, is the first impression of it that was given by Wajid Ali Shah.[186] Qalq and Shauqq were the associates of Wajid Ali Shah, and considering their 'gainful inferences' (*istifada*),[187] if they were considered to be followers of Wajid Ali Shah, it would neither be an insult, nor would it be wrong. The King's *Begum*, Nawab Alam Ara Alam, was also his disciple. Qalq learned

---

180. *'Masnavi Tilism Ulfat'* it is its first name (Tarikhi). (511 + 139 + 606 = 1256) but in the starting copies the verses in appreciation of the King indicate that Qalq has changed it later. On page 118 of Maarkaey *Chakbast wa* Sharar this masnavi is mentioned to be composed in 1266.

181. On page 105 of *Tazkiraey* Shauqq the date of composition of *Fareb e Ishq* 1261–63 is mentioned.There will be no harm if it is acknowledged as such.

182. Maulana Hali referring Dr. Abullais Siddiqi in *Lucknow Ka Dabistan e Shayari.* 462–63.

183. *Tazkiraey* Shauqq, 233, 238–39.

184. Maulana Hali, referring to Maulvi Abdul Haque, Muqadma, Masnavi *'Khwab o Khayal',* (page no. 'meem', and 'noon').

185. *Tazkiraey* Shauqq, 255–75.

186. Neither by the narration of Maulana Hali nor Maulvi Abdul Haque it is clear that they were aware of the Masnavis of Wajid Ali Shah. Dr. Abullaiss Siddiqi referring to *Daryaey Ta'shuqq* writes that "there is fusion of the style of Mir Hasan and Naseem" (Lucknow Ka Dabistan e Shayari, 65). Perhaps he did not come across Afsanaey Ishqq and Behre Ulfat and he was unable to write the dates of Daryaey Taa'shuqq, Tilisme Ulfat and Fareb e Ishq .

187. *Behre Ulfat.* Md. Wajid Ali Shah Akhtar. Matbaey Sultani Lucknow. (Khuda Baksh, Raza) 33.

The King writes; *Previously also I related two tales- Friends have taken away*

'Poor they' considered me simple hearted- All the friends took away those strange verses.

Contrary to the tradition of other poets calling himself as 'ignorant' and as the 'dust of the feet of all the poets of the world' was enough for person like him. Had some other composed it then he would have written*'raqeeb'* (rival) instead of 'ghareeb.'(Poor) but then it would have not been that master like style. (*kalamul mulook*).

the trick of fusing poetry with artificiality,[188] and took the '*beher*' of Behr e Ulfat. Shauqq learned the use of daily idioms in poetry from Wajid Ali Shah.[189] And to compensate for any flaws, he crossed the normal limits.

If one studies the life and composition of *Anis*, Wajid Ali Shah, and Shauqq, then among the qualities which are commonly found, the most prominent is the maternal and paternal lineage of their ancestors, which is rooted in Delhi. He did not visit Delhi, but he was in touch with the exalted ruling class (*Mehlat e Mualla*) until he was deposed. The masterpieces of his poetry had appeared by then. The collective attributes of these masterpieces include the fascinating language, spontaneity of idioms, the beauty of their simplicity, and their fineness of expression. None of their early compositions were free of the artificiality (*sannai*). *Anis* and Shauqq soon changed, but Wajid Ali Shah, though he tried, could not change. The fusion of poetry with craftsmanship and artificiality (*sannai*) is the hallmark of his compositions.[190]

The distinguishing quality of Shauqq is that he only started writing *masnavis* when he came of age.[191] Gradually it reached its pinnacle and became 'immortal.' His first *masnavi* is '*Fareb e Ishq*', which according to a commentator was composed at the age of 64 or 65. Up till this time, he neither thought of learning (*istifada*) from the *masnavis* of Mir, nor did he think the *masnavis* of Mir Hasan and Momin were worthy of being studied.

188. See the verses in appreciation of Wajid Ali Shah in *Talism e Ulfat.* The use of daily idioms and the versification of idea in composition for which the masnavis of Qalq and Wajid Ali Shah are considered mentionable, Qalq has appreciated Wajid Ali Shah for such qualities. The owner of Tarikh Adab Urdu says that Qalq regarded himself as the disciple of Wajid Ali Shah. See Tarikh Adab Urdu, Ram Babu Saxena. (Translator, Mirza Md. Askari, Lucknow) Naval Kishore Press, Lucknow. 1952. 262–63.

189. In *Nigar* (Monthly, Lucknow) October 1942 Janab Sahil Bilgrami has presented such verses from Behre Ulfatwhich can be said to be inferred from the composition of Shauqq.

190. *Ishq Nama* (1266) is the masnavi of medieval time and in spite of its craftsmanship it is highly commendable.

191. On page 39 of *Tazkiraey* Shauqq his date of birth is given as 1197and on page 55 year of his death is mentioned at the age of 91. This is because he died in 1288 (1871).

After the *masnavis* of Wajid Ali Shah were published,[192] he chose that same language for his own *masnavis*, which were a kernel of Wajid Ali Shah's *masnavis*. In an attempt to promote one's passion,[193] it is not advisable that the learner be given the status of the inventor.[194] Wajid Ali Shah, for his poetic language, can be regarded as the spiritual disciple of that family in which Mir Hasan, Mir Khaliq,[195] and poets like Mir Anis were born – and under the patronization of which they contributed to the 'bride of poetry (*Uroos e Sukhan*).'[196]

The peak periods of *Anis* and Wajid Ali Shah were the same. *Anis* specialized in writing elegies, while Wajid Ali Shah specialized in writing *masnavis*. To gain success in elegy writing, which was in the thoughts of *Anis*, it was necessary to have simple, eloquent, idiomatic, and commonly plausible language. This was the language of his family and he adopted that. Wajid Ali Shah, for *masnavi* writing, did not require the language which was trending at that time. There was no real pleasure in story telling either in that language, nor was it within the competence of an amateur to adopt that language. To forego deliberation and to achieve individuality the easy way out for Wajid Ali Shah was to resort to that language which was not prevalent among common poets. Such was the language of Wajid Ali Shah's family, and to use it in poetry he received guidance from the *masnavi* of Mir Hasan. The source of learning for both *Anis* and Wajid Ali Shah was that single person namely Mir Hasan.

---

192. *Lucknow Ka Shahi Stage,* Prof. Syed Masood Hasan Rizvi Adeeb. Kitab Nagar Lucknow. 1957. 123.

193. (Couplet) *All the innumerable Urdu experts regard you as the mystifying narrator. Your poetry is unique, it is the dictionary of Urdu language.* (Behre Ulfat).

194. *Takiraey* Shauqq, 26.

195. *Kulliyat* Akhtari; (Couplet) *Akhtar don't be surprised if one weeps out of jealousy; The salam of K*Haliq *be given the status of* Ghazal. Md. Wajid Ali Shah Akhtar. Matbaey Sultani. Calcutta.1278. (Khuda Baksh, Avadh, Raza).

196. The Preface writer of the Elegies of Anis (Publisher: Munishi Naval Kishore) says that since the time of Begum Saheba the members of the family of Anis were employed to write down the 'Begmati language' and this continued up till the time of Mir Khaliq.

For an intelligent and understanding vision, it is not necessary that the guide should be in the vicinity. Just like *Anis* learned from Mir Hasan, Wajid Ali Shah did too. It is quite believable that whenever Wajid Ali Shah made a mistake, the grandson of Mir Hasan used his elegies as an example, and gave a good lesson in elegy writing. Anyone who writes on Wajid Ali Shah would find a pleasant difference between the poetic *Ishq Nama* and the descriptions of events scenes and dialogue, as well as the metaphors and similes, of the three initial *masnavis*. This honour was received after hearing *Anis's* composition through him.

Anis considering the delicacies of pronunciation recited the elegy in a dramatic style which was the taste and style of his patron. (Here Wajid Ali Shah). At the same time, he wished that 'Sultan e Alam' (Wajid Ali Shah) would appreciate it.

O Anis! I am trebling with the fragility of old age
These verses will remain memorable in this world
Many great verses came out of my pen due to enthusiasm
The words are of the choice of 'Sultan' and the verses too of the choice of 'Alam'
This time and this congregation of mourning (aza) is memorable
There is gusto of old age and the agony of loneliness [197]

The buyers of precious stones do not distribute pebbles but among the precious stones of Wajid Ali Shah there is no glimmer or shine as found in the stones (composition) of Anis, but nevertheless they are precious and not mere pieces of glass.

The narration that Wajid Ali Shah and Anis adopted the language of their respective families and received lessons from Mir Hasan implies that in Lucknow, different families had their own language, and Mir Hasan's

197. It is the last verse (band) of Anis's marsia; '*Jab Qata ki masafat shabe Aftab ne.*' This elegy is said to be the work of his last days but there is no confirmation regarding this. The internal evidence in the fourth line of this 'maqta' cannot be overlooked.

language was superior to them. But if one thinks in this way, then this is not so different from thinking that *Anis* lived in Lucknow, spoke the language of Delhi, but received appreciation from the people of Lucknow. A mother tongue is not adopted; it is automatically imposed on a person. However if most people speak a different language, and if a person for some reason does not change his language (mother tongue) to match, then he can be said to adopt it as his mother tongue.

During the period of Nasikh and Aatish, the language of Lucknow passed through this tug of war. The language of poetry was different from the language of the common man, and as Hali puts it "the more he moved, the farther he became from the path of progress."[198] *Anis* was amused by this conflict (of languages) and because of the pride he took in the language of his ancestors he did not give up his own language. This was a taunt and a lesson for the poets who had given up their own language. Miles away from Delhi, adopting the "daily language, eloquence and mannerism" of the elite class of Delhi was possible, but people hardly appreciated this as they were unaware of it, and were tired of it. *Anis* had the opportunity to visit different cities, and attended the gatherings of poetic minded people, but he could not forget Lucknow.[199] This was only because there was an essence of the waters of Gomti in his language, and so it was not surprising that those who never had the opportunity to taste it, could not understand or appreciate it. The language of *Anis* is not only the refuge of the elite class of Delhi, but of the elite class of that Lucknow, which included Wajid Ali Shah, *Alam*, Shauqq, and many other selected families. There is no gain in being attached to only one school because "there is no considerable difference in the eloquence and articulacy of both the places."[200] While considering these differences, which were the grounds for the conflict, it becomes clear that *Anis* learned not from

---

198. *Muqaddamaey Sher o Shayari.* Khwaja Altaf Hussain Hali. Maktabaey Jaddid. Lahore. 1953. 198.

199. Yaadgar e Anis, 121–22.

200. *Muqaddamaey Sher o Shayari,* 195.

Delhi but from Lucknow.[201] The claim by *Anis* that he spoke his household language indicates that he kept his own language on a high pedestal, superior to the languages of Lucknow and Delhi. While connecting the legacy of *Anis* with Delhi, one should not neglect this poetic supremacy. Wajid Ali Shah also connected himself with Delhi:

The King speaks special Urdu
Akhtar the eloquent! This language is unparalled[202]

Just like a beggar, though receiving alms from humans remains grateful to Allah, *Anis* and Wajid Ali Shah learned from the Lucknow school, but, while they noticed the diversion of the Lucknow people towards another language, they moved towards Delhi, which had been the altar of respect for the bygone elderly class. Neither *Anis* nor Wajid Ali Shah was prejudiced against the beliefs which were held by others.[203]

GHAZAL COMPOSITION

'Ghazal' is the synonym for 'talking to the fair sex', and the portion of Wajid Ali Shah's Ghazal composition which falls under this category is commendable. The center point of his poetry was 'woman', [204] the spirit

---

201. In the dissertation of Ph.D. titled *"Anis Ki Zaban"* in Chapter 4 the learned thesis writer has explained this with the help of many illustrations and references.

202. Nazm Namvar, Md. Wajid Ali Shah Akhtar. Matbaey Sultani. Calcutta. 1287. (Raza, Ittihadiya, Khuda Baksh) page 257.

203. The fact that the masters of Lucknow formed a different school or the insistence by the masters of Delhi that they will not accept the suggestions or corrections made by the eastern lot (*purbi*) is something which needs thorough investigation.The author only want to assert that the two prominent personalities of Lucknow were promoting the healthy tradition of 'correction' (*isslahe sukhan*), the tradition which reached from Deccan to Delhi and was gradually vanishing .The byproducts of these traditions namely some well-known poets also became its victims and were divided into stereotype categories.

204. See the reason behind the composition of '*Afsanaey Ishq.*'

behind his composition was 'woman,'[205] the fan of his composition was 'woman',[206] and it would have been really surprising had the subject matter of his 'Ghazals' not been 'woman.' Much of his compositions are also on subjects other than 'woman', but that was his artistic poetry which does not enrich the language; the treasure of language will not become poorer if those parts are lost or destroyed. However, it would be a big loss if his Ghazals in which his own personality is reflected, were destroyed or lost.

At a time when '*pardah*' was a common trend, poetry in which the feminine gender was used was forbidden, and mentioning and glorifying women was considered highly objectionable, the bold expressions of Wajid Ali Shah about his wives, beloveds, and darlings was, in the words of Hali, "to introduce ladies of his own family and seraglio to the outsiders."[207] The innovative part of Wajid Ali Shah's poetry is that is it has both the dimensions of appreciation and admonition. At the same time, his innovation also comprised of the description of the personalities of his 'Begmats', their beauty, and his relations with them. This innovative quality, with the exception of Quli Qutub Shah, is hardly found in Urdu literature, and it is only this part of the treasure of Urdu poetry which can stand at par with Arabic and English compositions.[208] The opulence of Wajid Ali Shah manifested in other compositions, but his Ghazals contain a particular type of information not found anywhere else. For instance, the rebellion of the Begums of yesteryear is today's *Hazrat Mahal.* People want to know about her, they want to gather more and more information about her life and her personality, but

---

205. See the reason behind the composition of '*Daryaey Taa'shuqq.*'

206. See, *Adab Ka Maqsad,* 172, Tarikhe Firaq (Handwritten), 74–75.

Couplet:

Out of craziness I add wings to the fairies- (Hence) the fairies have flown my couplets to the Caucasus mountains

207. In '*Muqaddamaey Sher o Shayari*' (p. 212) the admonition by Hali though was for poets in general but it applies more aptly on the work of Wajid Ali Shah.

208. In present time much work is found in romantic poetry but during the nineteenth century not many specimen were found in English poetry.

the 'Ghazal' which carries this knowledge is still hidden from their sight. It does not contradict the claims of historians;[209] in fact it corroborates and elucidates them. There is no other way to contradict the following:

Hazrat Mahal is my sweetheart
She is the embodiment of beauty
Autumn falls on the garden
Hazrat Mahal is the beauty Queen
What to write about the golden body
I am myself enriched by Hazrat Mahal
The homes in the city are devastated
Hazrat Mahal my own land[210] *is uprooted*
The King of exquisiteness is enslaved
Hazrat Mahal deserves my chastisement (for arresting me by her charm)
You are the source of my comfort
Hazrat Mahal you are the messiah of poor
The Mirror *envies you, your hair is great*
*Hazrat Mahal you are fiercely ad*Mire*d*[211]
Tatar (Turks) is crushed by your beauty
Every time name of beloved is on my tongue
My dear darling Hazrat Mahal
Commendable qualities, great attributes
Fairy-faced, well-mannered Hazrat Mahal
Now the world will vanish with fear

209. These are some of the ancient and modern writings: *Tawarikh e Nadirul Asar* (page 136), Russell's 'My Diary of Indian Mutiny', *Hazrat Mahal Number of Nazzara* (p. 63), *Naya Daur* (page 72), Begum Hazrat Mahal (Anis Fatima, Barelvi). Book *'Eighteen Fifty Seven'* by S.N. Sen.

210. The plundering of Qaiser Bagh started with the downfall of the empire. Tarikh e Iqtidar (Handwritten), Volume 2, 42. (2/42).

211. See the picture of Hazrat Mahal in the Hindi book *'Gadar Ke Phool'*.

If you flutter your eye Hazrat Mahal
Where Where Where is she
O! the beloved of Akhtar, Hazrat Mahal[212]

Despite the discussion of a woman, there is nothing which can be objected to by Hali. Though Wajid Ali Shah had not always been so cautious and careful, he had always shown regard for the status of his subjects, and often for his own, but he has chosen a subject of common interest. In the above mentioned Ghazal, Wajid Ali Shah had made the real term of address a '*radif*' (repetition of the same word in a poem), and there is no shortage of Ghazal*s* where the name has been used as '*radif*'. The meaning of such words has been put to good use as in the following line:

Who knew he is the emperor for the last five generations,
The 'Raunaq' of Akhtar is captivated[213]
Death does not question the hardened in jail
Dear! Death is afraid of the lover during separation[214]
How to relate my story
How to express myself[215]
Every day the style of my verse is new
Dress which is old is not good
Akhtar! I have send Ghazal *for 'Achchi' (one of his* Begums *whose real name was Seemtan)*
Why to lie? Making stories is not good[216]

---

212. In *Sheva-e-Faiz,* 125–26. (The entire Ghazal is reproduced).

213. *Shevaey Faiz,* 107. Raunaq Ara was the real name of daughter Wazir Ali Naqi Khan. At the time of his dethronement the King resorted to poetry composition to please her. Wajid Ali Shah is the fifth King of Avadh and not that he was the King for the last five generations. Perhaps this was in reply to the line of Anis; "Panchveen pusht hai Shabbir ki maddhaey mein."

214. *Ibid,* 110.

215. *Ibid.*

216. *Ibid,* 408–09. Achchi Begum was the real name of Malka Seemtan. See Sheva-e-Faiz, 272.

There are ample examples of the tuning of words, the joining of two names, and creating melody in verses with the help of names. This is illustrated by the following:

This is the rosary of the good name
Say again Seemtan Seemtan
The pen enjoys the repetition
When it is written Seemtan Seemtan[217]
Fairy Seemtan Seemtan Seemtan
Cheers Seemtan Seemtan Seemtan
Long live
Dear Seemtan Seemtan Seemtan
Now Akhtar's eyes are not teary
Due to the separation Seemtan Seemtan Seemtan[218]
....
Why the officers, slaves and fairies be not proud
Khaas Mahal Saheba is fed up of me
Charming face and height, prettily dressed with good figure
Khaas Mahal Saheba is fair complexioned and beautiful[219]
Najmunnissa and Zaibunnissa are like the Sun and the Moon
Najmunnissa and Zaibunnissa are like the Moon crescent
There is double pleasure from each, two means four
Najmunnissa and Zaibunnissa are like the 'Tashdeed' of a word.[220]

---

217. *Ibid*, 272.
218. *Ibid*, 273–74.
219. *Ibid*, 317. '*Khaas Mahal Saheba*' was the pen name of Nawab Badshah Mahal Alam Ara Begum Alam.
One masnavi and one Diwan are her compositions. She died after the death of the King and she is buried in her self-constructed Imambarah in 24 Parganas, Metiaburj. It is under the possession of the Sunnis and the mosque also belongs to her.
220. Qamar Mazmun, Md. Wajid Ali Shah Akhtar. Matbaey Sultani. Calcutta. 1281h. 288–89.

(Tashdeed, a sign in Urdu where stress is laid on one alphabet)
The voice of heart is heard in the jail which sounds like
Maharani! Maharani! Maharani! Maharani!
Give me your memoir
O Jaani! O Jaani! O Jaani![221]

There are also examples where he makes meaningful use of a pen name, or any other attribute, in the form of '*radif*.' This is as follows:

The biggest name in beauty is Nanhi *Begum*
Nanhi *Begum is moon-faced, flower-like*[222]
Abadi Begum you ruined my heart
Do you like this my disaster?[223]

Or often it is addressed as follows:

1. Navrozi Begum my heart is gone
   It is gone to ashes[224]
2. Ghazala! this is my jungle of Ghazals
   My screams pierce the sky[225]
3. Connect my lips Seemtan
   My chest with yours[226]
4. Mehndi Begum! How to relate the plight of my bruised heart
   Your beloved remains restless the whole night[227]

---

221. *Ibid*, 468.
222. Nazm Namvar, 263.
223. *Mulk Akhtar,* Md. Waji Ali Shah Akhtar. Matbaey Sultani, Calcutta 1296. 42.
224. *Sheva-e-Faiz*, 14.
225. *Ibid*, 24.
226. *Ibid*, 299.
227. *Ibid*, 316.

Often, he was free of the bondages of '*radif*', as follows:

Sweet heart your body is so delicate
I cannot touch your beauty
Eyes are like lilies, cheeks like petals
Your teeth are like pearls, your forehead like Sun,
Pearls roll down when you talk
Your palm is like moon, your nails like sun
Your body flows like Mirror[228]
Whenever the rainy season arrives
There is cloud of affection over my heart
Cheek of the beloved was seen
But then the bride of night felt shy.[229]
Venus,[230] *Star, Sun, or Moon who are you?*
Stealer of my senses, cruel, Beauty who are you?
Ghost, wicked, Subtle, Graceful, Fairy, impious
Fun playing is not good, how to address you?
You express the 'raag khyal', show the joyous dance
Why you charm me from distance, come near and say who are you?

By using such artistic expressions, the poet, in a limited manner, has displayed various shades of emotions. The feelings, thoughts, poetry, and craftsmanship have been aptly displayed. Through the magic of language, it does not seem that a person wants to satisfy his lust, but that a poet has made the woman his subject of expression, and are often portrayed in some simple ensemble, formal attire, or in the nude form to unleash the sour and bitter realities of life. The craftsmanship of *Konark* and *Khajuraho* and the engraving of *Ajanta* and *Ellora*, by displaying the physical feminine charm,

---

228. *Sukhan Ashraf/ Kulliyat e* Akhtari, /Nazm Namvar 73–74.
229. *Sheva-e-Faiz,* 273–274.
230. Qamar Mazmun, 289–90.

have risen to the pedestal of fine art. Similarly, if one is in quest of elegant and graceful verses in Hindustani poetry then perhaps it is this composition of Wajid Ali Shah.

The reason behind the abundance of names in Sheva-e-Faiz and its diversion from '*Behre Muktalif*,' is that the poet, while composing, sometimes used the real name, sometimes the pen name, and sometimes the formal address or title. He has transformed even the hardest words in the form of '*radif*.' It is illustrated in the following way:

1. Huzoor e Alia, Malkaey Avadh, Akhtar Mahal, Nawab Raunaq Ara Begum Saheba.[231]
2. Mushfiqaey Jahani, Husn Ara, Tirchhi Jaan, Nawab Shehenshah Mahal Saheba.[232]
3. Shafiqatul Zamani, Banki jaan, Meh Laqa, Nawab Sardar Mahal Saheba.[233]
4. Malkaey Mulk, Tajunnissa, Nawab Mashuqq Mahal Saheba.[234]
5. Malkaey Mehertan, Afsarunnissa, Nanhi Begum, Nawab Nishat Mahal Saheba.[235]

The interesting exercise of composing the names, which, unlike the sad and listless poetry of Behre Mukhtalif, arouses emotions, is not limited to

---

231. On page 186 of Sheva-e-Faiz in the part of Manavis these words are written in the same manner. The above mentioned underlined words are used as 'radif' in the part of 'Ghazalyat' on pages 104, 121, 168, 318 and 320.

232. The entire name along with the titles is given on page 90 of Sheva-e-Faiz (Masnavi Part) and the Ghazals are given on pages 131, 37, 251, 256 (Ghazalyat Part).

233. The detail of the title is given on page 137 of Mahal Khanaey Shahi, and Ghazals are given on pages 40, 161, 261, 357 of *Sheva-e-Faiz,* (Ghazalyat part).

234. The detail of the title is given on page 127 of *Mahal Khanaey Shahi*, and Ghazals are given on pages 33, 107–14, 118 and 122 of *Sheva-e-Faiz* (Ghazalyat part).

235. The detail of the title is given on page 127 of *Mahal Khanaey Shahi*, and Ghazals are given on pages 34, 127, 203, 216, 248 of *Sheva-e-Faiz* (Ghazalyat part).

the names of the Begmats – the King rewarded and honoured his pupils and children as well. The following verses explain this:

Long Live Nazakat Ara Nazakat Ara may you flourish
May you get long life and opulence Nazakat Ara may you wear the crown of honour
May you grow under the banner of Panjatan e Pak
Nazakat Ara May You earn the support of all
May you live forever like the Sun, Moon, Venice and stars
Nazakat Ara May you live forever in this world
May you have the treasure of precious stones and the opulence
Nazakat ara May the perfume of wealth spread all over your life
May you get good luck and the crown of glory and loyalty
May the umbrella of pomp and wealth always cover your head Nazakat Ara
You are the apple of Akhtar's eye
May you shine like Sun in the world Nazakat Ara

The poet who composed the names of others with so much fervour and enthusiasm must have nurtured the wish that others too should sing about his attributes and qualities. Shaida, Hoor, Noor, and Jamshed considered this, but such composition had a price. However, some spontaneous and natural compositions were made by the family members, and these are well adorned. The brief *Diwan* of *Nawab* Sadar Mahal *Sadar* composed the names of Wajid Ali Shah, likely on his demand. The final lines deserve appreciation. It goes like this:

Congratulations! Sultan my Diwan is compiled
My wishes are fulfilled Sultan Congratulations
I made a garland for you by plucking flowers
You are the pride of spring and garden Congratulations Sultan
With the shine of your names 'radifs' are formed and the 'matla' is composed
Each of this Ghazal *is composed in the name of* Allah *congratulations Sultan*

These are pieces of my heart in the form of words
This is the collection of my heart's tunes and expressions Sultan Congratulations
After a long time I have send a bouquet to you
This is my presentation and gift to you Sultan Congratulations
How long the bird will tweet for the sad heart of Sadar
The flowers of loyalty are blooming Sultan Congratulations[236]

This is the original composition of Sadar Mahal, as is evident from the '*Tameeli*' *mushaira* of *Bani*, where she occupies the place of '*sadar*' beside *Mukhfi* and *Alam.*[237] After Wajid Ali Shah, she was regarded as the most qualified poet.[238] Her son Mirza Jalal was also a poet.[239] Wajid Ali Shah regards the use of names as a '*radif*' as his own innovation. The following verse explains this:

The whole name of the Princess should come in the verses
Khurshid Laqa this is the innovation of you Akhtar.[240]

But perhaps this is said in the flow of rhyming. Wajid Ali Shah is not an inventor but he is a revivalist. In *Diwan Dilli* there are Ghazals with the *radif* of '*amritlal*' and '*gobindlal.*' In the *Diwan Fateh ud Daulah* Barq, there are Ghazals with the following titles:

'Madah khwan hun Qiblaey Alam Siknder Jah ka'
'Chhan raha hai pairahan se Noor *jism e pak ka'*
'Gauhar afshan hai niyan e karam Sultan Alam ka'

---

236. *Badshah Nama,* Nawab Sadar Mahal Sadar.Matbaey Sultani. Calcutta. 1288. 187.

237. *Bani,* 244. The above verses are extracted from *Badshah Nama.*

238. *Avadh Pension Papers,* 36.

239. In the published composition of Shehzada Mirza Jalal only a Qataey Tarikh of *Malazul Kalmat* and masnavi entitled *'Naghma e Dard'* was found.

240. *Shevaey Faiz,* 37.

These can be ignored as they sketch masculine characters. However, the *Kulliyat e* Quli Qutub Shah cannot be ignored, and one copy was seen by Springer in the library of the *Avadh* emperors. Some 250 years before Wajid Ali Shah wrote about Haider Mahal, Khudadad Mahal, Qutub Mandir, Nanhi, Sanwli, Chhabeli, Mohan, Laalan, Mushtari and his other beloveds, [241] the Golconda ruler had written about his '*parizaads*' (beautiful women). A Ghazal in the radif of '*mehboob*' is associated with some beloved, the title of which was '*mehboob*.'[242] The Urdu patrons of the 19th century did not regard the Urdu of Deccan as 'Urdu'. However if we regard it as Urdu, then we should treat Wajid Ali Shah not as inventor who first started a tradition, but as a 'revivalist' who brought back earlier work. The oldest Ghazal*s* of Wajid Ali Shah come after the *Diwan* of Barq.[243] Wajid Ali Shah was inspired by Barq, to include proper names in his compositions, and from Quli Qutub Shah he learned the style of characterization in poetry.[244] However, compiling the *Diwan* in this style was his own innovation.

Other than the Ghazal*s* which were composed for 'Diwans,' '*Mushairas*' and 'Begmats', in every collection Ghazal*s* are also found which express the original feelings of the poet. A sensitive poet who was on a quest for opulence, splendor, and luxury could not escape the melancholy ambience which surrounded him. In the noise of laughter, their sobs and sighs may easily be lost, but one who is truly compassionate can still hear them. The reality of the lavishness and extravagance of Wajid Ali Shah's courtyard was different from what meets the eye.[245] An entire treatise would be required

---

241. *Kulliyat e* Quli Qutub Shah, 211–81.

242. *Ibid*, 260.

243. These are the Ghazals of *Diwan Mubarak*: (Couplet) *'Falak par rahe naam* Akhtar Mahal *k'a and 'Sardaron ki sardar hain Mehboobey Alam.'*

244. Nazm Namvar, 188; (Couplet) *'Buton ke husn ko kheencha hai parkare tassavur se-Qalam Aashiq ka hai behzaad ka mai naam kya karta.*

245. See *Savaneh Lucknow* (Handwritten), 30, Muaasir (Monthly, Patna) December 1942, Asadul Akhbar Issue 116. Other contemporary newspapers also have the similar news.

to explain this phenomenon, but an examination of only one couplet of Wajid Ali Shah is enough to say that his work was not fully free from pain and melancholy; nor was it anything different from the soreness of those times. Many Ghazals of *Sukhan Ashraf* gained new meaning by the time they reached Nazm Namvar. One of the couplets goes like this:

Same fans same gathering same opulence
Don't worry the burning flame! Another night will descend[246]

This couplet reminds of the days when a devout person like Amjad Ali Shah was at the helm of affairs. The religious empire of Md. Ali Shah and Amjad Ali Shah crushed the opulence and magnificence of Nasiruddin Haider. This was where Wajid Ali Shah was in the prime of his youth. Seeing his enthusiasm doused and his gusto snubbed, he consoled his heart in the following words:

O! The healer of pain don't worry
Treat your agonies, all the wishes will be fulfilled don't worry
Your stepping will enlighten every path
Don't worry greenery will once again descend upon the parterre

Soon after he ascended to the throne, all his delightful dreams of the future were realized. Now there was no need to delay the joy of splendor, and so one word was changed to make the desired expression. It goes as follows:

Same fans same gathering same opulence
Don't worry the burning flame! Another night descends[247]

But this night too fleeted away soon. Destiny contained the lonely nights of exile. Though he tried to brighten the dark nights with his love for luxury,

---

246. *Sukhan Ashraf* (Handwritten).
247. *Sukhan Ashraf* (Handwritten), 4.

in his heart of heart he knew that his original fervour could not be revived.[248] For his own satisfaction, there was an amendment to the same couplet, as follows:

Same fans same gathering same opulence
Don't worry the burning flame! This is the meeting of togetherness[249]

Wajid Ali Shah was not a pessimist, hence the Ghazal "*gham na kha*" (don't lament) shows his true nature.[250] He looked for ways to comfort himself in adverse situations. He always remained optimistic and hopeful about the future. He always strived to rise above present adversaries, talked about his disappointments while he was in exile, defiant and hopeful about the future, and then eventually let go of his worries. To understand Wajid Ali Shah, the following verses will go a long way:

1. *How cruel was the killer, how oppressed was the heart*
   Say the sharp sword how was my throat[251]
2. *This is the style of love, the end is inevitable*
   Who is to listen the advice, what the broken heart will do?
3. *Gardeners! This is the new style of flowers in the garden*
   At one glance the Bulbul will be heartbroken
4. *My attire which was not torn is now apart*
   The remedy for my bruising heart is here
5. *Sorrow and melancholy will be the remedy of the lover*
   The comfort of heart will be the endless sorrow
6. *Say if I recall your image or not*
   Should I do something to console my heart or not?[252]

248. *Bani,* 123–24.

249. Nazm Namvar, 124.

250. In the same metre (zameen) there is a Ghazal of Quli Qutub Shah which is the translation of Khwaja Hafiz's Ghazal "Yusuf e gumm gushta baaz aayad ba kunaan gham makhur."

251. *Gulistan e Aashiqaan/Kulliyat e* Akhtari, 17, 35.

252. Sukhan Ashraf/Kulliyat e Akhtari, 72, 76, 89, 108, 548.

7. *I am neither hopeful of happiness, nor I am afraid of grief*
I neither yearn for comfort nor do I apprehend cruelty[253]
8. *I am enriched by the downfall of beauty*
Black deeds turned my hair grey
9. *I was under some frenzy*
I became hopeless all my life
10. *Up till Spring the glow of my face did not go*
But when autumn came my youth vanished
11. *Neither the garden nor its freshness came to my mind*
But before I could regain sense I remembered the ravisher
12. *The abode of ravisher and the flower was uprooted*
The destroyer was still not satisfied
13. *I squeezed my heart while missing your face*
The petals fell down from the branches[254]
14. *If ever I meet you keep me close*
Howsoever take care of me
15. *Alas! I am caught amidst worries*
Alas! The crown and pomp is snatched away
16. *I am a captivated bird , desertion is my abode*
Instead of flowers my feet is shackled
17. *The plucker ! see the plight of the flower in the morning*
See the dew drops on the flowers[255]
18. *How in this tender age, time has bereaved me*
It is condoling my heart in this grief
19. *Sweet heart reply to my grieving letter*
The distance pains me give me some relief
20. *Don't recall the charm of the garden*
Don't complain against the captivator[256]

---

253. *Diwan Mubrak*/Nazm Namvar, 145, 157, 175.
254. *Sheva-e-Faiz,* 10, 30, 45, 395.
255. Qamar Mazmun, 259, 268,283.
256. Nazm Namvar, 121 222, 272.

21. *Captivator! Don't try to compete with me*
I am made up of the arrows of love
22. *Wishes for kiss are buried in my heart*
The vile sky has thrown me from top
23. *During agony, in pain and in sorrow*
The star of Akhtar will remain wandering[257]
24. *There is dearth of peace in my heart*
There is palpitation of an injured in my grave
25. *What the time will gain by tormenting me*
Who will trust the promise breakers?[258]

There are some verses by Wajid Ali Shah which are fully in the mode of Ghazal composition, as shown in the couplets below. Looking for such verses in his compositions is like searching for gold in a goldmine.[259]

Now I am embraced by love
Though it irked me yet I wish good luck for love
Balm could be applied if there were a few bruises
But Akhtar's body is fully scorched[260]

He had no interest in Sufism or philosophy. He often issued sermons or gave advice, but he was neither a preacher nor an advisor, all such things were the culmination of his experiences. He easily mastered compositions in small or big '*beher*' (lines), using in simple or complicated meters, but he did not use '*do ghazla*' or '*ghazla*', nor was he bound by rhyming restrictions.[261]

---

257. *Mulk Akhtar,* 105, 107.

258. *Malazul Kalmat* (Supplement), 295.

259. Nazm Namvar, 188. (Coupet) *Wat alif he does not know bay tey say – Akhtar is getting a bad name in* Ghazal *composition.*

260. *Sukha Ashraf/Kuliyat e* Akhtari, 63 & 101.

261. Kulliyat e Akhtari, 325. (Couplet) *'ye radifi qafiey hain Akhtar hoshiyar raho! Buss yahein tak khoob thha jo bandh gaye do chaar kaj.'* (These rhyme flows Akhtar beware! It is enough that you followed this so far).

While perusing his Ghazals if one forgets that it is the composition of a King then he will be more convinced of his power of expression and less of his poetic caliber, but if he is aware of the events and happenings of his real life then he will be convinced both of his power of expression and his poetic caliber. And this amalgamation of King's poetic ability and his power of expression is the hallmark of his Ghazal composition.

ELEGY WRITING

Wajid Ali Shah must have started writing elegies when he started composing Ghazals. Lucknow was echoing with the chants of *Anis* and Dabir. Wajid Ali Shah had a love for all genres of poetry, and would not have liked to fail even in writing elegies, *Asir* writes about this:

What to say about his elegies
The elegy reciters are reciting it
The subject and the composition are all proper
No doubt these elegies are very popular
He is naturally gifted for this
The pupil becomes the master
Had there not been these compositions
This art would not have been prominent[262] *(and popular)*

But in the published work of Wajid Ali Shah, we do not see any elegy which can be considered his own composition from that time, and so no comments on it can be made.

In the available elegies from *Kulliyat Soom* to *Riyazul Uqba*, there are about 70 elegies in which there are around 6,000 '*bunds*' (couplets). Over a period of 30 years, it would not be difficult for a prolific poet like Wajid Ali Shah to compose such a number of elegies. Sharar relates that while moving from his house to the Imambarah covering a distance of two furlongs, he

262. *Durrul Taj,* Md. Muzaffar Ali Khan Asir. Matbaey Sultani. Lucknow. 1270. 120–21.

could dictate elegies and '*salams.*' All the qualities and drawbacks which could be in a fast composition like this were present, and looking for the hallmarks of the work of Hali, *Shibli*, and Azad in such composition would be a sheer waste of time.

Wajid Ali Shah's elegies, not from the poetic viewpoint but from the viewpoint of the art of prosody, are quite worthwhile. A common man who found it difficult to comprehend the elegies of Dabir would face the same problem in understanding the work of Wajid Ali Shah. He rightly composes the traditions as these are based on his knowledge of facts. In view of critics, this was the main attribute of his elegies. But we don't resort to elegies to learn about the wedding story of Hazrat Qasim, the agonies of a three-day thirst, or the last rites of Imam Hussain. Our aim is to study the vision and poetic excellence relating to the happenings of Karbala, and this study helps us in refining and correcting our ethical and literary taste. In the elegies of Wajid Ali Shah we hardly come across such a point, which impresses us deeply. If the elegy writer becomes the teacher, sits on the pedestal (*mimber*: a raised place from where one gives sermons), and asks the gathering to cry and weep, then hardly anyone will listen. But if he gradually covers the phases of the battlefield and a life of luxury and reaches martyrdom, then the tragedy of life may create an impact upon the minds of the audience, who may then react tearfully.

Elegy is the fusion of historical facts, religious belief and poetic excellence. Historical facts in Wajid Ali Shah's elegy are up to the extent when he discovers an event in war literature. He composes it in the form of sixain (*mussaddass*), often making a reference to it and often without it. That tradition or event could also be false or wrong. However a devout poet does not care for this, the falsehood if any being easily put on the shoulder of the narrator as he himself composes this elegy with religious fervor. Anyone who has excessive faith in religious belief will be affected by the event of martyrdom, no matter under what heading or wordings it is brought to him. There are hardly descriptions of Miracles, appreciations of arrow, sword, flag and horse-riding, as the intricacies of art of war. The attempt to outline physical skill and valour are very rare in Wajid Ali Shah's elegies, and whatever there is cannot match the lightest expression of the school of *Anis* or Dabir. The poet has tried to create mysticism through the eloquence and articulacy of words but being devoid of ground reality it fails to impress. The power of words indicates the flaws in imagination, and poetry becomes a manifestation of prosody, a medium of spell. In this prosodic spell there is also a big flaw. In a sixain composing four proper lines and then looking for a '*bait*' (distich/couplet in a Ghazal) of the same style is a complicated job and requires deep insight. In the sixain of Wajid Ali Shah if two or three lines (*misra*) are found proper then the '*bait*' becomes weak. Perhaps this is due to the reason that the poet composes all the six lines in a sequence. Usually the sixain poets first compose the '*bait*' and then for '*misras*' (half of a couplet in a Ghazal) they go from downwards to upper portion of the poem or Ghazal.

In elegy writing, a descriptive portion (*chehra*) is written in a formal way. There is no such description in the brief elegies of Wajid Ali Shah and wherever it is composed, it is done by way of introducing some of his own thoughts or ideas. The poet, by relating to his own innocence, has tried to gain the sympathy of the audience and to create a melancHolic ambience.[263] This shows that he was aware of their psychology and that is why, other than the real tradition, he included two other short traditions so that the audience does not become restless. Such audience is no more, and the taste to recite elegies has also vanished. Now only those are there who only peruse the elegies and it will be enough if they patiently continue with this.

Apart from the meaningful quality of the couplet, the composition of the poet is regarded a trustworthy lexicon of the language.[264] Wajid Ali Shah's work is also worthwhile as he roped in the treasure of choosy words, everyday phrases and idioms in his Ghazals, *masnavis*, and elegies which is highly

263. *Toshaey Akhirat,* 4-.7 See two sixains on page 288 & 316 title verse of which are; (1) *Aijaz raqam Khmaey gulrang hai mera* and (2) *Jo yezdo jurad ki dukhtar ko laey pesh umr.*
264. *Muqaddamaey Sher o Shayari,* 122.

beneficial for those who make a deep study of the work and gain scholarly benefits from them.[265] Abundance of the use of synonyms and analogies, using a word in varied context, and the use of words pertaining to a particular idea[266] are the hallmark of his work which are impressive enough to attract a dictionary writer. As he was a free writer, often he overlooks the fact that the expression is against the style of his school or it is not in conformity with the tenets of poetry. But such flaws are very few and they contain 'an attractive style of eloquence' thus if his elegies are disregarded as the composition of a 'spoiled poet and elegy writer' then one may overlook even those good points for which the poet worked a lot.

NOHA COMPOSITION

'*Salam*' (complimentary poetry about religious personality) and '*noha* recitation'(lamentation/dirge) are the backbone of elegy writing. The elegy recitation (*marsia goeey*) was so dear to the writers of Wajid Ali Shah's period that they did not give much attention to '*salams*' and '*nohas*'. In this genre, the introduction of the Ghazal was considered highly objectionable because the impressive and touching feature of *salams* and *nohas* is considered its most important characteristic. *Salams* and *nohas* are usually associated with the poets of *Ithna Ashri* Shias[267] and while reciting them, they cast the same

265. *Markaey Chakbast wa* Sharar, 89, 96, 101, 111. *Nikat e Anand,* 57–58. Som lexicons like Amir*ul Lughat,* Noor*ul Lughat,* and *Mohzabul Lughat.*Volume 3, 236, 369, 305 etc.
266. Elegy on page 319–54 of *Toshaey Akhirat* with the first verse; *'Jab qaaf ko do zer toh Saaqib ho huveda'* and the elegy on page 1424–48 with the first verse *'Hai daag badal Maah e Falak kiss ke aza mein'* need special attention.
267. The Arabic term denotes the number twelve which here means that sect of Shia Muslims who believe in all twelve Imams starting from Hazrat Ali whom Shias believe to be the vicegerent of Prophet Muhammad (PBUH) as declared by the Prophet himself on several occasions. (Fatamid Law: Intr., XL. sqq. as quoted by A.A.A. Fyzee in his book Outlines of Muhammadan Law , 5th. Edn. 2008. page 24.) Also known as Twelvers, the Shia believe that the 12th. Imam is behind divine drape and will reveal on the Day of Judgment. (Translator).

spell as the poets of 'Sufism' while reciting '*sufi*' composition. The *salams* and *nohas* composed by Wajid Ali Shah are an example of the same passionate poetry. His command over language, innovative style, and religious fervor are characteristic features of his compositions, which are rarely found in the poets of that era. He was carried away by the appreciation of his work.[268] There is no match to his flow and simplicity when he composes spontaneously. Some verses from his 59-verse *Salam* are reproduced here:

Forest, mountain, light, Sun, Moon and the entire universe
Land and water, red and white, Imam is the owner of all
You! the Holy one, the Source of generosity, sea of valour
You! Fountain of kindness, pearl of Imamat, famous and popular
O! Pearl of the exalted river, Advisor of the Prophet's belief
The start (matla) of 'Ahmed's' Diwan, Salam on You by your appreciator
King of bravery, the killer of non-believer
King in exile, the friend of all
Progeny of the Prophet, Friend of Allah, *Pious*
The kernel of charity, The Prophet's dear, the famous
You! the dearest of Sibte Ahmed, Zehra and Ali
O! Brother of Hasan, apple of Prophet's eye
King of Kings of the World, Emperor of religion, dauntless
You the highest moon, the bright Sun
When my heart thinks of the shining face
The Sun shines on the sky
The beggar of the emperor of the Two Worlds is satisfied
You are the King of the poet, you are needed every time
Stars, Skies, Moon, Sun the sea and the good and the bad
The jinns the humans, the devils and the fairies all need you
O! The Moon of Fatima remember Akhtar surely

268. See the Salams of Mulk Akhtar especially on the rhyme and metre of Anis with the title verse namely '*Hum aasman se laey hain in zamenon ko.*'

Come to me along with Mehdi[269] *(for my salvation)*

In the above extract, there is an artistic display by the poet which is missing in the majority of his compositions. Like Ghazals, he insists on rhyming, but here he does not bother to adorn his feelings and thoughts. He also attempts to give descriptions through words as follows:

Bano said I die for you Sakina
Open your eyes and see your father Sakina
When the two earrings dangled in her ears
Strange Sakina stared at every face
'Baiyat' (to become someone's disciple) *was an excuse though killing was intended*
O Sakina! This is the blame on Shabbir,[270]
This was mandatory for the writer of destiny
Story of oppression was written for the heart
Crying and weeping is different from elegy
Name of Hussain is enough to impress
Alas! The portion which was kissed by Mustafa (Prophet PBUH)
This neck was the target of Shimr's (killer's name) *sword*
When in Karbala *evening fell* (Sham e Ghariban)
And the morning came
Zehra's star was shrouded with the cloud of martyrdom
The moonlight faded and the sunlight became barren
The Sun of deen (religion) *is eclipsed*
The light of the shining moon has faded
Friends! Continue with your tears
Daughter of Zehra is imprisoned in 'Shaam.'[271]

---

269. *Imaan,* Md. Wajid Ali Shah Akhtar. Matbaey Sultani. Calcutta. (Two Edns. 1288 & 1301). 102–8.
270. *Ibid,* 102–8.
271. *Ibid,* 158–59.

Lamenting on martyrs is usually associated with women, and even today in India, when there is lamentation, it is not in eloquent Urdu and is dominated by Hindi words. When Wajid Ali Shah composed lamentations starting with the words "*Bano ne kaha...*" or "*Zainab ne Kaha....*", he took particular care that it should not depict the common female style of lamentation. He knew that eloquence and richness of language at such a place would be undesirable. Following the advice of '*martaba dar nazr rakh kar*' (taking care of the status) would be unacceptable in matters of lamentation. However amidst the richness of language at such a place, and the common style of lamenting, the poet wandered. In this exercise he composed one '*salam*' in Hindi which is as follows:

Qasim the bridegroom was beheaded
Away from the bride he had a blood bath
Whom should the broken-hearted mother call
The dearest suffered the blow of arrow on his chest
The '*maang*' (hair parting) *was devastated, womb was destroyed*
The '*sindoor*' (vermillion) *was no longer auspicious*
When the mehndi was smeared on your palms
It was smeared with blood

No line of demarcation was drawn between '*noha*' and '*salam*' in Urdu, nor is any particular period fixed for their origin. However if this is done in the future, Wajid Ali Shah's *Diwan* will be of great use.

SONG WRITING (LYRICS)

In elegy and *nohas*, lamentation is the creation of the poet's mind. To make them impressive it is not at all necessary that they should contain the same words which were actually used. The poet is free to write as it suits him. As '*nohas*' and elegies are mainly associated with religion, some restrictions are inevitable. It is difficult to say how far Wajid Ali Shah succeeded in composing these lamentations. Other than lamentations, there is another genre which expresses feminine emotions, and is associated with Indian poetry. This is known as '*geet*' or songs. These emotions do not necessarily originate from real separation, nor do they have any connection with religion or spirituality. Thus:

> "Geets are a medium of melodious manifestation of feminism... it is the call of a woman, hence not only that it is passionate but instead of any imaginary figure it aims at a figure of real flesh and blood."[272]

A woman who is lost in love has no ability to think rationally and choose her words. She simply tries to impress and charm her lover, and employs all the means which would attract her lover. On rainy nights, the clouds float towards her, lightning creates a spell, the nightingale, peacock and cuckoo's songs reignite the fire of separation in her, and she is lost in the love of her lost lover. Her friends console her, Holi arrives, and she becomes hopeful of a reunion. But unaware of the responses of anyone, she becomes crazy about her lover, and out of this craze some words come out of her inner self and reach her lips. Such poetry has no similarity with Persian poetry, and its temperament, language, symmetry, and melody has nothing to do with the traditional poetry of Urdu.

Had Wajid Ali Shah regarded songs as an expression of emotions, or a means of conveying message like Kabir[273] and Meera Bai,[274] his songs would have been different from those which, due to his own restrictions, had lost any delight and impression. He did not compose songs merely for the sake of

---

272. *Urdu Shayari Ka Mijaz.* Wazir Agha. Seemant Prakashan, Delhi. (?). 163–64.

273. Kabir Das (1398–1513 CE) also known as Sant Kabir Saheb was a 15th. Century mystic poet, philosopher and spiritual teacher. Courtesy: Kabir - Wikipedia (Translator).

274. Mira Bai (born c. 1498 kudaki- Died 1547, Dwarka Gujarat). She was a Rajput Princess. She was a mystic and a poet. An image of Krishna was given to her during her childhood by a holy man whom ignited in her selfless devotion to Krishna. In cultural history she is known for song of devotion to Lord Krishna. Written and fact checked by the Editors of Encyclopedia Britannica. (2024) (Inserted by Translator)

it, but wanted to instill life into the music for which he thought that verbal expression was necessary. Hence the songs in *Najo*, *Dulhan*, and *Bani* are collected under various headings for various genres of music. For a long time, the language of the music of North India was '*brij*', and so in his songs, this is the predominant factor in which traces of Punjabi and Deccan Urdu are also found. He also tried to compose songs in Punjabi and plain Urdu, but was not very successful. His songs depict his musical expression more strongly, perhaps to compensate for the shortcomings in his poetic expressions. This means that he has more talent for music than for poetry. As one person put it, his '*thumris*' and '*daadars*' are more popular than his Ghazals.[275]

The romance of Radha and Krishna is an important topic in Hindustani songs. There are two dimensions of this romance: one is of '*sanjog*,' which depicts the physical union of Radha and Krishna, and the other of '*viyog*,' in which Radha is seen impatiently waiting for Krishna. Some of Wajid Ali Shah's *geets* depict this romantic background of Vrindavan, but in most of his songs a common Hindustani woman is seen. Deserted and forlorn, the woman sings in this manner:

The dark clouds come with lightning and sound
Blood is flowing from eyes,
The black cloud is coming listen! my beloved! I am yearning without you
The cuckoo sings and pierces my heart
The flowers decay... the common cuckoo harks and sings with lonely Akhtar[276]

A woman gives her heart to a soldier and sings:

You gallant guy your looks are bad
You snatch away my heart through sword...[277]

---

275. *Tarikh e Avadh,* Volume 5, 110.
276. *Najo,* 61.
277. *Bani,* 31.

The beetle sings about my darling, it is with my heart
Your face is like moon and you seduce me, I spend the night restlessly[278]

This woman enjoys the coquettish behavior of her lover, but she does not respond in a stereotypical way. She sings the following:

My sweetheart you touch my hand, I am unable to bear it
My bangles make sound, my arms become red, don't touch me.[279]
My dear (saiyyan) dye my chunri, my mind is getting sad
Dye it (so strongly) that the colour does not come out though the laundryman washes it for fifty times![280]
Repeat the name of 'girdhari' don't cheat with charming face

The woman in Wajid Ali Shah's *geets* is sometimes a gardener, a milk maid, a laundry woman, a water-bearer, or one of any other profession. The geets of '*mundhas*' (nuptial bower), of saying farewell to daughters (*rukhsati*), and of maternity do not belong to a particular community. In the *geets* of Wajid Ali Shah, these familiar voices are heard, and they present a familiar form of folk songs which are not only in harmony with the melody but also with their meaning.

From the viewpoint of language, one can say that the language of his *geets* is not pure (*shudh*). The most probable reason for this is that he was not proficient in Punjabi or in *Brij*, or maybe he intentionally adopted a middle path. Like the aforementioned *geets*, his other *geets* are also an amalgamation of *Brij*, *Avadhi*, Deccan, and Urdu. While this style is not new, some of the other *geets* have surpassed this amalgamation. In one *geet*, the initial part of the song (*aastai*) is in *Brij*, while the second line (*antra*) is in Persian. The amalgamation of two different languages is also found in the compositions of Amir Khusro. Wajid Ali Shah sought a fusion of two cultures:

278. *Ibid*, 27.
279. *Ibid*, 17.
280. *Ibid*, 17.

O! Native of Najaf *fill up the glass of Kausar*
There is jubilation with Ali Wali
Akhtar! What fun is going on[281]

Drawing a similarity between the festivals of '*Navroz*' and 'Holi' may be considered sacrilege, like the speaking of pure Hindi by the speakers of Lucknavi Urdu. Wajid Ali Shah did not care about all this when he arranged the '*rahas*' of Radha and Krishna. He was also not reluctant in fusing the words of these two languages in his songs. Ultimately, after centuries, such mixed language and culture has turned into a strong bond of mutual harmony.

MASNAVI WRITING

Intellectuals consider the recounting of events and facts to be an important part of poetry. The explanation goes as such:

> "In fact, relating the events tastefully is an important part of poetry which is not possible in a Ghazal. In this way, Mir Hasan, Naseem Lucknavi, and Mirza Shauqq were great chroniclers, but they do not affect the morals positively. Of course the compositions of Mir Anis especially the elegies of his last days ...are a wonder in Urdu literature."[282]

The poetry in various dramas from Greece, England, and India, and the epics of various nations and time periods can be presented as examples of this concept. However, though the *masnavis* of Wajid Ali Shah are artful, they are cursorily composed and contain no morals. This reference is only to remind one that relating events is part and parcel of such poetry. Such narration of events does not require an amalgamation of thoughts, art, and morals. The ability to think which is bestowed upon human beings is enough to transform them into poetry.

281. *Ibid*, 27.

282. *Zamana* (Monthly, Kanpur), March1911. Nazm Tabatabai, 233.

> "So long as a society is semi-cultured, and its knowledge and awareness is limited, life itself seems to be a story (or fable).The chronicle of life, which is a sequence of events and happenings, if related to a semi-cultured society then it often creates fear, surprise or enthusiasm which ultimately are the main ingredients of poetry."[283]

Wajid Ali Shah's *masnavis* contain such semi-cultured emotions and thoughts which did not convince cultured people, and even if they were convinced, they did not like it. The poet does not require objective knowledge to relate events because he is personally aware of them, and it is his own story. The secret of his success is that he had poetic competence, and for this he chose that form which suited his temperament the most. As Hali says:

> "Unless there is an urge for a thing in one's heart power of thinking is not generous in inspiring it."[284] "For poetic expression no situation or timing suits more than the passion which is spontaneously generated in one's heart."[285]

Before composing the *masnavis*, Wajid Ali Shah had great mental anxiety, and so one may not be surprised by the mastery with which he related these events. Other *masnavi* writers did not choose such subjects, nor did they look for such a suitable moment.

Regarding chronicle accounts (*Waqaya nigari*)[286] and masterful poetry, his three *masnavis*, *Ishq Nama*, *Huzn e* Akhtari and *Sabatul Quloob*, depict three natural inclinations of his mind. Out of these three *masnavis*, commentators are aware of only *Huzn e* Akhtari. Some have regarded it as one of the selected *masnavis* of Urdu literature,[287] some have regarded it as

---

283. *Muqaddamaey Sher o Shayari,* 108.

284. *Ibid*, 204.

285. *Ibid*, 203.

286. Relating certain events in such words that the reader gets a picturesque impression of the entire story. (Translator)

287. *Tarikh e Adab Urdu,* Ram Babu Saxena (Translator. Mirza Md. Askari. Naval Kissore Press. Lucknow. 1937. 259.

one of the five *masnavis* of the Lucknow School,[288] while some have regarded only this *masnavi* alone as mentionable.[289] But had anyone asked Wajid Ali Shah about *Huzn e* Akhtari, then he would have said that he himself finished *Huzn e* Akhtari and passed away before he could finish *Ishq Nama* and *Sabatul Quloob.*

Huzn e Akhtari is shrouded in melancholy, though he was a fan of luxury and opulence. The four other selected *masnavis* of Lucknow which are considered alongside *Huzn e* Akhtari are: *Sehrul Bayan*, *Gulzar Naseem*, *Zehre Ishq* and *Tilism e Ulfat.* But it is not proper to include *Huzn e* Akhtari with these, because they are all chronicle *masnavis* (*Dastani masnavi*). In such chronicle *masnavis*, the events are within the control of the writer, and he can mold and arrange the events according to his wishes. In historical *masnavis*, the writer cannot control events, and his mastery lies in the beauty of the selection, arrangement, and expression of these events.

Nazm Tabatabai presented moral grounds to cancel *Zehr Ishq* and other *masnavis.* The chronicle *masnavis*, no matter how morally strong they are, cannot meet the standard of relating events (Waqaey Nigari), especially when the composition of Anis is on one side of the scale. The composition of *Anis* is measured in pearls, and hence on the other side of the scale, those pearls will be put which are made available by other elegy writers, and there are none to suit the purpose. Here there is no room for the *masnavis* of Wajid Ali Shah either, but one with taste can say that the mastery and standard which is achieved by *Anis* in writing chronicles inspired Wajid Ali Shah. He was, to some extent, successful in imbibing those qualities in his own *masnavis.* Nazm Tabatabai would not be unaware of the *masnavi Ishq Nama*, but when *masnavi* of Mir Hasan was rejected on moral grounds, then regarding Wajid Ali Shah's *masnavi Ishq Nama*, the lesser said the better.

---

288. *Nazm Urdu,* Hakim Syed Abul ala Natiq Lucknavi, Zafarul Matabey, Lucknow 1941. 130.

289. *Urdu Masnavi Ka Irtiqaa,* Abdul Qadir Sarwari, Idaraey Abiyat Urdu, Hyderabad, 1940. 117–18.

An elegy writer must take care of historical facts, the etiquettes of poetry, and religious feelings. Regarding historical facts, there is no chance of any change or addition. The audience is already aware of such facts, and they only notice the presentation of the elegy writer. One who writes his biography is required to take care of his status and prestige, and he is the only person who is aware of all the events of his life. Hence, it is noteworthy which events of his life are reproduced and in what way. He is however not required to recite his story like an elegy writer. Thus, either a person is not ready to relate his own life story, or if he does do so, he should be prepared to pass through the trial.

An elegy writer, through his mastery, enlightens others. Some want to teach the lessons of poetry, some learn the lessons of morals and the poet himself gains name and fame, reward and requital (*sawab*).[290] An autobiographer neither intends to teach the lessons of poetry or morals, nor does he expect reward or appreciation. Whatever he writes, he writes out of passion, with poetic mastery, and with the hope that people will learn about his life and sympathize with him. It is a strange dimension of his fame, that people should take lessons from his life. It could not be presented as an ideal because he was a King and so it could only provide guidance for one who becomes a King. If one looks into the historical background, it is seen that the life of luxury and magnificence during Wajid Ali Shah's reign continued until the end, though there was a gradual downfall Wajid Ali Shah is a renowned 'lover'. Though he gained sympathy in this regard, he also faced resentment which continues till today. In the field of writing *masnavis*, there was a prominent change from previous trends, which ultimately reached the standard of *Zehre Ishq*.

The moon not only absorbs light from the Sun, but it also spreads it to others. Those living on the other side of the hill may perhaps not be aware of where the light is coming from, but those who enjoyed the moonlight can only explain its charm. Hali has repeatedly advised reading the compositions

290. One of the five principles of Islam to guide the behavior of a Muslim entailing punishment or reward. Sawab means a person gets salvation and achieves great reward for the good deeds he does. (Translator)

of Anis.[291] This advice also came with the warning that no one can achieve his zenith in elegy writing, nor should one resort to this genre.[292] It was not difficult for a knowledgeable evaluator, assessor, and critic like Hali to dive deep into the elegies of Anis and conclude that in his compositions, there are hidden secrets of poetry which will benefit and enrich the poets to come. However, he could not discover the intricacies of *Tilism e Ulfat* and *Bahar e Ishq*, and perhaps kept silent, thinking that strangely enough, the poets of Lucknow could not gain anything from *Anis*. Had Hali received the *masnavis* of Wajid Ali Shah, there would have been no need for him to go up to '*Khwab o Khayal*' for '*Bahar e Ishq*.' He would have found the qualities of *Anis's* work which were mentioned.[293] Everyone deciphers poetry based on their own competence. Whatever Wajid Ali Shah gained from *Anis* was based on his own boldness, and whatever Shauqq gained from Wajid Ali Shah was based on his own taste. Present intellectuals are aware of the incomplete lessons which Shauqq gained from Wajid Ali Shah, but the information is presented in a way that gives Wajid Ali Shah a bad name, and all the credit is given to Shauqq.*z* Shauqq is kept on such a high pedestal that no one dares to raise their fingers towards him.[294] *Ishq Nama* is the proof of Shauqq*'s* character.[295]

To save Shauqq*'s* name, it was propagated that the King himself used to write such *masnavis.*[296] People forgot the year of writing of *Fareb e Ishq*, and that it was written years before *Ishq Nama.* Perhaps this inspired the King; as Shauqq did not have the courage to pen down the real events, why should he not try it himself?

291. *Muqaddamaey Sher o Shayari,* 264–66.

292. *Muqaddamaey Sher o Shayari,* 272.

293. In the starting pages of *'Rooh e Anis'* the comments of Prof. Masood Hasan are worthwhile.

294. *Tazkira e* Shauqq, 113–16.

295. *Ishq Nama* (Hndwritten), Poetic. *Daastan* 28.

296. *Nayaz Fatehpuri* in appreciation of Nawab Mirza Shauqq.

To judge the *Waqiya Nigari* in Shauqq*'s masnavis*, the masnavis, the narration of Hali[297] and the statement of Shauqq himself are present.[298] In these *masnavis*, the men are speechless while the women are extremely talkative. Neither the upper class ladies nor the women of the red light district could compete with them. Shauqq enjoyed recording the idiomatic language of women, and in this regard he was inspired by Wajid Ali Shah's masnavis (*Daastani masnavi*). But Wajid Ali Shah was a playwright, and his dialogues were balanced. Shauqq was not a playwright. He neither cared for the standard of the women he was writing about, nor for the suitability of situation. Wajid Ali Shah's *masnavis* are a topic of research, and anyone who takes on this responsibility would realize that, though we are not very familiar with his *masnavis*, the King's contemporaries were not as unaware of it as is implied by the commentators.

Wajid Ali Shah's poetic excellence cannot be measured by his *masnavis* because in these *manavis* the events were imaginary, and this was his first composition. *Huzn e* Akhtari and *Haibat e Haidari* are incomplete and do not complement his temperament. Short *masnavis* were also composed, and in these the mastery of the poet could not be revealed. *Ishq Nama* and *Sabatul Quloob*, though complete and spontaneous, are imperfect and are translations – their basic source is Persian. But of all these *masnavis*, those which can be regarded as the sum total of the poet's life and the treasure of Urdu literature are *Ishq Nama* and *Sabatul Quloob*. These two *masnavis* are related to Wajid Ali Shah as legs are related to the human body. In terms of quality, *Ishq Nama* is unmatched in Urdu literature, and *Sabatul Quloob* is a work of wonder in eloquence and unwieldiness. But when a master like

---

297. *Muqaddamaey Sher o Shayari,*Khwaja Altaf Hussain Hali. Maktabaey Jaddi. Lahore. 1953. 286–87.

298. In the ending lines of *Bahar e Ishq* (Handwritten) statement of Shauqq that the masnavi was composed on the request of Nawab Anwar Ali Khan to include the phrases(mahawrat) of the women. There is no such statement for Fareb e Ishq or for Zehr *e Ishq* but their style of composition is the same.

Nasikh, while translating the *Hadith*, loses patience after composing about 200–400 couplets, then that poet's caliber and competence can be exemplary who in the same field composes about one lakh couplets. The bulkiness of *Sabatul Quloob*, and the mastery of *Ishq Nama* still require recognition, and the credit they deserve is long overdue. Unfortunately, one is unknown and obscure, while the other is ill famed.

THE LONGEST MASNAVI OF URDU LITERATURE

In the four or five century history of Urdu literature, many *masnavis* were composed. It is not easy to say that which is the longest one. It is quite possible that, like *Sabatul Quloob*, there are other *masnavis* which are still hidden from the common gaze. But so far, based on the comments given by the evaluators, *Sabatul Quloob* is given a place of pride as the longest ever Urdu *masnavi.*

Writer of '*Tarikh e Masnaviyat Urdu*'[299] has mentioned two long and worthwhile *masnavis* in the following words:

A. "Rustami who is one of the prominent poets of Deccan wrote a masnavi '*Khawar Nama*' on the request of elder daughter of Quli Qutub Shah son of Ibrahim Qutub Shah in which in about eighty thousand couplets relating the achievements of Hazrat Ali KaramAllahwajahu are composed."[300]

B. *Munshi* Amir*ullah* with the pen name Tasleem wrote about 6–7 *masnavis* which are memorable. In the last *masnavi* 'Shaukat *Shajahani*' there is narration of the journey to England of the ruler of Rampur which has 32,000 couplets."[301]

---

299. *Tarikh e Masnaviyat Urdu',* Maulvi Hafiz JalauddinAhmed Jafri, Matbaeu Anwar Ahmed. Allahabad. 13–14.

300. *Ibid.*

301. *Ibid.*

Both of these narrations require some investigation – perhaps he did not see the *masnavis* himself, and those who have seen them may have a different opinion. It goes as below:

A. Those who have a right to comment on the literature of Deccan opine that the number of couplets of *Khawar Nama* is not more than 24,000.

"Rustami's name was Kamal Khan...other than '*Qasaids*' and 'Ghazal*yat*' he also wrote a *masnavi* titled *Khawar Nama.* Only one copy of *Khawar Nama* is available, which is in London. In the *Khawar Nama* of Rustami (proprietor of the India Office), Ali Ibrahim wrote a note in Persian in 1889 in which the number of the couplets and images of the *Khawar Nama* are also given. In it 23,735 couplets and 150 images are mentioned. Though Rustami has translated this from Persian, but this cannot be called translation because *Khawar Nama* is the first longest epic *masnavi* of Urdu. The proof of Rustami's poetic competence and eloquence is evident from the fact that this bulky *masnavi* comprises some 24,000 couplets which he composed within a short period of two and a half years... Rustami himself composed the date of its writing," as below;

The Flight of the Prophet

Was in the year with one thousand plus fifty and nine (1059 A.H.) (1649 A.D.).

Rustami calculated this at that time.

Rustami's *Khawar Nama* was not been published so far.[302]

"The Khawar Nama of Rustami is considered as one of the longest masnavis of Urdu because there are about twenty four thousand couplets in it."[303]

302. Thesis of Prof. Nasiruddin Hashmi, '*Aligarh Tarikh Adab Urdu*', 285–87.

303. Dr. Mohiuddin Qadri Zor, *Dakkini Adab Ki Tarikh,* 46.

In addition, both the statements agree on the point that there are about 24,000 couplets in the *Khawar Nama*, which is less than half the length of the *Sabatul Quloob*.

By 'Shaukat *Shajahani*' is meant '*Safarnamaey Khusravi*', the *masnavi* of Tasleem. In this *masnavi* Tasleem, with reference to newspapers and letters, has accounted for the journey to Europe of Nawab Hamid Ali Khan Bahadur. Towards the end of the *masnavi* he writes about his attempts;

Ultimately in a short period of six months
This was transformed from prose to poetry
Labored very hard
Then retrieved thousands of precious pearls (excellent expressions)
Thus in the end the gist of my narration is
The account of Khusravi's journey which is the year (1312 A.H.).[304]

In the complete handwritten copy of the *masnavi*, there are about 264 pages. Every page has a 21-line format, with about 20 couplets. Thus, by this calculation, and if the headings are ignored, the number of couplets will not be more than 13,944. Tasleem, other than the *masnavi* mentioned above, has composed two other *masnavis* in the context of the nawabs of Rampur, which are its poetic history. The first is *Tawarikh e Badih*, which is about the events from the time of Nawab Ali Md. Khan Bahadur to that of Nawab Kalbe Ali Khan Bahadur. The second is *Tawarikh e Kaamil*, which relates events from the death of Nawab Kalbe Ali Khan Bahadur up to Nawab Hamid Ali Khan Bahadur's accession to the throne. These three parts were not compiled by Tasleem, but he composed them from the books which were provided to him. In the Preface of *Tarikh e Badih* he writes:

Hence after some days
I got a heartening statement

304. *Safarnamaey Khusravi* (Handwritten), 263–64.

When I checked it
I saw that it is fully correct and authentic
I then composed the prose matter
With all my hard labour and thinking[305]

Regarding these historical poems, a well-known writer says:

> "There are hardly historical *masnavis* in Urdu and there is no other such a long historical poetic book."[306]

There are 212 pages in *Tarikh e Badih*, and 186 pages in *Tarikh e Kaamil*. Both have a 23-line format.[307] In this way, the number of couplets come to (186 + 212)×23 = 9,154. If the couplets of *Safar Namaey Khusravi* are added to this, the total would still be less than in the *Khawar Nama*, which contains 23,735 couplets. In all the three *masnavis* of Tasleem, there are at most 23,098 couplets. There are 48,150 couplets in the first two volumes of *Sabatul Quloob*, which means there are more there than the combined total of the couplets in the *masnavis* of Rustami and Tasleem. There is no possibility of adding to the *masnavis* of Rustami and Tasleem, where the couplets are counted as above. In this count, even the headings have been included, increasing the number of lines from 21 to 23.

In Wajid Ali Shah's *masnavis* there is the possibility of an increase in the number of couplets like Volume 1, it is possible that some more handwritten copies of Volume 2 will be discovered that are more complete than the present ones. The compositions of all three of these poets are also worth mentioning because all of them have composed in '*Behre Mutaqaarib Mussaman*

305. *Tawarikh e Badih* (Handwritten) 15.
306. *Lucknow Ka Dabistan e Shayari*, 748.
307. Perhaps due to mistake of writing twenty three is written. In both the hand written copies there are 21-lined pages on which at the most twenty one couplets are written. In this way as per the count of pages instead of 9,154 only 8,358 pages are counted.

Makhdoof.'[308] Of them, two were professional writers. While one though was not a professional, he was well aware of the art, and must have written more pages than the previous two writers. Three poets from Lucknow, namely Mir*za Asghar Ali Naseem Dehelvi*, *Munshi Totaram Shayan*, and *Munshi Shadi Lal Chaman*, had collectively written a *masnavi* titled '*Alif Laila Nau Manzoom*,' which has been published. The printed copy is 23-lined with 1,234 pages. There are two couplets in every line. Apart from the headings, based on the number of pages, there could be up to 56,764 couplets. None of these compositions are even half of the size of Wajid Ali Shah's composition.[309] And if the compositions of all the three are compared with the *Sabatul Quloob*, then further investigation will be required to determine the correct number of couplets. The inclusion of headings will make a difference of thousands. However, in the *Sabatul Quloob*, one will have to include even those couplets which were once regarded to be the compositions of an outsider. *Sabatul Quloob* was an individual's work, while the others are the combined efforts of three people. Hence, such comparison will not be very truthful or effective. Just like Totaram ji completed the incomplete masnavi, similarly some other person may take over the task of completing Volume 2 of *Sabatul Quloob*.

THE MOST ILL-FAMED MASNAVI OF LUCKNOW

Ishq Nama, like *Huzn e* Akhtari and *Sabatul Quloob*, is not a composition from Bengal. Each and every line was composed on the soil of Lucknow by its ruler, in the local language. Its unpopularity is evident from its disappearance. Only two of copies are available in print, and both of these are incomplete. Many pages are missing from the beginning, middle, and end of the book.[310]

---

308. There are many 'behers' or meters in which poetry is composed. This is one of the techniques which denotes the prosodic meter of verse in Urdu poetry

309. *Naseem Dehelvi*, 17,710 couplets (First Volume); *Shayan*, 20,792 couplets in Second and Third Volumes; *Chaman*, 18,262 couplets (Only Third Volume).

310. *Hamari Zaban* (Weekly, Aligarh). Issue Dated 15th January 1966, 4.

For years, tolerated the brunt of the King's unpopularity and ill fame and now they are not willing to bring it in public as this will be considered a 'makruh' or undesirable act. (Makruh under Islamic law is an act which though not a sin but is rendered undesirable).

Apart from the literary viewpoint, their concealment of it by these people is, to some extent, justifiable. Though this *masnavi* can be appreciated for its qualities, for the frankness and guts of the writer, it is at the same time likely to cause misunderstandings. The luxuries of Wajid Ali Shah were publicized and then targeted by the critics due to his own bold account of his opulent life. Even if these parts were excluded, what would be left would not have been enough to make his life seem exemplary. Wajid Ali Shah was well aware of the fact that he was very popular among the masses and that people were crazy about him. However, if a person himself equips others with arms to rise against him, it will be said that either he is the biggest fool, or it would suit him to ask 'What harm they will cause by going against me?' We can form any opinion regarding the good and bad points of his poetic biography, and it will reflect our taste. The writer of *Masnavi* has written, in plain and direct terms, what he wanted to relate about his own life. While this narration discusses the luxuries of life, with bold scenes and talk of sex, it also portrays politeness, decency, respect for religion, and a fear of Allah. A farsighted eye sees both the roses and the thorns, and enjoys it. A blind man does not see either, and when the thorn pierces him, he pulls back his hand, and when he smells the perfume, he is impressed.

The subject of the *masnavi* is the evoking of sexual desires and sexual dialogue. It is unsuitable to call a *masnavi* with such a lascivious topic '*Ishq Nama*'. However, in the philosophy of emotions '*Ishq*' is a decent name for such sexual urges and sensuality, and when fused with other emotions, it has been regarded as holy and righteous:

> "People have defined 'Ishq' in different ways and terms but a study of human nature shows that that Ishq is but a special form of sexual urge. Today no matter in how many versions Ishq is seen and felt which though

apparently seems to be varied but in fact they all culminate in the same point of lasciviousness."[311]

For a poet with sordid taste, it would have been possible to name the *masnavi* '*Pari Khana*', 'Sarwar *e Khaqani*,' '*Aamal Nama*' or something similar. However, the tasteful way in which Wajid Ali Shah has expressed the different shades of this emotion is reflected in both the name and the starting couplets of the *masnavi.*[312] Instead of dithering with words like he did in '*Hamd*', '*Naat*', and '*Manqibat*' (his other *masnavis*), in this work, which was his magnum opus, he comes directly to the subject after only a few verses:

First I will sing to the glory of Khuda Kareem
The omniscient, the omnipotent and the Compassionate
Now I sing to the glory of Muhammad (PBUH)
And I appreciate and commend the lineage of Prophet
Ahmed (PBUH) who is the friend of Allah
He is aware of Allah *and* Allah *is aware of him*
Had 'Ishq' not been a requirement of Allah
Then Prophet would not have been His friend
Had there not been revelation of the ancient beauty
Then Kalim (ullah) would not have fainted on Toor (Mountain)
Therefore the stories of Ishq are strange
These all are the coquetry and Miracles *of 'Ishq'*
No living being is without it
It is the life of every iota of this world
Often it is in the form of blaze of the Sun

---

311. *Falsafaey Jazbat*, Maulana Abdul Majid Daryabadi. (Not more given) 209.

312. If the wisdom is complete, then every letter will have a different title (Anis). While compiling *Ishq Nama* (Persian) to *Ishq Nama* (Poetic) many changes were made in the headings, but the name of the book was not changed. This is also mentioned in the discussion of the Ishq Nama, (See, the Thesis, 420). Recalling two books with the same name forcefully endorses the suitability of the title. (*Ishq Nama*).

Often it is in the form of the sparkle of the Toor
It is like the tear in the eye and a scar in the heart
Like a flower in the garden or a lamp in the gathering (mehfil)
Often it is like a grain in the threshing ground
Often it is like the voice of a Bulbul
The curly tresses of Laila
Put a chain around Majnun's feet
Often it is the sparkle
Often it is the chisel of the mountain digger
It is present in every shade and form
It is like a pearl in the oyster and like ruby in stones
If it reaches the stone then it becomes a flame
If it reaches the sky then it becomes a star
Often it is like pupil of the eye
Often like a Mirror *in the company of the sweetheart*
It becomes magic when it reaches the eyes
It becomes a deer when it reaches the wilderness
Often it is like tresses in the form of the waves
Often it is like the eye of the whirlpool
Often it becomes the target of grief
Often it is spread on the shoulder like hair
Ultimately the 'Ishq' is the liveliness of every house
From earth to sky it is 'Ishq'

Though the poet associates '*Ishq*' with the land and sky, he still does not reveal when he felt the first bite of love. According to Maulvi Najmul Ghani Khan, Wajid Ali Shah had a romantic temperament since his childhood:

> "On his fifth birthday he enjoyed the lap of a forty-year-old heavy-bodied woman."[313]

313. *Tarikh e Avadh,* Volume 5, 47. This narrative is in fact not the statement of Maulvi Sahab because like verses most of the part of his biography is taken form Talism e Hind. But Maulvi Sahab instead of Talism e Hind presented "Wajid Ali Shah's masnavi" as a proof.

At the age of five, one cannot even distinguish the genders; his falling in love with a forty-year-old woman is a baseless claim. Had the historian taken this from Wajid Ali Shah's autobiography, and narrated it without any additions or amendments, more details about the incident would have been revealed. Wajid Ali Shah himself explains the moment of his sexual awakening in the following words:

My labor did not yield a result
I did not get the taste of love
Hence when I reached the age of eight
My eyes started staring at the beauty
I saw a new day that day
I got entangled in the situation
That a simply good looking woman
Her name was Rahiman and she was my governess
That lady was of the age of forty five or so
She had heavy and plump body
I was not in my full senses
Her lap was my bed
She took out new tunes from heart
Started spreading her hand everywhere
She displayed her fairy face
She turned a pious into a lover
There was a big difference between me and her
I was like cotton and she like fire, I like a glass and she like a stone
I was very much surprised at things
What to say how disturbed I was?
She frightened me as a master

He is not even aware of the name of this masnavi. At present either no proof is given or Maulvi Sahab's statement is presented as proof. See, Pari Khana, 11–12. *Tazkiraey* Shauqq, 138. *Hamari Zaban* (Weekly, Aligarh). Issue January 8, 1966.

She threatened as a teacher
No solution came with her acceptance
It left a mark on the wall[314]

This was not the first time he interacted with a mature woman at a young age. Turning young boys into lovers is a topic that has held the interest of many psychologists and sexologists, on which they have compiled their 'collections' (*Kulliya*). These collections profess that the more intelligent a child is, the sooner his sexual desires awaken, and the more beautiful a child is, the faster he turns to lasciviousness.[315] The reality of these '*kulliyat*' fully applied to Wajid Ali Shah. Then came a time in his life that, when recalling the events, he recounts with the words "*I was like cotton and she like fire, I like a glass and she like a stone.*" Rahiman passed away after a few years, but the flame she ignited was not doused throughout his life, and the so called 'glass' continued to break into small pieces. In his own words:

What to say how long this company remained
I came to the age of nine and ten
By the time I reached ten I could not get her whereabouts
Where she vanished, to what direction she went
But by then I had caught the fever of romance (ishq)
This frenzy continued unabated[316]

He relates not just one or two, but dozens of his illegal affairs with pleasure, but he also does not miss discussing his lawful connections. Here, we see a different side of Wajid Ali Shah's personality, one of natural virtue and dignity. He believed a wife is a wife, with gravitas and station, and cannot be a 'beloved' (*Mashuqa*). When he talks about his sweethearts, he mentions

314. *Ishq Nama* (Handwritten), Dastan.

315. Cann, Fronter, 519.

316. *Ishq Nama* (Handwritten), Dastan.

their age, figure, and their intimacy with brevity. But wherever he thought of maintaining respect and dignity, he did not disclose their profile or his intimacy with them. In the eagerness of marriage, he writes about thirty-eight couplets as an introduction, but when the bride arrives, the details are composed in only three couplets, as below:

There was henna ritual and marriage
Both met and the difference vanished
The rituals of the elite class
Were performed by my relatives
Where there was connection between husband and wife
The intimacy continued for six months[317]

Ironically, the women whose names are not mentioned in the *Ishq Nama* were those who left behind memorable imprints: Nawab Badshah Mahal Alam who is important in the history of Urdu literature, and Nawab Hazrat Mahal who is significant in the history of India.

An important point of attention is that when discussing cohabitation, the situation is described in a pleasant manner, and nowhere does the poet use lewd or bawdy expressions. Hali definitely always blamed those with 'shamelessness' who resorted to verbal debauchery. But had he perused *Ishq Nama* he would have surely appreciated decent expressions in Wajid Ali Shah's masnavi who though was well known for voluptuousness. The words, 'The mark was imprinted on the wall,' 'she herself became the quilt', and 'many targeted rightly' were such fine metaphors, that only an experienced reader could comprehend the symbolism. Shauqq relates the reality of cohabitation, though it is not necessary to explain each factor, as in the following verses:

317. *Ishq Nama* (Handwritten), Dastan.

Rubbed, lubricated made to sit
Pressed, embraced, cajoled, seduced[318]
Stood, sat down, held close, squeezed and caressed

In abusive language, there is so much of reality, but in literature even the abuses can be explained with decency. The *masnavis* which take us to moral ends must not resort to immoral or bawdy language. The explanation of the situation in the above two couplets indicates his language, which eventually becomes distasteful. Wajid Ali Shah explains the same situation in the following words:

The boat was jammed to the boat
Till morning the chests were joined[319]

A person with taste can easily understand which one of these is the artistic expression. Wajid Ali Shah had control over the use of symbolism and synonyms at proper places, which is evident in many parts of this *masnavi* and at innumerable places in his other compositions where, without any weight or hesitation, he continues to weave the words. This is craftsmanship, not just poetry.

Wajid Ali Shah is the hero of his tales (*Daastan*), but these tales are not imaginary; they are the combination of his own experiences. How honestly and sincerely the poet has narrated them is evident from his initial statements. After he has gained our trust, it is quite possible that we would accept his every legitimate point, provided it is not destroyed by the flaws of exaggeration. Wajid Ali Shah has taken care of this up to the end. After marriage, amidst the fervor of youth and opulence, he developed relationships with a good number of women. Some relationships were temporary, some were permanent, sometimes he had a crush on others, and sometimes others

318. *Bahar e Ishq* (Handwritten). See the narration of cohabitation.
319. *Ishq Nama* (Handwritten), Dastan, 28.

fell in love with him. But in these relationships, he was mindful of self-respect, family prestige, religious mandates, and decorum.

In the following verse, a prostitute comes; she dances, and has a crush on the King. She is afraid of her mistress, he is anxious about his father, but he does not look for excuses to meet the prostitute:

One day I invited her for 'mujra'
I was pleased with closeness
She was concerned about her mother
I was afraid of my father
On both sides there was the same anxiety
There was separation like Sun and the Moon[320]
Another married woman says that she saw the King in her dream:
The dream was strange
As if she was gifted with some wealth
Love showed the way to reunion
As if in the dream the king was like a beggar
There was much chatting in the dream
"The nights of separation were prolonged
Now I have neither patience nor tolerance
Come soon to my house
How long this hiding will continue?
Isn't it strange to forget love?
I don't want so much of indifference
O! You Inconsiderate! I want to hear from you"
When suddenly I awoke from dream
Then I saw there was nothing except me
Said "O Allah *what scandalous outrage!*
What happened within a moment?

320. *Ibid*, 46.

Where is the face which I had seen just now?
Where is the wealth I had just now?"[321]

Thus, a servant was engaged as a mediator:

Went to him and said "O! You
Will you do my work, I request
Show me that face again
Show me some solution"[322]

The servant took this message to the King:

Firoz gave me this message
Said "Excellency! Congratulations! For this month
Khuda gives me chance to maintain
The needy gets the need fulfilled."[323]

But the King was not interested in illegal relations, hence he says:

I said: "She has her husband
Don't shame me before God
Don't play with me like this
I have not played with (marital) ties yet."[324]

On another occasion, a young dancer was ready to give up her profession, provided the King was ready to accept her:

The next day she lost her patience
She uncontrollably made a request to me
"My Messiah! Have mercy on me

321. *Ibid*, 32.
322. *Ibid*, 32.
323. *Ibid*, 52.
324. *Ibid*, 28.

I am sick, give me medicine
No one gives such strange messages
But what to do? I am unable to control
Save me! I am dying
For God sake give me some relief
Bestow some favor on me
I have informed you (about my plight)
If you will delay then where will I be?
It is said that life is above everything
If you say I will unhesitatingly give my life
You can thrash me if I go back on my words
Neither my heart nor my life is more precious than you
The entire life I will be at your service
Have such mercy on me
That it will be remembered by the whole world."
That flower (woman) made such sweet talks
That I became her fan like (bulbul)
When I saw her pathetic condition
I was forced to have mercy on her
Though this heart is full of loyalty
But I always feared my father
This was a new problem for me
There was no medicine though my heart bruised[325]

Good poetry is that which gives the taste of prose. The above lines are so masterfully composed that there can be no better expression, not even in prose.

Because of these romantic stories and relationships, the King's clan became a host of '*mamtua* Begmats,'[326] who adorned his *Pari Khana.* In this

325. *Ibid*, 52.

326. Those wives of the King with whom he contacted *'Mut'a'* marriage. (Translator)

Pari Khana, if grace and beauty were at their zenith, then there were also some mischievous developments. The poet weaves these two contradictory dimensions of the *Pari Khana* in such an eloquent and graceful manner that it remains unparalleled in any other *masnavi* of Urdu literature. The following shows his mastery in painting the picture:

By God's grace there was heaven on earth
Pari Khana got a new gleam
In fact it was the Divine help
It actually pleased me a lot
Every style was mesmerizing
It was not Pari khana but like a tavern
The wine of beauty intoxicated so much
That everyone there forgot himself
At some corner woman smiled like flower
She was of jolly nature as per the gathering
At places there were hushed talks, and at places there were gestures
At places there were romance or pleasant scenes
There were explanations, or rudeness
At places there was fight on abuses
Often there were passing remarks, often peeping
There were amorous glances, warmth of love
Some lifted their dress
Some took care of 'dupatta'
Some frowned at the unwanted glances
While the self, the heart and the glances all were scattered
Often there was style and coquetry in everything
The gestures carried thousands of tales
There were riddles and puzzles
While some were fond of tales
Some shone like the star
Often every part of the body danced

Some left their tresses on face
Some had fixed glances
What to say all of them were clever
All of them were brutal
They were engrossed in their dances
They were surprisingly drenched in songs
The songs were like raining clouds
All the roads were obstructed
Someone was jolly, someone impatient,
They were able to make others laugh or weep
When I saw all this
The flower of joy bloomed
The people were very considerate
All the lovers were very romantic at heart
There was extravagance all the time
There was no sense (or feel) of day or night
When I was free of one (beloved)
Then the other was ready
When there was separation there was sickness
But when there was union, then came relief
Often the beloved was a fan of the lover
Often the beloved was very loving
With the thought of separation the senses were lost
Sitting together and eating together was the only charm
Who bothered for 'Kaaba' or temple?
Every play and entertainment was there (Pari Khana)
Without her company there was no joy
Even the fairy failed to impress.[327]

There was no need to search for words; it was as if the words were naturally in their proper place. This mesmerizing narration is seen not only

327. *Ishq Nama* (Hand written), Dastan, 61.

in description, but also in conversation. The narration about pleasant things like request sycophancy and adulation by members of '*Parikhana*' is over.

Hence, the following verse describes the shrewdness, infighting, and erratic attitude of the women in the feminine style and wording. In the background is the hot ambience of the *Pari Khana* in which the unruly Begmats are busy gossiping about each other:

Every one told the other out of jealousy
"If I am bad then you are also not pious
How you are good and virtuous
You are connected with the unnamed."[328]
Helplessly the King brings them together and enquires about their disloyalties:
I asked them with tears in my eyes
"What is the matter, tell me quickly
This insolence with such a master"
All of them touched their ears
Both Sarfraz and Hoor *said*
Huzoor! What disgraceful thing is this?
This is lie, there was ear poisoning unnecessarily
One who claims must come and prove
She should say what she wants to say
Must show and confront it
Huzoor! Where you see with your own eyes
You may punish me as you like
There are many talks (and rumors) in this world
Why to believe the backbiting
I was speechless with this argument
This was proper reasoning hence had no reply.[329]

328. *Ibid*, 81.
329. *Ibid*, 77.

Sarfraz Begum, who was accused of being unchaste, was angry with the King. The King was impatient to cajole her, but she refused to even meet him:

After all one day I came across that naughty woman
Only myself and she was there
Impatiently I started relating[330]
"O! Disloyal and unkind
How long you will remain strange like this?
How long this problem of mine will continue?
Now I am hopeful of love
It depends on the rivals
Whatever cruelty you want to do with me
If you want to destroy me then destroy fast
The empire of heart be devastated
Anything which is to happen tomorrow must happen today
If you will keep on worrying me like this
Then you will be worse than enemies
Presently you have control
Nigar! I want your attention"

Hoor *Begum*, who was so vehement about her innocence, was once seen with someone else. The brother of that man came to see the King, who was not aware of the details of the incident:

The three brothers became aware
They fell on my feet
I was surprised as to what is this?
(I) Said "Tell me is everything ok what is the problem?"
They wept like rainy clouds

330. (Couplet) *It was the common style of the elite. The expression and the earnestness was the same (Anis).*

They could not even speak properly
When I insisted strongly
They said "What to tell what is the incident?
May God take me out of this trouble
If death is to be given then I should be burned
My brother who is Haider Ali
What to say about him
(In) The Hoor *Mahal of the King*
He was captivated there
He is in captivation and he is surrounded by heavy crowd
*B*Ashir *and Firoz did all this"*
I asked him "Are you Taqseer?" He kept mum
What to relate the undesirable talks
But how to say whatever I could understand
My heart is pierced with the pangs of pain
Apparently I consoled him a lot
I controlled my anger much."[331]

Then morning came, and people gathered before the King with a letter in their hand. They were accompanied by the accused. The charge was made:

"The Hoor *of the Mahal has compromised with him*
If you see then it is all her fault
She wrote this letter to me
This I am going to read
If the secret is disclosed
Then I will give you two thousand gold" (rupees)
When the secret was disclosed before me
I felt much ashamed

331. *Ibid*, 117.

He threw one glance towards the letter, and another towards the accused:

Then Haider Ali *appeared*
He was in chains
There was a wave of grief in my heart
I became very angry and I spat on his face
But even then he ignored it
But all the four brother were expelled
The wrong must be punished
What to do there is no punishment for this wrong

Despite having high status and authority, if he forgave such wrongs, it was due to his kindness and high-level character, and not helplessness.

This family was brought to the palace. Note the narration of fury and justice in the King's own words:

But this is universal truth
That Allah *is the biggest emperor*
The accused is charged with sin
What the woman and the child have to do with the accused?
There is nothing improper here they are not starving for livelihood.[332]

The repetition of events and incidents in a limited setting is not at all surprising. The commendable fact is that, in spite of this monotony, the poet has created so much freshness and charm in his compositions that the audience and the readers of the *masnavi* do not feel that they have come across such tales before. As it was a biography, it was possible for the poet to mention the political, social, and cultural interests of his time, but to stay consistent with the title of the *Daatan* (*Ishq Nama*), only those events are mentioned which maintain the continuity of the subject. The birth of

332. *Ibid.*

children, the deaths of those that were dear, the construction of buildings and gardens, and the organization of meetings, are all narrated in a very concise manner. Such narrations make the reader aware of the background, while also revealing the poet's ability to describe varied subjects with mastery and flow. For instance, while he shows interest in charming and beautiful women, always looking for pretty faces, his gaze is also fixed on clay toys. He looks for satire and fun in these toys. This is clear from the following:

There were plays of the young ones
Toys of the innocent ones
He started selling these things so cheap
The old lady for one penny (damri)
The elite were so worthless
Mirza *for half aana and rich for one paisa*
The poor were brought down so much
That the chun chun (toy) for one-eight anna delighted the kids
Young kids were made into soldiers
With their sword of wood and shield of clay.[333]

And when the same poet, forgetting the pomp and show of the fairyland (*parikhana*), laments the death of his father, the colour of the sky is changed:

Suddenly the times changed
The crown of the empire fell off
The lamenting of the King was very strange
The pomp of crown and the empire vanished
The eye lashes were choked with blood
The world was dark and devastated
There was dust all over the heads

---

333. *Ibid*, 96.

The garden of Lucknow was devastated
Why not ! the resting deer flew in fear
All the houses were black colored
The morning was also devastated
The evening spread its fragrant tresses all over
The shriek of grief was so strong
Even the angels' ears were pierced
All the men and women started weeping badly
They beat their chest with 'maatam'
Even the stars on the sky were tearful
Forehead of the moon and the head of the Sun were open
The wind too was mourning
The earth scattered dust all over
The lamenting threw so much of noise
That the Gomti River became a stream of commotion
The birds were extremely sad
They came out leaving behind their nests
They came out while lamenting and beating their chest
There was melancholy and regret all over
Often there was the shriek of bulbul in the garden
Often there was weeping by the chukor in mountains
This behavior pierced the heart badly
Of the ruby in Badakhshan[334] *and cornelian in Yemen*[335]
The fervor of 'maatam' left a scar
On the flower in the garden and the lamp in the gathering
By listening to such soulful shrieks
The dead in their graves and the people in their homes were saddened
Every loyal was fully broken and tearful

334. A province in Afghanistan (Translator)

335. Republic of Yemen in West Asia (Translator). A reader if well versed in Urdu must go through the original composition to get the taste of poetry of class. (Translator).

In fact the court was burdened with sorrow
In fact the tragedy touched me so passionately
That I became a statue of sorrow from top to bottom
The tragedy rendered the world worthless for me
That I was so close to the great soul.[336]

After describing his own covetousness, the insincerity of women, and the disloyalty of servants, he takes the reader to a different world, where instead of immoral tales, he relates about the admonitory and lesson giving happenings with same fervor and sincerity with which he relates the vulgarity in the *masnavi.* It is not possible that a person of taste be affected by one and not by the other. After his father's death, the entire world seemed shattered. The untimely demise of dear ones showed him the temporary nature of the world and the momentary worth of life:

Where is stability in the life?
That this five day old life is transitory
Who is happy and contented here?
The worthlessness of life is the rule here
Every wave is giving this news
Let's go let's go let's go[337]

O! cupbearer (Saaqia) not only my heart is full of grief
The whole world is mourning
If dust is scattered over the land
The sky is pierced with the galaxy
On the skies it is not star or Sun
It is the scar of my heart
This is not the circle around the moon

336. *Ishq Nama* (Handwritten), Dastan, 102.
337. *Ibid*, 112.

In fact this is the crescent of sorrow
During night these are not stars
These are the tears of the inmates of the world
Why not to lament
Here life is too short[338]

Before concluding the *masnavi*, the poet gives a summary of his bitter experiences in the form of a few verses, as below:

In this special book which I have written
All its subjects are well selected
There is not an iota of lie in it
I have written frankly what actually was experienced by me.
The intellectuals must read it with learning attitude
Beware! I have informed fully
It is not only a story of pain and tragedy
It is like a lamp for the guidance[339]

But alas! In spite of this advice, the poet himself does not seem to benefit from it. The trend of romance continued even after this, and so the couplets of the *masnavi* kept on increasing.

Apart from the inconsistency of the composition, there is no good example of praise for the physical charms of the beloved. It appears as if the moment the poet faces their beauty, he is distracted. Instead of describing their real features, he considers formal metaphors and similes as the best way to convey their beauty:

There was the condition
As if it showed the rise of a bright Sun
The Sun before the brightness of which

338. *Ibid*, 113.
339. *Ibid*, 131.

The shine of the beauties vanished like the stars
Strange, coquettish playfulness, and naughty
The glance naughty and every style naughty
Heart stealing, life of the world and deceiving
Cruel, pitiless, spiteful and crown stealer
Jasmine-like body, pretty, tall and rosy face
Tune like the wishes of the flower
Eyes like the goblets
Which kill the lover within a moment
The eye brows bent on each other
As if the wrestlers are about to fight
The earlobes hung
This would douse the flame of the candle
If I start writing about the beautiful face
Then every line would be so shining
When even one word is written in appreciation
Then the ink will act like vermillion
The forehead depicted brightness
So much so that the fairy was ashamed to see it
The forearms and arms were round
That someone will take it as his slave
Hence all the body parts of the beauty
Were like a lump of brightness
There was 'missi' (black powder to adorn lips)
on the lips and 'surma' (kaajal type) *in the eyes*
It doubly attacked the lover
The youthful age was hardly of fifteen
God showed this day
The name of the month was 'umrao'
The name of the woman was Umda Khanam[340]

340. *Ibid*, 52.

In places, he expresses the power of his thinking through metaphors and similes:

When she stood up to dance
She displayed a show, a firework
She spread light in a strange manner
One side the heart was burnt, the other side fire was lit[341]
On the wall there were some four five pasted
Pictures of His Excellency emperors
The men were surprised to see it
They stood in awe against the wall[342]

And often, he was an artistic poet. For conciseness, inimitable ease, aesthetic and poetic beauty, and reality, his couplets were unique in the matter of depiction imagery, dialogue and sketching. But when it comes to describing the beauty of the beloved's physical charm, some qualities were missing. Instead, he appreciates beauty in a manner which could be applicable to anyone.

These extracts from his *masnavi* were not presented to make a critical evaluation of them, or to make them the center of discussion. Instead, the intention was to present examples which would reflect Wajid Ali Shah's mastery in composing the *masnavi.* While commenting on the Lucknow School or on the poetic competence of Wajid Ali Shah, critics did not bother to mention this *masnavi*, though there it has many qualities that are rarely found in the *masnavis* of other schools. It may be that the subject of the *masnavi* is coarse and lewd, or that the poet has a bad reputation, but as a piece of literary excellence the *masnavi* continues to have unique importance. Why destroy its literary value?

341. Dastan, *Ibid*, 46.
342. *Ibid*, 52.

From the viewpoint of history, biography, and literature, this *masnavi* invites attention. It is quite possible that after its analysis, we will conclude that this *masnavi* is missing one or more qualities, but even then the question of its value still exists. There are seven thousand couplets in the *masnavi*. Even if more than half of the couplets were deleted, there would be three thousand couplets which are perfect from the beginning up to the end, which must surely be of some worth. Are the intellectuals not interested in it? Or have they not seen the couplets at all? The published comments indicate that the couplets did not reach the public gaze. It is quite possible that most of the critics of today are not the historians of nineteenth century, who would peruse it with a view to denigrate it. The *masnavi*, with all its qualities, is not worthy of being rendered as the '*King of compositions*' (*mulukul kalam*), but at the same time, it is not so unworthy that it will be disregarded as being the '*composition of kings*' (*kalam ul muluk*). A day will come when this *masnavi* will become public, and then many narrations and comments regarding the Lucknow School and the emperors of Lucknow will have to be either amended or deleted.

Architectural Artifacts of Wajid Ali Shah

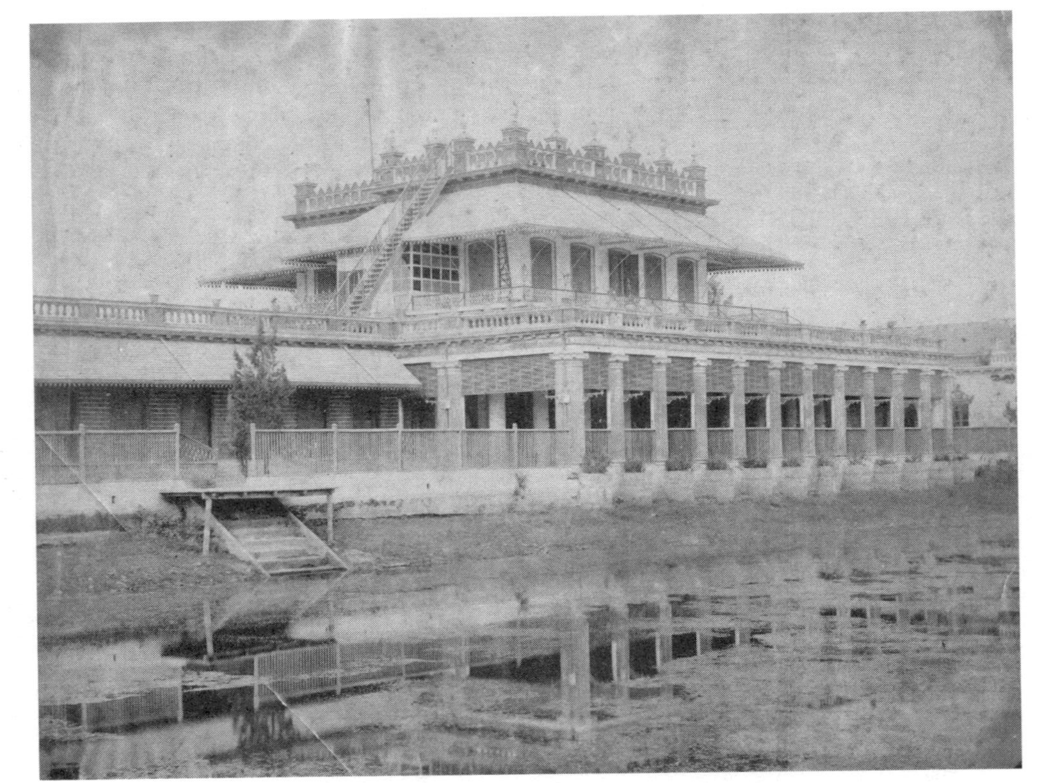

Sultan Khana: The magnificent building, initially the Kothi of the Maharaja of Burdwan, later became the official residence of Wajid Ali Shah after his release from Fort William in 1272h/1856, and thus came to be known as Sultan Khana (Shah Manzil).

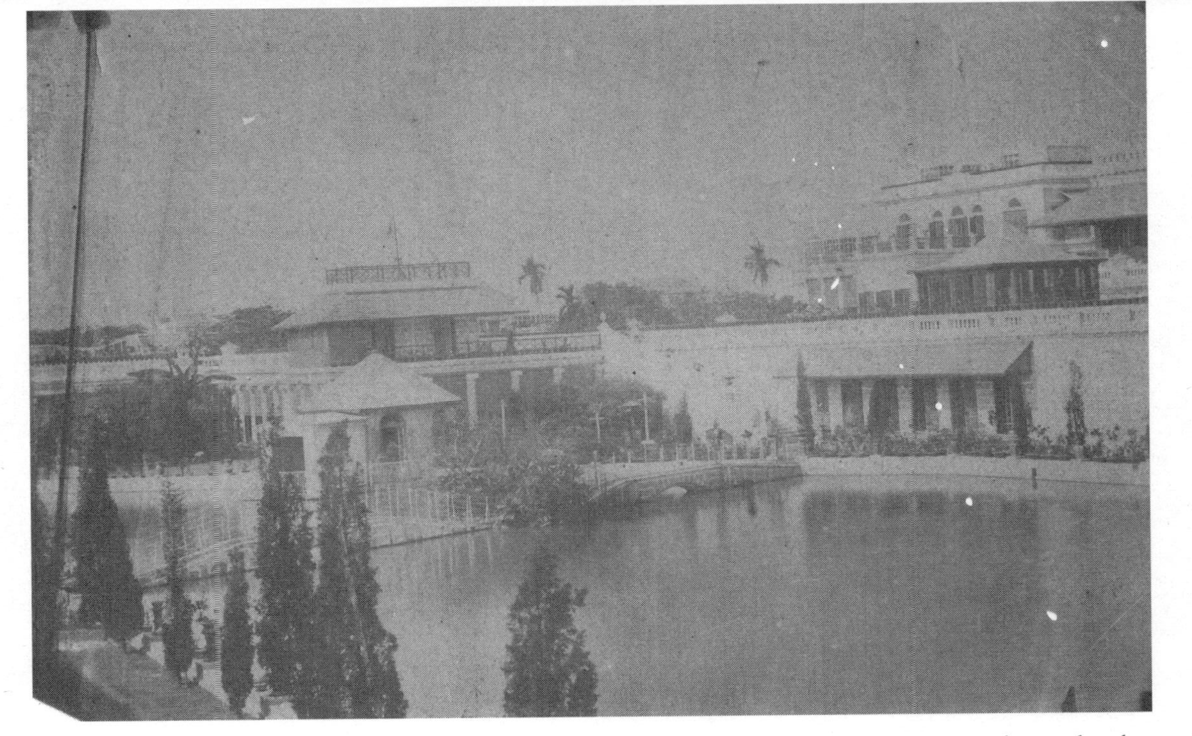

Extension Of The Eastern Side of Sultan Khana: Consequently, upon his release from Fort William, the King – having lost hope of returning to Lucknow – decided to reside in Calcutta. As a result, the Sultan Khana was extended on its eastern side. He expressed his desolation in Qamar Mazmun (1276h) in the following verse:

Now the Symbol of love be engraved here
Beauty of Lucknow City vanishes
The misfortune befalls now this calamity is my fate (wealth)
If Allah allows my countrymen will be replaced by my loyals

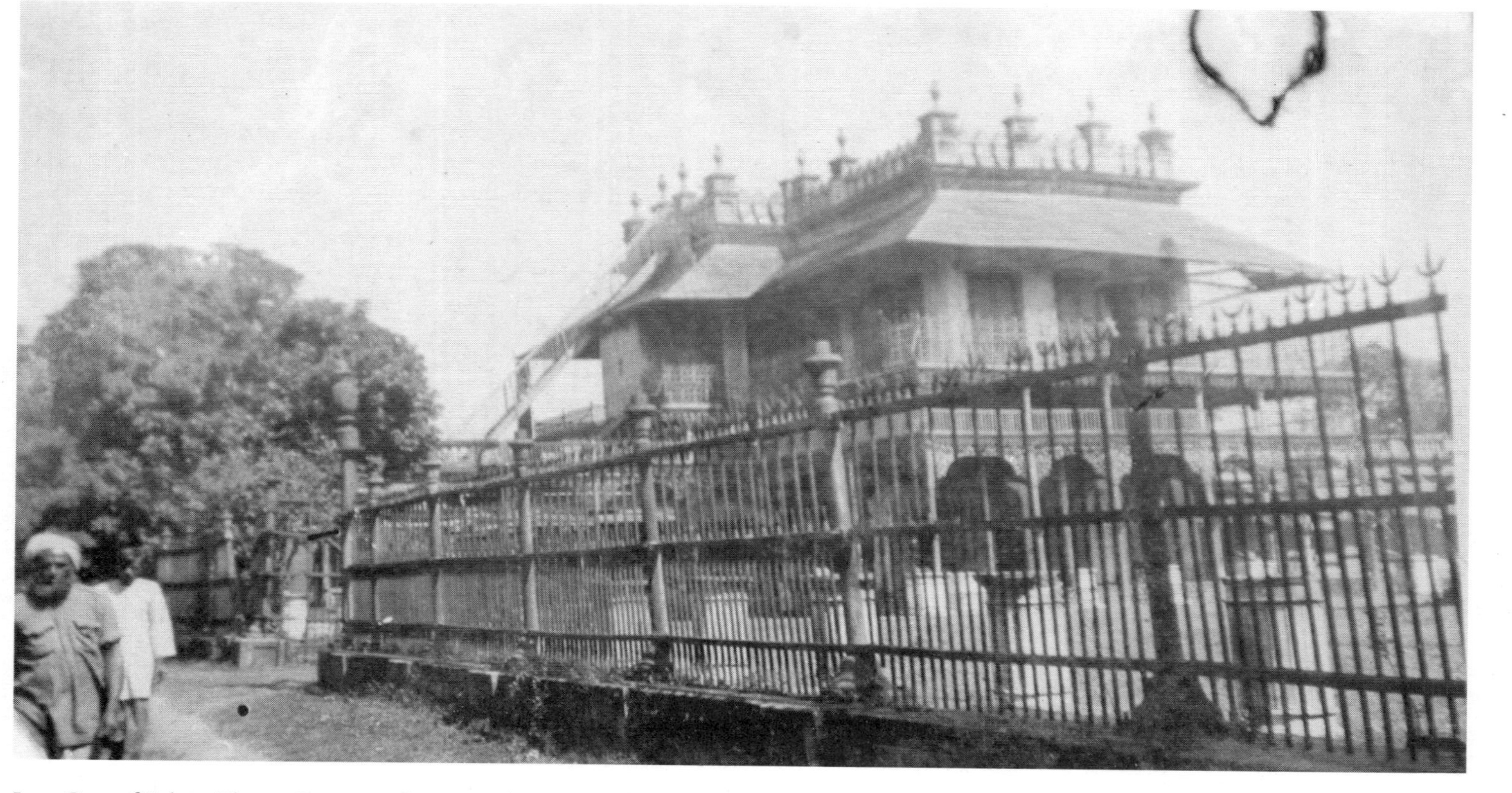

Iron Gate of Sultan Khana: Owing to the iron railings, the nearby road is now known as Iron Gate Road. The main road to which Iron Gate Road has been connected for centuries was called Garden Reach Road, named after the gardens of the Royal Palace. In September 2004, the Government of West Bengal renamed it Wajid Ali Shah Road.

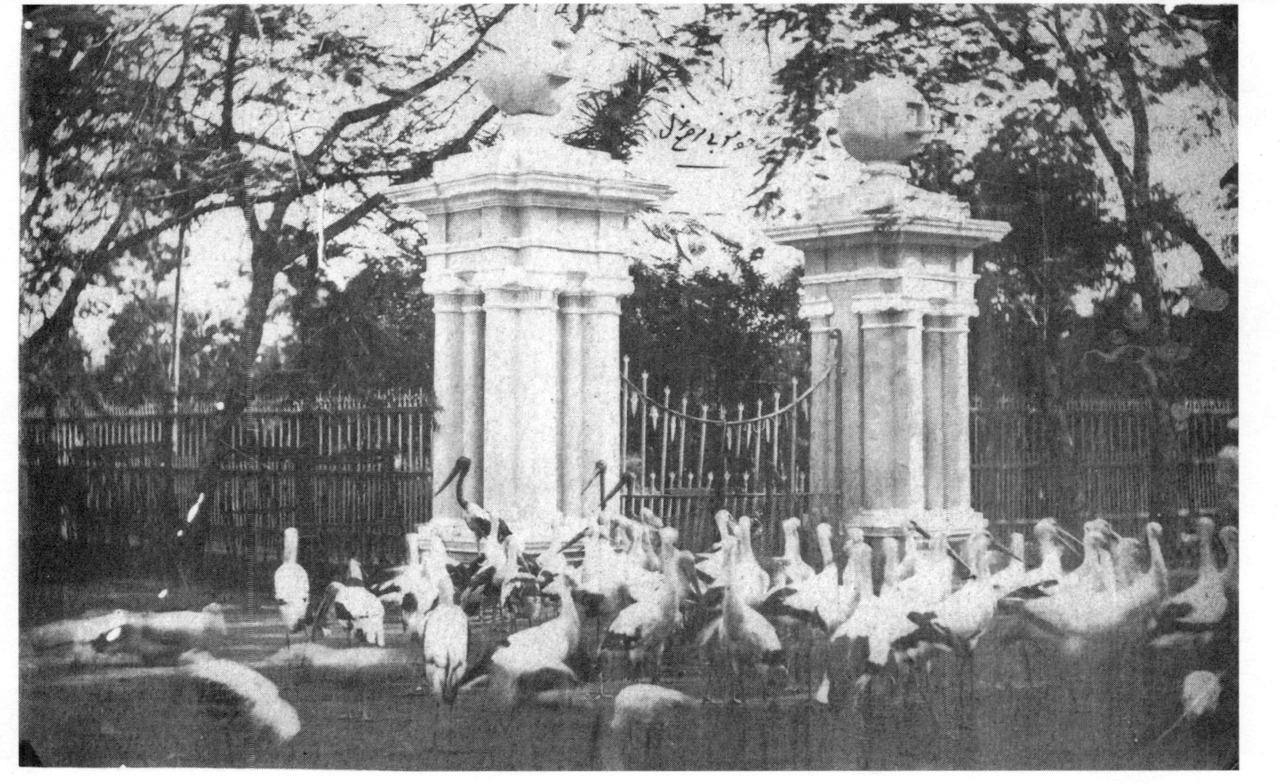

Murassaa Manzil Gate: It opened towards the zoo and the Snake House, featuring a unique artificial mountain and waterfall. It now houses the Electric House of Metiaburj, locally known as Batti Kal. Similarly, in the parterre in front of the present Sibtainabad Imambara, there were displays of various sea animals and other living creatures. During the British period, the stream was widened and ships were brought here for painting, repairs, and related work. Today, it houses the famous Garden Reach Shipbuilding Factory of the Government of India.

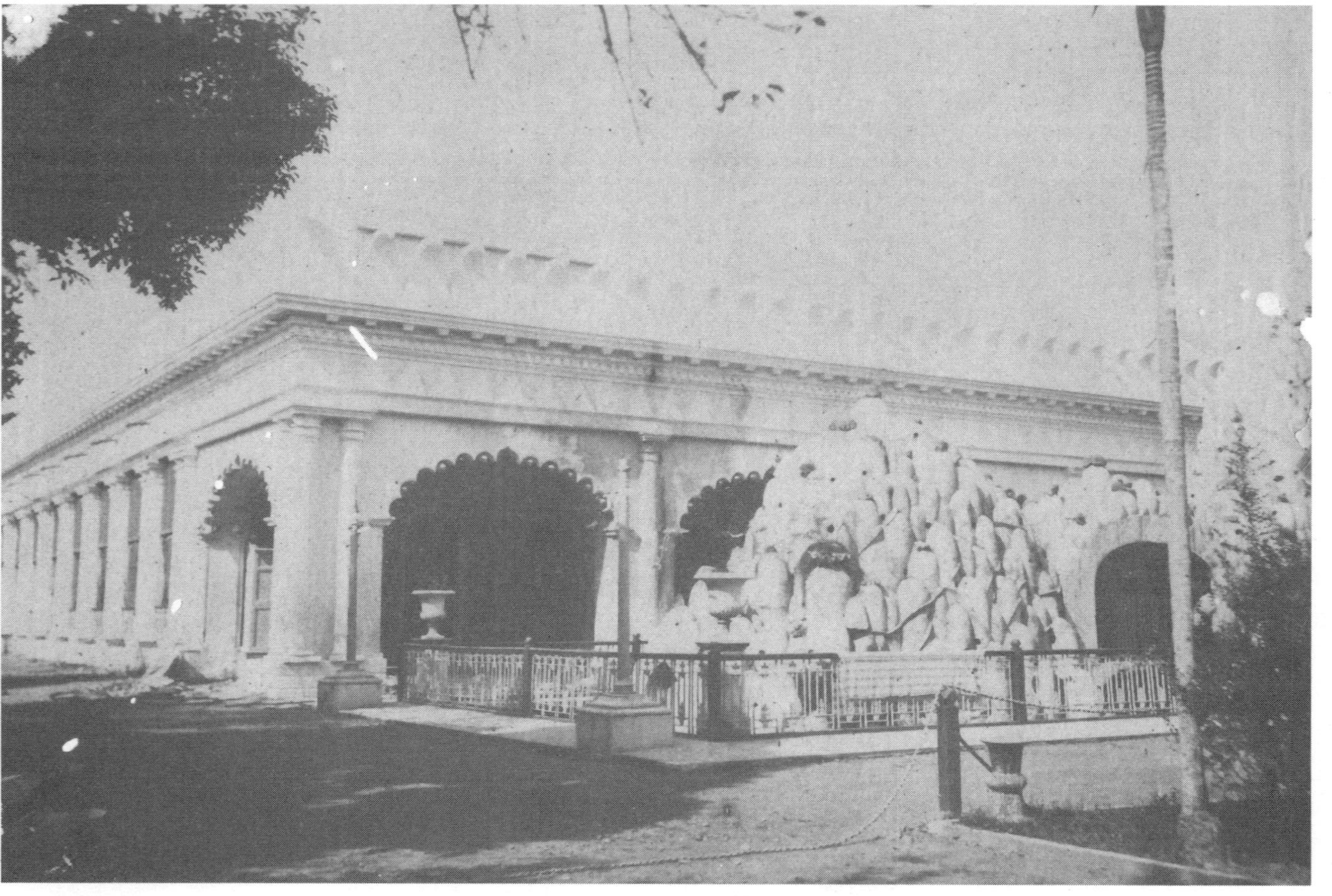

The Snake House

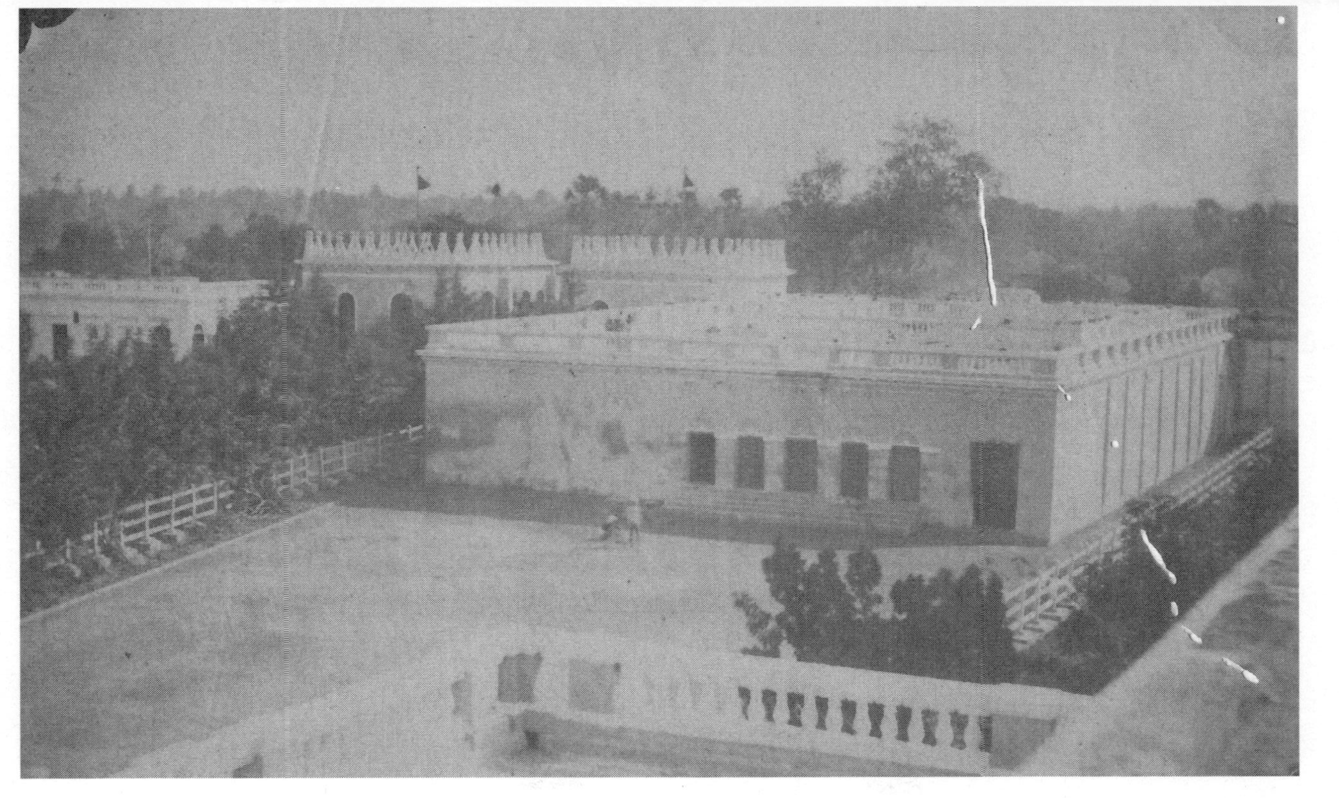

A Portion of Sultan Khan: When the royal buildings were auctioned, they were purchased by the Court of Wards on behalf of the King's nephew and son-in-law, Sir Mir Jahan Quder. However, the declining condition of the family, rapid industrial development in Calcutta, the damp climate of Bengal, and the upheavals of the post-Independence period completely altered the landscape of Metiaburj. The abandoned and ruined buildings of the Sultan Khana allegedly came to be regarded as the abode of jinns. During the Second World War, the Isfahani Jute Mill (Chattkal) was established, which is now known as the Calcutta Jute Mill. The Chashma-e-Husn, where the King's body was given ghusl, is now used for retting jute.

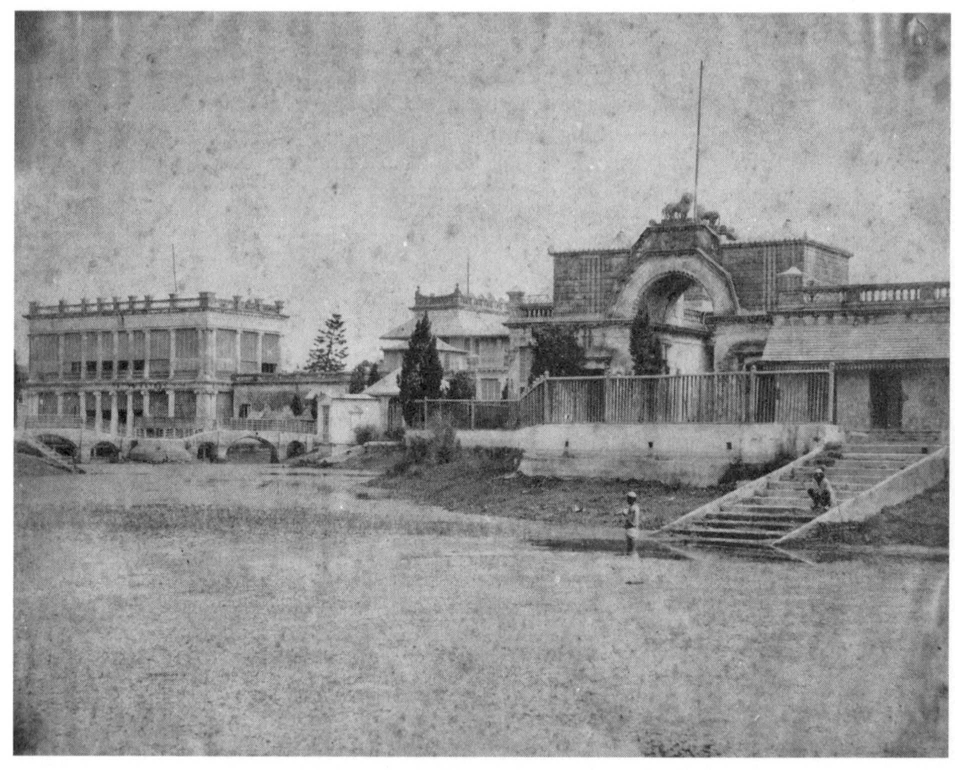

A glimpse of Qasrul Buka: Qasrul Baiza, the first Imambara (Tazia Khana) of Metiaburj, was purchased from the government by the King's daughter-in-law and renamed Qasrul Buka. For many years, however, its tomb was used as an advertising board for an adjacent cinema hall and a medical shop (in the photograph, only its black flags are visible, top left). Today, only the main Imambara and some portions of the structure survive.

All these photographs are memoirs of the pre–First World War period. At that time, the waves of the streams, rising up to the roof of the Sultan Khana, seemed to speak of the sorrowful tale of the deposed King. Alas, today the area is marked by shabby housing for the downtrodden and the tattered scenes of narrow, unsightly lanes.

It reminds one of Saqib's heart rending couplet:

In these premises in the year of farewell of the King there echoed
Lamentation, dirge, hymn, melancholy, glum and grief (1305/1887)

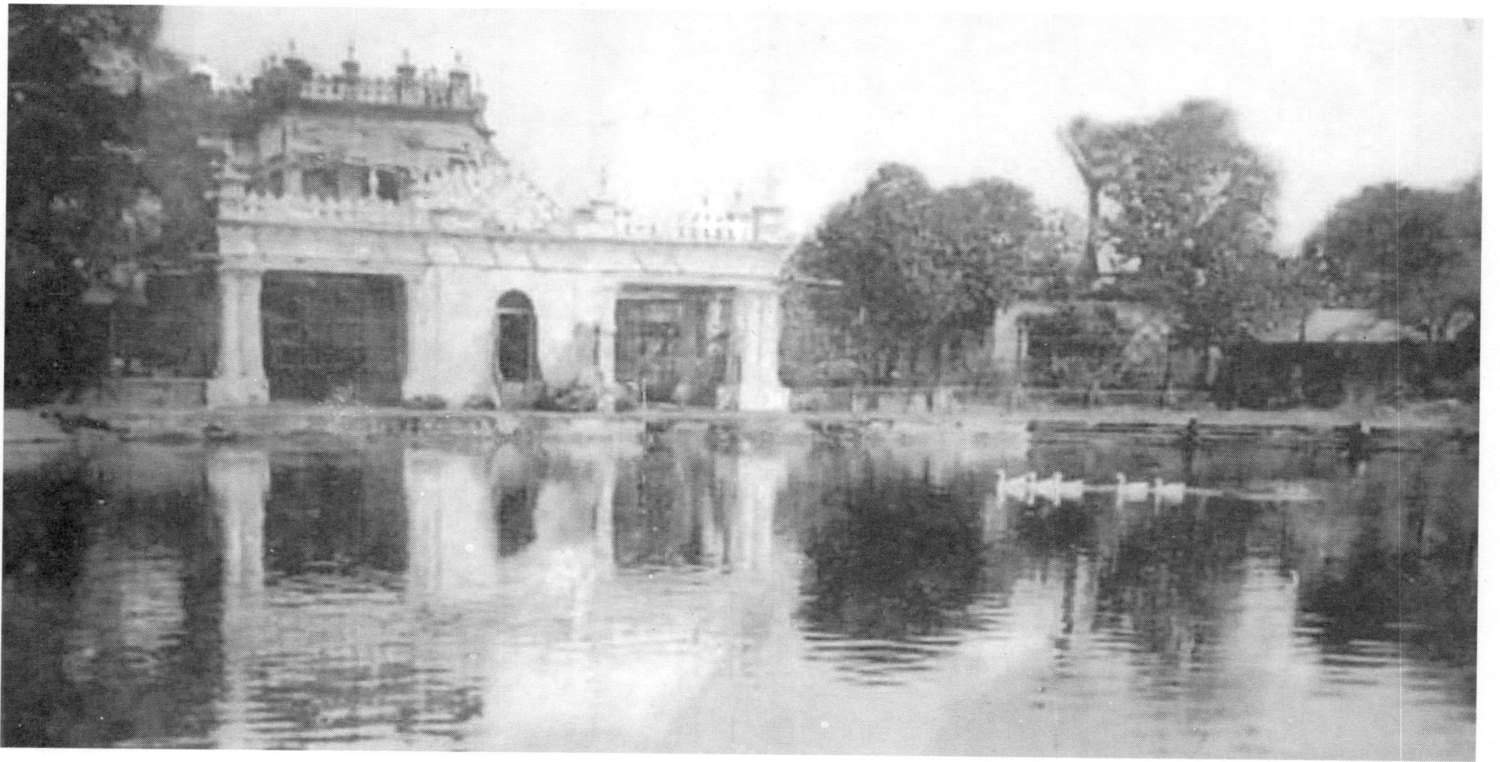

Shahi Mosque, Chashma e Husn and a section of Sultan Khana in the background: In this pond, the King's body was given 'ghusl' (the final ritual bath) on 21 September 1887 at 9:00 p.m.

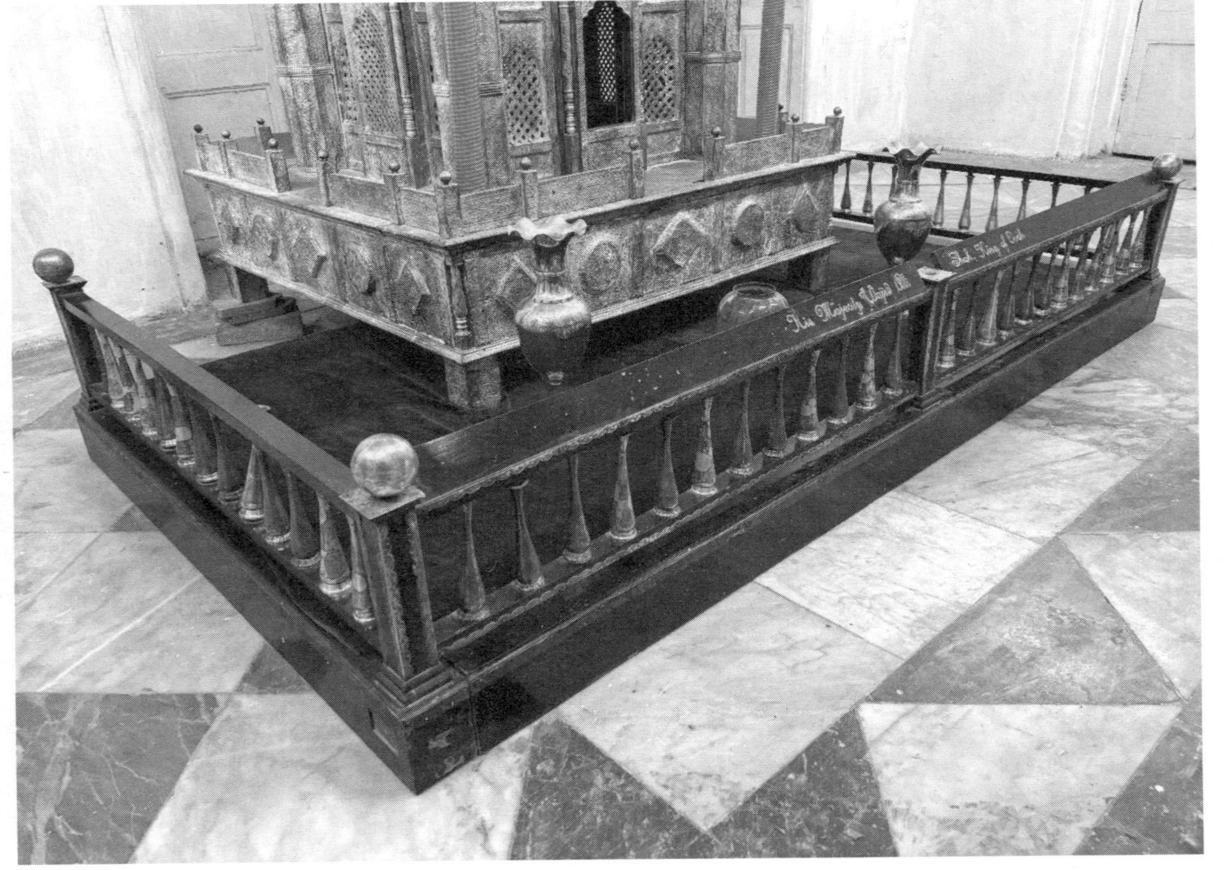

Grave of King Wajid Ali Shah, who passed away on 3rd of Muharram 1305 h at 2 a.m. (21 September 1887) and was buried here on 4th of Muharram (corresponding to 21 September 1887).

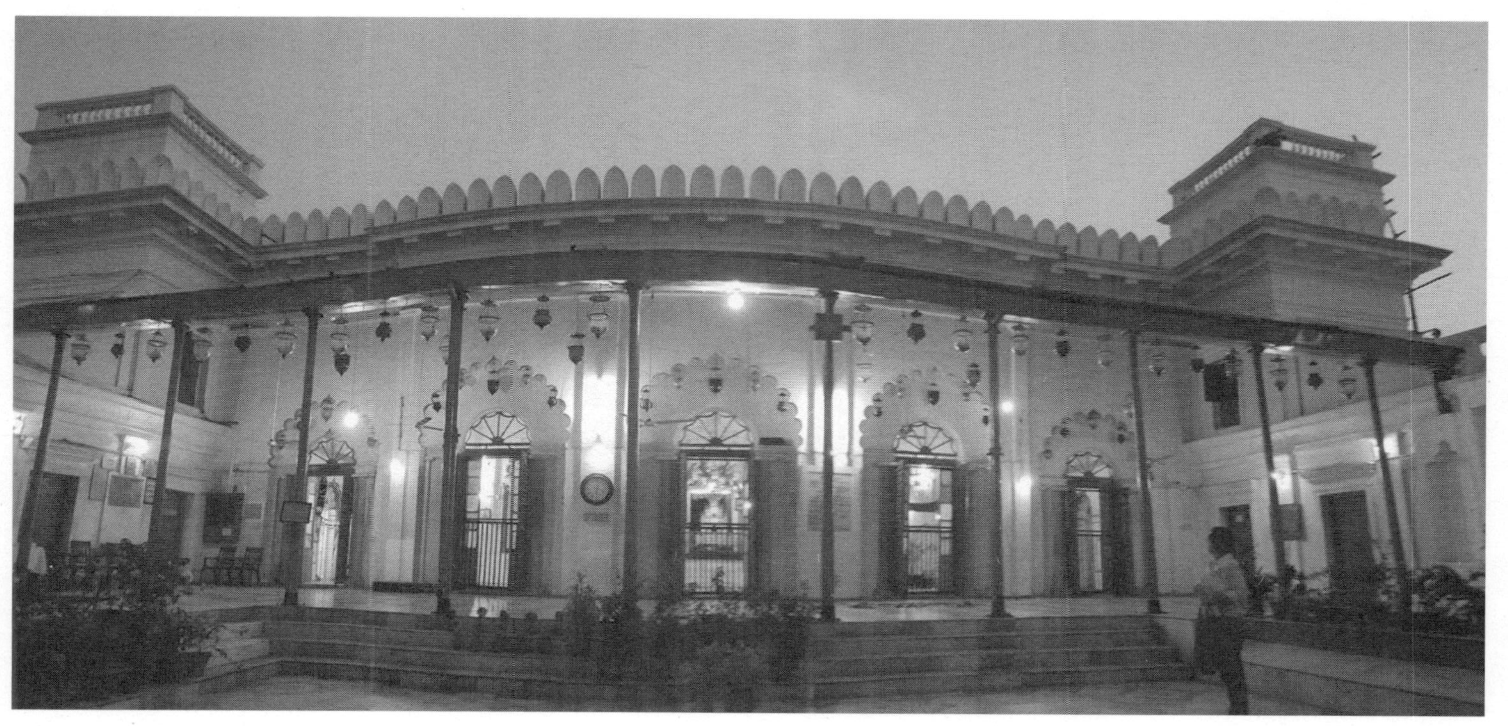

Sibtainabd Imambara: Built by Wajid Ali Shah in 1866 and situated at P34 Wajid Ali Shah Road, Metiaburj, Kolkata 700 024.

Epilogue

The popularity and fame of Wajid Ali Shah depends on his literary and cultural contributions, though due to the passage of time it has become difficult to understand the depth and dimensions of his services. Wajid Ali Shah's legacy is that of a ruler, but as one who was deposed in the interest of the public and under the pretext of being incompetent and a debaucher. Historians of the colonial era highlighted this side of his personality and documented facts randomly, often without due academic regard. In literary circles, commentators retrieve from such wirings and instead highlight the political aspect of his life. But if one sincerely studies his life then it is evident that his becoming a king was only a coincidence, and him being deposed was the result of political machinations. Nobody becomes a writer, poet or an artist by merely becoming a king nor do such attributes come to an end with the end of kingship. Wajid Ali Shah's literary and cultural interests took shape when there was no hope of him becoming a monarch – and after stepping down from the throne, these interests kept him engaged till his last breath.

Sixty-seven years of his prolific life is indicative of his creative propensities – a period five times more than his kingship. A reign demands administrative abilities, and the competence of Wajid Ali Shah could only be evaluated correctly had there not been restrictions on his freedom. However this is not the right time to discuss his kingly-know-how as presently the subject matter is his creative and artistic genius. When going through his magnum opuses, one can say that his creative genius was on par with this administrative competence. His interests were not only by way of pastime as it was in the case of other kings. Nature had made him a fan of its wonders and a lover of its diverse marvels. He himself was fine-looking and was a lover of beauty, whether it was physical, aesthetic or the beauty of melodies and sounds. His creations in the form of ghazals and thumris are markers of his creative skills but also speak of a deep melancholy that pervaded most of his life. His environment played an extraordinarily important role in nurturing his art. All of his creations start with an emotional note but they do not follow a constant path. Often a book begins with a sentimental touch but does not reach the expected end or is hastily pushed to a conclusion because there is some other pending work; although, it often culminates into an expected end with mastery and interest only to be restarted without any justifiable ground. Most artists are in quest of better creations; they are bound by their sentiments and accordingly their creations take shape. Those who work with sincerity and earnestness have their individual style, which reflects in their work.

The impression of Wajid Ali Shah's constructive and creative memoirs are found in the form of books, but that does not mean he did not give attention to any work other than writing or composition. His contributions in the field of dress designing, architecture, painting, dance and music are only in the form of 'discussions'. For instance the innovations he made in the 'rahas'[1] and its stages are well deserved to be called the 'Hindustani stage' of nineteenth century, the cursory information regarding which can be gathered from books. The details and style of the scene changes are something worth discussing. Those who witnessed the battle field sequences go on to describe that wherever an elaborate background was required, every care was taken to create the minor details on the stage and there was every effort in motion

1. Technically speaking the word 'rahas' can be read as a synonym of 'dance drama' or ballet in English language.

to recreate the happenings. But Wajid Ali Shah was self-effacing and did not highlight his achievements or his role in the 'rahas'. One reason for this could be his sentimental style of narration, which has been mentioned above, and the other was his humility, as a result of which though no matter how much others would appreciate his innovations, he himself was quite modest about them.

Wajid Ali Shah's innovative quality, which was so popular during his time and which is hardly remembered today, was the hallmark of his nature. Thus in his literary and cultural contributions, there is hardly anything that is a stereotype. For example, in Urdu and Persian, the pen runs from right to left and the books are also read in the same direction. There are also some principles which are followed in ghazal writing. If there are mistakes made, then they are corrected either by deletion or by striking the wrong word. And for a writer it is not possible to change their writing like one changes clothes. Wajid Ali Shah was fed up of these orthodox practices. It was not possible to do the writing in the reverse direction, that is from left to right, but it was possible to fill the left side of the page first and then continue on the right side like it is the practice in English and Hindi writing. It is now done in case of Urdu writing too, that is to write the poem in prose style where no blank space is left in the middle. The arrangement of verses were not in one direction but by turning the pages or by writing the second line shorter than the first and the third line shorter than the second, it would thus result into a triangular shape. He would also write two to three words in connection, or make unnecessary and intentional turns in pen while writing a word; often he would change the sequence of dots (nuqtas) or just delete them or use the sign of 'mudd' instead of dots. When mistakes were made, he wouldn't correct them, or if he were to correct them, he would replace the incorrect word or phrase with a drawing or painting. Due to this innovative style of Wajid Ali Shah, Urdu calligraphy got some sense of commercial art at a time when Urdu writing was unfamiliar to the need and use of it . Even today, there is no word in Urdu dictionary to describe this nature of art. For example if, say, 'the seed of wish' is composed as 'blooming', then with the help of sketches it should be shown as laden with fruits or flowers. Hence after composing *Afsanaey Ishq, Daryaey Taa'shuqq,* and *Behre Ulfat* this presentation style was manifested in the form of 'Shahi Rahas'. Whatever information regarding the details of these rahas is gathered, are from the discourse of commentators of that time and indicate that there is nothing in these rahas that make them short of dramas. It is true that Wajid Ali Shah and his associates did not name them as dramas because the way of their presentation was different from the traditional dramas that were shown in Kanpur and other places by the theatre companies of that time. Wajid Ali Shah intentionally differentiated his creations from regular performance art, which were often imitations of other artists's works. He wanted to assert an artistic differentiation with not calling his works dramas and naming them as 'rahas'. The first imperfect form of rahas was a group dance. As per the details given in *Sautul Mubarak* and *Bani,* several dancers pretending to be a familiar character presented it in the form of song and dance. It can be called a ballet as it has characteristics of one but there appears to be no connection between different forms in Wajid Ali Shah's work. There is another form of rahas in which there is, in fact, relations and mutual dialogue between the characters such as, the rahas of 'Krishan and Radha', which is found in *Bani* in full detail. It can be called a one-act play or opera as it has all the characteristics of one. In this type of rahas there was requirement of stage and theater to display it. The *Kamraey Sulaimani* and *Makan e Jashn e Khaqani* as mentioned by *Darakhshan* is the same stage and theater, which is well known to us. The third and much advanced type of rahas in which there is correlation, 'rabt', dialogue and dramatic way of presentation with all its complexities are the rahas of *Dastani Masnavis.* We have no hesitation in calling them drama as they have all the characteristics of one and there are also dialogues in it. Western stage of the nineteenth century was not as advanced so as to show, with beauty and perfection, complicated events and happenings live, accompanied with music and songs. Wajid Ali Shah dedicated all his means towards it and not only his 'pari khana' (or sets) or the stages of rahas were exquisite, but the gold crown and studded jewellery used therein were precious ones and they were a treat for the eye. It will not be proper to name the innovations of Wajid Ali Shah as group dance, ballet, opera or one-act play as such terminology from the artistic viewpoint had certain definitions at the time and could invite misunderstanding or criticism. But just like a child is born first and then he is named, similarly the various forms of Shahi Rahas came into being at such a time when they had no parallel in Urdu literature and there was a search for a proper nomenclature. It is not easy to look for proper terminology and convince everyone. Wajid Ali Shah invented two for his creations: 'rahas' and 'pari khana'.

He faced many difficulties in presenting his rahas which in today's time are commonly faced by film makers. For new rahas, every time new studios, new costumes, other logistic support and décor were incorporated. In film-making today, an entire team of experts make different arrangements, for instance there are hair stylists, costume designers, music directors, art directors, etc. As per the various commentators of that time all these activities, from the designing of unique costumes up to the innovative tunes and music, were undertaken by the king himself. However it can be said that no matter how many specialists and helpers were present, it was Wajid Ali Shah who supervised and directed them. He was deeply involved in acting, dance and music, costumes, jewellery, dialogue along with the construction of studios and their décor. His innovative and unique artistry prevailed and gained a fleet of fans and appreciators. It will not be out of place to say that while dealing with the artists and workers, the king experienced unusual relations with them and is often defamed for this.

One reason for not giving a Western or English name to his innovations was that in his opinion, Indian art and literature was not less than the Western art and literature, and even if there were some shortcomings, it could be compensated with attention and awareness. However there was diversion in this opinion of his when it came to the armed forces. He wanted to take his army up to the standard of the British Army as he rightly thought that a soldier who has bow and arrow cannot compete with a soldier who is equipped with firearms and ammunitions. But he thought that the exercise and training need not be named after English terminology. His innovation was again put to use there and entered the Persian terminology. In his own ways, he tried to compensate this. For example, in Botany and Zoology there are hundreds of names given to living beings and plants, while in Urdu there are no words in this field. Hence he invented hundreds of names which are listed in *Bani*. However, even innovation cannot compensate for every flaw. 'Neel Kanth' can be easily named as such as it has a blue patch on its neck but there are a good number of species of the same bird and the zoologists suggest different names for each of these species. The king tried to give different names termed by him as 'khitab' for different breeds, but it could have been a job better done by an institution, which was non-existent at that time.

Wajid Ali Shah has a prestigious position in the field of Hindustani dance and music. It was the patronage of culture-leaning and eminent personalities, that the standard of fading classical music was rescued in a decaying society. On the other hand, the establishment of an institution for the musical training and formation of a special kind of 'kathak' are some of the remarkable achievements of Wajid Ali Shah. Often institutions die within the lifetime of its founders but even among such are those that remain memorable, who sow saplings which grow into formidable trees after the extinction of the institutions. The kathak dance of Lucknow School, its *thumri,* and 'Lucknow Baj Sitar' are such blooming trees whose popularity keeps on increasing day by day. Those keen on these art forms, and those who decide and define their standards, stand up in respect and touch their ears in awe when they hear the names of Wajid Ali Shah, Kalka and Binda Din. The entry of beauty, décor and a pleasant romantic attraction in kathak happened in the era of Wajid Ali Shah. He has illustrated some 'gatein' (plight/condition) of it in *Bani*, which are found in the books of such arts with reference to Wajid Ali Shah. But it is not possible to illustrate the coquetry and amorous or romantic glance in pictures, which created a spell among the spectators. A kathak dancer illustrates emotions of grief, anger, ignominy magnetism and despair with perfection through the movement of eyebrows and eye balls, which are understood even by those who cannot hear the sound or understand the language. This dramatic style of expressing emotions and this language of silence is attributed to Wajid Ali Shah who was hard of hearing and in order to conceal this condition of his, he took support of exaggerated styles. When being entertained by these, one cannot imagine that a person having such a deep understanding and interest in music was audibly challenged. There is no authentic medical authority to support this but by the narratives of people who saw him up close, it is believed that he did suffer from this condition and it was because of this hurdle that he developed interest in various genre of music. He not only was very fond of dramatic expression of poetry and prose, but he made others a fan of these arts as well.

In the genre of prose and poetry, the dramatic expression is manifested in the selection of the style of dialogue delivery and subjects that are to be expressed. Among the innumerable compositions of Wajid Ali Shah, the composition titled *Mubahisaey Bainul Nafs wal Aql* is in Persian and while it may not appear important from the viewpoint of subject matter, it is indicative of the natural inclination of the writer. It is a well-known fact that a person excels in fields where their inherent capabilities shine. In his compositions, the manifestation of Wajid Ali Shah's natural interest was sufficient to give him a unique identity, and hence it was not necessary that he imitate or follow others. But his innovation and dramatic style, which on the one hand, are his prominent attributes have no other rival in his period. This becomes a double-edged sword for this does not earn him the status of an author bearing a unique style of writing (*Saheb e Tarz*). 'Saheb e Tarz' means that a writer has a unique style of presentation, which becomes their identity and they mostly stick to that style. But Wajid Ali Shah presented a diversion from this belief and instead of following others, he was often hesitant to follow his own style and regarded it as a practice of copying, like it happens in printed matters. He appeared to wander as a restless and unfulfilled soul. This habitual wandering reflected not a lack of thoughtfulness, but rather a preference for aesthetic perception over deliberate reflection. His fundamental and defining characteristic was his direct or indirect association with the histrionic arts. His dialogue style in letters, ghazals and masnavis and his dramatic style in kathak is although found in writers before and after him, but none of them hold that unique interest and indulgence with which the king nurtured the tradition.

The evaluation of Wajid Ali Shah's literary contribution is not possible without the literary, political, religious and social analysis of his times. This analysis is a difficult job which is very easily passed off by the writers of that era. In their writings there is traditionalism more than investigation and indulgence more than vision. For the sake of brevity and without getting into the controversies, one can divide his literary life into two periods. The first period is when he was the king or was about to become the king. In the second period, kingship had been taken away and only the title and its memoirs remained. During the initial periods of his literary life he wrote to satisfy his creative calling and to achieve a distinction among his contemporaries. The compositions of the second phase were to dispel his grief and to maintain and save those traditions which were fast vanishing under the impact of western culture. The compositions from both phases were abundant; however, not all of them were available, nor were they of equal literary merit. Nevertheless, it may be argued that such a vast body of literary creations were beyond the privilege or abilities even of kings. Thus, this inexhaustible reservoir of lived experience remained a source of profound knowledge for readers throughout the decades.

His mentionable compositions can be studied in the light of literary, political and social background. In the third and fourth decade of the nineteenth century, the inmates of Lucknow welcomed all those who were bent upon adding luster to the lively and formal ambience of Lucknow. New kingship and new enthusiasm were fast moving to give birth to a new culture. People had trust that the kingdom, which was established on the backing of the English, will sustain for long that they will stick to their promises, although they will continue to make gains and achieve wealth under the pretext of developing the empire. The generosity of Ghaziuddin Haider and Nasiruddin Haider brought prosperity and affluence to the empire. Congregations, meetings and gatherings depicted the progress and development of the empire. As the population was generally affluent and carefree, their aspirations, if any, centered on the pursuit of novel lifestyles and innovation. Wajid Ali Shah gained prominence during the period when Naasikh and Aatish in ghazal composition and Khaleeq and Zameer in elegy reciting received accolades from people who shaped taste and culture. There is impact of the style of these writers on the work of Wajid Ali Shah, but at the same time it has fusion of innovation and the characteristic features of that period. Followers of Aatish looked for everyday mannerisms and the introduction of idiomatic language in his compositions. The followers of Naasikh looked for subtle and refined thinking and a meaningful construction of words. Their mode of composing everyday dialogue, more than any other genre, was shaped by a style that expressed feminine sensibilities, commonly referred to as 'rekhti'. In elegiac writing, storytelling, and sketching, the scope remained limited and was not sufficiently compelling to inspire poets to adopt these techniques extensively in masnavi composition. However, Wajid Ali Shah succeeded in reviving and integrating these artistic forms in his very first composition, *Afsana e Ishq*. Although the most popular and enduring masnavi of the period was *Masnavi Gulzar e Naseem*, poets of the time increasingly favored Wajid Ali Shah's stylistic approach over it. This preference is evident in his masterful works such as *Afsana e Ishq*, its revised version *Darya-e-Ta'shuq*, *Behr e Ulfat*, and his autobiographical masnavi *Ishq Nama*, in which his creative genius attained its highest expression. The construction of dialogue in everyday language, combined with the adoption of a dramatic style marked by clarity in storytelling, sketching, and characterization, constituted a distinctive and highly appealing technique. Wajid Ali Shah did not seek to refine this method further; rather, he found ample scope to display his creative exuberance in compositions celebrating the physical beauty of the beloved, a tendency he fully exploited in *Saaqi Nama*. In the aforementioned masnavis, the fusion of poetry and craftsmanship represented a novel development for his contemporaries. Notably, Shauqq and Qalq further expanded these elements, thereby enriching the Lucknow School with several significant masnavis.

Ishq Nama is the autobiographical masnavi of Wajid Ali Shah which was composed in 1266h (1850 as per the Gregorian calendar). This masnavi which was published by Matbaey Sultani (Lucknow) is worth mentioning. From a historical point of view the real facts and events of the king's life are found nowhere except here. From a literary point of view no other masnavi among all the masnavis of Wajid Ali Shah can come near it, nor from the poetic viewpoint such a masnavi is ever found in Urdu literature. Amid the political upheavals of the nineteenth century, only the first part (haisiyat) of the masnavi received public attention, and it came to be regarded as evidence of Wajid Ali Shah's alleged opulence. Selected extracts were translated into English, published, and presented before the British Parliament as part of the Blue Book, and were also circulated in contemporary newspapers. Wajid Ali Shah was ultimately deposed, and this masnavi was cited as one of the grounds for his dethronement. His opponents argued that admirers of the king could conceal the work, and as a result it gradually disappeared from public view. Over time, it became exceedingly rare; today, only two published copies are known to exist, both incomplete, with most of their pages missing. Consequently, critical commentary on the text remains limited, as many scholars are unaware of its original title, and some even dispute its authorship, denying that it was composed by Wajid Ali Shah. Historical realities have thus been transformed into narratives, and contemporary scholarship continues to search for truth within these layered accounts.

In the context of the masnavi *Ishq Nama*, much of what has been written thus far about the life and poetic stature of Wajid Ali Shah warrants renewed examination. While political motives and objectives receded with the end of foreign rule, the masnavi endures, and as a self-narrated account by a king, it demands serious scholarly attention. The masnavis of *Nawab Mirza Shauqq* though have no historical importance and they are also not morally up to the mark, but due to the beauty and elegance of expression they are still studied, and people are surprised to see the clarity of language of a Lucknow poet. However, a close reading of *Ishq Nama* is likely to surprise readers by revealing how actual life events are rendered with remarkable accuracy, clarity of incident, and narrative transparency. Elements that appear overt or indulgent in masnavis such as *Bahar-e-Ishq* and *Khwab-o-Khayal* are transformed, in Wajid Ali Shah's language, into refined and aesthetically controlled poetic expression. In *Ishq Nama*, the poet makes his personal emotional awareness and intimate experiences the subject of an autobiographical narrative; yet, while remaining faithful to lived reality, he consistently preserves elegance and dignity of expression. Conversational narration and storytelling form the very spirit of this masnavi, and it is these qualities that give it precedence over a large number of masnavis in Urdu literature.

Out of the approximately one lakh couplets across Wajid Ali Shah's various masnavis, aside from the shorter works composed around a particular letter or incident, each masnavi possesses distinctive features. With his first three masnavis—*Afsana-e-Ishq*, *Darya-e-Ta'shuq*, and *Behr-e-Ulfat*—the trend of composing idioms related to women and engaging in poetic dialogue began in Lucknow. Prior to these works, apart from *Gulzar-e-Naseem* and *Sehrul-Bayan*, no other noteworthy masnavis were produced within the Lucknow School.

Ishq Nama and *Huzn-e-Akhtari* function as autobiographical masnavis ('aap biti'), the former portraying a life of mirth and the latter revealing one of suffering and anguish. In both, Wajid Ali Shah's frank, free, honest, and candid expression is unparalleled in Urdu masnavi literature.

In the masnavis *Chanchal* and *Urooz*, he explored the arts of music and prosody. A study of these works demonstrates that the king's engagement with poetry extended beyond writing: he composed his verses to music with equal ease, exhibiting rare skill and artistry in the process.

Haibat e Haidari and *Sabatul Quloob* are the poetic translations of Persian books. *Haibat e Haidari* contains an explanation of Persian verses and *Sabatul Quloob* is the poetic translation of Persian prose, and it is done with such great skill that in the religious literature of Urdu neither such candid and correct translations are found nor in matter of bulkiness there is any parallel of *Sabatul Quloob*. There are two copies of *Sabatul Quloob* of which one is incomplete. In both these copies there are forty-eight thousand one hundred and fifty couplets (48,150) and in these the events and anecdotes of the Prophets are composed. This masnavi is a memoir of the religious fervor and lingual expertise of the writer. The longest masnavis of Urdu are not even near *Sabatul Quloob* in size and length, even though the period of their composition is almost the same. A formidable hindrance in matter of translation of *Sabatul Quloob* was the true translation of the Holy Quran and Hadith. Naasikh tried this in masnavi *Mufazzal* but soon he was fed up of it. Wajid Ali Shah translated with much constancy and steadiness that even when his life came to an end, his work did not. In the vast extent of *Sabatul Quloob* the treasure of words and methods can only be measured when it is analyzed in the light of prosodic, translatory and lingual principles. Wajid Ali Shah's language is authentic, yet due to his diversions it cannot be called the last word. Without hesitation, he composed in the traditional style and, motivated solely by innovation, did not refrain from modifying words and terminology.

Wajid Ali Shah's ghazals are not qualitatively the level of his masnavis and the salams composed by him are regular at best. It has been said of Mir's ghazals that 'the higher is of the highest standard, and the lower is of the lowest.' A similar observation applies to the masnavis of Wajid Ali Shah. Unlike ghazals, masnavis impose relatively few restrictions on rhyme (qafia paimaey), yet in ghazals—and especially in salams—even minor deviations in rhyme become glaringly discordant. Wajid Ali Shah exercised caution in his ghazals; irregular meters and unusual rhymes are rarely found in these compositions. However, in his pursuit of uniqueness, he sometimes overlooked the sanctity of meter in elegies and salams. While minor lapses in elegiac composition may be tolerated, abrupt or forced rhymes in salams can jar the refined sensibilities of the reader. Nevertheless, those portions of Wajid Ali Shah's work that remain free from such flaws are particularly admirable and deserve recognition. Commentators have indiscriminately opined on the six diwans of Wajid Ali Shah but such comments are based on many understandings. There are seven diwans of Wajid Ali Shah namely: *Guldastaey Ashiqan, Sukhan Ashraf, Diwan Mubarak, Sheva-e-Faiz, Qamar*

Mazmun, Nazm Namvar and *Imaan.* One collection namely *Mulk Akhtar* which has hitherto been named as *Diwan* is in fact not a diwan but it is a collection of his compositions. Among these, there are some more like *Daftar e Humayun, Najo, Dulhan* and *Bani* in which 'thumris, 'dadras', 'dharpad' and geet are collected and in the other three there are varied compositions. *Toshaey Aakhirat* is the collection of his sixty-nine elegies. There are some other elegies. This surprising treasure of Wajid Ali Shah's poetic composition is the proof of his proficiency. But among all these creations he will be always remembered for the works like *Sheva-e-Faiz, Imaan* and the collection of songs (*geet*). The prominent feature of *Sheva-e-Faiz* is that no such diwan is compiled in the history of Urdu poetry. Wajid Ali Shah has addressed his begmats in these ghazals and in most of these he has used the names of these Begums as 'radif.' While the ghazals themselves may not be revolutionary in the description of beauty or characterization, they are noteworthy collectively for their association with the fair sex. After the *Diwan Hussaini* of Hashim Burhanpuri, no other Diwan comprises of *Nohas* and *Salams* except the diwan *Imaan.* Both *Sheva-e-Faiz* and *Imaan* are the memorable compositions of his innovative style. The collection of songs like *Najo Dulhan,* and *Bani* have found place of pride in the diaries of musicians. 'Navras' of Ibrahim Aadil Shah is also a famous diary, but it is only due to Wajid Ali Shah these collections were saved in printed form, and which continues to cater to the taste and liking of the fans of music and literature. These collections are in fact the books of lessons of his school of music. Even in that era, when audiences sought melodious and pleasing tunes, these collections satisfied their craving. Remarkably, they continue to exist today and remain equally valuable and inspiring. Even to date these books exist and are equally beneficial.

Wajid Ali Shah possessed a natural inclination towards poetry. He showed little interest in prose, and when he did engage in it, it was typically out of necessity and composed in Persian. At first he was translating *Hayatul Quloob* in *Riyazul Quloob* in Urdu prose but he found himself more interested in poetry. In Bani, the section of copies (naql) is rendered in Urdu, as Wajid Ali Shah intended it for readers who were not commonly literate in Persian.

Wajid Ali Shah's five mentionable writings namely: *Majmuaey Wajidia, Sautul Mubarak, Jawab e Blue Book, Mubahisaey Bainul Nafs wal Aql* and *Sahifaey Sultania* were in Persian because at that time the status of Persian as a language of the learned was on par with Urdu. *Majmuaey Wajidia* is a fountain of information regarding Wajid Ali Shah's student life. It also serves as a window into the curriculum of elite students of that era. The sections containing idioms, phrases, associative ideas (talazma), and riddles hold considerable literary value. Recognizing their relevance to everyday language, an Urdu translation was subsequently published by Matbaye Sultani. In *Sautul Mubarak* too in a way there are lessons of music. The last portion of free verse which contains description of rahas was entered in *Bani* after being translated into Urdu. Only the Urdu translation of *Jawab-e-Blue Book* was available, and it remained the sole published copy. The rebuttal to the charges brought by the English was provided by Wajid Ali Shah himself. Notably, the rational, concise, and coherent response he offered surpassed even the explanations provided by lawyers and historians. Wajid Ali Shah was always mindful of religious affairs and *Mubahisaey Bainul Nafs wal Aql* and *Sahifaey Sultania* are the candid proof of it. He published it in the later years of his life, and it found considerable demand within religious circles, enjoying wide acceptance at the time, though today it has largely lost its significance.

The collection of letters between Wajid Ali Shah and his begmats are the only surviving evidence of his prose writing. Shah's compilation was a bold and innovative step, considering the times. Nobody had compiled such letters in Urdu literature before him. In letter writing, there are two roles of Wajid Ali Shah: first as a letter writer and the second as its compiler. As a writer there would hardly be any other during that period who within a period of two to three years wrote about two and a half thousand letters in Urdu – mostly written when he was confined in Fort William. During this period of exile and loneliness, and for the relief of phyiscal needs and spiritual demands (muanqa), he resorted to this practice. The prominent feature of these letters is its boldness, simplicity, straightforwardness, minimalism and the conversational style which escaped the attention of intellectuals. The three letters *Tarikh e Ghazala, Tarikh-e-Mumtaz* and *Tarikh e Mazzahab* are addressed to three of his begums. Doubtlessly if there were great number of begums then the number of letters would also be ample. When the letters were being written at that time, Wajid Ali Shah did not even think that one day he would compile these and discuss his own love affairs. By the time he thought of putting them together, much were destroyed in the devastation of Qaiser Bagh and wreckage of Lucknow. The letters including *Tarikh e Khaas, Tarikh e Mushgala,* and *Tarikh Deher* are found in the list of *Bani* which indicates that up to 1292h these were available in the royal library, but later could not be traced.

However, this trend was short-lived. Once he was reunited with his begums in Metiaburj, the need for letter writing naturally diminished. Nevertheless, Wajid Ali Shah can be credited with initiating the practice of romantic letter writing in Urdu, which ceased abruptly when his personal interest waned. The letters compiled by Wajid Ali Shah namely *Tarikh e Noor, Tarikh e Jamshedi, Tarikh e Badr,* and *Tarikh e Firaq* have one big benefit as they contain the names of the writers of these letters who in their own way attempted to innovate ways and styles of writing letters. The letters attributed to the begums are often cited by commentators as examples of the so-called 'Begmati language.' However, of all the letters that have been recovered, not a single one can be conclusively said to have been written by them. The begums were largely analphabetic and it is evident not only from their own letters but also from Wajid Ali Shah's collections, which clearly dispel any claims that these writings originated from the begums themselves. Apart from this secondary importance and relevance of his letters, the letters of Wajid Ali Shah and begmats are valuable documentation of Lucknavi language, culture, society, politics, literature and history of that period. The letters are also valuable as the contents reveal that Wajid Ali Shah was like a common man who thought it his duty to wish his palace staff and to give his associates and companions the lesson of tolerance and contentment.

The letters of Wajid Ali Shah and his books had enough material to refute the baseless charges made against him and to dispel the misunderstandings.

Historians and commentators never dove deep, even though, at the time, Wajid Ali Shah himself did not leave any stone unturned to circulate his books among the commoners. Many were published and those which could not be, at least did not deserve to be destroyed. But unluckily, Wajid Ali Shah was devoid of the favourable environment needed for the proliferation of his artistic qualities. The slow violence of time even erased those imprints, which often gave the indication of a plundered caravan. Had the people who wrote about the incapability and hopelessness of Wajid Ali Shah also mentioned the shrewdness and cleverness of the plunderers, then the coin which was the currency of the time would not have been left one-sided.

If we expect from Wajid Ali Shah why he was not a soldier like Tipu Sultan, a king like Akbar the Great, an architect like Shahjehan, a poet like Mir Anis and Ghalib then we would always be disappointed. But if we keep aside the orthodox lens, see and study Wajid Ali Shah as a student of history, civilization, literature, poetry, music, dance, drama and religion, then in his single persona one will be bound to admit the magnitude of his ideas and his genius.

Bibliography

MANUSCRIPTS

(Urdu/Arabic/Persian/English)

Abbas Mirza, *Al Hasn ul Mateenfi Tarikh e Salateen*, Society, 1281.

Afsana e Ishq, Lucknow: Sultani Publications.

Akhbar Deodhi Badsha e Awadh, Tagore, 1254 A.H.

'Anis Ki Zaban Waqar e Husn', Azad, 1963.

Bahadur 1280–(Asifia)

Bayaz Maulvi Aulad Hussain Shair, Raza.

Bayaz Mehtab Uddaulah Darkhsahn, Asifia.

Bayaz Wazir ul Sultan Nawab Mohammad Amir Ali Khan Bahaduramir (found in the possession of Dr Zubair Siddiqui)

Gauhar Ali Mushir, *Masnavi Mushir*, Khuda Bakhsh, 1276.

G.D. Bhatnagar, 'Awadh Under Wajid Ali Shah', University of Lucknow, 1968.

Ghulam Raza, *Usool ul Naghmat Al Asafi*, Raza.

Guzraneda Munshi Muzaffar Ali Khan Asir, Munshi Amir Ahmad, *Dastoor ul Amal Awadh*, Raza.

Hakim Tassaduq Hussain Khan, *Bahar Ishq*, Khuda Bakhsh, 1276.

Mohammad Wajid Ali Shah Akhtar, *Behr e Hidayat*, Lucknow: Sultani Publication, Lucknow, 1267. (Imambara, Tagore)

Ibrahim Adil Shah Sani, *Navras*, Salar Jung, 1004–1012.

Iqtidaruddaulah Mohtashanmul Mulkmehdi Ali Khan, *Tarikh e Iqtidariya.*

Kaukun Darri, on the order of Mohammad Wajid Ali Shah Akhtar, Imambara.

Lalji Wald Seetal Prashad, *Mirat ul Awza*, Raza.

Lalji Wald Seetal Prashad, *Sultan ul Hikayat*, Raza, 1270.

Maharaj Jig Opal Saqib, *Nadarat ul Saqib*, 1290.

Majmua e Hujuyat, Hatif Lucknavi, Safi, 1913.

Majmua e Maroozat, Madar ul hamlisan ul Sultan wafa Shuaar Mehmoodud daulah Hamid ul Mulkmunshi Mohammad Safdar Ali Khan Bahadur, Ittihadiya, 1281.

Majmua e Ruqaat e Begmat, Compiled by Syed Taskeen Kazmi, Hyderabad.

Mir Ali Ausat Rashk, *Diwan e Rashk (Vol. 3)*, Azad.

Mirza Mohammad Taqi, *Aaftab e Awadh*, Tagore, 1874–75.

Mohammad Abdullah Khan Zaigham, *Yadgar Zaigham*, Idaara.

Mohammad Imtiaz Ali Khan, *Mukhzan e Asrar e Sultani*, Asfia.

Mohammad Imtiaz Ali Khan, *Tohfa e Sultani*, Raza.

Mohammad Rafi Aali Rizvi, *Tarikh e Benares*, Raza.

Mohammad Raza Khan Aashiq, *Rashk Mah e Tamam*, Khuda Bakhsh.

Mohammad Wajid Ali Shah Akhtar, *Afsana e Ishq*, Salar Jung.

Mohammad Wajid Ali Shah Akhtar, *Najo*, Salar Jung.

Mohammad Wajid Ali Shah Akhtar, *Gulzaar e Hussaini*, Imambara, 1291.

Mohammad Wajid Ali Shah Akhtar, *Huzn e Akhtar*, Raza, 1306.

Mohammad Wajid Ali Shah Akhtar, *Ishq Nama (Poetic) Author's Manuscript*, Anjuman, 1266, (Mahmudabad).

Mohammad Wajid Ali Shah Akhtar, *Ishq Nama (Persian)*, Memoodabad, 1265.

Mohammad Wajid Ali Shah Akhtar, *Majmua e Wajidiy e Sultani*, Amir.

Mohammad Wajid Ali Shah Akhtar, *Malk Akhtar*, Imambara, 1295.

Mohammad Wajid Ali Shah Akhtar, *Marsia Aafaq Mein Hai Rashk e Atarad Apna Qalam*, Kutb Khana Sakar Amdat ul Ulema.

Mohammad Wajid Ali Shah Akhtar, *Marsia Sarosh e Ghaib Ne Mujh Ko Ye Sada e Gham*, 1302.

Mohammad Wajid Ali Shah Akhtar, *Mubaahis e Bainul Nafs Wal Aql*, Nuskha 1, Imambara, 1290.

Mohammad Wajid Ali Shah Akhtar, *Nabi*, Imambara, 1292–94.

Mohammad Wajid Ali Shah Akhtar, *Riyaz ul Quloob*, Salar Jung.

Mohammad Wajid Ali Shah Akhtar, *Sabat ul Quloob*–Vol 1 Nuskha 1

Do Nuskha 2 (Azad)

Do Nuskha 3 (Imambara)

Mohammad Wajid Ali Shah, *Sabat ul Quloob (Vol. 2)*, Imambara.

Mohammad Wajid Ali Shah Akhtar, *Saif e Sultania*, Imambara, 1286.

Mohammad Wajid Ali Shah Akhtar, *Shev e Faiz*, Imambara, 1276.

Mohammad Wajid Ali Shah Akhtar, *Sukhan e Ashraf*, Amir.

Mohammad Wajid Ali Shah Akhtar, *Tarikh e Badr*, Idaara, 1276
Mohammad Wajid Ali Shah Akhtar, *Tarikh e Firaq*, Khuda Bakhsh, 1276.
Mohammad Wajid Ali Shah Akhtar, *Tarikh e Jamshedi*, 1276.
Mohammad Wajid Ali Shah Akhtar, *Tarikh e Noor*, Khuda Bakhsh, 1276.
Mohammad Wajid Ali Shah Akhtar, *Deh Majlis (Vol. 1)*, Imambara, 1284,
Mohammad Wajid Ali Shah Akhtar, *Deh Majlis (Vol. 2)*, Imambara, 1289.
Mohammad Wajid Ali Shah Akhtar, *Deh Majlis (Vol. 3)*, Imambara, 1293.
Mohammad Wajid Ali Shah Akhtar, *Deh Majlis (Vol. 4)*, Imambara,
Mohammad Wajid Ali Shah Akhtar, *Qamar Mazmun (Author's Manuscript)*, Imambara.
Mufatih Khaqani, On the Orders of Mohammad Wajid Ali Shah Akhtar, Imambara.
Munshi Amir Ahmad Minai, *Nasr e Murassadar Madh e Qaiser Bagh*, Raza.
Munshi Amir Ullah Kamil, *Tawarikh e Kamil*, Raza, 1308.
Munshi Amir Ullah Tasleem, *Safar Nama e Khusravi*, Raza, 1312.
Munshi Amir Ullah Tasleem, *Tawarikh e Badi*, Raza, 1303.
Munshi Zahir Uddin Bilgrami, *Asrar e Wajidi*, Tagore, 1266–78 A.H.
Munshi Zahir Uddin Bilgrami, *Huliya e Asrar e Wajidi*, Raza.
Munshi Zahir Uddin Bilgrami, *Maahit ul Ghana*, Imambara, 1276.
Munshi Zahir Uddin Bilgrami, *Tarikh e Lucknow*, Raza.
Mussavidat e Sultani, Tagore.
Nijat Hussain Khan Azimabadi, *Sawah Ne Lucknow*, Patna University Library, 1259.
Risala Der Mausiqi, Raza.
Ruqaat e Begumat e Awadh, Raza.
Saadat Khan Nasir, *Khush Maarka e Zeba*, Khuda Bakhsh.
Syed Ali Hussain Lucknavi Al Mukhatib Ba Monisuddaulah, *Mualja e Kabutaran*, Society.
Syed Hidayat Hussain Ibn Janab Syed Ali Naqi Sahab, Muvahib Sujania, Imambara.
Syed Ibn Ibrahim Ibn Mumtaz ul Ulema, *Amlul Amal*, Imambara.
Syed Israr Hussain Khan, *Qadeem Hunar Wa Hunarmandan e Awadh*, Lucknow: Sarfraz Qaumi Press, 1936.
Syed Jalal Uddin Haider, *Afsana e Lucknow*, Imambara, 1290.
Syed Jalal Uddin Haider, *Shikwa e Farang*, 1293.
Tek Chand Bahar, *Bahar e Ajam*, Ittihadiya.

PUBLICATIONS

(Urdu/Arabic/Persian/English)

Aale Ahmad Suroor, *Aligarh Tarikh e Adab Urdu*, Aligarh: Aligarh Muslim University.
Abdul Salam Khurshid, *Urdu Drama*, Lahore: Maktab e Urdu.

Abdul Qadir Sarwari, *Urdu Masnavi Ka Irtiqa*, Hyderabad: Idara e Adbiyaat Urdu, 1940.

Abdul Rauf Ishrat Lucknowi, *Aab-e-Baqa*, Lucknow: Nami Press, 1918.

Abdul Rauf Ishrat Lucknowi, *Shahan e Awadh*, Delhi: Hamidiya Press.

Abu Nasir Mohammad Khalidi, Maulvi Mahmood Ahmed Khan, *Taqweem Hijri Wa Eisvi*, Delhi: Anjuman Tarraqqi Urdu Hind.

Abul Lais Siddiqi, *Lucknow Ka Dabistan e Shairi*, Lahore: Gilani Press, 1955.

Abul Lais Siddiqi, Maulana Abdul Salam Nadvi, *Lucknow Ki Aakhri Shama*, Aligarh: Education Book House.

Ahkam e Adalat e Alvia, Lucknow: Sultani Publication, 1259.

Alig Bari, *Company Ki Hukumat*, Lahore: Maktab e Urdu, 1944.

Allamah Mohammad Baqir Majlisi, *Hayat ul Qulub*, Compiled by Maulvi Syed Tasaduq Hussain, Lucknow: Naval Kishore Publication.

Anand Nath Verma, *Nakat e Anand*, Delhi: Bombay Job Press, 1941.

Asad Ali Khan Qalaq, *Tilism e Ulfat*, Lucknow: Majmaul Uloom Publication, 1296.

Ataullah Palwi, *Tazkira e Shauq*, Lahore: Savera Art Press, 1956.

Babu Hatt Prashad Akbarabadi, *Tawarikh e Awadh*, Fatehgarh: Matba Dilkusha Publication, 1860.

Baharistan e Awadh, Translated by Maulvi Abdullah Ashiq, Delhi: Source Faiz Press, 1366.

Debi Prasad Furqat, *Latif e Furqat*, Lucknow: Mehdia Publication, 1273.

Diwan Munshi Roshan Lal, *Khulaa Sae Tarikh e Awadh*, Sitapur: Subah Sadiq Publication, 1890.

Durga Prasad Sandelvi, *Bostan e Awadh*, Lucknow: Ahmedi Publication, 1892.

Faridun Qadr Mirza Mohammad Hazbar, *Diwan e Huzbar*, Kanpur: Nizami Publication, 1297.

Garcin de Tassy, *Khutbat e Garcin de Tassy*, Edited by Maulvi Abdul Haq, Aurangabad: Anjuman Taraqqi Urdu Hind, 1935.

Garcin de Tassi, 'Maqalat e Garsan,' Translated by Yusuf Hussain Khan and Aziz Ahmad, Delhi: Anjuman Tarraqi Urdu Hind.

Ghulam Haider Saghir Lucknavi, *Aaien e Akhtar (2nd Edition)*, Lucknow: Awadh Press, 1912.

Guldasta e Awadh, Compiled by Munshi Bulaqi Das, Delhi: Mayur Press, 1906.

Haft Qulzum, Edited by Ghaziuddin Haider, Lucknow: Sultani Publication.

Hakim Syed Abul Ala Natiq Lakhnavi, *Nazm Urdu*, Lucknow: Zafarul Mutbeh, 1941.

Hamid Hasan Qadri, *Dastan e Tarikh e Urdu*, Agra: Laxmi Narayan Agarwal Publication, 1941.

Hasb ul Hukm Amjad Ali Shah, *Aamal ul Saliheen*, Lucknow: Sultan ul Mutab E.

Intizam Ullah Shahabi, *Begamat e Awadh Ke Khutoot*, Delhi: Faruqui Press, 1366.

Jalal Uddin Ahmad Jafri, *Tareekh e Masnaviyat e Urdu*, Allahabad: Anwar Ahmed Publication.

Kalam ul Muluk, Compiled by Shehzadi Chitra Ara Begum, Lucknow: Nizami Press.

Khan Bahadur Shaikh Siddiq Ahmad, *Tarikh Anjuman e Hind Awadh*, Lucknow: Naval Kishore Press, 1937.

Khaqan e Sarwar, Compiled by Khwaja Mohammad Wali Jaan Aasi, Lucknow: Gulshan e Faiz Publication, 1317.

Khwaja Ahmad Faruqi, *Classiki Adab*, Delhi: Azad Kitab Ghar.

Khwaja Arshad Ali Khan Qalaq, *Mazhar e Ishq*, Lucknow: Naval Kishore Publication, 1872.

Khwaja Badshah Sahab Saghir Lucknavi, *Gulshan e Ishq,* Anwar Muhammadi Publication, 1291.

Khwaja Mohammad Abdur Rauf Ishrat, *Khutoot e Akhri Shah e Awadh*, Lucknow: Naval Kishore Publication.

Khwaja Mohammad Mir Asar, *Khwab O Khayal (2nd Edition)*, Karachi: Anjuman Taraqqi Urdu Pakistan, 1950.

Khwaja Rashad Ali Khan Qalaq, *Safar Ashoob*, Lucknow: Karnama Publication, 1289.

Kulliyat Muhammad Quli Qutub Shah, Compiled by Syed Mohin Uddin Qadri Zor, Hyderabad: Sabras Kitab Ghar, 1940.

Lala Devi Dayal, *Phal*, Delhi: Imperial Book Depot, 1908.

Lala Sri Ram, *Khum Khana e Javed (Five Volumes),* Delhi: Mukhzin Press.

Madrasa e Qaiseriya, Calcutta: Metia Burj, 1887.

Mardan Ali Khan Rana, *Guncha e Rag*, Lucknow: Naval Kishore Publication, 1863.

Masnavi e Nasikh, Compiled by Habibullah Khan Ghaznafar, Allahabad: Kitabistan, 1931.

Maulana Abdul Halim Sharar, *Guzishta Lucknow*, Lucknow: Nasim Book Depot.

Maulana Abdul Majid Daryabadi, *Falsafa e Jazbaat*.

Maulana Altaf Hussain Hali, *Hayat e Javed*, Lahore: Punjab Academy, 1957.

Maulana Syed Ali Naqi Sahab, *Janab Ghufran Muab*, Lucknow: Sarfraz Qaumi Press, 1378.

Maulana Syed Ali Naqi Sahab, *Janab Rizwan Muab,* Lucknow: Sarfraza Qaumi Press, 1959.

Maulvi Abdul Ghafoor Khan Bahadur Nasaakh, *Sukhan e Shuara*, Lucknow: Naval Kishore Publication, 1874.

Maulvi Abdul Halim Sharar, *Jaan e Alam*, Lahore: Idara e Farogh e Urdu, 1951.

Maulvi Abdul Haq, *Chand Hum Asar*, Compiled by Sheikh Chand, Delhi: Anjuman e Taraqqi Urdu Hind.

Maulvi Abdul Haq, *Chand Hum Asar (4th Edition: Revised & Extended)*, Karachi: Urdu Academy, 1953.

Maulvi Abdul Haq, *Chand Hum Asar*, Karachi: Urdu Academy, 1961.

Maulvi Hamid Ullah Sahab Nadvi, *Urdu Makhtootat (Jama Masjid)*, Bombay: Urdu Research Institute.

Maulvi Mirza Mohammad Ali, *Mufid ul Azhan*, Calcutta: Sultani Publication, 1286.

Mir Mehdi Hasan Ahsan Luchnowi, *Waqiyat e Anees*, Lucknow: Muta Bae Ashal Matabae, 1905.

Mirza Asghar Ali Khan Naseem Dehlvi, *Alif Laila*, Lucknow: Naval Kishore Publication.

Mirza Fida Ali Khanjar Lakhnavi, *Mahal Khana e Shahi*, Lucknow: Nami Press, 1934.

Mirza Hatim Beg Ali Meher, *Almas e Darakhshan*, Agra: Ilahi Publication, 1895.

Mirza Jahan Qadr Nayyer, *Kitab ul Marasi*, Hyderabad: Shamsul Mutab E.

Mirza Jahan Qadr Nayyer, *Majmua e Nazm*, Hyderabad: Usman Press, 1333.

Mirza Mehdi Ali Khan Qubool, *Faizan ul Fikr*, Lucknow: Sultani Publication, 1272.

Mirza Mohammad Abbas Hussain Hosh, *Savaneh Umri*, Lucknow: Munshi Ganga Prasad Publication, 1308.

Mirza Mohammad Ali Khan Qubul, *Zikr ul Masoomeen*, Lucknow: Sultani Publication, 1272.

Mirza Mohammad Hadi Aziz Lakhnavi, *Tarikh e Abbas*, Lucknow: Nizami Press.

Mirza Mohammad Jalal, *Naghma e Dard*, Calcutta: Ripon Press, 1888.

Mirza Mohammad Raza Barq, *Diwan e Barq*, Lucknow: Sultani Publication, 1269.

Mirza Mohammad Wasa, *Guldasta e Aashiqan*, Lucknow: Muhammadi Publication, 1259. (Anjuman, Khuda Bakhsh)

Mirza Rajab Ali Beg Suroor, *Fasana e Ibrat*, Lucknow: Najmul Uloom Karnama Publication, 1884

Mirza Rajab Ali Beg Suroor, *Sarwar e Sultani*, Lucknow: Masihai Publication, 1268.

Mirza Zaki Ali Khan Zaki Lucknavi, *Akhtar Jinan*, Lucknow: Jafri Publication, 1305.

Mohammad Abdul Ahad Rabit, *Tahqiq ul Awzan*, Lucknow: Sultani Publication, 1271.

Mohammad Abdullah Khan Zaigham, *Yadgar e Zaigham*, 1303.

Mohammad Ahad Ali, *Muraqqa e Awadh*, Lucknow: Al Nazir Press, 1912.

Mohammad Ahad Ali, *Shabab Lucknow*, Lucknow: Al Nazir Press, 1912.

Mohammad Ali Khan Mohsin, *Ghunch Mazaq e Mohabbat*, Lucknow: Naval Kishore Publication, 1885.

Mohammad Ashfaq Ali Khan, *Naghmat ul Hind*, Lucknow: Nizami Press.

Mohammad Hasan Raees, *Zia e Akhtar*.

Mohammad Khan Bahadur Goya, *Sair ul Mohtashim*, Jawhar: Sarkar Gulshanabad Publication.

Mohammad Masih Uddin Khan Bahadur, *Safeer e Awadh*, Lucknow: Al Nazir Press, 1929.

Mohammad Muzaffar Ali Khan Asir, *Riyaz e Mussanif*, Lucknow: Ali Baksh Khan Publication, 1271.

Mohammad Najmul Ghani Khan Rampuri, *Tarikh e Awadh (1st Edition, Three Volumes)*, Moradabad: Matbaul Uloom, 1913.

Mohammad Najmul Ghani Khan Rampuri, *Tarikh e Awadh (2nd Edition, Five Volumes)*, Lucknow: Naval Kishore Publication, 1919.

Mohammad Shafi Rizvi, *Sharah e Nisah e Akhtari*, Lucknow: Awadh Gazette Publication, 1276.

Mohammad Shafi Shirazi, *Maaraka e Chakbast O Sharar*, Lucknow: Naval Kishore Publication, 1942.

Mohammad Taqi Ahmad, *Wajid Ali Shah*, Lucknow: Adab e Urdu Press, 1945.

Mohammad Wajid Ali Shah Akhtar, *Bani*, Calcutta : Sultani Publication, 1877. (Khuda Bakhsh)

Mohammad Wajid Ali Shah Akhtar, *Beh Re Mukhtalif*, Culcutta: Mustafai Publication, 1277.

Mohammad Wajid Ali Shah Akhtar, *Beh Re Ulfat*, Lucknow: Sultani Publication. (Khuda Bakhsh, Raza)

Mohammad Wajid Ali Shah Akhtar, *Daftar Gham W Behrul Alam*, Calcutta: Sultani Publication, 1290. (Society)

Mohammad Wajid Ali Shah Akhtar, *Darya e Taashuq*, Lucknow: Sultani Publication. (Khuda Bakhsh)

Mohammad Wajid Ali Shah Akhtar, *Darya e Taashuq*, Lucknow: Naval Kishore Publication. (Azad)

Mohammad Wajid Ali Shah Akhtar, *Diwan e Mubarak*. (Saalar Jung)

Mohammad Wajid Ali Shah Akhtar, *Haybat e Haidri*, Calcutta: Sultani Publication, 1292. (Azad, Imambara)

Mohammad Wajid Ali Shah Akhtar, *Huzn e Akhtar*, Compiled by Mahbub Ali, Lucknow: Daara e Adbia, 1922.

Mohammad Wajid Ali Shah Akhtar, *Huzn e Akhtari*, Calcutta: Sultani Publication, 1276. (Azad, Calcutta)

Mohammad Wajid Ali Shah Akhtar, *Imaan (2nd Edition)*, Calcutta: Sultani Publication, 1288, 1301. (Safi)

Mohammad Wajid Ali Shah Akhtar , *Irshad Khaqani*, Lucknow: Sultani Publication, 1269. (Azad)

Mohammad Wajid Ali Shah Akhtar, *Jauhar e Urooz*, Calcutta: Sultani Publication, 1290.

Mohammad Wajid Ali Shah Akhtar, *Jauhar e Urooz*, Calcutta: Sultani Publication, 1293.

Mohammad Wajid Ali Shah Akhtar, *Jawab e Blue Book*, Lucknow: Beni Prasad Nawaz Ganj.

Mohammad Wajid Ali Shah Akhtar, *Jawab e Blue Book*, Lucknow: Siddiq Book Depot

Mohammad Wajid Ali Shah Akhtar, *Jawab e Blue Book*, Lucknow: Kutub Khan e Nadir.

Mohammad Wajid Ali Shah Akhtar, *Kulliyat e Akhtari*, Calcutta: Sultani Publication, 1278. (Khuda Bakhsh, Saalar Jung, Azad, Raza)

Mohammad Wajid Ali Shah Akhtar, *Kulliyat e Soom*, Murshidabad.

Mohammad Wajid Ali Shah Akhtar, *Mubasah e Bayn ul Nafs Waal Aql*, Calcutta: Sultani Publication, 1291.

Mohammad Wajid Ali Shah Akhtar, *Malaz ul Kalmat*, Calcutta: Sultani Publication, 1297. (Azad)

Mohammad Wajid Ali Shah Akhtar, *Majmua e Wajidia*, Lucknow: Sultani Publication, 1266. (Raza)

Mohammad Wajid Ali Shah Akhtar, *Majmua e Wajidia e Sultani*, Lucknow: Sultani Publication, 1267. (Tagore)

Mohammad Wajid Ali Shah Akhtar, *Marasi*, Calcutta: Sultani Publication.

Mohammad Wajid Ali Shah Akhtar, *Mulk Akhtar*, Calcutta: Sultani Publication, 1296. (Imambara)

Mohammad Wajid Ali Shah Akhtar, *Najo*, Calcutta: Sultani Publication, 1286.

Mohammad Wajid Ali Shah Akhtar, *Nasah e Akhtari*, Lucknow: Naval Kishore Publication, 1275. (Azad)

Mohammad Wajid Ali Shah Akhtar, *Nazm Namvar*, Calcutta: Sultani Publication, 1287. (Raza, Ittihadiya, Azad, Khuda Bakhsh)

Mohammad Wajid Ali Shah Akhtar, *Qamar Mazmun*, Calcutta: Sultani Publication, 1281. (Imambara)

Mohammad Wajid Ali Shah Akhtar, *Riyaz ul Uqba*, Calcutta: Sultani Publication, 1300. (Imambara, Safi)

Mohammad Wajid Ali Shah Akhtar, *Sahifai Sultani*, Calcutta: Sultani Publication, 1289. (Azad, Imambara)

Mohammad Wajid Ali Shah Akhtar, *Sheva e Faiz*, Calcutta: Sultani Publication, 1277. (Tagore, Murshidabad, Azad)

Mohammad Wajid Ali Shah Akhtar, *Soorat ul Mubarak*, Lucknow: Sultani Publication, 1269. (Raza)

Mohammad Wajid Ali Shah Akhtar, *Sukhan e Ashraf*, Lucknow: Sultani Publication.

Mohammad Wajid Ali Shah Akhtar, *Tareekh e Ghazala*, Compiled by Syed Wasi Bilgrami, Agra: Mufeed e Aam Publication, 1914. (Azad)

Mohammad Wajid Ali Shah Akhtar, *Tareekh e Mumtaz*, Compiled by Mohammad Baqar, Lahore: Urdu Markaz, 1952. (Azad)

Mohammad Wajid Ali Shah Akhtar, *Tosha e Akhirat*, Calcutta: Sultani Publication, 1299. (Imambara)

Mufti Mir Abbas, *Jawahar e Abqarya*, Lucknow: Sultani Publication, 1271.

Munshi Muzaffar Ali Khan Bahadur, *Durratul Taj*, Lucknow: Sultani Publication, 1270.

Mulla Biman Ali Raji Kirmani, *Humla e Haidri*, Bombay: Mashhadi Mohammad Raza Publication, 1264.

Munshi Amir Ahmad, *Mahamid Khatim ul Nabin*, Ahmed Khan Sufi Publication, 1889.

Munshi Amir Ahmad, *Yadgar e Intikhab*, 1297.

Munshi Amir Ahmad, *Sharah e Hidayat ul Sultan*, Lucknow: Sultani Publication, 1268.

Munshi Tota Ram Shayaan, *Tilism e Hind*, Lucknow: Naval Kishore Publication, 1874.

Munshi Mohammad Qudrat Ullah, *Hadiqa e Qudrat e Sultan e Alam*, Agra: Aftab Qudrat Publication, 1281.

Munshi Mohammad Qudrat Ullah, *Qaiser Shah e Awadh*, Agra: Aftab Qudrat Publication, 1864.

Munshi Musaffar Ali Khan Asir, *Guldasta e Imamat*, Lucknow: Sultani Publication, 1271.

Munshi Naval Kishore, *Tawareekh e Nadir ul Asra*, Lucknow: Naval Kishore Publication, 1863.

Munshi Radhe Lal Mohani, *Tareekh e Farmaravayan e Awadh*, Lucknow: Naval Kishore Publication, 1878.

Munshi Ram Sahai Tamanna, *Afzal ul Tawarikh*, Lucknow: Tammanai Publication, 1879.

Munshi Ram Sahai Tamanna, *Ahsan ul Tawarikh*, Lucknow: Tammannai Publication, 1259.

Muzaffar Ali Khan Asir, *Diwan e Asir*, Lucknow: Naval Kishore Publication, 1286.

Nadir Bahu Nawab Sardar Begum, *Wakf Nam Imambrah Qasrul Buka*, Calcutta: Kalimi Publication, 1917.

Najmul Ghani Khan Majmi Rampuri, *Akhbaar ul Sanadeed*, Lucknow: Nawal Kishore Publication, 1918.

Nasir Uddin Hashmi, 'Detailed List of Manuscripts of Kutub Khana Nawab Salar Jung', Hyderabad: Ibrahimia Publication, 1957.

Nasir Uddin Hashmi, *Urdu Makhtootat (Kutub Khana e Asfia)*.

Nawab Masood Jung Bahadur, *Intiqab e Zarrin (3rd Edition)*, Budaun: Nizami Press, 1937.

Nawab Sadr Mahal, *Badshah Nama*, Calcutta: Sultani Publication, 1288.

Nawab Zaigham Ud Daulah, *Tarikh e Qaisri*, Lucknow: Mazahar ul Ajaib Publication, 1308.

Pari Khana, Translated by Tahseen Sarwari, Karachi: Naya Rahi Publication.

Qamar Raees, *Urdu Drama*, Aligarh: Sir Syed Book Depot, 1961.

Qazi Mohammad Saeed, *Fehrist Numaish Idara e Tahqeeqat e Urdu*, Patna.

Rais Ahmad Jafri, *Wajid Ali Shah Aur Unka Ahad*, Lucknow: Kitab Manzil, 1958.

Ram Babu Saxena, *Tareekh e Adab Urdu*, Translated by Mirza Mohammad Askari, Lucknow: Naval Kishore Press, 1952.

'Report Of Anjuman e Muhammadi (1907-1910)', Calcutta: Star Press, 1910.

Sadıq Alı Khan Dehlvi, *Sarmaya e Ishrat*, Delhi: Iftikhar Publication, 1286.

Safi Lakhnavi, *Lakht e Jigar*, Calcutta: All India Shia Conference,1928.

Sayyad Kamal Uddin Haider, *Qaisar ul Tawarikh (3rd Edition)*, Lucknow: Naval Kishore Publication, 1907.

Sayyad Murtaza Hussain, *Mushaira Aalam e Arwah*, Lucknow: Nasim Book Depot, 1955.

Shaikh Aman Ali, *Riyaz e Sahar*, Lucknow: Karnama Publication, 1291.

Shamsur Rahman, *Urdu Khutoot*, Delhi: Kitabi Duniya, 1947.

Sheikh Mohammad Jaan, *Sukhan be Misaal*, Compiled by Wasl Lucknavi, Lucknow: Tsvir Alam Press, 1901.

Sheikh Tasadduq Hussain, *Begmat e Awadh*, Lucknow: Kitab Nagar, 1956.

Shorish Kashmiri, *Us Bazar Mein (3rd Edition)*, Lahore: Mutbuat Chattan.

Syed Abdullah, *Shoara e Urdu Ke Tazkire*, Lahore: Maktaba e Jadid, 1952.

Syed Ali Akbar, *Sabikat ul Zeheb*. Lucknow: Ithna Ashri Publication, 1309.

Syed Anir Fatima Barelvi, *Sattawan Ke Hero*, Aligarh: Muslim University Press, 1949.

Syed Badshah Hussain, *Urdu Mein Drama Nigari*, Hyderabad: Shamsul Mutabey, 1935.

Syed Ghulam Ali Khan, *Imad us Saadat*, Lucknow: Naval Kishore Publication, 1864.

Syed Israr Hussain Khan, *Qadeem Hunar Wa Hunarmandan e Awadh*, Lucknow: Sarfraz Qaumi Press, 1936.

Syed Masood Hasan Rizvi Adeeb, *Lucknow Ka Shahi Stage*, Lucknow: Kitab Nagar, 1957.

Syed Mohammad Ali Arsh Nomani Malihabadi, *Ruqaat e Badr*, Hyderabad: Qasim Press, 1323.

Syed Mohammad Hadi Lucknavi, *Wazadaran e Awadh*, 1908.

Syed Mohammad Rafi Ali Mohani, *Taj O Nishan*, Moradabad: Nayyer e Azam Book Agency, 1321.

Syed Mohammad Sajjad Hussain Rehani, *Sawaneh Shah e Awadh*, Meerut: Tuti Hind Publication, 1887.

Syed Mohsin Ali Mosvi Mohsin, *Sarapa Sukhan*, Lucknow: Naval Kishore Publication, 1874.

Syed Moin ul Haq, *Akhbar e Rangeen*, Karachi: Pakistan Historical Society, 1962.

Syed Muzaffar Ali Khan Asir, *Gulistan e Sukhan*, Lucknow: Sultani Publication, 1271.

Syed Noorul Hasan Hashmi, *Adab Ka Maqsad*, Lucknow: Hindustan Kitab Ghar, 1956.

Taqweem e Sultani, translated and compiled by Syed Kamaluddin Haider, Lucknow: Sultani Publication, 1265.

Urdu Encyclopaedia, Edited by Abdul Waheed, Lahore: Firoz & Sons, 1962.

Wazir Agha, *Urdu Shairi Ka Mizaj*, Delhi: Seemant Prakashan, 2000.

Wazir ul Sultan Mohammad Mir Ali Khan Bahadur Amir, *Amir Nama*, Calcutta, 1870.

Wazir ul Sultan Mohammad Mir Ali Khan Bahadur Amir, *Wazirnama,* Kanpur: Nizami Publication, 1293.

Ziyapash Sahabposh, *Hindustan Mein Shiite Ki Tarikh*, Karachi: Darul Tasnif, 1957.

ENGLISH BIBLIOGRAPHY

Abdul Wali, *Sorrows of Akhtar*, Calcutta, 1924.

Act 19 of 1887. Government of India Press.

Ahmad Muhammad Taqi, *Tarikh Badshah Begum*, Lucknow, 1938.

Aloys Sprenger, *A Catalogue of the Arabic, Persian and Hindu'sta'ny Manuscripts, Of the Libraries of the King of Oudh (Vol. 1)*, Calcutta, 1854.

Appeal No. 221, Calcutta High Court, 1900.

Ashirbadi Lal Srivastava, *Shuja-ud-Daulah (Vol. 2)*, Lahore: The Minerva Book Shop, 1945.

Ashirbadi Lal Srivastava, *The First Two Nawabs of Oudh*, Lucknow: The Upper India Publishing House, Ltd., 1933.

Captain James Paton, *The British Government and the Kingdom of Oudh 1764–1835*, Edited by Bisheshwar Prashad, University of Allahabad, 1944.

Captain R. Smyth, 'Map of Calcutta', Samuel Smith & Co., 1854.

Captain William White, *The Prince of Oudh Mirza Kaiwan Jah or the Dethroned King of Oudh in Chains*, London, 1838.

Captain William White, *The Prince of Oudh or the Claim of Nawab Ekbal-ood-Dowlah Behadoor to the Throne of Oude*, London, 1838.

Charles T. Metcalfe, *Two Narratives of the Mutiny in Delhi*, London: Westminster Archibald Constable & Co., 1898.

Edward H. Hilton, *The Tourist's Guide to Lucknow*, Lucknow, 1913.

Emma Roberts, *Scenes and Characteristics of Hindostan*, London: W. H. Allen and Co., 1835.

Fanny Parks, *Wanderings of a Pilgrim, In Search of the Picturesque (Vol 1.)*, London: Pelham Richardson, 1850.

Fritz Kahn, *Our Sex Life: A Guide and Counsellor for Everyone*, London: William Heinemann Ltd, 1939.

George Dodd, *The History of the Indian Revolt*, London, 1859.

H. C. Irwin, *The Garden of India; or, Chapters on Oudh History and Affairs*, London: W. H. Allen, 1880.

Hon. Federick J. Shore, *Notes on Indian Affairs (Vol. 1)*, London: John W Parker, 1837.

Ikramuddin Kidwai and K. R. Qanungao, *Lucknow: Past and Present*, University of Lucknow, 1951.

J. F. Blumhardt, *A Supplementary Catalogue of Hindustani Books in the Library of the British Museum: Acquired During the Years 1889-1908*, London, 1909.

J. F. Blumhardt, *Catalogue of Hindustani Printed Books in the Library of the British Museum*, London, 1889.

J. F. Blumhardt, *Catalogue of the Hindustani Manuscripts in the Library of the India Office*, London, 1926.

John Malcolm Ludlow, *British India: Its Races and Its History*, Cambridge: Macmillan & Co., 1858.

John William Kaye, *A History of the Sepoy War in India 1857-1858*, London: W. H. Allen & Co., 1876.

Malcolm Lewin, 'Has Oudh Been Worse Governed by Its Native Princes Than Our Indian Territories by Leadenhall Street?' London: James Ridgeway, 1857.

Martin Richard Gubbins, *An Account of the Mutinies in Oudh*, London: Richard Bentley, 1858.

Michael Edwardes, *The Orchid House: Splendours and Miseries of the Kingdom of Oudh 1827-1857*, London: Cassell & Co., 1960.

Mohammad Masih Uddin Khan Bahadur, *Oude, Its Princes, and Its Government Vindicated*, London, 1857.

Nagendranath Gupta, *Reflections and Reminiscences*, Bombay: Hind Kitabs Ltd. Publishers, 1947.

Oude: Papers Relating To, London: Harrison and Sons, 1855-1857.

'Oudh Pension Papers', Calcutta: Government of India Publication (B.S. Press), 1913.

Rai Bahadur Prayag Dayal, *Catalogue of the Coins of the King of Oudh*, Allahabad, 1939.

Reginald Heber, *Narrative of a Journey Through the Upper Provinces of India (Vol. 1)*, London: John Murray, 1828.

Robert Wilberforce Bird, *Dacoitee in Excelsis: Or, the Spoliation of Oude*, London, 1857.

S. A. A. Rizvi, *Freedom Struggle In Uttar Pradesh: Source Material*, Lucknow: Information Department of Uttar Pradesh.

Safi Ahmad, *British Aggression in Oudh*, Lucknow, 1964.

Sidney Hay, *Historic Lucknow*, Lucknow: Pioneer Press, 1939.

Sir Henry M. Lawrence, *Essays on Indian Army and Oude*, Serampore: Friend of India Press, 1859.

Sir Joseph Fayrer, *Recollections of My Life*, London: William Blackwood and Sons, 1900.

Sir W. H. Russell, *My Diary in India in the Year 1858–59*, London: Routledge, Warne & Routledge, 1860.

Sir W. H. Sleeman, *A Journey Through the Kingdom of Oudh in 1849–50 (Vol. 1)*, London: Richard Bentley, 1858.

T. G. P. Spear, *The Nabobs: A Study of the Social Life of the English in Eighteenth Century India*, London: Oxford University Press, 1932.

Thomas Letts, 'City Plan of Calcutta (3rd. Edition)', Surveyor General of India, Calcutta: Letts and Sons, 1892.

William Hoey, *History of Asafud Daulah, Nawab Wazir of Oudh*, Oudh Government Press, 1885.

William Knighton, *The Private Life of An Eastern King, together with Elihu Jan's Story or The Private Life of an Eastern Queen*, Edited by S. B. Smith, London: Oxford University Press, 1921.

C. NEWSPAPERS & MAGAZINES

Urdu/English

Aaj Kal, Delhi, 1953–1967.

Adeeb, Allahabad, 1910.

Adeeb-e-Urdu, Lucknow, 1922.

Ahsan Marharvi, 'Masnavi Husn e Akhtar Aur Khususiyat e Musannif', *Hindustani*, Allahabad, 1931.

Al-Nazir, Lucknow, 1930.

Amir Hasan Gorgani, 'Wajid Ali Shah Ke Zamanae Qayam Kalkatta Ke Baaz Aham Mamlaat', *Nigar*, Lucknow, March 1963.

Awadh Punch, Lucknow, 1885 –1887.

Dilgudaaz, Lucknow, 1877–1933.

Hamari Zaban, Aligarh, 1964–1967.

Ibadat Baarelvi, 'Wajid Ali Shah Ki Ek Nadir Masnavi', *Mah-e-Nau*, Karachi, March 1965.

Lisan ul Asar, Kanpur, 1910.

Naya Daur, Lucknow, 1955–1965.

Nazzara, Lucknow, 1962–1963.

Nuqoosh, Lahore, 1956–1966.

Payam-e-Amal, Lahore, 1964.
Qazi Abdul Wadud, 'Asadul Akhbar (Agra)', *Muasir*, Patna, 1942–1943.
Saheefa, Lahore, 1964–1965.
Shams Bangala, Calcutta, 1907–1908.
Zamana, Kanpur, 1909–1912.

English

Amrita Bazar Patrika, Calcutta,1887.
Indo–Iranica, Calcutta, Vol 18, June–December 1965.
Marg, Bombay, September 1957, September 1959.
Raj Herald, Lucknow Periodical [now defunct], 1934–1935.
Statesman and The Friend of India, Calcutta, 1885–1887.
The *Calcutta Review*, Calcutta, Vol 1, 3, 25,1844–1845, 1855.
The *Englishman*, Calcutta, 1856–1857.
The *Indian Daily News*, Calcutta,1887.
'The Journal of the U.P. Historical Society', Vol 9, July 1936.
The *Pioneer*, Allahabad, 1887.

REFERENCES FULL FORM OF ABBREVIATIONS OF LIBRARIES USED IN THE BOOK

Amir, Amir-ud-Daula Public Library, Lucknow.
Anjuman, Anjuman-i Taraqqi-i Urdu, Aligarh.
Asfia, Andhra Pradesh State Library (State Central Library), Hyderabad.
Azad, Maulana Azad Library, Aligarh.
Idara, Idara-e-Adabiyat-e-Urdu, Hyderabad.
Ittihadiya, Ittihadiya Library [now defunct], Calcutta.
Khuda Bakhsh, Khuda Bakhsh Oriental Public Library, Patna.
Mahmudabad, Kutub Khana Riyasat Mahmudabad, Lucknow.
Murshidabad, Palace Library (Hazarduari Palace), Murshidabad.
Raza, Raza Library, Rampur.
Salar Jung, Salar Jung Museum, Hyderabad.
Society, Asiatic Society of Bengal, Calcutta.
Safi, Safi Daarul Mutaley [now defunct], Nadan Mahal, Lucknow.
Tagore, Tagore Library, Lucknow.
Yateem Khana, Yateem Khana Islamia (Calcutta Muslim Orphanage), Calcutta.

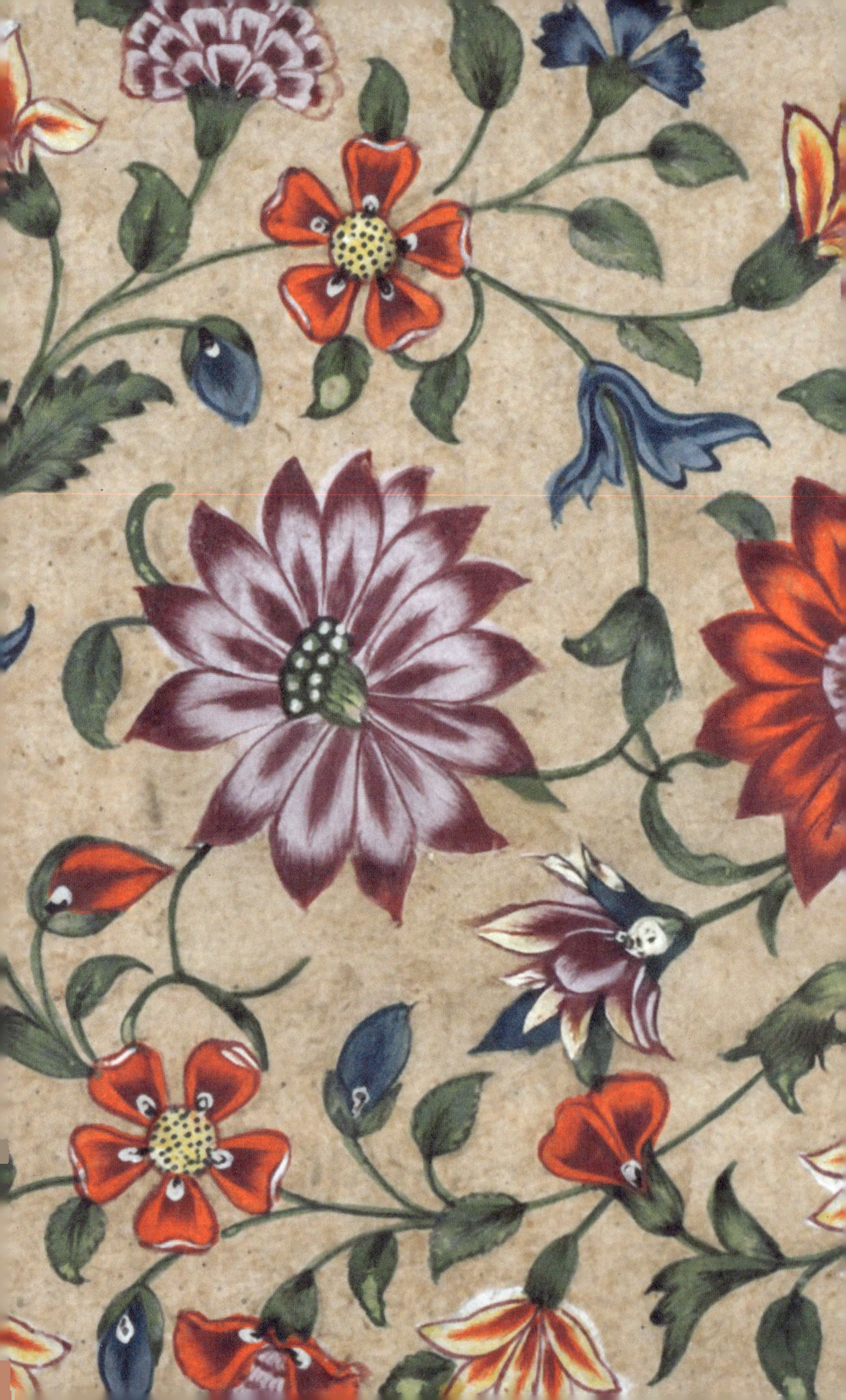